CRIMINAL JUSTICE IN AMERICA

FIFTH EDITION

Developed by

Marshall Croddy

Bill Hayes

Constitutional
Rights
Foundation

601 South Kingsley Drive
Los Angeles, California 90005
(213) 487- 5590
www.crf-usa.org

Developed by
Marshall Croddy and Bill Hayes

Board Reviewers
Marshall P. Horowitz, Lisa Rockwell,
Patrick Rogan, K. Eugene Shutler,
Douglas Thompson, Lois Thompson

Editor
Bill Hayes

Contributing Writers
(Various Editions)
Bill Hayes, Marshall Croddy, Todd Clark,
Teri Engler, Lucy Eisenberg, Damon Huss,
Sandy Kanengiser, Carlton Martz, Betsy
Salzman, Eden Kusmiersky, Coral Suter,
Charles Tremper, Michelle Ng, Roy Kim,
Shruti Modi, Anjelica Sarmiento, Sophia Khan,
Marianna Muratova

Researchers
(Various Editions)
Rick Bhasin, Luke Delgado, and Michael Sokolson

Production
Andrew Costly, *Designer*

Library of Congress Cataloging-in-Publication Data

Criminal justice in America / developed by Marshall Croddy and Bill Hayes ; edited by Bill Hayes ;
written by Bill Hayes ... [et al.]. -- 5th ed.
    p. cm.
  Includes bibliographical references and index.
  ISBN 978-1-886253-46-9 (pbk.)
  1. Criminal justice, Administration of--United States. I. Croddy, Marshall. II. Hayes, Bill, 1945-

HV9950.C745 2012
364.973--dc23

                              2012013906

The development of these materials was financially assisted through the United States Office of Juvenile Justice and Delinquency Prevention.

Printed in ROK

CRIMINAL JUSTICE IN AMERICA

Summary of Contents

CRIMINAL JUSTICE IN AMERICA
TABLE OF CONTENTS

Introduction

INTRODUCTION

No matter who you are, crime affects your life. As a student, your school might be vandalized or your wallet stolen. Statistically, chances are good that sometime in your life you will be a crime victim. As a taxpayer, you will be required to contribute money in the fight against crime or to repair the damage it does. As a voter, you will be asked to choose candidates based in part, at least, on their views about solutions to crime. Everyone agrees that crime is a serious problem. Few agree about its causes or solutions.

Although the debate over the causes and solutions to crime will probably never end, society has evolved a criminal justice system for dealing with crime. Two areas of jurisprudence are essential to understanding this system: criminal law and criminal procedure.

Criminal Law

Criminal law focuses on defining crime itself. For what type of conduct does our society punish people? After all, if society had no standards for human behavior, we would not have any crime, let alone a crime problem.

Today, our criminal law is contained in a wide array of statutes and ordinances enacted by federal, state, county, and city government. Each law spells out the elements of the crime in question and the punishment for those who break it.

The process of defining and applying criminal law never stops. Legislatures repeal out-of-date laws, modify existing laws, and enact new ones. Criminal trial courts interpret the meaning of various laws and apply them to particular cases. Criminal appeal courts review the decisions of trial courts and set precedents for trial courts to follow. Thus, the body of criminal law keeps changing.

Criminal Procedure

Criminal procedure comes into play when police start investigating a particular crime. It focuses on the steps taken and decisions made in the investigation, accusation, trial, verdict, and sentencing of a criminal defendant. It is the process by which we decide the what, when, where, how, and who questions of criminal justice.

Criminal procedures also are designed to protect a defendant from being falsely accused or convicted of a crime. The U.S. Constitution requires "due process of law," offers protection from "unreasonable searches and seizures," and forbids "cruel and unusual punishment." These, and many other constitutional provisions, have done much to shape our criminal procedure.

Criminal procedure has other functions also. Court rules attempt to assure an orderly and consistent decision-making process. Rules of evidence are designed to ensure that the facts of the case presented to a jury are relevant, accurate, and not overly prejudicial. There are also rules of conduct for judges, lawyers, and juries.

Like criminal law, criminal procedure is everchanging. Legislators enact new laws, judges and courts adopt new rules, and the Supreme Court interprets and applies the Constitution.

Criminal Justice

This book will have a lot to do with criminal law and procedure. They are important parts of criminal justice. Yet, there is much, much more to consider. Criminal justice also raises vital questions for each of us about fairness, security, and rights in a free society.

As you explore the selections in this book, you will meet the people who investigate crime and enforce our laws. You will learn about judges and courts and their struggle to protect individual rights while determining guilt or innocence. You will see the darker side of the criminal justice system and find out how society deals with people after they have been found guilty beyond a reasonable doubt. You will visit prisons and prisoners, guards, and parole officers, and in doing so you will discover the problems they face on a daily basis.

The Problem of Crime

Beyond criminal law and procedure and the system that investigates, apprehends, and punishes lawbreakers, you will study crime itself. Social scientists who engage in this study are called **criminologists**. They try to find answers to some difficult questions. Why do people become criminals? How serious is our crime problem? How can crime be reduced? Although you won't be a professional criminologist after studying this book, you will have a much better understanding about important issues of criminal justice.

Unit 1
CRIME

Friday evening, 9:30 p.m. . . .

In an underground parking garage downtown, a young man staggers to a pay phone on the wall and leans against it to hold himself up. Finally he gets the strength to call 911. A few seconds later, a voice comes on the line.

"Emergency services."

"My name is Sam Peterson," the man stammers. "I've just been robbed."

Meanwhile, in a middle-income residential area, a young husband and wife arrive home from a movie. They notice that the glass in the back door has been smashed in. Inside, they find a horrible mess, with furniture tipped over and china broken on the floor. The television and DVD player are gone. They both start to tremble. A place that they believed was private and safe had been torn open and violated.

A major crime happens somewhere in America every few seconds. But this isn't just a statistic. Behind each crime are people: victims who are hurt, criminals who often live violent and destructive lives, and those who must deal with the aftermath – the police, social workers, attorneys, judges, and legislators.

In this unit, we will look at criminal acts, defenses to criminal charges, criminals, and crime victims. What acts does our society, through its laws, define as crimes? What must be proved before a person is convicted of a crime? Who are the criminals and why do they do it? What is it like to have your life changed in an instant by someone else's wrongdoing? By considering these questions, you will learn a lot about crime and its consequences. And you will be able to take an intelligent part in a great debate going on in our society: What should we do about crime?

CHAPTER 1
CRIMES

Crime is a sociopolitical artifact, not a natural phenomenon. We can have as much or as little crime as we please, depending on what we choose to count as criminal.
– Herbert L. Packer, professor of law, *The Limits of the Criminal Sanction* (1968)

THE BASICS OF CRIME | ELEMENTS OF A CRIME | MURDER | THEFT | INCHOATE CRIMES
CRIMES AGAINST THE JUSTICE SYSTEM | HATE CRIMES | CYBERCRIME

The Basics of Crime

Although it is not likely that a criminal will carefully consider the text of the law before he murders or steals, it is reasonable that a fair warning should be given to the world in language that the common world will understand, of what the law intends to do if a certain line is passed. To make the warning fair, so far as possible the line should be clear.
– Justice Oliver Wendell Holmes Jr., *McBoyle v. U.S.* (1931)

Criminal cases differ from civil cases. In most civil cases, individuals sue one another seeking compensation for injuries done to them. In criminal cases, the state prosecutes individuals for injuring *society*. Instead of seeking compensation from defendants, the state seeks to punish them. A criminal case focuses on whether a defendant has committed a crime against society and what sentence is appropriate to punish the defendant for the crime.

But what conduct should society outlaw? In many instances, this question is easy to answer. Almost everyone would agree that murder, rape, and arson should be prohibited. Debates arise, however, over other acts. Should prostitution or the use of drugs be made criminal? What about gambling or private sexual activity? What conduct should society prohibit? These debates raise questions about where criminal laws come from in the first place.

The Sources of Criminal Law

Our criminal laws spring from two major sources, laws passed by legislatures and what is called **common law**. Common law is judge-made. Instead of being created by a legislature, it is based on legal precedents — court decisions — set by judges in earlier cases. English common law is an important root of our current legal system. Originally, the criminal laws in England were mostly unwritten. If a judge heard a case

and believed that certain conduct was anti-social, he made it a crime and punished the offender accordingly.

Definitions of crimes and defenses developed in the decisions of the English courts. These later became part of the common law adopted in early America. In turn, American courts began contributing to the common law. Over the years, a rather unwieldy body of law developed.

Common law has one serious problem. If it isn't written down in some simple way, how do people know if they are breaking the law? William Penn, the founder of Pennsylvania, made this point when he was tried in London in 1670 for unlawful assembly. (He had attended a Quaker meeting.)

> **Penn:** I desire you would let me know by what law it is you prosecute me . . . .
> **Judge:** Upon the common law.
> **Penn:** Where is that common law?
> **Judge:** You must not think that I am able to run up so many years, and over so many adjudged cases, which we call common law, to answer your curiosity. . . .
> **Penn:** It is too general and imperfect an answer, to say it is the common law, unless we knew both where and what it is. For where there is no law, there is no transgression . . . .

All states and the federal government today have written criminal codes. Most jurisdictions have replaced common-law crimes with written statutes. Some states still recognize the power of the courts to punish common-law crimes when no criminal statute exists, but this power is rarely exercised. Most states and the federal government deny courts this power. In these jurisdictions, only conduct expressly forbidden by a criminal statute is a crime.

Thus, the primary source of criminal law today is legislative enactment. By the second half of the 19th century, legislatures had seen the problem of relying on common law and had begun to enact comprehensive criminal codes. Many of these codes included all of the elements of the old common law.

An influence on modern codes is the American Law Institute's *Model Penal Code*. Written by prominent judges, lawyers, and legal scholars, it is an attempt to improve criminal law by producing a code that is clearer, simpler, and more up-to-date than the common law. Many states have enacted parts of the *Model Penal Code* into law. A few states (New Jersey, New York, Pennsylvania, and Oregon) have adopted almost all of it.

Classification of Offenses

The common law divided crimes into two categories — felonies and misdemeanors. Common law felonies were murder, manslaughter, rape, sodomy, mayhem, robbery, arson, burglary, and larceny. All other crimes were misdemeanors.

Under modern criminal law, the distinction between felonies and misdemeanors is spelled out by statute. Most states define a felony as any crime punishable by death or by imprisonment in a state prison. A crime punishable by time in a local jail is a misdemeanor. Other states distinguish by length of imprisonment, not place of imprisonment. For example, a felony is often defined as a crime punishable by one year or more in prison.

FOR DISCUSSION

1. What characteristics distinguish criminal from civil cases?
2. What are the two sources of criminal law? How are they different?
3. Today, most states have done away with common-law crimes. Only acts specifically defined in statutes as illegal can be punished. What would happen if some criminal managed to find a loophole? What if an individual did something obviously harmful to others that was not specifically outlawed by statute? Should the courts be allowed to recognize a new crime to fill the gap? Explain your answer.

CLASS ACTIVITY

Felony or Misdemeanor?

In this activity, students evaluate whether certain actions should be crimes, and if so, whether they should be felonies or misdemeanors.

1. Form pairs. Each pair should:
   a. Read and discuss **Criminal Acts?** below. Each of the persons described is an adult.
   b. Answer the following questions for each act:
      - Should the act described be a crime? Why or why not?
      - If so, should it be a felony or misdemeanor? Why?
2. Reconvene as a class and share group answers.

Criminal Acts?

a. Margaret tells the police that an officer who stopped her on the street was verbally abusive to her. She is lying.
b. Sam sees a young boy struggling in a pond and calling for help. Sam does nothing and the boy drowns.
c. Dick is married to Suzanne and Mary.
d. Ruby promises to give Harry $1,000 if he graduates from college. He graduates and she refuses to give him the money.
e. Robert holds a toy pistol to Ashley's head and demands all of her cash and jewelry. She believes it's a real gun and hands over the goods.
f. Pedro calls a local pizza parlor and orders five pizzas to be delivered to a phony address.
g. Jane's country is at war. She shoots and kills an enemy soldier.
h. John lets his dog run wild around the neighborhood, even though he knows that the dog scares young children and constantly knocks over garbage cans looking for food.

Elements of a Crime

In any case of injustice, it makes a great difference whether the wrong is done on impulse or whether it is committed deliberately and with premeditation; for offenses that are committed on impulse are less culpable than those committed by design and with malice.
– Cicero (106–43 B.C.), Roman statesman, *On Duties*

The criminal justice system carefully defines exactly what a crime is. The system also takes care in defining what must be proven to convict a person of a crime. Almost every crime has four basic elements:

1. **A prohibited act.** At common law, this was called the *actus reus* (Latin for "guilty act"). The law does not punish people for having criminal thoughts alone. There must be an act, which is today almost always defined by a statute. In murder, for example, the act is killing someone. In a few rare cases, *failing to act* is a crime when a person has a legal duty to act. For example, if a parent lets a child die of a long illness without seeking medical help, it can be a crime.

2. **Criminal intent.** At common law, this was called *mens rea* (Latin for "guilty mind"). This can be the most difficult element to prove. It will be discussed in more detail below.

3. **Concurrence of the act and the intent.** The person has to intend the act when it is committed. For example, Sluggo wants to kill Nancy. Then he changes his mind and forgets all about it. A month later, he accidentally drives his car into her and kills her. This is not legally murder because the intent to kill is not linked to the act.

4. **Causation.** The act has to cause the harmful result. For example, Marge, intending to kill Homer, puts poison in a doughnut. As he reaches for the doughnut, Homer slips, hits his head, and dies. Marge cannot be found guilty of murder because she did not cause Homer's death.

Criminal Intent

Criminal laws generally punish only those who have criminal intent, a guilty mind. But what constitutes a guilty mind, the so-called *mens rea*, depends on the crime. The criminal intent required for most crimes usually falls into one of four categories:

1. **Specific intent.** This is the easiest type to define. It means the person intended just the result that happened. The person did it on purpose. Certain crimes, such as theft, require specific intent. To convict John of theft, for example, the prosecution must prove not only that John took Mary's car, but also that he did not intend to return it.

2. **General intent.** This means that the person either knew the result would happen or consciously disregarded the extreme likelihood that it would happen. For example, John picks up a gun on New Year's Eve and shoots it toward a crowd of people. A bullet hits Mary and kills her. He didn't kill Mary on purpose, but he must have known he would kill, or was likely to kill, someone. This would meet the general intent requirement of second-degree murder.

3. **Criminal negligence.** This means that a person does an act unintentionally but with an extreme lack of care. For example, John is drag racing down a city street when Mary, a pedestrian, steps in front of his car. Mary is killed.

A crime is made up of:			
Criminal Act	**Criminal Intent**	**Concurrence of Act and Intent**	**Causation**
Conduct prohibited by law	KINDS 1. Specific 2. General 3. Criminal Negligence 4. Strict Liability	Act and intent must be linked.	Result must be caused by the act.

4. **Strict liability.** This means no mental state is required at all. Anyone doing the act is guilty regardless of intent. Almost all common-law crimes required some mental state. But bigamy is an example of a common-law crime that required no intent. For example, if John mistakenly believes he has divorce[d] and he marries Mary, [he is con]victed of bigamy. Other ex[amples of strict] liability crimes include [safety,] safety, and traffic offense[s]. [For example,] if Joe runs a red light, he is guilty whether or not he saw the light.

CLASS ACTIVITY

Did They Commit Crimes?

In this activity, students analyze five cases to determine whether criminal conduct has taken place.

1. Form groups of four. Each group should:
   a. Read and discuss the five cases that follow.
   b. Refer to the explanations above of the four basic elements of a crime — (1) act, (2) intent, (3) concurrence of act and intent, and (4) causation.
   c. Assign one element of a crime to each person in the group. Have that person say whether that element is present in each case, and then discuss whether the whole group agrees. To find the definition of a crime, refer to the glossary (at the back of the book).
   d. When the discussion is completed, assign one case to each student for reporting back to the whole class. Be prepared to explain and discuss each element.
2. Reconvene as a class and share the answers.

CASE 1: Tim

Marcos and his friends, Tim and Jill, were having a beer together at their local bar. When Tim went to the jukebox to play more music, Marcos asked Jill to dance. Tim became jealous and punched Marcos in the face. Tim has been charged with battery.

CASE 2: Karen

Karen told everyone that she hated Emily for stealing her boyfriend. Karen said she wanted to hurt Emily. Two months pass and Karen nudges a flowerpot off her second-floor patio as Emily stands below. The flowerpot hits Emily and gives her a concussion. Karen swears that she forgot all about her threats and didn't mean any harm. Karen is charged with battery.

CASE 3: Ray

Mr. Ray Anderson sat on his front porch cleaning his rifle. Many children were playing on the sidewalk in front of his home. When Anderson turned the gun over, it went off, killing one of the children in the crowd. He has been charged with involuntary manslaughter.

CASE 4: Susan

Susan was shopping in her favorite department store. She saw a sweater that she liked, stuffed it into her book bag, and ran out of the store. A security guard caught her. Susan has been charged with shoplifting.

CASE 5: Gayle

Gayle shoots Mary in the big toe. Mary goes to the hospital to have her toe examined and treated. One week later, Mary dies of blood poisoning that she got from an unsterilized medical instrument. Gayle is charged with murder.

Murder

Murder most foul . . . most foul, strange and unnatural.
– William Shakespeare (1564–1616), poet and playwright, *Hamlet*

No crime seems to fascinate people more than murder. Religions teach the basic tenet, "Thou shalt not kill." Yet throughout the ages, storytellers have told and retold tales of murder — Cain and Abel, the Greek tragedies, Shakespeare's *Macbeth*, and thousands of mystery novels, movies, and crime TV shows. In our country, the most severe penalty our society can inflict — death — is reserved for murderers.

Like all crimes, murder is made up of particular elements. These must be proved before a person can be convicted.

Murder at common law and under many modern statutes is the unlawful killing of a human being with *malice aforethought*. Malice aforethought is the intent, or *mens rea*, element of this crime. It doesn't mean what you might expect it to. Malice aforethought is sometimes defined as an *actual or implied intention* to kill with no provocation by the victim.

Actual intent is found when the defendant consciously meant to cause another's death. Implied intention exists when the defendant *either*:

(1) intended to cause great bodily harm *or*
(2) should have known that the act would result in death or great bodily harm.

Consider some examples:

- If Barbara hates Michael, decides to kill him, and picks up a knife and does so, malice aforethought is present. In this case, Barbara's malice aforethought was an *actual* intent to kill Michael and she could be charged with murder.
- If Barbara decides to hurt Michael badly, stabs him in the chest and kills him, malice aforethought is also present. This time the intent to kill is *implied*, because she did not specifically intend to kill, but only cause great bodily harm.
- If Barbara hates Michael, decides to scare him, pushes him in front of oncoming traffic at a street corner, and Michael dies as a result, malice aforethought is also established. In this case, though Barbara didn't intend to kill or even seriously injure Michael, she should have known her actions would cause him to die or suffer great bodily harm. Under the law, Barbara had *implied* intent to kill Michael.

Degrees of Homicide

Over the years, the law has developed degrees of criminal homicide. The punishment a convicted person may receive depends on the degree of the homicide. The worst degrees of homicide are commonly called murder and the lesser degrees, manslaughter.

First-degree murder is a deliberate and premeditated killing done with malice aforethought.

This is a cold-blooded murder. "Deliberate" means it was done with a cool mind, capable of reflection. "Premeditated" means the person actually reflected on the murder before committing it. And "malice aforethought," of course, means that the killer had the intent to kill. It takes all three elements — deliberation, premeditation, and malice aforethought — to establish the *specific intent* for first-degree murder.

Second-degree murder is a killing done with malice aforethought, but without deliberation and premeditation. This covers all murders that are not in the first degree.

Felony murder is any killing done while a person is committing a felony. If the killing is done while committing certain felonies, such as robbery, rape, arson, or burglary, it is classified as first-degree murder. Killings done while committing other felonies are considered second-degree murder.

Voluntary manslaughter is an intentional killing committed without malice aforethought. The killer must:

- be seriously provoked by the victim,
- act in the heat of the anger, *and*
- not have had an opportunity to cool off.

The provoking act does not excuse the killing, but it makes the crime a lesser degree than second-degree murder.

Involuntary manslaughter is an unintended killing that takes place during a crime that is a misdemeanor ("misdemeanor manslaughter"). It can also be a killing caused by criminal negligence.

Vehicular homicide is a crime recognized by many states. It covers killings from automobile accidents when the driver is criminally negligent.

FOR DISCUSSION

1. The penalties for these forms of homicide in every state are increasingly harsh: *Involuntary Manslaughter — Voluntary Manslaughter — Second-Degree Murder — First-Degree Murder*

   If one person is killed in each of these cases, why do you think the punishments get harsher? Is this fair? Explain.

2. Howard tries to murder someone, but fails and harms no one. Fred is guilty of involuntary manslaughter when he accidentally kills a person. Which person should be punished more harshly — Howard or Fred? Why?

CLASS ACTIVITY

Death in the School Halls

In this activity, students examine a hypothetical killing and determine what crime was committed.

1. Divide into groups of four and read the following case:

   One day in gym class, Adam made fun of the way Rick was shooting a basketball. Rick told Adam to shut up or else he would take care of him. Adam couldn't help making another comment on the way Rick was shooting. Rick grabbed Adam and beat him up.

   Adam ended up with a broken nose and a black eye, and he decided to get even. He dug his father's pistol out of the attic, loaded it, and headed off to school to find Rick. He waited at Rick's locker for almost an hour, but Rick never showed up. Adam became impatient. Nervously he checked the gun again to make sure that all the chambers were loaded. Just then the school bell rang out, startling Adam into firing the gun by accident. The bullet ricocheted off a locker and hit a student who was walking out of class. She was killed instantly.

2. In each group, assign one person to each of the following crimes: murder, felony murder, voluntary manslaughter, and involuntary manslaughter. Each person should:

   - Decide whether the crime described above fits the crime assigned to him or her.
   - Be prepared to explain why or why not.

3. Discuss the case in your group. Go through the crimes, one by one, and the person responsible for that crime should explain whether the case fits that crime or not. Discuss why or why not.

4. Reconvene as a class and compare each group's findings.

Theft

All bad men are not thieves, but all thieves are bad men.
– Aristotle (384-322 B.C.), Greek philosopher, *Rhetoric*

Stealing is one of the most commonly committed crimes. The law recognizes many forms of stealing. The differences depend on how the stealing is done.

Larceny is the usual legal word for theft. It means taking without permission someone else's property and intending not to give it back. For example, if someone walks by your desk and takes your wallet, that person has committed larceny. There are usually two categories of larceny, or theft:

1. **Grand theft** means stealing property worth over a certain amount. The amount varies from state to state, but it is usually around $500. Grand theft is a felony. If your wallet contained $1,000, stealing it would be grand theft.
2. **Petty theft** means stealing property worth less than the grand theft amount. Petty theft is a misdemeanor.

Burglary is the unlawful entry into any building with the intent to commit a crime, usually theft. At one time in common law, burglary meant breaking into a home at night to steal. That definition has been expanded to include illegally entering any building at any time of day to steal or commit any crime. Some states have expanded it to include breaking into cars. If a thief broke into your office to steal your wallet, the crime would be burglary.

Robbery, unlike burglary, is a crime against the person. It is forcible stealing — the taking of a person's property by violence or by threatening violence. If someone grabs you, demands your wallet, and then takes it and runs away, that person has committed robbery.

Armed robbery means using a dangerous weapon to take something from a person. Even pretending to have a weapon is considered armed robbery in most states. If someone pulls a knife on you and steals your wallet, that person has committed armed robbery. Armed robbery is a more serious offense than simple robbery, and it carries a stiffer penalty.

Other Forms of Stealing

Larceny, burglary, and robbery are the three main categories of stealing. But as the common law developed in England and America, courts and legislatures added additional categories.

Embezzlement is when people take property they have been entrusted with. For example, you give John $200 to hold for you while you go swimming, and he decides to keep it. He has embezzled the money. Embezzlement differs from larceny in that the person takes possession of the property legally.

Fraud is knowingly misrepresenting a fact to get property from another person. For example, John tells you a worthless coin is gold (which he knows is false) and sells it to you for $100. John has defrauded you of $100. Fraud is sometimes a crime in itself and more often an element of other crimes, such as larceny by trick, false pretenses, forgery, and writing bad checks.

Extortion is making a threat with the intent of getting property (usually money) from another person. One form of extortion is blackmail. For example, Elsa threatens to tell your friends that you spent time in jail unless you pay her $1,000. She is extorting money from you.

An extortionist can threaten violence. For example, if Elsa says she will kill you unless you give her $1,000 by Friday, she has committed extortion. But if the threat is of immediate harm, the crime is robbery. For example, if she points a gun at you and demands money, she is committing robbery, not extortion.

Receiving stolen property is against the law in every state. The crime requires that the person knows or should have known that the property is stolen. For example, Sam goes over to his neighbor Ed's house and sees Ed filing the serial numbers off five brand-new high-definition TVs in his garage. Ed generously gives Sam one of the televisions. Sam is guilty of receiving stolen property

---

ASK AN EXPERT

Invite a criminal lawyer to your class to explain the elements of different crimes.

even if Ed never told Sam the television was stolen. Sam should have known they were stolen.

Today, a number of states have classified embezzlement, fraud, extortion, and receiving stolen property under a general law against theft. Others retain them as separate laws against stealing.

FOR DISCUSSION

1. The penalties for these forms of stealing in every state are increasingly harsh: *Theft — Burglary — Robbery — Armed Robbery* If a wallet containing only $20 is stolen in each of these cases, why do you think the punishments get harsher? Is this fair? Explain.

2. What is the difference between robbery and extortion? Between larceny and embezzlement?

3. Why do you think states outlaw receiving stolen property? Do you think they should? Explain.

4. Do you think a robber who uses a realistic-looking toy gun should be charged with armed robbery? Why or why not?

ACTIVITY

What's the Crime?

In this activity, students analyze a hypothetical to determine what crimes have been committed.

1. Divide into pairs.
2. Each pair should:
   a. Read **Thievesville, U.S.A.**, below.
   b. Imagine that the state in which Thievesville, U.S.A., is located has laws against **larceny**, **burglary**, **robbery**, **armed robbery**, **embezzlement**, **fraud**, **extortion**, and **receiving stolen property**.
   c. Determine which of these crimes, if any, each person committed. Review the article for information on each crime.
   d. Write down the offender, which law the offender broke, and why.
   e. Prepare to report the answers to the whole class.
3. The pairs should report, and the class should discuss the answers.

Thievesville, U.S.A.

Amy, Bob, Carol, Dave, Eden, Frank, and Gina all live in separate houses in the same neighborhood. Determine which laws, if any, each of these persons broke.

Early every morning Amy goes from house to house stealing newspapers. She gets about 20 every day.

She takes them to the corner newsstand run by Bob and sells them to him for a nickel apiece.

She takes the dollar she earns and deposits it in the bank. She always goes to her favorite teller, Carol. Carol has a policy of taking 5 cents of every deposit for herself. She only makes a few dollars a day (all in nickels), but over the years the money has added up to $1,200. She doesn't dare put it in the bank. She keeps it at home under her mattress.

One day Dave is out searching for his newspaper when he sees that Carol has left one of her bedroom windows open. He seizes the opportunity, crawls in, finds the bulging mattress, and steals her money.

As Dave crawls out the window, Eden sees him. She writes Dave a note, "I saw you. If you don't pay me $1,000, I'll tell the police."

Dave thinks he better pay Eden off. Late at night, he takes $1,000, puts it in a bag, and walks toward Eden's house. But Frank is lurking in the bushes. Frank sneaks behind Dave and jabs his finger in Dave's back, saying, "I've got a gun. Just drop the bag on the ground and leave. Don't turn around." Dave does as he's told.

When Dave gets home, he realizes he has to raise some cash fast to pay off Eden. He calls his neighbor Gina, who he's heard is an investment wizard. He tells her he only has $200 and needs $1,000 soon. She says, "No problem. I've got an investment paying 5–1, guaranteed. It's a sure thing." Dave gives Gina $200. She puts it with all the other "investments" she's received recently and flies to Rio to live where none of her "investors" can find her.

Inchoate Crimes

inchoate (in KŌ it) adj. Incomplete, in the beginning stages. From the Latin word "incohare," to begin.

Imagine that Sylvia plans a bank robbery and assembles a team to commit it. According to plan, Greg drives John to the bank. John enters the bank, armed with a gun, and robs the bank. When he leaves, Greg drives them away. They will meet with Sylvia later. Who can be charged with bank robbery?

Under the common law, the answer was John and Greg. John would be the **principal in the first degree**, the person who carried out the crime. Greg would be the **principal in the second degree**, who was at or near the crime scene and helped commit the crime. Sylvia would be charged with the inchoate, or incomplete, crime of **accessory before the fact**, because she didn't take part at the crime scene but helped prepare for the crime.

Today, in most jurisdictions, these distinctions are gone. All three would be charged with bank robbery. John is the principal, and Sylvia and Greg are his accomplices. An accomplice is someone who aids another in committing a crime. The person may help before the crime, for example, by planning the crime. Or the person may help during the crime, for example, by driving the get-away car.

An accomplice is just as guilty of committing the crime as the principal, the person who actually carries out the crime. The U.S. Code reads: "Whoever commits an offense against the United States or aids, abets, counsels, commands, induces or procures its commission, is punishable as a principal."

Most states have adopted similar laws. The inchoate crime of accessory before the fact has disappeared in most states. But other inchoate crimes still exist.

Accessory After the Fact

An accessory after the fact is someone who helps a felon after the crime has been committed. Imagine that right after the bank robbery, Greg swings by David's house, and asks David to store the money bags for him. Greg then goes to Bill and asks if he can hide out at his house. If David or Bill agrees, they can be accessories after the fact.

Several things must be proven for the crime of being an accessory after the fact. First,

In 2005, rapper Lil' Kim was tried for conspiracy, perjury, and obstruction of justice for lying to a federal grand jury about what she knew about her friends' involvement in a shootout. She was convicted of conspiracy and perjury, but acquitted of obstruction of justice.

the defendant must help the criminal avoid getting caught or convicted. Second, the felony must have already been committed. The defendant must help Greg *after* the bank robbery. (If it is before, the person may be an accomplice to the crime.) Third, the defendant must know about the crime and intentionally help the criminal.

Attempt

An attempt is an inchoate crime consisting of three elements. First, a person must intend to commit a crime. Second, the person must take steps toward committing the crime. Third, the person must not actually commit the crime.

Imagine that Hugo sees Chuck leave his bicycle unlocked. When he grabs the bike, Chuck's friend Phil stops him from taking it. To convict Hugo of attempted theft, it must be shown that he intended to take the bike and not give it back. This is the intent required for theft. The second and third elements, that he took steps to steal the bike and that he failed to steal it, are clear in this case.

The law of attempt raises many questions. One is how close the person must go toward committing the crime. The common law rule was that the person must have done everything he could to commit the crime. The reason the person did not commit the crime was out of his control. Most courts today require far less. Some ask: Would a reasonable person, seeing what the accused did, believe he was trying to commit a crime? Others require that the person took a "substantial step toward committing the crime." Still others require that the accused's actions strongly corroborate his "criminal purpose."

Another question involves impossibility. Is it attempted murder if a man points a gun at another's head, pulls the trigger, and then discovers the gun is unloaded? Is it attempted smuggling if a woman takes baby powder, which she wrongly believes is cocaine, and carries it into the United States? What if instead of "cocaine," she carries coffee in the mistaken belief it is also against the law? Questions such as these have perplexed courts and led to different conclusions.

Courts often look to the purpose of attempt laws when deciding difficult cases. The major purpose of attempt laws is to prevent crime. People disposed to commit crime pose a danger. Letting the police act before a crime is committed can prevent much harm. Punishing those who try and fail to commit a crime recognizes that these people have tried once and may try again.

In addition to attempt laws, most states have passed specific laws aimed at people preparing to commit crimes. For example, most states outlaw the possession of explosive devices, burglary tools, and master keys to vehicles.

Conspiracy

Another inchoate crime is conspiracy. A conspiracy is an agreement between two or more people to commit a crime. Like other crimes, it has an act and intent requirement.

The act is the agreement. Some jurisdictions also require that at least one of the conspirators do an overt act in furtherance of the conspiracy. Thus if John and Mary agree to kidnap Sally, some jurisdictions also require an overt act. For example, John may send Mary an e-mail telling her when Sally leaves for work and comes home. This is enough to qualify as an overt act. Unlike attempt, conspiracy does not require a substantial step toward committing the crime.

The intent required for conspiracy consists of two things. First, the conspirators must understand what they are agreeing to. Second, the conspirators' purpose must be to achieve the goal of committing the crime.

Like attempt laws, one purpose of conspiracy laws is to punish people disposed to commit crimes. Another, more important purpose is to punish criminal enterprises. In the 1961 case of *Callanan v. U.S.*, the U.S. Supreme Court explained why criminal conspiracies are so dangerous:

[C]ollective criminal agreement — partnership in crime — presents a greater potential threat to the public than individual delicts [offenses]. Concerted action both increases the likelihood that the criminal object will be successfully attained and decreases the probability that the individuals involved will depart from their path of criminality. Group association for criminal purposes often, if not normally, makes possible the attainment of ends more complex than those which one criminal could accomplish. Nor is the danger of a conspiratorial group limited to the particular end toward which it has embarked. Combination in crime makes more likely the commission of crimes unrelated to the original purpose for which the group was formed. In sum, the danger which a conspiracy generates is not confined to the substantive offense which is the immediate aim of the enterprise.

In 1970, the federal government passed an important conspiracy law aimed at curbing organized crime. RICO, the Racketeer Influenced and Corrupt Organizations Act of 1970, makes it illegal for anyone

employed by or associated with any enterprise . . . to conduct or participate, directly or indirectly, in the conduct of such enterprise's affairs through a pattern of racketeering activity . . . .

In other words, the person must be connected to an "enterprise." The enterprise may be a criminal organization, or it may be a legitimate organization. (Lawmakers were particularly concerned about organized crime infiltrating legitimate businesses.) The person must conduct the enterprise's affairs through a "pattern of racketeering." For a pattern to exist, the person must commit at least two crimes related to racketeering within a 10-year period. The act lists a number of crimes related to racketeering. Among them are kidnapping, gambling, arson, robbery, bribery, extortion, dealing in obscenity, drug trafficking, counterfeiting, embezzlement, fraud, obstruction of justice, and human trafficking. The crimes must be related to one another and pose a threat of continued criminal activity.

A defendant convicted under RICO stands to serve a long prison term, pay a large fine, and lose his interest in the enterprise and all his ill-gotten gains (which are forfeited to the government).

Federal prosecutors strongly favor RICO. They believe it has put a dent in organized crime. Critics see RICO as unnecessary. If someone commits crimes, that person can be prosecuted under other laws for those crimes. If the crimes happen to be part of a criminal enterprise, the persons in the criminal enterprise can be (and often are) prosecuted under existing conspiracy laws.

Others criticize RICO as federalizing law enforcement. They believe most of the crimes prosecuted under RICO should be left to state and local authorities.

Solicitation

Imagine that Harry wants to rob a bank, but does not want to carry it out himself. He tells Jill he will plan the robbery if she will go to the bank with a gun. Let's look at several possibilities:

a. Jill agrees and is caught as she enters the bank. Jill and Harry are guilty of attempted bank robbery (and conspiracy to rob a bank).

b. Jill agrees and stakes out the bank. Jill and Harry are guilty of conspiracy to rob a bank.

c. Jill agrees, and she robs the bank. Jill and Harry are guilty of bank robbery (and conspiracy to rob a bank).

d. Jill refuses. Jill is innocent, but Harry is guilty of solicitation.

Solicitation is an inchoate crime that consists of asking, ordering, or encouraging another to commit a crime. The person making the solicitation must intend that the other person commit the crime.

The Doctrine of Inchoate Crimes

The following four general rules, known as the doctrine of inchoate crimes, apply to the inchoate crimes discussed (attempt, conspiracy, accessory after the fact, and solicitation):

1. **To commit an inchoate crime, a person must do something.** Thinking about committing the crime is not enough. Attempt requires the most action: a substantial step toward actually committing the crime. Solicitation requires the least: a request that a crime be committed. Conspiracy requires just a little more: an agreement and an overt act.

2. **Inchoate crimes require intent.** Conspiracy and attempt require the intent to do the crime. Solicitation requires the intent to have someone else do it. Accessory after the fact requires the intent to aid and abet the crime.

3. **With the exception of conspiracy, people cannot be convicted of an inchoate crime if they are convicted of the actual crime.** For example, John helps Lou rob a bank and hide out. If John is convicted of the bank robbery, he cannot be convicted of being an accessory after the fact in the same robbery. He can, however, be convicted of bank robbery and conspiracy to commit bank robbery.

4. **Inchoate crimes usually carry lesser penalties than those for the actual crime.** In some cases, however, they carry the same penalty.

FOR DISCUSSION

1. What are inchoate crimes? How do they differ from most crimes? Explain.

2. What crimes have people in the boldface type committed in the examples below?

   a. **Sam, Pam**, and **Cam** agreed on a plan to rob a bank and split their take among the three of them. Cam scouted the bank to determine the best way to rob it.

   b. After shooting a man, Alan ran to Herman's house and told him what he had done. **Herman** hid Alan's gun in his house.

   c. **Robin** decided to kill Chester. Police caught her as she was planting a bomb in his car.

   d. **Roy** offered Michael $10,000 to kill David. Michael turned him down.

e. **Susan** worked in a warehouse. When she left one night, she turned off the burglar alarm, which allowed her boyfriend to enter the building and steal thousands of dollars worth of goods.

3. Do you think accomplices should be treated as having committed the crime? Or do the old common-law distinctions make sense? Explain.

4. In your opinion, which of the following people has committed the worse crime? Why?
   a. Sam intends to burn down a house but is stopped by police just before he starts the fire.
   b. Jane carelessly throws away her cigarette into a yard and accidentally burns down a house.

5. Wilma, Xavier, Yolanda, and Zeno agree to and do rob several banks. They are charged with three counts of bank robbery. Do you think they should be charged with one or three counts of conspiracy to rob a bank? Explain.

6. Imagine that Ann and Betty, the only conspirators, are charged with conspiring to rob a bank. Can the jury convict Ann but not Betty of conspiracy? Explain.

7. Under the Model Penal Code, a person convicted of attempt receives the same punishment as a person who completed the same crime. Do you think this should be the law in your state? Explain.

ACTIVITY

An Attempt or Not?

States typically do not write an attempt law into every crime. Rather, they craft one law of attempt that applies to all crimes. Because the one law must fit many different crimes, the law is usually quite general. The courts decide how it applies to specific crimes. For example, below is Georgia's law on criminal attempt:

Georgia Code: Crimes and Offenses: 16-4-1. Criminal attempt. A person commits the offense of criminal attempt when, with intent to commit a specific crime, he performs any act which constitutes a substantial step toward the commission of that crime.

In this activity, students act as judges, decide six cases, and determine whether each amounts to an attempt under Georgia law.

1. Form groups of three or five students.
2. Each group should:
   a. Read and discuss each case below.
   b. Using the reading on attempt, decide whether or not each case is an attempt.
   c. Be prepared to report to the class its decisions and reasons for them.
3. The groups should report and the class should discuss each case.

CASE 1: Staples. Edmund Staples planned to break into a bank and steal its money. He rented an office in the same building as the bank, but a floor above. He knew that the bank's vault was directly below his office. He brought in drilling tools, acetylene gas tanks, and a blow torch, and on Saturday when he knew no one was going to be in the bank, he drilled holes in the floor. But he did not drill all the way through. Instead he stopped, realizing that his idea of robbing a bank was absurd. He returned periodically to the office with the intent to finish the heist, but he changed his mind every time. Eventually, the landlord became suspicious, went into the office, saw the holes, and called the police. Staples was arrested and charged with attempted burglary of the bank. (*California v. Staples*, 1970)

CASE 2: Mandujano. Undercover police officer Cavalier met Roy Mandujano in a bar. Pretending to be a drug trafficker, Cavalier asked him for a one-ounce sample of heroin. Mandujano agreed to supply a sample, but said his regular drug shipment had not yet arrived,

(Continued on next page.)

so he needed $650 to buy it from another source. Cavalier supplied the money, and Mandujano went off while Cavalier waited at the bar. Mandujano eventually returned empty-handed, stating he couldn't find his contact. He returned Cavalier's money and told him to call him back at 6 p.m. when his regular shipment was due. When Cavalier called back, Mandujano did not answer. Mandujano was later arrested and charged with attempt to distribute heroin. (*U.S. v. Mandujano*, 1974)

CASE 3: Kordas. Police received a Harley-Davidson motorcycle "for educational purposes." They altered its vehicle identification number and other things to make the motorcycle appear stolen. Working undercover, a police officer then sold the motorcycle to Michel Kordas, who believed it was stolen. Kordas put the motorcycle in his van and drove away. Police arrested Kordas and charged him with attempt to receive stolen property. (*Wisconsin v. Kordas*, 1995)

CASE 4: Rizzo. Charles Rizzo and three other men were planning on robbing a bank employee who was supposed to be carrying a company's payroll worth $1,200 from the bank to the company. Rizzo was to identify the bank employee, and the others were to hold him up. The day of the robbery, the four men drove from the bank to the different locations of the company, looking for the bank employee. Rizzo never spotted the bank employee. By the time the men reached their last stop, the police were following them. When Rizzo went inside to see if the bank employee was there, the police arrested him. He and the others were charged with attempted robbery. (*New York v. Rizzo*, 1927)

CASE 5: Wilson. Wilson had a check for $2.50. The check was stamped with the words "Ten Dollars or Less." Even so, instead of depositing the check as is, Wilson wrote a "1" in front of the "2.50" and tried to pass it off as $12.50. Wilson was charged with attempt to commit forgery. (*Wilson v. Mississippi*, 1905)

CASE 6: Jackson. Vanessa Hodges, Robert Jackson, and two others planned to rob a bank. They planned to enter the bank when it opened on Monday, grab the weekend deposits, and leave. On the day of the robbery, the group drove to the bank, but arrived late. The bank was already open and filled with too many bank patrons and other potential witnesses. The group decided to rob the bank the following week. A day or two later, however, Hodges was arrested on unrelated charges and revealed the group's plan to the police. In response, FBI agents staked out the bank. When the group (minus Hodges) arrived, one of the members spotted an FBI agent, and the car left the scene. FBI agents pursued and arrested the group. Inside the car, agents found a suitcase with guns and masks. One of the charges against members of the group was attempted bank robbery. (*U.S. v. Jackson*, 1977)

A major political scandal followed the 1972 break-in at Democratic headquarters in the Watergate Office Complex in Washington, DC. The insert shows President Nixon at right and from left to right his aides H.R. Haldeman, Dwight Chapin, and John Ehrlichman. The main scandal involved attempts to cover up what happened through perjury and obstruction of justice.

Crimes Against the Justice System

Though the bribe be small, yet the fault is great.
– Edward Coke (1552–1634), English judge, politician, and legal scholar, *Third Institute*

The criminal justice system trusts police officers, attorneys, judges, jurors, witnesses, and other officials to act honestly and without improper interference from others. It has laws to punish those who act to betray that trust.

Contempt of Court

Courts have long had the power to cite people for contempt when they show disrespect, disrupt the courtroom, or fail to follow a court order. Contempt can be civil or criminal.

Civil contempt normally involves court orders. The court may, for example, order a party to pay alimony or to turn over evidence. If the party refuses, the court may hold the person in contempt. This may mean the court will fine the person for each day the person fails to comply. Or the court may jail the person until the person complies with the order. The purpose of civil contempt is not to punish the person but to get the person to follow the court order.

When people are jailed for civil contempt, they usually quickly agree to comply with the court order, but not always. In 1992, a divorce court in Pennsylvania ordered H. Beatty Chadwick to turn over $2.5 million. He refused and fled. When he was caught in 1995, he was jailed for civil contempt. He could have gotten out of jail by turning over the money, but he refused to do so. In 2002, he asked a federal appeals court to order his release. In *Chadwick v. Janecka*, the court ruled that his detention did not violate the U.S. Constitution:

> Because the state courts have repeatedly found that Mr. Chadwick has the present ability to comply with the July 1994 state court order, we cannot disturb the state courts' decision that there is no federal constitutional bar to Mr. Chadwick's indefinite confinement for civil contempt so long as he retains the ability to comply with the order requiring him to pay over the money at issue.

Chadwick was not freed until 2009, when a Pennsylvania court ruled that holding him in jail any longer would not serve any purpose.

Unlike civil contempt, criminal contempt is a crime, and its purpose is to punish those who disrupt or attack the integrity of the courts. The U.S. Code declares that federal courts have the "power to punish by fine or imprisonment, or both" the following:

(1) Misbehavior of any person in its presence or so near thereto as to obstruct the administration of justice;
(2) Misbehavior of any of its officers in their official transactions;
(3) Disobedience or resistance to its lawful writ, process, order, rule, decree, or command.

States also have laws against criminal contempt. For example, article 215 of the New York Penal Code goes on for more than a page listing acts that amount to criminal contempt of court. Among them are "disorderly, contemptuous, or insolent behavior," "refusal to be sworn as a witness," refusing to answer questions, and "disobedience or resistance to the lawful process."

Probably the most famous cases of criminal contempt occurred at the 1969–70 "Chicago Seven" trial. At the height of the Vietnam War, rioting had broken out on the streets of Chicago during the Democratic National Convention of 1968. The seven (initially eight) defendants were charged with conspiracy and intent to start a riot. During the federal trial, the defendants engaged in acts of silliness (e.g., blowing kisses to the jury, wearing judicial robes to court), disrespect (e.g., not standing when the judge entered), and outright hostility (e.g., yelling insults at the judge). While the jury was deliberating, the judge found the defendants and their two lawyers guilty of 159 counts of criminal contempt and sentenced them to years in prison. On appeal, the contempt convictions were reversed. The appeals court agreed that a judge had the power to punish a person on the spot for criminal contempt committed in the judge's presence. But the court held that because these sentences were longer than six months, the defendants deserved a jury trial on the contempt charges.

Perjury

Another crime important to the criminal justice system is perjury. Imagine Peter is on trial for robbing a liquor store. Peter's wife, Judith, takes the stand and tells the jury that on the night of the robbery, Peter was home watching a movie with her. Judith is lying. Peter was not at home that evening, but believing that Peter would never commit robbery, she wants to be Peter's alibi to prevent a conviction.

By lying under oath, Judith has committed perjury. All states and the federal government have laws against perjury. Under the U.S. Code, perjury occurs when a person takes an oath in cases that "a law of the United States authorizes an oath to be administered" and willfully makes statements that he believes or knows to be untrue.

The U.S. Supreme Court in the 1973 case of *Bronston v. U.S.* addressed the question of whether misleading, evasive, or unresponsive testimony can amount to perjury if the statements themselves are factually true. Samuel Bronston, the owner of a movie production company, was testifying in his company's bankruptcy case. He was asked these questions:

Q. Do you have any bank accounts in Swiss banks, Mr. Bronston?
A. No, sir.
Q. Have you ever?
A. The company had an account there for about six months, in Zurich.

The issue surrounded his answer to the second question. The answer was true, but it failed to fully answer the question. It was later discovered that Bronston had maintained a large personal Swiss account, which was closed before he testified. Prosecutors believed that Bronston's answer to the second question, though factually true, was intentionally misleading. Bronston was tried and convicted of perjury.

A unanimous Supreme Court reversed Bronston's perjury conviction. The court held that the perjury statute did not cover evasive truthful answers. When a witness evades answering, the lawyer should ask specific questions. The perjury statute cannot be invoked

> simply because a wily witness succeeds in derailing the questioner — so long as the witness speaks the literal truth. The burden is on the questioner to pin the witness down to the specific object of the questioner's inquiry. If a witness evades, it is the lawyer's responsibility to recognize the evasion and to bring the witness back to the mark, to flush out the whole truth with the tools of adversary examination.

A related crime is the **subornation of perjury**. Returning to our example of Peter and Judith, imagine that Peter had asked Judith to lie. By persuading Judith to commit perjury, Peter has committed subornation of perjury. Under the U.S. Code, a person can be convicted of suborning perjury if he persuades another

1950: Alger Hiss. This State Department official was tried and convicted of perjury for statements he made under oath to the House Un-American Activities Committee, which was investigating allegations of espionage.

1975: Watergate Scandal. During the 1972 presidential election, police caught burglars connected to the Committee to Re-Elect President Nixon trying to enter the Democratic National Committee's headquarters. An investigation ensued, and a number of high-ranking members of the Nixon administration were convicted of trying to obstruct the investigation. Among those convicted of perjury were former Attorney General **John Mitchell**, Assistant to the President **John Ehrlichman**, and several others.

1977: Richard Helms. As director of the CIA from 1966 to 1973, he honored a request from President Nixon to support a military coup against Chilean President Salvador Allende. During the public hearings before Congress, he denied the CIA's involvement in the covert operations. He was convicted of perjury.

1987: Michael Deaver. President Reagan's former deputy chief of staff, Deaver was convicted of perjury for statements he made under oath to Congress and to a federal grand jury investigating his lobbying with the administration.

2002: Chris Webber. This NBA player was charged with lying to a grand jury about receiving money from a University of Michigan basketball program booster. Webber pleaded guilty to one count of criminal contempt for lying.

2005: Lil' Kim. The rapper was convicted of three counts of conspiracy and one count of perjury for lying to a federal grand jury about her friends' involvement in a 2001 shooting outside a radio station in New York City.

2007: Lewis Libby. A former adviser to Vice President Dick Cheney, Libby was convicted of two counts of perjury, one count of obstruction of justice in a grand jury investigation, and one count of making a false statement to federal investigators for his involvement in leaking the identity of a CIA operative.

2011–2012: Major League Baseball Steroid Scandal. Two star players were charged with perjury in the recent scandal over the use of steroids. **Barry Bonds** was charged for his testimony before a federal grand jury. The jury deadlocked on the perjury charge, but convicted him of obstruction of justice. **Roger Clemens** faced six felony counts involving perjury, false statements, and obstruction for testimony he made before Congress. A mistrial was declared in his first trial, but a jury acquitted him of all charges when he was retried.

person to perjure herself and she actually commits perjury.

In 1934, Congress passed the False Statements Act, which created a new perjury-like federal crime. As amended in Title 18, § 1001 of the U.S. Code, the act currently makes it a crime to lie to the FBI and certain representatives of other government agencies even if the person making the statement did not take an oath.

Perjury laws and the False Statements Act require that the falsehood be "material." A statement is material if it has any tendency to influence or sway the outcome of a case. Thus someone lying about his age would not be material unless the person's age was important to the case.

Witness Tampering

Imagine that Kendall, an eyewitness to a murder, is set to testify against the alleged murderer. Since cooperating with the investigator, Kendall has been receiving anonymous phone calls and letters, threatening her if she testifies.

The anonymous caller has committed witness tampering, which is against federal and state law. For example, the U.S. Code outlaws, among other things, using physical force or the threat of physical force to get a witness not to testify.

In a 2009 federal case, Robert Simels, a prominent defense attorney, was convicted of witness tampering. Simels was recorded telling a government informant that he wanted to "eliminate" or "neutralize" witnesses against his drug kingpin client (who was also convicted of witness tampering and drug charges). Simels was sentenced to 14 years in prison.

Jury Tampering

Imagine that Gary and Leon, attorneys for a defendant being tried for murder, stood outside the courtroom when the trial broke for lunch. Knowing that they were in the presence of jurors, Gary and Leon discussed evidence showing that their client was not at the crime scene on the morning of the murder. Have Gary and Leon done anything wrong?

All states and the federal government have laws against jury tampering. Similar to witness tampering, jury tampering can occur in various manners. The U.S. Code forbids anyone who "corruptly, or by threats or force, or by any threatening letter or communication, endeavors to influence, intimidate, or impede any grand or petite" jurors from carrying out their duties. It also outlaws any acts that are intended to "influence, obstruct, or impede, the due administration of justice," such as influencing the outcome of a jury trial by deliberately disseminating information within the earshot of the jurors, (as in the case of Leon and Gary).

Obstruction of Justice

Black's Law Dictionary defines obstruction of justice as any "interference with the orderly administration of law and justice." This means that obstruction of justice can encompass many of the crimes we have already discussed. In fact, jury tampering and witness tampering are in the part of the U.S. Code titled "Obstruction of Justice." This part of the code lists specific acts as obstruction of justice, such as stealing court records. Aside from these specific acts, this part of the U.S. Code also has what is known as an "omnibus clause." This clause punishes anyone who "corruptly . . . influences, obstructs, or impedes, or endeavors to influence, obstruct, or impede, the due administration of justice." According to a federal court,

> The omnibus clause was intended to ensure that criminals could not circumvent the law's purpose by devising novel and creative schemes that would interfere with the administration of justice but would nonetheless fall outside the scope of . . . [the law's] specific prohibitions. (*U.S. v. Tackett*, 1997)

To prove obstruction of justice under the omnibus clause, the government must establish that (1) a judicial proceeding is pending,

WITNESS PROTECTION PROGRAMS

An intimidated witness must make a difficult decision. The witness can refuse to testify and face contempt of court or even obstruction of justice charges. Or, the witness can choose to testify and risk being harmed or killed. The police can provide temporary protection, which is normally all that is necessary. Witness intimidation usually ends once the witness testifies. But in some cases, more permanent protection may be needed. A witness protection program can meet this need.

Set up by the Organized Crime Control Act of 1970, the federal witness protection program provides protection for witnesses of serious or organized crimes. Witnesses and their families are relocated, given new identities, and provided housing, medical care, basic living expenses, and employment training. The program allows witnesses to testify and be safe. In exchange, however, the witnesses must give up their existing lives and move, cutting off contact with friends and loved ones. The U.S. Marshals Service runs the program.

Several states also offer their own witness protection programs. The California witness protection program, for example, reimburses local police departments for expenses incurred in protecting and relocating witnesses. It has spent more than $10 million protecting witnesses in recent years.

(2) the defendant knows about the judicial proceeding, and (3) the defendant acted in such a way intending to corruptly influence or impede the proceeding. Notice that the person does not have to succeed in influencing the case.

People have been convicted under the omnibus clause for hiding witnesses and altering, destroying, or hiding evidence. More controversial have been convictions for evasive testimony. In 2011, baseball player Barry Bonds was tried for perjury and giving evasive testimony to a grand jury investigating steroid use. A jury could not agree on the perjury charges, but did convict him of obstruction of justice under the omnibus clause for his evasive testimony. Below is Bond's evasive testimony. It is an answer to a question about his trainer, Greg Anderson.

> Q. Did Greg ever give you anything that required a syringe to inject yourself with?
>
> A. I've only had one doctor touch me. And that's my only personal doctor. Greg, like I said, we don't get into each others' personal lives. We're friends, but I don't — we don't sit around and talk baseball, because he knows I don't want — don't come to my house talking baseball. If you want to come to my house and talk about fishing, some other stuff, we'll be good friends. You come around talking about baseball, you go on. I don't talk about his business. You know what I mean?

Bribery

A final crime important in protecting the criminal justice system is bribery. According to Black's Law Dictionary, bribery occurs when a person gives something of value, such as gifts or money, to public officials with the intention of influencing such officials. The crime includes those offering the bribe as well as those receiving it. In the criminal justice system, bribery cases can involve judges, jurors, witnesses, police, lawyers, and others.

Below is a sampling of recent bribery cases:

- In March 2011, a Texas judge pleaded guilty in federal court to receiving $257,300 in bribes to secure favorable rulings. One bribe kept a child molester on the streets.

- In separate cases in 2011, three Memphis, Tennessee, police officers pleaded guilty in federal court to receiving thousands of dollars in bribes from nightclub owners to warn them of undercover investigations.
- In April 2010 in Colorado, a juror returned to his seat in the jury box and found a note that said, "Please don't find me guilty. I will pay $5,000. I am very frightened. Please don't give this to anyone." The defendant disappeared, and a warrant for her arrest has been issued for attempting to bribe a juror.

To establish a bribery case, the government must prove that the person offering the bribe intended to influence an official action. The government does not have to prove that the official accepted the bribe. (In some states, if the bribe is not accepted, then the person is only guilty of attempted bribery.) In the case of the person receiving the bribe, the government must show that person took it with the "corrupt intent" of it influencing the person's public duty.

States have enacted similar laws against bribery. A few states have separate laws for those offering the bribe and those receiving the bribe.

FOR DISCUSSION

1. Courts often say that a person held in civil contempt "has the keys to the cell." What does this mean? Do you agree with the federal court's decision in *Chadwick v. Janecka*? Explain. What is the difference between civil and criminal contempt? Which do you think is the better remedy?
2. What is obstruction of justice? Do you think Barry Bonds should have been convicted of obstruction of justice for the statement he made? Explain.
3. What are perjury and subornation of perjury? Do you agree with the Supreme Court's decision in *Bronston v. U.S.*? Explain. Do you think lying to an FBI agent should be a crime?
4. If you witnessed a violent gang crime and were called to testify, what fears would you have? Would you accept an offer to go into the witness protection program? Explain.
5. What is the purpose of all the laws discussed in this article? Which of these laws do you think is the most important in upholding this purpose?

Section 1001

The federal crime of lying to federal officials is the newest and most controversial of the crimes against the justice system. Unlike perjury, this crime does not require that the person made the statement under oath. Below is the statute.

18 U.S. Code § 1001. Statements or entries generally

(a) . . . [W]hoever, in any matter within the jurisdiction of the executive, legislative, or judicial branch of the Government of the United States, knowingly and willfully — . . . (2) makes any materially false, fictitious, or fraudulent statement or representation; . . . shall be fined under this title, imprisoned not more than 5 years . . . , or both.

In this activity, students role play appeals courts and decide some actual cases dealing with this statute.

1. Divide into small groups.
2. Each group should:
   a. Read and discuss each of the three cases, below.
   b. Decide whether each defendant is guilty under the statute.
   c. Be prepared to report its decisions and reasons for them to the class.
3. Ask the groups to report their decisions. Hold a discussion on each case.

Brogan. Brogan was an officer in the union representing the employees of JRD Management Corporation. Investigating Brogan for taking bribes, FBI agents knocked on his door and asked him if he had ever accepted cash or gifts from the company. Brogan lied and denied doing so. Brogan was later convicted of bribery and of violating § 1001 by lying to the agents. On appeal, Brogan argued that Congress did not intend § 1001 to apply to a simple denial of guilt. (*Brogan v. U.S.*, 1998)

Turner. Turner directed the Division of Physical Services in Illinois from 1999 to 2005. During that time, Turner actively covered up that three of his employees were falsifying their time cards and getting paid for time that they didn't work. Eventually, the FBI investigated and persuaded one employee to turn over recorded conversations and other evidence. Acting on this evidence, FBI agents asked Turner if he had been covering for these employees, Turner denied any coverup, and even after recorded conversations were played for him, he still denied the allegations. Turner was convicted of embezzlement and violating 18 U.S.C. § 1001. On appeal, Turner argued that because the FBI already knew that he participated, his denial was not material, as it could not persuade the agents conducting the investigation, and therefore he was not guilty of violating § 1001. (*U.S. v. Turner*, 2008)

Yermian. Working for a defense contractor, Yermian needed access to classified information to do a particular job for the contractor. He was required to fill out a security questionnaire provided by the Department of Defense to obtain a security clearance. In response to a question about whether he had ever been charged with any crime, Yermian did not mention that he had been convicted of mail fraud. He was charged with violating § 1001. At trial, Yermian argued that he thought the questionnaire was going to his employer, not the federal government. The trial court ruled it was irrelevant whether he knew it was going to the federal government. Yermian appealed, claiming § 1001 required such knowledge. (*U.S. v. Yermian*, 1984)

Hate Crimes

In our culture, cross burning has almost invariably meant lawlessness and understandably instills in its victims well-grounded fear of physical violence.

– Clarence Thomas, U.S. Supreme Court justice, dissenting in *Virginia v. Black* (2003)

- In 2010, two young men in Pennsylvania were convicted of beating an illegal immigrant to death. While beating him, they repeatedly yelled at him, "This is America. Go back to Mexico."
- In 2009, a white supremacist and Holocaust denier went to the U.S. Holocaust Memorial Museum in Washington, D.C., and opened fire with a rifle, killing a security guard.
- On Election Night 2008, four men in New York City, angry at the election of Barack Obama as president, went on a rampage against people of color. They beat a teenage Muslim with a pipe and bat, assaulted a mentally disabled man, and ran down with their car a white man who they mistakenly believed was black.

Each of these brutal crimes had one thing in common: They were motivated by hate. These incidents and others around the country have drawn increased attention to the problem of hate crimes.

Currently the federal government and 45 states have hate-crime laws. Some of these laws define a hate crime as any crime committed against a person or a person's property motivated because of the person's race, religion, nationality, or ethnicity. Others also prosecute crimes motivated by bias against gender, sexual orientation, and disability as hate crimes.

In 2010, according to the FBI's Uniform Crime Reports, almost 8,000 hate crimes were reported around the United States. About half were motivated by racial bias. Prejudice against religion, sexual orientation, and ethnicity or nationality accounted for about 1,000 incidents apiece. Crimes against persons, such as assault or threats and intimidation, made up about 60 percent of the reported offenses. Most of the remaining incidents were property crimes, particularly vandalism.

It is difficult to accurately compare one year with another or to study trends in hate crimes. The federal government has only been collecting statistics on these crimes since 1991. Some places do not report hate crimes as a separate type of crime, but each year more agencies have started reporting them. From 1995 to 2008, hate-crime reports increased substantially. In 2009, reports dropped slightly and remained about the same in 2010. A lively debate exists over the trend in hate crimes.

R.A.V. v. City of St. Paul (1992)

Some critics of hate-crime legislation argue that these laws violate the First Amendment's protection of free speech. This amendment gives every American the right to express opinions or hold ideas even if they are racist or bigoted. On several occasions, the U.S. Supreme Court has been asked to determine whether hate-crime laws violate the Constitution.

In 1989, St. Paul, Minnesota, passed a city ordinance making it a crime to place on public or private land a hate symbol, such as a burning cross or Nazi swastika. About a year later,

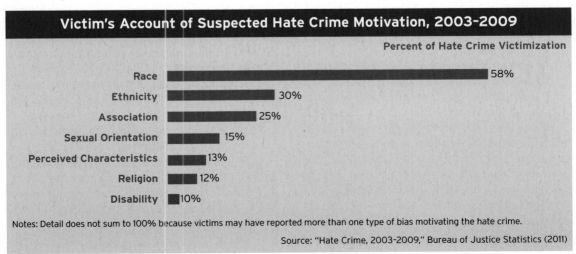

Victim's Account of Suspected Hate Crime Motivation, 2003-2009

Percent of Hate Crime Victimization

- Race: 58%
- Ethnicity: 30%
- Association: 25%
- Sexual Orientation: 15%
- Perceived Characteristics: 13%
- Religion: 12%
- Disability: 10%

Notes: Detail does not sum to 100% because victims may have reported more than one type of bias motivating the hate crime.

Source: "Hate Crime, 2003-2009," Bureau of Justice Statistics (2011) police arrested a group of white juveniles for a series of cross burnings. In one instance, the youths taped chair legs together into a crude cross and set it ablaze inside the fenced yard of a black family.

In an appeal that reached the U.S. Supreme Court, attorneys for the juvenile defendants argued that the St. Paul law violated the First Amendment. The city responded that by prohibiting such acts as cross burnings, the ordinance served "a compelling governmental interest" to protect the community against hate-motivated threats.

In June 1992, a unanimous Supreme Court agreed with the juvenile defendants. Writing the opinion for the court, Justice Antonin Scalia stated that although government may outlaw activities that present a danger to the community, it may not outlaw them simply because they express ideas that most people or the government find despicable.

Scalia also pointed out that other laws existed to control and punish such acts as cross burnings. In this case, the city could have prosecuted the juvenile offenders under laws against trespassing, arson, vandalism, and terrorism. (*R.A.V. v. City of St. Paul*)

Virginia v. Black (2003)

In 2003, the Supreme Court decided a case involving a Virginia law against cross burning. The law made it a felony "for any person . . . , with the intent of intimidating any person or group . . . , to burn . . . a cross on the property of another, a highway or other public place." It further stated: "Any such burning . . . shall be prima facie evidence of an intent to intimidate a person or group." (This meant that if the prosecution proved the defendant burned a cross, the prosecution had shown that the defendant intended to intimidate a person or group. The defense would have to bring evidence proving otherwise.)

The court considered together the cases of three defendants convicted under the Virginia law. One defendant was Barry Black. Leading a Ku Klux Klan rally of about 30 people, Black burned a cross. The rally was on private property, was held with the permission of the landowner, and was relatively isolated. It took place about 300 to 350 yards from a highway.

The other two defendants were Richard Elliott and Jonathan O'Mara. They had driven a truck onto the property of an African-American family, put up a cross about 20 feet from the house, and set it on fire.

The Supreme Court noted that the Virginia law was different from the St. Paul ordinance in *R.A.V.* The latter made it a crime to put a hate symbol on public or private land. These symbols are protected by the First Amendment. The Virginia law forbid cross burning *with the intent to intimidate people.*

The court noted that the First Amendment does not protect all speech. For example, it does not protect "true threats." The court explained that:

> "True threats" encompass those statements where the speaker means to communicate a serious expression of an intent to commit an act of unlawful violence to a particular individual or group of individuals. . . . Intimidation . . . is a type of true threat, where a speaker directs a threat to a person or group of persons with the intent of placing the victim in fear of bodily harm or death.

The court pointed out that burning a cross can "convey a message of intimidation . . . And when a cross burning is used to intimidate, few if any messages are more powerful." The First Amendment does not protect threats and intimidation.

But the court also noted that cross burnings are not always intended to intimidate someone. The cross burning may simply convey a message of hate. This message, though despicable, is protected by the First Amendment.

The court ruled that the law must distinguish between cross burnings that are meant as threats and those that are not. It therefore struck down as unconstitutional the part of the Virginia law that made cross burnings alone evidence of intimidation. The court said that the prosecution must prove that the cross burning was intended to intimidate someone.

The court therefore overturned the conviction of Black. His rally was not meant to intimidate anyone, but to instill a message of hate in his audience. The First Amendment protects his right to spread this message.

But the court returned the cases of Elliott and O'Mara to the trial court. They could be retried and convicted under the Virginia law if the prosecution proved they intended to intimidate the family.

President Obama meets with relatives of murdered hate-crimes victims after the passage of the 2009 Hate Crimes Prevention Act.

Wisconsin v. Mitchell (1993)

Other hate-crime laws are different. Instead of creating special hate crimes, these statutes add extra penalties for any crime committed out of hate. For example, Wisconsin's hate-crime statute increases the maximum penalty for an offense whenever a criminal "intentionally selects the person against whom the crime . . . is committed . . . because of the race, religion, color, disability, sexual orientation, national origin or ancestry of that person. . . ."

On October 7, 1989, Todd Mitchell, 19, and a group of other young black men violated the law in Kenosha, Wisconsin. After seeing the movie *Mississippi Burning*, which concerns Ku Klux Klan terrorism against blacks in the South during the 1960s, they decided to attack a 14-year-old white boy, Gregory Reddick. Mitchell asked his friends, "Do you feel hyped up to move on some white people?" He then pointed to Reddick and said, "There goes a white boy. Go get him!"

About 10 members of the group, but not Mitchell himself, ran across the street, beat up Reddick, and stole his tennis shoes. Severely beaten, Reddick remained in a coma for four days and suffered permanent brain damage.

As the instigator of the attack, Mitchell was tried and convicted of aggravated battery, which normally carries a penalty of two years in prison. But the jury found that Mitchell had selected his victim because of his race. Consequently, the judge applied Wisconsin's hate-crime enhancement law and added two more years to Mitchell's sentence.

Mitchell appealed his sentence, claiming that the state's enhancement law violated the First and 14th amendments. Since the enhancement law is based on a criminal's motives, Mitchell argued that motives are based on thoughts and beliefs, which are protected by the First Amendment. Mitchell further argued that the law violates the 14th Amendment's guarantee of equal protection because it treats criminals who are motivated by prejudice differently from criminals not so motivated, even though their crimes are identical.

Attorneys for the state argued that the law in this case differed from the one in *R.A.V. v. City of St. Paul*. This law did not prohibit specific speech, symbols, or beliefs. It only applied to criminal acts (i.e., selecting a victim), which are not protected by the First Amendment. They pointed out that during sentencing, judges commonly consider many things, including a criminal's motives. Further, they claimed that the state had a "compelling governmental interest" in eliminating prejudiced criminal behavior.

In 1993, the U.S. Supreme Court upheld the Wisconsin hate-crime penalty-enhancement law. Writing for a unanimous court,

Chief Justice William Rehnquist ruled that a criminal's prejudiced motives may be used in sentencing, although "a defendant's abstract beliefs, however obnoxious to most people, may not be taken into consideration by a sentencing judge." The chief justice also stated that "the statute in this case is aimed at conduct unprotected by the First Amendment." (*Wisconsin v. Mitchell*)

In 2000, the Supreme Court decided another case that limited how enhancement penalties could be used. The court struck down a New Jersey hate-crime law that allowed a trial judge to extend a maximum prison term if the judge found *by a preponderance of the evidence* that the crime was a hate crime. The Supreme Court ruled that the Sixth Amendment required a jury to make such a determination *beyond a reasonable doubt.* (*Apprendi v. New Jersey*)

As the cases show, the line between punishing hate and protecting speech and free thought can be difficult to draw. On one side, our Constitution seeks to assure tolerance and equal protection for all citizens no matter what their race, ethnicity, religion, or gender. On the other hand, our Constitution contains protections for individual beliefs, no matter how distasteful they might be. As the U.S. Supreme Court has determined, the state may not make the expression of hate a criminal matter, but it can punish criminal acts motivated by hate more harshly.

The Debate Over Hate Crimes

Now that the Supreme Court has set guidelines for hate-crime legislation, states and the federal government are considering adopting more such laws. In 1968, Congress passed the first federal hate-crimes law, outlawing violence based on the victim's race, color, religion or national origin. In 2009, it expanded the law to include gender, sexual orientation, and disability.

Supporters see these laws as extremely important in our diverse society. They believe hate crimes deeply hurt all levels of the community — individuals, families, groups, and society at large. Hate crimes intentionally send a message that minorities are unwelcome and unsafe. Supporters argue that hate-crime laws will help prevent much violence and will convey our society's intolerance for these crimes.

Opponents view hate-crime legislation as well-meaning but unnecessary and even counterproductive. They argue that anyone who commits a serious crime is already punishable under current state laws. These laws protect everyone equally. They see no reason to pass laws that set up special classes of victims. Further, they contend that hate-crime laws will primarily affect those who commit lesser crimes by sending more of them to prison. They believe that sending someone to prison is likely to make them more racist, because many prisons harbor racist gangs. Thus, they say, the law may actually increase hate crimes.

In addition, opponents see no need for federal intervention into an area of law that states have traditionally handled. In recent years, the federal government has enacted much crime legislation. Opposition has grown to this federalization of criminal law. And the Supreme Court recently has struck down a number of federal crime laws.

The Constitution limits the powers of Congress. Congress can only enact laws based on those powers given to it in the Constitution. Federal crime laws are usually based on Congress' power to regulate interstate commerce. For most of the 20th century, the Supreme Court liberally interpreted what constituted "interstate commerce," allowing laws to be passed regulating the environment, the work place, and civil rights.

In recent years, however, a divided court has refused to go along with this interpretation. The justices have started overturning federal laws based on the commerce clause if they find the law is only remotely related to interstate commerce. Thus the court has struck down the Gun-Free School Zones Act (*U.S. v. Lopez*, 1995) and part of the Violence Against Women Act (*U.S. v. Morrison*, 2000). These opinions leave doubt as to whether the court will find federal hate-crime legislation constitutional. In the words of the court majority opinion in *Morrison*, the "Founders denied the National government and reposed in the States . . . the suppression of violent crime and vindication of its victims."

It should be noted that following the *Lopez* decision, Congress and the president re-enacted the Gun-Free Schools Act. To get around the Supreme Court's objection, it made the law apply only to guns that have moved in interstate commerce (which practically all guns have).

FOR DISCUSSION

1. What are hate crimes? Why is it difficult to determine if they are increasing or decreasing? How serious do you think the problem of hate crimes is in the United States? Explain.
2. The article mentions three different hate-crime laws ruled on by the Supreme Court. What are these laws? How are they different? How did the Supreme Court rule on each? Do you agree with the decisions? Why or why not?
3. Do you think the federal government should have hate-crime laws? Explain.

CLASS ACTIVITY

Hate-Crime Bill

In this activity, students role play a legislative session on a proposed hate-crime law.

1. Imagine that the following law is being proposed in your state:
   > Anyone who intentionally selected the victim of the crime because of the victim's race, gender, religion, color, disability, sexual orientation, national origin, or ancestry shall have his or her sentence increased by 30 percent over the normal sentence.
2. Divide into groups of three. Every student in each triad should have one of these three roles: state legislator, supporter of the bill, opponent of the bill.
3. The legislators, supporters, and opponents should meet separately to prepare for the role play. The supporters and opponents should think up their best arguments and the legislators should think of questions to ask each side.
4. Regroup into triads and begin the role play. The legislator should let the supporter speak first and then have the opponent speak. The legislator should ask questions of both. After both sides present, have the legislators move to the front of the room, discuss the proposed law, and vote. Each legislator should individually state his or her opinion on the bill.
5. Debrief by asking what were the strongest arguments on each side.

Cybercrime

There has . . . been [a] noticeable increase in account takeovers. This can be directly related to the continued rise of the Zeus Trojan and other malware variants created to capture login credentials to financial websites. These account takeovers result in fraudulent transfers from the victim's account to an account under the control of the perpetrator.
– Verizon's 2011 *Data Breach Investigations Report*

The Internet keeps growing. More people from around the world go online every day. People send e-mail, chat, use social media, play games, and conduct business with people on the other side of the world. People also commit crimes.

In many ways, the Internet provides a perfect place to commit a crime. Criminals can remain anonymous and prey on victims far away. Police have no crime scene to search for clues and they may have to track criminals halfway around the world.

If police do manage to find the criminal, problems may arise. Although many traditional crimes like fraud and theft occur on the Internet, new crimes, exclusive to the Internet, also take place. The United States has developed laws against these crimes, but many places haven't.

An international treaty against cybercrime exists. In 2001, the Council of Europe, a group of European nations, created a Convention on Cybercrime. The convention does not make specific acts against international law. Instead, it spells out types of computer misconduct. Countries that sign and ratify the treaty agree to create national laws criminalizing this misconduct and to investigate these crimes. The council has invited all nations in the world to join the treaty. So far more than 30 European nations have signed and ratified it. The United States is the only country outside of Europe that has ratified it, and its laws criminalize the misconduct suggested by the treaty.

Many nations have not yet signed the treaty and have not enacted criminal penalties for cybercrimes. Thus a person could work at a computer in a faraway place, hurt many people around the world, and that country may not even outlaw what the person did.

Hacking

Hacking is electronically breaking into or disrupting computer systems. Once inside a system, hackers do different things.

Some hackers steal. The thefts can involve almost anything — from money to credit card numbers to intellectual property like books, music, art, and computer code. Five hackers in Ukraine infected the computers of companies, churches, cities, and individuals with malware called Zeus. The malware captured bank account numbers, passwords, and other bank login information. More than $70 million was transferred from accounts to about 3,000 "mules," people in the United States recruited to send the funds to the hackers. In 2010, the FBI announced that Ukrainian authorities had arrested the hackers and the FBI had so far arrested 39 of the mules.

In 2004, hackers broke into many computer networks of corporations and the U.S. government. The hackers got into systems that were supposed to be highly secure and got "root" or "super-user" access. That meant they controlled the system and could do anything they wanted. One corporation, Cisco Systems, reported that a hacker stole programming code for software that controls traffic on the Internet. The hacker posted the code on the Internet so that other hackers could find vulnerabilities in the code. The only suspect is from Sweden, was 16 years old when the attack took place, and Swedish authorities convicted him of other computer crimes.

Malware can do many harmful things. Some programs take over large numbers of computers and send out spam from them. "Click-jacking" malware misdirects Internet users to phony sites. "Scareware" announces that the computer is infected with a virus, but by making a payment (using a credit card), the virus can be removed.

In 2011 in England, three teenagers and a 21 year old were convicted and sentenced to serve up to five years in prison each for operating the Ghostmarket web site. The site sold malware, Social Security numbers, and login information and passwords to PayPal and bank accounts. It was believed to be the largest English-language criminal hacker site on the Internet.

Hackers often vandalize and destroy. Some spread computer viruses, worms, and Trojan horses, which can erase files on computers. For

Companies spend billions of dollars on computer security each year.

example, the "IloveYou" virus appeared on people's computer's as an e-mail attachment from someone they knew. When a person opened the attachment, the virus erased files on the person's computer and sent the "IloveYou" attachment to everyone in the person's e-mail address book. In this manner, the virus quickly spread to computers around the world, causing millions of dollars in damage. Other hackers vandalize by breaking into web sites and leaving "graffiti." For example, hackers placed hardcore, violent pornographic images on many people's Facebook pages.

Still others try to shut down web sites. Using so-called "denial of service" attacks, which overload a site's computers, hackers have managed to shut down such popular sites as Twitter, Yahoo, e-Bay, and E*Trade. An even more dangerous threat would be an attack that shuts down a power grid. This has not yet happened, but experts are worried about such acts of cyberterrorism.

Other hackers do nothing except enter the site and look around. Even this, however, is illegal. The federal government's Computer Fraud and Abuse Act outlaws entering without authorization any computer system run by government, banks, or those involved in interstate commerce, such as those on the Internet. It also bans viruses and computer attacks. For a first offense, an unauthorized person entering a computer system without intending to cause harm can get one year in prison. Those intentionally damaging computers or stealing information for commercial gain can get five years. Every state has similar laws.

Hackers fall into three categories — often called "white hats," "black hats," and "gray hats." The white hats do nothing illegal. They are hired by companies to improve computer security. They try to infiltrate a company's computer system and expose security lapses. "A white hat does it when asked, under contract, with a 'get out of jail free' card," explained Charles Palmer, manager of network security and cryptography at IBM Research.

"We'll do the job, evaluate it, and tell the customer what we're doing." On the other extreme are the black hats, who are clearly criminals. They steal, vandalize, and disrupt.

In the middle are the gray hats. These are the hackers of computer folklore. They follow a so-called "hacker ethic." This ethic bans stealing and vandalism. But it allows accessing computers without permission, which is illegal. They also push the borders of illegality by publishing on the Internet hacking programs and security holes they find in computer systems. In fact, the denial of service attacks that shut down Yahoo and other sites used a program called Tribal Flood created by a gray-hat computer hacker in Germany nicknamed Mixter.

10 TIPS FOR SAFEGUARDING YOUR DATA

Hackers often steal data from individuals' computers. Hackers exploit vulnerabilities in computers and install malware, capable of tracking keystrokes and sending account numbers back to them. Below are steps that experts recommend you take to keep your data safe.

1. **Use security software and a firewall.** Keep them up to date and make sure you have real-time protection against viruses and spyware. In case your smart phone is stolen, make sure you have installed apps that can let you remotely wipe all data, lock it, and track where it is.
2. **Update all your software.** Hackers exploit security holes in all types of software, which updates fix.
3. **Use strong passwords.** Avoid using actual words like "password" and sequential numbers such as "123456." Use random upper and lowercase letters, numbers, characters, and punctuation marks. The longer, the better (at least 10 characters). A simple way to create memorable passwords is to use the first letter of each word in a song or poem you know. Don't use the same password everywhere.
4. **Check your credit reports.** Each year you can get a free report from one of the three credit reporting agencies. Every four months, visit **www.AnnualCreditReport.com** and download a report.
5. **Beware of phony links.** This is particularly a problem with e-mail and with shortened URLs used in Twitter and Facebook. Check these links using anti-virus software or an online link scanner.
6. **Don't reveal private information.** Don't put it on Facebook. Don't respond to e-mails asking (or that lead you to web sites asking) for your Social Security number, account numbers, PIN numbers, passwords, birthdate, mother's maiden name, or other personal information. Keep this information secure.
7. **Avoid public WiFi.** Hackers can see everything you do, and you are in danger of getting malware installed on your computer. If you have WiFi at home, select the highest security option and change the default password to a new, strong password.
8. **Only log on to secure pages.** They are marked **https** or **shttp**, not http. Your browser may also show a lock symbol to indicate high security.
9. **Keep paper documents private.** Don't let identity thieves get their hands on your bills, account statements, and credit card solicitations. Shred what you throw away. Keep the rest locked away.
10. **Monitor your accounts.** Check your accounts online. When bills and statements arrive, look at them right away.

Mixter and other gray hats believe they are performing a public service by posting such programs on the Internet. They say that they are exposing security flaws and giving everyone an equal chance to come up with countermeasures. Mixter argued: "It would be unfair to provide them to just a small circle of security experts who would possibly only consult some few elected companies. The only fair way is getting the information out to everyone, because generally, everyone on the Net can be affected by security issues." He criticized those who used his program to shut down the sites, calling the attacks "stupid and pointless." But he also thought the attacks were "an inevitable price to pay to be able to develop countermeasures and fixes."

Many disagree that gray hats are performing a public service by breaking into computer systems or posting hacking programs, like Mixter's Tribal Flood, on the Internet. John C. Dvorak of *PC Magazine* compares a web site to a business and the Internet to "a road leading to that business. My business unlocks the doors during the day and keeps them locked at night. If people break in at night, they are considered burglars and are prosecuted as such. Breaking into computer systems is similar, and people are now prosecuted for breaking into them. In many states, you can also be prosecuted for owning burglary tools" (like lock picks). Dvorak compares posting hacking programs to designing and giving away a new lock pick that can open most door locks. Few, he says, would consider this a public service.

These are just a few examples of crime on the Internet. Other current concerns about the Internet include fraud, hate crimes, child pornography sites, and chat rooms in which adults lure underage children into sex. As the Internet grows, the list of crimes will also grow. The web may be a virtual world, but the crime on it is real.

FOR DISCUSSION

1. What do you think are the greatest dangers of cybercrime? Why?
2. Do you think that an international treaty on cybercrime is important? Explain.
3. What are the differences between white-, gray-, and black-hat hackers? Do you think that what gray-hat hackers do should be against the law? Explain.

CLASS ACTIVITY

Free Speech?

Some people think that the Internet should be a bastion of free speech and that anything should be allowed. Others agree that free speech is important, but say that it has limits. They point out that the U.S. Supreme Court has upheld some limits on freedom of speech. In this activity, students look at some examples of material on the Internet and decide whether they think it is free speech that should be allowed on the Internet.

1. Form small groups. Each group should:
   a. Discuss each of the **Six Examples of Material on the Internet**.
   b. Decide for each whether it should be protected as free speech.
   c. Prepare to report its decisions and the reasons for them to the class.
2. Regroup as a class and have groups report back.
3. Debrief the discussion using the questions below.

Six Examples of Material on the Internet

1. Instructions for making a bomb
2. Racist remarks
3. Sexually explicit photographs
4. A threat to kill a person
5. The code for a highly destructive computer virus
6. Downloadable illegally made copies of a new movie

Debriefing Questions

1. Why is freedom of speech important?
2. Do you think some speech should not be protected by the First Amendment? Explain.

CHAPTER 2
DEFENSES

[T]he Constitution guarantees criminal defendants "a meaningful opportunity to present a complete defense."
– Justice Sandra Day O'Connor, *Crane v. Kentucky* (1986), quoting *California v. Trombetta* (1984)

AN OVERVIEW OF DEFENSES | SELF-DEFENSE | THE INSANITY DEFENSE | ENTRAPMENT

An Overview of Defenses

An Oklahoma man, charged with armed robbery, elected to defend himself. He handled his case well until the store manager identified him as the robber, at which point the defendant leaped to his feet, accused the woman of lying, and exclaimed, "I should have blown your . . . head off." He then paused, sat down, and muttered, "If I'd been the one that was there."
– Rodney R. Jones, attorney, and Gerald F. Uelmen, law professor, *Supreme Folly* (1990)

In our criminal justice system, persons accused of a crime are innocent until proven guilty beyond a reasonable doubt. In our system, defendants do *not* have to prove they are innocent.

During a trial, the criminal defendant and the defense lawyer do everything they can to prevent the prosecutor from proving guilt. Most defenses consist of raising reasonable doubt about the prosecution's case. A defense attorney will cross-examine prosecution witnesses. The attorney may bring out inconsistencies or contradictions in a prosecution witness's story, raise doubts about a witness's believability, or show that a witness's identification of the defendant is not reliable. The prosecution must establish to a jury or judge every element of the crime beyond a reasonable doubt. If the defense can keep the prosecution from doing this, the defense wins.

The defense may call its own witnesses, including the defendant, to poke holes in the prosecution's case. It may also call experts to testify, for example, that a bullet did not come from the defendant's gun, the tire tracks were not from the defendant's car, or the DNA did not belong to the defendant. The defense may present an **alibi** for the defendant, showing that the defendant was nowhere near the crime scene on the day in question.

The defense tries to raise reasonable doubt about the prosecution's case. In some instances, it may put on an affirmative defense.

Defendants in our society also have further protections. Our criminal law recognizes some special legal defenses, known as **affirmative defenses**. If the defendant successfully establishes one of these defenses, it does not matter whether the prosecution can prove the elements of the crime or not. The defendant is not guilty. Affirmative defenses are usually grouped under two categories: justifications and excuses. Justification means that the act was not wrong: It was justified under the circumstances. An excuse defense argues that although the act was wrong, the defendant had a good excuse.

The legality of carrying pepper spray for self-defense varies from state to state.

Justification Defenses

Self-Defense. This is the most important justification defense. If Bob attacks Jose, Jose has the right to defend himself. This defense is explained in a separate article on page 40.

Necessity. If someone burns a patch of weeds on public land to stop a raging forest fire, that person may raise the defense of necessity against a charge of arson. The person has broken the law, but has done so to prevent a greater evil. The defense of necessity requires that the defendant (1) did not intentionally cause the circumstances surrounding the illegal act, (2) could not accomplish the same objective using a better (and legal) alternative, and (3) chose the lesser evil. Thus the defense would fail if the defendant had started the forest fire, or if he had a large tank of water available to stop the fire, or the forest fire was about to die out and his fire started a new forest fire.

Excuse Defenses

Duress. If a bank robber puts a gun to a friend's head and forces the friend to help him rob the bank, the friend may raise the defense of duress. To be successful in this defense, defendants must show that they (1) were under an immediate threat of serious bodily harm or death, (2) had a well-grounded belief that the threat would be

carried out, and (3) had no reasonable chance to escape or frustrate the threat.

This defense was raised in the trial of Patty Hearst, an heir to the Hearst newspaper fortune. While a student at the University of California, Hearst in 1974 was kidnapped by a terrorist group, the Symbionese Liberation Army. According to Hearst, she was kept blindfolded in a closet for two months and was sexually and physically abused. After two months of torment, she was forced, she said, to join the group and take part in a bank robbery. She was captured in September 1975 along with other members of the group. Tried for bank robbery and felonious use of firearms, she raised the defense of duress. The prosecution, however, offered evidence that she had had access to loaded firearms and opportunities to escape. She was convicted and sentenced to seven years in prison. In 1979, President Jimmy Carter commuted her sentence, and she was released from prison.

Insanity. Bob is insane and has a delusion that he is swatting flies. In fact, he is attacking people on the street. At his trial for assault, he may raise the defense of not guilty by reason of insanity. Definitions of legal insanity vary, and the defense is highly controversial. In the most common definition, people are criminally insane if, as a result of mental illness, they did not know what they were doing or that it was wrong. The insanity defense is discussed in a separate article on page 43.

Entrapment. If the police induce John to commit a crime he would not have committed otherwise, he may raise the defense of entrapment. This defense is explained in a separate article on page 45.

Ignorance of the law. The common law rule is that "ignorance of the law is no excuse." This rule still applies to most crimes. For example, if a bank robber says that he did not know that robbing a bank was a crime, it would not matter. He would still be guilty. Everyone is supposed to know that robbing a bank is illegal. Society demands that people understand what is against the law.

The problem arises with laws that few people know about or understand. In modern times, the number of criminal laws has greatly increased, and the laws are more complex. Even so, the general rule has remained in place. But some decisions have backed away from strictly applying the rule.

In 1994, the U.S. Supreme Court decided *Ratzlaf v. U.S.* The case involved a man, Ratzlaf, who owed a gambling debt of $160,000 to a Reno, Nevada, casino. When Ratzlaf came with $100,000 in cash, the casino told him it had to report all cash transactions of $10,000 and above to state and federal authorities. The casino also informed him that if he gave the casino a cashier's check, it would not have to report it. The casino supplied him with a limousine and an employee to go to a bank. The bank informed him that it had the same reporting requirements. So Ratzlaf had the limousine drive him from bank to bank so that he could deposit just under $10,000 in each bank and withdraw the amount in cashier's checks. He gave these checks to the casino. Ratzlaf was charged, convicted, and sentenced to prison for violating the Money Laundering Control Act of 1986. This act stated, in part, that "No person shall for the purpose of evading the reporting requirements . . . structure . . . any transaction with one or more domestic financial institutions." The act punished those who "willfully" violated this provision.

Ratzlaf argued that he did not know what he had done was illegal. The trial court and appeals court said his ignorance was no excuse as long as he knew about the reporting requirements. The Supreme Court, however, ruled that to willfully violate the provision, Ratzlaf had to know that what he did was illegal. The court stated: "We do not dishonor the venerable principle that ignorance of the law generally is no defense to a criminal charge." But the court went on to say that when Congress added the requirement of willfulness, it made ignorance of the law an excuse to that crime.

Mistake of fact. If Jay's girlfriend at a party asks him to get her purse and Jay grabs the wrong purse, he could raise the defense of mistake of fact against a charge of theft. Jay had no intent to steal. But if Jay's mistake was that he thought he was stealing Maria's purse instead of Karen's, Jay would not have a defense of mistake of fact. Jay intended to steal. He just got the wrong purse.

MISSISSIPPI STATUTE OF LIMITATIONS

Mississippi Code Section 99-1-5

The passage of time shall never bar prosecution against any person for the offenses of murder, manslaughter, aggravated assault, kidnapping, arson, burglary, forgery, counterfeiting, robbery, larceny, rape, embezzlement, obtaining money or property under false pretenses or by fraud, felonious abuse or battery of a child . . . , touching or handling a child for lustful purposes . . . , sexual battery of a child . . . , or exploitation of children . . . . A person shall not be prosecuted for conspiracy . . . or for felonious assistance program fraud . . . unless the prosecution for such offense be commenced within five (5) years . . . . A person shall not be prosecuted for any other offense not listed in this section unless the prosecution for such offense be commenced within two (2) years . . . . Nothing contained in this section shall bar any prosecution against any person who shall abscond or flee from justice, or shall absent himself from this state or out of the jurisdiction of the court, or so conduct himself that he cannot be found by the officers of the law, or that process cannot be served upon him.

Intoxication. A person may get intoxicated from drugs or alcohol and do something the person would not do if sober. The general rule is that intoxication is no excuse for a crime. If a person knowingly drinks alcohol or ingests drugs, that person has taken the risk of going out of control.

The exception is when the person unknowingly ingests drugs or alcohol. Involuntary intoxication is a defense. It applies to people who are forced to take an intoxicant, who are slipped the intoxicant without their knowing it, or who take prescribed medication without knowing of the risks.

Statute of Limitations Defense

Another affirmative defense is neither a justification nor excuse defense. The statute of limitations bars prosecution of criminal defendants if legal action starts too long after the commission of the crime. Legal action must be brought within a period that begins from the date of the criminal act, or defendants can raise this defense and bar the criminal proceedings against them.

The limitations period differs based on the crime and jurisdiction. Most misdemeanors have statutory periods of two or three years. More serious felonies, such as rape and robbery, may have longer statutory times of six to 10 years. Some jurisdictions do not have any statute of limitations for serious felonies. No jurisdiction has a statute of limitations for murder.

The reason for the defense is fairness. The passage of time may obscure evidence and turn eyewitness accounts into distant faded memories. Supporters of statutes of limitations argue that it would be unfair to charge a defendant with a crime based on old and stale evidence.

A couple of things can stop the statute of limitations from running out. If the defendant flees the jurisdiction, the statute does not run while the defendant is in hiding. If a charge is brought against the defendant within the statutory period, the statute is stopped.

DNA evidence has also affected the statute of limitations defense. Law regarding DNA evidence is still in its infancy, but because DNA evidence does not fade over time, as eyewitness accounts do, it is viewed as reliable even many years after the crime. Under Title 18, Section 3297 of the U.S. Code, a defendant cannot raise the statute of limitations defense if he is identified by DNA testing. Instead the limitations period restarts from the date the test identifies the defendant.

Under California law, the statute of limitations stops running when an arrest warrant is issued that "names or describes the defendant with the same degree of particularity required for [a] complaint." In the 2010 case of *California v. Robinson*, the California Supreme Court ruled that an arrest warrant that described the defendant solely by his DNA profile was sufficient to stop the statute of limitations.

FOR DISCUSSION

1. What are some ways that a defense attorney can try to establish reasonable doubt?
2. What is an affirmative defense? What are the main justification defenses? The main excuse defenses?
3. In these situations, do you think each of the following affirmative defenses would work? Should it work? Explain.
   a. Brad is an accountant. He learns that the FBI is investigating a client for fraud. The client calls and orders him to shred his files. Brad does not know it is against the law to shred the documents. Charged with obstruction of justice, he makes the defense of ignorance of the law.
   b. Emily has never had a drink of alcohol. Friends take her to a bar for her 21st birthday. She gets drunk and punches another woman. Charged with battery, she makes the defense of intoxication.
   c. Ethan is a schizophrenic. With medication his disease is under control. One day he decides not to take the medication, and he becomes delusional and robs a bank. He does not know what he is doing and that it is wrong.
4. Do you think serious felonies should have a statute of limitations? Explain.

Which Defense Is Valid?

In this activity, students look at hypothetical situations and decide which defense might be raised in the situation.

1. Divide into pairs. Each pair should:
   a. Read each of the hypothetical situations below.
   b. Decide which of the defenses mentioned in the article best applies to each situation.
   c. Discuss and decide whether you think the defense should work in that situation.
   d. Be prepared to explain your decisions and the reasons for them.
2. Reconvene as a class and compare the findings from each group.
3. Debrief the activity using the debriefing questions, below.

Hypothetical Situations

a. Ned is at a church social and drinks what he believes is non-alcoholic punch, but someone has spiked the punch with vodka. Ned gets drunk and walks home late at night singing loudly. He is arrested for disturbing the peace.

b. Jack, a federal agent, knows that Sam, a terrorist, has planted a nuclear weapon somewhere in an American city. The bomb will detonate in one hour and kill thousands unless it is found and defused. Jack tortures Sam until he tells Jack where it is. The bomb is found and defused. Jack is arrested for assault and battery.

c. Sylvia has been gambling for years. In five years, she won more than $400,000 playing poker. She did not declare this money when filing her tax returns because she did not know she had to. She is charged with income tax evasion.

d. Officer James, in plain clothes, approaches Keri on the street and offers to sell her a "hot" radio for a cheap price. Keri at first refuses, but the officer persuades her to buy it. He arrests Keri for receiving stolen property.

e. Mark, who has been in and out of mental hospitals for years, hears a voice ordering him to kill Satan, who is disguised as his next door neighbor Phil. Mark kills Phil and is charged with murder.

f. Fred goes next door to his neighbor and asks for half a cup of flour. The neighbor, a drug dealer, thinks Fred means he wants cocaine and gives him half a cup. When Fred leaves his neighbor's house, he is stopped by a police officer and charged with possession of cocaine.

g. Peter was walking down the street. Without warning, a man began hitting him with a rolled-up newspaper. Peter pulled out a gun and shot him. Peter is charged with assault with a deadly weapon.

h. Nelson tells Lisa, a saxophone player, that he will "make sure she never plays the saxophone again" unless she shoplifts a portable digital audio player. She is caught and charged with shoplifting.

Debriefing Questions

1. Which of the affirmative defenses seems most reasonable? Why?
2. Do you think any of them should be eliminated as defenses? Explain.

Self-Defense

It is difficult to the point of impossibility to imagine a right in any state to abolish self defense altogether, thereby leaving one a Hobson's choice of almost certain death through violent attack now or statutorily mandated death through trial and conviction of murder later.
– Judge Francis D. Murnaghan Jr., *Griffin v. Martin* (1986)

Imagine that you are alone in your apartment asleep at 3 a.m. You wake up and realize your bedroom window is sliding open inch by inch. A tall shadowy figure steps into the room. In terror, you pick up a lamp by your bed and hurl it. The lamp shatters against the man's head and he slumps to the floor.

Can you be charged with battery? Yes, it's possible, but it's not likely. Even if you were prosecuted for battery, you would have a strong claim of self-defense. This is the most important justification defense.

Defense of Self

Generally, you have a right to use whatever force is necessary to defend yourself from an unlawful attack. For a proper claim of self-defense, you must establish three things:

1. You reasonably believed that the force was required for your own protection — even it that belief turns out to be mistaken.
2. The threatened harm was about to happen and the attacker was willing and able to injure you. (The threat was an imminent threat.)
3. The force used in self-defense was reasonable — that is, no more than was necessary to prevent the victim from inflicting harm.

The law is much stricter about using *deadly* force in self-defense. Deadly force may only be used when you reasonably believe, based on the circumstances, two things:

1. The attacker was about to kill you or inflict great bodily harm.
2. The deadly force was the only way of preventing the harm.

The law of self-defense was first developed before police forces existed, when people were expected to provide for their own physical safety. Even so, people confronted with deadly force were expected to attempt to reach a safe location prior to defending themselves. They were obligated to "retreat to the wall of the castle" or to some other point that prevented them from retreating further. A minority of jurisdictions still require a person to attempt to withdraw from a conflict, though even in these states, retreat is never required unless it can be made in complete safety. There is, further, a longstanding rule that people are never required to retreat when attacked in their own homes.

Defense of Others

Imagine that Max sees Peter hitting Sam. Can Max come to Peter's defense? In general, defending others is the same as defending yourself. But a few states say you only have the same right of defense as the person you are defending. So if Peter is defending himself from Sam's attack, Max would have no right to defend Sam. Sam was the aggressor and he therefore has no right to self-defense. In these states, Max could not claim self-defense either. The common law referred to this as the "alter ego" rule.

Most states, however, do not follow the "alter ego" rule. Max can claim self-defense if he has a reasonable (but mistaken) belief that Paul was under attack *and* the force he used was reasonable under the circumstances.

Defense of Property

Imagine that Max is not trying to defend a person. Instead, he is trying to stop Rob from stealing his bicycle. As long as Max reasonably believes that Rob is stealing his bike, he can use whatever force is necessary, up to deadly force. He cannot use deadly force unless Rob is threatening him with deadly force. In other words, he must be acting in self-defense.

Defense of Home

The rules about deadly force change when people are defending their home. A home is a sanctuary, a "castle." An old common law rule was that people could use deadly force if they believed the force was necessary to prevent an imminent and unlawful entry into their home. So if a burglar was breaking into Jasmine's home, she could shoot him. She could also shoot a drunken neighbor who mistook her house for his house and tried to enter. She could even shoot the drunken neighbor if she knew who he was if she reasonably believed it was the only way to stop him from entering.

Most states do not follow the old rule. Most now allow people to use deadly force in

Most states limit when people can use deadly force on intruders.

defense of a home only if they reasonably believe that (1) the intruder is about to unlawfully enter the home, (2) the intruder intends to commit a felony or injure an occupant of the home, and (3) deadly force is necessary to stop the intruder.

Domestic Abuse as a Defense

Questions about self-defense often arise in cases involving domestic violence. Domestic abuse can occur over a period of years. Some husbands beat their wives, go to bed, and threaten to beat them some more when they wake up. If a woman in such a situation attacks her husband in his sleep, can she validly claim self-defense? Most states say no. The threat is no longer imminent. It ended when he fell asleep.

The issue of appropriate force is also problematic. If a woman uses deadly force to stop her husband from beating her, has she used too much force? The law requires that the attacker be about to kill her or inflict great bodily harm.

Most courts allow defendants to introduce evidence of abuse. But defendants still must show they had the right to use deadly force in self-defense.

FOR DISCUSSION
1. What is required for a valid argument of self-defense? Why are the rules tougher for the use of deadly force? Do you think they should be? Explain.
2. What is the alter-ego rule? Do you think it should be the law? Why or why not?
3. What was the common law rule for defending your home? What is the modern rule? Which do you think is better? Why?
4. What problems do victims of domestic abuse face in arguing self-defense? Do you think the law of self-defense should be changed for victims of domestic abuse? Explain.

Stand Your Ground?

In 2005, Florida enacted a new self-defense law called "Stand Your Ground." The law contained several controversial provisions, including the two sections discussed below.

One section of the law removed the duty of retreat when people are attacked *outside their homes*. This duty previously existed in Florida law. As long as the person is not engaged in illegal behavior and has a right to be in that place, the person "has the right to stand his or her ground and meet force with force, including deadly force if he or she reasonably believes it is necessary to do so to prevent death or great bodily harm to himself or herself or another or to prevent the commission of a forcible felony." Thus this section lets people use deadly force even if they can safely leave the situation or can otherwise protect themselves.

Another section involved the use of deadly force by a person lawfully in a *home* or *vehicle*. It allows such a person to use deadly force if the person "knew or had reason to believe" that an intruder was making or had made "an unlawful and forcible entry" into the "dwelling, residence, or occupied vehicle." This is the only requirement. It does not require a showing that the person feared harm or that the deadly force was necessary.

The proponents of this law say that they are going to get every state legislature in the nation to pass a similar law. So far, they have managed to get more than 20 other states to pass similar laws.

Imagine that this law has been proposed in your state. You are members of a legislative committee deciding on this law. **You are considering only the two sections of the law dealing with the use of deadly force outside the home *and* in a home or vehicle.**

1. Form groups of five or six. Each group will serve as a legislative committee.
2. Each committee should:
   a. Reread the article, especially the **Defense of Self** and **Defense of Home** sections.
   b. Discuss the pros of the proposed new law.
   c. Discuss the cons of the proposed new law.
   d. Decide whether or not to adopt each section of this law.
   e. Be prepared to present its decision and the reasons for it.
3. The committees should report to the class.
4. Hold a class discussion and then vote on the two sections.

The Insanity Defense

The insanity defense is a key part of our criminal justice system, which is founded on the belief that [people] normally choose whether or not to obey the law. Certain people . . . cannot make that choice, however, either because they are too young or because of severe mental retardation or mental illness.

– Elyce Zenoff, professor of law, from an interview in *U.S. News & World Report* (1982)

Defendants will be acquitted if they can prove that when they committed the crime, they were legally insane. This defense has existed for hundreds of years and has always been controversial.

But public debate intensified after President Ronald Reagan was shot in 1981, and his attacker was found not guilty by reason of insanity. The defendant in that case, John Hinckley Jr., purchased a gun and stalked the president for some time. He wrote a letter to a famous actress telling her what he planned to do. Millions of Americans watched in horror as videotapes of the shooting played over and over again on national television. "How could this person be found not guilty?" they demanded.

For criminal law, "insanity" has a special meaning. Even in this context, legal scholars and lawmakers have disagreed about what constitutes insanity for a defense to a criminal charge. Over the years, several different legal tests for determining insanity have been developed, but none has been universally accepted as valid.

1. **The *M'Naghten* Rule.** Under this traditional approach, defendants must show that because of their mental illness, either they did not know what they were doing or they did not know it was wrong (*M'Naghten Case*, 1843). About half of the states and the federal courts use the *M'Naghten* rule.

   Critics of the *M'Naghten* rule point out that it does not protect defendants who cannot control themselves. Thus defendants can be convicted under the *M'Naghten* rule even if they cannot avoid committing the crime because of mental illness.

2. **The Irresistible Impulse Rule.** In some states, defendants will be acquitted if they can prove that the crime was committed

Controversy arose over the insanity defense following its successful use in the trial of John Hinckley Jr., who attempted to kill President Ronald Reagan.

because of an insane impulse that controlled their will. This test of insanity often supplements the *M'Naghten* approach. (*Parsons v. Alabama*, 1887)

3. **The *Durham* Rule.** To prove insanity under this rule, defendants must show that the crime was "the product of mental disease or mental defect" of some sort. Because of the vagueness of this rule, only one state follows it today, New Hampshire. (*Durham v. U.S.*, 1954)

4. ***Model Penal Code* Test**, also known as the substantial capacity test. A much stricter rule than *Durham*, this test is used in almost half the states. This was the test used in the Hinckley case. Under the *Model Penal Code* approach, defendants are insane if because of a mental disease or defect, they:
   - lacked substantial capacity to appreciate the criminality of their conduct, or
   - lacked substantial capacity to conform their conduct to the requirements of the law (*Model Penal Code* Sec. 4.01 [1]). Some jurisdictions omit this second part of the test.

Under any of these tests, defendants who are successful with this defense will be found not guilty by reason of insanity. Often this means the defendants will be committed to mental hospitals. They will not be released in many jurisdictions until they can prove beyond a reasonable doubt that they are sane or that they no longer pose any threat to society.

In Hinckley's case, since 1982 he has been confined in a mental hospital in Washington, D.C. He has received psychiatric treatment and anti-psychotic drugs. He is currently off medication, and doctors report his mental condition is greatly improved. In 1999, he was allowed to leave the hospital grounds on supervised visits. Since that time, judges have allowed him to visit his mother's house under her supervision, and the periods he has been allowed at her home have increased over time.

The insanity defense is rarely used. One study showed that only 1 percent of all defendants at trial raised the defense. It also revealed that the defense was successful in just one-quarter of these cases. In other words, defendants were found not guilty by reason of insanity in about 0.25 percent of all cases taken to trial.

Guilty But Mentally Ill

At least 20 states have developed a new verdict — **guilty but mentally ill**. The meaning of this verdict varies.

In most of these states, "guilty but mentally ill" means the defendant was *not* legally insane, but was mentally ill when committing the crime. It means that the defendant's defense of insanity has fallen short, but the jury recognizes that the defendant has mental problems. These jurisdictions have not replaced the insanity defense.

In a few states, guilty but mentally ill *replaces* the verdict of not guilty by reason of insanity. The verdict in these states means that the defendant was legally insane when committing the crime.

The effect of the verdict is the same in most states. The defendant will receive a standard prison sentence, but may serve it in a mental hospital. If the person recovers from the mental illness, the person will serve the remainder of the sentence in prison.

A few states have entirely eliminated all insanity defenses. It is no longer a valid defense in Idaho, Kansas, Utah, and Montana. In these states, however, the defense can introduce evidence showing that the defendant did not have the state of mind (*mens rea*) required for the crime.

CLASS ACTIVITY

The Insanity Defense

In this activity, students apply the four insanity tests to a hypothetical case.

1. Divide into groups of four. Each group should:
   a. Assign each person in the group one of the insanity tests described in the preceding section.
   b. Read **Mark's Statement**, below.
   c. Have each person apply his or her assigned insanity test to Mark to see if it fits.
   d. Have the whole group discuss whether each test fits.
2. Reconvene as a class and compare the findings from each group.

Mark's Statement

During his trial for murdering a friend, defendant Mark made the following statement:
   I knew that it was wrong, but I couldn't help myself. During the night of April 30, Beelzebub, grand duke of Hell, came to me with biddings from the master. He told me to kill my friend. I resisted, but his will was too strong and finally I had to do what I was told.

Debriefing Questions

1. Which insanity tests fit Mark's case? Which do not?
2. If Mark's statement reflects his actual belief, do you think he should be found not guilty by reason of insanity? Why or why not?
3. Which insanity test, if any, do you think is best? Why?

FOR DISCUSSION

1. Which of the definitions of legal insanity do you think is best? Why?
2. What purpose would it serve to punish criminally insane persons? Do you think they deserve punishment?
3. Do you think the law should permit a verdict of not guilty by reason of insanity? Why or why not? If not, what should the law do about people who are criminally insane? Explain.

Debate on Insanity

Choose a pro or con position on the following statement:

The insanity defense should be abolished.

Research this issue. On the Internet, a good place to start is Constitutional Rights Foundation's Research Links or *Criminal Justice in America* Links. (Both are at **www.CriminalJusticeInAmerica.org**.) At your school or community library, do an online search through their periodical index. Write a two- or three-page essay supporting your opinion. These can be used for a class discussion or debate.

Entrapment

The first duties of the officers of the law are to prevent, not to punish crime. It is not their duty to incite to and create crime for the sole purpose of prosecuting and punishing it.
– Judge Walter H. Sanborn, *Butts v. U.S.* (1921)

A defendant can be acquitted if the defense proves the police entrapped the defendant into committing the crime. The first U.S. Supreme Court case upholding an entrapment defense took place during Prohibition. An undercover federal agent was invited to the home of Randall Sorrells, a North Carolina factory worker. The men talked for a couple of hours, learning that they had served in the same infantry division in World War I. The agent asked Sorrells if he could get him a jug of whiskey. Sorrells declined, saying he "did not fool with whisky." The agent persisted and finally Sorrells relented. He left his house and returned a half hour later with a jug. When Sorrells handed over the whiskey in exchange for $5, the agent arrested him for violating the National Prohibition Act. At trial, Sorrells raised the defense of entrapment, but the trial court did not let the jury decide the issue of entrapment. Sorrell was convicted, and he appealed.

In *Sorrells v. U.S.* (1932), the Supreme Court ruled that Sorrells should have been allowed to show that he was "a person otherwise innocent whom the government is seeking to punish for an alleged offense" induced by "the creative activity of its own officials."

Over the years, two separate tests for entrapment have developed. The **subjective test** is used by federal and most state courts. It requires that the police lure the defendant into committing the crime *and* the defendant was **not** predisposed to commit the crime. It is subjective because it inquires into the defendant's predisposition.

A few states use the **objective test** for entrapment. It requires that the police lure the defendant into committing the crime by doing something that creates a "substantial risk that such an offense will be committed by persons other than those who are ready to commit it." This test does not look at whether the defendant was predisposed to commit the crime.

Several famous cases have featured the issue of entrapment. The federal government's **Abscam** operation in the early 1980s is an example of an entrapment defense that failed. The FBI invented a phony Arab sheik, Kambir Abdul Rahmen, to

Unit 1: Crime   45

Automobile entrepreneur John DeLorean poses with one of his sports cars. In 1983, DeLorean stood trial for trafficking in cocaine. He claimed the police entrapped him, and the jury acquitted him.

try to bribe one U.S. senator and seven representatives. The FBI filmed the sting operation and used the films as evidence in the trials for accepting bribes. The defendants argued that the FBI had entrapped them, but this defense failed. Why?

The FBI had received reliable information that these particular congressmen were corrupt. "Sheik Rahmen" did not approach just any congressmen. He chose ones who were reported to show criminal intent already. The FBI, said the courts, had merely given them an opportunity to do something they already had the intent to do.

On the other hand, the **John DeLorean** case at about the same time, demonstrates an entrapment defense that succeeded. DeLorean was an auto company executive who left Ford in the late 1970s to set up his own sports car company in Northern Ireland. His new gull-wing DeLorean sports car, named after himself, came out during a gasoline crisis and did not sell well. It was well known that his company was in deep trouble.

FBI agents claimed that an informant told them DeLorean was searching for illegal ways to keep the company afloat. In an elaborate sting operation, similar to Abscam, undercover operators approached him with a scheme to import $24 million in cocaine. They videotaped him accepting the deal and brought him to trial in 1983.

DeLorean's lawyers argued that he had a clean record, that the government's witnesses were unreliable, and that the FBI had lured and entrapped him into the crime. Despite the videotape, the jury found him not guilty. One juror said, "The way the government acted in this case was not appropriate."

In a similar development in 1992, the Supreme Court threw out the conviction of a man they felt had been entrapped. Postal inspectors thought that a Nebraska man named **Keith Jacobson** was predisposed to buying child pornography. They sent him an offer in the mail and he did not respond. For the next 26 months, they repeatedly sent him offers to buy child pornography. Finally, he bought two magazines, and they arrested him. He was convicted, but the Supreme Court on a 5–4 vote overturned the conviction. The court said that the government had "overstepped the line between setting a trap for the 'unwary innocent' and the 'unwary criminal' . . . and . . . failed to establish that [Jacobson] was

COMMON STING OPERATIONS

A sting is an undercover police operation that sets up a situation to catch criminals in the act. Most of these operations require video and audio surveillance. Some of the most common stings are:

Prostitution and drugs. Police pose as prostitutes to catch clients or pose as clients to catch prostitutes. Similarly, police act as drug dealers or buyers to catch drug users and dealers.

Fake pawnshops. Police open a pawnshop to catch people selling stolen property.

Decoy cars. Police place and stake out a car in a place known for auto theft. Some decoy cars have tracking devices or even lock, trapping the thief, when the thief enters them.

Fake web sites. Police create web sites offering child pornography.

Phony ads. Police place an ad listing a number of people as winners of the lottery. The list is actually of people with outstanding warrants for their arrest. When the people arrive to collect their winnings, they are arrested.

independently predisposed to commit the crime." (*Jacobson v. U.S.*)

A more recent entrapment case involved the war on terrorism. **Hemant Lakhani**, 69, a British citizen, was caught in an international sting operation by Russian, British, and U.S. intelligence services. A clothing merchant, Lakhani was approached by agents claiming to be Russians who could supply weapons and agents claiming to be Somalis interested in buying shoulder-launched missiles to shoot down U.S. airliners. He was arrested in New Jersey after receiving a missile (a dud) from an agent. He was charged with providing material support to terrorists and selling arms without a license. His lawyer at the trial argued that Lakhani had been entrapped. He pointed out that Lakhani was the only person involved who was not an agent. He said to the jury: "Ask yourself, would any of this have occurred without the government?" The government's witnesses described Lakhani as eager to take part. In 2005, a jury rejected his entrapment defense and convicted him of all the charges.

FOR DISCUSSION

1. What are the differences between the Sorrells, Abscam, DeLorean, Jacobson, and Lakhani cases. Do you think each of the cases was decided properly? Explain.
2. What is the difference between the objective and subjective tests for entrapment? Which do you think is better? Why?
3. Do you think the defense of entrapment makes sense? Why or why not?

CLASS ACTIVITY

Were They Entrapped?

In this activity, students decide several entrapment cases.
1. Form small groups.
2. Each group should:
   a. Read and discuss the cases below.
   b. Decide whether or not the defendant in each case has been entrapped.
   c. Decide which test for entrapment is better: the subjective or objective test.
   d. Be prepared to report its decisions and reasons for them to the class.
3. Reconvene the class, groups should report their decisions, and the class should discuss them.

CASE #1: An undercover federal agent offered to supply a hard-to-obtain chemical necessary for making methamphetamine, an illegal drug. He asked for half of the drugs produced. The defendants, who had manufactured meth in the past, agreed to the deal. After manufacturing the meth, defendants were arrested by the agent. (*U.S. v. Russell*)

CASE #2: Lively had used cocaine at age 14, but stopped. At 18, she drank to excess and tried to stop by attending Alcoholic Anonymous / Narcotics Anonymous meetings where she met Desai, a police informant. (The police paid for his apartment, utilities, car, and living expenses.) According to Lively, Desai and she began a romantic relationship, and she moved in with him. She alleged that Desai pressured her for two weeks to buy cocaine for "Rick," an undercover officer. She made two deliveries to him and was arrested. The defendant had no previous drug arrests. (*Washington v. Lively*)

CASE #3: Sherman met Kalchinian, a government informant, at a doctor's office where they both were being treated for drug addiction. They kept running into each other at the doctor's office or the pharmacy and began talking about their struggles with drugs. Over time, Kalchinian began complaining that his treatment was not working. He repeatedly asked Sherman to get drugs for him. Sherman refused and said he was trying to stay clean. Eventually, however, Sherman agreed after hearing Kalchinian's stories about how he was suffering. Kalchinian found a drug source, and Sherman bought drugs and sold them to Kalchinian. (Sherman kept some for himself and began using again.) Kalchinian then went to the Bureau of Narcotics and told agents that he had found another seller. They gave Kalchinian money, and he bought more drugs from Sherman. Sherman was arrested, tried, and convicted of selling narcotics. For his efforts, Kalchinian received a lighter sentence on a pending drug charge against him. (*Sherman v. U.S.*)

CHAPTER 3
CRIMINALS

Every society gets the kind of criminal it deserves.
– John F. Kennedy (1917-1963), U.S. president

HISTORY OF VIOLENT CRIME IN AMERICA | HOW MUCH CRIME IS THERE?
YOUTH, GANGS, AND VIOLENCE | WHITE-COLLAR CRIMINALS | SWINDLERS AND CON ARTISTS

History of Violent Crime in America

When I was young, I could play in the park at night. Now it's all drug dealers. You could leave all your doors unlocked. Now you can't walk down your own street without getting robbed.

For 30 years beginning in the 1960s, crime rates rose in America. Then in the 1990s, crime rates began to drop, and they have continued to fall. Many view the decrease as a trend toward a normal low rate of crime. Many older people look back on their past as a time when streets were safe and crime happened somewhere far away. Indeed, statistical evidence shows that the decades from the 1930s through the 1950s were less crime-ridden. Yet those decades may be exceptions in American history. If you take a careful look back into our history, you will find that violent crime has played a large role in American life.

During the 1700s, robbery and other violent crimes were already troubling the English colonies of America. Land was growing scarce. The English were fighting a series of wars and demanding high taxes from colonists to pay for them. In turn, the colonies suffered high rates of unemployment and poverty. Crime flourished in this environment.

Adding to the crime problem, criminals from England's jails, both men and women, were deported to America as indentured servants. Before the American Revolution, more than 50,000 of these lawbreakers had arrived. Some ran away immediately and joined the growing criminal population.

Philadelphia, one of America's first important cities, was known as the "crime capital of the colonies" during the early 1700s. Robbery, rape, murder, and arson occurred with frightening regularity.

By the mid-1700s, New York City was challenging Philadelphia for the dubious title of "crime capital." Its population was exploding. Along with the increasing population, came a rise in violent crime. A New York newspaper editorial complained, "It seems to have now become dangerous for the good People of this City to be out late at night without being sufficiently strong or well armed."

In the countryside and on the frontier, gangs of thieves and robbers preyed on farmers. Gangs in the North Carolina backwoods provoked citizens to take the law into their own hands. In 1767, citizens formed the first American vigilante group, which attacked and punished gang members.

Crime in the 1800s

During the 1800s, many American cities grew rapidly. Workshops and new industries attracted immigrants from England and Northern Europe. By 1800, New York had passed Philadelphia and Boston to become the biggest city in the country, with 60,000 people. Further waves of immigrants came to escape famines and wars in Europe. With the rise of heavy industry and mining in New England and the industrial Midwest, many companies actively recruited in Europe for laborers.

Many of the new immigrants had to squeeze into crowded tenements in urban areas. Cities like New York gained a reputation for overcrowding and criminal violence. In the decade before the Civil War, more than 3,000 homeless children roamed the streets of New York. Many of them became pickpockets and street robbers. One civic leader wrote in 1842: "Thronged as our city is, men are robbed in the streets . . . . The defenseless and the beautiful are ravished in the daytime and no trace of the criminals is found."

Before the Civil War, few cities in America had anything like a police department to keep order. Boston had a night watch, but it was mainly a fire lookout. Watchmen were afraid to enter many neighborhoods at all. In some

An 1857 engraving depicts a battle between two rival gangs — the Dead Rabbits and the Bowery Boys — in New York City.

places, vigilantes were the only organized resistance to criminals.

More murders took place in New York than London, a far bigger city. One English traveler wrote, "Probably in no city in the civilized world is life so fearfully insecure." The same fear plagued other cities. In Philadelphia during the mid-1800s, bands of robbers began to prey on wealthy citizens, stripping them of their cash.

In the West, men often wore guns wherever they went. Horse and cattle theft became a major problem. Los Angeles was only a sleepy village of about 8,000, but in one 15-month period in the 1850s, 40 murders occurred. In much larger San Francisco to the north, there were entire neighborhoods where few dared go after dark.

Ethnic Urban Gangs

In many cities, jobless immigrants formed violent gangs in ethnic slum neighborhoods. In Philadelphia, lower-class Irish and black groups formed gangs. With names like the Bleeders, Garroters, Rangers, Tormentors, and Killers, the gangs sometimes fought bloody battles on a spot known as the Battle Ground. Gang members as young as 10 carried clubs, knives, brass knuckles, and pistols. They attacked lone pedestrians, younger children, or members of other ethnic groups.

In New York, well-organized adult street gangs controlled the immigrant areas of Five Points and the Bowery. Made up mostly of young Irish immigrants, gangs called the Dead Rabbits, Plug Uglies, and Shirt Tails grew famous for mugging people. In the nearby Fourth Ward, the Daybreak Boys murdered 20 people between 1850 and 1852. Political parties recruited squads of toughs from these gangs to intimidate voters.

Probably the most violent New York street gang at this time was called the "Whyos." The Whyos came from Mulberry Bend, another slum neighborhood. They robbed people and burglarized homes and stores throughout the city. At one time, the Whyos had more than 500 members, all of whom supposedly had killed at least one person. Dandy Johnny Dolan, the gang's leader, invented a copper device for gouging an eye out and kept an eye as a trophy.

In cities of the Northeast, urban rioting broke out often from the 1830s through the 1850s. The pressures on the urban slums boiled over. There were ethnic riots, labor riots, election-day riots, anti-black riots, and anti-Catholic riots. In that period, Baltimore alone had 12 major riots, Philadelphia had 11, and New York had eight. This burst of lawlessness spurred the development of police forces in most cities.

Post-Civil War Violence

More than 600,000 people died in the Civil War. This is more than any other war in our history. The passions that gave rise to the war also left a legacy of hatred and violent revenge following the war. The most vicious and widespread postwar violence targeted blacks. During the period of Reconstruction, freed slaves served in state legislatures in the South. Former slaves educated themselves, voted, and many started businesses or began farming their own small fields. In response to these developments, some Southern whites created the Ku Klux Klan and other groups to terrorize blacks and help end the social changes of Reconstruction. In a reign of terror in Louisiana in the 1870s, a group called the White League killed more than 3,500 blacks, many by **lynching** — a form of mob violence that executes an accused person without a legal trial. Most of the lynchings were hangings.

The Klan engaged in lynchings of poor blacks and their supporters for decades. In incidents all over the country, almost 2,000 African Americans were lynched and murdered from 1882 to 1903.

Outlaws in the West

After the Civil War, violence in the West took a new turn. The Reno brothers of Indiana were the first train robbers, and dozens of small gangs followed their example. The most famous robbers were the James brothers — Jesse and Frank. They had been Confederate guerrillas, and after the war they turned to robbing trains and banks, terrorizing Union states from Missouri to Minnesota. They killed 16 people.

In the 1870s, Billy the Kid, who was born in a New York slum tenement, roamed the Southwest, gambling, killing, and hiring out as a cattle rustler. Sheriff Pat Garret finally tracked him down and shot him. According to legend, Billy the Kid had killed 21 men, one for each year of his life. The actual number was probably smaller.

John Wesley Hardin from Texas killed his first victim at age 15. The victim was a black teen who had beaten him at wrestling. He went on to kill more than a dozen others, including one because he had badmouthed Texas. Hardin was shot and killed in 1895 and became another outlaw legend, though today we would probably think of him as a psychopathic serial murderer.

Even more violent were the range wars. Throughout the Western states, cattle and land barons hired armies of gunmen to guard or expand their private empires. In some cases, the cattlemen had the law squarely on their side. But often their gunmen fought battles and used violence to settle scores. Texas had the Sutton-Taylor feud, the Horrell-Higgins feud, the Jaybird-Woodpecker feud, and several others. Montana had the Johnson County War, which pitted European immigrant homesteaders against a cattle baron. Arizona had the worst range war of all. In the Pleasant Valley War, the cattle-raising Grahams fought the sheep-raising Tewkesburys with hired armies. The conflict raged for six years and was fought literally "to the last man."

Racial Violence

The end of the century marked the beginning of a long era of race riots. As early as 1871, a white mob in Los Angeles went on a rampage and hanged 20 Chinese workers from street lamps. Near the turn of the century, mobs in Eastern cities began descending on black neighborhoods to lynch any black man unlucky enough to be caught. Major race riots against blacks erupted in Atlanta in 1906, Springfield, Illinois, in 1908, and in many other cities.

Prohibition and Organized Crime

The 20th century saw the rise of organized crime. In 1920, the 18th Amendment to the Constitution made the manufacture, transport, or sale of alcoholic beverages illegal. The era of Prohibition, one of this country's most violent crime periods, extended from 1920 until the 18th Amendment was repealed in 1933. Prohibition created the conditions for thriving illegal businesses.

In Chicago, gangsters set up illegal beer-brewing and distribution businesses, plus a network of bribed police and politicians to protect them. The business proved so lucrative that rival gangs fought for control. Between 1923 and 1926, the Chicago beer wars killed more than 200 people. By 1927, the mobster Al Capone had come out on top. His beer business took in over $60 million a year, which would be well over $1 billion in today's dollars.

During the early 1930s, various crime organizations sought to form alliances to control gambling, prostitution, narcotics, and other illegal money-making activities. Gangster rivalry and greed, however, led to many underworld murders.

Depression and World War II

Near the beginning of the Great Depression, violent crimes reached a peak. In 1933, the murder rate was 9.7 murders for every 100,000 Americans. The murder rate would not be this high again until the late 1970s.

A curious thing happened as the Depression worsened and unemployment skyrocketed: The crime rate went down. Despite widespread news coverage of Depression-era bank robbers like John Dillinger, "Pretty Boy" Floyd, and Bonnie and Clyde, violent crime actually declined. The murder rate, for example, dropped 50 percent between 1933 and the early 1940s. Other serious crimes fell by a third.

Why did crime decrease during a time of great hardship for almost all Americans? According to some historians, the Depression

IS THERE MORE CRIME THAN THERE WAS A YEAR AGO, OR LESS?

	MORE	LESS	SAME	NO OPINION
	%	%	%	%
2010	66	17	8	9
2009	74	15	6	5
2008	67	15	9	9
2007	71	14	8	6
2006	68	16	8	8
2005	67	21	9	3
2004	53	28	14	5
2003	60	25	11	4
2002	62	21	11	6
2001	41	43	10	6
2000	47	41	7	5
1998	52	35	8	5
1997	64	25	6	5
1996	71	15	8	6
1993	87	4	5	4
1992	89	3	4	4
1990	84	3	7	6
1989	84	5	5	6

NATIONAL POLL OF PEOPLE IN THE U.S.
Source: Gallup Poll

brought Americans closer together, because almost everyone was in the same boat. In addition, the birthrate had dropped in the 1920s, which meant that the youth population — 18 to 29 year olds — declined in size. Younger adults commit the most crimes, especially violent crimes. World War II unified Americans even more.

The Postwar Years

Following World War II, many people started families. The "baby boom," which lasted from 1946–1964, produced a huge increase in the birth rate.

The 1950s stayed relatively calm, but the turbulent 1960s saw an increase in many kinds of violence. A dozen civil-rights activists were murdered in the South, and the Vietnam War caused thousands of anti-war activists to take to the streets in demonstrations that sometimes turned violent. In the mid-1960s, major urban riots exploded in African-American communities in Los Angeles, Newark, Detroit, and other cities where urban problems had been festering.

Street crime also began to increase. The children of the baby boom were growing up.

The 18–29 age group grew rapidly. Many crime experts believe that this surge of young people in the population contributed significantly to the increase of crime in the 1960s and 1970s.

In the early 1980s, the sudden appearance of crack cocaine caused a tremendous rise in drug addiction and associated crimes. Drug-dealing gangs plagued many Latino and African-American communities. With unemployment and homelessness rising, reports of street crime skyrocketed. Crime so concerned ordinary citizens that it spawned whole communities barricaded with walls, barred windows, and burglar alarms.

Then in the early 1990s, crime started plummeting. By the end of 2010, the crime rate had dropped to its lowest point in 40 years. Part of the explanation is that the population is growing older. Experts have advanced other reasons for the decline: More police on the streets, more criminals behind bars, and better policing. These factors may account for some reduction in crime, but crime fell in parts of the country that didn't have more police, more prisoners, or better policing. Some experts believe the booming economy caused the drop. But others point out that the economy and the crime rate both soared in the 1960s, and the crime rate did not go up when the economy plunged into recession in 2008. Some experts believe that the dwindling use of crack cocaine produced the drop. Two researchers have even put forth a controversial theory that the legalization of abortion in 1973 caused crime to drop two decades later. They argue abortions stopped many unwanted children, who are more likely to turn to crime, from being born. But others respond that abortion was illegal when crime was low in previous decades.

Since the percentage of 18–29 year olds in the population is projected to fall, some Americans think the crime rate will continue to drop. Others predict the future will bring greater violent crime. No one knows for sure. But one fact remains: Violent crime has almost always existed at a high level throughout American history.

FOR DISCUSSION

1. Why do you think that violent crime has existed at such a high level throughout American history?
2. Why do you think American outlaws like Jesse James and Billy the Kid have so often been portrayed as heroes? Is there anyone like them today who is portrayed as a hero?

3. How do you account for so much mob violence directed against African Americans throughout our history?

4. Why did the crime rate go down in the 1930s? Why did it go up again in the 1960s? Why do you think it began falling in the 1990s? What direction do you think it is heading today? Why?

5. List as many causes of crime in American history as you can. Discuss the list and select the five most important. Explain your reasons.

CLASS ACTIVITY

Now and Then

The problem of crime in America varies from place to place and from generation to generation. In this activity, students interview a parent or older person and compare this person's experience with crime growing up to their own.

1. All students should:
   a. Read and answer for themselves the **Interview Questions**, below, on a sheet of paper.
   b. Find a parent or older person to interview. Ask the same questions and record the person's answers on another sheet of paper.
   c. Write a two or three paragraph essay comparing their responses to those of the person they interviewed.
   d. Staple all the pages together to be turned in.
2. Before students turn in their papers, they should share their findings with the class.

Interview Questions

1. When were you born?
2. As a young person, where (did, do) you live?
3. (Did, do) you feel safe in your neighborhood? Describe crimes, if any, that took place in your neighborhood.
4. (Did, do) you feel safe at school? Describe crimes or major incidents of misbehavior that took place in your school.
5. What crime story from the media most impressed you when you were growing up?
6. Do you think it was safer then or now? Why?

How Much Crime Is There?

People's fear of crime doesn't come from looking over their shoulders. It comes from looking at their television screens.
– Robert Lichter, director of the Center for Media and Public Affairs, *Los Angeles Times* (1994)

How do we know how many murders, rapes, robberies, burglaries, and other crimes there are each year? Where do crime statistics come from? There are two main sources: (1) the Uniform Crime Reports (UCR) and (2) the National Crime Victimization Survey (NCVS).

Since 1930, police departments from across the country have sent crime data to the Federal Bureau of Investigation for inclusion in its Uniform Crime Reports. The UCR lists eight so-called index crimes — four violent crimes and four property crimes. They are homicide, forcible rape, robbery, aggravated assault, burglary, larceny-theft, motor vehicle theft, and arson. Almost every police department in the United States reports its crimes for inclusion in the UCR.

The UCR has at least two built-in weaknesses. First, it does not attempt to account for all crime — only for crime reported to the police. If someone does not report a crime, it cannot possibly get included in the UCR. Second, it relies on police departments to relay the information accurately. This may not always happen.

To get a fuller picture of crime, the Department of Justice started an annual National Crime Victimization Survey in 1973. (Until 1991, it was called the National Crime Survey.) Twice a year, the survey polls 42,000 households, representing about 75,000 people over age 12. Following a detailed questionnaire, poll takers ask individuals if they have been victims of rape, robbery, assault, larceny, burglary, or car theft. Unlike the UCR, the NCVS reflects both reported and unreported crimes.

But the NCVS has problems also. First of all, it doesn't track some crimes. It cannot count homicides because murder victims cannot be interviewed. It doesn't include crimes against businesses, such as robberies and burglaries, because it only interviews households. It only interviews people over age 12, so it doesn't count crimes against young children. Of the crimes it does count, the interview could be flawed.

The Trend of Crime

Since the UCR and NCVS measure different data, they come up with different numbers for most crimes. As would be expected, the NCVS consistently reports far higher numbers than the UCR, except for auto theft. NCVS reports only slightly higher numbers of auto thefts than the UCR.

What do the UCR and NCVS say about the trend of crime? Is it increasing, decreasing, or staying the same? Is it worse than in previous years or better? If 10 years ago, fewer robberies took place than today, would it mean that crime got worse during this period? Not necessarily. The population today is greater than it was 10 years ago. To make comparisons between two different times, you need to know the **crime rates** — the amount of crime per person. The UCR calculates these rates as the number of crimes for every 100,000 persons. The NCVS usually calculates them for every 1,000 persons age 12 or older (for violent crimes) or for every 1,000 households (for property crimes).

The NCVS shows that the rate of violent crime has fallen sharply in the last 10 years. In 1973, the rate of violent crime was 47.7 per 1,000. It reached a peak of 52.3 per 1,000 in 1981, declined to 42.0 in 1986, rose steadily to 51.2 in 1994. Then it began plummeting. By 2009, it had fallen to 17.1.

The UCR paints a slightly different picture. It shows crime rising almost steadily from 1973 to 1992. From that point, the crime rate starts declining.

Most experts tend to trust crime trends from the NCVS over the UCR. But experts also believe the UCR statistics for homicide are highly accurate. The NCVS does not cover homicide. The UCR homicide statistics follow almost the same pattern as the NCVS statistics for other violent crimes. They rise to a peak of 10.2 homicides per 100,000 in 1980, drop to 7.9 in 1985, rise to 9.5 in 1993, and then start declining. By 2000, the rate had dropped to 5.5. It hovered around that rate until 2008 when it began dropping again. In 2009, the rate had fallen to 5.0. Other homicide studies back up these figures.

Although crime has been falling for about 30 years, most of the public does not know it. For many years, the Gallup Poll has asked Americans whether there is more or less crime in the U.S. today than a year ago. Almost without exception, they have responded there is more crime (see "Is there more crime than there was a year ago, or less?," page 51).

FOR DISCUSSION

1. What are the differences between the Uniform Crime Reports and the National Crime Victimization Survey? Which do you think more accurately paints a picture of crime in America? Why?
2. Why do you think the UCR and NCVS report similar numbers of car thefts each year? Why do you think the other crimes are not similar in number?

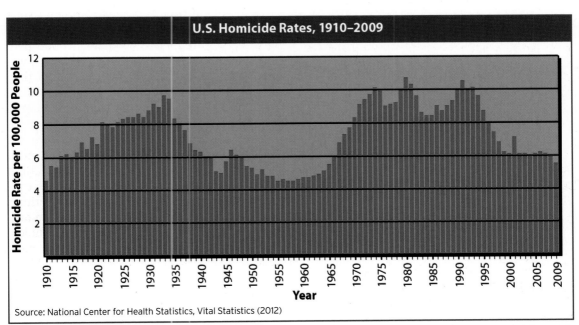

U.S. Homicide Rates, 1910–2009

Homicide Rate per 100,000 People / Year

Source: National Center for Health Statistics, Vital Statistics (2012)

3. Why do you think experts believe UCR homicide statistics are so accurate?
4. What do you think could account for the difference in the UCR's and NCVS's trends in violent crime since 1973? Which do you think is more accurate? Why?

5. Even when crime is declining, why do you think most Americans believe crime in the U.S. is getting worse?

CLASS ACTIVITY

Crime Victim Survey

How has crime affected the people who live in your community? In this activity, students survey people to find what experiences members of the community have had with crime.
1. Form small teams.
2. Each team should:
   a. Prepare several copies of a crime victim survey using the suggested questions below as a guide. Leave room for brief responses for each question.
   b. Have each student on the team target a person with a different occupation in the community, e.g., a storekeeper, homemaker, religious leader, business supervisor, fast-food employee. Students should survey the targeted persons.
   c. Summarize and compare the responses from the surveys. Try to account for any differences, based on different occupations.
3. All the teams should compare their surveys and list results on the board. Do you find similarities among the answers given by people with similar occupations? Why or why not? Do you find similarities based on other factors?

Crime Victim Survey
1. Have you ever been a victim of a crime such as bike theft, burglary, assault, etc.?
2. Have any members of your family been victims of crime?
3. Have any nearby neighbors ever been victims of crime?
4. Do you feel unsafe alone at night in your own neighborhood?
5. Do you believe a crime problem exists at the local schools?
6. Have the people in your family been forced to change how they lead their lives because of crime?
7. Do you think the police in your community are doing an adequate job of protecting you and other citizens from crime?
8. Compared to one year ago, do you think the crime problem in your community has gotten worse, stayed the same, or improved?

Debriefing Questions
1. Were there any surprises in the results? How do you explain the surprises?
2. Make a list on the board of the kinds of crimes reported in the survey. Do you think other areas in your town or other towns would have a different list? Why or why not?
3. Discuss ways your family and neighbors attempt to protect themselves from crime. For example, you might consider special locks, bars on the windows, watchdogs, guns in the home, neighborhood patrols, etc.
4. What crimes occur most frequently at school? What could be done to prevent them?
5. What are the police in your area doing to prevent crime? What should they be doing?

Youth, Gangs, and Violence

Most gang homicides are not random, nor are they only disputes over drugs or some other crime. The vast majority of violent incidents involving gang members continue to result from fights over turf, status, and revenge.

– Violence Prevention Coalition of Greater Los Angeles, "Violence Prevention Fact Sheet" (2007)

About 40 percent of all people arrested are under the age of 25. About three-fourths of those arrested are males. In fact, males account for more than 80 percent of all violent-crime arrests.

One of the most common violent criminals is the street robber. In his book *Criminal Violence, Criminal Justice,* Charles Silberman described the typical street robber as a male minority teenager or young adult from a poor family. This type of robber takes money from people impulsively if the opportunity arises. Rarely does he plan a holdup.

Sometimes street robbers steal because they want money for drugs, food, or goods. Sometimes they just need to impress someone. At other times, the street robber acts out of boredom. The victims of street robbers are often weak or vulnerable. They could be an old person walking alone or a drunk who has passed out on a park bench. Almost always they belong to the same ethnic group as the robber.

Youth Gang Violence

Youth gangs are not new to our cities. Throughout American history, gangs of young men have come together in immigrant and poverty areas of cities. In the late-19th and early-20th century, Eastern cities such as Boston, New York, and Philadelphia saw the rise of numerous gangs. Their members usually came from newly arrived or first-generation groups — Irish, Jewish, and Italian. In the early 1900s, the sociologist Frederick M. Thrasher studied the youth gangs of Chicago and found over 1,000 of them. These early gangs mainly took part in street crime. Later some developed ties to political machines and formed the basis of organized crime in America.

The Latino street gangs of Los Angeles arose in the 1920s during a huge wave of Mexican immigration from poor rural farms. In the 1930s and 1940s, these early gangs solidified into the *pachuco* lifestyle. They wore special clothes, called zoot suits, had nicknames, and spoke their own slang, called *Calo.* Feeling shut out of American society, they became heavily territorial, each defending a small neighborhood or *barrio.* They acquired names like Los 39s and Clarence Street Locos. Many of these groups have survived in the same area for more than 80 years. Puerto Rican youths in New York formed similar gangs, as portrayed by the Sharks in the popular 1961 film *West Side Story.*

To some degree these gangs were social clubs, but they also took part in street crime, drugs, and long-running turf warfare. In fact, by the 1970s, this turf warfare had given rise to the characteristic gang crime — the drive-by shooting. Gang members as young as 13 would lean out the windows of cars to avenge some wrong by shooting at an enemy gang member. Often the shots hit the wrong target, a guest at a wedding party or a tiny child playing on a lawn.

Outlaw motorcycle gangs developed in some poor white communities in the 1950s. As shown in the 1950 film *The Wild One,* these bikers were less interested in defending turf than in appearing like a marauding band of pirates. Later, motorcycle gangs became associated with drug trafficking and other crimes.

Outlaw motorcycle gangs were often marked by a vicious anti-black, anti-Latino racism. In the 1970s and 1980s, some impoverished white communities saw the development of similar groups who called themselves skinheads. They modeled themselves on British punk gangs who shaved their heads. Often identifying with punk music and voicing overt racism, the skinhead groups produced an embittered subculture of hatred and violence.

African-American youth gangs had a different history. They arose in the 1950s to protect local turf, much like the Latino gangs. In the period of political protest of the 1960s, some of these gangs turned to radical politics. The Blackstone Rangers in Chicago became Black P. Stone (the "P" stood for power). After the Watts riots of 1965, the Slausons became the nucleus for the Los Angeles Black Panthers. These politicized groups did not survive long into the 1970s. Black P. Stone,

Childhood Risk Factors For Joining a Gang

Factors predicting that children ages 10-12 will join a gang between ages 13 and 18

Risk Factor	Number of times more likely to join a gang
Neighborhood	
Availability of marijuana	3.6
Neighborhood youth in trouble	3.0
Low neighborhood attachment	1.5
Family	
Family structure	
One parent only	2.4
One parent plus other adults	3.0
Parental attitudes favoring violence	2.3
Low bonding with parents	ns
Low household income	2.1
Sibling antisocial behavior	1.9
Poor family management	1.7
School	
Learning disabled	3.6
Low academic achievement	3.1
Low school attachment	2.0
Low school commitment	1.8
Low academic aspirations	1.6
Peer group	
Association with friends who engage in problem behaviors	2.0
Individual	
Low religious service attendance	ns
Early marijuana use	3.7
Early violence	3.1
Antisocial beliefs	2.0
Early drinking	1.6
Externalizing behaviors	2.6
Poor refusal skills	1.8

Notes: (1) To clarify the meaning of the chart using the first risk factor, youth from neighborhoods where marijuana was most available were 3.6 times more likely to join a gang compared with other youth. (2) "ns" means the factor was not a significant predictor. (3) "Externalizing behaviors" mean aggression, oppositional behaviors, and inattentive and hyperactive behaviors.

Source: "Early Precursors of Gang Membership: A Study of Seattle Youth," OJJDP (2001)

for example, changed again and eventually became a drug-dealing gang called El Rukn.

In the early 1970s, Los Angeles saw the beginning of a new federation of gangs called the Crips. Unlike other gangs, the Crips spun off subgroups called "sets" in many areas around Southern California. An archrival group called the Bloods also developed, spinning off its own sets, until many Los Angeles neighborhoods became a patchwork of gang territories. The two super-gangs sported official colors — blue for the Crips, red for the Bloods — and each set had a hand sign, like a letter of the deaf alphabet, to identify itself. Gang members, known as gang-bangers, also used pro football and basketball jackets to announce their identities.

The black gangs might have settled into the pattern of earlier gangs — street crime, turf wars, and petty vendettas. But in the early 1980s, crack cocaine hit the streets. The normal powdered form of cocaine cost about $100 a gram. Crack, however, could be bought as cheaply as $5. This cheap and highly addicting drug instantly transformed cocaine use into a widespread and deadly problem. With millions of dollars to be made overnight, many sets of the Bloods and Crips turned themselves into drug-dealing networks to rake in the profits.

This flood of cash plus ties to Latin American drug suppliers brought along a huge increase in violence. Gang members now used automatic weapons like the Uzi or AK-47. Some sets of the Crips and Bloods started sending out exploration parties to set up business in cities across the country. The drug network spread.

On the Eastern seaboard, Jamaican immigrants formed similar crack-dealing gangs called posses, and they too started to spread outward from Boston, New York, and Washington, D.C. The Untouchables from Miami and El Rukn from Chicago did the same. By the late 1980s, gangs of second-generation Vietnamese, Cambodian, and Chinese immigrant youth were also jumping into the crack trade.

Crack addiction created many social problems. With more addicts searching for small amounts of ready cash to buy crack, reports of street crime and theft continued to rise. The number of drug- and gang-related murders increased. Crack addiction also increased prostitution rates and the use of injected drugs like heroin. These were major factors in the spread of AIDS.

By 2000, the crack epidemic had slowed and the number of gang-related killings dropped. But the number of transnational gangs increased. A transnational gang is one that operates across national boundaries. Many of these gangs formed when members, not legally in the U.S., were convicted of crimes and deported to Mexico and Central America. They had learned about gangs in the United States and used their knowledge to set up gangs in other countries.

Two such gangs are the 18th Street Gang and the Mara Salvatrucha 13 (MS-13), both originally formed in Los Angeles. The 18th Street gang is primarily Latino, but includes members from all racial and ethnic groups. The MS-13 is mainly composed of those with Central American ancestry. The two gangs combined are estimated to have about 40,000 members across the nation and in other countries, most of them in many separate, independent *clikas*, or cliques. The gangs engage in robbery, kidnapping, murder, and trafficking humans, weapons, and drugs across the border.

Young people join gangs for different reasons. For some inner-city youths, it may seem safer to be in a gang (although statistics show that gang members are at least 60 times more likely to be killed than those in the general population). For others, the gang offers a way to make money (although studies have shown that even in the most successful drug gangs, most gang members, aside from those at the top, make little money). For many, gangs provide a substitute for a functioning, supportive family.

One researcher has classified gangs into three types: corporate, territorial, and scavenger. Corporate gangs try to make money. These gangs tend to be highly organized and almost everything they do concerns making money. Territorial gangs are less organized and focus on protecting their turf. They may respond with violence to anyone who intrudes on their area. Scavenger gangs are the least organized. The members who band together are usually low achievers and violence prone. Most outbursts of gang violence tend to be driven by vendettas and revenge.

In the worst neighborhoods, the fear is pervasive, even among gang members. David M. Kennedy, who has advised troubled communities across the nation, says:

> Even the *gang* kids are scared to death. They get shot at, they get shot, their friends have been shot, they've got real enemies out there. . . . The fear . . . makes them join gangs, it makes them get guns, it makes them carry guns, it makes them use violence to show they shouldn't be messed with.

FOR DISCUSSION

1. List some of the factors that might push a young male toward violence. Do these factors also affect young females? Why do you think young males, as a group, are more violent than young females?
2. Does gang activity exist in your community? How has it changed in recent years?
3. What do you think should be done to stop gang violence? Explain.

White-Collar Criminals

White collar crime may be defined approximately as a crime committed by a person of respectability and high social status in the course of his occupation. Consequently, it excludes many crimes of the upper class, such as most of their cases of murder, adultery, and intoxication, since these are not customarily a part of their occupational procedures. Also, it excludes the confidence games of wealthy members of the underworld, since they are not persons of respectability and high social status.

– Edwin H. Sutherland, criminologist, *White Collar Crime* (1949)

The average loss from a street crime — a burglary or mugging or theft from a car — is less than $500. White-collar criminals, however, take far more from their victims. White-collar crime refers to acts like bank and securities fraud (such as obtaining credit on a false basis, selling stocks with false information, putting false entries in accounting records).

White-collar criminals don't rely on violence or breaking and entering. They take advantage of their positions of power and violate the trust of others. They steal money and property and also endanger the trust people have in our economic system.

Enron

One major fraud involved Enron, a corporation based in Houston, Texas. Enron began in 1985 as a natural gas pipeline company. But as states and the federal government deregulated energy utilities, Enron became an energy trading company. If a utility company needed energy (natural gas or electricity), Enron found another utility that could supply it.

As its stock price rose, Enron decided to branch out and trade in many other things, some of them extremely risky investments. When these deals did not go well, Enron went into debt. To cover up the debt, it created offshore partnerships with companies that held the debt for Enron. It also falsified financial records on many of its trades, claiming much greater revenue than it actually received. The apparent revenue increases made Enron's stock appealing to investors.

Every company that offers its stock to the public must report its financial statements to the Securities and Exchange Commission (SEC), a federal regulatory agency. Financial statements must be audited by an independent company certifying their validity and accuracy. Enron's dealings were shady, but its auditor, Arthur Andersen, the nation's largest accounting firm, did not uncover the massive frauds. Enron not only paid Andersen $25 million a year to perform audits, it also paid Andersen $27 million a year for other accounting services.

Enron kept reporting rising profits, and its stock price soared. It was the nation's seventh largest company in 2000, reporting more than $100 billion in business that year.

The next year was far different. A deal fell through to distribute movies over the Internet. It was revealed that a bankrupt energy company owed Enron more than $500 million. The Securities and Exchange Commission began investigating Enron's offshore deals. As Enron's shaky financial condition was revealed, its stock price plummeted. By the end of 2001, Enron declared bankruptcy.

Thousands of employees lost their jobs. Many had invested their pensions in now-worthless Enron stock. In fact, many individual investors, mutual funds, and pension funds had invested in the stock.

Some Enron executives were charged, tried, and convicted of violating federal fraud statutes. Kenneth Lay, Enron's founder was convicted of six counts of wire and securities fraud, but died before being sentenced. Jeff Skilling, Enron's chief operating officer, was convicted of 19 counts of fraud and sentenced to 24 years in prison.

Many other Enron executives pleaded guilty, including Andrew Fastow, the chief financial officer and architect of most of the fraudulent deals. He was sentenced to 10 years in prison.

The accounting firm of Arthur Andersen was charged with obstruction of justice. Its executives admitted directing employees to shred Enron documents in accordance with its document retention policies after learning of the SEC's investigation of Enron. More than two tons of paper were shredded. The firm was charged under a statute that makes it a crime to "knowingly" and "corruptly" persuade another person to "withhold" or "alter" documents to be used in an "official proceeding." The trial judge instructed the jury that even if Andersen's executives believed their conduct was lawful, the jury could still convict the firm. The jury found the firm guilty, and the firm went out of business.

In 2005 in *Andersen v. U.S.*, a unanimous Supreme Court ruled that the judge's instruction was wrong and reversed the conviction. Writing for the court, Chief Justice William Rehnquist stated: "Only persons conscious of wrongdoing can be said to 'knowingly . . . corruptly persuad[e].' "

Other major financial institutions were implicated in the scandal. Four bankers from Merrill Lynch were convicted of fraud for one of Enron's offshore deals.

In response to the Enron scandal, the federal government passed the Sarbanes-Oxley Act in 2002. The act set up a new agency to regulate firms that audit corporations and made it against the law for firms to audit a corporation's books *and* perform other accounting work for the same corporation. It also set strong penalties for anyone who "knowingly" destroys, alters, or falsifies documents to "impede, obstruct or influence" a federal "investigation" or bankruptcy. Finally, it requires chief executive officers and chief financial officers to certify the accuracy of their financial statements. Anyone who certifies a statement knowing that it is not true faces penalties up to 20 years in prison and $5 million in fines.

Bernard Madoff

Another, more recent fraud was committed by Bernard "Bernie" Madoff. Just before it was exposed in December 2008, Madoff's company claimed to have $65 *billion* in assets, double the amount of assets on the books of financial giant Goldman Sachs.

The reason Madoff's fraud grew so large was that people trusted and respected him. He was seen as an innovator and visionary on Wall Street.

In the early 1960s, he had set up a small brokerage house, Bernard L. Madoff Investment Securities LLC. (LLC stands for "limited liability company." It is not a corporation.) Wall Street then had two major stock exchanges, the New York and American, which traded major stocks. Madoff's company specialized in trading "over the counter" stocks, those of companies not listed on the two exchanges.

Madoff began trading after hours, when the two major exchanges closed. His company developed software for conducting trades quickly and efficiently.

Bernard Madoff, center, was sentenced to 150 years in prison for fraud.

When NASDAQ, the first electronic stock exchange, opened in the early 1970s, it used the software Madoff's company had developed. Madoff even later served as the chairman of NASDAQ, an honorary position.

Aside from trading, Madoff's company also created a fund for people to invest in. It was this fund that became the fraud. Madoff claims his fraud began in the early 1990s, but many believe it began long before. Nobody knows why Madoff turned to fraud. He was proud of being considered a financial genius, capable of getting returns for his fund even in bad times. The fraud probably began during a bad time with him fudging numbers at first, and it later turned into a huge Ponzi scheme.

A Ponzi scheme works by taking money from investors, promising them a high rate of return. When investors want their profits, they get paid by money from newer investors. To work, the scheme requires a constant flow of new money into the fund. (The name Ponzi comes from Charles Ponzi, who defrauded people using this method in the 1920s.)

When people invested money in Madoff's fund, he put their money into his personal bank account. There was no fund. He developed software that could show investors and regulators where the fund's money was supposedly invested. It allowed him to send out thousands of monthly statements to investors.

Madoff's scheme differed from most Ponzi schemes in two ways. First, he did not promise investors outlandishly high returns. His returns were high, but most important, they were consistent. Madoff made it seem like his fund was a safe investment, always going up. Second, he did not pursue investors. He made his fund seem like an exclusive club, and investors came looking to invest in it.

Madoff managed to get charitable foundations, university endowments, mutual funds, and hedge funds to invest in his fund. He seemed to have an endless amount of new money coming in until the stock market collapsed in 2008.

When the market fell, mutual funds, hedge funds, and other large investors wanted their money from Madoff because they needed to pay people who were withdrawing money from their funds. Much more money was going out of Madoff's fund than coming in. Madoff realized he was done. He told his sons what he had been doing and that he was going to consult an attorney and eventually turn himself in. But the sons consulted their own attorney and were told they could not wait for their father to turn himself in because the fraud was ongoing. They went to the authorities, and Madoff was arrested the next day, December 11, 2008.

In March 2009, Madoff entered a guilty plea to all the charges against him — 11 federal felonies (among them, securities fraud, wire fraud, and mail fraud). He admitted to the court that he had committed a massive fraud and implausibly stated he had acted alone. Three months later, the judge sentenced him to 150 years in prison.

Others in Madoff's company have pleaded guilty to fraud charges. His accountant, who supposedly singlehandedly audited Madoff's "huge" fund since 1991, pleaded guilty to nine federal felonies. Madoff's second in command also pleaded guilty.

Exactly two years after Madoff's arrest, his son Mark committed suicide. Several investors also committed suicide. Pension funds, university endowments, and charities lost huge amounts of money. Some charities were forced to close down. Many thousands of investors lost their savings.

As early as 1999, one financial analyst had reported Madoff to the SEC. The analyst stated he could tell that something was wrong with Madoff's company within five minutes of examining its records. Madoff's returns always went up, never down. The analyst repeatedly tried to get the attention of the SEC, the media, and others in the financial industry. But he was ignored.

FOR DISCUSSION

1. At the time, Enron's fraud was called the "corporate crime of the century." Describe the fraud.

2. At Enron and other companies accused of massive fraud, chief executives, paid millions of dollars a year to run the companies, have claimed they knew nothing about the fraud. Do you think it is likely to be true? If it were true, should the executives be held accountable somehow? Explain.

3. What role did the accounting firm Arthur Andersen play in the Enron scandal? Do you agree with the Supreme Court's decision in *Andersen v. U.S.*? Explain.

4. What is a Ponzi scheme? Why do you think Madoff's scheme was so successful?

5. Why didn't the Sarbanes-Oxley Act apply to Madoff's firm? If it had, do you think it would have made a difference?

6. Do you think the criminal justice system should treat white-collar criminals less harshly than violent criminals? Explain.

7. Do you think tighter economic regulations can help prevent white-collar crime or is there little that can be done to prevent it? Explain.

Swindlers and Con Artists

Fraud and deceit abound in these days more than in former times.
– Edward Coke, English judge, politician, and legal scholar, *Twynes Case* (1602)

Not all swindles involve banks and huge sums of money. Smaller swindles — called con games, scams, or buncos — cost Americans billions of dollars each year. Con games can vary from small schemes that take a few dollars from schoolchildren up to elaborate plots to steal large sums from the rich.

P.T. Barnum, the great showman, said, "There's a sucker born every minute." In fact, almost any of us could be suckered at one time or another. Con artists tend to be bright, articulate people. They are clever actors and patient at waiting for the right moment to strike. In addition, they often work in groups to help bamboozle their victims. Often someone called a "shill," who seems to be an innocent bystander, begins the process of drawing in the victim. Complex con games can involve several other people called "cappers" who also pretend to be innocent. In fact, they are all part of the swindle team.

Some con games prey on people's desire to help and be good neighbors. In one such scam, a person pretends to be your new neighbor who has locked his keys inside his house and needs to call a cab to get to an important

Some Con Game Slang

big store an elaborate confidence game involving a fake office and many people. The film *The Sting* shows a good example.

blowoff the last move in a con game.

capper an apparent bystander who is actually an accomplice of the swindler. Also, a steerer.

fish the victim. Also the mark, the pigeon, the customer.

green a naive victim.

hang paper to write a fraudulent check.

hurrah the point in a con game where the victim is totally committed.

red inking the threat to eliminate the victim from some elaborate scheme just as he or she gets greedy.

salt a mine placing a few real gems in a worthless mine, or something similar.

squeeze a crooked wheel game such as roulette.

stall the point in a swindle where the victim is momentarily delayed in order to increase his or her greed.

touch the money taken from a victim.

appointment across town. You loan "cab fare" to the "neighbor" and never see him again.

Most con games, however, rely on the victim's desire to get something for nothing. The swindler offers huge rewards at some later date in exchange for some of your money right now. Dallas police investigator W.E. Orzechowski once said, "Con men basically are using the same old schemes, time after time, and they still work." The best bet to avoid a con game is to remember: If it seems too good to be true, it almost certainly is. Everyone should say no to schemes suggested by strangers.

The following section describes several classic swindles, and a few new ones developed for the telephone and Internet age. To help you keep the bad guys straight, in each case we will call the swindler "Bunco" and the accomplice "Capper."

Pigeon Drop

Mr. Bunco approaches a well-dressed elderly woman named Ms. Green at a bus stop. While chatting in a friendly way, Mr. Bunco spots an envelope on the sidewalk. He peeks into the envelope and says it contains $6,000. Now Ms. Capper arrives and joins the conversation. Mr. Bunco asks both women what they should do with the money. Soon they all agree to share the money, but Ms. Capper recommends that Mr. Bunco go to a nearby lawyer for advice.

Mr. Bunco returns and says the lawyer told him the three should share the $6,000. But Mr. Bunco reports that the law requires a neutral party to hold the money for six months. He says the lawyer has agreed to hold the $6,000 if they will each put up $1,000 to show good faith.

The minute poor Ms. Green adds her $1,000 to the envelope, the swindlers find a way to go off with it. They may even leave her with the original envelope — full of worthless paper.

Bank Examiner Swindle

Mr. Bunco visits Maria, a young housewife, and identifies himself as a bank examiner. He picked her out as a victim by watching her fill out a deposit slip at the bank. Mr. Bunco tells Maria that he believes one of the tellers at the bank is embezzling money. He asks Maria to help him trap the teller and offers her a reward of $500. After she agrees, Mr. Bunco asks Maria to withdraw a large sum of money from her account. "Bring the money home," he says.

"One of our security people will come by and pick up the bills to examine the serial numbers." Maria withdraws the money, but of course it is picked up by Ms. Capper, who disappears with it.

Phony Prize or Sweepstakes Offers

This is a common telemarketing, or telephone, fraud. Mr. Bunco telephones Henry and informs him he has won second prize in a sweepstakes or lottery. His prize is $250,000, but before Henry can receive it, he must pay $10,000 in taxes. When Henry wires him the money, Mr. Bunco calls Henry with even better news. The first place winner has been disqualified and Henry now can win the $1 million grand prize. All he has to do is pay $70,000 more in taxes. Henry wires more money, and he never hears from Mr. Bunco again.

Other Telemarketing Scams

Telemarketing swindles like the luxury tax scam have become big business, stealing billions of dollars a year. Often a room full of callers work these swindles. When authorities begin to investigate, the whole operation can move on easily. Here are some common telemarketing schemes that either steal money directly or offer a service at hugely inflated prices:

- Schemes to fix bad credit or get a credit card for a fee
- Phony offers of educational grants for a fee
- Magazine subscriptions that are overpriced or never appear
- Work-at-home offers that promise huge incomes
- Fake offers of loans for a fee paid in advance
- Phony travel and vacation offers
- Fake calls from a bank or credit card company to get personal information

If you are approached by a caller like this, try to get an address or telephone number and then call the police, the district attorney's office, a local consumer protection agency, or the National Fraud Information Center at (800) 876-7060.

ASK AN EXPERT

Invite a police officer from the bunco squad to discuss with your class different con games and swindles.

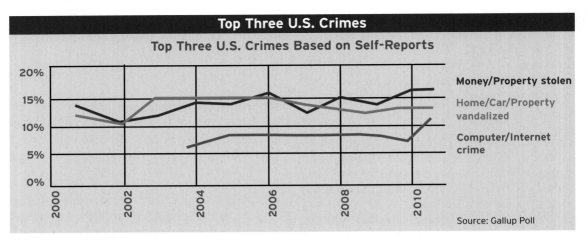

Top Three U.S. Crimes

Top Three U.S. Crimes Based on Self-Reports

- Money/Property stolen
- Home/Car/Property vandalized
- Computer/Internet crime

Source: Gallup Poll

Internet Fraud

With the growth of e-commerce, many telemarketing scams have moved to the Internet. Scammers set up web sites and telephone banks and send bulk e-mail, known as spam, asking people to contact them. Just like telemarketing fraud, scammers offer phony merchandise, prizes, magazine subscriptions, and investment opportunities. In addition, the Internet offers con artists new opportunities. Here are a few common Internet frauds:

Auctions. The Federal Trade Commission reports more fraud from auctions than anywhere else on the Internet. Mrs. Bunco offers to sell a new television on an auction web site. She gives a mail drop as her address. When the money arrives, Mrs. Bunco never sends a television.

In more than 90 percent of all Internet fraud cases, payment is made offline — by check or money order. "Requesting cash is a clear sign of fraud," said Susan Grant, director of the Internet Fraud Watch. "Pay the safest way. If possible, pay by credit card because you can dispute the charges if there is a problem."

Phishing. Mr. Bunco sends out spam claiming to be from a bank, credit card company, or Internet service provider. The e-mail has a phony link to the company's web site. It is actually to Mr. Bunco's web site, which is designed to look like the real company's site. When people click on the link, the web site tells them that their accounts need updating (particularly passwords and credit card information). When customers respond, Mr. Bunco goes on a spending spree with their credit card numbers.

Nigerian money scam. Ms. Bunco sends spam in which she claims to be an official of a foreign government who needs help getting a huge sum of money (or diamonds) out of the country. She offers to give a share of the money to the person who helps her. She has pictures and documents galore. When people respond, she acts desperate, saying she needs money for some purpose, perhaps to bribe an official. She always needs a little more money. People send it thinking they are going to get a share of a fortune.

FOR DISCUSSION

1. Are you familiar with any of these swindles? Which ones seem most tempting to victims? Why?
2. Why do victims fall for swindles? How can they avoid them?

ACTIVITY

More Cons

There are many more con games and swindles than have been mentioned in this book. In this activity, students find and report on different schemes. Each student should:

1. Research and find a different con game or swindle. To find one, talk to people, go to the library, or research on the Internet. A good place to start on the Internet is at *Criminal Justice in America* Links (**www.CriminalJusticeInAmerica.org**).
2. Write a one-page paper describing the con game, how it works, and who its victims are.

CHAPTER 4

CRIME VICTIMS

Americans are fascinated by murders and murderers but not by the families of the people who are killed — an amazingly numerous group, whose members can turn only to one another for sympathy and understanding.
– Eric Schlosser, "A Grief Like No Other" in *The Atlantic* (1997)

WHO ARE THE VICTIMS? | VICTIMS OF VIOLENT CRIMES | VICTIMS OF PROPERTY CRIMES
HELPING VICTIMS OF CRIME | THE PUSH FOR VICTIMS' RIGHTS

Who Are the Victims?

Broad studies have revealed certain trends within crime and victimization patterns. Adolescents are most likely to be victimized. Men become crime victims more often than women do, and blacks experience more crime than other racial groups.
– **National Institute of Justice web site, "Victims and Victimization" (2012)**

Suzanne Rossetti, 26, was driving home from the theater at Arizona State University in Phoenix. On the way, she stopped at the market, where she accidentally locked her keys inside her car. Two young men got the door open for her with a coat hanger and then asked her for a lift. She agreed, but once in the car, they turned vicious almost immediately.

The young men forced Suzanne to drive them to her apartment. There they beat and raped her for several hours. Then they drove her into the desert and threw her off a cliff. When they heard her moans down below, they climbed down after her. She pleaded with them to leave her alone.

"I'm dying anyway," she begged.

"Damn right you are," one of them growled. He picked up a rock and crushed her skull.

Shocking stories like these have frightened most of us. *The streets just aren't safe at night. I've had my third car stereo stolen. I hate putting bars on my windows, but what choice do I have?* Opinion polls consistently show that Americans express great concern over the crime rate and the effectiveness of the criminal justice system.

Down through the years, this concern has sparked many studies of the causes of crime and many proposals for possible solutions. In recent decades, attention has shifted to the *victims* of crime. Who are they? How can we help them through the tangle of the legal system? What can be done to protect them? And what can be done to help them recover from the effects of the crime?

First, who are the victims? They come from all walks of life and all age groups. But studies show that the most common victim of violent crime is a black male teenager from a low-income family. And the most common victim of theft is a white male teenager from a low-income family. Most studies show that criminals tend to victimize members of their own race.

Being a victim can be deeply disturbing. It can take years to recover, and some victims never recover. This is not just true of violent crime. Fraud can wipe out a victim's life savings. A bank swindle can take away a home that an elderly couple worked all their lives to pay for.

Crimes against property like fraud, burglary, and theft are the most common crimes in the United States. Violent crimes such as murder, rape, and robbery are less common. But they probably cause more anxiety and fear. Violent crime can leave a victim crippled, physically or emotionally. It's hard to imagine the effect if it hasn't happened to you. Some victims never want to leave the safety of their homes again.

In the following sections, we will examine some victims of violent and property crimes. First we will find out what **victimology** — the study of victims — tells us about victims of these crimes. Then we'll listen to some victims describe the effect crime had on their lives.

Victims of Violent Crimes

Without warning, Silva pulled out a hunting knife and began moving about the room with demonic speed, stabbing six people in a matter of seconds. Among these were Martin, stabbed in the thigh and the arm, the woman behind the counter, stabbed in the chest and abdomen while phoning the police, and Anna, stabbed in the side as we pulled each other toward the door. I had gone no more than a few steps down the sidewalk when I felt a hard punch in my back followed instantly by the unforgettable sensation of skin and muscle tissue parting. Silva had stabbed me about six inches above my waist, just beneath my rib cage. Without thinking, I clapped my hand over the wound before the knife was out, and the exiting blade sliced my palm and two fingers.

– Bruce Shapiro, "The Violent Politics of Crime" in *Harper's Magazine* (1995)

Violent crimes, such as murder, rape, robbery, and assault, are also known as **crimes against the person.** In these crimes, the criminal either uses force or threatens to use force against the victim. Below, we will take a closer look at victims of two kinds of violent crime — robbery and domestic violence.

Average Annual Rate of Violent Victimization Per 1,000 Persons, 1993-2008

	Percentage of Population	Victimization Rate
Sex		
Male	48.8%	15.7
Female	51.2	14.2
Race		
White	67.9%	13.6
Black	11.9	20.8
Hispanic	14.0	15.6
American Indian or Alaskan Native	0.5	42.2
Asian or Pacific Islander	4.7	6.3
Two or more races	1.0	52.6
Age		
12-14	4.7%	27.5
15-17	4.8	23
18-20	5.1	33.9
21-24	6.5	26.9
25-34	16.3	18.8
35-49	24.7	12.6
50-64	22.7	10.9
65 or older	15.1	2.4

Source: "Crimes Against Persons Age 65 or Older, 1993-2008," Bureau of Justice Statistics (2010)

The Robbery Victim

In a robbery, the criminal takes property by force or by threat of force. In this scary crime, victims can lose their property, suffer injuries, and even die. Statistically, the chances of being killed are small: Almost 99.8 percent of all robbery victims survive. About one-third of all victims suffer injuries, mostly minor. Only 2 percent receive wounds serious enough to stay overnight in a hospital. Strangely, victims are most likely to be hurt by unarmed robbers, probably because these robbers often attack their victims to establish control in the robbery. Victims are most likely to be killed, however, by robbers armed with guns. Victims who resist are more likely to be injured or killed than those who do not resist.

The most likely victim is a male between the ages of 12 and 24. As a person's age increases, the likelihood of being robbed declines. People over 65 make up the age group least likely to be robbed.

What is it like to be robbed? The following is excerpted from a robbery victim's statement.

Harry's Story

"My dad and I were walking to meet my brother at a cafe where we went to lunch a lot. As we walked up, we saw the owner down the street waving and jumping up and down. We waved back. Later, we found out he was trying to warn us not to go in. He had been in the bathroom when the robbery started and had climbed out a window and run down the street.

"When my dad opened the cafe's door, a guy grabbed him and pulled him in. I turned and started to walk away, but a guy came out, pointed a sawed-off shotgun at me, and ordered me into the cafe. I did what he said. Inside, he threw me on the ground and pressed the shotgun against my head. All the customers in the cafe — about 25 people — were lying on the ground. There were seven robbers, all with guns. They went around from person to person grabbing wallets and jewelry. One man didn't like how they had talked to his wife. When he objected, a guy hit him with his gun. I lay there thinking, 'I hope the cops don't come until these guys get outside.' I was afraid of being taken hostage.

"They took my wallet, refused my old watch, and tried and failed to get my ring off. It stuck on my finger. They didn't want to spend any more time in the cafe, so they left. We had come in near the end of the robbery.

"The next day I had a large knot on my head. I don't understand why. The guy had just pressed his gun against my head. He didn't hit me. My dad had lost a ring he had owned his whole life. My brother to this day has never gone back to the cafe. The robbery shook up the owner so much that he sold the cafe to someone else."

The Domestic Violence Victim

Typically, when people use the phrase "domestic violence," they are referring to spousal abuse (also known as intimate partner violence), which can be committed by spouses, ex-spouses, boyfriends and girlfriends. The term also has a broader definition that includes family violence, child abuse, elder abuse, and abuse by residents of the same household.

Much violent crime takes place at home and is committed by family members or intimates. Half of all 911 calls are related to domestic violence. In most cases, however, nobody calls the police and the incident goes unreported. Of the more than 1.3 million Americans suffering from intimate partner abuse each year, about 75 percent of those victims are women. If victims decide to leave their abusive partners, they remain at risk of suffering serious or lethal violence. One study showed that 65 percent of all murdered female abuse victims were separated from their abusers at the time of death.

Domestic violence is a terrifying crime, violating a person's most basic zone of safety — the home. The following is an excerpt from a statement made by a survivor of domestic violence.

Denise's Story

"When I met Al, he was handsome, polite, and totally charming. I fell for him immediately. He was divorced and had a 4-year-old daughter, who lived with his ex-wife. I didn't know that he had broken his previous wife's jaw and she had a restraining order against him.

"We went out for a year and then we got married. We had a son the next year and a daughter the following year. Al was fine at first. But things gradually grew worse. When he'd get upset, he would tell me I was fat (I've always been thin) or that I was disgusting or stupid. Sometimes when he didn't like the food I'd serve him, he'd throw it out the window or feed it to the dog. At his daughter's 7th birthday party, I had ordered two pizzas. When Al saw them, he got mad. They weren't the right

kind. In front of all the kids, he threw the pizzas on the ground and started swearing at me.

"This was just the beginning. I became afraid whenever he got upset. He would often strike out. He'd grab the kids and spank them. Sometimes he would twist my arm behind my back. Other times he hit me. But after hurting me or the kids, he always apologized — sometimes spending lots of money on trips for the family or special gifts. I began to believe his outbursts were my fault and tried harder to be a better wife and mother.

"In the time we were married, I had many broken fingers, a broken arm, and numerous stitches. I wore dark glasses and makeup to cover black eyes. It got so bad that I started missing work. Although I was trying to hide it, people knew what was going on. My boss told me, 'If you don't get help, you're going to lose your job.'

"I started seeing a counselor. This helped. One day, after eight years of marriage, I bundled up the kids, went to a shelter, and got a restraining order. We lived in the shelter for three months. After that, I got a new job in another city. I haven't seen Al in five years."

FOR DISCUSSION

1. Why do you think many women do not report rapes or instances of domestic violence? Would you if you were a victim of these crimes? Why or why not?
2. What do you think would help victims of violent crimes recover from the crimes? Explain.
3. Victims of violent crimes sometimes report that witnesses do not call the police or try to help them. Why do you think people might not respond when they hear screams or see crimes?

Victims of Property Crimes

Lower income households were more likely than higher income households to experience property crime.

– Bureau of Justice Statistics, *National Crime Victimization Survey* (2011)

Property crimes, such as theft, burglary, and fraud, involve stealing property. They differ from violent crimes because the criminal *neither* uses force *nor* threatens to use force. If the criminal uses force, the crime is a violent crime — a crime against the person — not a property crime.

According to FBI statistics, losses from property crime add up to more than $15 billion a year. Every family in the country suffers — some from direct loss, some from high insurance rates, and some just from fear and insecurity. In the following sections, we will take a closer look at victims of two kinds of property crime — burglary and identity theft.

The Burglary Victim

Burglary is the unlawful entry into a building with the intent to commit a crime, normally theft. Almost 4 million burglaries occur every year, resulting in reported losses of $3.5 billion. Crime surveys reveal that victims report about half of all household burglaries to the police. Although not a violent crime, burglaries often greatly upset the victims, because the criminal has intruded into the privacy of the home. The following story is excerpted from a statement given by a burglary victim.

Helen's Story

"I was coming home from work on a Monday. My front door was unlocked. I walked in, and the first thing I noticed was my new tablet computer was missing. I thought, 'How dare she (my younger sister) take it out of this apartment without asking me!' Then I noticed clothes scattered in the hallway and thought, 'She must be doing the laundry, but why does she have to dump it in the hallway?' It wasn't until I walked into the bedroom that it dawned on me that we had been burglarized. The stuff in our nightstands was scattered on the bedroom floor. I ran into the living room to look for my TV and DVR. They were gone. I ran around the apartment — anything and everything of value they took. I was in shock and felt so helpless. When I called the police, I had

Every state today offers an assistance program for crime victims.

to repeat everything twice because I was crying and talking at the same time.

"The burglars had picked the lock to enter the apartment. So I replaced my deadbolt lock with a new one, which, according to the police, was 'practically unpickable.' I replaced the tablet computer, TV, and DVR. A month later on another Monday, I came home to find my apartment burglarized again. They had not picked my unpickable lock. They had broken down the door with a crowbar. They took everything I had replaced and looked through places they had missed the first time. The police took fingerprints both times and came up with a suspect. But they haven't caught him yet.

"After the second burglary, I no longer felt safe. The thought of being invaded a third time was too much. So within a month, my sister and I moved to a new apartment in a different neighborhood."

The Identity Theft Victim

Identity theft is a type of fraud. A criminal steals a person's credit card or Social Security number, assumes the victim's identity, and quickly spends as much money as possible. The criminal may pay for goods, get loans, apply for new credit cards, rent houses, get a job, and even declare bankruptcy — all in the victim's name. This crime was rare just a decade ago. Now, more than 11 million people fall victim to it each year.

Unlike most fraud, the victim never meets the criminal. The victim doesn't discover anything is wrong until it is too late. A credit card company may call asking about unusual activity on the account. Or the victim may be denied credit because of all the bills the criminal has accumulated.

The victim is not responsible for most of these debts. But payment will be demanded. The victim must spend countless hours contacting and convincing merchants that the person who ran up the bills was not the victim. Identity theft leaves victims' credit in shambles. It may take years for them to restore it. This is one victim's story:

Maureen's Story

"On a Sunday afternoon we received a phone call questioning an unusual pattern of activity on our credit card. Neither my husband nor I had authorized or made the charges to the account. I was told our credit card would be canceled. Two months later we received a phone call from J.C. Penney's credit department advising us that an account had been opened using my husband's name and Social Security number. We were advised by J.C. Penney's to immediately contact the three major credit reporting bureaus [Trans Union, Experian, and Equifax] to place fraud alerts on our credit reports.

"In speaking to the three credit bureaus, I discovered there had been 25 inquiries into our credit report in the previous 60 days. I requested that each credit reporting agency send me a copy of our credit reports, and I spent the next three days frantically making phone calls to the merchants who had made inquiries. I also contacted the Federal Trade Commission's Identity Theft Hotline, which assigned a reference number to our case."

[Subsequently, Maureen learned that several different suspects were fraudulently using her and her husband's personal information and had gotten a cell phone account, two new cars, and three bank loans totaling $45,000.]

"Our efforts to restore our good names and good credit have been extensive. I have made hundreds of phone calls. I've sent dozens of notarized letters to the merchants. We have submitted numerous affidavits, notarized statements, and notarized handwriting samples. We have filled out over 20 different sets of forms and statements in order to comply with the merchants requests for further information. It's like filling out your income tax return 20 different times, using 20 different forms, and following 20 different sets of instructions.

"I have logged over 400 hours of time trying to clear our names and restore our good credit. The impact of being a victim of Identity Theft is all encompassing. It affects you physically, emotionally, psychologically, spiritually and financially. We now have adverse ratings on our credit reports. We are also receiving phone calls from collection specialists wanting to know why we are overdue on the payments for our two new cars. I try to nicely explain to these collection specialists that we are victims of Identity Theft and we did not purchase these vehicles. Once you become a victim of Identity Theft your life is forever changed. We do not know how many more accounts may still be outstanding, we do not know if a collection specialist is calling when our phone rings, we do not know if our good names and financial reputations will ever be truly restored."

FOR DISCUSSION

1. Many victims speak of not being the same person after being victimized. Why do you think this is so? What has changed for them?
2. Many victims of burglary describe the crime as an invasion of their privacy. What do you think they mean by this?
3. Have you ever had anything stolen? If so, how did it affect you? Do you worry that it may happen again?
4. States make receiving stolen property a crime. Do you think it should be? Why or why not?
5. What sorts of crimes do you think people are most likely to report to the police? Least likely? Why do you think some people don't report crimes to the police?

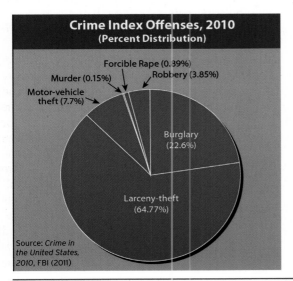

Crime Index Offenses, 2010
(Percent Distribution)

Forcible Rape (0.39%)
Murder (0.15%)
Robbery (3.85%)
Motor-vehicle theft (7.7%)
Burglary (22.6%)
Larceny-theft (64.77%)

Source: *Crime in the United States, 2010*, FBI (2011)

Helping Victims of Crime

The victim of a robbery or an assault has been denied the "protection" of the laws in a very real sense, and society should assume some responsibility for making him whole.
– Arthur J. Goldberg, secretary of labor, Supreme Court justice, and ambassador, *New York University Law Review* (1964)

Some ancient legal codes called for compensating crime victims. The Code of Hammurabi (c. 1750 B.C.), for example, forced the criminal to pay as much as five times the value of the damage caused. If the criminal couldn't be caught, the state would compensate the victim.

Early English and American law forced criminals to make direct payments, called **restitution**, to victims. Gradually, however, criminal law shifted away from helping victims and focused exclusively on punishing lawbreakers. The only way for a victim to get restitution was to sue under civil law. Unfortunately, this was usually impossible. Either the criminal had escaped or the criminal was poor and couldn't pay the victim.

It was only in the 1960s that we again began looking for ways society could help crime victims directly. In 1963, New Zealand passed the first victim-compensation legislation. This pioneering act set up a board to pay cash awards to crime victims. In an influential 1964 *New York University Law Review* article, former Supreme Court Justice Arthur J. Goldberg wrote that "Government compensation of victims of crime . . . is long overdue . . . ." The idea spread quickly to England in 1964 and then to California in 1965. Today, every state has a victim-compensation program.

One State's Model

During a street mugging, a man is assaulted and hit several times in the face. The mugger takes the man's wallet with $35 in it and flees. Bruised, scared, and with broken glasses, the man is taken to a nearby emergency room for treatment. The New York Office of Victim Services (OVS) would pay for the replacement of the eyeglasses, the lost cash, and the emergency room bill if the man did not have insurance.

A young woman, age 16, sitting in the park becomes the victim of a random shooting. Rushed to the hospital, she dies after several days. OVS would pay for any unreimbursed medical expenses, funeral costs up to $6,000, and counseling for her parents and brothers and sisters.

The state of New York offers monetary aid to families who have suffered financially from violent crime. Crime victims, their dependents, or immediate family members can apply for compensation. OVS will pay for medical expenses, mental health counseling, job retraining, funeral or burial expenses, lost earnings, and loss of support. It will also compensate for losses of cash or essential personal property if the victim has suffered a personal injury. The limits on the amounts of the awards are as follows:

Medical expenses	unlimited
Counseling	unlimited
Vocational rehabilitation	unlimited
Funeral or burial	$6,000
Lost earnings	$30,000 ($600/week)
Loss of support	$30,000 ($600/week)
Crime-scene cleanup	$2,500
Loss of cash or essential personal property	$500 ($100 for cash)
Attorney fees	$1,000
Emergency	$2,500

The New York plan compensates for losses caused by crimes of violence, such as assault, rape, murder, and hit-and-run. It also compensates elderly or disabled crime victims. The board will not pay for losses that have already been covered by insurance.

The New York plan also requires the victim to cooperate with the police and prosecution. And the board checks to make sure that the victim did not contribute to the incident in some significant way. This is particularly important in cases involving drugs or substance abuse.

These are the main standards that the New York Office of Victim Services checks before making an award:

(1) a violent crime occurred, resulting in an injury (or an uninjured victim is disabled or over 60 or under 18 years of age);
(2) the victim cooperated with authorities; and
(3) the victim did not contribute to the crime.

The main problem with the New York plan and other victim compensation programs is money. Many state compensation boards are behind in the settlement of claims because of lack of funds and inadequate staffing. In fact, many programs would be overwhelmed if every eligible person applied for benefits. With increased public awareness of the programs, more funds will be needed in order for them to meet their goals.

Other Victim Programs

Cash payments aren't the only way victims can be assisted. Government agencies and private organizations offer many other services: shelters for battered women, rape counseling, crisis intervention programs, child-abuse intervention, and medical counseling.

In many cities, the prosecutor's office or a private help organization has a unit to aid victims when they first come into contact with the criminal justice system. This service is aimed at comforting victims, notifying them of court dates, and even helping them find transportation to court.

Many communities have programs that offer crime victims free or low-cost legal advice, psychological counseling, or employment assistance. And some agencies provide help in replacing items stolen or destroyed in crimes. It can be a great comfort to a crime victim to have someone's help in as simple a task as replacing a stolen ID or a broken door lock. The primary goal of most victim assistance programs is to help the victim get through the crisis with dignity and get back to as normal a life as possible.

Restitution

In addition to compensation programs, court-ordered restitution has made a comeback. Today every state and the federal government give courts the authority to order a convicted defendant to pay restitution to the victim. Courts can, for example, order offenders to pay for the items they stole, the property they damaged, and the medical expenses the victim incurred.

Restitution serves several purposes. It helps compensate the victim and places that burden on the person responsible for the harm, the offender. It also helps the offender recognize what he has done and take responsibility for it. One study even found that offenders who paid restitution were less likely to offend again.

Courts frequently order defendants to pay restitution for property crimes, when defendants are not sent to prison, and when defendants can afford to pay. Some states require a restitution order in all criminal cases.

A 2011 report from the National Center for Victims of Crime, however, found that many offenders ordered to pay restitution fail to do so.

A study released in 2005 by the Government Accountability Office examined five high-dollar white collar financial fraud cases and found that only about seven percent of the restitution ordered in those cases was collected, up to eight years after the offenders' sentencing.

The experience at the state level is equally discouraging. In Iowa, for example, outstanding court debt, including restitution, amounted to $533 million as of 2010. . . . In Texas, a 2008 examination found that more than 90 percent of offenders discharged from parole between 2003 and 2008 still owed their victims restitution.

FOR DISCUSSION

1. What is the difference between state victim compensation and restitution for victims? Which do you think is better? Why?
2. Do you think courts should order restitution in all cases? Explain.

CLASS ACTIVITY

Crime Victims Board

In this activity, students role play members of a Crime Victims Board similar to the New York model. It is their responsibility to review applications for crime victim compensation and decide which, if any, should be approved.

1. Form small groups of four students each.
2. Each group should:
   a. Review the standards used for making awards in New York on page 68.
   b. Read each of the cases below and decide, based on the standards, whether compensation should be awarded.
   c. For each case, write down the following:
      (1) The case number.
      (2) Whether the group approves or denies an award of compensation.
      (3) The reasons for the decision.
      (4) The total amount of the award.
      (5) The amount of award money allocated to medical expenses, vocational rehabilitation, funeral or burial, lost earnings, loss of support, and loss of cash or essential personal property.
   d. Be prepared to discuss and support its recommendations.

Case No. 1

William Hall was at the Shady Oak Bar playing a game of pool with the suspect, Ken Ross. William had a $50 bet on the game. He lost the pool game, and the two men began arguing over the bet. According to witnesses interviewed by police, William threw a punch at Ken and missed. Ken picked up the pool cue and struck William in the mouth, causing him to lose several teeth.

William claims that he did not try to strike Ken and that they had no argument.

The District Attorney's office refused to prosecute Ken because of insufficient evidence.

William is claiming $1,500 in medical damages and $600 in lost wages.

Case No. 2

Robert Samuelson, owner of the Valley Drug Store, was shot and killed during a robbery of the store. His widow, Ruth, is claiming a wage loss of $50,000 per year for five years due to her husband's death. Funeral expenses totaled $7,000.

Ruth will receive her husband's estate, which is valued at $100,000. In addition, she receives Social Security benefits of $900 per month.

Case No. 3

Rocky Pineda was playing with his two children at Allstone Park, when he was approached by two young men. One of them had a gun and demanded money. Rocky attempted to explain that he could not speak much English. He tried to take his children and run when one of the young men shot him in the back. He died a few moments later from the gunshot wound. The suspects were never found.

The funeral expenses were $7,000, to be paid by Maria Pineda, his widow. She is eight months pregnant and has no health insurance to cover her medical expenses. She is claiming a $30,000 wage loss due to her husband's death.

Case No. 4

Susan Jones was sitting in the Whaling Ship Bar with two of her girlfriends. They were listening to music and having a drink. Three men sat down at their table and began to talk. After a while, they all started dancing and continued drinking.

One of the men, Mike, offered Susan a ride home. She accepted. When they arrived at her apartment, she invited him in for coffee. He followed her into the kitchen, grabbed a knife, and then forcibly raped her and cut her several times with the knife.

Her medical insurance covered her hospital bills. She stayed away from work for three weeks because of the psychological trauma. She is claiming $3,000 for seeing a psychiatrist and $1,800 in lost wages.

Debriefing Questions

1. Which claims did groups deny? Why?
2. Are the standards for awarding compensation fair? Why or why not? How would you change the standards?
3. If you could write your state's law regarding compensating victims, what would your laws provide?
4. Although most states do not, a few require serious financial hardship for compensation awards. Do you think the requirement makes sense? Why or why not?
5. What are the benefits of victim compensation laws? What are their drawbacks? Do you think states should have such laws? Why or why not?

The Push for Victims' Rights

Over the last 20 years, more than 30,000 victim-related laws have been passed at the state and national level. . . .[Many] states have even gone so far as to pass amendments making victims' rights part of their constitutions.
– Justice Solutions web site, "Implementing Victims' Rights" (2012)

Since the 1960s, concern has grown about how the criminal justice system treats crime victims. Citizens have banded together to form groups to represent crime victims and their families.

These groups have often complained that crime victims are injured twice — first by the criminal and then by an insensitive criminal justice system. They claim that too often victims have been ignored or even subtly blamed for the crime. Many victims have found themselves caught up in police investigations and judicial proceedings that they don't really understand. They have been moved from hearing to hearing at the convenience of attorneys or judges or the police. In the early 1980s, the President's Task Force on Crime said, "Somewhere along the way, the system began to serve lawyers and judges and defendants, treating the victim with institutionalized disinterest."

Advocates of crime victims have pressed for reforms in the criminal justice system. They have been joined by many groups, including women's groups interested in helping victims of rape and domestic violence. They have met with remarkable success.

Federal Programs

The federal government has passed several acts designed to address the needs of crime victims. In 1982, Congress enacted the Victim and Witness Protection Act. In addition to protecting crime victims and witnesses, the act was meant to serve as a model for legislation for state and local governments and to ensure that the federal government helps victims and witnesses without infringing on anyone's constitutional rights. The following are some specific features of the act:

- The crime's impact on the victim should be considered in deciding penalties.
- Anyone threatening or harming a witness should be punished severely.
- Court orders should be used to restrain anyone from harassing a witness.
- A victim is entitled to restitution from the criminal.

In 1984, Congress passed the Victims of Crime Act of 1984. This act set up a Crime Victims Fund, which provides grants to local victim

States With Victims' Rights Amendments

Purple states are those with Victims' Rights Amendments

Source: National Victims' Constitutional Amendment Passage (2012)

compensation programs. Today, it supplies almost 40 percent of the funds in these programs. The money comes from fines and forfeitures paid by federal criminals. Government payments to individual crime victims now range from $100 to $50,000 or more. The majority of the grant money goes to victims of rape and family violence.

In 1990, Congress enacted the Victims' Rights and Restitution Act. It set into law basic rights for victims of federal crimes. The Victims Rights Clarification Act of 1997 made clear that victims could attend trials and testify at sentencing hearings.

Responses from States

Many states have passed what are called **victims' bills of rights** into law. These laws focus on procedures within the criminal justice system. They attempt to make the victim an important part of the process. Michigan, for example, in 1988 passed a constitutional amendment. It gave crime victims rights such as the right to:

- Keep the accused's trial from being unnecessarily delayed.
- Be protected from retaliation.
- Be notified of court proceedings.
- Attend all court proceedings that the accused has the right to attend.
- Confer with the prosecution.
- Make a statement to the court at sentencing.
- Get restitution.
- Receive information about the sentence and release of the accused.

By the year 2012, 33 states had adopted victims' rights amendments to their state constitutions.

Although almost everyone favors helping crime victims, some amendments have drawn fire when they intrude on the rights of criminal defendants. For example, crime victims no longer have to testify at preliminary hearings in California. This was approved by voters in 1990 as part of Proposition 115, California's Crime Victims Justice Reform Act. Investigating police officers may read what the victims said in the police report. This means defendants no longer have the opportunity to cross-examine their accusers at preliminary hearings. (These hearings determine whether the prosecution has enough evidence to hold the defendant for trial.) Some critics argue that denying criminal suspects the right to see and contradict their accusers may well result in unjust prosecutions. They point out that more than 90

percent of all criminal cases end in plea bargains and never go to trial. The preliminary hearing is the only formal presentation of evidence in most cases. They say that the idea of using unchallenged accusers goes against the grain of the entire Anglo-American judicial system. Supporters of the law point out that the police report is only read at the preliminary hearing — not at trial where defendants can still cross-examine their accusers. They believe that it's important to spare the victim from making any unnecessary court appearances. This law was upheld on appeal in California courts. (*Whitman v. Superior Court*, 1991)

Another controversy involves victim-impact statements made at sentencing hearings. After a defendant is convicted, courts often conduct sentencing hearings. These are required in death-penalty cases when the court must weigh mitigating and aggravating factors in the crime. Victim-impact statements allow victims (and their families) to tell the court how they suffered from the crime. Critics have argued that courts should not consider these statements. They say that the victim is not on trial and that the victim's character should not be either an aggravating or mitigating factor.

The U.S. Supreme Court has grappled with this issue. In 1987 in *Booth v. Maryland*, the court ruled that victim-impact statements in death-penalty cases violated the Eighth Amendment's ban on cruel and unusual punishments. The court said the statements inflamed juries and led to erratic results. But four years later in *Payne v. Tennessee*, the court reversed itself. The court stated that sentencing hearings had always examined the harm done by defendants. "Victim-impact evidence," said the court, "is simply another method" for the court to get this information.

Proposed Constitutional Amendment

For the last several sessions of Congress, lawmakers have proposed a victims' rights amendment to the U.S. Constitution. It would require passage by two-thirds of both houses of Congress and ratification by three-fourths of the state legislatures. The amendment, if passed, would give victims of violent crimes the right to:

- Be given notice of and to attend any public hearing.
- Be heard at the hearings and to submit statements at any hearing determining release from custody, a negotiated plea, a sentence, or parole.
- Notice of any release or escape from custody.
- Not have unreasonable delays in the trial.
- Restitution from the convicted offender.
- Consideration for the safety of the victim in determining any release from custody.

Supporters of the amendment believe it will finally enshrine in the Constitution basic rights for victims of crime. These will be rights that no state may deny. They view the amendment as restoring the balance between the rights of criminal defendants and victims.

Critics of the amendment think it provides nothing that most states don't already guarantee by law. Most troubling to the critics is that the law forces *all* states to comply. Others worry about the amendment's vagueness and how courts will have to interpret what these rights mean.

FOR DISCUSSION

1. Do you agree with California's policy of permitting police officers at preliminary hearings to read what the victims said in the police reports instead of having the victim testify? Explain.
2. Some victims' rights groups propose that statements made by victims during post-crime counseling sessions should not be used in court or made available to the defense. Do you agree with this policy? Why or why not?
3. The Supreme Court has ruled that victim-impact statements may be used at death-penalty hearings. Can you see any dangers in doing this? Would you support stronger penalties for killing a nun as opposed to killing a prostitute? Why or why not?
4. Make a list of the problems that crime victims face. How can society address these problems?
5. What is the proposed victims' rights amendment to the U.S. Constitution? What are some arguments in favor of it? What are some arguments opposing it?

CLASS ACTIVITY

Victims' Rights Amendment
In this activity, students role play state legislatures deciding on a proposed amendment to the U.S. Constitution.
1. Imagine that Congress has passed the victims' rights amendment to the U.S. Constitution described in the article. Three-fourths of the state legislatures must now ratify this amendment.
2. Form pairs. Each pair will represent a state legislature considering the victims' rights amendment. Each pair should:
   a. Discuss the amendment's pros and cons.
   b. Decide how its state will vote (if the pair cannot agree, the vote is "no").
   c. Prepare to present its position to other "state legislatures."
3. Regroup as a class and different pairs should present pro and con arguments on the amendment.
4. Vote and conduct a discussion using the debriefing questions, below.

Debriefing Questions
1. What do you think were the strongest arguments in favor of the amendment? The strongest arguments against it?
2. Do you think the amendment, as proposed, is a good idea? Explain.

Sources for Unit 1

ALI Model Penal Code Sec. 4.01 (1). · Alperovitch, D. "Revealed: Operation Shady RAT," McAfee, 2011. URL: www.mcafee.com · Anderson, J. "Gang-Related Witness Intimidation," *Nat. Gang Center Bulletin*, 2/2007. · *Attorney General Guidelines for Victim & Witness Assist.*, OVC, 2011, NCJ 235121. · Avila, J. *et al.* "Lawyer Freed After Longest-Ever Term for Contempt." ABC News, 7/17/2009. URL: http://abcnews.go.com · *Best Practices To Address Community Gang Problems*, 2nd ed. OJJDP, 2010, NCJ 231200. · "Black Victims of Violent Crime," BJS, 2007, NCJ 214258. · Blumstein, A. *et al. The Crime Drop in America.* NY: Cambridge UP, 2006. · "Bribery." US Legal, 2010. URL: http://uslegal.com · Bureau of Justice Statistics. 2012. URL: http://bjs.ojp.usdoj.gov · *Calif. Youth Violence Prevention Scorecard.* Calif. Wellness Foundation. URL: www.tcwf.org · Chemerinky, E., "Striking a Balance on Hate Speech." Assoc. of Trial Lawyers of America, 2003. · *Civil Gang Injunctions.* BJA-Sp., 2009, NCJ 227644. · *Confronting the New Faces of Hate.* Leadership Conf. on Civil Rights Ed. Fund, 2009. · "Contempt of Court." Dept. of Justice. URL: http://www.justice.gov · Convention on Cybercrime. URL: http://conventions.coe.int · *Crime in the U.S., 2010.* Wash., D.C.: FBI, 2011. · "Crime's Decline — Why?" *NIJ Journal*, 10/1998. · "Crime Victims Fund," OVC, 2010, FS 000319. · *Criminal Rico.* 5th ed. U.S. Dept. of Justice, 2009. · "Criminal Victimization, 2010," BJS, 2011, NCJ 235508. · *Criminal Victimization in the U.S., 1973–90 Trends.* Wash., D.C.: BJS. 1992. · *Criminal Victimization in the U.S., 2008–Statistical Tables*, BJS, 2011, NCJ 231173. · "Cybercrime Against Businesses, 2005," BJS, 2008, NCJ 221943. · *Cybercrime,*NIJ-Sp., 2009, NCJ 231832. · "Cybercrime Grows Up," NIJ-Sp., 2007, NCJ 220990. · Denise's story. Printed with permission. · *Directory of Family & Domestic Violence Statistics, 2011.* NCJ 237029, 2011. · Donohue, J. *et al.*, "Impact of Legalized Abortion on Crime." *Quarterly J. of Economics*, 2000. URL: http://ssrn.com · Doyle, C. *Obstruction of Justice.* CRS Report for Congress, 2007. · Dressler, J. *Understanding Criminal Law.* 5th ed. Newark, NJ: LexisNexis, 2009. · Dvorak, J., "A Brick Through the Window," *PC Mag.*, Apr., 4, 2000. · Egley, A., "Nat. Youth Gang Survey Trends From 1996 to 2000." Wash., D.C.: OJJDP, 2002. · *Ensuring the Quality, Credibility, and Relevance of U.S. Justice Statistics.* Nat. Academies P, 2009. · "The Evolving Federal Role in Bias Crime Law Enforcement & the Hate Crimes Prevention Act of 2007." *Stanford Law & Policy Rev.*, Vol. 19, 2008. · "Expanding Police Ability to Report Crime," NIJ, 2009. NCJ 225459. · "Federal Justice Statistics, 2009," BJS, 2011, NCJ 234184. · "Findings From the Eval. of OJJDP's Gang Reduction Program," OJJDP, 2010, NCJ 230106. · Findlaw, "Civil Contempt of Court" & "Criminal Contempt of Court." 2011. URL: http://public.findlaw.com · Florida, R. "Why Crime Is Down in America's Cities," *Atlantic*, 7/2/2011. URL: www.theatlantic.com · Flood, J. *et al.* "Rico: The Crime of Being a Criminal," *Columbia Law Rev.*, 5/1987. · "Gang Prevention," OJJDP, 2010, NCJ 231116. · "Gang Units in Large Local Law Enforcement Agencies, 2007," BJS, 2010, NCJ 230071. · *Gender & Violent Victimization, 1973–2005*, NIJ-Sp., 2009, NCJ 229133. · Goldberg, A. "Equality & Government Action," Volume 39, *NYU Law Rev.*, 1964. · Goodnough, A., "Florida Expands Right to Use Deadly Force in Self-Defense." *NY Times*, 4/27/2005. · Harrell, E. "Violence by Gang Members, 1993–2003." Wash., D.C.: NCJ, 2005. · Harry's story. From H. Karabel. Printed with permission. · "Hate Crime, 2003–2009," BJS, 2011, NCJ 234085. · "Hate Crime in America," NIJ, 2007, NCJ 218259. · *Hate Crime Statistics, 2010.* Wash., D.C.: FBI, 2012. · Helen's story. From H. Kwon. Printed with permission. · Henriques, D. *The Wizard of Lies: Bernie Madoff & the Death of Trust.* NY: Henry Holt, 2011. · Herrington, L. "Statement of Chairman," *President's Task Force on Victims of Crime*, 1982. · "Highlights of the 2009 Nat. Youth Gang Survey," OJJDP, 2011, NCJ 233581. · Hill, K. *et al.*, "Early Precursors of Gang Membership." Wash., D.C.: OJJDP, 2001. · "History of Street Gangs in the U.S.," BJA, 2010, NCJ 230569. · Homicide trends in the U.S., BJS, 2012, URL: http://bjs.ojp.usdoj.gov · "Homicide Trends in the U.S., 1980–2008," BJS, 2011, NCJ 236018. · *IC3: 2010 Internet Crime Report.* URL: www.ic3.gov · "Identity Theft," NIJ, 2007, NCJ 218778. · *Identity Theft*, NIJ-Sp., 2007, NCJ 219122. · *Internet Security Threat Report*, Symantec, 2011. URL: www.symantec.com · Intimate Partner Violence. CDC, 2012. URL: www.cdc.gov · Karmen, A. *Crime Victims*, 8th ed. Pacific Grove, Calif.: Wadsworth Pub., 2012. · Kendall, A. "Obstruction of Justice," *American Criminal Law Rev.*, Vol. 45 No. 2, 3/2008. · Kennedy, D., "Pulling Levers," *NIJ Journal*, 7/1998. · LaFave, W. *Criminal Law.* 5th ed. St. Paul, MN: West Pub., 2010. · Lichtblau, E., "Trying to Thwart Possible Terrorists Quickly, F.B.I. Agents Are Often Playing Them." *NY Times*, 5/30/2005. · Magnuson, E. "The Curse of Violent Crime" *Time*, 3/23/1981. · Markoff, J. *et al.*, "Internet Attack Is Called Broad & Long Lasting." *NY Times*, 5/10/2005. · Maureen's story. Excerpted & edited from Maureen Mitchell's 3/7/2000 statement to the U.S. Senate Subcommittee on Technology & Terrorism. URL: www.senate.gov · Maxson, C., *et al.*, *Can Civil Gang Injunctions Change Communities?* Wash., D.C.: NIJ, 2005. · "McAfee: In the Dark: Crucial Industries Face Cyberattack," Center for Strategic & International Studies, 2011. URL: www.mcafee.com · McLaughlin, J. *et al.* "Obstruction of Justice," *American Criminal Law Rev.*, Vol. 44 Nbr. 2, 3/2007. · Mediati, N. "Secure Your Life in 12 Steps," *PC World*, 6/2011. · "Mobilizing Communities to Address Gang Problems,"BJA-Sp., OJJDP-Sp., 2009, NCJ 234964. · Morrison, S. "When Is Lying Illegal? When Should It Be?" *John Marshall Law Rev.*, Vol. 43, 2009. · Office for Victims of Crime. URL: www.ovc.gov · "PandaLabs Uncovers Alarming Statistics on Cyber-Crime Black Market." URL: http://press.pandasecurity.com · Pasternak, A. "How Criminals Steal Passwords, Bank Websites, & the Internet." 2011. URL: www.huffingtonpost.com · "Predicting a Criminal's Journey to Crime," NIJ, 1/2006, NCJ 212264. · "Profile of Intimate Partner Violence Cases in Large Urban Counties," BJS, 2009, NCJ 228193. · *SB 436.* Florida Legislature. URL: www.myflorida.gov · Sebok, A. "Florida's New 'Stand Your Ground' Law." 5/2/2005. URL: writ.news.findlaw.com · *Self-Reported Law-Violating Behavior from Adolescence to Early Adulthood in a Modern Cohort*, NIJ-Sp., 2006, NCJ 217588. · Shrestha L. "The Changing Demographic Profile of the U.S.," *CRS Report for Congress*, 2006. · Silberman, C. *Criminal Violence, Criminal Justice*, NY: Random House, 1978. · Singer, R. *et al. Criminal Law: Examples & Explanations.* NY: Aspen, 2004. · Sloan, A. "Who Killed Enron." *Newsweek*, 1/21/2002. · Sloan, A. *et al.* "No Accounting for It." *Newsweek*, 2/25/2002. · Sourcebook of Criminal Justice Statistics 2011. BJS. 2012. URL: www.albany.edu/sourcebook · Starbuck, D., *et al.*, "Hybrid & Other Modern Gangs." Wash., D.C.: OJJDP, 2001. · *Teen Dating Violence*, NIJ-Sp., 2011, NCJ 235368. · Thrasher, F., *The Gang*, U. of Chicago P., 1963. · Tillman, B. "Who's Afraid of Sarbanes-Oxley?" *Information Management J.*, 11/1/2002. · *2011 Data Breach Investigations Report*, Verizon, 2011. URL: www.verizonbusiness.com · "Ukraine Detains 5 Individuals Tied to $70 Million in U.S. eBanking Heists," KrebsOnSecurity, 2010. URL: http://krebsonsecurity.com · "U.S. Gang Problem Trends & Seriousness, 1996–2009." Institute for Intergovernmental Research, 2011. · "Victimization During Household Burglary," BJS, 2010, NCJ 227379. · "Victims of Identity Theft, 2008," BJS, 2010, NCJ 231680. · Vilbig, P. "The Great Enron Disappearing Act." *NY Times*, 3/11/2002. · *Violence & Victimization Research Division's Compendium of Research on Violence Against Women, 1993–2009*, NIJ, 2009, NCJ 223572. · "Violence by Intimates," Wash., D.C.: BJS, 1998. · Werdegar, M. "Enjoining the Constitution," *Stanford Law Rev.*, 1/1999. · Westen, P. "Impossibility Attempts." *Ohio State J. of Criminal Law.* Vol. 5:523, 2008. · "Your Security," *Consumer Reports*, 6/2011. · Zalman, M. *Criminal Procedure.* 6th ed. Boston: Prentice Hall, 2011.

Unit 2
THE POLICE

Police officers do not have an easy job. When enforcing the law, they deal with society's problems — quarreling spouses, drug and alcohol addiction, serious traffic accidents, and senseless violence. They must face danger and make lightning-quick decisions.

To be effective, the police need community support. Many of their contacts with the public help build this support — the police find a child, solve a crime, return stolen property to its owner. But other contacts may erode public support. Some of us have received traffic tickets or had other minor unpleasant encounters with the police. We grumble and go on our way. Others of us report serious problems of police misconduct, including harassment, beatings, and other abuses of authority.

When abuses do occur — whether through error, indifference, or overzealous enforcement — the criminal justice system must act to correct them. In a democracy, part of enforcing the law is upholding the constitutional rights of all citizens. Police authority cannot go unchecked. What that authority should be and whether it is properly used in particular situations are issues that can make police work difficult and sometimes controversial.

In this unit, we go behind the badge to explore law enforcement in our society. In doing so, you will encounter interesting questions: What might it be like to be a police officer responding in the line of duty? What are people's attitudes about the police and how might that affect police work? How do our laws affect police investigations and arrests? What are the proper limits of police authority? This unit will give you a better picture of police in our society.

CHAPTER 5
POLICE AND SOCIETY

The police are the public and the public are the police.
– Sir Robert Peel (1788-1850), British prime minister and the "father of modern policing"

From Volunteers to Professional Police

Though citizens can do a great deal, the police are plainly the key to order maintenance. For one thing, many communities . . . cannot do the job by themselves. For another, no citizen in a neighborhood, even an organized one, is likely to feel the sense of responsibility that wearing a badge confers.
– George L. Kelling and James Q. Wilson, "Broken Windows" in *The Atlantic*, March 1982

Nearly every civilization has had some form of law enforcement. Anthropologists have discovered written records of laws and law enforcement more than 5,000 years old.

Citizen Volunteers in England

In early English history, it was considered each citizen's duty to defend king and country from foreign invaders and local lawbreakers. In some cases, citizens received rewards for capturing criminals. Individuals or even entire villages could be fined for not assisting the king in enforcing the laws of the land.

As English towns grew in size, the need arose for regular law-enforcement officers. Able-bodied men began to take turns looking out for the safety of their neighbors. These volunteers, called constables, depended heavily on other citizens to help them.

Over the years, towns were grouped into counties, or shires. Each shire had a shire reeve, or sheriff, responsible for getting the citizens of the shire to enforce the law properly.

During the 1300s, large towns and cities organized citizen-volunteer groups to protect the streets at night. This form of policing, called the night watch, was eventually adopted in the American colonies.

City Police Forces in the U.S.

From colonial times until the 1800s, citizen volunteers enforced the law in most American cities. Often, volunteer night watchmen carried rattles or noisemakers to warn off criminals. According to jokes at the time, the rattling noise was caused by the night watchmen themselves who shivered and shook with fear.

In 1829, Sir Robert Peel organized a force of paid law-enforcement officers, called peelers or bobbies, to patrol London. About 10 years later, Boston established the first round-the-clock police force in the United States. In 1844, New York City formed a 24-hour professional police department. By 1870, most American cities had police forces patterned after those organized in Boston and New York.

While U.S. cities organized police departments, rural areas were also developing law-enforcement agencies. Rural police forces followed the form of the old English shire-reeve system. In many parts of the country, they evolved into agencies headed by county sheriffs.

The need for law enforcement on the frontier led to the establishment of the first *state* police force, the Texas Rangers. Later, other states established their own statewide police forces. Today, state law-enforcement agencies include highway patrols, bureaus of narcotics, fish and game departments, and civil defense bureaus. Each of these agencies responds to different law-enforcement needs.

The *federal* government has developed various agencies to handle its law-enforcement responsibilities. The Internal Revenue Service investigates tax evasion. The Bureau of Alcohol, Tobacco, and Firearms monitors these products. These agencies fall under the control of the Treasury Department. The newly formed Department of Homeland Security oversees agencies such as Immigration and Customs Enforcement, U.S. Coast Guard, and the Secret Service (which, among its other duties, investigates counterfeiting and protects the life of the president).

The Department of Justice, headed by the attorney general of the United States, directs

On the far right is legendary lawman John Reynolds Hughes (1855–1947). A Texas Ranger, he pursued outlaws throughout the state.

such agencies as the Drug Enforcement Administration and the Federal Bureau of Investigation (FBI).

The FBI operates throughout the nation. But it may only investigate *federal* law violations. For example, the FBI investigates kidnappings, bank robberies, civil-rights violations, and crimes committed on federal territory and property. Most law enforcement in the United States, however, is handled by state and local police.

Policing Today

Unlike most countries in the world today, the United States does not have a national police agency that enforces the laws throughout the country. Rather, more than 40,000 independent law-enforcement agencies exist at the local, state, and federal levels of government. Each agency has its own special function and enforces specific laws in a well-defined geographical area. For example, fire inspectors enforce local fire codes, and health department inspectors enforce a city or town's health and sanitation ordinances. Sheriff deputies patrol counties to enforce county ordinances and state law. Local police enforce a state's and city's criminal laws.

Today, the public often views the police primarily as crime fighters. In reality, although the police do fight crime, they also spend substantial time on many other tasks within the community. They settle disputes, monitor public protests, control traffic, respond to medical emergencies, and handle many forms of social work (such as dealing with crime victims and their families, meeting with community members, and directing people to agencies that can help them).

To understand the police, it helps to consider the pressures and fears affecting officers. Their duties have become more dangerous and more complex in recent times. Many factors have contributed to this: the increase in the availability of dangerous weapons, a more critical news media, a more critical general public, and budgetary problems, including a lack of funds to hire enough officers. Police must cope with the realities of law enforcement in a democratic society. Under law, they must protect the constitutional rights of the public. In enforcing the law, they must also obey the law.

FOR DISCUSSION

1. How does the organization of police forces in the United States differ from most other countries? Why do you think these differences exist?

2. Could our crime problem be better handled if there were one large police agency to enforce all criminal laws throughout the United States? What would be the advantages of having such a force? What would be the disadvantages? Do you think the United States should have this kind of police force? Why or why not?

3. Read the **Police Officer's Oath** on page 81. It describes the ideals of law enforcement. Do you agree with these ideals? If not, what would you change? Why?

Local Police

To protect and to serve.
– Motto of the Los Angeles Police Department

In an emergency, most people call their local police department. Almost every community has one. Departments range in size from one-person departments in rural areas to the almost 40,000 sworn officers that make up New York City's force, the largest in the nation. More than three-quarters of all law-enforcement officers belong to local police departments.

Unlike larger departments, those with only a few members cannot offer services around the clock seven days a week. Their members must do work that would be done by special units elsewhere.

Although large cities account for only 1 percent of all police departments, they employ almost a quarter of all officers. The budgets for these large departments reflect their size. New York City spends almost $4 billion annually on its department.

Large police forces have many units and a set of regulations and policies, known as standard operating procedures, for all officers to follow. Most departments are organized with a military-type structure. The chain of command starts with the police commissioner or police chief and runs down through inspectors, captains, lieutenants, and sergeants, to the patrol officers on the street. This chain of command can be quite effective in setting policies and operations. But in day-to-day encounters on the street, police do not usually wait for commands from above. They must act using their own discretion. Officers must be well-trained so that when they act, their actions fall within the department's regulations and policies.

Most large departments divide the workload into five basic units:

1. **Operations unit** patrols the streets and investigates crimes. It is the largest unit in any department.
2. **Services unit** helps support the operations unit by training officers, keeping records, maintaining equipment, and (in the largest departments) running a crime laboratory.
3. **Administration unit** manages payroll, personnel, and finances.
4. **Internal Affairs unit** polices the police. It investigates any reports of wrongdoing by officers.
5. **Community Outreach unit** works on improving police-community relations. In recent years, many police departments have placed greater emphasis on improving relations and have developed special units for this purpose.

With most officers in operations, many departments have specialized operational divisions. As a general rule, the larger the department, the more special divisions it will have. The special divisions include:

Patrol. Most officers belong to the patrol unit. These uniformed officers patrol the streets, keep the peace within their assigned areas, and respond when a crime or other emergency is reported. Their very presence on the street helps prevent crime.

A patrol officer's job can be divided into three functions, which often overlap. The first is law enforcement, activities directly related to catching suspected criminals. A citizen reports a crime. Police respond. They make an arrest. They investigate the crime. These are the things people think police do most. But the other two functions take up much more of a patrol officer's time.

10 Largest Local Police Departments

Name of department	Population served	Full-Time Sworn Officers	
		Number	Per 10,000 residents
New York Police	8,220,196	35,216	43
Chicago Police	2,824,434	13,336	47
Los Angeles Police	3,870,487	9,504	25
Philadelphia Police	1,435,533	6,778	47
Houston Police	2,169,544	4,892	23
Wash. DC Police	588,292	3,913	67
Phoenix Police	1,541,698	3,231	21
Dallas Police	1,239,104	3,122	25
Miami-Dade Police	1,082,395	3,120	29
Detroit Police	860,971	3,049	35

Source: "Local Police Departments, 2007," Bureau of Justice Statistics (2010)

The second function is order maintenance. A person complains that a neighbor's stereo is too loud. Two people are having a dispute on the street. A large group of people assembles in one place (for a parade, demonstration, or sporting event). An accident is blocking traffic. A homeless person is sleeping on a crowded sidewalk. A mentally ill person is causing a disturbance. Patrol officers must take care of these situations.

The final function is service. Someone asks for directions. A mother reports that her small child has wandered off. A motorist is stranded on the highway. Service is a large part of the job. Patrol officers are usually the first to arrive at any emergency. They may have to do first aid. They may even take someone to the hospital. When people don't know who else to call, they call the police.

Detectives. After a period of working as a patrol officer, an officer may be assigned to the detective division. Detectives do not necessarily outrank patrol officers. But they have more prestige, they often get paid more, their hours are more flexible, and they work in plainclothes. They are strictly involved in one police function — law-enforcement investigations.

Although patrol officers investigate some crimes and usually initiate all investigations, detectives investigate serious crimes — robbery, rape, homicide. Special detective units may be set up for homicide, robbery, bunco, vice, auto theft, sex crimes, and narcotics.

They investigate crimes by collecting physical evidence, interviewing witnesses, contacting informants, checking criminal files, and talking with lab technicians and forensic scientists. In some cases, police stake out locations or even work undercover (especially in drug and vice operations).

If a suspect is arrested, detectives help prepare the case for prosecution. If any suspect agrees to talk, they conduct the interrogation.

Traffic. From 3 to 10 percent of many departments consist of traffic officers. They enforce traffic laws, investigate accidents, and keep traffic moving. Most traffic stops are routine, ending with a ticket or warning. Some, however, uncover criminal suspects and can become violent.

Juvenile. Many departments have juvenile units. Officers in these units undergo special training in dealing with juveniles and in laws related to them. Officers exercise great discretion in deciding whether to take a juvenile into custody and whether the juvenile should be processed through the justice system.

Gang. The gang unit is relatively new to most police departments. The oldest active unit dates back to 1975, and most units were created after 2000. Today, police departments with more than 100 officers usually have a unit specializing in gangs. Gang units monitor gang graffiti, track gang members, infiltrate gangs, patrol gang areas, investigate gang-related crimes, and even keep track of gang communications on the Internet.

On the Job

As most police departments remain open around the clock seven days a week, police must work all hours and days. They usually work eight-hour shifts, which rotate from day, swing, and graveyard. Some departments have longer shifts — 10 hours a day, four days a week, or 12 hours a day, three days a week. Officers can expect to work many holidays, especially New Years and the Fourth of July, which may require the force to be on alert.

POPULATION SERVED	CHIEF	SERGEANT	ENTRY-LEVEL OFFICER
Average Minimum Base Starting Salaries in Local Police Departments, by Size of Population Served			
All	$63,500	$49,750	$37,150
1,000,000 or more	188,350	87,450	61,700
500,000-999,999	148,500	69,450	52,950
250,000-499,999	134,400	71,450	54,700
100,000-249,999	128,300	71,550	53,800
50,000-99,999	113,450	69,250	51,050
25,000-49,999	98,650	65,600	48,650
10,000-24,999	82,300	57,300	43,900
2,500-9,999	62,000	48,100	37,100
Under 2,500	40,550	34,800	28,550

Source: "Local Police Departments 2007," Bureau of Justice Statistics (2010)

Police work is growing increasingly more complex. In the 1950s, an officer needed street smarts, good judgment on using force, and moral strength to resist the temptations that often arise on the job. A good officer today still needs all these qualities. In addition, the officer must know criminal law and procedure, be able to collect evidence properly, be familiar with forensic science, know how to interact with different people, be able to mediate disputes, and know how to analyze and solve crime problems.

All departments require that applicants have at least a high school education. In 1973, National Advisory Commission on Criminal Justice Standards and Goals recommended that every police agency require police officers to have completed four years of college. Today, about 30 percent of all officers belong to departments that require some college education.

Other requirements are usually a minimum age of 21, good physical condition, and no criminal record. Applicants must also pass an entrance examination and tests for drug use, mental fitness, and physical strength and agility. Most departments also conduct extensive background checks. To attract more women, most departments have done away with minimum height and weight requirements.

Policing has traditionally been a low-paying job, but in the 1960s many police officers started joining unions. Today about two-thirds of all officers belong to unions. Most states outlaw strikes by police. Even so, a few police strikes have taken place. Job actions like "blue flu" epidemics (officers calling in sick) and "ticket droughts" (officers not writing tickets) have occurred in many cities. Unionization has raised salaries, improved working conditions, and put grievance procedures in place.

Starting salaries average between $27,000 and $45,000, depending on the department's size. Average salaries for a sergeant range between $33,000 and $96,000, again depending on the department's size. But most police earn more than their base salary because of overtime work and salary incentives. In addition, many departments pay generous pension and disability benefits.

Minorities and Women

In 1950, only 2 percent of all police were minorities. Many departments openly refused to hire them. No department in the United States had a woman patrol officer.

Local Police Officers			
Race and Ethnicity		**Male and Female**	
74.7%	white	88.1%	male
11.9%	black	11.9%	female
10.3%	Hispanic		
3.6%	other		

Source: "Local Police Departments 2007," Bureau of Justice Statistics (2010)

The civil rights movement helped change this. In 1972, Congress passed the Equal Employment Opportunity Act. It banned public employers from discriminating on account of race, national origin, religion, or gender. Most of the largest police departments have been sued under the act. Many cities are under court order to improve their hiring practices.

In addition, minorities in many cities have gained political power. They have used this power to ensure that departments have fair hiring practices.

By 2007, more than one-quarter of all police officers were minorities. The percentage of African Americans on police forces reflected their proportion of the population. Women made up 12 percent of all police. In cities of 1 million or more, they composed 18 percent of the force.

No one today argues against the ability of minorities to perform police duties. Some, however, express such doubts about women. The main argument is that they are not strong or tough enough for police work. But studies have proven otherwise. Women make as many arrests as men, and they do well in work evaluations. Some even argue that they may make better officers than men because they're less confrontational and more adept at mediating disputes.

FOR DISCUSSION

1. Some departments only hire officers who live in the area the police department serves. Why do you think they do this? Do you think it is a good idea? Explain.

2. Do you think police should have college degrees? Why or why not?

3. In 1973, the National Advisory Commission on Criminal Justice Standards and Goals recommended that police departments should try to get a workforce that reflects the ratio of minorities in the community. What are pluses and minuses of such a policy? Do you agree with it? Explain.

4. Do you think police forces should recruit women officers? Explain.

Police Call

What is it like to be a police officer responding to a call for assistance? What is police work like? In this activity, students role play interactions between police and citizens.

1. **Preparation:** In preparation for the activity, contact your police department and arrange for an officer to visit your class on the day of the activity. The officer's role will be to observe and help debrief the role plays. You may wish to conduct the activity over a two-day period and have the officer only present on the second day. Also, you may want to hold the activity in a large multi-purpose room or auditorium, if one is available.

2. **Form Groups:** Form the class into four groups of equal size.

3. **Group Selection:** In each small group, select two members to play police officers and one or two members to act as group spokespersons. The remaining members role play citizens. Send the police officers to a circle in the center of the room.

4. **Police Group Assignment:** The visiting police officer should take part in the group's preparations. At the center circle, the students taking the role of police officers should:
   a. Select a patrol partner.
   b. Read and discuss the **Police Officer's Oath** and **Departmental Regulations** to determine how they will conduct themselves on a police call.

5. **Citizen Group Assignment:** Assign one of the **Police Calls** below to each group. Each should then take about 10 minutes to decide how it will role play the situation. (Group members should try to act as realistically as possible. For example, how would youngsters caught shoplifting react to the store owner and police? Passively and quietly, or loud and defensively?) Also, one member of the group should prepare to call the police for help by giving a minimum amount of information about the assigned **Police Call**. For example, "Come quick . . . there is a robbery in progress at Green's Drugstore."

6. **Role playing:** When all the groups are ready, conduct role plays one at a time in front of the class. In turn, a member from each should call for help based on the assigned **Police Call**. A team of police officers responds to each call. The role play may begin or be in progress as the police arrive. The visiting police officer should comment after each role play.

7. **Debriefing:** After the activity, conduct a class discussion including the visiting police officer. Use the following questions as a guide:
   a. What have you learned about the kinds of jobs police officers are called upon to do?
   b. How did you feel when you played the police officer's role? The suspect's role? The role of a citizen in need of help?
   c. What different kinds of incidents have you been involved in or heard about that were not included in the simulation? How many involved violent crimes?
   d. What part do you believe fear plays in the interactions between police and community members? When do you think police officers are most afraid? What might cause police to be afraid? What causes others to fear the police? What could be done to reduce fear?
   e. What effect might police officers' fear have on their attitudes toward civil liberties? Politics? Suspects? Explain.
   f. Does fear of the police keep people from breaking the law? Why or why not?
   g. Try to describe the ideal police officer. Use examples from the game, from your own experiences, or from stories you have heard.
   h. Do you believe society might expect too much from the police? Why or why not?

8. **Follow-up:** As a follow-up activity, you might create additional "police calls" based on similar or typical incidents and have groups role play them for the class.

Police Officer's Oath

"As a law-enforcement officer, my fundamental duty is to serve humanity; to safeguard lives and property; to protect the innocent against deception, the weak against oppression or intimidation, and the peaceful against violence and disorder; and to respect everyone's constitutional rights to liberty, equality, and justice."

(Continued on next page.)

Departmental Regulations

On patrol, the police must try to enforce society's laws fairly, be polite and courteous to all citizens, follow procedures established by the courts and their superiors, solve many problems not connected with fighting crime, and respond to each call quickly and efficiently.

Cautions:

• Always be on guard to protect yourself, your partner, and other citizens from attack and injury.
• Handcuff anyone you take into custody.
• Be prepared for unusual public reactions when you are present.
• Treat all people firmly and fairly.
• Treat all people equally: The law is blind to race, sex and religion, and status.

Police Call: Group One

The police will be called to investigate a shoplifting incident.

   Design an incident in which a shopkeeper has reported catching a youth shoplifting, and the police are called to the scene. Keep in mind the following questions:

1. How do you think a young person feels to be caught shoplifting?
2. Should the police arrest the youth or do something less drastic, such as taking the youth home and talking to the parents, etc.? Explain.
3. Should people report all crimes that they know about? Why or why not?
4. What else could the shopkeeper have done instead of calling the police?

Police Call: Group Two

The police will stop a car with a broken tail light. The car, full of young people, is cruising suspiciously in a shopping district late at night.

   Design an incident in which the police stop a car cruising suspiciously. Keep in mind the following questions:

1. What would give the police the right to stop the car?
2. Should the police treat the people in the car differently depending on their age, gender, or ethnic group?
3. How do you think innocent people will feel and act when they are stopped by the police?

Police Call: Group Three

The police will be called to calm a domestic quarrel between a husband and wife.

   Design an incident in which a husband and wife fight violently enough for the neighbors to call the police. Keep in mind the following questions:

1. Considering that most murders happen in the home between people who know each other well, what special precautions should the police take?
2. How should police draw the line between private family matters and legitimate law-enforcement concerns?
3. Since many homes have at least one gun, how might the police protect themselves?

Police Call: Group Four

The police will be called to a bar on a drunk-and-disorderly call.

   Design an incident involving a drunk, disorderly man in a bar who has threatened another person with violence. Keep in mind the following questions:

1. Does it make a difference to the police what neighborhood the bar is in?
2. Since much violent crime involves people who have been drinking, what precautions should police take?
3. If the drunk resists arrest, what should the police do?
4. If the call had said that the drunk was armed with a gun, how differently do you think the police would have reacted to the situation?

CHAPTER 6
METHODS AND INVESTIGATIONS

The heart of problem-oriented policing is that this concept calls on police to analyze problems, which can include learning more about victims as well as offenders, and to consider carefully why they came together where they did. The interconnectedness of person, place, and seemingly unrelated events needs to be examined and documented. Then police are to craft responses that may go beyond traditional police practices. . . . Finally, problem-oriented policing calls for police to assess how well they are doing. Did it work?
– National Research Council, *Fairness and Effectiveness in Policing* (2004)

COMMUNITY POLICING | SUPPRESSING GANG AND DRUG-RELATED VIOLENCE
CRIMINAL INVESTIGATIONS

Community Policing

Community policing is a broad term generally meaning an approach to law enforcement that's proactive instead of reactive. Cops walk beats, and become more of a part of the communities they serve. It focuses more on prevention than confrontation and aggression.
– Radley Balko, journalist, "Law and Order" in *The Atlantic* (2009)

From the 1930s through the 1960s, most police departments in America went through a reform process that left them more disciplined and more professional. They began training programs designed to teach officers the latest policing techniques. They grew independent from political influence and corruption. Their hiring practices required that applicants have more education and go through a battery of psychological tests and background checks.

Also, by the 1950s, the police had come to rely heavily on squad cars, radio, and other technology. Their primary activity was responding to emergency calls. In some cities, corruption scandals drove this change. Reformers felt that beat cops were too close to local criminals and too easy to corrupt through bribery. But economics accounted for much of the change. Through mobility and technology, reformers believed effective policing could be maintained with fewer officers.

The system that developed did away with foot patrols in favor of squad cars. Often called **proactive policing** or **motorized rapid response**, this approach relied on radio to direct cruising police cars to emergency calls. This meant that most officers had little contact with their communities, except when they were arresting suspects or investigating crimes. And what officers did see of a community was often from the window of a car.

By the 1980s many people were criticizing the shortcomings of rapid motorized response. They felt this system left the police too divorced from the community and created a bitter "us and them" feeling on both sides. Cities began to experiment with different systems. They sent many officers back on beat patrols on foot, or horseback, or even bicycle. They set up neighborhood mini-stations. They also tried to develop Neighborhood Watch programs of local residents who would watch over their communities and tell the police of any problems they could see developing.

The point of most of these new programs was to get patrol officers to think in terms of patterns of criminal activity, not single radio calls for help. Officers would be visible continuously in an area, not just sent periodically into a community. And most of all, the officers would work actively to win local cooperation and look for causes of crime. This new type of policing was called community-oriented policing, or problem-oriented policing. It consists of three basic ideas.

1. Strengthening the community. The goal of community policing is to help make the community stronger. In a strong neighborhood, people care about what happens. They know one another and watch out for each other. They may sometimes call the police, but citizens do most of the "patrolling" when they are out and about in the community.

2. "Broken Windows" theory. In 1982, James Q. Wilson and George L. Kelling wrote a highly influential article in the *Atlantic Monthly* titled "Broken Windows." It advocated that police find out what bothers community members and focus on solving these problems. The problems often turn out to be seemingly unimportant things — graffiti, panhandlers, derelicts drinking on the corner — what Wilson and Kelling called "quality of life" issues. They explained this strategy by giving the example of a car left on the street with a broken window. They say that if the car is left in this condition, soon other windows will be broken and eventually the car will be torn apart. The unrepaired broken windows send a signal of neglect. Similarly, they claim that disorderly behavior, when ignored, leads to worse behavior and eventually violent crime. This is because people view the neighborhood as out of control and stop going out. The street is taken over by drug dealers, prostitutes, and hoodlums.

3. Problem-oriented policing. Community policing stresses problem solving. The police must not just respond to incidents. For example, when residents of a Los Angeles neighborhood complained about graffiti, the police did not merely try to catch the taggers. They helped organize neighborhood groups into painting out graffiti immediately and thus discouraging tagging.

Many police departments across the country have adopted community policing. Its growth was aided by the Violent Crime Control and Law Enforcement Act of 1994, which set up funding for 100,000 community police officers over six years. The methods of community policing vary from city to city.

New York's Emphasis on Accountability

The New York Police Department has a computer system that tracks crime block by block. Precinct commanders are held accountable for controlling crime in their precinct. Since 1994, the top brass of the New York Police Department has met frequently with precinct commanders, examining the computerized crime statistics for each precinct. Commanders discuss what has worked and what hasn't. With the hot spots of crime mapped out, commanders send out patrol and plainclothes officers to make arrests on quality-of-life crimes in these areas.

New York City Crime Statistics 1993-2011

Number of Crimes

	1993	2011	% Change
Murder	1,927	515	-73.3
Rape	3,225	1.415	-56.1
Robbery	85,892	19,745	-77.0
Felonious Assault	41,121	18,583	-54.8
Burglary	100,936	18,822	-81.4
Grand Theft	85,737	38,766	-54.8
Grand Theft Auto	111,622	9,305	-91.7

Source: NYPD CompStat Unit (2012)

The arrests have paid off. At first, police found many people were carrying weapons when they were arrested for drinking in public or other so-called quality-of-life crimes. Fewer people today risk carrying a gun, and fewer guns on the street has resulted in fewer murders. Anyone arrested is questioned about other criminals and crimes. Intelligence about what was taking place in the criminal community has grown.

With better intelligence, police started focusing on the criminal support system — the fences who sell stolen property, the chop shops that buy stolen cars, the gun dealers who supply weapons to criminals. Without the support system, crime fell.

With its full-scale attack on crime and quality-of-life issues, crime dropped dramatically. In 1993, New York had 1,927 murders. By 2010, the number had fallen to 532 murders, a 73-percent drop.

San Diego's Neighborhood Policing

With a much smaller department than New York's, the San Diego Police Department has taken a different approach to community policing. Its Neighborhood Policing program encourages a problem-solving partnership between citizens and police.

Citizens play an active role in crime prevention and detection. The SDPD has revitalized Neighborhood Watch programs, with community coordinators, watch coordinators, and block captains working together. Citizens can be alerted by e-mail of crimes committed in their neighborhood.

More than 1,000 citizens have volunteered for more active roles. Some serve on citizen patrols, which go through neighborhoods looking for problem areas and suspicious activity. Others work at police stations, freeing officers to go out in the community.

The police now have more time to work on solving crime problems. Officers are trained to identify a crime problem, learn as much as possible about it, develop a carefully planned response, and evaluate their response. In one case, officers discovered that the design of a trolley station contributed to the high rate of crime there. They presented the information to the transit board, which agreed to redesign the station.

Crime has since dropped at the station, as it has in San Diego in recent years. In 1990, 135 murders took place. By 2010, the number had dropped to 29. The number of incidents of all violent crime has plunged from 12,047 in 1990 to 5,616 in 2010. San Diego claims to be the second safest large city in the United States.

Critics of Community Policing

Not everyone favors community policing. Some doubt that the drop in many cities' crime rates can be attributed to community policing, because crime has dropped everywhere — even in places without community policing. They point to failed experiments such as Houston's "Neighborhood Oriented Policing." Disenchanted officers openly ridiculed it as "Nobody on Patrol." A new mayor was elected who vowed to end it, and it was abandoned in 1992. The mayor and new police chief's answer was more police on patrol. Houston's crime rate dropped. But a new police chief in 1996 returned to community policing, and crime has continued to fall.

Critics of community policing say that communities must make a choice: Either they can have police respond rapidly to crime, or they can have community policing. It would cost too much to have both. Community policing costs more than rapid-response policing, because more personnel is required than it takes to just respond to 911 calls and other reports of crimes.

Further, many police officers view community policing as social work that detracts from what they view as the real job of the police — to make arrests and solve crimes. They dismiss community policing as a misguided experiment that wastes personnel.

Finally, many in police leadership positions believe they are the experts on law enforcement. They are reluctant to share their power with non-experts in the community. Indeed, some citizens say that police departments only pay lip service to community policing instead of actually getting involved with a neighborhood and its residents.

FOR DISCUSSION

1. What are the advantages and disadvantages of community policing?
2. What are the advantages and disadvantages of motorized rapid response?
3. Why might some police officers prefer working in a department that uses community-oriented policing? Why might others prefer a department that uses motorized rapid response?
4. New York and San Diego exemplify two different styles of community policing. What are the pros and cons of each?
5. Which type of policing would you prefer in your community? Why?

ACTIVITY

Checking Out Community Policing

In this activity, students research and report on local or national efforts at community policing.
1. Form teams.
2. Each team should:
   a. Find a police department in your area that is putting into practice at least some part of community policing. (If there is none in your area, choose one of the major plans, such as New York, Chicago, San Diego, or Seattle and use the Internet or library to conduct your research.)
   b. Look up articles in your local newspaper or local magazines about the system. Summarize the articles on a sheet of paper.
   c. Talk to someone in the police department about his or her experiences.
   d. Prepare a report on the successes and failures of the local strategy. Divide the report so everyone gets to contribute.
3. The teams should present their reports to the class.

Suppressing Gang and Drug-Related Violence

[In the state of nature, there is] continual fear, and danger of violent death, and the life of man, solitary, poor, nasty, brutish, and short.
– Thomas Hobbes, English philosopher, *Leviathan* (1651)

Crime has fallen nationally. Even places once considered dangerous are far safer today. New York City's Central Park, in the middle of Manhattan, is an example. In the past, few dared to enter the park after dark. In 1980, more than 700 robberies occurred in the park. In 2011, fewer than 20 took place. No murder has occurred in the park in more than a decade.

Although violent crime is down in most places, it remains high in certain neighborhoods and communities across the nation. These neighborhoods are poor, their residents are mainly minorities — black and Latino — and they are terrorized by gangs, which control the streets. With gangs in control, businesses fail, property values go down, and many residents leave if they can afford to.

Outsiders drive to these neighborhoods to buy drugs on the street or from drug houses or apartments. Much of the violence is between gang members, but stray bullets can kill anyone — an old woman sitting near a window, a child at a school bus stop.

Police often respond to these shootings by flooding the neighborhood with police, stopping people who look suspicious, frisking them for guns, and making a lot of arrests. When the police eventually leave, the gangs resume control of the streets, and the drug market reopens.

What is most frustrating to police is that many people in these crime-ridden neighborhoods refuse to cooperate with them. Those who do cooperate are often viewed as "snitches."

The gang members who control the streets express bravado, saying the prospect of prison does not faze them. Many claim they expect to die young.

In recent years, many attempts have been made to suppress gang and drug-related violence. Below are several that have gained a lot of attention.

Chicago's Gang Congregation Ordinance

In 1992, the city of Chicago passed an ordinance that banned "criminal street gang members" from loitering in public places. The

Police have adopted various methods to stop gangs from terrorizing neighborhoods.

law defined loitering as remaining "in any one place with no apparent purpose." Under this law, a police officer could order people loitering in public to disperse and leave the area if the officer reasonably believed one of them was a gang member. Anyone not promptly obeying the order violated the law. In three years, police dispersed about 90,000 people on Chicago streets and arrested more than 40,000 who refused to move on. The law, however, was challenged in court.

In 1999 in *Chicago v. Morales*, the U.S. Supreme Court ruled 6–3 that the law violated due process and was unconstitutional. A basic requirement of due process is that a law must clearly describe what is forbidden. The court found that the crime of loitering was too vague for people to recognize when they were breaking the law. In January 2000, Chicago enacted a new ordinance, which it hopes will pass constitutional tests. It bans "gang loitering" in certain parts of the city. "Gang loitering" is defined as remaining in one place "under circumstances that would warrant a reasonable person to believe that the purpose or effect of that behavior is to":

(1) "establish control over identifiable areas,"

(2) "intimidate others from entering those areas, or"

(3) "conceal illegal activities."

Street-Gang Injunctions

Beginning in the late 1980s, several California cities got court orders, known as injunctions, against gangs. Under laws in most states, courts can grant injunctions to shut down "public nuisances." A nuisance suit is not a criminal action, but a civil lawsuit. If a court grants an injunction, however, anybody who violates it can be held in contempt of court and fined or jailed. A "nuisance" is something that interferes with people enjoying their property or personal interests. A "public nuisance" affects a whole community or neighborhood and endangers public health or safety. Nuisances are long-running abuses, not single incidents.

In 1993, the city of San Jose got an injunction against more than 30 alleged gang members. Every night for several years, they had allegedly taken over Rocksprings, a neighborhood they didn't live in. They allegedly sold drugs, played loud music, fought with rival gangs, and made the residents virtual prisoners in their own homes. The injunction ordered the gang members not to use certain drugs, carry weapons, destroy property, or trespass. All these things were illegal. But the injunction also banned the gang members from doing things in the neighborhood that were legal. It ordered them not to gather in groups, wear clothes with certain symbols, or carry a beeper. In the years following the injunction, crime in the neighborhood dropped dramatically.

Several of the alleged gang members, however, challenged the injunction in court. They argued it violated due process to penalize them without a criminal trial. They also said the injunction violated their First Amendment right to peaceably assemble and associate freely. In 1997 in *Gallo v. Acuna*, the California Supreme Court upheld the injunction. The court stated: "To hold that the liberty of the peaceful, industrious residents of Rocksprings must be forfeited to preserve the illusion of freedom for those whose ill conduct is deleterious to the community as a whole is to ignore half the political promise of the Constitution and the whole of its sense." One of the justices who disagreed with the opinion argued that the injunction should be limited to illegal acts only. He said in his dissent that the court "would permit our cities to close off entire neighborhoods to Latino youths who have done nothing more than dress in blue or black clothing or associate with others who do so . . . . In my view, such a blunderbuss approach amounts to both bad law and bad policy." The U.S. Supreme Court refused to hear an appeal from this decision.

Many prosecutors view civil gang injunctions as showing promise in combating gang violence. Research thus far, however, is inconclusive on their effectiveness. One study looked at the impact of an injunction in San Bernardino, a city in Southern California. The city had seen a 23 percent rise in crime at a time when crime was falling in most of California. The injunction targeted the Verdugo Flats gang, which had long claimed Westside San Bernardino as its turf. Published in 2005, the study surveyed residents 18 months before and six months after the injunction. Although crime increased in the city during that period, residents reported a decrease in gang intimidation, fear of gangs, and fear of crime. It failed to show, however, "larger improvements in neighborhood quality." Another study in 2009 examined the results of an injunction in Santa Ana, another Southern California city. The study found, "The injunction generated an increase in reports of violent crime and a decrease in property crime reports, with no effect on overall crime or public order crime."

Boston's Operation Ceasefire

Operation Ceasefire was developed in 1996 as part of an anti-violence strategy in Boston. A research group led by then-Harvard professor David Kennedy looked into the city's problem of gang violence. It found that fewer than 1 percent of all young people belonged to street gangs. Yet this small number accounted for *at least* three-fifths of all youth homicides. Most of the violence was prompted by vendettas, feuds, and "respect" issues.

The researchers also found that 75 percent of all young murderers and victims had lengthy criminal records, an average of 10 arrests apiece. Because gang members committed so many crimes and had records, they were particularly vulnerable to increased attention from law enforcement. If law enforcement focused on a single gang, it could, for example, look into probation and parole violations, serve open warrants, stop making plea bargains for existing cases, and hand over to federal authorities cases that would normally be prosecuted by the state.

Personnel from many agencies — local and federal police and prosecutors, probation officers, youth corrections, gang outreach — formed the Ceasefire Working Group. To begin Operation Ceasefire, the most violent gang in the city was targeted. Members with outstanding warrants were arrested. Probation and parole officers visited the homes of gang members, searched for drugs and guns, and more arrests were made. Federal prosecutions were started. Prosecutors made the cases a priority.

Then the Ceasefire Working Group started meeting with gangs. It informed gang members that any violence attributed to their gang would result in a similar crackdown on all members of that gang. This was the message:

When a gang kills someone, or shoots guns, or terrorizes the neighborhood, this group steps in. We'll focus on everyone in the gang. We'll arrest drug dealers and shut the drug markets down. We'll serve warrants. We'll call in probation and parole. Nobody's going to smoke a joint or drink in public, nobody's going to have any fun. We'll talk to the judges and make sure they know what's going on. We'll talk to your parents. It's up to you whether you get this attention. This group, no violence, no harm, no foul. It's not a deal, it's a promise. Somebody else might come get you for dealing drugs, you take that chance. We go where the violence is.

Aside from the warning, gangs were told that the city could also offer services — job training, protection from enemies, but they must stop the violence. And they heard from members of their own community how desperately they wanted the violence to stop.

The Ceasefire Working Group pointed out what had happened to the first gang it had cracked down on. The gangs were asked: "Who's next?" Law enforcement did not have the personnel to crack down on every gang, but it didn't have to. No gang wanted to be next.

Only one other gang crackdown was needed. Violence plummeted. By the end of 1998, the number of homicides in Boston had dropped by 50 percent. Ceasefire was dubbed the "Boston miracle."

ESTIMATED NUMBER OF GANGS, 1996-2009

Year	Estmated Number of Gangs
1996	30,800
1997	30,500
1998	28,700
1999	26,200
2000	24,700
2001	23,500
2002	21,800
2003	20,100
2004	24,000
2005	26,700
2006	26,700
2007	27,300
2008	27,900
2009	28,100

Source: *National Youth Gang Survey Analysis*, National Gang Center (2010)

Many other cities successfully copied Boston's Ceasefire strategy, including Minneapolis, Minn.; Indianapolis, Ind.; Stockton, Calif.; and New Haven, Conn. In each of these cities, the number of homicides plunged.

By 2005, however, the rate of violence climbed in Boston to pre-Ceasefire levels. Almost the same thing happened in the other cities with Ceasefire: With the success of the program, less attention was paid to it. Team members were moved to work on other projects. New police chiefs came with new priorities. As David Kennedy explained, "It wasn't a miracle. If the work doesn't get done, it won't work." Boston and other cities have returned to the Ceasefire model, and violence is again declining.

High Point's Drug Market Intervention

Ceasefire is designed to reduce violence. Although violence is reduced, gangs can remain in charge of the streets, and the drug markets can still continue.

The Drug Market Intervention is the next step beyond Ceasefire: It aims at shutting down the drug markets. A major component of the intervention is to address the poisonous relationship that often exists between the police and the community in high-crime neighborhoods.

The police have often given up on most residents in these neighborhoods, seeing them as corrupted by drugs, uncaring about crime, and unwilling to cooperate with the police. The police view the drug dealers as violent, irrational, and incapable of changing.

In turn, neighborhood residents view the police as an occupying force. At best, they see the police as uncaring, ineffective at stopping crime, and constantly harassing them with stops and searches. At worst, they view the police as part of a racist conspiracy to arrest and lock up the men in the neighborhood.

Finally, the drug dealers see themselves as victims, with racism confining them to a life of drug dealing and crime. The police are simply part of a plot to keep them down.

All these attitudes are wrong, and they fuel antagonism between the police and community.

The Drug Market Intervention was first developed in High Point, a small city of 95,000, located next to the much larger city of Greensboro, North Carolina. High Point had successfully adopted the Ceasefire model, and when a new police chief, James Fealy, came to the city in 2002, he wanted to do something about the drug markets. Working with Ceasefire's Kennedy and the U.S. attorney's office, the High Point Police Department (HPPD) developed the intervention. The intervention took much planning and discussion with police and community members to get everyone on board.

High Point had four open drug markets, all in poor neighborhoods. The department decided to close them one at a time. The worst market was in the West End, a neighborhood of about five square blocks. HPPD identified 16 active dealers in the neighborhood. This surprisingly low number of active drug dealers is typical. Most people in crime-ridden neighborhoods are not involved in drug dealing or in any illegal activity.

HPPD sent undercover officers to the West End, and over time they managed to buy drugs from all 16 dealers and record the transactions. Four of the 16 dealers were considered dangerous and violent. They were arrested and prosecuted.

The cases against the remaining 12 were put on hold. The 12 were notified in person and given a letter from the police chief that they were in trouble for drug dealing, but they might be able to avoid arrest and get help if they attended a special meeting at the police department. A promise was made that they would not be arrested at the meeting. They were asked to bring friends or relatives, people influential in their lives, with them. These "influentials" are an important part of the intervention, because these are people they trust. (See full text of the letter, below.)

Nine of the 12 showed up, accompanied by family and friends. Community members spoke, saying the drug dealing had to end, it was wrong and was destroying the neighborhood, and the nine were getting a rare opportunity to avoid prosecution and get help. They explained that everyone in the room wanted them to succeed. Prosecutors spoke, explaining what would happen to them if they were convicted on drug charges. Then each was shown the evidence against him. The police explained that the charges were going to be put on hold, but if they went back on the streets to sell drugs, the charges would be brought against them. Finally, the nine were offered help by service providers in the community — education, housing, jobs, transportation. Most of them signed up for services.

TEXT OF THE LETTER FROM HPPD CHIEF JAMES FEALY

As Chief of Police with the High Point Police Department, I am writing to let you know that your activities have come to my attention. Specifically, I know that you are involved in selling drugs on the street. You have been identified as a street level drug dealer after an extensive undercover campaign in the West End area.

I want to invite you to a meeting on May 18, 2004, at 6:00 PM at the Police Department. You will **not** be arrested. This is not a trick. You may bring someone with you who is important to you, like a friend or relative. I want you to see the evidence I have of your involvement in criminal activity, and I want to give you an option to stop before my officers are forced to take action. Let me say again, you will not be arrested at this meeting.

If you choose not to attend this meeting, we will be in contact with you along with members of the community. Street level drug sales and violence have to stop in High Point. We are giving you one chance to hear our message before we are forced to take action against you.

The meeting deeply influenced all who attended. By not arresting the dealers and encouraging them to get help, the police showed they were not part of a racist conspiracy to lock everyone up. The police saw that community members and parents wanted the criminality to end. The drug dealers could no longer use the excuse that the police were forcing them into a life of selling drugs. The choice was theirs: Take the help that was offered or keep dealing drugs and get arrested.

The next day, May 19, 2004, the West End drug market was empty. No sellers returned to the streets. The open drug market, which had existed for more than 20 years, was gone. As of 2012, the market has not returned. No homicide, shooting, or rape has occurred in the West End since the meeting. The streets became safe for people to go out again. The community now trusts the police and is cooperating with them to keep the drug markets closed.

The other three markets in High Point were shut down in the same way. Violent crime in High Point is significantly lower. The intervention has not ended drug use, just the open drug markets. Drugs exist in communities across America, but most communities do not have drug dealers on the streets hawking drugs to strangers. Drugs can ruin individual lives. Open drug markets can destroy communities.

Other cities across the United States are adopting Ceasefire and the Drug Market Intervention strategies. Both were designed as deterrent strategies. In fact, all criminal laws are meant to deter wrongdoing by letting people know they will be punished if they break them. The Ceasefire and Drug Market Intervention strategies make sure the deterrent message gets out. These strategies actually tell offenders not to harm anyone (Ceasefire) or sell drugs (Drug Market Intervention) and warn them what will happen if they do.

FOR DISCUSSION

1. What is an open drug market? What dangers does it pose?
2. Which of the four strategies mentioned in the article do you think would be the most difficult to implement? Why?
3. What is deterrence? Which strategies in the article are deterrent strategies? How does each attempt to deter wrongdoing? Which do you think is most effective? Why?

Criminal Investigations

Investigators should approach the crime scene investigation as if it will be their only opportunity to preserve and recover . . . physical clues. They should consider other case information or statements from witnesses or suspects carefully in their objective assessment of the scene. Investigations may change course a number of times during such an inquiry and physical clues, initially thought irrelevant, may become crucial to a successful resolution of the case.
– *Crime Scene Investigation*, U.S. Department of Justice (2000)

The goal of criminal investigations is not simply to catch criminals. Investigators must also collect evidence that can be used in court to convict them. If investigators don't follow proper procedures, they open themselves up to courtroom attack by defense attorneys. In some cases, if police don't follow proper procedures, the court will not even allow the evidence to be introduced.

Two of the most common investigatory techniques are searches and interrogation, or questioning, of suspects. Courts have set out special rules for these techniques. Chapter 8 will discuss them in detail, but we will touch on them here. We will mainly, however, take a look at some other techniques and issues of criminal investigation.

The Crime Scene

Patrol officers are almost always the first to arrive at a crime scene. They pursue suspects at the scene and make arrests. Or, more typically, they interview victims and witnesses and make a report. For most crimes, they are the only investigating officers. If the crime is serious or if patrol officers believe the case merits further investigation, they will call in detectives.

By the time detectives arrive, patrol officers have already conducted a preliminary investigation and secured the crime scene. Securing the scene helps preserve the physical evidence. In an 1892 story, fictional detective Sherlock Holmes lamented about a crime scene: "Oh, how simple it would all have been had I been here before they came like a herd of buffalo and wallowed all over it." Today's detectives have powerful tools for combing a crime scene. They, even more than Holmes, place great importance on sealing off crime scenes from spectators and other officers. They cannot risk

A crime scene must be sealed off so that investigators can find, examine, and document evidence.

picking up fingerprints, footprints, and hair left behind by spectators and other officers who enter the area.

The main job of detectives on the scene is to document it. They take statements from witnesses. They note conditions at the time of the crime. Were curtains open or closed? Were the lights on or off? Where was each piece of furniture? Many departments photograph and videotape crime scenes. All documentation goes into the case file.

Detectives must carefully mark all evidence taken from the scene — whether hair, blood, or the suspected murder weapon. They usually place items in special plastic envelopes. They seal each envelope, write the date and time, and sign it. Most evidence either goes to police evidence lockers or to crime labs. Each new person who takes custody of the envelope must also write the date and time and sign it. In this way, a **chain of custody** is established. When the evidence is introduced at trial, each custodian can be called to testify about what happened to the evidence while it was in that person's custody. The police can prove that the evidence wasn't tampered with. If police cannot establish a chain of custody, the evidence may not be allowed in evidence.

Lineups, Showups, and Throw-downs

If people witness a crime, detectives will try to get them to identify the suspect. They may call out a sketch artist to draw a picture of the suspect, based on descriptions of witnesses. Many departments today use software to create pictures of suspects. They also may call witnesses down to the precinct to look through books of mug shots.

If police catch a suspect, they will want eyewitnesses to identify the suspect. Beyond providing a strong basis for arrest, eyewitness identification resounds in the courtroom. "It's the most theatrical moment of the trial," says UCLA law professor John Wiley Jr. "Everybody in the jury box looks at the witness, looks at the [eyewitness's] finger and follows the line right to the defendant." Eyewitness identifications can make a case.

Yet experts have known for years that eyewitnesses are sometimes unreliable. Innocent people have gone to prison because witnesses wrongly identified them. Studies have shown that mistaken eyewitness testimony is the leading cause of wrongful convictions.

Even witnesses who express absolute certainty can be mistaken. Our brains are not videotape recorders storing information perfectly.

Police often interview those near a crime scene.

Psychologist Elizabeth Lofthus has explained: "Every time we recall an event, we must reconstruct the memory and with each recollection the memory may be changed. . . . Thus our representation of the past takes on a living, shifting reality."

So investigators must be careful when getting identifications, particularly when an eyewitness makes the first identification of an offender. Studies have shown that eyewitnesses will stick with their first identification even when they are later shown the actual offender.

Investigators typically use three methods for witnesses to identify suspects — lineups, showups, and throw-downs. In a lineup, five or six people, one of whom is the suspect, stand on a stage so witnesses can view them. In a showup, the witness is shown a single suspect. In a throw-down, detectives show pictures for the witness to choose from.

All three methods can be highly suggestive. A showup gives the witness no possibility of choosing anyone but the suspect. A lineup can be just as suggestive if only one suspect resembles the description given by the witness or if officers hint who the "right one" is. Throw-downs can be equally as suggestive if officers give hints, fail to offer an array of photographs, or fail to say that the perpetrator may not be among the photographs.

In the late 1960s and early 1970s, the U.S. Supreme Court made several rulings on lineups, showups, and throw-downs. In 1967 in *U.S. v. Wade*, the court held that a person indicted for a crime has the right to have an attorney present at a lineup. The court believed the attorney's presence would help prevent irregularities. Five years later, however, the court in *Kirby v. Illinois* refused

to extend the right to counsel for lineups held prior to an indictment.

The same year as *Kirby*, the court in *Neil v. Biggers* refused to overturn a conviction because the identification was based on a showup. The court stated that although showups were highly suggestive to witnesses, the "totality of the circumstances" showed that the identification was reliable. The court noted that the witness had not identified others at previous lineups, showups, and throw-downs and that the suspect met the witness's prior description. The court had ruled similarly in the 1968 case of *Simmons v. U.S.* where witnesses made in-court identifications arguably based on previous exposure to a suggestive photographic array. The court held that "convictions based on eyewitness identification at trial following a pretrial identification by photograph will be set aside . . . only if the photographic identification procedure was so impermissibly suggestive as to give rise to a very substantial likelihood of irreparable misidentification." If there is not such a likelihood, then the evidence can be admitted and the jury is allowed to determine whether it is reliable.

In 2008, the California Commission for the Fair Administration of Justice issued a report, making recommendations for improving the justice system in California. One of the problem areas it identified was mistaken eyewitness testimony.

The commission made a number of recommendations for improving eyewitness identifications and lessening the chance of bias in identifications. Among the recommendations were: Showups should be avoided. Every witness should be separated from other witnesses when making identifications. Police should arrange that everyone in lineups or throw-downs resemble each other. They should tell the witness that the perpetrator may not be in the lineup or throw-down. The person conducting the lineup or throw-down should not know who the suspect is. The witness should view one person or photo at a time and respond with "yes," "no," or "unsure" to each person. When the identification process ends, police should record the witness's level of certainty.

In 2011, the New Jersey Supreme Court made a ruling on eyewitness identifications that changed that state's methods of conducting identifications. In the case, police followed most of the procedures recommended by the

California commission for a throw-down. But when the witness, who had been drinking and smoking crack at the time of the crime, could only narrow his choice to two pictures, detectives investigating the case briefly talked to the witness alone. When the person conducting the throw-down again went through the pictures, the witness positively identified the suspect.

In a lengthy opinion, the court carefully went through the research on eyewitness identifications and how they can be wrong. The court ordered new procedures in New Jersey to ensure better identifications. First, if a defendant believes bias or suggestiveness have tainted an identification, the defense can demand a pretrial hearing to present evidence of bias or suggestiveness. The prosecution must present its own evidence on the reliability of the identification. If after weighing the evidence, the court finds that the defense has proven "a very substantial likelihood of irreparable misidentification, the court should suppress the identification evidence." Otherwise, the evidence will be admitted. But if it is admitted, the jury must be instructed on the factors that might make eyewitness evidence unreliable. In the case at hand, the court ordered the trial judge to conduct a hearing on whether the evidence was reliable. (*New Jersey v. Henderson*)

Informants

Many police officers develop a network of informants, who give intelligence about what is going on in the criminal community. Most informants are low-level criminals involved in so-called "victimless crimes" — drugs, gambling, prostitution. Informants can provide information that an officer could get only by going undercover and working for months to gain the trust of criminals. Police can put the word out that they want information about a particular case or person. Informants often supply it.

Police commonly use informants to get search warrants. The Fourth Amendment protects against unreasonable searches and seizures. It requires warrants be issued only on "probable cause." This means that before a judge may issue a warrant, police must produce evidence of criminality that a reasonable person would believe. This is usually done in a sworn, written statement by a police officer. The statement describes the place to be searched and things to be seized. It also sets forth the evidence of criminality. Often

this evidence consists of the officer stating that a reliable informant has told the officer facts about a crime. The U.S. Supreme Court has held that such evidence is enough for a search warrant as long as the "totality of the circumstances" in the sworn statement show a "fair probability that contraband or evidence of a crime will be found in a particular place." (*Illinois v. Gates*, 1983)

Informants usually ask for something in return. Some informants get paid in cash. Police departments often have funds for informants. Other informants get charges against them dropped. Many police agencies agree not to arrest each others' informants as a professional courtesy.

Some critics condemn the use of informants for several reasons. Most informants are criminals, and critics question their reliability. Critics claim that informants often say what police want them to say. In addition, they point out that informants don't make good witnesses at trials because juries tend not to believe them. Informants themselves don't want to testify, because they don't want to be branded as a "snitch" and risk getting hurt by other criminals.

Critics particularly disapprove of jailhouse informants, those already in jail who testify that a cellmate has confessed. The U.S. Supreme Court has ruled that police cannot deliberately elicit incriminating statements from indicted defendants without their attorneys (*Massiah v. U.S.*, 1964). This means that if a person in jail has been charged with a crime and is represented by an attorney, the police cannot send informants into the person's cell to get a confession on that charge. But if cellmates without prior police contact offer information to police, their testimony can be used in court. Critics point to many celebrated cases of jailhouse informants helping convict innocent defendants.

Most police defend the use of informants as a necessary evil. They point out that many guilty defendants have been convicted this way. Most also agree, however, that the practice must be closely controlled to prevent abuses.

FOR DISCUSSION

1. What is a chain of custody? Why is it important?
2. What are lineups, showups, and throwdowns? Which do you think is the most reliable? Why?
3. What problems might arise from using informants? What can be done to prevent these problems?

CLASS ACTIVITY

Is This the One?

In this activity, students analyze police procedures for identifying suspects.

1. Form pairs.
2. Each pair should:
   a. Read each of the cases below.
   b. For each case, discuss and answer:
      (1) Why might this identification be unreliable?
      (2) What should the police have done to make it more reliable?
      (3) Do you think the identification should be admitted in court? Explain.
3. The pairs should report back and discuss each case with the whole group.

Case #1: Hospital Visit. An attacker in the victims' home slays the husband and severely wounds the wife. Police bring a suspect to the hospital handcuffed to a police officer. The suspect is the only African American in the room. An officer asks the wife whether the suspect is "the man." After the suspect repeats "a few words for voice identification," the wife identifies him as the attacker. At trial, the wife identifies the suspect. (*Stovall v. Denno*, 1967)

Case #2: Hallway. An undercover officer buys heroin from a dealer in a hallway lit only by natural light. The two stand two feet apart for about three minutes. Afterward, the officer describes the dealer to another officer as "a colored man, approximately five feet eleven inches tall, dark complexion, black hair, short Afro style, and having high cheekbones, and of heavy build." The other police officer thinks he recognizes the suspect from the description. He leaves a police photograph of the suspect for the undercover officer, who sees it two days later and identifies it as the picture of the dealer. In court, the officer identifies the suspect. (*Manson v. Brathwaite*, 1977)

Case #3: Lineups. At an initial lineup, the witness fails to identify the suspect. Police arrange a showup, at which the witness makes a tentative identification. Finally, at another lineup, the witness makes a definite identification of the suspect. (*Foster v. California*, 1969)

Case #4: Parking lot showup. A woman calls police and reports seeing from her apartment a man rampaging through a parking lot. Police arrive, stop a man, and an officer goes to the witness's apartment to talk to her. When police ask her to describe the man, the witness points out her window to the man standing next to the police officer in the parking lot. The witness later fails to identify the man in a throw-down at the police station. (*Perry v. New Hampshire*, 2012)

CHAPTER 7
FORENSIC SCIENCE

Every human being carries with him from his cradle to his grave certain physical marks which do not change their character, and by which he can always be identified — and that without shade of doubt or question. These marks are his signature, his physiological autograph, so to speak, and this autograph can not be counterfeited, nor can he disguise it or hide it away, nor can it become illegible by the wear and mutations of time. This signature is not his face — age can change that beyond recognition; it is not his hair, for that can fall out; it is not his height, for duplicates of that exist; it is not his form, for duplicates of that exist also, whereas this signature is this man's very own — there is no duplicate of it among the swarming populations of the globe. This autograph consists of the delicate lines or corrugations with which Nature marks the insides of the hands and the soles of the feet.
– Mark Twain, *Pudd'nhead Wilson* (1894)

THE ORIGINS OF FORENSIC SCIENCE | MODERN CRIME LABS
CURRENT ISSUES IN FORENSIC SCIENCE

The Origins of Forensic Science

We balance probabilities and choose the most likely. It is the scientific use of the imagination.
– Arthur Conan Doyle, *The Hound of the Baskervilles* (1902)

The word *forensic* has its root in the Latin word *forum*. In ancient Rome, the forum was a public place where citizens discussed politics, a marketplace where they traded goods, and the venue for criminal trials. Today, the word *forensic* can apply to anything related to the law.

Forensic science, then, applies scientific investigation to the law. Sometimes, the term *medico-legal* is used as a synonym for *forensic*, because of the close connection between medical and legal investigation. Likewise, the term *criminalist* is synonymous with forensic scientist. Often, scientists working in crime labs have received training and certification in criminalistics as a field of study.

The use of science in criminal investigation has a long history. The earliest known text on using medical procedures to investigate crime appeared in China in the 13th century. Titled *Hsi Duan Yu* (The Washing Away of Wrongs), it is a guide to investigating suspicious deaths. For example, it describes how to examine a corpse's neck cartilage to tell whether the person died by drowning or by strangulation.

As advances were made over the centuries in science, medicine, and technology, so did law enforcement apply those advances to solving crime. The development of photography in the 19th century allowed police officers to retain daguerrotypes (early photographic prints on copper plates) of people they arrested. Today, these photographs are taken digitally and known as "mug shots." Ultraviolet, infrared, and laser photography are used in the examination of questioned documents, or documents thought to be fraudulent or forged. The development of microscopy not only enabled doctors to view microbes, but it also helped criminalists examine fiber and hair evidence and enhanced the analysis of fingerprints.

Fingerprinting itself is perhaps one of the most famous methods of the forensic scientist. In 1685, anatomy professor Marcello Malpighi recognized the intricate patterns in skin of the human fingertip. These are highly individualized and considered unique to each individual. Malpighi coined the terms *loops* and *whorls* to describe the features of fingerprint patterns. Loops come in several varieties and are tiny ridges that double back on themselves, forming wave-like patterns in the skin. Whorls are ridges that resemble small whirlpools. These terms are still used today. In 1910, Thomas Jennings was the first person in the United States to be convicted due to fingerprint evidence found at the scene of a murder. Later, the infamous bank robber John Dillinger was so afraid of the FBI's ability to match fingerprints that he burned his own fingertips with acid to avoid capture. Enough remained to match to his prints on file with the FBI.

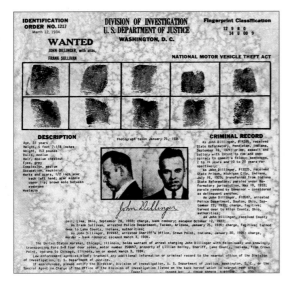

The fingerprints and mug shots of bank robber John Dillinger, who died in a shootout in Chicago in 1934.

Developments in medicine have revolutionized forensic science. In 1901, the Austrian-born American biologist Karl Landsteiner discovered that not everyone's blood was of the same type. Blood could be classified, in fact, into the four types of A, B, AB, and O. Landsteiner called it the ABO blood group system, and it allowed doctors to make safe blood transfusions from donor to patient. The ABO system revolutionized both medicine and serology, the forensic study of bodily fluids left at a crime scene. The serologist, for example, can examine dried blood left at a scene to determine if it matches a sample from a criminal suspect. In 1915, Dr. Leon Lattes at the University of Turin, Italy, developed a way to apply ABO blood analysis to clothing and other materials. Blood also contains DNA (deoxyribonucleic acid), which, as we will see, offers criminalists a means of performing DNA profiling. Medicine, combined with advances in biology and chemistry, has also enabled the growth of toxicology, or the study of poisons, including alcohol and drugs in a person's body.

The first comprehensive text on the use of physical evidence to solve crime was published by Hans Gross, an Austrian lawyer and judge, in 1893. Titled *Criminal Investigation*, the book even described the weaknesses of eyewitness testimony when compared to physical evidence. In a later book, *Criminal Psychology*, Gross appears to have coined the term *criminalist* to describe a forensic scientist.

The world's first crime lab appeared in Lyon, France, in the early 20th century. A physician and professor of criminology named Edmond Locard established the lab, staffed by law-enforcement officers who conducted criminal investigations.

Locard's lab used the most advanced technology of the time. In 1911, he achieved notoriety by using the lab to prove that a suspect in a counterfeiting case had dust from counterfeit coins in his pocket. Today, this type of investigation would be done in a trace evidence unit of a crime lab.

Locard was an avid reader of Arthur Conan Doyle's stories of Sherlock Holmes, a character who became the prototype of the modern criminal investigator. Locard sometimes even assigned the Holmes stories to his own students. Conan Doyle created Holmes as a deductive, logical, methodical, and keenly observant detective.

Holmes is well remembered as the detective smoking a pipe and telling Dr. Watson about "elementary" conclusions. He can also be remembered as the investigator looking into his microscope or performing analysis of blood samples in his home at 221B Baker Street, London. Indeed, the stories of Sherlock Holmes made popular the idea of using forensic science to solve crimes.

Sherlock Holmes' influence on the real world of forensic investigation has been significant. His fictional crime lab inspired Edmond Locard to create his own pioneering lab. Thousands of others have read or viewed movies about Holmes. In 2002, the Royal Society of Chemistry in England honored Holmes' use of forensic science by making him an honorary fellow, even though he was fictional. The writings of Conan Doyle have helped people understand the importance of forensic science in today's criminal investigations.

FOR DISCUSSION

1. Advances in photography led to the use of "mug shots" and enhanced forensic analysis of questioned documents. What other ways could photography be used by law enforcement?

2. Which scientific advance in history do you think has had the greatest impact on modern forensic science?

Modern Crime Labs

Physical evidence cannot be wrong, it cannot perjure itself, it cannot be wholly absent. Only human failure to find it, study and understand it, can diminish its value.
– Edmond Locard (1877-1966), French criminologist

Because of rapid developments in technology, particularly the computer, crime laboratories play an increasingly important role in investigating crimes. Today's computers allow huge amounts of data to be stored, compared, and retrieved quickly. Crime labs across the country have developed databases and continually link them to one another.

The first crime lab in the United States was established by the Los Angeles Police Department in 1923. Today, about 400 accredited crime laboratories exist in this country. Every state and many large police departments run crime labs. Criminalists, with specialties in many different fields, work at these labs.

Created in 1932, the FBI Laboratory is the nation's largest crime lab. It examines evidence from other federal, state, and local agencies as well as from FBI cases. The FBI divides its crime lab into units, each specializing in one area, like firearms, explosives, or hairs and fibers. One piece of evidence may be examined by several different units. All the units work together as a team, sharing their piece of the puzzle and trying to put together as much information as they can discover about a crime or criminal. The following are some of the FBI crime lab units:

DNA Units look at DNA, the genetic code in every human cell. DNA can be found in blood, sweat, mucus, semen, saliva, and other human tissue. Since no two people have identical DNA, it can be used to identify perpetrators of crimes and to exonerate innocent people accused of crime. Laboratory DNA units analyze DNA from crime scenes and also operate the Combined DNA Index System (CODIS). CODIS holds three DNA databases, national, state, and local, containing more than 10 million DNA profiles taken from offenders, crime scenes, and missing persons. Crime labs across the nation can store and search these databases using CODIS software. For example, the brutal murder of 80-year-old Alice Virginia Mosconi went unsolved for four years. In 2005, a DNA database matched DNA at the crime scene to Joaquin B. Hill, an inmate in a California

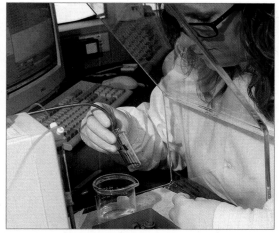

A woman analyzes evidence at the Orange County Crime Lab in California.

prison. Hill was tried and convicted of the murder based on the DNA evidence.

The **Latent Print Unit** analyzes fingerprints. According to specialists, everyone has different fingerprints, and they remain the same throughout life. This makes them excellent for identification. Since 1924, the FBI has had a fingerprint unit. Today, experts have many methods for combing crime scenes for fingerprints, palm prints, footprints, and even lip prints. They can find prints using lasers, alternative light sources, and chemicals as well as dusting for prints with powders. Once they've discovered prints at a crime scene, experts compare them with the known prints of victims and suspects. In October 1993, Polly Klaas, a 12-year-old girl, was kidnapped from her home. Local police worked with FBI crime-scene experts to collect and analyze evidence. Using fluorescent powder, special goggles, and an alternative light source, agents found a partial palm print on the girl's bunk bed. But the print didn't do much good without a suspect to match it to. Two months later, police learned that a car had been stuck on a nearby road on the night of the kidnapping. From a computer, detectives found out that the car belonged to Richard Allen Davis, who had a police record and prints on file. The palm print matched. When Davis read about the match in a newspaper, he called a detective and confessed to kidnapping and killing Polly Klaas. Davis was convicted and sentenced to death.

The **Firearms-Toolmarks Unit** investigates guns, ammunition, evidence with residue from gunshots, tools, motor vehicle numbers, and serial numbers. The unit maintains a collection of

Estimated Year-End Backlog at the Nation's Crime Labs, 2005

Type of Function	Backlog as of January 1, 2005	New Requests during 2005	Requests Completed in 2005	Estimated Backlog at Year End
Controlled substances	112,693	1,086,672	976,687	222,6781
Biology screening	18,545	62,127	51,429	29,243
Firearms/toolmarks	26,316	84,453	75,889	34,880
Latent prints	44,123	237,049	211,019	70,153
DNA analysis	24,030	67,009	52,812	38,227
Toxicology	16,200	389,446	383,441	22,205
Questioned documents	931	6,793	6,605	1,119
Computer crimes	246	1,881	1,865	262
Other functions	9,726	68,114	60,728	17,112
Total	**252,810**	**2,003,544**	**1,820,475**	**435,879**

Notes: (1) "Controlled substances" are illegal narcotics and prescription drugs. (2) "Biology screening" looks for traces of bodily fluids (blood, saliva, semen, and urine). (3) "Toxicology" covers poisons, alcohol, and other harmful substances. (4) "Other functions" includes fire debris, polygraph, shoe/tire print, digital imaging, etc. (5) All of these estimates are conservative: The actual backlog may be greater than estimated.

Source: "Census of Publicly Funded Forensic Crime Laboratories, 2005," Bureau of Justice Statistics (2008)

firearms, ammunition, and their distinctive markings. Its ballistics experts can tell what kind of a gun fired a bullet. If police have an alleged murder weapon, lab experts fire it into a tank of water. The water stops the bullet without disfiguring it. Experts then compare the bullet fired into the tank to those found at the crime scene. If the bullets match, they have found the murder weapon. Experts can also tell by the pattern of gunshot residue on the victim whether the shooter fired from close range. In addition, the unit examines marks made by tools. Every tool leaves its own distinct marks and can be identified. In one case, the unit showed that a series of bank robberies in Virginia were done by the same criminals because of the tool markings on the safe deposit boxes they pried open. A tip to one of the screwdrivers broke off at one robbery. When the suspects were arrested, police found the screwdriver. From this evidence, they were convicted.

The **Questioned Documents Unit** studies anything that has to do with paper. The unit has many specialties, from determining what a piece of paper is made of to analyzing handwriting and breaking codes. It deals with machines that use paper, including typewriters, computers, copy machines, and printers. It also handles footprints and tire tracks since they leave marks behind on a surface, much like writing or typing on paper. It maintains collections of anonymous letters, bank robbery notes, fraudulent checks, office equipment, shoe prints, and tire tracks. The unit has solved many cases by studying indentations

left by writing. In one case, a suspect had drawn a map to show her accomplice in a murder where to wait for the victim. The map was found, but it had to be connected to the suspect. When her belongings were searched, the police found a blank notebook. Agents studied the marks left by the machine that cut the paper and found that the map fit perfectly between the 12th and 14th pages. On the 14th page, they found indentations showing the map the woman had drawn. This linked the suspect to the crime.

The **Trace Evidence Unit** examines hairs, fibers, ropes, cordage, feathers, plants, woods, soils, glass, and building materials. It usually gets evidence first so that tiny fibers, hairs, or other debris can be collected before they fall off and are destroyed. The evidence is taken to a sealed-off room where the temperature and humidity are controlled. Examiners carefully scrape it off with a metal spatula. Any hairs, fibers, or other debris fall on a clean sheet of paper and examiners mount them on microscope slides for study. The unit maintains huge collections of fibers, wig hair, human and animal hairs, feathers, ropes, woods, and seeds. Using the collections for comparison, examiners can sometimes re-create entire crime scenes. They can figure out what criminals were wearing and the color, length, and style of their hair. In the case of serial killer Ted Bundy, agents matched nearly 100 clothing fibers between Bundy and one of his victims. The match helped the jury connect Bundy to the crime and he was convicted.

The **Regional Computer Forensics Laboratory** (RCFL) is a national network of 16 digital forensics laboratories. RCFL examines digital evidence in cases of terrorism, child pornography, financial crime, fraud, and other crimes. The unit's criminalists recover digital information from digital cameras, DVD-Rs, CD-Rs, computer hard drives, and other digital sources. Sometimes, the criminalist must locate and retrieve data from a hard drive that had been deleted by a suspect before arrest. The criminalist generally creates a copy, or "forensic duplicate," of the digital information from the source (e.g., digital photos on a hard drive) to preserve the original evidence while analyzing the copy. Because digital information can be copied without loss of quality, the criminalist is able to look at an exact version of the source information. Finally, the criminalist writes a report about the data and the process of retrieval for use by investigators. In one case, the Rocky Mountain RCFL examined the computer of a man under investigation for a series of rapes and sexual assaults in Colorado. On his computer, the RCFL found the names of the Colorado victims and other victims in the state of Washington. They also recovered over 400 photos of an attack in Washington from one of the suspect's own digital camera memory cards, which led to his conviction in 2011.

FOR DISCUSSION
1. Which unit do you think is most important? Why?
2. Do you know of any other aspects of crime labs not mentioned in the article?

CLASS ACTIVITY

DNA From Everyone Arrested?

DNA would be a more powerful weapon for law enforcement if more people's DNA profiles were available on a database. At present, most people's DNA is not on file. The procedure for getting a DNA profile is simple and non-intrusive. A technician simply brushes a cotton swab against the inside of a person's mouth. The sample is sent to a crime lab, which makes the profile. England now requires everyone arrested to give a DNA sample. By the end of 2011, the FBI had recorded over 10.2 million offender profiles in its National DNA Index (NDIS). In 2004, the people of California voted in favor of a Ballot Proposition 69. It mandates that DNA be collected from anyone arrested for a felony or other specified crimes. As a result, California has had over 1.3 million offender profiles in the NDIS, with 22 labs participating statewide.

Some people believe that every jurisdiction in the United States should require those arrested of felonies to give DNA samples. Representative Maeghan Maloney, a lawmaker in the Maine legislature, argues, "This would do two things. One, it exonerates people who are innocent, and two it has been able to find people who are not innocent. . . . DNA has almost become like fingerprinting. We should be using this tool like we use fingerprinting."

The American Civil Liberties Union opposes this. Barry Steinhardt, associate director of the ACLU, stated: "While DNA databases may be useful to identify criminals, I am skeptical that we will ward off the temptation to expand their use. In the last ten years alone we have gone from collecting DNA only from convicted sex offenders to now including people who have been arrested but never convicted of a crime. There have even been proposals to store newborns' DNA for future use by law enforcement."

In this activity, students evaluate the pros and cons of requiring DNA from those arrested on felony charges.
1. Form small groups. Each group should:
   a. Discuss the pros and cons of requiring DNA from everyone who is arrested for a felony.
   b. Decide whether to support or oppose this proposal.
   c. Prepare to discuss its decision and the reasons for it with the class.
2. The groups should report to the whole class.
3. Students should conclude the activity by voting on whether they think this proposal should be adopted in their state.

Current Issues in Forensic Science

Among existing forensic methods, only nuclear DNA analysis has been rigorously shown to have the capacity to consistently, and with a high degree of certainty, demonstrate a connection between an evidentiary sample and a specific individual or source.
– National Academy of Sciences (2009)

In 1953, two scientists walked into a pub near Cambridge University in England. One of them announced, "We have found the secret of life." The two scientists were James Watson and Francis Crick, and they had uncovered the structure of DNA, arguably the greatest scientific discovery of the 20th century. DNA contains the genetic code that determines the physical characteristics of living things.

Watson and Crick's discovery revolutionized the science of biology, opening up the study of genetics and leading to countless studies, papers, and other discoveries by scientists around the globe. In 1962, they, along with another scientist, received the Nobel Prize for their work.

The discovery of DNA has also revolutionized forensic science. No two people have identical DNA. Each human cell holds the complete genetic blueprint for an individual, each cell containing 3 billion "base pairs," the building blocks of DNA. Current technology cannot chart all these pairs, but instead charts a few selected areas. From a small amount of blood, saliva, semen, skin, fingernail, or hair, scientists can make a DNA profile. The DNA profile from a suspect can be compared to DNA found at the crime scene. If they don't match, then the suspect is cleared. In recent years, DNA has played a major role in clearing innocent suspects and freeing wrongly convicted prisoners.

If the suspect's and crime scene's DNA do match, this does not necessarily mean the DNA at the crime scene belongs to the suspect. Since the profile charts only a few sections of DNA, conceivably other people could share the same DNA profile. Scientists calculate the odds. The odds can sometimes run as high as 1 in 20 billion and make the match almost certain. Contamination can be a problem if people collecting and storing DNA evidence do not follow proper procedures. Once DNA evidence gets to a lab, poor lab procedures can cause mistakes.

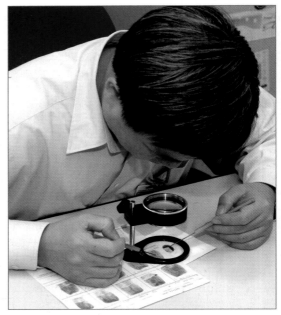

Fingerprint examiners look at fingerprints on computer databases and on fingerprint cards.

The National Academy of Sciences has issued three reports on the forensic use of DNA, the first two making recommendations for improvements and the last one in 2009 concluding that "DNA evidence is scientifically sound" and procedures and standards have been well defined. The 2009 report concluded:

DNA analysis . . . has been subjected to more scrutiny than any other forensic science discipline, with rigorous experimentation and validation performed prior to its use in forensic investigations. As a result of these characteristics, the probative power of DNA is high.

In fact, the scientific precision of DNA has called into question the reliability of other forensic sciences, particularly those that purport to match a suspect to evidence to the exclusion of everyone else in the world. One example is fingerprint evidence.

Fingerprinting

Fingerprint evidence has been used in the United States for more than 100 years. Before DNA evidence was developed, fingerprinting was considered the most reliable forensic science. In fact, DNA profiles were at first called "DNA fingerprints" to indicate how reliable DNA evidence was.

Fingerprint evidence is based on the idea that every individual has a unique set of fingerprints, which remain the same over a lifetime. Latent fingerprints, those not visible to the naked eye, can be lifted (using powder, chemicals, tape, or special light), photographed, and compared to known fingerprints on file.

The known fingerprints on file come from scans or inked impressions of people's fingerprints (10-print cards). The known prints are put into computer databases, the largest being the FBI's Integrated Automated Fingerprint Identification System, which holds more than 50 million prints. The FBI's system cannot automatically make matches to latent prints, but it does narrow down the possible matches. Expert fingerprint examiners decide whether latent prints match the known prints in the database. This can be incredibly difficult because latent prints vary by the condition of the skin making the print, how the finger touched the object, the surface of the object touched, the size of the print, and other factors.

The technique examiners use is called ACE-V, which stands for the four steps in the process — Analysis, Comparison, Evaluation, and Verification. Examiners first analyze the latent and known prints to see whether a comparison can be made. If the prints are suitable, then they are compared to see if there are similarities. If similarities exist, the similarities are evaluated to determine whether a match exists. If it does, the latent and known prints are sent to another examiner to verify that the prints do match.

The major organization for fingerprint examiners is the International Association for Identification (IAE). It offers certification of examiners, but many examiners are not certified. The IAE says examiners may only testify to three possible conclusions regarding a fingerprint. The print is either (1) a match, (2) not a match, or (3) the evidence is inconclusive. It has stated:

> [A]ny . . . latent print examiner who provides oral or written reports, or gives testimony of possible, probable, or likely friction ridge [fingerprint] identification shall be deemed to be engaged in conduct unbecoming such . . . certified latent print examiner.

For many years, the FBI considered fingerprint identification the "gold standard" of forensic science, and examiners across the nation have given testimony expressing certainty in their identifications.

Over the years, several fingerprint identifications have been shown to be wrong. The fingerprint community has blamed these errors on incompetent examiners, claiming that if a competent examiner makes the identification, the error rate is zero.

In 1997, Stephan Cowans was convicted on a number of charges, including attempted murder, and sentenced to prison. The perpetrator had shot and wounded a Boston police officer, and to escape, he had invaded a home and briefly taken people hostage. Two eyewitnesses, including the wounded police officer, identified Cowans in throw-downs and lineups. Boston police also matched Cowans to a thumb print the perpetrator had left on a mug in the home he invaded. The perpetrator had also left behind a baseball cap and sweatshirt. In 2004, DNA testing of the mug and clothing proved that Cowans was not the perpetrator. When the fingerprint was re-examined, it was discovered that it belonged to a family member who lived in the house. Cowans was released from prison. This was the first case of DNA evidence disproving fingerprint evidence. In response to the case, the Boston Police Department shut down its fingerprint unit and now sends fingerprint evidence to the state crime lab.

Experts blamed the wrong fingerprint identification on incompetent examiners. Far more troubling to the fingerprint community is the case of Brandon Mayfield. Following a terrorist attack in Madrid in 2004 that killed almost 200 people, the Spanish National Police sent the FBI latent prints found on a plastic bag.

The FBI ran the best latent print, that of an index finger, through its Automated Fingerprint Identification System and came up with 20 people's prints as possible matches. The FBI did background checks on all 20. After examining the prints, a leading FBI fingerprint expert declared the print matched Brandon Mayfield's print. Mayfield was an attorney in Portland, Oregon, who was a Muslim and active in Portland's Muslim community. The FBI sent the print to another leading expert, who had previously worked for the FBI. He verified the identification. The FBI then sent it the print to another FBI expert who also verified the match.

When the FBI sent Mayfield's prints to Spain, however, the Spanish police saw dissimilarities between the prints and concluded they did not match. The FBI sent agents to Madrid, but the Spanish police remained firm in their conclusion.

The FBI continued its investigation of Mayfield. It submitted a sworn statement to a federal district court that the print was a "100% positive identification" of Mayfield. The court appointed its own expert to examine the prints, and that expert also verified the match.

Ultimately, the FBI arrested Mayfield. He was held for two weeks until Spanish police announced they had arrested a suspect whose fingerprints matched those on the plastic bag. Mayfield received an apology and later a $2 million settlement. (For more details on the case, see pages 359–360.)

In short, four fingerprint experts, three of them leading FBI latent print examiners, had wrongly identified Mayfield. The FBI issued a statement that the mistake was made because the Spanish police had sent a digital image of the print that was "of substandard quality." An investigation by the inspector general of the Department of Justice rejected this explanation. It concluded the primary factors were that the prints were "extraordinarily similar" and the FBI "Laboratory's overconfidence in the superiority of its examiners" to those of the Spanish police. The investigation noted mistakes the examiners made. "Among other things, the examiners applied circular reasoning, allowing details visible in Mayfield's known prints to suggest details in murky or ambiguous details [of the digital print] that were not really there." Although the investigation did not find Mayfield's religion contributed to the initial mistaken identification, it did conclude that "facts developed during the field investigation, including his Muslim religion, also likely contributed to the examiners' failure to sufficiently reconsider the identification after legitimate questions about it were raised."

The 2009 National Academy of Sciences Report

Congress asked the National Academy of Sciences to evaluate the state of forensic science. In 2009, the National Academy issued a more than 300-page report titled *Strengthening Forensic Science in the United States: A Path Forward*. It looked at many areas of forensic science and made recommendations on improving them.

One area it examined was fingerprint evidence. The report noted that historically fingerprint "analysis has served as a valuable tool, both to identify the guilty and to exclude the innocent." It found "some scientific evidence" that fingerprints "are unique to each person and persist unchanged throughout a lifetime." But it warned, "Uniqueness does not guarantee that prints from two different people are always sufficiently different that they cannot be confused . . . ."

As to the ACE-V process (Analysis, Comparison, Evaluation, and Verification) that examiners follow, the report concluded:

ACE-V does not guard against bias; is too broad to ensure repeatability and transparency; and does not guarantee that two

---

THE FIRST FORENSIC USE OF DNA

In 1986, two separate murders of teenage girls took place near Leicester in England. Both girls had been raped and strangled. Fearing a serial predator was on the loose, police went on a manhunt. Soon, investigators focused on a 17-year-old suspect who had displayed great interest in one crime scene.

Using the technology of the time, serologists analyzed blood samples that police thought would link the suspect to the crime. The test results were negative. Police knew about a local geneticist named Alec Jeffreys who had developed a technique to map DNA. Police asked Jeffreys for help in creating DNA profiles based on the suspect's blood sample and from semen found at the crime scenes. Jeffreys agreed, and his analysis exonerated the 17-year-old suspect.

His analysis also established that the same person had committed both rapes and murders. Police then asked all local males between the ages of 17 and 34 to provide blood samples for DNA analysis. If a sample matched the profile created by Jeffreys, the police would have a new suspect. The police collected thousands of samples, but none matched the profile.

After many months, however, a local bakery employee tipped off police that a coworker told her he had taken the blood test in place of someone else. When police questioned him, he named his fellow baker, Colin Pitchfork, as the man he had taken the test for. When Pitchfork was tested, his DNA matched. This led to Pitchfork's 1988 conviction for the rape-murders. The case thus involved both the first person ever to be exonerated and the first person ever to be convicted based on DNA evidence.

---

analysts following it will obtain the same results. For these reasons, merely following the steps of ACE-V does not imply that one is proceeding in a scientific manner or producing reliable results.

The report cited recent research showing that "experienced examiners do not necessarily agree with even their own past conclusions when the examination is presented in a different context some time later."

The report called on examiners to document each step they take and the reasons for their conclusions so that others can better study their work. It also called for further scientific research on fingerprints.

The report evaluated many different types of forensic science. In general, it concluded that those forensic sciences that arose from science rather than crime scene investigation are, not surprisingly, more scientific. DNA science has "benefitted from extensive basic research, clinical applications, federal oversight, vast financial support from the private sector for applied research, and national standards for quality assurance and quality control."

Other forensic sciences such as toxicology and drug analysis, based on the science of chemistry, have great reliability. But the report concluded that those forensic sciences such as fingerprints, writing analysis, toolmarks, bite marks, and hair comparison that have grown up in crime labs require more independent scientific study.

The report made 13 recommendations for improving forensic sciences. Among them were these:

Establish an independent National Institute of Forensic Science. The institute would set best practices for forensic scientists, set standards for accreditation of labs and certification of criminalists, and fund scientific research to address issues of reliability and validity of forensic sciences. It should be outside any law-enforcement arm of the government and should develop close associations with research universities.

Make it mandatory that all crime labs be accredited and all forensic scientists be certified. Currently, great differences exist throughout the country in the quality of crime labs and their staff: "Forensic science facilities exhibit wide variability in capacity, oversight, staffing, certification, and accreditation across federal and state jurisdictions."

Conduct more "research . . . on human observer bias and sources of human error in forensic examinations." Scientists recognize that people making observations can easily make mistakes, and they have developed methods to minimize the risk of such mistakes in scientific inquiries. Similar methods must be developed for forensic examinations. The report stated:

A body of research is required to establish the limits and measures of performance and to address the impact of sources of variability and potential bias. Such research is sorely needed . . . in most of the forensic disciplines [such as fingerprint analysis] that rely on subjective assessments of matching characteristics. These disciplines need to develop rigorous protocols to guide these subjective interpretations and pursue equally rigorous research and evaluation programs.

Set a goal to replace all the coroner systems in the United States with medical examiners. The report noted that "more than 80 years ago, the National Academy of Sciences . . . called for the abolishment of the coroner's office . . . ." Coroners are elected or appointed officials. Unlike medical examiners, they are not necessarily medical professionals. The report noted that recently in Indiana, an 18 year old with minimal experience was elected as a deputy coroner. "Currently, 11 states have coroner-only systems, 22 states have medical examiner systems, and 18 states have mixed systems — in which some counties have coroners and others have medical examiners."

The 'CSI Effect'

Since 2000, millions of Americans have watched a television program called *CSI: Crime Scene Investigation*. The show depicts the work of criminalists in Las Vegas as they solve murders by closely examining physical evidence. One of the most watched TV shows for more than a decade, it has inspired *CSI: Miami*, *CSI: NY*, *Numb3rs*, and other shows that glamorize and often overstate the scientific work of criminalists. These shows often portray forensic science as far more advanced than it is and much more reliable than studies, such as the 2009 report of the National Academy of Sciences, indicate that it is.

Given its popularity, *CSI* has also caused concern among criminal attorneys and judges. Many prosecutors say that the show has made jurors expect scientific evidence to be presented in every case and will vote to acquit a defendant if the prosecution presents no scientific evidence. Similarly, defense attorneys worry that jurors may overestimate the reliability of forensic science whenever it is offered by the prosecution. These suspected effects on juries are known as the "*CSI* Effect."

Is the *CSI* Effect real? Recent studies have tried to find out. One was conducted by a doctoral candidate and a professor of psychology at Arizona State University. They were looking at two questions:

[D]o *CSI* viewers give forensic science more weight than it deserves? Or, by having had their expectations raised, have they become more skeptical?

They prepared a short simulated trial transcript of witness testimony. One prosecution witness was a forensic expert who testified about using a microscope to determine that the defendant's hair matched a hair found on a ski cap. Without this testimony, the prosecution's case was relatively weak. Researchers asked 48 university students to read the transcript and answer questions, including whether they watched *CSI*-type shows, their opinion of the case's scientific testimony, and whether they would vote to convict or acquit the defendant. The study found that *CSI* viewers were far more skeptical of the expert's testimony than non-*CSI* viewers. But it also found no difference between viewers and non-viewers on whether they would vote to convict the defendant.

In another, larger study, Michigan Judge Donald Shelton joined with criminology researchers at Eastern Michigan University to examine the *CSI* Effect. In a 2006 study and a follow-up study in 2009, the researchers surveyed more than 2,000 potential jurors. They asked them about their television-watching habits, their expectations for scientific evidence, and about their opinions in specific crime scenarios.

The studies found no significant difference between *CSI* and non-*CSI* viewers. But it did find that almost half of all jurors — both *CSI* and non-*CSI* viewers — expected scientific evidence in every case. But the studies

showed that most jurors still appeared to trust . . . eyewitnesses and will rely on factual testimony to find that the government has met its burden, even in the absence of scientific evidence. Thus, jurors are not necessarily prepared to acquit defendants due to a lack of scientific evidence alone. In cases where there are no eyewitnesses and the government relies on circumstantial evidence, . . . jurors are much more likely to acquit if the government's case does not include some scientific evidence.

The researchers believe that the jurors' high expectation for scientific evidence comes not from watching *CSI*, but simply from living in the modern high-tech, interconnected world.

[I]nformation technology . . . quickly makes scientific discoveries and advancements part of our popular culture. The dissemination of technological developments is fast and widespread through various media, including the Internet, fiction and non-fiction television programs, film, and traditional news sources like television, newspapers and magazines.

FOR DISCUSSION

1. Why is DNA evidence considered very reliable? What could cause DNA evidence to be unreliable?
2. What happened in the Brandon Mayfield case? Why do you think the mistake was made?
3. Why is it important that forensic science be based on science?
4. What were the main recommendations of the 2009 National Academy of Sciences report? Do you agree with them? Explain.
5. What is the *CSI* Effect? Do you think it is real? Explain. If it is real, what do you think can be done about it? Explain.

CHAPTER 8
POLICE AND THE LAW

The forefathers, after consulting the lessons of history, designed our Constitution to place obstacles in the way of a too permeating police surveillance, which they seemed to think was a greater danger to a free people than the escape of some criminals from punishment.
– U.S. Supreme Court Justice Robert H. Jackson, *U.S. v. Di Re* (1948)

CRIMINAL PROCEDURE | THE LAW OF SEARCH AND SEIZURE | HAS A SEARCH OR SEIZURE TAKEN PLACE? |
IS THE SEARCH OR SEIZURE REASONABLE? | THE MOTOR VEHICLE EXCEPTION |
THE STOP AND FRISK EXCEPTION | OTHER EXCEPTIONS | INTERROGATION AND CONFESSIONS |
MIRANDA'S AFTERMATH | THE EXCLUSIONARY RULE

Criminal Procedure

As applied to a criminal trial, denial of due process is the failure to observe that fundamental fairness essential to the very concept of justice.
– U.S. Supreme Court Justice Owen J. Roberts, *Lisenba v. California* (1941)

Police officers must study two areas of law. One is **criminal law**, which you learned about in Unit 1. It defines which acts are illegal. Because police enforce the criminal law, they must know it. The second area of law that police must study is criminal procedure.

Criminal procedure deals with procedures for arrests, trials, and appeals. It sets out the rules for processing someone through the criminal justice system. Because illegal arrest or investigation procedures may jeopardize a criminal case, the police must pay close attention to criminal procedure.

Criminal procedure comes from a variety of sources, including federal and state statutes. Most important, it comes from the U.S. and state constitutions. Appellate courts interpret these statutes and constitutions when criminal defendants appeal their convictions claiming that their constitutional rights have been violated. Deciding these cases, appellate courts produce rules that police and criminal trial courts must follow. As the highest appellate court in the land, the U.S. Supreme Court often decides whether particular criminal procedures meet the U.S. constitutional standards of the Bill of Rights, particularly the Fourth, Fifth, and Sixth amendments.

Originally, the Bill of Rights only applied to the federal government. But after the Civil War, the 14th Amendment was added to the Constitution. Its due process clause declares that no state shall "deprive any person of life, liberty, or

RIGHTS INCORPORATED BY THE 14TH AMENDMENT

Rights	Amendment	Supreme Court Decision	Date
Just Compensation	Fifth	*Chicago, B, & Q RR v. Chicago*	1897
Freedom of Speech	First	*Gitlow v. New York*	1925
Freedom of the Press	First	*Near v. Minnesota*	1931
Counsel in Capital Cases	Sixth	*Powell v. Alabama*	1932
Freedom of Assembly & Petition	First	*DeJonge v. Oregon*	1937
Free Exercise of Religion	First	*Cantwell v. Connecticut*	1940
No Establishment of Religion	First	*Everson v. Board of Education*	1947
Public Trial	Sixth	*In re Oliver*	1948
No Unreasonable Searches & Seizures	Fourth	*Wolf v. Colorado*	1949
No Cruel & Unusual Punishments	Eighth	*Robinson v. California*	1962
Counsel for Felonies	Sixth	*Gideon v. Wainwright*	1963
Privilege Against Self-Incrimination	Fifth	*Malloy v. Hogan*	1964
Confrontation of Witnesses	Sixth	*Pointer v. Texas*	1965
Impartial Jury Trial	Sixth	*Parker v. Gladden*	1966
Speedy Trial	Sixth	*Klopfer v. North Carolina*	1967
Compulsory Process in Obtaining Witnesses	Sixth	*Washington v. Texas*	1967
Trial by Jury	Sixth	*Duncan v. Lousiana*	1968
No Double Jeopardy	Fifth	*Benton v. Maryland*	1969
Counsel for Crimes with Jail Terms	Sixth	*Argersinger v. Hamlin*	1972
Right to Bear Arms	Second	*McDonald v. Chicago*	2010

property, without due process of law. . . ." This means that states cannot deprive people of certain rights. But what rights does the 14th Amendment's due process clause include?

The Supreme Court struggled with this question for years. But in the 1930s, the Supreme Court ruled that the clause **incorporates** those guarantees in the Bill of Rights that are "rooted in the tradition and conscience of our people." (*Palko v. Connecticut*, 1937.) Since that time, the Supreme Court has decided on a case-by-case basis which rights in the Bill of Rights were fundamental and were therefore rights that every state had to grant to individuals.

In a series of landmark cases beginning in the 1960s, the Supreme Court applied almost all the rights found in the Fourth, Fifth, and Sixth amendments to the states. Not only did the court apply these rights to the states, it also strengthened them. When speaking of the court, it should be noted that not every justice on the court agreed with all of these decisions. Some justices complained that strengthening the constitutional rights of individuals made law enforcement too difficult. But the majority stressed the need for the police to respect rights. The court made so many profound changes that the era marked a revolution in criminal procedure.

Following the 1960s when the rights of criminal suspects and defendants rapidly expanded, the court changed. New justices were appointed to the court forming a new majority. Although these justices did not directly overturn the decisions of the 1960s, they often restricted them. So while the court minority complained that the court was eroding basic rights, the new majority stressed the need for crime control.

This tension on the court reflects the tension between the two, often conflicting, goals of the criminal justice system: protecting society from criminals and protecting the constitutional rights of those being processed through the system. Criminal procedure attempts to achieve both.

FOR DISCUSSION

1. What is the difference between criminal law and criminal procedure?
2. How do appellate courts create rules of criminal procedure?
3. What are the two, often conflicting, goals of the criminal procedure? How might they conflict? Which do you think is more important? Why?

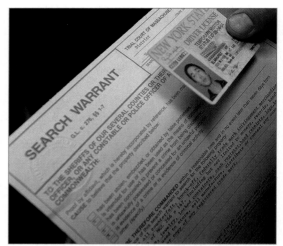
For most searches, police must obtain a warrant.

The Law of Search and Seizure

The right of the people to be secure in their persons, houses, papers, and effects, against unreasonable searches and seizures, shall not be violated, and no Warrants shall issue, but upon probable cause, supported by Oath or affirmation, and particularly describing the place to be searched, and the persons or things to be seized.
– Fourth Amendment to the U.S. Constitution (1791)

One of the most important and complex areas of criminal procedure comes from the Fourth Amendment. This amendment affects how police officers investigate crimes and gather evidence, because the Supreme Court has ruled that illegally seized evidence may not be used at trial.

All police searches, seizures of evidence, and arrests must comply with this amendment. Courts have interpreted the amendment's meaning in hundreds of search-and-seizure cases. These interpretations have grown into a full body of law, known as the law of search and seizure. Although the law is complicated, determining whether a search or seizure is legal comes down to two basic questions:

- Has a governmental search or seizure taken place?
- If so, was the search or seizure reasonable?

In the sections that follow, you will learn how to answer these questions for most searches or seizures.

Has a Search or Seizure Taken Place?

[T]he application of the Fourth Amendment depends on whether the person invoking its protection can claim a "justifiable," a "reasonable," or a "legitimate expectation of privacy" that has been invaded by government action.
– U.S. Supreme Court Justice Harry Blackmun, *Smith v. Maryland* (1979)

To be a search or seizure under the Fourth Amendment, it must be (1) done by a government employee or agent **and** (2) it must fit the courts' definition of a search or seizure. We will examine each of these issues.

Did a government employee or agent conduct the search or seizure?

The first step in analyzing search-and-seizure problems is to determine who conducted the search or seizure. The Fourth Amendment protects citizens from actions by government officials. The Fourth Amendment does not usually cover actions by private individuals. If, for example, your neighbor breaks into your house, finds evidence of a crime, and turns it in to the police, your rights under the Fourth Amendment would not have been violated. If you were prosecuted, this evidence could be used against you at trial. Of course, the police could also arrest the person who broke into your house for burglary, and you could sue the person in civil court.

Note, however, that if the police had requested your neighbor to break into your house, then Fourth Amendment protections would come into play. The neighbor would be considered an agent of the government.

Was it a search or seizure as defined by the courts?

The Fourth Amendment protects people from unreasonable searches and seizures of their "persons, houses, papers, and effects." But what is a "search"? What is a "seizure"? The next consideration is to decide whether a government official's conduct amounted to a search or seizure.

In the landmark case of *Katz v. U.S.* in 1967, the Supreme Court defined a search as any governmental intrusion into something in which a person has **a reasonable expectation of privacy**. This privacy interest covers places and things such as houses, yards, garages, apartments, diaries, briefcases, and mail.

Executing a search warrant, police place seized property in plastic bags.

The court has held, however, that there is no reasonable expectation of privacy in places or things that are in **plain view**. For example, a person growing a four-foot-high marijuana plant in a front bay window cannot claim that a search was conducted if a police officer spots it from the street. But officers who detect things in plain view must do so from places they have a legal right to be in. For instance, if an officer climbs over an eight-foot fence surrounding a yard and spots marijuana growing in a back corner, a search has taken place. People normally have a reasonable expectation of privacy in their private property that cannot be seen except by trespassing.

But the court has held there is no reasonable expectation of privacy for **open fields** away from a residence. Even though they are private property, they usually are readily accessible to the public. Thus police walking through open fields are not conducting a search.

A similar rule applies to **abandoned property**. For example, if a person placed letters containing incriminating statements into the trash, the police could retrieve them from the garbage dump without having conducted a search. There is no reasonable expectation of privacy in such items.

The idea of "seizure" is somewhat easier to understand. A seizure is any taking into possession, custody, or control. Property may be seized, but so may people. An arrest is one form of seizure, because in making an arrest, the police take someone into custody. Thus arrests fall under the requirements imposed by the Fourth Amendment.

FOR DISCUSSION

1. What is the difference between a search and a seizure?
2. The Supreme Court has ruled that the police have **not** conducted a search if the object is in plain view, in an open field, or has been abandoned. Why does the court say this in each instance? Do you agree? Why or why not?
3. Why do you think the Fourth Amendment protects only against intrusions by the government? Are these intrusions more dangerous than intrusions by individuals? Why or why not?
4. For each of the following, decide whether a search or seizure has taken place and explain why or why not. Don't be concerned whether it was legal.

a. A police officer arrests Mary Clark for shoplifting.
b. Lois Kindel, a custodian at the Shadyville Police Department, believes her neighbor deals drugs. She tells police but they have no evidence. She agrees to keep a close watch on her neighbor. One day she spots a marijuana plant, which has grown taller than her neighbor's fence.
c. Officer Sanchez climbs a hill in a public park and spots three stolen cars in a nearby backyard surrounded by a 10-foot-high fence.
d. On surprising George Meyers, a known narcotics dealer, police observe him swallow several capsules. They take him to the hospital and have his stomach pumped.
e. The police stop Anna and question her for a few minutes about where she's been and what she has been doing the past few days. (Anna has been arrested twice in the last year for prostitution but has never been convicted.)

CLASS ACTIVITY

Is It a Search?

In this activity, students analyze and research cases to determine whether a search or seizure has taken place.

1. Form groups of 10. Each group should:
   a. Discuss each of the cases below and decide if a search or seizure has taken place in each case.
   b. Each group member should be assigned one of the cases cited to look up. The cases can be found on the Internet or at a law library. A good place to start Internet research is Research Links or *Criminal Justice in America* Links (both are at **www.crf-usa.org**). Law libraries can be found at law schools and at courthouses. (To find the cases, law librarians can help.)
2. After researching, students should meet in one of 10 groups according to the case they looked up. In this "expert" group, students should:
   a. Discuss the case and prepare to report on it to the class.
   b. One person should be assigned to report on the facts of the case, another to report on what the court majority decided and why, another on what the court dissenters believed and why, and finally each member should state how he or she would have decided the case and why.

Cases

a. Unable to see over Mike's 10-foot-high fence, police hire a plane and fly over the house at 1,000 feet and see marijuana plants growing in the backyard. See *California v. Ciraolo* (1986) and *Florida v. Riley* (1989).

(Continued on next page.)

b. Police install a device at the phone company office that keeps track of the numbers that Gilbert dials from his home phone. See *Smith v. Maryland* (1979).

c. Suspecting drug dealing, police have the trash collector turn over Bill's trash to them instead of throwing it in the trash truck. See *California v. Greenwood* (1988).

d. The FBI listens to Joe's conversation by attaching an electronic eavesdropping device to the outside of the public telephone booth he uses at 11 a.m. every day. See *Katz v. U.S.* (1967).

e. Investigating a shooting, police legally enter an apartment looking for weapons and the shooter. While inside, an officer spots a high-priced stereo, which seems out of place in the rundown apartment. The officer picks it up, jots down the serial number, puts it down, calls headquarters, and finds out the stereo is stolen. See *Arizona v. Hicks* (1987).

f. Oliver posts "no trespassing" signs around his land and locks the gate to his property. Police go onto a highly secluded part of his land about a mile from his house and find marijuana plants growing. See *Oliver v. U.S.* (1984).

g. A Border Patrol agent boards a bus in Texas. As he walks down the aisle, he squeezes the luggage that passengers have stored above their seats. When he squeezes Steven's bag, he feels a suspicious "brick-like" object, which the agent believes to be a "brick" of methamphetamine. See *Bond v. U.S.* (2000).

h. Suspecting that Danny was growing marijuana in his house, federal agents scan the house with a thermal imager to see whether it was emitting abnormal amounts of heat consistent with lamps for growing marijuana. See *Kyllo v. U.S.* (2001).

i. Police stop Roy for a traffic violation. During the stop, an officer walks a drug-sniffing dog around the car, and the dog "alerts" the officer to drugs in the trunk. See *Illinois v. Caballes* (2005).

j. Without Jones' knowledge, police install a GPS device on his car and track where he goes in his car for a month. The tracking shows Jones makes frequent visits to a particular address, linking him to a drug conspiracy. See *U.S. v. Jones* (2012).

k. Police receive an unverified tip that Jardines is growing marijuana in his home. Police take a drug-sniffing dog to Jardines' front door, and the dog "alerts" officers that drugs are in the house. See *Florida v. Jardines* (2013).

Debriefing Questions

1. What is the test used by the Supreme Court to determine whether a search has taken place?
2. Do you think this is a good test? Explain.
3. Do you think the Supreme Court has applied this test satisfactorily in these cases? Why or why not?
4. A few police departments have begun using drones, which can observe people for 20 hours straight, flying high above noiselessly and out of sight. Is using a drone a search?

Is the Search or Seizure Reasonable?

The Fourth Amendment and the personal rights which it secures have a long history. At the very core stands the right of a man to retreat into his own home and there be free from unreasonable governmental intrusion.
– U.S. Supreme Court Justice Potter Stewart, *Silverman v. U.S. (1961)*

After a court determines that a search or seizure has taken place, then it must determine whether it was reasonable. There are two basic questions to answer to determine whether a search was reasonable:

1. Was the search or seizure conducted pursuant to a valid warrant?
2. If not, does one of the court-recognized exceptions to the warrant requirement apply?

Was the search or seizure conducted pursuant to a valid warrant?

In general, courts have held that a search or seizure is unreasonable without a **warrant**. A warrant is a court order issued by a judge authorizing a search, an arrest, or a seizure of evidence. Warrants must specifically describe the place to be searched and the items or persons to be seized. In 2004, the U.S. Supreme Court in *Groh v. Ramirez* ruled that it is not enough that the application for the warrant described these things. The search warrant itself must describe them so that the person whose belongings are being searched can inspect the warrant.

Before issuing a warrant, a judge must receive evidence presented under oath — usually supplied by a police officer. The evidence must show that there is probable cause to believe that:
(1) a crime has been or is about to be committed, *and*
(2) the person, place, or thing to be searched or seized is related to that crime.

Probable cause means that the evidence must be strong enough that an independent person would have good reason to believe it.

Once the police get a search warrant, they must carry out the search promptly — usually within 72 or 96 hours, depending on the state. Many states allow police to execute warrants only during daytime hours except in special cases. Police must normally follow the **knock-and-announce rule**. A common law rule considered part of the Fourth Amendment, this rule requires police to knock, announce their presence, and wait a reasonable time before entering a home to execute a search or arrest warrant. But police can forgo this formality if they have reason to believe that a fugitive is hiding out, a threat of violence exists, or evidence is being destroyed. In most jurisdictions, the police may forcibly enter a place when no one will let them in.

When officers seize property under a search warrant, they must prepare for the court a list of the items they seize.

If police do not obtain a warrant, does a court-recognized exception to the warrant requirement apply?

The courts do not require police to obtain a warrant before every search and seizure (though probable cause is still required in almost all cases). Over the years, courts have created exceptions to the warrant requirement. They have made these exceptions for several reasons:
- To protect the safety of officers and the public.
- To ensure that evidence will be seized before it can be hidden or destroyed.
- To help apprehend suspects or prevent their escape.

In determining whether a warrantless search or seizure is reasonable, courts weigh the need for immediate police action against the invasion of individual privacy involved. The next three articles discuss the major exceptions to the warrant requirement.

FOR DISCUSSION
1. What is a search warrant? What do police officers have to prove before they can get a warrant from a judge?
2. Why do you think courts require police officers to obtain warrants? Why are search warrants important?
3. When do you think it might be reasonable for a police officer to make a search without a warrant? Explain.

THE STATE OF TEXAS   §   **SEARCH WARRANT**

COUNTY OF HARRIS   §

TO THE SHERIFF OR ANY PEACE OFFICER OF HARRIS COUNTY, TEXAS

G R E E T I N G S:

WHEREAS, I am a District Court Judge in and for Harris County, Texas, and WHEREAS, E.G. Chance, a peace officer employed by the Houston Police Department Narcotics Division, hereafter called Affiant, came before me this day with a sworn affidavit (which is attached hereto and is specifically incorporated by reference for all purposes along with the sworn affidavit of LAPD Officer Orlando Martinez), requesting a search warrant; and WHEREAS I have made inquiry of the basis of said beliefs of the Affiant and find that; the affidavit sets forth substantial facts establishing that probable cause does exist for the issuance of a search warrant, that the person, place or thing to be searched and seized is not one which is prohibited nor beyond the authorization of this magistrate, and that the search is requested upon proper grounds.

THEREFORE, YOU ARE COMMANDED to search the business at **6826 West Montgomery Road Houston, Harris County, Texas**, and search for, seize and examine all items including but not limited to, billing records, medication orders, transport receipts, billing receipts, medical records and computerized medical records, for implements and instruments used in the commission of a crime and for property or items constituting evidence of the offense of manslaughter that tend to show that Dr. Conrad Murray committed the said criminal offense.

It is Ordered that any items recovered may be removed from Harris County, where it was seized to any county in the State of California;

HEREIN FAIL NOT, as the peace officer to whom this warrant is delivered, you shall execute it without delay and within three whole days and due return make by faithfully completing the form attached hereto designated for said purpose.

SIGNED, ENTERED and ORDERED this the 20th day of July, 2009, at 10:50 o'clock a.m., to attest to which I subscribe my name.

Hon. Judge SHAULA J.
District Court
Harris County, Texas

RECORDER'S MEMORANDUM
This instrument is of poor quality
at the time of imaging

A warrant to search a Texas office of Dr. Conrad Murray, who later was convicted of involuntary manslaughter for the death of singer Michael Jackson.

The Warrant

In this activity, students create and evaluate search warrants.

The Fourth Amendment states that "no Warrants shall issue, but upon probable cause, supported by Oath or affirmation, and particularly describing the place to be searched, and the persons or things to be seized."

Imagine that you are police officers. Sam is suspected of stealing a television set from a store. You have sufficient evidence for probable cause that (1) Sam stole the set and (2) the set is in Sam's house. You are going to apply for a warrant to search Sam's house and seize the stolen television set.

1. Form pairs.
2. Each pair should take the role of police officers and apply for a search warrant for Sam. Each pair should:
   a. Read **Instructions for Applying for a Search Warrant**, below.
   b. Think up a set of facts that would allow you as police officers to search Sam's house.
   c. Using your made-up facts, write an application for the search warrant following the **Instructions for Applying for a Search Warrant**, below. Remember your facts must be clear enough for a third party — a judge — to understand.
3. Once the pairs have created their applications for search warrants, each pair should exchange its warrant application with another pair. Now the pairs should role play judges and determine whether or not to grant a search warrant based on the application. Each pair should:
   a. Read the warrant application.
   b. Make sure the warrant is signed and dated and states the four things required for a warrant (listed below in **Instructions for Applying for a Search Warrant**).
   c. Determine whether the fact statement establishes probable cause (a) for the crime, (b) that Sam has committed the crime, (c) that the items to be seized are connected to the crime, (d) that the items are in the house to be searched.
   d. If the application fulfills all the requirements, then create and sign a search warrant on a sheet of paper using the search warrant on page 111 as a guide. If the application does not fulfill all the requirements, state the reasons on another sheet of paper.
4. When the judges finish, ask pairs to report on whether the warrant applications were successful.

Instructions for Applying for a Search Warrant

To apply for a warrant, you must fill out an application. The application is an affidavit (a sworn statement made under penalty of perjury). This is what the Fourth Amendment means by an "Oath or affirmation." The affidavit must state:

1. Your name and that you are a police officer.
2. The address of the house you want to search.
3. The specific items that you expect to find when you search the house.
4. Facts supporting a finding of probable cause. This statement of facts must show evidence that:
   a. A crime has been committed (in this case theft).
   b. Sam, the owner of the house, committed the crime.
   c. The items to be seized are connected to the crime.
   d. The items are in the house to be searched.

The evidence might be from eyewitnesses, informants, circumstantial evidence, or your own observations. You must show that the evidence is reliable.

To finish, sign and date the affidavit and swear under penalty of perjury that what you have stated is true.

The Motor Vehicle Exception

[T]he Fourth Amendment has been construed . . . as recognizing a necessary difference between a search of a store, dwelling house or other structure in respect of which a proper official warrant readily may be obtained, and a search of a ship, motor boat, wagon or automobile, for contraband goods, where it is not practicable to secure a warrant because the vehicle can be quickly moved out of the locality or jurisdiction in which the warrant must be sought.
– U.S. Supreme Court Chief Justice William Howard Taft, *Carroll v. U.S.* (1925)

Late one evening, a reliable informant telephoned Detective Marcum and told him that an individual known as "Bandit" was selling drugs. The informant had just seen Bandit complete a narcotics sale and Bandit had told him that he had more drugs in the trunk of his car. The informant gave the detective a detailed description of Bandit, described his car as a maroon Chevrolet Malibu, and told Marcum the address where it was parked.

Detective Marcum, along with two other police officers, immediately drove to the address and found a parked maroon Malibu. A license check disclosed that the car was registered to Albert Ross. A computer check on Ross revealed that he fit the informant's description and was known to use the alias "Bandit." The officers cruised through the neighborhood, but did not see anyone matching Ross' description.

When they returned to the address, they saw the maroon Malibu going down the street. They pulled alongside the Malibu, saw that the driver matched the informant's description, and stopped the car. They ordered Ross out of the car. While the officers were searching him, Detective Marcum noticed a bullet on the car's front seat. Marcum took Ross' keys and opened the trunk, where he found a closed brown paper bag. He opened the bag and discovered many cellophane envelopes containing white powder.

Later at the police station, the officers thoroughly searched the car again. They discovered a red leather pouch in the trunk. Unzipping the pouch, they found $3,200 in cash.

The police laboratory later determined that the powder in the cellophane envelopes was heroin. Ross was charged with possession of heroin with intent to distribute.

The Supreme Court has carved out a motor vehicle exception to the warrant requirement for police searches.

The police had never obtained a search warrant, and Ross claimed the searches were unreasonable. He made a motion to suppress the heroin and the cash from evidence at his trial.

The U.S. Supreme Court decided *U.S. v. Ross* in 1982. In a 6–3 decision, the court ruled that the searches and seizures were reasonable and did not violate Ross' Fourth Amendment rights. Police officers who have legitimately stopped an automobile (as they did in this case) and who have probable cause to believe that contraband is concealed somewhere within it (as they did in this case) may conduct a warrantless search of the vehicle.

In addition, when police have probable cause to search a vehicle, they may conduct a warrantless search of every part of the vehicle and its contents. This includes all containers and packages that may conceal whatever the police are searching for. But it excludes containers that could not hold what they are looking for. For example, probable cause to believe that undocumented aliens are being transported in a van will not justify a warrantless search of a suitcase in the van. Justice White argued in dissent:

> The majority . . . not only repeals all realistic limits on warrantless automobile searches, it repeals the Fourth Amendment warrant requirement itself. By equating a police officer's estimation of probable cause with a magistrate's, the Court utterly disregards the value of a neutral and detached magistrate . . . .The court simply ignores the critical function that a magistrate serves. And although the Court purports to rely on the mobility of an automobile and impracticability of obtaining a warrant, it never explains why these concerns permit the warrantless search of a container, which can easily be seized and immobilized while the police are obtaining a warrant.

Justice Marshall also disagreed with the decision. In his dissenting opinion, he warned that the majority ruling would have "profound implications for the privacy of citizens traveling in automobiles."

The *Ross* case removed the warrant requirement for **motor vehicle searches**. The court made this exception because, if the police had to wait to get a warrant, motor vehicles could easily be moved and any evidence in them concealed or destroyed. (Of course, before searching any vehicle, police must still have probable cause to believe it was used in the commission of a crime or it contains evidence of a crime.)

FOR DISCUSSION

1. Did Detective Marcum's opening of Bandit's car trunk constitute a search? What about the brown paper bag? The cellophane envelopes? Explain your answers.

2. Assume that opening the trunk, brown bag, and cellophane envelopes were searches. Do you think they were reasonable under the circumstances or should the officers have secured a warrant first? Why?

3. Was unzipping the red leather pouch at the police station a search? If so, was it reasonable under the circumstances or should the officers have obtained a warrant first? Why?

4. Why did the court carve out an exception to the warrant requirement in automobile searches? What reasons did the dissenters give in opposing it? Do you agree with the decision in *Ross*? Why or why not?

Cases After Ross

Since the *Ross* case, the U.S. Supreme Court has made a number of decisions on automobile searches. In this activity, students role play justices of the Supreme Court and decide some important automobile search cases.

1. Form small groups. Each group will role play the U.S. Supreme Court.
2. Assign each group one of the **Automobile Search Cases**, below.
3. Each group should:
   a. Discuss and decide these questions about its assigned case:
      (1) How is this case similar to the *Ross* case? How is it different?
      (2) Does the automobile search in this case violate the Fourth Amendment? Explain.
   b. Be prepared to report its answers and reasons for them to the class.
   c. If time permits, read and discuss the other cases so group members can weigh in on the discussion of them.
4. Have the groups assigned to each case report on their decisions and hold a class discussion on each case.

Automobile Search Cases

California v. Carney (1985). Carney met a young person in downtown San Diego. A Drug Enforcement Administration agent followed them to a nearby motor home, which DEA agents had heard was being used to trade marijuana for sex. Agents waited outside the motor home. When the young person left, agents stopped him. He told agents that Carney had given him marijuana to have sex with him. They returned to the motor home and had the young person knock on the door. When Carney answered, they showed him their badges. With probable cause but without Carney's consent or a warrant, they entered the motor home, found marijuana, and arrested Carney.

California v. Acevedo (1991). A federal drug enforcement agent sent police in Santa Ana, Calif., a package of marijuana he had intercepted. The police took the package to a nearby Federal Express office and waited for someone to claim it. The next morning, Jamie Daza picked up the package, and with police following him, took it to his apartment. One officer went to get a search warrant while others watched the apartment. An hour later, Charles Acevedo entered the apartment, stayed for about 10 minutes, and emerged with a brown paper bag. Acevedo walked to his car, put the paper bag in the trunk, and began to drive away. Police stopped him, opened the trunk and the bag, and found marijuana.

Wyoming v. Houghton (1999). Wyoming Highway Patrol officers pulled over a car for speeding and having a faulty brake light. One officer noticed that the driver had a hypodermic syringe in his shirt pocket. He asked the driver to step out of the car and asked him about the syringe. The driver admitted that it was for taking drugs. Officers had the two passengers, both females, get out of the car and asked for their identification. One of them, Sandra Houghton, lied to officers, giving a false name and saying she had no identification. The officers began searching the car. On the back seat was a purse, which Houghton said belonged to her. An officer opened the purse, found her wallet, and pulled out her identification. He kept searching the purse and found a brown pouch, which Houghton said was not hers. Inside the pouch was a syringe containing 60 ccs of methamphetamine. The officer also found track marks on her arms. She was arrested.

Arizona v. Gant (2009). Police in Tucson, Ariz., went to a house where, according to an anonymous tip, drugs were being sold. Rodney Gant answered the door, identified himself, and told the officers that the owner would be back later. After they left, police found that there was an arrest warrant for Gant for driving with a suspended license. The officers returned at night and arrested a woman in a car in front of the house for having drug paraphernalia. They also arrested a man near the back of the house when he provided a false name. After they put the two in separate patrol cars, they saw Gant drive up, park in the driveway, get out of his car, and walk toward the officers. They arrested him and put him in another patrol car. Officers then searched Gant's car, finding a gun and a bag of cocaine.

The stop-and-frisk exception does not require probable cause, only reasonable suspicion.

The Stop and Frisk Exception

This case presents serious questions concerning the role of the Fourth Amendment in the confrontation on the street between the citizen and the policeman investigating suspicious circumstances.
– U.S. Supreme Court Chief Justice Earl Warren, *Terry v. Ohio* (1968)

In 1968, the Supreme Court decided *Terry v. Ohio*. This case carved out an exception to both the warrant and probable cause requirements. A series of cases has elaborated on this exception.

The case arose when a plain-clothes police officer observed three men on a street corner in Cleveland, Ohio. He believed they were "casing" a nearby store for an armed robbery. For 10 minutes, he watched the men take turns walking in front of the store and returning to the corner to discuss what each had seen. When the men started to go in the store, he stopped them. He identified himself as a policeman and asked them their names. When one of them mumbled something, he grabbed him and turned him around so all three men faced him. Believing they were armed, he patted them down for weapons. He found guns on two of them. The officer arrested the two men for carrying concealed weapons.

Convicted on the charges, the men appealed, ultimately to the U.S. Supreme Court.

The men claimed that the search was illegal because the officer did not have probable cause to stop and search them.

The Supreme Court agreed that the officer did not have probable cause. But in an 8–1 decision, the court upheld the stop and frisk as reasonable under the circumstances. Writing for the majority, Chief Justice Earl Warren stated that the stop and frisk had to comply with the Fourth Amendment. This amendment protects against unreasonable searches and requires probable cause for search and arrest warrants.

Warren noted that stopping the two men was not an arrest. The officer was simply investigating their suspicious behavior. Warren stated: "It would have been poor police work indeed for an officer of 30 years' experience in the detection of thievery from stores in this same neighborhood to have failed to investigate this behavior further." The court held that "where a police officer observes unusual conduct which leads him reasonably to conclude in light of his experience that criminal activity may be afoot . . . ," the officer has a right to stop the persons.

Warren further noted the dangers of stopping criminal suspects, especially those armed with guns or knives. So the court concluded that if "the persons with whom he is dealing may be armed and presently dangerous . . . he is entitled for the protection of himself and others in the area to conduct a carefully limited search of the outer clothing of such persons in an attempt to discover weapons which might be used to assault him."

Thus a brief stop and frisk does not require **probable cause** — evidence strong enough to give a careful person good reason to believe it. A stop or frisk requires **reasonable suspicion** — evidence that would make an experienced police officer suspicious.

For example, the following would be a proper stop and frisk: The police see Fritz run out of a dark alley at 3 a.m. They stop him, ask him who he is and what he has been doing, and frisk his outer clothing. In doing so, the officers detect what feels like a large metal object in his coat pocket. They reach inside and pull out a gun.

The following, however, would be an unreasonable search: The police see Fritz run out of a dark alley at 3 a.m. They stop and frisk him. In doing so, the officers detect what feels like a plastic bag in his coat pocket. They reach inside and pull out a small bag of marijuana. (Because of the nature of the object, it could not possibly have been a dangerous weapon.)

Is an Anonymous Tip Grounds for Reasonable Suspicion?

Several recent cases have further clarified the *Terry* decision. In one, Miami police received an anonymous phone call reporting that a young man was carrying a concealed gun at a bus stop. The caller described the young man as black and wearing a plaid shirt. Police responded a few minutes later. They found three young men at the bus stop. One (J.L.) was wearing a plaid shirt. Police did not know the men or notice them doing anything unusual. Based on the tip alone, police frisked J.L. and found a handgun. He was arrested and convicted of carrying a concealed weapon.

In 2000 in *Florida v. J.L.*, a unanimous Supreme Court ruled that the search was illegal because it was not based on reasonable suspicion. The officers' suspicion was not reasonable because it did not come from any observations of their own, but only on a call made by an unknown person. Such callers, the court noted, are extremely unreliable.

What About Running From Police?

Teenager Sam Wardlow was standing in front of a house in a high-crime neighborhood at about noon. When four police cars rounded the corner, he took off running. Officers caught him, patted him down, and found a loaded gun. Arrested, charged, and convicted of a weapons crime, Wardlow appealed. He argued that the police had no right to stop him. A state appellate court agreed, ruling that officers did not have reasonable suspicion to make a stop and frisk. The Illinois Supreme Court affirmed, determining that sudden flight in a high-crime area does not create a reasonable suspicion justifying a stop because flight may simply be an exercise of the right to "go on one's way" (as the Supreme Court had noted a person had a right to do in *Florida v. Royer*).

In a 5–4 decision in *Illinois v. Wardlow* (2000), the U.S. Supreme Court upheld the stop and frisk, declaring that the officers' actions did not violate the Fourth Amendment. The court ruled that, given the circumstances, the officers had reasonable suspicion that criminal activity was taking place. Being in a high-crime area is a factor, said Chief Justice William Rehnquist, writing for the court majority. But it is not enough by itself for reasonable suspicion. "Nervous, evasive behavior is another pertinent factor in determining reasonable suspicion . . . and headlong flight is the consummate act of evasion. . . . Such a holding is consistent with the decision in *Florida v. Royer* . . . that an individual, when approached, has a right to ignore the police and go about his business. Unprovoked flight is the exact opposite of 'going about one's business.' "

The dissent, written by Justice Stevens, argued that there was not sufficient grounds for reasonable suspicion. Stevens noted that there are many innocent reasons why people may run at the sight of police, especially in a high-crime neighborhood. For example, they may run to stay out of danger. Stevens stated that running at the sight of police in a high-crime area "arguably makes an inference of guilt less appropriate, rather than more so."

Does It All Add Up to Reasonable Suspicion?

A Border Patrol agent in southern Arizona noticed a minivan driving toward him on a deserted, unpaved road off the main highway. Smugglers often drove on this road to get around a nearby border checkpoint, and they usually drove minivans. The timing was also suspicious. It was about 2 p.m. when agents were returning to the checkpoint to change shifts, normally leaving the roads around the checkpoint unpatrolled. When the driver saw the border patrol agent, he slowed down from about 50 to 25 miles per hour. Passing the agent, the driver did not wave or even look at the patrolman, which most people do on deserted roads. Five people were in the car. A woman passenger and three children in the back seat. Two of the children had their knees elevated, as if their feet were on top of some cargo.

Suspicious, the agent made a U-turn and followed the minivan. The children waved awkwardly and in unison to the agent, as if they were told to do so. The driver was heading toward the checkpoint, but turned onto a canyon road before reaching it. The agent called in the license number of the minivan and discovered it was registered to an address four blocks from the Mexican border in an area known for smugglers.

Based on all this information, the agent pulled the minivan over. Receiving permission from the driver to search the van, the agent discovered more than 100 pounds of marijuana. (The children in the back seat had their feet on a bag containing some of it.) At his trial, the driver claimed the agent did not have reasonable suspicion for the stop, but the trial court ruled that he did. The Court of Appeals reversed the trial court, saying that only a few of the factors gave the agent any suspicion, and these few did not add up to reasonable suspicion to make the stop.

The prosecution appealed to the U.S. Supreme Court. In 2002 in *U.S. v. Arvizu*, the Supreme Court upheld the stop. Chief Justice William Rehnquist, writing for a unanimous court, stated that the Court of Appeals had mistakenly examined each factor in isolation. When determining reasonable suspicion, said Rehnquist, a court must look at the "totality of the circumstances." "Undoubtedly, each of these factors alone is susceptible to innocent explanation, and some factors are more probative than others. Taken together, we believe they sufficed to form" reasonable suspicion for making the stop.

Do People Have to Identify Themselves?

After the *Terry* decision, many states enacted so called "stop and identify" laws. Nevada's law reads in part:

1. Any peace officer may detain any person whom the officer encounters under circumstances which reasonably indicate that the person has committed, is committing or is about to commit a crime.

   . . .

3. The officer may detain the person pursuant to this section only to ascertain his identity and the suspicious circumstances surrounding his presence abroad. Any person so detained shall identify himself, but may not be compelled to answer any other inquiry of any peace officer.

In 2004, the U.S. Supreme Court decided a case challenging the constitutionality of this law.

A sheriff's officer in Humboldt County, Nevada, responded to a report of a man striking a woman in a truck. The officer saw a truck parked by the side of a road. A man was standing outside the truck. A young woman was sitting in the driver's seat. The officer approached the man and told him there was a report of a fight between the two of them. The man responded he didn't know anything about that. The officer asked him for identification. The man, who appeared intoxicated, responded, "I don't, I don't think, I think I've . . ." The officer kept asking for identification. The man seemed confused about why the deputy was talking to him. Several times he told the deputy that the truck was legally parked. The officer kept asking him for identification. The man refused. He kept asking why the officer needed it. Finally, he said, "I don't want to talk. I've done nothing. I've broken no laws. Take me to jail, I don't care." The man put his hands behind his back and told the officer to arrest him. Eventually, the officer did.

The man's name was Dudley Hiibel. The young woman in the car was his daughter. They had been arguing, and she may have hit him before she pulled over. Hiibel was not charged with any crime related to intoxication or assault. He was charged with obstructing an officer from carrying out his duties. In other words, he was charged because he did not give his name to the officer. He was convicted and fined $250. He appealed on the grounds that the law requiring him to identify himself violated his Fourth and Fifth Amendment rights.

The U.S. Supreme Court in a 5–4 decision in *Hiibel v. Nevada* upheld the Nevada law. Writing for the majority, Justice Anthony Kennedy said that the law met Fourth Amendment standards under the *Terry* decision. He noted: "Our decisions make clear that questions concerning a suspect's identity are a routine and accepted part of many *Terry* stops. . . . Obtaining a suspect's name . . . serves important government interests. Knowledge of identity may inform an officer that a suspect is wanted for another offense, or has a record of violence or mental disorder. On the other hand, knowing identity may help clear a suspect and allow the police to concentrate their efforts elsewhere."

Kennedy also found that the law did not violate Hiibel's Fifth Amendment rights. The Fifth Amendment prohibits people from being forced to incriminate themselves. Kennedy pointed out that Hiibel's refusal was not based on any "fear that his name would be used to incriminate him . . . . As best we can tell, petitioner refused to identify himself only because he thought his name was none of the officer's business."

Writing in dissent, Justice Breyer pointed to cases following *Terry* in which the court had stated that an officer making a *Terry* stop may ask "a moderate number of questions to determine his identity and to try to obtain information confirming or dispelling the officer's suspicions. But *the detainee is not obliged to respond*." Breyer argued that the court had stated "no good reason now to reject this generation-old statement of the law." The decision, said Breyer, violates a person's right to remain silent under the Fifth Amendment and the Fourth Amendment's basic protections from police intrusions.

FOR DISCUSSION

1. The lone dissenter in *Terry* was Justice William O. Douglas. He said that if it was necessary to create a standard other than probable cause, then the Constitution should be amended. Otherwise, he said, the court was creating an unconstitutional standard. Do you agree with Douglas? Why or why not?
2. What did the court decide in *Florida v. J.L.*? Do you agree? Explain.
3. How were the reasons for stopping J.L. different from those for stopping and questioning Hiibel?
4. Do you think the circumstances in *Wardlow* gave officers reasonable suspicion that criminal activity was going on? Explain.
5. *Arvizu* was decided shortly after September 11, 2001. Some critics say this explains the unanimous decision. Do you think the reasonable suspicion was overwhelmingly clear? Explain.
6. What was the decision in *Hiibel*? Do you agree with it? Explain.

CLASS ACTIVITY

The Next Decision

More than 20 states have stop-and-identify laws. The Arizona reasonable-suspicion statute in *Hiibel* only required that people give their names when asked by police. Some states require more of those stopped with reasonable suspicion. When asked, suspects must give their names and an explanation of what they are doing and where they are going.

Imagine that a law like this exists in Tim Smith's state. He is stopped by police who have reasonable suspicion that he is involved in criminal activity. They ask him his name, and he tells them. But when they ask him what he is doing there, he responds, "None of your business," and he refuses to say more. Police arrest him under the law. The case is appealed to the U.S. Supreme Court.

In this activity, students role play members of the court and decide whether the law violates Smith's Fourth and Fifth Amendment rights.

1. Form small groups of five to nine students. Each group is the U.S. Supreme Court and should:
   a. Select a chief justice to direct the discussion.
   b. Discuss the cases mentioned in the article and how they apply to this case.
   c. Decide whether Smith's Fourth Amendment rights are violated.
   d. Decide whether Smith's Fifth Amendment rights are violated.
   e. Be prepared to discuss its decisions and reasons for them to the whole class.
2. Each court should report its decisions and reasons. Hold a class discussion on the case.

Other Exceptions

[S]earches conducted . . . without prior approval by judge or magistrate, are per se unreasonable under the Fourth Amendment — subject only to a few specifically established and well delineated exceptions.

– U.S. Supreme Court Justice Potter Stewart, *Katz v. U.S.* (1966)

There are other situations in which searches and seizures may be conducted without a warrant:

Searches Incident to Lawful Arrests. In *Chimel v. California* (1969), the U.S. Supreme Court held that searches and seizures incident to lawful arrests may be done without a warrant. The court said: "When an arrest is made, it is reasonable for the arresting officer to search the person arrested in order to remove any weapons that the latter might seek to use in order to resist arrest or effect his escape [and to] seize any evidence on the arrestee's person in order to prevent its concealment or destruction." These so-called *"Chimel* searches" may extend to everything within the area of the arrested person's immediate control. Questions sometimes arise as to whether the arrest itself was lawful. If it was not, any search conducted along with it would not be valid.

Examples:

Reasonable Search: Didi is arrested outside of Elliot's Department Store for shoplifting. Without a warrant, the police search the book bag she is carrying.

Unreasonable Search: Didi is arrested outside of Elliot's Department Store for shoplifting. The police go to her home, a block away, and search her bedroom. (The search is not *incident* to the arrest. The police could have obtained a warrant if they had probable cause to believe there was evidence of a crime in the house.)

Consent. The police may search without a warrant if the person "knowingly and voluntarily" consents. (But these searches are not reasonable if the police use deception or fraud to get the person's consent.) Sometimes an individual may consent to a search of someone else's property if the consenting party owns or shares the property with the one being searched. For example, a husband could consent to the search of the home he shares with his wife. But the Supreme Court has ruled that the police do not have consent, when both spouses are present, if just one consents and the other refuses to consent. (*Georgia v. Randolph*, 2006)

Examples:

Reasonable Search: The police stop Luis on the highway for driving with a broken brake light. They ask him to open his glove compartment. Luis opens it and the officers look inside.

Reasonable Search: Without a warrant, the police go to Meg's house and ask her parents if they can search her room for illegal drugs that they believe she has been selling at school. Meg's parents let the officers in to search.

Unreasonable Search: Mike and Murray are roommates in a two-bedroom apartment. The police go to their apartment and ask Mike to let them search Murray's bedroom and file cabinet. Mike consents to the search. (Though they share the common areas of the apartment, Mike has no right to consent to a search of Murray's private space.)

Exigent Circumstances. Police do not need a warrant in exigent circumstances, events that require immediate action. The courts have ruled that police do not need a warrant in the following exigent circumstances:

- **Hot Pursuit.** Police in hot pursuit of a fleeing criminal suspect do not need a warrant to enter a place where they saw the suspect go.

Examples:

Reasonable Search: Police approach a suspect to arrest her for drug dealing. When she sees they are police, she darts inside her house. They enter the house and see that she has spilled two bags containing a white powder, which turns out to be heroin. (*U.S. v. Santana*, 1976)

Reasonable Search: The police see Josie knock down an old lady, hit her with a lead pipe, and take her purse. They chase Josie into a building about a mile away and see her run into apartment #10B. When she refuses to answer, the officers kick down the door.

Unreasonable Search: Mrs. Thackaberry reports that someone broke into her mailbox and stole her Social Security check. The police suspect Josie, a known robber of the elderly. They trail her for a few days and finally follow her into an apartment building where she often goes. The police knock on the door to #10B, but Josie won't let them in. The police

Airport searches, including those done by drug-sniffing dogs, are another exception to the warrant requirement.

kick down the door. (There is no "hot pursuit" in this case. The police were only following a lead and could have gotten a warrant.)

- **Emergency Situations.** Police do not need a warrant to conduct a search or seizure in emergency situations.

Examples:

Reasonable Search: Officers are called to a loud party. Through a window, they see a juvenile being held by adults. The juvenile escapes and punches one of the adults. The police enter the house. (*Brigham City v. Stuart*, 2006)

Reasonable Search: An officer on the beat hears a woman's loud screams and the sound of shattering glass coming from a trailer home. He radios for help and then opens the front door to see what is happening.

Unreasonable Search: The police are concerned about gang violence at Jackson High School. Three students have been killed already. The police hear that a fight between two rival gangs is supposed to take place on Friday. The day before, they ask the principal of Jackson High to assemble all students in the gym. Without a warrant, the officers then open all the lockers with a passkey and search for dangerous weapons. (The police are not reacting to an immediate emergency.)

- **Imminent Destruction of Evidence of a Crime.** Police do not need a warrant when they reasonably believe that evidence is about to be destroyed.

Examples:

Reasonable Search: Officers chasing a drug suspect lose sight of him in an apartment house. They wrongly believe he has entered a particular apartment, which smells of marijuana smoke. When they knock on the apartment door and say "police," they hear movement in the apartment. Believing the suspect is destroying evidence, they kick down the door and find others with drugs. (*Kentucky v. King*, 2011)

Unreasonable Search: Police knock on a door, hear nothing, and break down the door. (The police have no reason to believe evidence is being destroyed.)

Other Exceptions

The courts have found a number of other exceptions to the warrant requirement. They include:

- **Airline searches** of passengers and carry-on baggage by means of metal detectors, physical pat-downs, or drug-sniffing dogs.

ASK AN EXPERT

Invite a prosecutor, defense attorney, or police officer to visit your classroom and briefly discuss search-and-seizure law with you. Then have the resource expert take part in the class activity **Applying the Checklist**. The attorney can help pairs of students and discuss each case when the activity ends.

- **Border searches** by immigration control officers within areas reasonably close to U.S. international boundaries.
- **Customs searches** at borders, ports, and international airports by U.S. customs agents.
- **Searches in detention facilities** (such as prisons and jails). Courts will allow any search policy unless "substantial evidence" proves the policy is an "unnecessary or unjustified response to" security problems. In 2012, the Supreme Court upheld a policy of conducting strip searches of everyone entering detention, including those charged with minor crimes. (*Florence v. County of Burlington*)

FOR DISCUSSION

1. What reasons does the court consider in making exceptions to the warrant requirement? What are the dangers in making exceptions?

2. The court has carved out several exceptions: motor vehicle searches, stop and frisks, searches incident to a lawful arrest, consent searches, searches done in hot pursuit, searches in emergency circumstances, border searches, and airline security searches. What is the reason for each of these exceptions? Do you disagree with any of these exceptions? Why or why not?

A SEARCH AND SEIZURE CHECKLIST

This checklist provides a summary analysis of whether the Fourth Amendment has been violated. Use the checklist to help you determine the legality of searches and seizures.

Has a search or seizure taken place?
- Did a government employee or agent conduct the search or seizure?

  [If NO, then no violation]

- Was it a search or seizure as defined by the courts?

  - Did the person have a reasonable expectation of privacy?

    [If NO, then no violation]

  - Was the item . . .

    ___in plain view?

    ___in an open field?

    ___abandoned?

    [If YES to any of these, then no violation]

Was the search or seizure reasonable?
- Was the search or seizure conducted with a valid warrant?

  [If YES, then no violation]

- If not, does one of the court recognized exceptions to the warrant requirement apply?

  ___Motor Vehicles

  ___Incident to a Lawful Arrest

  ___Stop and Frisk

  ___Consent

  ___Exigent Circumstances (hot pursuit, emergency, or destruction of evidence)

  ___Border Searches

  ___Airline/Security Searches

  [If YES, then no violation]

CLASS ACTIVITY

Applying the Checklist

In this activity, students apply the **Search and Seizure Checklist** to evaluate the legality of some hypothetical search and seizures.

1. Form pairs.
2. As a pair, do the following:
   a. Review the checklist on page 122 and what you have learned about search-and-seizure law.
   b. Analyze the following cases and decide if any Fourth Amendment violations have occurred.
   c. Be prepared to explain your answers and discuss any differences of opinion that may arise.
3. Regroup as a class and discuss each case.

Case 1: Hans Metcalf. Smith and Houston, special investigators from the district attorney's office, had been following Hans Metcalf, a suspected bookie. They saw him enter a telephone booth with a briefcase in his hand and make a short call. He then left the phone booth, but without his briefcase. Smith and Houston rushed to the phone booth, opened the briefcase, and found several bundles of betting slips. Just then, Metcalf returned to retrieve his briefcase and he was arrested.

Case 2: Vivian Madison. Mary Krensy was angry with her roommate, Vivian Madison. She went to the police and offered to show them where Vivian was hiding 50 stolen holiday turkeys. The police accompanied her to the garage both women shared and discovered 50 turkeys reported stolen from the Henderson Poultry Company. The police confiscated the poultry and placed Vivian under arrest.

Case 3: Dan Lewis. Officer Hanano was on patrol late at night. Suddenly, she spotted a house trailer behind, but not attached to, a car with no license plates. On closer inspection, she noticed a thin wisp of smoke escaping from one of the trailer windows. She walked to the door and knocked a few times. A voice called back, "Go away!" The officer forced opened the door and found a young man preparing a liquid substance in a makeshift laboratory. Officer Hanano arrested the man, whose name is Dan Lewis, for the manufacture of illegal drugs.

Case 4: Betty Kim. Acting on an informant's tip that Betty Kim was receiving stolen property, Detective Drebs went to her apartment to talk to her. She invited him in, but when he started to poke around the living room she screamed, "I said you could talk, not search the place. Get out!" He grabbed her, put handcuffs on her, then frisked her. He found a scout knife in her pants pocket and arrested her for disturbing the peace and carrying a concealed weapon. He then searched the living room and found a stolen stereo receiver.

...le lesson of history, ancient ...1 system of criminal law en-... ...omes to depend on the "con-fession" wu... ...the long run, be less reliable and more subject to abuses than a system which depends on extrinsic evidence independently secured through skillful investigation.

– U.S. Supreme Court Justice Arthur Goldberg, *Escobedo v. Illinois* (1964)

Another important area of criminal procedure comes from the Fifth Amendment to the U.S. Constitution. Part of this amendment says "(no) person . . . shall be compelled in any criminal case to be a witness against himself. . . ." This means that unless you agree to talk to the police, they may not force you to answer questions about a crime they think you committed. Unlike the Fourth Amendment, which balances your right to privacy against the police's need to act, your Fifth Amendment right not to talk to police is absolute. If you invoke it, the police may not legally make you talk.

The Supreme Court did not apply the Fifth Amendment to the states until 1964. But even before this, it struck down cases where confessions were not made voluntarily. The court determined that these cases violated the due process clause of the 14th Amendment. This clause declares that no "State shall deprive any person of life, liberty, or property, without due process of law. . . ." Due process of law guarantees fair procedures and basic liberties. Among the cases that the court struck down as violating due process were:

- *Brown v. Mississippi* (1936). Trying to get a confession, deputies hung the defendant from a tree twice. Then they whipped him. Whipping him a second time, they told him they would not stop until he confessed, which he finally did. Then they took him to jail.
- *Ward v. Texas* (1942). So that no friend or attorney could contact the defendant, the police took him out of the county to three different jails in three days. Questioned continuously, the defendant at one point said he would make whatever statement the police wanted even though he claimed not to have committed the crime. Finally, he confessed.

- *Ashcraft v. Tennessee* (1944). Police put the defendant in an interrogation room on Saturday night at 7 p.m. and questioned him in relays so they would not get tired. On Monday at 9:30 a.m., the defendant confessed. During the 36-hour interrogation, police had given the defendant only one five-minute break.
- *Malinski v. New York* (1945). Instead of taking the defendant to jail, police took him to a hotel room. They told him to remove his clothes. They questioned him for three hours while he was naked. Then allowing him to put on his underwear, they questioned him for seven more hours until he confessed. Then after letting him dress, they took him to jail.
- *Leyra v. Denno* (1954). After questioning the defendant for days and allowing him little sleep, police brought in a doctor trained in hypnosis. The police had wired the room so they could listen in. During his one-and-one-half hour visit, the doctor repeatedly suggested that the defendant confess. Eventually the defendant did. The doctor then brought officers into the room and had the defendant repeat the confession.
- *Spano v. New York* (1959). Although the defendant refused to talk and asked for his lawyer, police continued to question him for eight straight hours. Police sent in a childhood friend, a policeman with four children, who falsely told the defendant he would be fired unless the defendant confessed, which he ultimately did.
- *Lynum v. Illinois* (1963). Police told the defendant that if she confessed, nothing would happen to her, but if she did not, her children would be taken away from her. She confessed.

It wasn't until 1964, in *Malloy v. Hogan*, that the Supreme Court ruled that the Fifth Amendment protection against self-incrimination applied to the states. But courts still faced the difficult task of determining on a case-by-case basis whether confessions were coerced or voluntary. So in 1966 in the landmark case of *Miranda v. Arizona*, the Supreme Court laid down clearer guidelines for police and courts to follow.

Miranda v. Arizona (1966)

In this case, Ernesto Miranda was arrested at his home and taken to a police station. A

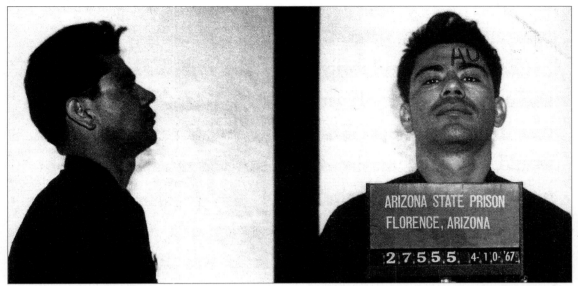

The U.S. Supreme Court overturned Ernesto Miranda's conviction because police failed to tell him that he didn't have to talk with them. He was retried and convicted a second time without his confession entered into evidence.

witness identified him, and two detectives took him into a special room. After two hours of interrogation, the officers got Miranda to sign a written confession.

At his trial, Miranda was convicted of kidnapping and rape and was sentenced to 20 to 30 years in prison. But police had never told him of his right not to talk to them. He had never been told of his right to a lawyer. These rights are guaranteed by the Fifth and Sixth amendments. When the Supreme Court heard this case, it decided that any interrogation of suspects in custody is unconstitutional unless the police clearly tell suspects before any questioning begins that:

- They have the right to remain silent.
- Anything they say may be used against them in court.
- They have a right to a lawyer.
- If they want a lawyer but can't afford one, the court will appoint one before any questioning.

Also, after giving these warnings, police may not go on interrogating unless suspects "knowingly and intelligently" waive their rights. That is, suspects must completely understand their rights and waive them. If police fail to do this, nothing that suspects say can be introduced as evidence against them at their trials.

The Supreme Court believed that police questioning of suspects in the station house was inherently coercive. In other words, the court believed that the station house surroundings and police interrogation put tremendous pressure on suspects to say what the police wanted them to say. It felt that the only way to prevent coerced confessions was to make sure suspects knew their rights. Thus police need to tell suspects that they do not have to say anything and that they can have a lawyer with them during questioning. The court concluded that if police do not give a suspect this information, they violate the suspect's Fifth Amendment rights.

FOR DISCUSSION

1. The article lists six Supreme Court decisions invalidating confessions because they violated due process — *Brown*, *Ward*, *Ashcraft*, *Malinski*, *Leyra*, *Spano*, and *Lynum*. Would you trust the confessions as being reliable in any of these cases? Explain. Would you consider any of the confessions voluntary? Why or why not?

2. What does the quotation (at the beginning of the article) from Supreme Court Justice Arthur J. Goldberg mean? Do you agree? Why or why not?

3. What are the *Miranda* warnings? When do police have to give these warnings? What are the warnings supposed to prevent? Do you agree with the decision in *Miranda*? Explain.

Miranda's Aftermath

Miranda has become embedded in routine police practice to the point where the warnings have become part of our national culture.

– U.S. Supreme Court Chief Justice William Rehnquist, *Dickerson v. U.S.* (2000)

Miranda requires the police to read suspects **in custody** their rights before any **interrogation**. Police do not need to get people to waive their rights if they are not in custody or not being interrogated. Since *Miranda*, the court has clarified its decision by focusing on what "in custody" and "interrogation" mean. It has also carved out an exception and looked at other challenges to *Miranda*.

To be in custody, a person's freedom must be significantly restrained. The court has held that most people stopped briefly by police are not in custody, because they will soon be on their way. Thus routine traffic stops and even stop and frisks do not normally require *Miranda* warnings. (*Berkemer v. McCarty*, 1984)

In *Thompson v. Keohane* (1995), the court stated an objective test for "in custody": Given the circumstances, "would a reasonable person have felt he or she was not at liberty to terminate the interrogation and leave"?

In *Rhode Island v. Innis* (1980), the high court defined interrogation as "words or actions on the part of police officers that they should have known were reasonably likely to elicit an incriminating response." In that case, police officers talked to each other as they drove the defendant to the police station. One mentioned that it would be too bad if children attending a nearby school for the handicapped found the abandoned shotgun that Innis had supposedly used to rob one taxi driver and kill another. Innis, who had previously requested a lawyer after hearing his *Miranda* rights, spoke up and directed the officers to the gun (a major piece of evidence in his later conviction for robbery and murder). The court ruled that the officers' remarks did not constitute interrogation so his rights were not violated.

New York v. Quarles (1984)

In 1984 in *New York v. Quarles*, the Supreme Court carved out a major exception to *Miranda*. In that case, police chased a rape suspect through a supermarket. Finally catching and handcuffing him, they found he had an empty shoulder holster. An officer asked him where the gun was. Nodding toward some empty boxes, the suspect said, "The gun is over there." The police retrieved a loaded .38 caliber handgun from a box. Since the suspect had not been given any *Miranda* warnings, his incriminating statement and perhaps the gun should have been excluded from evidence. But the court created a **public safety exception** to *Miranda*. It ruled that the police do not have to give *Miranda* warnings when their questions are "reasonably prompted by a concern for the public safety." Since the loaded gun in the store caused reasonable concern for public safety, the court ruled that the evidence was admissible.

Dickerson v. U.S. (2000)

In 2000, the Supreme Court decided a case that directly challenged *Miranda*. It was based on a law more than 30 years old. In 1968, two years after the *Miranda* decision, Congress enacted the Omnibus Crime Control and Safe Streets Act of 1968. Section 3501 of this act purports to overturn *Miranda* for federal cases. It permits a confession to be given in evidence "if it is voluntarily given." Section 3501 lists several factors for a court to consider in determining whether a confession is voluntary. *Miranda* warnings are one of these factors, but are not considered necessary for a voluntary confession.

For 30 years, prosecutors and police ignored Section 3501, believing it unconstitutional. They reasoned that Congress cannot overturn a Supreme Court decision on constitutional law.

But a law professor at the University of Utah, Paul Cassell, thought Section 3501 was constitutional and waged a campaign to get it upheld. He noted language in *Miranda* that said Congress or states could adopt substitutes for *Miranda* warnings as long as the procedures were "at least as effective in apprising accused persons of their right of silence and in assuring a continuous opportunity to exercise it." Cassell argued that Congress had done this in 1968.

In 1999, a federal appeals court adopted Cassell's argument. The case involved Charles Dickerson, a defendant who claimed the FBI had not read him his rights before he confessed. The trial judge, although noting that the confession was voluntary, threw out the confession. When the judge refused to hear new evidence that the FBI had given the defendant his *Miranda* warnings, prosecutors appealed. The appeals court reversed the trial judge's decision, reasoning that

CONFESSIONS FROM INNOCENT PEOPLE

As strange as it may seem, innocent people sometimes confess to crimes they have not committed. A national study of exonerations published in 2005 in the *Journal of Criminal Law & Criminology* found that false confessions were the second most common cause of wrongful convictions. (The most common cause was mistaken eyewitness identification.) A recent book titled *True Stories of False Confessions* recounts almost 40 such confessions and offers various causes for false confessions. One cause can be police coercion, but innocent people can confess even without being coerced. Young people can be particularly susceptible to making a false confession. The same is true of those who are mentally challenged or suffer from mental illnesses. Probably the most famous false confession, also recounted in the book, was the New York Central Park jogger case in 1989. A woman jogging in New York's Central Park was brutally raped and beaten. Knocked unconscious, she had no memory of the attack. Police rounded up five teenagers who had been in the park, and after being questioned, four of them confessed. No physical evidence linked them to the crime, but they were convicted and sent to prison. They served 12 years before another person admitted to sexually assaulting the Central Park jogger..

Below is another story told in the book. It took place in Escondido, a small California city about 30 miles northeast of San Diego.

At 6:30 a.m. on January 21, 1998, Stephanie Crowe's body, covered in blood, was found lying in the doorway of her room. A 911 call was placed, paramedics arrived, and within an hour, homicide investigators from the Escondido Police Department were examining the scene. They found no signs of a forced entry to the house.

Stephanie was 12. When a child is killed at home, the most likely suspects are those in the home. After speaking to the parents, investigators became suspicious of Stephanie's 14-year-old brother Michael.

Several things pointed to Michael. He had appeared calm the day Stephanie was found dead. Investigators discovered he had a deep fascination with violent video games. And Michael had gone downstairs at 4:30 on the morning of Stephanie's death and claimed he did not see her body in the hallway. Medical examiners placed her time of death several hours earlier.

Investigators began questioning Michael at the police station. On different days, they questioned him for long periods. He repeatedly declared his innocence, but investigators did not believe him.

Investigators asked Michael to take a Computer Voice Stress Analyzer test to see if he was lying. They informed him his voice showed deception when he was asked if he knew who took Stephanie's life. Michael continued to deny knowing who killed his sister.

Investigators then lied about finding blood in his room, linking Michael to the murder. Michael still declared his innocence.

Investigators then led him to believe he had blacked out, which would explain why he could not remember killing his sister. They falsely told him this was common when people did horrible things. They urged him to write a letter to Stephanie asking for forgiveness. He complied, writing that he felt it was a blessing he could not remember killing her and that "if I did do this then I must be insane." Upon reading this letter, the investigators pressed Michael for details about the killing and told him he had a choice to make: Either he could let them continue investigating, which would lead to murder charges against him, or he could confess, tell them what had happened, and get psychiatric help. Michael said he wanted to confess, but said he would have to lie to do so. Investigators told him he was under arrest for Stephanie's murder and lied to him saying his parents never wanted to see him again. Upon hearing this, Michael confessed, citing jealousy and rage as motives for the murder.

Michael was indicted for murder along with two of his friends. (Police managed to get a confession from one of the friends.) None of them had anything to do with the murder. All three were completely innocent. Just before their trial began, DNA testing showed that Stephanie's blood was on the clothing of a mentally ill drifter who had been wandering the neighborhood and alarming neighbors the night of Stephanie's murder. The three boys were released, and the drifter was later convicted of voluntary manslaughter.

A U.S. Border Patrol agent reads a suspect his *Miranda* warnings.

the confession was voluntary and therefore admissible under Section 3501.

The U.S. Supreme Court, however, overturned the appeals court decision in *Dickerson v. U.S.* By a 7–2 vote, the court ruled that *Miranda* was based on the Constitution and that Congress does not have the power to overturn the decision. It therefore ruled that Section 3501 was unconstitutional. It further rejected the argument that Section 3501 provided an effective substitute for *Miranda* warnings. The court stated that Section 3501 was simply a return to the "totality of the circumstances" test of voluntariness, which existed prior to *Miranda*. This test, said the court, did not adequately protect a defendant's constitutional rights.

Missouri v. Seibert (2004)

In 2004, the Supreme Court decided a case that revolved around its 1985 decision in *Oregon v. Elstad*. In that case, police had gone to the house of 18-year-old Michael Elstad to arrest him for burglary. One officer took Elstad's mother into the kitchen to explain why they were arresting her son. The other officer talked with Elstad in the living room. The officer told him they believed he was involved in a burglary of a neighbor's house. Elstad replied,

"Yes, I was there." The officer had not given him a *Miranda* warning.

The police took him to the station, gave him the warnings, and he again made the same statement and confessed to the crime. The trial court excluded the statement Elstad made at home, but allowed in evidence the statements he made after the warning. The Supreme Court in a 6–3 decision agreed that this was proper. It held that a prior voluntary statement made without *Miranda* warnings does not prevent a suspect from making a confession after being given the warnings.

Following this decision, it was reported that many police departments began interrogating suspects without issuing *Miranda* warnings. After suspects made incriminating statements, they would give them the warnings. The case of *Missouri v. Seibert* raised the question of whether this practice was constitutional.

Patrice Seibert's 12-year-old son, Jonathan, had cerebral palsy. He could not walk, talk, or feed himself. When Jonathan died in his sleep, Patrice feared that she would be charged with neglect because Jonathan had bedsores. She was present when her two sons and their friends planned to burn the family's mobile home to hide the facts surrounding Jonathan's death.

They decided to let Donald Rector, an 18-year-old mentally disabled boy who lived with the family, die in the fire. They did not want it to appear that Jonathan was unattended.

Five days later, the police awakened Seibert at 3 a.m., arrested her, and took her to the police station. The arresting officer did not give her the *Miranda* warnings. Instead, he questioned her for 30–40 minutes, squeezing her arm and repeating "Donald was also to die in his sleep." After Seibert admitted that the plan was for Donald to die in his sleep, the officer left her alone for 20 minutes, then returned, gave her the *Miranda* warnings, and had her sign a waiver of her rights.

He then resumed questioning, reminded her of the confession she had made, and got her to repeat what she had previously said. The officer admitted at trial that he had deliberately withheld the *Miranda* warnings. He testified that he was using a technique that he had been taught: to question first, then give warnings, "and then repeat the question until I get an answer that she's already provided once."

A 5–4 majority of the Supreme Court in *Seibert* concluded that the interrogation technique that police used on Seibert was a deliberate "end run" around *Miranda*. The basic question on the "question-first" technique, Justice David Souter wrote in the court's opinion, is whether the warning will be effective and will allow the suspect to make a rational decision to stay silent or talk. The answer, he wrote, is clearly "no." Souter added, police were being trained to use the "question-first" strategy because it achieved the desired result, "which is to get a confession the suspect would not make if he understood his rights at the outset." The court concluded that, "because the question-first tactic effectively threatens to thwart *Miranda*'s purpose . . . and because the facts here do not reasonably support a conclusion that the warnings given could have served their purpose, Seibert's postwarning statements are inadmissible."

Berghuis v. Thompkins (2010)

In 2010, the Supreme Court decided a case on what constituted a valid waiver of *Miranda* rights. Thompkins was apprehended in Ohio as a suspect in a shooting outside a Michigan mall. Police let him read a paper with the *Miranda* warnings, read him the warnings, and asked him to sign the paper that he understood his rights. Thompkins refused to sign. After that, the police began questioning him. The questioning lasted about three hours. Thompkins was almost completely silent for the duration of the questioning. But occasionally in response to a question, he would look up, nod his head, or say "no," "yeah," or "I don't know."

Near the end of his interrogation, an officer asked, "Do you believe in God?"

Thompkins answered, "Yes."

The officer then asked, "Do you pray to God?"

Again Thompkins answered, "Yes."

Finally, the officer asked, "Do you pray to God to forgive you for shooting that boy down?"

Once again, Thompkins answered, "Yes."

The police asked Thompkins to sign a confession, but he refused, and the interrogation ended 15 minutes later.

Over objections from the defense at trial, the prosecution introduced Thompkins' answer about praying for forgiveness. Thompkins was convicted of first-degree murder, assault with intent to commit murder, and several gun charges. He was sentenced to life without parole. He appealed his conviction claiming he had never waived his *Miranda* rights.

In a 5–4 decision, the U.S. Supreme Court ruled that Thompkins had waived his *Miranda* rights. Writing for the court majority, Justice Anthony Kennedy noted that the *Miranda* decision itself does say a defendant must expressly waive his rights. Specifically, *Miranda* says:

> If interrogation continues without the presence of an attorney and a statement is taken, a heavy burden rests on the government to demonstrate that the defendant knowingly and intelligently waived his privilege against self-incrimination and his right to retained or appointed counsel. . . .

An express statement that the individual is willing to make a statement and does not want an attorney followed closely by a statement could constitute a waiver. But a valid waiver will not be presumed simply from the silence of the accused after warnings are given or simply from the fact that a confession was in fact eventually obtained.

Kennedy pointed out, however, that later cases have ruled that defendants had waived their rights without making an express or written waiver. "The main purpose of *Miranda*," according to Kennedy, "is to ensure that an accused is advised of and understands the right to remain silent and the right to counsel."

Kennedy stated three reasons why Thompkins had waived his *Miranda* rights. "First, there is no contention that Thompkins did not understand his rights; and from this it follows that he knew what he gave up when he spoke. Second, when he answered the officer's question, that meant he waived his right to remain silent. "If Thompkins wanted to remain silent, he could have said nothing in response . . . or he could have unambiguously invoked his *Miranda* rights and ended the interrogation. . . . Third, there is no evidence that Thompkins's statement was coerced."

FOR DISCUSSION

1. When do police have to give *Miranda* warnings? Do you think a person should be considered in custody when police pull them over for a traffic stop? Explain. What is the test for whether a person is in custody? Do you agree with the court's decision in *Rhode Island v. Innis*? Why or why not?
2. According to the *Miranda* decision, why should the incriminating statement in the *Quarles* case be excluded from evidence? The court majority in *Quarles* said that the public safety exception did not give the police the right to coerce confessions from suspects. According to the *Miranda* decision, was Quarles' incriminating statement made in a coercive situation? Why or why not?
3. Both the majority and dissenting opinions in *Quarles* agreed that the decision would "lessen the desirable clarity" of the *Miranda* rule. Why is it desirable that the rule be clear?
4. Do you think Section 3501 is constitutional? Explain.
5. Do you agree with the court's decision in *Seibert*? Why or why not?
6. Do you agree with the majority opinion that Thompkins waived his right to remain silent? Explain.
7. When *Miranda* was decided, its critics claimed that suspects would stop making confessions. This claim has proved false. Suspects confess today as often as before *Miranda*. In fact, one commentator has stated that "next to the warning label on cigarette packs, *Miranda* is the most widely ignored piece of official advice in our society." Do you think *Miranda* sufficiently protects suspects' Fifth Amendment rights? Do you think it goes too far? Explain.
8. Many police departments now commonly record — either on audio or video — all interrogations. Do you think this should be a requirement everywhere? Explain.

CLASS ACTIVITY

Taking the Fifth

In this activity, students use their knowledge of the Fifth Amendment to argue actual cases that have come before the Supreme Court.

1. Form triads. Each student in each triad should be assigned a number — one, two, or three. All ones will role play a justice of the Supreme Court. All twos will role play defense attorneys. All threes will role play attorneys for the government. Each triad should be assigned one of the cases below — a, b, c, d, e, f, g, or h.

2. The class should regroup so students can consult with one another while preparing for the role play. Students arguing for the government should sit on one side of the room, students arguing for the defendants on the other side, and the student justices in front. Each group should follow its group's instructions, listed below.

3. Regroup into triads and begin the role play. The defense will present its case first. Each side will have two minutes to make its presentation. The justice can interrupt to ask questions. After both sides present, each justice should stand and prepare to present a decision on the case.

4. When every justice is ready, go around the room and have each justice read the facts of the case and present his or her decision and reasons for it.

5. Conclude the activity with a discussion using the debriefing questions on page 132.

Attorneys' Instructions

As attorneys, you are responsible for presenting the court with sound arguments supporting your side.

If you represent the government, you will argue that the incriminating statements should be allowed in evidence at the trial.

If you represent the defendant, you will argue that the incriminating statements should be excluded at trial.

Carefully read your case. Then review the section above on *Miranda* and the cases following it. How do these cases apply to your case?

To prepare your argument, write a clear, brief statement of your position. Include:

*   At least one fact from the case that supports your position.
*   An explanation of how that fact supports your position.
*   One previous court decision that supports your position.
*   An explanation of how that decision supports your position.
*   One reason why your position is fair to the government or defendant.
*   One reason why a court decision in your favor will benefit society.

Make an outline ordering this information so that you can include all of it in a two-minute presentation.

Justices' Instructions

When preparing to hear arguments, Supreme Court justices review the cases and the law with their clerks and develop questions they want to ask the attorneys. Working with other justices, read each case. Take notes while you discuss the following:

*   How do *Miranda* and the cases following it apply to your case?
*   What questions would you like to ask the attorneys about your case?

Remember: When you decide your case, you must consider the previous Supreme Court cases interpreting the Fifth Amendment, but you are not bound by them.

Cases

The issue in each case is the same: **Can the defendant's confession or incriminating statements be introduced in evidence at the trial?**

(Continued on next page.)

a. *Yarborough v. Alvarado* (2004). Police ask 17-year-old Alvarado to come to the police station for an interview with a detective. His parents bring him and wait for him. For two hours, the detective questions him about a shooting. Twice during the interview, the detective asks Alvarado if he needs a break. Alvarado confesses to being involved in the shooting. The detective lets Alvarado go home with his parents.

5:4
admissible

b. *Illinois v. Perkins* (1990). Police suspect that Perkins, an inmate in jail on another charge, has committed a murder. They put an undercover agent in Perkins' cell. After gaining Perkins' trust, the agent asks him if he has ever killed anyone. Perkins confesses to the murder.

8:1
admissible

c. *Duckworth v. Eagan* (1989). Duckworth confessed to a crime after receiving *Miranda* warnings from police. Police had deviated from the standard warnings in one way. They had told Duckworth: "You have a right to talk to a lawyer for advice before we ask you any questions, and to have him with you during questioning. You have this right to the advice and presence of a lawyer even if you cannot afford to hire one. *We have no way of giving you a lawyer, but one will be appointed for you, if you wish, if and when you go to court.* If you wish to answer questions now without a lawyer present, you have the right to stop answering questions at any time. You also have the right to stop answering at any time until you've talked to a lawyer." (Emphasis added.)

5:4
admissable

d. *Arizona v. Mauro* (1987). Arrested for killing his son, Mauro declined to answer any questions without a lawyer. The police let his wife in to talk with him, but they conspicuously placed a tape recorder on the table between them, which recorded incriminating statements.

5:4
admissable

e. *Edwards v. Arizona* (1981). Arrested for burglary, robbery, and murder, Edwards was read his rights and said he was willing to answer questions. While being questioned, he said he wanted to make a deal, but first he wanted an attorney. He was returned to his cell. The next day, other officers saw Edwards and got him to waive his Miranda rights and confess.

9:0
inadmissible

f. *Fare v. Michael C.* (1979). Police gave *Miranda* warnings to Michael, a 16-year-old boy accused of murder. When asked if he wanted a lawyer during the interrogation, Michael asked if instead he could call his probation officer. When the police told him they would not call the probation officer right away, Michael somewhat reluctantly agreed to talk and eventually incriminated himself.

6:3
admissable

g. *Oregon v. Mathiason* (1977). Weeks after a burglary, police sent Mathiason a note asking him to call. He called and made an appointment at his convenience to come into the station. On his arrival, an officer informed him he was not under arrest, but led him into a conference room. The officer falsely told Mathiason that police had found his fingerprints at the burglary scene. Mathiason confessed to the crime. The officer then let Mathiason leave without arresting him that day.

6:3
admissable

h. *Beckwith v. U.S.* (1976). Arriving at Beckwith's house at 8 a.m., IRS agents asked Beckwith if they could ask him some questions. He invited them in and they interviewed him for three hours. During the interview, he made incriminating statements. He was later arrested for tax fraud.

admissable

Debriefing Questions

1. Which of the justices' decisions expand the *Miranda* decision? Which restrict it? Why?
2. What were some strong arguments presented by the attorneys for the government for each case? What arguments would have improved their cases?
3. What were some strong arguments presented by the attorneys for the defendants? What arguments would have improved their cases?
4. What were some key questions asked by the justices? What other questions should they have asked?
5. Which decisions do you agree with? Why?

The Exclusionary Rule

Since in no case shall the right of the people to be secure against unreasonable searches and seizures be violated, the contention that unreasonable searches and seizures are justified by the necessity of bringing criminals to justice cannot be accepted. It was rejected when the constitutional provisions were adopted and the choice was made that all the people, guilty and innocent alike, should be secure from unreasonable police intrusions, even though some criminals should escape.

– California Chief Justice Roger Traynor, *California v. Cahan* (1955)

"Criminals always get off on technicalities." You have probably heard this before or even thought it yourself. But do you know what these "technicalities" are? Generally, they refer to the individual rights protected by the Constitution, particularly provisions of the Fourth and Fifth amendments. When these rights have been violated by an illegal search, seizure, or interrogation, an accused person may invoke the exclusionary rule. This is done by making, in court, a motion to suppress any illegally obtained evidence.

The **exclusionary rule** is a special remedy created by the courts to compel police to respect the constitutional rights of suspects. Under the rule, no illegally obtained evidence — whether papers, objects, or testimony — may be presented in court to convict a defendant whose constitutional rights have been violated. This does not mean that the accused will automatically be set free. But in some cases, this evidence makes up the bulk of the government's case. In such cases, the charges may have to be reduced or dropped altogether.

The exclusionary rule is based upon two theories:

- **Judicial integrity.** Courts are supposed to uphold the law. If they allow illegally obtained evidence to be used at trial, they fail to uphold the law. They condone, even encourage, illegality. How can citizens respect our judicial system if the system accepts illegal practices?

- **Deterrence.** Excluding tainted evidence is the only effective way to prevent police abuse of constitutional rights. If illegally obtained evidence may not be introduced in court, police will not resort to illegal searches and seizures.

The rule has applied to *federal* criminal cases since 1914. The Supreme Court did not at first apply the rule to the states. Instead, the court let states decide how to uphold constitutional rights — whether by the exclusionary rule or by other methods. But in 1961, the Supreme Court decided that the exclusionary rule was required to assure that police would obey the Constitution. In *Mapp v. Ohio*, it applied the exclusionary rule to state criminal trials.

Mapp v. Ohio (1961)

Dollree Mapp, lived with her young daughter in a two-story house in Cleveland. On May 23, 1957, police arrived at her house and demanded entry. Although they gave Mapp no explanation, they later said they were responding to a tip about a recent bombing. After phoning her attorney, Mapp refused to let the officers in without a warrant. They left. Three hours later, they returned, still without a warrant, but with reinforcements. They pounded on the door. When Mapp did not come to the door immediately, the police broke into the house.

When they entered, Mapp was coming down the stairs. She demanded to see a warrant. An officer waved a piece of paper at her, but it was not a warrant. She grabbed it and stuffed it down her blouse. The officers forcibly retrieved it and handcuffed her. Then they dragged her upstairs to her bedroom and searched through her belongings and personal papers.

Meanwhile, Mapp's attorney arrived, but the officers would not let him in the house. They continued searching through the rest of the house. After searching everywhere, officers found some obscene materials tucked away in a basement trunk. Mapp was arrested, tried, and convicted of possessing these materials.

During Mapp's trial and her subsequent appeals, the state never denied that the search was illegal. Instead, the state argued that the illegal search was irrelevant. Mapp had obscene materials in her basement. She had broken the law and was guilty as charged. Her conviction should not be overturned because of an illegal search.

The Supreme Court disagreed. Ruling that "nothing can destroy a government more quickly than its failure to obey its own laws," the court threw out Mapp's conviction and returned the case to a lower court for further proceedings. In doing so, the court extended the exclusionary rule to all criminal trials in the country — both state and federal.

FRUIT OF THE POISONOUS TREE

If police find evidence during an illegal search, the exclusionary rule bars prosecutors from using this evidence at trial. But what if the illegally obtained evidence leads police to other evidence? For example, police conduct an illegal search of an office building and find cocaine in Dan's office. When Dan comes to work, they read him his *Miranda* rights and question him. He confesses to possessing and selling cocaine. The cocaine cannot be used as evidence at Dan's trial because of the illegal search. But can the confession be used? Police have complied with *Miranda*. But if Dan can show that police never would have had reason to question him except for their illegal search, then the confession would be excluded from the trial under the "fruit of the poisonous tree doctrine." This doctrine holds that if illegally obtained evidence (the poisonous tree), leads police to new evidence (the fruit), this new evidence may not be used in court against the person whose rights have been violated.

Courts have recognized several exceptions to this doctrine, and in recent years the Supreme Court has liberally interpreted these exceptions:

- **Independent source.** If police did not have to rely on the illegal evidence to find the new evidence, then the new evidence could be used at trial. For example, if a witness had told police that Dan dealt drugs, then they would have had reason to question him and the confession would be admitted. (*Silverthorne Lumber Co.* v. U.S., 1920, *Segura v. U.S.*, 1984, and *Murray v. U.S.*, 1988)
- **Inevitable discovery.** If police would have found the evidence eventually, then the evidence can be admitted in court. In *Nix v. Williams* (1984), police were searching for a body. They illegally obtained a confession that indicated where the body was. The body could be used as evidence at the trial because the court ruled the police would have found it eventually.
- **Cleansed taint.** If the connection between the illegal action and the new evidence is weak, then the new evidence will be allowed at trial. For example, if Dan's confession had not taken place the day of the search but had been volunteered by him a week later, a court might allow the confession as evidence. (*Wong Sun v. U.S.*, 1963)

For Discussion
1. What is the fruit of the poisonous tree doctrine? Do you agree with this doctrine? Why or why not?
2. What are the exceptions to the doctrine? Do they make sense? Why or why not?

The court stated that the constitutional right against invasions of privacy by police should not be an empty promise. The court said it could no longer permit this right

> to be revocable at the whim of any police officer who, in the name of law enforcement itself, chooses to suspend its enjoyment. Our decision, founded on reason and truth, gives to the individual no more than that which the Constitution guarantees him, to the police officer no less than that to which honest law enforcement is entitled, and, to the courts, that judicial integrity so necessary in the true administration of justice.

The Exclusionary Rule Since *Mapp*

The *Mapp* decision affected police behavior immediately. Police, who had rarely bothered to get warrants, started applying for them. In New York City, for example, police had requested no search warrants in 1960, the year before the *Mapp* decision. The year after *Mapp*,

the police requested more than 800 search warrants. The exclusionary rule, with its threat of suppressing illegal evidence, pushed police into seeking warrants.

But the *Mapp* decision did not end legal debate over the exclusionary rule. The Supreme Court has considered the issue many times. In recent years, the court has carved out several exceptions to the rule:

- If criminal defendants testify in their own defense, evidence illegally seized can be used to challenge the defendants' testimony. (*Harris v. New York*, 1971, *Michigan v. Harvey*, 1990, and *James v. Illinois*, 1990)
- Evidence gathered by police acting in good faith can be admitted if the police have reasonably relied on a search warrant issued by a judge that turns out to be technically defective or, through a judge's error, turns out not to be based on probable cause. (*U.S. v. Leon*, 1984, and *Arizona v. Evans*, 1995)

- Evidence found due to a police error in record keeping can be admitted as long as the error is not on purpose or a common practice (*Herring v. U.S.*, 2009). In *Herring*, the police arrested Herring and searched his van based on an arrest warrant that had been revoked months before.
- Evidence discovered after police violate the knock-and-announce rule can be admitted. (*Hudson v. Michigan*, 2006)

Critics of the exclusionary rule believe it hampers the fight against crime. Some argue that too many criminals escape conviction because either prosecutors reject cases with "tainted" evidence or courts exclude the evidence in motions to suppress. Others simply say the rule makes no sense. U.S. Supreme Court Justice Benjamin Cardozo reflected this opinion in 1926 when he asked: "Is it right the criminal is to go free because the constable has blundered?"

Supporters of the rule point out that motions to suppress evidence based on the exclusionary rule rarely succeed and thus affect few criminal prosecutions. This is partly because police today do a good job of following proper procedure. In response to critics who claim the procedures themselves hinder law enforcement, supporters point out that these procedures are required by the Constitution. The exclusionary rule simply helps ensure the police follow the Constitution.

FOR DISCUSSION
1. What is the exclusionary rule? Why was it established? What two justifications are given for it?
2. Do you think it is necessary? Why or why not?
3. What exceptions has the Supreme Court carved out to the exclusionary rule? Do you think each of them should be an exception? Explain.

CLASS ACTIVITY

A Second Look at the Exclusionary Rule
Critics of the exclusionary rule have set forth a variety of proposals to change the rule. These proposals include:
- Abolishing the exclusionary rule and allowing all relevant evidence to be used in court.
- Abolishing the exclusionary rule but establishing other civil and criminal remedies for citizens when the police violate their rights (e.g., a person could bring a civil suit against the officer for invasion of privacy in cases of unreasonable searches and seizures).
- Extending the good-faith exception to all situations where police act in good faith and in the reasonable — although mistaken — belief that their actions were legal.

Critics of the exclusionary rule claim it needs to be changed to prevent criminals from avoiding punishment when police make technical violations of the law. Its supporters argue that any change would encourage police lawlessness.

In this activity, students evaluate the pros and cons of the exclusionary rule and proposed changes to it.
1. Form small groups. Each group should:
   a. Discuss the pros and cons of the exclusionary rule.
   b. Discuss the advantages and disadvantages of the proposed changes to the rule listed above.
   c. Discuss whether there are other alternatives that would respect people's Fourth and Fifth Amendment rights but not place too heavy a burden on police.
   d. Decide whether the group favors changing the rule and if so, what change the group supports.
   e. Prepare to discuss its decision and the reasons for it with the class.
2. The groups should report back. Any new alternatives to the exclusionary rule should be written on the board.
3. Students should conclude the activity by voting on whether they think the exclusionary rule should be changed. If they vote to change it, they should vote on the alternatives.

CHAPTER 9
THE LIMITS OF POLICE AUTHORITY

There is a paradox in the fact that a democratic society needs protection both by police and from police. On a broader scale, this is one of the major challenges of democratic government. President James Madison argued that "you must first enable the government to control the governed; and in the next place, oblige it to control itself."
– Gary T. Marx, professor emeritus of sociology, MIT, "Police and Democracy" (1999)

RACIAL PROFILING | POLICE CORRUPTION | USE OF FORCE | POLICING THE POLICE
YOU AND THE POLICE

Racial Profiling

[T]he scope of racial profiling in America has expanded greatly since 9/11. Today "driving while black or brown" has been joined by "worshipping while Muslim," "walking while South Asian," and "flying while Middle Eastern."
– Benjamin Jealous, president of the NAACP, "Profiles of the Profiled" (2004)

For many years, blacks and other minorities have complained that police often target minority drivers, pulling them over for minor infractions or no reason at all and often subjecting them to humiliating car or body searches. Christopher Darden, an African American and former prosecutor, has been stopped many times by police. He said that "to be pulled over for no good reason is very offensive. But then to be asked for consent to search your vehicle just ratchets things up another notch. And in those situations where you've been forced out at gunpoint or you've been asked to spread out on the street, to lay out on the pavement, makes you boiling with anger."

John Lambeth of Temple University conducted a study to determine whether blacks were being targeted on the New Jersey Turnpike. He found that African Americans made up 13.5 percent of highway users and 15 percent of the speeders, but he found that they represented 35 percent of those stopped by police. They were almost five times more likely to be pulled over as other drivers. Similar results were found in studies conducted in Maryland and Florida.

Other minority community members complain that they too are stopped and questioned by authorities for no good reason. Latinos protest that they are targeted at Border Patrol checkpoints within the United States. Arab-Americans claim that they are often detained for long periods by airport security, especially since the September 11, 2001 terrorist attacks.

Pulling over a car, or stopping a person, solely on the basis of the driver's race violates the 14th Amendment to the U.S. Constitution, which guarantees equal protection under the law. If proven, it would invalidate an arrest or the use of any evidence seized from the driver. Federal civil rights laws outlaw it and several states have passed laws specifically against this practice.

The more difficult question arises over police officer discretion in deciding who to pull over. In the 1996 case of *Whren v. U.S.*, the U.S. Supreme Court unanimously ruled that police may stop a car for any traffic or equipment violation even if they have a different motivation for making the stop, such as the suspicion of drug trafficking.

Some experts point to "profiling" as the major cause of disproportionate traffic stops and searches on minorities. Profiles are systems used by police to predict criminal behavior. Some use scientific methods and statistics to develop a list of factors that make up a profile of a potential suspect. They might include age, location, type of car, time of day, driving patterns, route of travel, and whether the driver is alone. Profiles can also target white citizens. For example, a police officer might be more likely to pull over a late-model car for a minor traffic violation if it were driven by a white youth at night in an inner-city neighborhood where drug dealing occurs. In this case, the driver might fit a profile of someone who is likely trying to buy drugs.

Since 1999, 27 states have passed laws requiring police to keep track of the race and

ethnicity of everyone they stop. The data is forwarded to experts to analyze whether and to what extent officers are targeting people on the basis of race or ethnicity. These laws are widely supported by minority leaders. Walter Wilson, legislative director of the National Association for the Advancement of Colored People, has stated: "The NAACP believes that comprehensive data collection is critical to the process of ending racial profiling. Without data collection, there is no progress on this issue."

Other states and the federal government are considering such laws. But strong opposition to these laws has come from police groups. They argue that stopping people is already hazardous and forcing officers to ask people about their race and ethnicity will needlessly lengthen stops and inflame the situation. They also don't think the statistics will prove anything because people stopped will probably reflect the racial makeup of the community they are stopped in. They believe that instead of collecting data, all allegations of officers targeting minorities should be thoroughly investigated.

Although it is clearly illegal to single out a person solely on the basis of race, many people favor profiling when race or ethnicity is one of several factors. (This is sometimes called "partial racial profiling.") They argue that it is an effective law-enforcement tool. Bernard Parks, former chief of the Los Angeles Police Department, has stated: "We have an issue of violent crime against jewelry salespeople. . . . It's a collection of several hundred Colombians who commit this crime. If you see six in a car in front of the Jewelry Mart, and they're waiting and watching people with briefcases, should we play the percentages and follow them? It's common sense." Parks is an African American. He sees nothing wrong with using race as one factor in a profile.

Randall Kennedy, a law professor at Harvard, opposes using race as a factor in profiles. He doesn't think that police necessarily use this practice because they have racist motives. He thinks they may believe it is an effective law-enforcement tool, and Kennedy believes they may be right. But Kennedy points out that many innocent people get stopped by police using these profiles. And, he says, they often don't just get stopped once, but many times. This, he says, causes great anger and alienation. "Alienation of that sort gives rise to witnesses who fail to cooperate with the police, citizens who view prosecutors as 'the enemy,' . . . and jurors who yearn to 'get even' with a system that has, in their eyes, consistently mistreated them. For the sake of better law enforcement, we need to be mindful of the deep reservoir of anger toward the police that now exists within many racial minority neighborhoods. Racial profiling is a big part of what keeps this pool of accumulated rage filled to the brim."

The Effect of September 11 on Profiling

The terrorist attacks of September 11, 2001 spurred some to rethink whether racial profiling might be a proper police tactic. Because terrorist attacks are so devastating, police must focus on preventing them before they occur. The perpetrators of the September 11 attacks were Arab males. Is it proper for police to single out Arab males?

According to a November 2010 Washington Post poll, 70 percent of Americans support "profiling people . . . in order to determine who gets selected for extra security screening at airports." The current practice allows screeners to do random searches and to search those who appear suspicious. But it does not allow racial profiling. Presidents George W. Bush and Barack Obama and most members of Congress have opposed using racial profiling at airports.

New York Post columnist Dick Morris supports profiling at airports. He argues: "We know that a long and depressing list of terrorist attacks — culminating in 9/11 — have been executed by Arab men between the ages of 17 and 40. There is every reason to stop all such men who seek to board airplanes and subject them to intensive searches."

Frank Keating, the former governor of Oklahoma and a former FBI agent, does not believe ethnicity should be the sole factor, but it should be allowed to be a factor in profiles. He criticized airport security for preventing officials from looking closer "if someone is speaking Arabic or reading the Koran or praying . . . ." He said: "Random searches contribute nothing to safety at all."

Stuart Taylor, a columnist for *National Journal*, explained that he opposed racial profiling in most cases, but not in cases of terrorism. He stated: "There's a big difference between pulling someone over in the rain to hunt for drugs in a harassing way . . . and stopping somebody going through an airport for a few minutes to make sure he's not carrying a bomb . . . ." He went on to say: "Unless you can thoroughly search everyone, which would be great, but it would take hours and hours and hours, it makes sense to search with special care those people who look like all of the mass murder suicide hijackers who did the deeds on September 11th."

Abed Hannoud, a Michigan prosecutor and member of the Arab American Political Action Committee, also believes in profiling based on behavior and background. He says that "profiling can work if it's done right. In the case of Arab Americans, it is done wrong." He says that he has been stopped in airports because his U.S. passport lists Lebanon as his country of origin. He points out that terrorists can disguise themselves and buy U.S. passports that say anything they want. "So the narrow view of security, the narrow view of focusing on some passport of some nationalities misses the point. It is dangerous, besides hurting Arab Americans and offending us."

Frank Wu, a professor at Howard University Law School, opposes profiling at airports. He counters: "Even if we were to take an absurd number, let's say a thousand people of Arab descent within the United States are terrorists, that's still a fraction of 1 percent of the Arab population [in the United States]. The other 99 percent are law-abiding citizens like you or me. Having racial profiling sweeps too broadly . . . . It's simply wrong."

In 2004, Amnesty International USA, a human rights group, issued a report on racial profiling. It found that since September 11, 2001, racial profiling by "police, immigration, and airport security procedures has expanded . . . ." The report stated that racial profiling has "frequently distracted law enforcement officials and made them blind to dangerous behaviors and real threats." It cited the example of the Washington DC-area sniper attacks in 2002. The profile called for a white, disaffected male acting alone or with another. The actual killers were black and had been stopped by police several times, but let go. One FBI agent stated: "A black sniper? That was the last thing I was thinking."

FOR DISCUSSION

1. A bank is robbed and the suspect is described as an Asian woman driving a red sports car. Police start looking for such a suspect. Is this a racial profile? Explain.

2. Amnesty International in its 2004 report defined racial profiling as "the targeting of individuals and groups by law enforcement officials, even partially, on the basis of race, ethnicity, national origin, or religion, except where there is trustworthy information, relevant to the locality and timeframe, that links persons belonging to one of the aforementioned groups to an identified criminal incident or scheme." Do you think this is a good definition of racial profiling? Explain.

3. Do you think profiling is an effective law-enforcement tool? If so, are its benefits worth its costs? Explain.

4. Should police ever be allowed to consider race when deciding whether to stop someone? Explain.

CLASS ACTIVITY

What Should Be Done About Profiling?

To find out more about racial profiling, some states have passed laws requiring police to collect data on the race and ethnicity of everyone they stop. Other states and the federal government are considering doing the same. Opponents of data collection support other measures such as police videotaping every traffic stop or police distributing their card to everyone they stop so that people can easily file complaints. In this activity, students role play advisers to a state governor who is considering introducing legislation on racial profiling.

1. Form small groups. Each group should:
   a. Discuss the problem of racial profiling and various proposals for addressing it.
   b. Decide which proposal, if any, to support. (Students may create their own proposal.)
   c. Prepare to report its decision and the reason for it back to the class.

2. The groups should report back and the class should discuss the various proposals. Conclude the activity by voting as a class on the proposals.

Police Corruption

[A]n appreciable number [of New York City police officers] do not engage in any corrupt activities. Yet, with extremely rare exceptions, even those who themselves engage in no corrupt activities are involved in corruption in the sense that they take no steps to prevent what they know or suspect to be going on about them.
– *Knapp Commission Report on Police Corruption* (1973)

Police work provides many opportunities for corruption. A driver pulled over by police may hand an officer $20 along with his license hoping the officer will let him go without a ticket. A restaurant owner may give police free meals in exchange for them providing extra protection for her restaurant. Bookmakers, prostitutes, and drug dealers may offer payoffs for officers who ignore their operations.

Throughout the history of police in America, many officers could not resist some of these temptations. In the early days, police were loosely controlled and corruption flourished. Most got their jobs as political patronage, and many routinely did favors for their political bosses. The Progressive era at the beginning of the 20th century did away with much political patronage. But many reformers also called for strict enforcement of prostitution, gambling, and liquor laws, which in turn often led to bribes, protection money, and other corruption. The Prohibition era in the 1920s saw increasing numbers of law-enforcement officers accept payoffs to leave alone the thriving underground liquor industry, which was usually controlled by mobsters.

In our time, the war on drugs has made drug dealing both dangerous and highly lucrative. With so much money at stake, criminals sometimes have lured officers into accepting bribes and helping their criminal enterprises. Some officers have stolen drugs and money discovered in dealers' residences. A few have even dealt drugs themselves. Almost every large city police force has experienced a major drug scandal in recent years.

For Personal Benefit

Corruption can be defined as misusing one's official powers for gain. Often police corruption is for personal benefit. Officers get money, favors, food, sex, goods, or services in return for doing something they shouldn't do.

One of the most widely publicized cases of corruption was revealed by New York detective Frank Serpico in the late 1960s. (His story was made into a feature-length film starring Al Pacino.) Serpico witnessed widespread corruption and payoffs within the department. For years, he repeatedly reported the corruption to higher-ups and even to the mayor's office. Although some officials paid attention, nothing happened until he told his story to the *New York Times*. When officers learned what he had done, they considered him a "rat" and shunned him. The city formed the Knapp Commission in 1969 to investigate. The commission's report gave some insight into how corruption can remain unchecked in any police department. It divided corrupt officers into two groups — the "grass eaters" and the "meat eaters."

Meat eaters actively seek bribes or other favors. They may extort money from people they stop (in exchange for letting them go) and even commit crimes like dealing drugs, burglary, robbery, or murder for hire. They are the ones who, when caught, make the headlines. But they make up a small percentage of corrupt officers.

Grass eaters compose the overwhelming majority of corrupt officers. They do not actively seek bribes or other favors. But if something is offered to them, they will accept it. Although they seem less dangerous than the meat eaters, they can cause serious damage by creating an atmosphere in a department that corruption is acceptable. They help build up the "blue wall of silence" that keeps other officers from reporting any corruption, however flagrant.

For Departmental Benefit

Not all corruption is done for personal benefit. It may be done in a misguided attempt to make sure justice is served or the department or unit looks good. An officer may testify, for example, that he saw a gun lying in plain view in the defendant's apartment when, in fact, he found the gun in the defendant's desk drawer. The officer knows that if he tells the truth, the gun will be excluded from evidence. More dangerous, and much less common, are instances of police planting evidence to make sure a suspect is convicted.

A scandal in the Rampart division of the Los Angeles Police Department was, at least in part, an example of this type of corruption. In 1999, an officer was charged with stealing an eight-pound bag of cocaine from a police evidence room. In return for a lighter sentence, he started accusing other members of his elite anti-gang unit of intimidating witnesses, committing perjury, planting evidence, beating suspects, and even shooting people without justification. The scandal tainted many cases, leading to more than 100 convictions being reversed. In 2001, the federal government imposed a consent decree, ordering reforms in the department. In April 2005, city officials announced they would pay $70 million to settle lawsuits stemming from the actions of the corrupt officers.

What Can Be Done?

Various proposals have been suggested for ridding police forces of corruption. Some are more practical than others.

Get rid of victimless crimes. This is a radical solution that has little chance of being adopted — at least in the short term. Most corruption grows out of so-called "victimless crimes" — drugs, prostitution, gambling. These are crimes that all the parties consent to. A segment of the population desires these goods or services. And the criminals who service this segment are more than willing to pay off police — sometimes with huge sums. Get rid of these crimes and much police corruption will disappear.

Monitor police officers better. Another reason corruption takes place is because the badge gives police great authority and they must use their own discretion in exercising it. In some departments, supervisors don't know what their officers are doing and don't care as long as they make arrests. One way to ensure this doesn't happen is to hold supervisors accountable for having corrupt officers in their ranks. New York did this following the Knapp Commission. Another corruption scandal (which produced yet another commission) broke out in the 1990s. But it was far less pervasive than the corruption exposed by Serpico and the Knapp Commission.

Make internal review stronger. Almost every department has an internal affairs unit to investigate police. If this unit is strong, corruption will be lower. Some departments have adopted a policy that internal affairs must investigate every complaint by a citizen. If officers know in advance that complaints will be investigated and taken seriously, fewer will dare to be corrupt.

Break down the blue wall of silence surrounding corruption. Most people go into policing thinking they can help their community. Few officers start off being corrupt. They usually learn it on the job and it develops over time. It progresses from accepting a meal to taking money for not writing a ticket to accepting bribes from gamblers and finally from drug dealers. To break down the wall of silence, departments must teach and continually reinforce that corruption is unacceptable and hurts the department. They must encourage, not discourage, the reporting of misconduct.

FOR DISCUSSION

1. In your opinion, which type of corrupt officer is more dangerous — a grass eater or a meat eater? Why?
2. Which type of corruption — that for personal benefit or for departmental benefit — do you think is more dangerous? Why?
3. What do you think can be done to prevent police corruption? Explain.

CLASS ACTIVITY

Preventing Corruption

In this activity, students evaluate different proposals for preventing police corruption.

1. Form small groups. Each group should:
   a. Discuss the pros and cons of the proposals for getting rid of police corruption, listed under **What Can Be Done?** on this page.
   b. Discuss whether there are other policies that would help prevent corruption.
   c. Decide which proposals should be adopted.
   d. Prepare to present its proposals and the reasons for them to the class.
2. The groups should report back. Any new proposals for preventing corruption should be written on the board.
3. Students should conclude the activity by voting on the various proposals.

Use of Force

The use of deadly force to prevent the escape of all felony suspects, whatever the circumstances, is constitutionally unreasonable. It is not better that all felony suspects die than that they escape.
– U.S. Supreme Court Justice Byron R. White, *Tennessee v. Garner* (1985)

One of the most controversial aspects of police work is the use of force. Controversy does not arise over whether police should be allowed to use force. Police are authorized to use force to enforce the law and make arrests. Questions arise when an officer uses a gun, a baton, or even restraining holds in particular situations. Did the officer need to use force? Was the force excessive? Did the force amount to brutality?

As a general rule, police may use whatever level of force is reasonable and necessary to make an arrest. For instance, shooting an unarmed person who has stolen an apple from a fruit stand would not be reasonable. Clubbing an unresisting suspect with a nightstick is not necessary.

In training programs, police officers learn how much force may be used in specific cases. They practice adjusting the level of force to the circumstances. For each situation — whether it is an arrest, crowd control, or citizen confrontation — they are taught to begin with the lowest level of force necessary. They should only escalate the level of force if the situation requires it. For example, if a suspect quietly submits to an arrest, a simple pat-down search and handcuffing are all that is necessary. But if the suspect suddenly throws a punch, a higher level of force is probably required, such as using a physical-restraint technique. All of this works well in theory. On the street, other

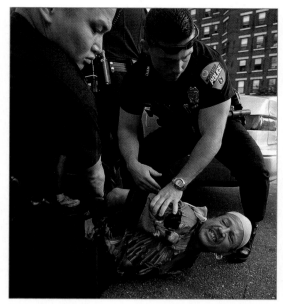

Police may only use reasonable and necessary force to make an arrest.

factors — including fear, anger, darkness, and split-second changes — can make deciding what force is reasonable and necessary much more difficult.

Police use of deadly force, especially firearms, is often highly publicized and controversial. Deadly force is commonly defined as "force that poses a high risk of death or serious injury to its human target, whether or not death or serious injury actually result." State criminal codes spell out laws governing the use of deadly force. Some police agencies and departments have even stricter standards for their officers. The following factors, among others, are used in determining whether deadly force is justified in a particular situation:

- The officer is making an arrest for a felony violation. (In general, deadly force is not justified in apprehending a person suspected of committing a misdemeanor or lesser offense.)
- The officer has made the reason for the arrest known to the suspect.
- The officer believes that deadly force is necessary to prevent death or great bodily injury to the officer or another person.
- The officer believes that the deadly force does not create a substantial risk to innocent persons.
- The criminal used deadly force or probably will use it if arrest is delayed.

ASK AN EXPERT

Does your police department have a written policy regarding the use of deadly force? If so, ask for a copy and see how it does or does not incorporate the basic requirements as outlined above.

If your police department does not have a written policy, interview officers and find out what, if any, formal or informal guidelines they follow in the use of deadly force.

Also, for most people firearms come to mind when they hear the phrase "deadly force." Find out if other forms of deadly force are used by police in your area.

Types of force used or threatened by police, 2008

Residents experiencing use or threat of force during most recent contact with police

Demographic characteristic	Number	% of those with police contact
Total	574,000	1.5%
Sex		
Male	390,000	1.8%
Female	184,000	1.0
Race		
White	347,000	1.2%
Black	130,000	3.4
Hispanic/Latino	68,000	1.6
Other	30,000	3.5
Age		
16-19	78,000	2.4%
20-29	253,000	2.5
30-39	122,000	1.5
40-49	61,000	0.8
50-59	33,000	0.5
60 or older	27,000	0.6

Source: *Contacts Between Police and the Public, 2008*, Bureau of Justice Statistics (2011)

In 1985 in *Tennessee v. Garner*, the Supreme Court ruled the Fourth Amendment puts a constitutional limit on the police's use of deadly force. In that case, police investigating a burglary saw an unarmed teenage boy run out of a house. Giving chase and calling for him to halt, they saw the boy start to climb a chain-link fence. Realizing that the boy would escape if he made it over the fence, an officer shot and killed him. The officer had acted in accordance with Tennessee law. The law gave police authority to use *any means necessary* to arrest a fleeing felon.

The Supreme Court ruled the law did not meet the constitutional standards of the Fourth Amendment. The court held it was not reasonable to use deadly force to arrest someone unless that person posed a threat to another person.

In 2007, the Supreme Court decided another deadly force case in *Scott v. Harris*. One night, police in Georgia tried to pull over Victor Harris for speeding. But Harris sped away, leading police on a wild high-speed chase along two-lane roads. Officer Scott joined the chase. Six minutes and 10 miles into the chase, Scott received permission to ram Harris' car from behind. Harris' car spun out of control, went down an embankment, and flipped over. Seriously injured, Harris was rendered a quadriplegic. Harris sued, claiming his Fourth Amendment rights were violated because police had unreasonably used deadly force.

The Supreme Court ruled against Harris. The court pointed out that the chase endangered many innocent people, pedestrians, drivers, and the police. If the police had just stopped chasing Harris, the court believed there was no guarantee that Harris would slow down. He might just believe the police were trying another tactic to catch him. Nor did the court want to issue a rule saying police could not pursue speeding motorists because such a rule would encourage others to speed away from police. Therefore, the court concluded: "A

WHEN IS IT WRONG FOR THE POLICE TO USE FORCE?

Police may use whatever force is reasonable and necessary to make an arrest. Often it is not reasonable or necessary for police to use force. Professor Albert Reiss has listed six examples when an assault by an arresting police officer would be wrong:

- When the officer does not attempt to arrest the person after using force to subdue the person.
- When the person does not resist arrest.
- When the person resisting arrest can be easily restrained by other methods.
- When many other officers are on the scene and can easily control the person.
- When the person is handcuffed and does not try to escape or resist violently.
- When the use of force goes on after the person stops resisting.

police officer's attempt to terminate a danger-ous high-speed car chase that threatens the lives of innocent bystanders does not violate the Fourth Amendment, even when it places the fleeing motorist at risk of serious injury or death."

FOR DISCUSSION

1. Why might deciding what force is reason-able and necessary be difficult for a police officer in the field?

2. Do you think the Supreme Court's decisions in *Tennessee v. Garner* and *Scott v. Harris* are consistent with each other? Do you agree with the decisions in each case? Explain.

3. In *California v. Gilmore* (1988), Gilmore, a private citizen, found a man trying to bur-glarize his house. The man ran, but Gilmore yelled three times for him to halt and then fired his gun and killed the man. Gilmore was convicted of manslaughter, but a California Court of Appeals reversed his conviction. It stated that *Tennessee v. Garner* only limits what police officers may do, not private citizens, because the Fourth Amendment only applies to government of-ficials. Under California law, any killing "necessarily committed in attempting, by lawful ways and means, to apprehend any person for any felony committed" is justifi-able. So the court found the killing justifi-able. Do you think private citizens should be able to shoot non-violent fleeing felons? Do you think police should be able to? Who should have more right to use force — police or private citizens? Why?

CLASS ACTIVITY

Split Second

If you were a police officer in a dan-gerous situation, how do you think you should respond? In this activity, students decide how they would respond as officers in different situations.

1. Form pairs.
2. Each pair should:
   a. Read the cases below.
   b. Decide how to handle each case and how much force, if any, is rea-sonable and necessary.
   c. Review the list of factors (page 144) that police officers might take into account when deciding how much force to use. Discuss:
      (1) Which factor, if any, went into your decisions in the cases?
      (2) Did any additional factors go into your decisions?
   d. Be prepared to discuss the cases and answers with the class.
3. The teams should report and discuss their findings with the class. Close the activity with a discussion using the de-briefing questions on page 144.

Cases

#1: Eulia

Eulia, a 39-year-old black woman, had a dispute with a gas company serviceman. The serviceman appeared at Eulia's home to turn off the gas because of an unpaid bill. She attacked the serviceman and struck him several times with a shovel. The serviceman left and called the police.

When two police officers arrived at Eulia's home to arrest her for the aggravated as-sault, Eulia screamed at them and threw some dishes on the floor. The noise at-tracted several curious neighbors to her front porch to see what was going on. While the officers talked to Eulia from a corner of the kitchen, she suddenly picked up an 11-inch knife from the counter and prepared to throw it at them.

(Continued on next page.)

#2: Tony

Tony, a tall, thin, 17-year-old boy, was speeding and swerving his car back and forth between the lanes on the highway late one night. Two police officers stopped him and asked to see his driver's license. Tony, who had obviously been drinking, became enraged and verbally abusive.

One of the officers, a 20-year veteran of the police force, attempted to handcuff him, but Tony pushed him away, grabbed a crowbar from his back seat, and waved it at the other officer. "I'll kill you if you come near me again," he screamed.

Possible Factors Police Might Consider

1. Suspect's sex
2. Suspect's age
3. Suspect's race
4. Suspect's demeanor
5. Suspect's height
6. Suspect's weight
7. Suspect's mental condition
8. Your weapon
9. Suspect's weapon
10. Time of day
11. Visibility
12. Location
13. Distance between suspect and officers
14. Cover for officers
15. Cover for suspect
16. Possibility of suspect's escape if deadly force is not used
17. Presence of bystanders
18. Availability of backup
19. Number of suspects
20. Number of officers

Debriefing Questions

1. What was the minimum use of force suggested for each case? What was the maximum?
2. After hearing all the team reports, would you modify the approach you suggested? Why or why not?
3. What factors from the list were most commonly used in making a decision? (List them on the board.) Which factors were least commonly used?
4. What factors should affect an officer's decision to use force in a particular situation? Why?

    Note: In a study, 50 police officers were asked to respond to hypothetical cases just as you did here. A majority of the officers considered the following factors important:

    1. Suspect's weapon
    2. Location
    3. Number of suspects
    4. Cover for officers
    5. Presence of bystanders
    6. Availability of backup
    7. Distance between suspect and officer

    From this study, it appeared that most officers focused on location and the suspects' actions, not the suspects themselves. Other factors, such as suspects' race, sex, height, and weight, did not have as much bearing on the officers' decisions.

Policing the Police

But who will guard the guardians?
– The Roman writer Juvenal (A.D. 50-130)

Who polices the police? This question has repeatedly come up, especially in minority communities, after incidents of alleged police brutality. Among the most notorious incidents are:

- In the early morning of New Year's Day 2009, Bay Area Rapid Transit Police were notified of a fight on a metro car arriving in Oakland, California. Officers rushed to the car and pulled several people off the train. One of them was Oscar Grant. A crowd gathered and cursed at the officers as they tried to control the chaotic situation. Grant was forced to lie on his stomach while two officers tried to handcuff and arrest him for resisting arrest. One of the officers, Johannes Mehserle, stood up, pulled his gun, and shot Grant in the back. Grant, who was unarmed, died hours later. Several people had videoed the incident, and the videos were shown repeatedly on television throughout the San Francisco area. Mehserle was charged with murder, but due to all the publicity, the trial was moved to Los Angeles. At the trial, Mehserle claimed that he was reaching for his Taser, but in the confusion, he mistakenly pulled his gun. The jury apparently believed him and returned a verdict of involuntary manslaughter. Sentenced to two years in prison, Mehserle was released in June 2011. Two lawsuits were filed against BART, asking for millions of dollars in damages.

- IIn 2004, Sayyid Qadri, 22, was stopped by police for making an illegal turn in Evanston, Illinois. Seeing that his license had expired, police handcuffed him and took him to the station. The station had video surveillance cameras throughout it. The cameras captured officers taking Qadri, still handcuffed, into a bathroom stall where there was no camera. A few moments later, Qadri emerged, covered in blood. A wound on his face required six stitches. All charges against Qadri were dropped. The two officers faced felony charges, but the judge dismissed the charges on the second day of the trial. The city settled Qadri's lawsuit by paying him $300,000.

PAUL CONRAD

"I have the right to remain silent. Anything I say can be used against me in court. If I cannot afford a lawyer, one will be provided . . ."

- In 1999, four plainclothes officers of the New York Police Department's Street Crimes Unit saw Amadou Diallo, an African immigrant, standing in the entrance hall to his apartment. Police thought he was a burglar and yelled at him to freeze. Diallo tried to open his door. When he reached for his wallet, police thought he had a gun. They opened fire, shooting 41 rounds and killing Diallo. Diallo was unarmed and had no criminal record. The four officers were charged with second-degree murder and five lesser offenses. In February 2000, a jury found the four defendants not guilty on all charges. Diallo's family settled a lawsuit against New York City for $3 million.

- In 1997, several New York police officers arrested Abner Louima, a Haitian immigrant. They mistakenly thought he had assaulted an officer during a brawl outside a nightclub. Louima charged that police beat him in the patrol car and that two officers in the station house rammed a broomstick up his rectum. Louima sustained serious injuries. Federal authorities took over the investigation. One officer pleaded guilty to violating Louima's civil rights and was sentenced to 30 years. Another officer was convicted of perjury and sentenced to five years in prison. Two other officers had their convictions overturned on appeal. Louima settled a lawsuit against New York City for $8.7 million.

National Poll of Police Officers on the Code of Silence

	Strongly Agree	Agree	Disagree	Strongly Disagree
The code of silence is an essential part of the mutual trust necessary to good policing.	1.2%	15.7%	65.6%	17.5%
Whistle blowing is not worth it.	3.1	21.8	63.5	11.7
An officer who reports another officer's misconduct is likely to be given the cold shoulder by his or her fellow officers.	11.0	56.4	30.9	1.8
It is not unusual for a police officer to turn a blind eye to improper conduct by other officers.	1.8	50.6	43.3	4.4
Police officers always report serious criminal violations involving abuse of authority by fellow officers	2.8	36.2	58.5	2.5

Source: "Police Attitudes Toward Abuse of Authority: Findings From a National Study," National Institute of Justice (2000)

- In 1991, a citizen videotaped several Los Angeles police officers beating Rodney King following a high-speed chase. The Los Angeles County district attorney filed charges against four officers. But in April 1992, a jury acquitted them of all charges. This provoked rioting and outrage in Los Angeles and other cities. It also prompted the federal government to bring criminal charges against the four officers for violating King's civil rights. At the federal trial, two of the officers were convicted. In August 1993, they were sentenced to 30 months in prison.

Many members of minority groups have long complained about police brutality and harassment on the street. What can be done about police officers who behave improperly?

Criminal Charges

In cases of severe misbehavior, officers can be charged with crimes, such as in the cases above. If officers use excessive force, they can face, depending on the circumstances, charges of assault under color of authority, assault with a deadly weapon, or even manslaughter or murder. Except in the most blatant cases, however, it can be very difficult to convict a police officer for using excessive force. Police reform experts point to the following as likely reasons for this difficulty:

Prosecutors may resist bringing charges against police. Prosecutors work with police on a daily basis. They depend on officers to investigate crimes and testify at trials. When an officer is accused of using excessive force, other police officers tend to rally around the accused officer. Because prosecutors have working relationships with police, many avoid prosecuting police except in obvious cases of excessive force.

Proving excessive force can be difficult. Since police are authorized to use force, the prosecutor does not merely have to prove that the officer assaulted the victim. The prosecutor must show that the officer used excessive force. Many of these incidents happen at night with few witnesses other than the victim and the police. And as with all criminal trials, the prosecution must convince all 12 jurors that no reasonable doubt exists that the officer used excessive force.

Many jurors tend to identify with the police. Like most Americans, jurors worry about crime. They see the police as the thin blue line between them and the criminal element. Knowing how hazardous police work is, they are thankful for the protection police offer them. Since police work is so important and so dangerous, most jurors tend to give the police the benefit of the doubt at trial.

Advocates for the police see the matter in quite a different light. They believe that criminal prosecutions for excessive force are normally inappropriate. They argue that police work is highly regulated and that incidents of abuse are extremely rare. In addition, they claim that criminal laws and departmental rules regulating excessive force are difficult to apply in the field, where officers sometimes work under life-and-death circumstances. Finally, they argue that police are expected to protect citizens, be tough on criminals, and deal with the most dangerous elements in society, often with inadequate resources and little public support.

Civil Lawsuits

What about civil lawsuits? Are they more effective at policing the police? The number of lawsuits against police officers has risen steadily over the last 30 years. Some cities pay out millions of dollars annually to plaintiffs alleging police brutality. Because of their high cost, these suits must have some effect on encouraging cities to root out problem officers.

But for an individual with a complaint against the police, filing a lawsuit is seldom an option. Since few people can afford to pay lawyer fees, those choosing to sue must find a lawyer who will take the case on a contingency fee. This means the lawyer will not charge the client unless the client wins. Since lawyers want to get paid, they will only take cases that they have a reasonable expectation of winning. Lawyers know these cases must be very strong. For although civil suits do not share all the obstacles of a criminal trial, they do share one — jurors, most of whom are concerned about crime, may tend to see the case from the police's point of view. This means that civil suits, like criminal cases, are likely to succeed in dealing with only the most outrageous misbehavior by the police.

Police Boards

So what can individuals with complaints against the police do? One option is to file complaints against the officers. Most police departments have a set procedure for taking citizen complaints. But methods for handling these complaints vary.

In some cities, the police department itself handles complaints against police officers. Other police officers or the chief of police investigate the charges. In larger police departments, an internal-affairs section staffed by special officers investigates citizen complaints and disciplines police officers who violate the law or police department regulations. These are the ways the police "police" themselves.

In recent years, the number of citizen complaints against the police has increased. Complaints range from relatively minor matters, such as failing to investigate a crime properly, to more serious cases involving police corruption or police brutality. Some complaints charge the police with mistreating people in custody.

Many people have seen a need to give citizens more control over police behavior. Some cities have used **citizen review boards** for this purpose. Composed of community members, these boards investigate reports of police misconduct and recommend what action should be taken. Citizen review boards may or may not have the power to carry out their recommendations.

Controversy, however, surrounds these boards. Police often oppose creating these boards. They feel that their job is dangerous and not easily understood by the public. They admit that misconduct sometimes occurs and citizen complaints must be treated seriously. But they usually insist that justice is more likely to be obtained if an accused officer is investigated by other officers who know what police work is really like. Furthermore, many police officers believe citizen controls may hamper police work and that outsiders may be hostile to the police.

On the other hand, many citizens argue that in our society civilians must exercise direct control over police behavior. Without effective civilian control, the police may apply their own standards and abuse may be more acceptable. If this occurs, citizens will lose respect for the police and for the law that the police are expected to enforce.

FOR DISCUSSION

1. There are several ways of disciplining problem officers — criminal prosecutions, civil lawsuits, departmental action, and citizen review boards. What are the strengths and weaknesses of each?
2. Who should police the police? How should it be done? Explain your answer.

CLASS ACTIVITY

A Board of Rights

In this activity, students simulate a review board on police misconduct and decide hypothetical cases.

1. Form groups of four members each. Each group will function as a Police Board of Rights whose purpose is to decide about possible disciplinary action against officers receiving complaints from citizens. Each board will deal with the same two cases. In each case, the board must:
   a. Determine the guilt or innocence of the officers.
   b. If guilty, decide the punishment the officer should receive.

   These cases have been thoroughly investigated by the police department's Internal Affairs Division and the accused officers are fully aware of the charges against them. You and the other Board of Rights members are all high-ranking police officers. You have already heard the evidence for and against the accused officers and you have discussed the contents of each officer's personnel file. (A summary of the events of each case and the evidence before you is given below.)

   The board must evaluate the evidence and decide on the guilt or innocence of the officers accused in the two cases.

2. Each group should:
   a. Select a chairperson.
   b. Read the materials on the two cases to be presented to the board on pages 148–150. Review each case thoroughly with all the members of the group.
   c. Using the questions listed under **Recommendations**, discuss each case, vote on the guilt or innocence of the accused officer, and decide on an appropriate penalty, if necessary. The chairperson should record the answers to the questions and the recommendations of the group. Minority opinions should also be noted by the chairperson.
   d. If the board determines that an accused officer is innocent, it should recommend that the complaint be dropped. If the board finds an officer guilty, it should decide on one of the following penalties:
      (1) Reprimand (warning to be placed in the officer's file).
      (2) Suspension up to six months with loss of pay.
      (3) Removal from the force.
   e. After deciding, prepare a brief report discussing the reasons for the decision and be prepared to discuss them with the class.

3. All the boards should report their decisions and reasons to the class. Conclude the activity by holding a discussion using the debriefing questions on page 150.

Case #1: Officers Mark Thomas and Stephen Campbell

Description of Events:

Mark Thomas has been on the force for six years and Stephen Campbell for five years. They are good friends. Recently, they met in a cocktail lounge at about 1 a.m. Both were just off duty and still in uniform. They had five or six beers, and Officer Campbell bought several drinks for one of the off-duty waitresses.

The two officers had a running joke about Officer Thomas wanting to buy Officer Campbell's gun. Campbell had brought the gun that evening to sell it to Thomas. Thomas kept offering more money than Campbell was willing to accept, and the matter became a joke between them as they passed the gun back and forth under the table.

Meanwhile, Officer Thomas and the waitress had some disagreeable words because the waitress felt Thomas had insulted her. Thomas contends he did not mean to insult her and was only joking.

(Continued on next page.)

Later, when Officer Thomas left the lounge, he pretended he was going to steal a decorative keg of beer from the cocktail lounge. Thomas claims he was only joking and had no intention of stealing the keg. But the waitress grabbed the keg and took it back to the bar. The waitress was upset, and Officer Campbell was unable to calm her down.

The next day, the waitress complained to the police department that the two officers had been at the bar waving guns around. She stated it was "a regular O.K. Corral without the shots fired." She also accused Officer Thomas of trying to steal the beer keg. In her written complaint, she said both Thomas and Campbell were drunk.

The waitress and her girlfriend were later interviewed together by Internal Affairs Division investigators, and so they could not be used to corroborate one another's stories. The parking lot attendant was not interviewed, nor were other witnesses found who could verify whether the officers were drunk. The bartender claimed the two officers were not drunk, but by law he must not serve intoxicated persons. So it serves his self-interest to claim they were sober. The waitress has a record of being under psychiatric care. All evidence indicates, however, that she is completely sincere and truthful.

Three charges currently exist against the two officers. They are listed below. The recommendation of the captain in charge of these officers was 15 days suspension without pay for Thomas, and 10 days for Campbell. Both officers have appealed their case to the Board of Rights contending that the punishment is unjust and the investigation was improperly handled.

Personnel Records:

Officer Mark Thomas has received only one previous complaint. This was from a motorist who objected to the traffic ticket he received and said that Officer Thomas was rude and did not call him "sir" when he spoke to him. Officer Thomas' evaluation from his superiors describes him as energetic, high spirited, and a good marksman.

Officer Campbell has received no previous complaints and has been found an excellent officer by his superiors.

Recommendations:

Based on your review of this information, do you think that Officer Mark Thomas should be found guilty of any of the three charges listed below?
(1) Exposing a firearm unnecessarily in public.
(2) Misappropriation of property (beer keg).
(3) Disturbing the peace.

Should any penalty be applied? If so, what? Do you feel that Officer Stephen Campbell should be found guilty of any of the charges listed above? If so, what penalty should be applied in this case?

Case #2: Officers Sam Allen and Mary McCrea
Description of Events:

Officers Allen and McCrea were summoned about 2 a.m. to a wealthy area of town by a resident. The resident complained of a disturbance from a loud party going on next door. The resident also stated that three people wearing black leather motorcycle jackets who apparently were attending the party had come to his door, obviously drunk. One of the three reportedly carried a kitchen knife and asked to borrow a "cup of sugar and maybe some blood."

As the officers approached the caller's house, they saw a young man, about 21, standing by three motorcycles. When the man saw the officers, he joined a young woman and began walking toward the front door of the house. The officers followed them and ordered them to stop.

Officers could hear a stereo playing music seemingly at full volume inside the house. But the two people in front said that nearly everyone had gone home except maybe for "two or three people in the back yard." It was clear to the officers that the two were under the influence of alcohol or narcotics or both.

(Continued on next page.)

When asked what had been going on, the two people replied that some people had "just been listening to music" and "having a good time." The officers explained that a neighbor had called about a disturbance and someone using a knife in a threatening manner. The officers overheard the girl say, "I wonder if Dusty was at it again."

Officers Allen and McCrea asked to speak to the owner of the house but were told that he was not at home. Then the officers asked to speak to the host or hostess and were informed that it was an open party, and there was no host or hostess. The two did not know who lived at the house. They went inside leaving the officers on the front lawn.

Just then, three people wearing black leather motorcycle jackets appeared from the side of the house. Officer Allen ordered the group to halt. He and Officer McCrea approached them. The trio was somewhat belligerent and, when questioned about the neighbor's call, said they knew nothing.

Officer Allen asked for their names. One of the group identified himself as Dusty Adams. The officer asked the group to remain until they could be identified by the complaining neighbor. They refused and said they were going to leave. At this point, Officer Allen ordered the three to stand spread-eagle with their hands on the stone wall next to the driveway. All of them began to curse.

While Officer McCrea held her gun, Officer Allen began to frisk the group. He found a kitchen knife in the boot of one. As he searched the second man, Dusty Adams turned saying, "Hey, man, listen, you don't want any trouble do you?"

"Keep your hands on the wall or we'll shoot," said Officer Allen. Adams took a step away from the wall. Officer McCrea fired, wounding Adams in the shoulder. No weapon was found on his person.

Subsequently, a complaint was filed against Officer McCrea charging that she overreacted and used unreasonable force. Internal Affairs investigated the complaint and referred it to the Board of Rights.

Officers Allen and McCrea contended that under the circumstances they had probable cause to act as they did and probable cause to believe that Dusty Adams was reaching for another weapon when he moved suddenly and removed his hands from the stone wall. Furthermore, the officers stated that the suspects had been warned, and that under the circumstances the officers had not acted unreasonably. The captain has recommended that no disciplinary action be taken against officers Allen and McCrea.

Personnel Records:

Officers Allen and McCrea have been on the force for three and two years respectively. Both are highly regarded by their superiors. Neither has received any previous complaints.

Recommendations:

In your opinion should Officer Sam Allen or Officer Mary McCrea be found guilty of using unreasonable force? If so, what should the penalty be?

Debriefing Questions

1. What was the most difficult part of deciding these cases? Why?
2. What factors might make the job of a police rights board difficult and controversial? Why?
3. What if your group had been made up only of citizens concerned about police behavior? Would you have decided any of these cases differently?

You and the Police

In 2008, an estimated 16.9% of U.S. residents age 16 or older had face-to-face contact with police.
– "Contacts Between Police and the Public, 2008"
Bureau of Justice Statistics (2011)

Some time you may have a difficult contact with the police. They may want to question you. You may be subject to arrest. It might be because of your conduct or just because you happen to be in the wrong place at the wrong time.

It is important to remember that the police work for you as a citizen of your community, whatever your age, race, or job. The police are required to respect your rights. You, in turn, should respect their authority and understand the difficulties of their job. Mutual respect can go a long way toward easing tension in a difficult situation.

The following is general advice on what to do if the police stop you. In any particular situation, you should always rely on your best judgment and, when possible, the advice of a lawyer.

If You Are Stopped by a Police Officer

1. Be courteous and cooperative. Avoid hostility, profanity, or aggressive movements. Do nothing to cause an officer to believe you are a threat.
2. Give your name and address, or show an I.D. if requested.
3. The police can search you for concealed weapons by patting your clothing. Do not physically resist, but you have the right to tell the officer that you do not agree to any search of yourself, your car, or your surroundings. By making it clear that you do not consent to any search, you can protect your right against unlawful searches. The police may search you or your surroundings anyway. Do not try to stop them physically. You can question the legality of the search in court. If the police say that they have a warrant, ask to see it.
4. If you believe the police have violated your rights, you have the right to file a complaint.

If You Are Arrested or Held

1. Never run away, strike an officer, or physically resist, whether you are innocent or guilty. If you resist or try to escape, the police can use whatever force is reasonable and necessary to stop you.
2. You are entitled to your *Miranda* rights, which include the right to remain silent. You are required to tell the police nothing except your name and address. Giving explanations or stories or trying to excuse your conduct will rarely benefit you unless your lawyer advises you to do so.
3. Ask to see a lawyer immediately. If you cannot pay for a lawyer, you have the right to request the police to get you a lawyer before you talk to officials.
4. After arrest, use your right to make a telephone call to a relative, trusted friend, or lawyer for assistance. If you are under age 18, you may not be permitted to make telephone calls. Ask to see a lawyer. You generally have the right to go into court the next court day after your arrest, and you can ask to be released on bail, although the law may differ for minors.
5. Do not make any decisions in your case until you have talked to a lawyer and understand what your choices are.

FOR DISCUSSION

1. How can you best assure mutual respect between you and the police?
2. Do you think mutual respect between you and the police is important? Why or why not?
3. Why is it important not to resist police?

Sources for Unit 2

Anti-Terror Lessons of Muslim-Americans, NIJ-Sp., 2010, NCJ 229868. · "Arrest-Related Deaths in the U.S., 2003–2009," BJS, 2011, NCJ 235385. · Baum, L. *The Supreme Court.* 8th Ed. Wash., DC: CQ P, 2010. · *Benefits & Consequences of Police Crackdowns*, COPS, 2006, NCJ 201916. · Bouza, A. *The Police Mystique.* NY: Plenum P, 1990. · Braga *et al.* "Problem-oriented Policing, Deterrence, & Youth Violence." *J. of Research in Crime & Delinquency*, Vol. 38, 2001. · *Calif. Commission on the Fair Administration of Justice, Final Report.* State of Calif.,. 2008. · Carter, D, "Drug-Related Corruption of Police Officers." *J. of Criminal Justice* 18(2), 1990. · Casselman, A. "Identical Twins Genes Are Not Identical." *Scientific Amer.*, 4/3/2008. · "Census of State & Local Law Enforcement Agencies, 2008," BJS, 2011, NCJ 233982. · "Changing Environment for Policing, 1985–2008," NIJ, 9/2010, NCJ 230576. · "Characteristics of Drivers Stopped by Police, 2002, BJS, 2006, NCJ 211471. · "Citizen Complaints About Police Use of Force," BJS, 6/2006, NCJ 210296. · Cole, S. "More than Zero," *J. of Criminal Law & Criminology*, Vol. 95, No. 3, 2005. · *Community-Based Violence Prevention*, NIJ-Sp., 2010, NCJ 230758. · *Community Policing Explained*, COPS, 2007, NCJ 220015. · *Community Policing*, COPS, 2009, NCJ 227424. · "Contacts Between Police & the Public, 2008," BJS, 2011, NCJ 234599. · "Characteristics of Drivers Stopped by Police, 2002," BJS, 2006, NCJ 211471. · "Crime Statistics," NYPD, URL: www.nyc.gov/html/nypd · "CSI Effect," NIJ, 2008, NCJ 221501. · "Death Investigation," Wash., DC: NIJ, 1999. · Durose, M. *et al.*, "Contacts between Police & the Public." Wash., DC: BJS, 2005. · *Effects of Problem-Oriented Policing on Crime & Disorder*, NIJ-Sp., 2008, NCJ 224990. · "Electronic Control Devices," NIJ-Sp., 2007, NCJ 220991. · *Event Dynamics & the Role of Third Parties in Urban Youth Violence*, NIJ-Sp., 2009, NCJ 227781. · *Eyewitness Evidence.* NIJ, 2003. NCJ 188678. · Farnworth, M., "Safe at Home?" *San Diego Mag.*, 9/2004. · "Federal Law Enforcement Officers, 1998," Wash., DC: BJS, 2000. · *The Fingerprint Sourcebook*, NIJ, 2011. · Fisher, D. *Hard Evidence.* NY: Simon & Schuster, 1995. · Fletcher, C. *Every Contact Leaves a Trace.* NY: St. Martin's P, 2006. · "Gang Units in Large Local Law Enforcement Agencies, 2007," BJS, 2010, NCJ 230071. · Gross, S. *et al.* "Exonerations in the U.S., 1989 through 2003." *J. of Criminal Law & Criminology*, Vol. 95, No. 2, 2005. · Harcourt, B. "Rethinking Racial Profiling." *U. of Chicago Law Rev.*, Vol. 71, Fall 2004. · Hickman, M. "Traffic Stop Data Collection Policies for State Police, 2004." Wash., DC: BJS, 2005. · ___, "50 Largest Crime Labs, 2002." Wash., DC: BJS, 2004. · *Investigative Uses of Technology.* NIJ, 2007, NCJ 213030. · Kelling, G. *"Broken Windows" & Police Discretion*, Wash., DC: NIJ, 1999. · Kennedy, D. *Deterrence & Crime Prevention.* Routledge, 2008. · ___. *Don't Shoot.* NY: Bloomsbury USA, 2011. · ___. "Pulling Levers," *NIJ Journal*, No. 236, 7/1998. · Kennedy, D. *et al.* "The High Point Drug Market Intervention Strategy," COPS, NCJ 234157, 2009. · Kim, Y. *et al.* "Examining the 'CSI-effect' in the cases of circumstantial evidence & eyewitness testimony," *J. of Criminal Justice*, Vol. 37, No. 5, 2009. · ___. "An Indirect-Effects Model of Mediated Adjudication." *Vanderbilt J. of Entertainment & Tech. Law*, Vol. 12, No. 1, Fall 2009. · Koppl, Roger. "CSI for real," Reason Foundation, Policy Study 364, 2007. · Law Enforcement, BJS, 2012, URL: http://bjs.ojp.usdoj.gov · *Less Lethal Weapon Effectiveness, Use of Force, & Suspect & Officer Injuries.* NIJ-Sp., 2008, NCJ 224081. · "Local Police Departments, 2007," BJS, 2010, NCJ 231174. · "Making Sense of DNA Backlogs, 2010," NIJ, 2011, NCJ 232197. · Martz, C. "Miranda Update." *Bill of Rights in Action*, Winter 1990. · ___. "The 14th Amendment & the 'Second Bill of Rights.'" *Bill of Rights in Action*, Spring 1991. · Maxson, C. *et al.* *Factors That Influence Public Opinion of the Police.* Wash., DC: NIJ, 2003. · McGough, M. "The Lazarus File." *Atlantic*, 6/2011. · "Police Integrity, Responsibility, & Discipline," NIJ, 2011. NCJ 235606. · "Role of Medical Examiners in Law Enforcement," *The Police Chief*, 11/2007. NCJ 221149. · *Multi-Method Evaluation of Police Use of Force Outcomes*, NIJ-Sp., 2009, NCJ 231176. · Nat. Research Council. *Fairness & Effectiveness in Policing.* Wash., DC: Nat. Academies P, 2004. · Newton, J. *et al.* "LAPD Condemned by its Own Inquiry Into Rampart Scandal," *LA Times*, 3/1/2000. · *NIJ Controlled Substances Case Processing Study*, NIJ-Sp., 2011, NCJ 233830. · "One Week in Heron City: A Case Study (Case A) & (Case B): A Case Study," NIJ, 2009, NCJ 227664. · Packer, H. "Two Models of the Criminal Process" in *The Limits of the Criminal Sanction* Stanford: Stanford UP, 1968. · Peterson, J. *et al.* "Census of Publicly Funded Forensic Crime Laboratories." Wash., DC: BJS, 2005. · "Police Attitudes Toward Abuse of Authority." Wash., DC: NIJ, 2000. · "Police Discipline," NIJ, 2011, NCJ 234052. · "Police Innovation & Crime Prevention," NIJ-Sp., 2006, NCJ 218585. · *Police Organization & Management Issues for the Next Decade*, NIJ-Sp., 2006, NCJ 218584. · "Police Use of Force, Tasers & Other Less-Lethal Weapons," NIJ, 2011, NCJ 232215. · "Policing in Arab-American Communities After September 11," NIJ, 2008, NCJ 221706. · "Profile of a Terrorist." Online NewsHour, 9/26/2001. URL: www.pbs.org · *Promoting Cooperative Strategies To Reduce Racial Profiling*, COPS, 2008, NCJ 224525. · "Racially Biased Policing," COPS, 2005, NCJ 211225. · *A Review of the FBI's Handling of the Brandon Mayfield Case.* Office of the Inspector General. U.S. Dept. of Justice. 2006. · Roane, Kit R., "The Verdict." *U.S. News & World Report*, 3/6, 2000. · Saks, M. *et al.* "The CSI Effect," 47 *Jurimetrics J.*, 2007. · "San Diego Historical Crime Actuals, 1950–2011," SDPD, URL: www.sandiego.gov/police · Schuster, B. "Police Lineups," *NIJ Journal*, No. 258, 10/2007, NCJ 219603. · Seabrook, J. "Don't Shoot," *New Yorker*, 6/22/2009. · Skolnick, J. *et al.* *Above the Law.* Free Press, 1993. · Snyder, H. "Arrest in the U.S., 1980–2009," BJS, 2011. NCJ 234319. · Steadman, G. "Survey of DNA Crime Laboratories, 2001," BJS, 2002. · *Sting Operations*, COPS, 2007, NCJ 220724. · *Stop Snitching Phenomenon.* COPS, 2009, NCJ 226881. · *Strengthening Forensic Science in the U.S.*, NIJ-Sp., 2009, NCJ 228091. · Study of factors in police use of force cited in *Journal of Police Science & Administration*, Northwestern U. School of Law, 3/1981. · Sullivan, T. "Police Experiences with Recording Custodial Interrogations," Northwestern: Center on Wrongful Convictions, No. 1, Summer, 2004. · "Threat & Humiliation." NY: Amnesty Int., 2004. · "2007 DNA Evidence & Offender Analysis Measurement," NIJ-Sp., 1/2010, NCJ 230328. · Warden, R. *et al.* *True Stories of False Confessions.* Northwestern UP, 2009. · Weiser, B. "In New Jersey, Rules Are Changed on Witness IDs," *NY Times*, 8/25/2011. · Weitzer, R. *et al.* *Rethinking Minority Attitudes toward the Police*, Wash., DC: NIJ, 2004. · Wilson, J. *et al.* "Making Neighborhoods Safe," *Atlantic*, 2/1989. · ___, "The Police & Neighborhoods Safety," *Atlantic*, 3/1982. · "Women in Law Enforcement, 1987–2008," BJS, 2010, NCJ 230521. · Zalman, M. *Criminal Procedure.* 6th ed. Boston: Prentice Hall, 2011.

Unit 3
THE CRIMINAL CASE

On July 6, shots ring out in a quiet residential community. A human life is taken and a suspect arrested . . . .

So begins the criminal case of *People v. Evans*. Although fictional, it is like real-life events that take place each day in cities and towns throughout the United States. There is only one important difference.

This time, you and your class will be on the scene from beginning to end – and not just as observers. You will step into the roles of lawyers, judges, and jurors in a criminal case. You will study the police report, meet the defendant and hear his side of the story, help the prosecutors prepare their case, rule on motions, and select a jury. Eventually, you will see the trial itself unfold and participate in finding the truth about the events on that hot July evening. Ultimately, your actions and decisions will take the case to a final verdict. When you are finished, you will have taken a behind-the-scenes look at how the criminal justice system handles a criminal case and the philosophies and procedures that shape the system.

CHAPTER 10
COURTS AND THE CASE PROCESS

Trial courts search for truth and appellate courts search for error.
– Saying

THE TWO SYSTEMS OF CRIMINAL COURTS | SPECIAL COURTS
JUDGES AND JUDICIAL INDEPENDENCE | CRIMINAL LAWYERS
THE RIGHTS OF CRIMINAL DEFENDANTS | THE CRIMINAL CASE PROCESS | USING THIS UNIT

The Two Systems of Criminal Courts

But there is one way in this country in which all men are created equal — there is one human institution that makes a pauper the equal of a Rockefeller, the stupid man the equal of an Einstein, and the ignorant man the equal of any college president. That institution, gentlemen, is a court. It can be the Supreme Court of the United States or the humblest J.P. court in the land, or this honorable court which you serve. Our courts have their faults, as does any human institution, but in this country our courts are the great levelers, and in our courts all men are created equal.

– Harper Lee, *To Kill a Mockingbird* (1960)

In the United States, the criminal courts belong to two separate systems — the state and federal. The state courts try defendants charged with state crimes and the federal system deals with those charged with federal crimes. Far more criminal trials take place in state courts, because states have traditionally handled most criminal offenses. In recent years, however, the federal government has created more federal crimes and, as a consequence, has increased the workload of the federal courts.

The Federal Courts

The federal court system consists of three basic levels. On the first level are the District Courts, which handle trials in the federal system.

A single judge presides over a criminal trial. The Sixth Amendment to the U.S. Constitution gives every criminal defendant the right to a trial by jury. For many criminal trials, defendants choose to have a jury, but often they waive this right and let the judge hear the case alone. In jury trials, the jury listens to testimony by witnesses and views other evidence presented. The judge rules on the law — ruling what evidence can be admitted, ruling on different motions from defense and prosecution, and instructing the jury on the law in the case.

If a defendant is convicted in a federal trial court, the defendant may appeal to the next level of courts — the U.S. Courts of Appeals. There are 13 of these courts, each usually having jurisdiction over a particular part of the United States. Each court has from six to 30 judges. The courts normally hear appeals in panels of three judges.

Appeals courts, also known as **appellate courts**, do not try cases. They review what the trial court has done and rule on matters of law. They rely on the record of evidence presented in the trial court and usually receive written legal arguments, known as briefs, from attorneys for

Criminal Court Systems	
STATE	**FEDERAL**
State Supreme Court	U.S. Supreme Court
Intermediate Court of Appeal	Circuit Court of Appeals
State Trial Court	District Court
The federal judicial system, and most state systems, have three levels of courts.	

the prosecution and defense. In cases that concern important legal issues, an appeals court might also receive *amicus curiae* (friend of the court) briefs from groups interested in the outcome. The appeals court often hears oral arguments from both sides. Then the judges retire and discuss the case among themselves. They vote and one judge is assigned to write the **opinion of the court**, which states the facts of the case, the issue, the court's decision (known as the **holding**), and the reasons for the holding. If a judge disagrees with the holding, he or she may write a **dissenting opinion**. Sometimes judges may also write **concurring opinions** when they agree with the holding but disagree with the court's reasoning or want to add something that is not in the opinion of the court.

On the highest level is the nine-member U.S. Supreme Court. It hears appeals from the prosecution or defense on federal appellate court decisions. It also can hear appeals of state supreme courts' decisions on issues of U.S. constitutional law.

The U.S. Supreme Court has what is known as discretionary jurisdiction. This means that the court does not have to take every appeal. Parties must petition to have their appeals heard by the court. If four of the nine justices agree that the court should hear a case, then the court grants what is called a **writ of certiorari**, and the court will hear the appeal. The court grants few appeals. Of the thousands of petitions filed each year, the Supreme Court typically grants fewer than 100.

In making their decisions, appeals courts and ultimately the U.S. Supreme Court interpret what the Constitution and other federal laws mean. Decisions can actually overturn laws if the court believes they conflict with the Constitution. Their written opinions add to the body of law.

The State Systems

Each state has its own criminal court system. Many states have two types of trial courts — courts of limited and unlimited jurisdiction. Courts of limited jurisdiction try only misdemeanors and lesser offenses. They may also hold pretrial felony hearings. They are often called municipal, magistrate, or police courts. Courts of unlimited jurisdiction commonly hear felony cases. Depending on the state, these courts are usually called superior, district, circuit, or general-sessions courts.

If convicted, defendants may appeal their cases to appellate courts. Most states have two levels of appeals courts — an intermediate level and the state supreme court. But some states have only a state supreme court. Like the U.S. Supreme Court, many state supreme courts have discretionary jurisdiction. They choose which cases they will hear by granting writs of certiorari.

If a state supreme court hears an appeal, it has the last word on interpretations of state law and the state constitution. Defendants cannot appeal further unless they charge violations of the U.S. Constitution. Then they may ask the U.S. Supreme Court to hear their cases.

FOR DISCUSSION
1. "We don't have two systems of criminal justice. We have 51." Do you agree? Explain.
2. What is discretionary jurisdiction? Why do you think the U.S. Supreme Court and many state supreme courts have this type of jurisdiction?
3. Under what circumstances could the U.S. Supreme Court overrule a state supreme court's interpretation of its state's law? Explain.

Special Courts

By giving addicts a sustained period of sobriety and the tools to help maintain that sobriety, drug courts . . . save money that would otherwise be spent on health care, prisons and law enforcement.

– Judge Peter Anderson, "Treatment With Teeth" (2003)

In 1899, a special court opened in Chicago for juvenile offenders. As you will learn in Unit 5, this court eventually spread to other jurisdictions and expanded into a separate justice system for juvenile offenders. Today, each state has a separate juvenile justice system.

In recent decades, other special courts have opened for particular offenders and offenses. Some are experimental, and others are more fully developed. All are being closely examined to see whether they are effective.

Drug Courts

Drugs are often related to crime. Many offenders are on drugs when they commit crimes, and a large percentage of people in prison are there on drug-related charges. Drug courts are designed with the goals of rehabilitating offenders, reducing their substance abuse, and lowering the number of repeat offenders.

First established in 1989 in Florida, drug courts divert non-violent substance-abusing offenders from prison and jail into treatment. Combining treatment services with comprehensive supervision by courts, the programs attempt to break the cycle of addiction, criminal behavior, and incarceration. Programs usually last between six months to one year, and participants must complete the entire program, attending frequent court hearings and remaining drug- and arrest-free.

To be eligible for drug court, defendants typically must be charged with drug possession or a non-violent offense and must have tested positive for drugs or have a history of addiction. Courts generally follow two models: deferred prosecution programs (defendants are diverted into the drug court system prior to pleading to a charge) and post-adjudication programs (defendants plead guilty and enter the program while their sentences are deferred or suspended). Judges are less formal and frequently interact with participants. They also

can offer incentives or penalize offenders, when necessary.

Thus far, studies have shown that drug courts save money and reduce recidivism (repeat offending). In some counties, the aggregate cost savings exceed $7 to $9 million per year. Today, more than 2,000 drug courts operate in all 50 states. More than 120,000 people are treated annually in drug courts.

Mental Health Courts

Many defendants and people in prisons are mentally ill. The insanity defense is rarely successful, and the criminal justice system must deal with mentally ill offenders. Mental health courts focus on criminal defendants who have mental disabilities.

The first mental health court began in the 1980s in Indiana. Judge Evan Dee Goodman set up a court at Wishard Memorial Hospital. In addition to arranging inpatient treatment, Judge Goodman often diverted defendants into outpatient treatment. Mental health courts began to spread across the United States, and today, more than 120 mental health courts exist.

The staff of a mental health court usually includes a judge, prosecutor, public defender, probation officers, and case managers from the mental health treatment system. Courts typically establish criteria for what types of mental health issues and crimes the court will consider. To be accepted into a program, participants must agree to plead guilty and to undergo treatment. After a length of treatment is determined, case managers usually connect participants with treatment services in the community. The treatment services vary widely, depending on each individual's needs and the community resources available. The court monitors each person's progress, and the offender must strictly adhere to the program's requirements or face sanctions, such as jail time.

So far, studies show that participants have lower rates of new criminal charges while under court supervision than individuals with mental illnesses who go through the traditional court system. Participants also have lower rates of recidivism after one year, and their mental health shows improvement. No studies have found that participants are more likely to be re-arrested.

In 2004, Congress passed the Mentally Ill Offender Treatment and Crime Reduction Act. It lets the U.S. attorney general provide grants to state and local governments for mental health courts.

Veterans Courts

With the recent wars in Afghanistan and Iraq, many veterans are returning home and trying to adjust to civilian life. Studies estimate that between 20 and 50 percent of these veterans may suffer from post-traumatic stress disorder (PTSD) and other mental disorders. PTSD is particularly difficult to deal with, and men and women trained for combat often deny even having it. Many try to self-medicate with alcohol and drugs, and some end up in trouble with the law.

Judge Robert Russell launched the first veterans court in Buffalo, New York, in 2008. The program is intended to give veterans with PTSD, brain trauma or chemical dependency a path toward recovery without forcing them to serve a sentence. Veterans plead guilty to the crime but have the sentence stayed, pending completion of the program. After an initial screening and assessment by the court, they are placed in a treatment program geared to veterans. Volunteer mentors support and monitor the participants to make sure they adhere to a strict schedule of rehabilitation programs and court appearances. Compliance is monitored through these regularly scheduled court hearings, during which participants can be sanctioned for noncompliance or rewarded for their success. As a result, so far 90 percent of participants complete the program, and the recidivism rate is zero.

The idea behind the Buffalo's Veterans Court has spread. Today, more than 50 veterans courts operate in 20 states.

Concerns and Criticism

Special courts can offer reduced burdens on taxpayers, keep families united, and promote public safety. Many critics urge caution to see what further studies say about the benefits of these courts. Also, since the courts offer defendants a chance to avoid punishment, questions arise over whether the courts should only permit misdemeanor offenders or non-violent offenders to participate. Many courts do limit participants in this way, but others allow felony offenders. Other critics object to the special treatment these courts provide. They believe for equal justice, all offenders should be treated the same.

FOR DISCUSSION
1. How are these special courts similar? Different?
2. What benefits do you see? Drawbacks? Do you think each is a good idea? Explain.

Judges and Judicial Independence

It is essential to the preservation of the rights of every individual, his life, liberty, property, and character, that there be an impartial interpretation of the laws, and administration of justice. It is the right of every citizen to be tried by judges as free, impartial, and independent as the lot of humanity will admit.
– Massachusetts Constitution of 1780, pt. 1, art. 29

Judges are expected to be neutral and fair in deciding cases.

When trial judges preside over criminal trials, they make many legal rulings: Should this evidence be admitted? Should that objection be sustained? What law applies to this case? On appeals, appellate court judges review these rulings. All judges — trial and appellate — are supposed to be fair and impartial. When judges interpret and apply the law, they must base their decisions on statutes, Constitutional law, and prior court cases. They must never be swayed by politics or popular opinion. This is what is meant by the rule of law. Our democracy depends on an independent judiciary.

The U.S. Constitution attempts to ensure judicial independence. All federal judges are appointed by the president, confirmed by the U.S. Senate, and serve for life. There is only one way under the Constitution that federal judges can be removed: The U.S. House of Representatives can vote to impeach any federal judge for "treason, bribery or other high crimes or misdemeanors." The judge is then tried by the Senate. To remove the judge, two-thirds of the Senate must vote to convict. Only 14 federal judges in our history have been impeached by the House and just eight convicted by the Senate. All have been convicted for criminal or inappropriate behavior. None has ever been convicted for making unpopular decisions or for holding an unpopular judicial philosophy.

State Judges

Most judges in the United States are not members of the federal judiciary. Most belong to the various state courts, which differ in how they select judges.

About 20 states hold direct elections for judges. This means that judges run for office. This allows voters to elect judges in their district, but it has drawbacks. Judges must raise money for campaigns, often from lawyers who will appear before them. That can give the appearance that lawyers are paying for favoritism. Judicial campaigns in themselves are problematic. Judges can't make campaign promises that they will rule in a certain way. That would make the judge biased. Bringing judges into the political process can make them seem less neutral in the courtroom.

For these reasons, most states have moved away from direct election of judges. In these states, the judges are appointed. In a few states, the governor or legislature makes the appointments. In more than 20 states, however, the governor makes selections from a list prepared by a judicial commission, which searches for the most qualified judicial candidates.

Most of these states, however, still require judges to face voters. Appellate judges usually go on the ballot in the next general election after being appointed. These are called retention elections because voters get to decide whether or not to retain the judges. No opposing candidates appear on the ballot. Voters must choose "yes" or "no." If voters retain them, the judges serve a set term, usually 12 years. At the end of their term in office, they may again stand for election. Trial judges also go before the voters in the next general election after their appointment. But their terms are shorter, typically six years. And in some states, opponents can run against them.

In addition, in many states, voters can recall judges that they believe do not belong on the bench. People opposing a judge must get a certain number of signatures on recall petitions. Then the judge's name is put on the ballot and voters decide whether they want to retain or recall the judge. If a majority votes to recall the judge, then the judge must be replaced — either by election or appointment, depending on the state.

The appointment system generally has shielded judges from politics. It allows judges to serve long terms with a limited degree of accountability to voters. And judges are retained in the vast majority of these elections. But in recent years, some recall and retention elections have provoked controversy. Some elections have even seen special interest groups mounting campaigns against judges. The late

Bernard Witkin, a noted legal scholar, warned:
> What we're seeing is a new way to approach judicial elections, challenging judges' qualifications on the basis of particular decisions that affect particular groups. . . . If we reach the point where . . . we end up telling the court, "If you don't do as we want, we'll remove you," then the courts won't be worth saving.

FOR DISCUSSION

1. What is judicial independence? Why is it important?
2. What are the differences between the way state and federal judges are selected and removed?
3. What do you think the best system of selecting and removing judges would be? Why?

CLASS ACTIVITY

Retention Election

In this activity, students take the role of voters in a state retention election for several justices of the Supreme Court, the highest appeals court in the state.
1. Form small groups. In each group, students should:
   a. Discuss each of the justices described below.
   b. Decide whether to vote "yes" to retain or "no" to remove each justice.
   c. Prepare to report each decision and the reasons for it to the class.
2. After the groups have made their decisions, they should report back and discuss each justice, indicating the reasons for voting to retain or not. Conclude the activity by holding a discussion using the debriefing questions.

Justices

All the justices have much experience as both lawyers and judges and have served at least one term of 12 years. The State Bar Association rates each as "highly qualified," the highest ranking. Each of the justices has drawn some public criticism for the incidents related below.

Justice #1: Joyce Harris. Justice Harris wrote the majority opinion last term overturning the conviction of a defendant accused of child molestation. The court ruled that police had illegally seized evidence. Without this evidence, prosecutors say they will be unable to retry the defendant.

Justice #2: Samuel Grodin. In the last 12 capital punishment appeals before the court, Justice Grodin has voted to overturn the death sentence nine times. Despite Justice Grodin's votes, the court upheld all 12 death sentences.

Justice #3: John Chen. Justice Chen is known as a law-and-order conservative. He rarely votes against death sentences or against overturning any case on the grounds that police did not conduct a proper search or interrogation.

Debriefing Questions

1. Review the reasons people gave for retaining or not. What do you think are valid reasons for voting for and against judges? Why?
2. Did you have enough information to vote? If not, what additional information would you need?

Criminal Lawyers

Any culture that has had its Jeffersons, Lincolns, and Darrows also must have a healthy notion of the lawyer's role in society.
— Matthew A. Hodel, trial attorney, *ABA Journal* (1991)

Lawyers are highly educated professionals. To become lawyers, students typically must graduate from a four-year college and complete three years of law school (obtaining a juris doctorate, or J.D., degree). After law school, they must pass a bar examination in the state in which they want to practice law. This is usually a two to three day examination on all aspects of the law. In addition, almost every state requires that they pass the Multistate Professional Responsibility Examination (MPRE). They also must undergo background checks, and those with criminal records must be cleared and found fit to practice law by a state bar committee. Once they pass the bar exam, MPRE, and background checks, they may practice law in the state. Members in good standing of a state bar may apply to be admitted to practice before federal courts as well.

Although members of the bar may practice in all areas of the law, few general practitioners exist today. Most specialize in one area — corporations, labor relations, real estate, wills and trusts, taxation, personal injury, civil litigation, and other fields. Few practice criminal law, probably less than 5 percent of all attorneys. The criminal bar is divided into prosecutors and defense attorneys.

Prosecutors

Prosecutors are government employees. They represent the public and present the government's case against the defendant in criminal cases. At trial, the prosecutor must prove the defendant's guilt beyond a reasonable doubt.

At the federal level, prosecutors work out of about 90 U.S. attorney offices across the country. Each office is headed by a U.S. attorney, appointed by the president and confirmed by the Senate. U.S. attorneys serve under the U.S. attorney general, the cabinet member who heads the Department of Justice.

Since most criminal prosecutions take place in state criminal courts, there are thousands of prosecutor offices for cities, counties, and states. Most are headed by an elected state, district, or city attorney. In rural areas, the

The criminal justice system depends on attorneys to vigorously prosecute and defend cases.

prosecutor's office may consist of one lawyer. The nation's 75 largest counties, however, account for more than half of all prosecutions. Los Angeles County has the largest office, with almost 1,000 deputy district attorneys and an annual budget of more than $300 million. Large offices have specialized units for prosecuting cases involving drugs, juveniles, child abuse, homicide, domestic violence, gangs, career criminals, arson, and white-collar crime.

Aside from presenting cases, prosecutors must decide whether to bring charges, what the charges are, and whether to change or drop charges. They are officers of the court, which means they have a duty to protect the integrity of the justice system.

All jurisdictions have professional codes of professional responsibility for lawyers. Most of them are based on the Model Rules of Professional Conduct of the American Bar Association (ABA), the leading organization of lawyers. This code states that the prosecutor

has the responsibility of a minister of justice and not simply that of an advocate. This responsibility carries with it specific obligations to see that the defendant is accorded procedural justice, that guilt is

CHARACTERISTICS OF PUBLIC DEFENDERS OFFICES

Types of Offices	Number of States	Population Served	Number of Cases Received	Number of Offices	Number of Litigating Attorneys	Total Expenditure
U.S. Total	50	240 million	5.6 million	957	15,026	$2.3 billion
State-based	22	73 million	1.5 million	427	4,321	$833 million
County-based	28	167 million	4 million	530	10,705	$1.5 billion

All states have public defender offices. Some are run at the county level and others by the state.

Source: "County-based and Local Public Defender Offices, 2007," Bureau of Justice Statistics (2010)

decided upon the basis of sufficient evidence, and that special precautions are taken to prevent and to rectify the conviction of innocent persons.

This means that they must only prosecute those they believe are guilty. In addition, they must turn over to the defense any evidence that tends to exculpate, or clear, a defendant. (*Brady v. Maryland*, 1963)

Further, prosecutors must not argue in bad faith. In the 2005 case of *In re Sakarias*, Sakarias and an accomplice, Waidla, were accused of committing a brutal murder. Tried separately, each was convicted of first-degree murder and sentenced to death. At Waidla's trial, the prosecutor argued that Waidla had struck the fatal blows with the hatchet. But at Sakarias' trial, the same prosecutor argued that Sakarias had struck the fatal blows with the hatchet. The California Supreme Court reversed Sakarias' conviction and ordered a new trial. The court stated: "By intentionally and in bad faith seeking a conviction or death sentence for two defendants on the basis of culpable acts for which only one could be responsible, the People violate 'the due process requirement that the government prosecute fairly in a search for truth . . . .' "

Defense Attorneys

Defense attorneys prepare and present defendants' cases at pretrial hearings, at trial, and on appeal. The U.S. Supreme Court has also ruled that a criminal defendant has the right to have a lawyer present at any interrogation (*Escobedo v. Illinois*, 1964) and post-indictment lineup (*U.S. v. Wade*, 1967). To present defendants' versions of the facts, defense attorneys try to find supportive witnesses and call them to testify at trial. They attempt to raise reasonable doubts about defendants' guilt and may present affirmative defenses.

Defense attorneys can be either private attorneys or public employees. Historically, most defense attorneys were private attorneys who required payment from their clients. If a criminal defendant could not afford a lawyer, then the defendant might have to go to court without one.

A series of U.S. Supreme Court decisions changed this situation and, in the process, changed the defense bar. In 1932 in *Powell v. Alabama*, the Supreme Court ruled that states must supply attorneys for indigent (poor) defendants in death-penalty cases. In 1938 in *Johnson v. Zerbst*, the court ruled that the federal government must provide lawyers for indigent defendants in all federal cases. In 1963 in *Gideon v. Wainright*, the court extended the rule to all felony cases in state courts. In 1972 in *Argersinger v. Hamlin*, the court further extended the rule to any misdemeanor that could result in the defendant spending time in jail. The decisions rested on the Sixth Amendment, which states in part that in "all criminal prosecutions, the accused shall enjoy the right . . . to have the assistance of counsel for his defense." The court reasoned, as Justice Hugo Black wrote in *Gideon*, that "any person hauled into court, who is too poor to hire a lawyer, cannot be assured a fair trial unless counsel is provided for him."

Following these decisions, the defense bar changed. It is no longer dominated by attorneys in private practice. The federal government, states, and counties set up systems to provide counsel to defendants who could not afford private attorneys. One system is the **assigned counsel** system, which is often used in rural areas. A judge appoints private counsel from a list. The lawyers are reimbursed by the government. Another system is **contract counsel**. Private firms under contract with the government provide legal services. The third system, the **public defender**, is the most widely used system. Public defenders work full-time for the government. Their job is to defend indigent defendants. They often work under heavy caseloads.

The public defender system has received criticism on several counts. Some say the heavy caseload causes public defenders to dispose of cases quickly instead of working wholeheartedly for defendants. Others claim that by working day-after-day with the same judges and prosecutors, public defenders may feel that they are on the same team and not vigorously do battle in court.

But many praise the work of public defenders as zealous advocates for their clients. They point out that many public defenders have far more experience and knowledge of the criminal courts than private attorneys, who may not even be specialists in criminal law. They also believe that because public defenders know prosecutors and judges well, they know which tactics and arguments will be most persuasive.

Whether attorneys are public defenders or in private practice, defending people accused of crime is difficult. Many people don't understand the important role defense attorneys play. Questions often arise, such as, "How can they defend those people?" or "How can they defend someone they know is guilty?" The answer is that everyone — guilty or innocent — is entitled to a fair trial.

Our justice system is an adversarial system. For it to work, both the state and defense should have able advocates. The state must prove that a person is guilty beyond a reasonable doubt. This may mean that guilty people will go free, but our system is set up on the old maxim: "Better that 10 guilty persons escape than that one innocent suffer." (This maxim appears in William Blackstone's *Commentaries on the Laws of England*, written in the 1760s.) The entire power of the government — the police and prosecutor's office — is lined up against the defendant. The defense attorney protects the rights of the defendant and in so doing protects the rights of everyone.

The ABA states in its Code of Professional Responsibility that "a lawyer should represent a client zealously within the bounds of the law." In short, an attorney should represent all defendants fully and forcefully.

EGREGIOUS MISCONDUCT

In a 2008 report, the California Commission on the Fair Administration of Justice looked into misconduct by prosecutors and defense attorneys. Overall, it found misconduct was rare, but warned the judges and lawyers should be vigilant and report misconduct, particularly seven types of misconduct the commission labeled as egregious, or obviously wrong.

1. Lying to a court.
2. Appearing in a judicial proceeding while under the influence of illicit drugs or alcohol.
3. Engaging in willful unlawful discrimination in a judicial proceeding.
4. Willful *Brady* violations. [Intentionally not turning over evidence favorable to the defense]
5. Willful presentation of material perjured testimony.
6. Willful unlawful disclosure of victim or witness information.
7. Failure to properly identify oneself in interviewing a victim or witness.

Defense attorneys, like prosecutors, are officers of the court. As the ABA notes, there are limits on what defense lawyers can do. They cannot, for example, advise a client to break the law or put anyone on the witness stand who the lawyer knows will lie. In 1986 in *Nix v. Whiteside*, the Supreme Court was asked to rule on these limits. A defense attorney told his client that if he took the stand and told a false story, the attorney would have to report him to the court. The defendant took the stand and did not lie. He was convicted, but he appealed claiming that his lawyer had denied him effective counsel by forbidding him to commit perjury. The Supreme Court ruled that the attorney had acted properly.

FOR DISCUSSION

1. What does it mean that prosecutors and defense attorneys are "officers of the court"?

2. Do you think defense attorneys should defend people they know are guilty? Why or why not?

3. Do you think indigent criminal defendants should be provided lawyers? Explain.

4. In 1979 in *Scott v. Illinois*, the Supreme Court refused to overturn the misdemeanor shoplifting conviction of a man who was tried without a defense attorney because he could not afford one. The statute he was convicted under authorized up to a year in jail but the trial judge sentenced him to pay a $50 fine. The Supreme Court ruled 6–3 that since the judge imposed no prison time, the sentence could stand. Do you agree with this decision? Explain.

5. The California Commission on the Fair Administration of Justice listed seven examples of egregious misconduct. Which do you think is the worst? Why?

CLASS ACTIVITY

Prosecutorial Misconduct

Most prosecutors and defense attorneys perform their jobs professionally and competently. But allegations of misconduct sometimes arise. In this activity, students examine cases that the defense appealed on grounds of prosecutorial misconduct.

1. Divide the class into small groups.
2. Each group should read and discuss the three cases. For each case, the group should discuss and answer these questions:
    a. What do you think the defense is alleging as prosecutorial misconduct?
    b. Do you think it is misconduct? Why or why not?
    c. If you think it is misconduct, then . . .
        (1) Should the prosecutor be penalized? Explain.
        (2) Do you think that based on the misconduct the defendant deserves a new trial (or sentencing hearing in Case #3)? Explain.
3. Regroup and ask the groups to report their answers. Hold a class discussion on each case.

Cases

1. *U.S. v. Sanchez* (2011). Arturo Sanchez was on trial for transporting cocaine across the border. Sanchez admitted to transporting drugs, but claimed he did it under duress. On the witness stand, Sanchez testified he had carried the drugs only because a Mexican drug cartel had threatened to hurt his family if he did not. The prosecutor ended his closing argument to the jury with this sarcastic statement:

> [W]hy don't we send a memo to all drug traffickers, to all persons south of the border and in . . . California — why not our nation while we're at it. Send a memo to them and say dear drug traffickers, when you hire someone to drive a load, tell them that they were forced to do it. Because . . . they'll get away with it if they just say their family was threatened. Because they don't trust Mexican police, and they don't think that the U.S. authorities can help them. Why don't we do that?

Sanchez was convicted.

(Continued on next page.)

2. *Bordenkircher v. Hayes* (1978). Paul Lewis Hayes was indicted by a Kentucky grand jury for passing a forged check in the amount of $88.30. He and his attorney met with the prosecutor seeking a plea agreement. If convicted on the charge, Hayes faced a prison term of two to 10 years. The prosecutor offered him a five-year sentence if he would plead guilty. He also said that if Hayes did not plead guilty and "save the court the inconvenience and necessity of a trial," he would go back to the grand jury and ask it to indict Hayes under the Kentucky Habitual Criminal Act, under which Hayes would face a life sentence if convicted because of his previous felony convictions. Hayes rejected the plea bargain, and the prosecutor returned to the grand jury and had Hayes indicted under the Kentucky Habitual Criminal Act. Hayes was convicted and sentenced to life.

3. *Coe v. Bell* (1998). Coe was convicted of a brutal rape and murder. At the sentencing hearing, the prosecutor made the following statement in arguing for the death penalty:

> I'm not a biblical scholar, ladies and gentlemen, and I don't pretend to be. But I would simply emphasize to you that the whole cornerstone of our law, the law of this land, the law of society is based upon those scriptures where it was established from, and the Bible and the scriptures themselves are replete with those circumstances where capital punishment has been applied. It's applied in reference to both the Old Testament and the New Testament. Whosoever sheddeth man's blood, by man shall his blood be shed. Terms are mentioned regularly throughout the Old and the New. And I just want to ask you to put your mind at rest if that in any way has created any conflict because there's certainly foundation for capital punishment in the Bible and in the scriptures themselves.

The jury sentenced Coe to death.

The Rights of Criminal Defendants

No freemen shall be taken or imprisoned or disseised or exiled or in any way destroyed, nor will we go upon him nor send upon him, except by the lawful judgment of his peers or by the law of the land.
– Chapter 39 of the Magna Carta (1215)

The chart on page 165 lists the constitutional rights and protections that criminal defendants have. Other parts of this book have explained many of them. We will briefly touch on those protections discussed elsewhere in the book and explain in more detail those not mentioned elsewhere.

Habeas Corpus

Most of the rights and protections are in the Bill of Rights, the first 10 amendments to the U.S. Constitution. But several are in the body of the Constitution itself. Article I, Section 9, guarantees the privilege of the writ of habeas corpus. The word "writ" comes from English common law. It means a court order. "Habeas corpus" in Latin literally means "you have the body." A writ of habeas corpus is a court order to an official (a prison warden or a military commander) holding someone in custody. It orders the official to deliver the person to the court. The writ allows the court to decide whether the person is being held illegally, and if so, to order the executive branch to release the prisoner. Many criminal appeals, especially death-penalty cases, are petitions for a writ of habeas corpus.

Ex Post Facto Laws

The Constitution bans ex post facto laws. An ex post facto law is a law that punishes someone for an act committed before the law came into effect. For example, imagine that Jay climbs a tree in front of the Capitol building. It is not against the law to do this, but Congress passes a law saying that it is now, and was then, against the law. This would be an ex post facto law.

The 1798 Supreme Court case of *Calder v. Bull* explained the four types of ex post facto laws:

1. "Every law that makes an action, done before the passing of the law, and which was innocent when done, criminal; and punishes such action."

2. "Every law that aggravates a crime, or makes it greater than it was, when committed."
3. "Every law that changes the punishment, and inflicts a greater punishment, than the law annexed to the crime, when committed."
4. "Every law that alters the legal rules of evidence, and receives less, or different, testimony, than the law required at the time of the commission of the offence, in order to convict the offender."

In 2003, the U.S. Supreme Court ruled that the ban on ex post facto laws applied to statutes of limitations. Most crimes, except murder, have a statute of limitations setting a time limit on when criminal charges may be filed. California extended its limit on child molestation cases and prosecuted a case that had been banned under the old statute of limitations. The Supreme Court in *Stogner v. California* ruled that this case violated the ex post facto clause.

Bills of Attainder

The Constitution also prohibits bills of attainder. A bill of attainder is an act by a legislature imposing punishment on an individual or group without the benefit of a court trial. For example, if a state legislature passed a law imposing a fine on a specific individual for polluting a stream, this would be a bill of attainder.

In 1943, Congress passed the Urgent Deficiency Appropriation Act. Its Section 304 excluded several federal workers, specifically named in the law, from receiving any money from the government. Congress believed these workers were disloyal to the U.S. In *U.S. v. Lovett*, the U.S. Supreme Court struck down this law as a bill of attainder:

Section 304 . . . accomplishes the punishment of named individuals without a judicial trial. The fact that the punishment is inflicted through the instrumentality of an Act specifically cutting off the pay of certain named individuals found guilty of disloyalty makes it no less galling or effective than if it had been done by an Act which designated the conduct as criminal.

Searches and Seizures

The Fourth Amendment bans unreasonable searches and seizures. If police violate a defendant's Fourth Amendment rights and illegally seize evidence, it may not be introduced at trial.

Grand Jury

The Fifth Amendment contains several important protections. One of them requires that anyone held for a federal felony must be indicted by a grand jury. A grand jury is a group of citizens charged with determining whether the prosecution has probable cause that the defendant committed a crime. It meets in secret, and the prosecutor presents evidence to it. If it decides that probable cause exists, it indicts the defendant. In 1884 in *Hurtado v. California*, the U.S. Supreme Court decided that states do not have to use a grand jury as long as they provide the defendant with a hearing determining probable cause.

CONSTITUTIONAL PROTECTIONS

Article 1, Section 9
　　Writ of habeas corpus
　　No bills of attainder
　　No ex post facto laws

Article 3, Section 1
　　Jury trial*

Fourth Amendment
　　No unreasonable searches or seizures

Fifth Amendment
　　Indictment by a grand jury
　　No double jeopardy
　　No self-incrimination
　　Due process**

Sixth Amendment
　　Speedy trial
　　Public trial
　　Impartial jury*
　　Notice of any accusation
　　Confrontation of witnesses
　　Compel witnesses to testify
　　Assistance of counsel

Eighth Amendment
　　No excessive bail
　　No excessive fines
　　No cruel and unusual punishments

14th Amendment
　　Equality under the law
　　Due process**

*The right to a jury trial in a criminal case is protected by both Article 3 and the Sixth Amendment.
**Due process is guaranteed by both the Fifth and 14th amendments.

Double Jeopardy

Another Fifth Amendment protection is against double jeopardy. It basically means that if a defendant is found not guilty of a crime, then the state cannot retry the defendant for the same crime.

In 2005 in *Smith v. Massachusetts*, the U.S. Supreme Court ruled on a question of double jeopardy. Smith was charged with armed assault with intent to murder, assault with a dangerous weapon, and possessing a firearm. When the prosecution rested its case, the defendant asked the trial court to dismiss the firearm charge. One element of the firearm charge was that the gun had a barrel less than 16 inches in length. The defense noted that the state had not introduced evidence of the barrel's length. The prosecution had introduced testimony that the gun was a .32 caliber pistol. The judge ruled that this was not sufficient evidence of the barrel's length and acquitted the defendant of the charge. When the defense rested, the prosecution showed the judge a case holding that evidence of the type of gun was sufficient to prove the barrel's length. The judge reinstated the charge, and the jury found him guilty of it. On appeal, the Supreme Court ruled 5–4 that when the judge acquitted the defendant, this was a final determination, and the defendant could not be tried again.

There are many examples of a defendant being tried twice for the same crime that are not cases of double jeopardy. When judges declare mistrials, such as when a jury cannot agree on a verdict, defendants can be retried. When defendants appeal their cases and win, they can be tried again. For example, if an appeals court rules that the trial court erred in admitting certain evidence and reverses the defendant's conviction, the prosecution can retry the defendant.

When state and the federal laws outlaw the same conduct, both may prosecute a person for that conduct. In 1922 in *U.S. v. Lanza*, the U.S. Supreme Court ruled that this was not double jeopardy. The court said: "We have here two sovereignties, deriving power from different sources, capable of dealing with the same subject-matter within the same territory."

Double jeopardy does not stop a criminal defendant from being sued in a civil lawsuit. For example, if a CEO is found not guilty of fraud in a criminal trial, the government could not charge him again for the same crime. But private parties could still file lawsuits against the CEO asking for money damages.

Self-Incrimination

The Fifth Amendment also protects against self-incrimination. The courts have ruled that a criminal defendant does not have to talk to police. Nor can a prosecutor force the defendant to testify. In fact, the U.S. Supreme Court has ruled that the prosecutor may not comment "on the accused's silence" and the judge may not instruct the jury that "such silence is evidence of guilt." (*Griffin v. California*, 1965)

Jury Trial

Written before the Bill of Rights was added, Article 3, Section 1, of the U.S. Constitution guarantees the right to a jury in all criminal trials. The Sixth Amendment details many of the protections criminal defendants have at trial.

Impartial Jury

One Sixth Amendment guarantee is an impartial jury. In *Duncan v. Louisiana* (1968), the Supreme Court explained that a jury, composed of fellow citizens, is a "safeguard against the corrupt overzealous prosecutor and against the compliant, biased, or eccentric judge."

To ensure that a jury is impartial, the judge and attorneys question prospective jurors. To keep publicity from prejudicing a jury, a judge may sequester (or isolate) the jury, move the trial to another place, continue (or delay) the trial, or even impose a gag order on attorneys to prevent them from trying the case in the media. In 1966 in *Sheppard v. Maxwell*, the Supreme Court reversed the murder conviction of a doctor in Cleveland, Ohio. The trial judge had done little to weed out prejudiced jurors or to shield the jury from the media circus that took place during the trial. The Supreme Court held that when there is a "reasonable likelihood" that a fair trial will not occur, judges must act to protect their courts from outside influence.

Speedy Trial

Another Sixth Amendment protection is a "speedy . . . trial." The Supreme Court has set no definite time limit on when trials must begin, but it determines whether defendants have received a speedy trial on a case-by-case basis. In 1972 in *Barker v. Wingo*, the court stated that it would look at four factors: (1) the "length of delay," (2) "the reason for the

Time From Arrest to Adjudication for Felony Defendants

Most serious arrest charge	Median number of days
All offenses	92
Violent offenses	139
Murder	364
Rape	228
Robbery	144
Assault	121
Other violent	141
Property offenses	85
Burglary	86
Theft	92
Motor vehicle theft	61
Forgery	80
Fraud	92
Other property	74
Drug offenses	75
Trafficking	112
Other drug	50
Public-order offenses	92
Weapons	88
Driving-related	114
Other public order	80

Source: "Felony Defendants in Large Urban Counties, 2006," Bureau of Justice Statistics (2010)

delay," (3) whether the defendant demanded a speedy trial, and (4) harm to the defendant especially from "oppressive pretrial incarceration," "anxiety and concern," and impairing the defense. Most states have speedy trial statutes setting forth time limits on holding trials (and reasons why the limits may be broken, such as the defense requested the delay).

Public Trial

The Sixth Amendment also guarantees a "public trial." Open trials prevent the government from secretly taking away people and trying them. It lets everyone examine whether a fair trial is taking place.

The Supreme Court has held that the right does not just belong to a criminal defendant. The press and public have a right to attend trials. The Supreme Court has held that in rare instances trials may be closed. In 1984 in *Waller v. Georgia*, the court stated that "the right to an open trial may give way in certain cases to other rights or interests, such as the defendant's right to a fair trial or the government's interest in inhibiting disclosure of sensitive information. Such circumstances will be rare, however, and the balance of interests must be struck with special care."

Notice of the Accusation

The Sixth Amendment also gives defendants the right to be informed of the charges against them. Unless they know the charges, defendants cannot prepare a defense.

The charges must state clearly what the crime is. The Supreme Court held in 1881 in *U.S. v. Carll* that it is not enough for an indictment to "set forth the offense in the words of the statute, unless those words of themselves fully, directly, and expressly, without any uncertainty or ambiguity, set forth all the elements necessary to constitute the offense intended to be punished." In the 1948 case of *Cole v. Arkansas*, the Supreme Court stated that "notice of the specific charge, and a chance to be heard in a trial of the issues raised by that charge, if desired, are among the constitutional rights of every accused in a criminal proceeding in all courts, state or federal."

Confrontation of Witnesses

The Sixth Amendment also gives defendants the right to question witnesses testifying against them.

In 2004, the Supreme Court decided a confrontation case in *Crawford v. Washington*. Crawford was tried for assault and attempted murder for stabbing a man who allegedly had raped his wife. Crawford claimed it was self-defense, but his wife had given a somewhat contradictory statement to police. Under Washington law, the prosecution could not call his wife to testify. So the prosecution introduced the wife's tape-recorded statement. Crawford challenged this evidence saying it violated his right to confront all witnesses.

A unanimous Supreme Court sided with Crawford. It stated that the trial court had admitted the wife's statement against the defendant even though "he had no opportunity to cross-examine her. That alone is sufficient to make out a violation of the Sixth Amendment."

Compel Witnesses to Testify

The Sixth Amendment gives defendants the right to compel others to testify at the trial.

This is normally done with a subpoena, a court order served on a witness. If the witness fails to comply with the subpoena, the witness can be held in contempt of court and jailed.

Defendants need this power in order to present a defense. The Supreme Court explained the need for defendants to compel witnesses in the 1967 case of *Washington v. Texas*:

> The right to offer the testimony of witnesses, and to compel their attendance, if necessary, is in plain terms the right to present a defense, the right to present the defendant's version of the facts . . . . Just as an accused has the right to confront the prosecution's witnesses for the purpose of challenging their testimony, he has the right to present his own witnesses to establish a defense.

Assistance of Counsel

The final right guaranteed by the Sixth Amendment is the right to a lawyer. Lawyers know the law, defendants' rights, and how to try criminal cases. Without the right to a defense attorney, defendants cannot be guaranteed a fair trial. The Supreme Court has ruled that criminal defendants have a right to have a lawyer as soon as they are brought into custody. It has also ruled that the government must supply attorneys for defendants who cannot afford them.

The Supreme Court has also ruled that "the right to counsel is the right to the effective assistance of counsel" (*Strickland v. Washington*, 1984). If a defendant appeals a conviction because of ineffective counsel, the defendant must prove two things:

1. The defense attorney's "representation fell below an objective standard of reasonableness."
2. There "is a reasonable probability that, but for counsel's unprofessional errors, the result of the proceeding would have been different."

Excessive Bail

When defendants are arrested and taken into custody, they often can be released by posting bail, an amount of money that will be returned when the defendant appears for trial. The 1951 Supreme Court case of *Stack v. Boyle* explained the purpose of bail: "This traditional right to freedom before conviction permits the unhampered preparation of a defense, and serves to prevent the infliction of punishment prior to conviction."

The Sixth Amendment gives defendants the right to be represented by an attorney.

The Eighth Amendment requires that bail not be excessive. The court in *Stack* ruled that bail is excessive if it is "set at a figure higher than an amount reasonably calculated to" make sure the accused appears at trial.

The Supreme Court has not interpreted the Eighth Amendment as giving all criminal defendants a right to bail. People accused of murder typically do not receive bail.

The federal Bail Reform Act of 1984 let judges refuse to set bail if the defendant posed a danger to the community. This practice is known as preventive detention, and its opponents claim it punishes people for future acts without trials. The Supreme Court in 1987 in *U.S. v. Salerno* upheld the Bail Reform Act, saying that it had many procedural safeguards to prevent abuse.

Excessive Fines

After a defendant is convicted, a court may impose a fine as a sentence. The Eighth Amendment requires that the fine not be excessive.

The Supreme Court has issued few opinions on excessive fines. One opinion ruled that the excessive-fines clause did not apply to civil lawsuits between private parties.

Another opinion ruled that it did apply to civil asset-forfeiture cases. These are actions taken by the government to seize property involved in criminal activity. In the 1993 case of *Austin v. U.S.*, Austin had been convicted of possessing two grams of cocaine with intent to distribute. He was sentenced to seven years in state prison. Federal agents seized his mobile home and body shop in a civil asset-forfeiture case. The Supreme Court decided that this might be an excessive fine and ordered the trial court to find more facts and rule on the case.

In 1998, the Supreme Court decided *U.S. v. Bajakajian*, Bajakajian was caught at the airport boarding a plane to Italy with $357,144 in cash in his baggage. He was convicted under the federal law against taking more than $10,000 in cash without reporting it. Prosecutors sought to have him forfeit the entire $357,144. The Supreme Court held that this would be an excessive fine "grossly disproportional to the gravity of his offense." The court noted that the money was not related to any illegal activity, and the defendant was carrying it to pay a lawful debt.

Cruel and Unusual Punishments

The Eighth Amendment bans "cruel and unusual punishments."

In 1878 in *Wilkerson v. Utah*, the Supreme Court listed a number of punishments that clearly would be cruel and unusual: torture, disemboweling alive, beheading, drawing and quartering, and burning alive.

Most Supreme Court cases on the Eighth Amendment concern the death penalty. The court has upheld the death penalty. But it has ruled that it is cruel and unusual to exact this punishment on the mentally retarded and on people who were under 18 when they committed the crime. It has also ruled that the death penalty can only be applied to murderers, not lesser offenders.

Equality Under the Law

The 14th Amendment guarantees "equal protection of the laws." It bans discrimination based on race, ethnicity, sex, or religion.

One of the most famous equal protection cases involved a challenge to the death penalty. A statistical study found that blacks in Georgia who had killed whites had been sentenced to death far more often than whites who had killed blacks. In 1987 in *McCleskey v. Kemp*, the Supreme Court in a 5–4 vote found that because the defendant had not proven discrimination in his particular case, the equal protection clause was not violated.

Due Process

Both the Fifth and 14th amendments guarantee "due process of law." "Due process" demands fair procedures and includes all the traditional protections accorded by English common law. It includes each of the rights and protections discussed in this article (and listed on the chart on page 165). It also includes such traditional principles as a person is considered "innocent until proven guilty" and the prosecution must prove a defendant "guilty beyond a reasonable doubt."

FOR DISCUSSION

1. What is a writ of habeas corpus? Why do you think it is important?
2. What is double jeopardy? Do you think *U.S. v. Lanza* was correctly decided? Explain.
3. What is due process of law?

CLASS ACTIVITY

Which Rights Are Most Important?

In this activity, students rank the due process rights.
1. Form small groups.
2. Each group should do the following:
   a. Discuss the rights on the chart on page 165.
   b. Rank what it considers the five most important rights in order of importance. (Exclude due process from the list because it includes all of these rights.)
   c. Be prepared to report its decisions and the reasons for them to the whole class.
3. Regroup the class and have the groups report back. Hold a class discussion on the rankings. Conclude by giving each student five votes and see which rights the class considers most important.

The Criminal Case Process

The trial of a case [is] a three-legged stool — a judge and two advocates.
– U.S. Supreme Court Chief Justice Warren Burger (1907–1995)

Every year, state and federal criminal justice systems handle thousands of criminal cases. Most cases are routine: A crime occurs, and a suspect is identified, arrested, and charged. If the defendant pleads guilty, which most do, a trial does not take place. Aside from realizing that police departments are overworked, courts are overburdened, and prisons are overcrowded, the general public knows little about the daily routine of criminal justice activity.

What does capture public attention is the big case. A sensational murder or a multi-million dollar fraud case can make headlines in our daily newspapers for months. Reporters clamor for interviews with the prosecution and defense teams, TV-news programs detail the day's courtroom events, and the defendant's name becomes a household word.

Although these big cases are not typical, they do give us a dramatic glimpse of the criminal justice process. These cases introduce us to a vast array of courthouse characters, legal terminology, procedural steps, and legal issues. At any point along the way, we might throw up our hands and ask, "What's the point of all this? Did he do it or didn't he do it?" Since no one can read a suspect's mind and no one can peer back into the past to find out exactly what happened, we need some system to find the truth.

The Adversarial System

Central to truth-finding in our criminal case process is the adversarial process. In it, opposing attorneys introduce evidence to neutral fact finders — the judge or jury. Ultimately, the fact finder must decide the facts of a particular case and come to a verdict.

In this process, the attorneys are advocates and adversaries. They try to present facts in a light most favorable to their side and point out weaknesses in their opponents' case. Through well-planned strategies and legal arguments, they try to convince the court to see "truth" as they do. In a criminal case, the opposing sides are the prosecution and the defense.

The basic goal of the prosecution is to protect society from crime by making sure the guilty are tried, convicted, and punished. By filing charges against a particular defendant, the prosecutor is alleging that the individual has committed a crime. At trial, the prosecutor must prove the allegation beyond a reasonable doubt.

The basic goal of the defense is to challenge the prosecutor's case by raising all reasonable doubts about the defendant's guilt. Defense attorneys must also make sure that the defendant gets every relevant right and benefit guaranteed under the law and Constitution.

By pitting these two sides against one another, it is believed that the truth will come out. For example, if the prosecution's robbery case depends on an eyewitness's identification of the defendant, the defense might go to great lengths to question the memory or eyesight of the witness. The defense can be assured of a similar strict examination of any evidence it produces. Under the adversarial system, the judge or jury must decide which version is true.

The fact finder must examine all the evidence produced at trial. Before determining whether or not a defendant is guilty, the fact finder must weigh the evidence and establish facts. Are the witnesses believable? Are the lab tests accurate? Are the connections between the various pieces of evidence logical and supportable? What other explanations for the alleged events are possible? Indeed, the quest for truth pervades a criminal trial.

Because the adversarial process involves humans, it is not foolproof. Memories fail, witnesses see the same event in different ways, reasonable people differ about what is true. Sometimes, biases and prejudices arise, lies are told. In extreme cases, truth can get lost when an advocate goes too far in trying to win. An emotional argument can sway a jury in spite of the facts. Important evidence can be concealed.

To protect against these problems, our criminal-case process has developed sophisticated checks and balances. Some protect the process itself, while others protect the defendant. Judges and jurors can be removed for bias or prejudice. Witnesses are sworn to tell the truth and can be punished if they lie. Lawyers must follow rules of evidence and are bound by ethical rules against knowingly presenting false testimony. Criminal defendants in serious cases can count on representation by an attorney, a trial by jury, the right to confront accusers, a speedy and public trial, and the right to appeal. They are also protected against having to post an excessive amount for bail or having to testify against themselves. These protections come from the U.S. Constitution and the constitutions and laws of the various states.

Facts, Facts, Facts

Basic to every criminal case are facts. When used to prove a point before a court, they are called **evidence**. Evidence comes from the testimony of witnesses or from physical items related to the crime. Woven together, evidence can tell a story of guilt or innocence.

As you will discover, facts are important at every stage and to every person in the criminal-case process. Consider just a few examples. A police officer must have sufficient facts to show probable cause to arrest a suspect or conduct a search. A judge examines these facts before issuing a warrant. A criminal trial judge may be called upon to decide whether facts offered in evidence are relevant to the case.

The facts in the case of *People v. Evans* will be important throughout this unit. They are found, among other places, in the Police Investigation Report, in the defendant's story, and in the witnesses' statements. Sometimes you will be using facts as attorneys do. For example, in one activity you will take the role of prosecutors and, based on the facts, decide whether to bring a particular charge. In another, you will cross-examine witnesses to establish or refute facts contained in their testimony.

Other times you will take a more impartial attitude toward the facts. For example, as jurors you will decide what the facts are and whether taken together they amount to the defendant's guilt beyond a reasonable doubt.

FOR DISCUSSION
1. What is the main purpose of the criminal-case process?
2. What is the adversarial system? How does it aid truth-finding in a criminal case? What might be some weaknesses in the system?
3. What are some checks and balances found in the criminal-case process?

Just the Facts

In this activity, students analyze the facts of a hypothetical criminal case in which a defendant (D) is charged with assault with a deadly weapon.

Each student should:

1. Read the **Prosecutor's Facts** and **Defense's Facts**.
2. Write a summary of the sequence of events as the prosecution might see them.
3. Do the same from the defense's point of view.
4. Write answers to the following questions:
   - To prove a case beyond a reasonable doubt, which facts must the prosecution establish clearly? Which facts must the prosecution cast doubt upon? Why?
   - If the facts described in point b of **Defense's Facts** are proven false, could the defense still prevail? Why or why not?
   - Why would the examination of witnesses under oath be crucial to this case?

Prosecutor's Facts

a. D owns a .38 caliber Smith & Wesson handgun registered in his name.
b. D's handgun was found by the investigating officers at the scene of the shooting on August 1.
c. A fingerprint expert testified that D's fingerprints were all over the handgun found at the scene. The gun had no other fingerprints on it.
d. One witness testified that two hours before the assault, he heard D threaten to shoot the victim.
e. The victim's neighbor, who reported the crime, testified that he heard shots fired at 7:35 p.m. on August 1.

Defense's Facts

a. D testified that his handgun was stolen from his house about July 29. No police report was made because D did not discover it missing until August 2.
b. D's business partner testified that D was having dinner with her between 6:45 and 8:30 p.m. on August 1.

Using This Unit

This unit has four major features:

The Criminal Justice Case Guide

The chart on page 173 shows you each important step in a criminal case. It starts when a crime is committed and continues until a court imposes a sentence. Because procedures vary in different jurisdictions, your state's procedures may vary slightly from this guide.

Key Steps

These special sections are found throughout the unit and provide more detailed information about the various steps outlined in the Criminal Justice Case Guide. A typical key step will give a particular procedure's purpose and describe what happens during that procedure.

Case Notes

These reading selections tell you about the Evans murder case. In them, you will meet all the main characters, discover facts, and learn law about the case.

Activities

Each activity focuses on the criminal case — an issue or event — and *you* will be on the firing line. Sometimes you will be asked to take the role of an attorney, sometimes a judge or juror. By the time the unit is over, you will have argued constitutional questions, evaluated evidence, examined witnesses, made judicial rulings, and come to a verdict in the case of *People v. Evans*.

The Criminal Justice Case Guide

INVESTIGATION AND ARREST

- Incident

- Warrant

- Arrest

PRETRIAL

- First Court Appearance

- Probable Cause Hearing – Indictment or Information

- Arraignment

- Pretrial Motions

TRIAL

- Jury Selection

- Opening Statement

- Presenting Evidence

- Closing Arguments

- Instructions to the Jurors

- Jury Deliberation

- Verdict

POST TRIAL

- Sentencing Hearing

- Post-trial Motions

- Appeals to Higher Court

CHAPTER 11

INVESTIGATION AND ARREST

A liberal is a conservative who has been arrested.
– Tom Wolf, novelist, *The Bonfire of the Vanities* (1987)

ARREST | POLICE CRIME INVESTIGATION REPORT | STATE CRIMINAL CODE
IN THE DEFENSE OF THOMAS EVANS

Key Step: Arrest

What It Is:

An arrest is the taking of a criminal suspect into custody to charge the suspect with a crime.

What Is Required:

An arrest must be based on probable cause and must be made:
- with a valid warrant;

or

- without a warrant under one of the judicially recognized exceptions to the Fourth Amendment warrant requirement.

Who May Arrest:

Depending on the jurisdiction, arrests may be carried out by:
- Law-enforcement officials.
- Private citizens. (Many jurisdictions, however, restrict the rights of a private citizen to make an arrest. In some jurisdictions, you may only arrest people for certain offenses, for example, felonies and misdemeanors, but not for violating ordinances. In other jurisdictions, you may not make a citizen's arrest for a misdemeanor unless the misdemeanor is committed in your presence. In a few jurisdictions, you may not make a mistake: If it turns out that the suspect did not actually commit the offense, then the arrest is not valid and you can be sued for false arrest. It is important to find out the law in your own state.)

Case Notes: Police Crime Investigation Report

Date of Investigation: July 6–7

Investigating Officer: Lt. Tony Jackson

Crime Description: At approximately 7 p.m. on Tuesday, July 6, Joyce Ann Miller, age 4, was hit in the head and chest by a shotgun blast at a range of about 10 yards. The victim died instantly.

Arrest: At 11:45 p.m. on July 7, I arrested Thomas Wade Evans and booked him for murder in the first degree.

Report of Investigation:
1. On Monday evening, July 5, the arrestee, Thomas Wade Evans, age 18, went to a party at the home of his girlfriend, Gail Duran. Witnesses at the party report that almost everyone there, including the suspect, consumed a lot of beer. A fight broke out at about 3 a.m. Witnesses could not identify everyone who was involved in the fight, but told me that suspect Evans was clubbed over the head with a beer bottle by another guest named Oscar Hanks. Friends took Evans to the hospital for treatment. Five stitches were required to close the wound.
2. On Tuesday, July 6, at about 5 p.m., Evans visited the apartment of a friend, Joel Robertson. Robertson stated that Evans was still angry about being hit during the fight the night before. Robertson also said that Evans remarked, "I'm going to get that guy once and for all. That man is going to pay in a big way." Evans also asked Robertson how to work one of his shotguns. Robertson is a hunter who owns several guns.

Estimated Number of Arrests
United States, 2010

	Number of Arrests	% of Total Arrests
Murder and non-negligent manslaughter	11,201	0.1
Forcible rape	20,088	0.2
Robbery	112,300	0.9
Aggravated assault	408,488	3.1
Other assaults	1,292,449	9.9
Burglary	289,769	2.2
Larceny-theft	1,271,410	9.7
Motor vehicle theft	71,487	0.5
Arson	2,207,335	16.8
Forgery and counterfeiting	78,101	0.6
Fraud	187,887	1.4
Embezzlement	16,616	0.1
Stolen property (buying, receiving, possessing)	94,802	0.7
Vandalism	252,753	1.9
Weapons; carrying, possessing, etc.	159,020	1.2
Prostitution and commercialized vice	62,668	0.5
Sex offenses (except forcible rape and prostitution)	72,628	0.6
Drug abuse violations	1,638,846	12.5
Gambling	9,941	0.08
Offenses against the family and children	111,062	0.9
Driving under the influence	1,412,223	10.8
Liquor laws	512,790	3.9
Drunkenness	569,718	4.3
Disorderly conduct	615,172	4.7
Vagrancy	32,033	0.2
All other offenses	3,720,402	28.4
Suspicion	1,166	0.01
Curfew and loitering law violations	94,797	0.7
Total Arrests	**13,120,947**	

Source: *Crime in the United States, 2010*, FBI (2011)

3. At about 6:30 p.m. on July 6, Evans visited the home of Gail Duran. Duran told me that Evans was still angry about what had happened the night before. She also said that Evans told her he knew who had hit him. Evans invited Duran to go for a ride with him, and she agreed. He asked Duran to drive his car while he sat in the back seat giving her directions. Duran stated that Evans directed her to Fourth Street. When he spotted a red Toyota truck parked in front of one of the houses, he told her to slow down. At this point, according to Duran, she noticed for the first time that Evans was handling a shotgun. She said she became very nervous. Suddenly, according to Duran, there was a loud explosion inside the car. Startled, Duran stepped on the gas pedal and quickly drove away. She stopped on a quiet street nearby. Evans then got into the driver's seat and took her home. Duran stated that Evans told her on the drive back to her home that all of a sudden the shotgun had gone off by itself. He also stated that he did not think he had hit anything.

4. The only eyewitness to the shooting of Joyce Ann Miller was her mother, Karen Miller. At about 7 p.m. on July 6, Miller told her daughter to close the front gate to the yard. Miller watched as her daughter went to close the gate. Miller then noticed a black car driving slowly on the street in front of her house. She also saw a long gun barrel pointing out of its rear window right at her daughter. Before she could say or do anything, Miller stated, there was a loud blast, and Joyce Ann collapsed. Miller and

her neighbors rushed to help Joyce Ann. Paramedics were called, but Joyce Ann was pronounced dead on arrival at Central Receiving Hospital. Miller stated that she had no idea who killed her daughter and could offer no description of the occupants of the black car except that she thought the driver was a young woman.

5. The Miller residence is located three doors to the east of Oscar Hanks' residence on Fourth Street.

6. That evening at 10:05 p.m., I received an anonymous phone call at the police station. The caller said, "If you want to know who murdered that little girl, you better check out what happened at Gail Duran's party last night." After interviewing a number of witnesses at the party, including Joel Robertson and Gail Duran, I arrested Thomas Wade Evans at 11:45 p.m. on July 7. I read the suspect his *Miranda* rights and booked him for the first-degree murder of Joyce Ann Miller.

FOR DISCUSSION

1. To arrest Evans, Lt. Jackson must have had **probable cause**. Probable cause means that the officer has enough evidence to cause a reasonable person to believe that a crime was committed and that the suspect committed it. Murder is often defined as the unlawful killing of a human being with **malice aforethought**. "Malice aforethought" refers to the state of mind of the person doing the killing. Malice aforethought can mean that the killer, with no serious provocation from the victim, either:
   * intended to kill,
   * intended to inflict great bodily harm, or
   * intended to do any act where there was an obvious risk that death or great bodily injury might result.

   What evidence did Lt. Jackson have that might give him probable cause to arrest Evans on a charge of murder? Explain your answer.

2. According to the information gathered by Lt. Jackson, do we know for sure what happened inside the Camaro at the moment the shotgun was fired. What else *could* have happened? What are some other ways the shooting could have taken place?

Case Notes: State Criminal Code

In the state where Joyce Ann Miller was killed, the following criminal laws define the various forms of criminal homicide.

Section 274: Degrees of Murder

Any killing committed *with* malice aforethought.

(a) Murder in the First Degree: All killings that are premeditated.

(b) Murder in the Second Degree: All other killings with malice aforethought.

Section 298: Manslaughter

Any killing committed *without* malice aforethought.

(a) Voluntary Manslaughter: All *intentional* killings committed as a result of serious *provocation* or *extreme anger*.

(b) Involuntary Manslaughter: All *unintentional* killings that are the direct result of committing:
   1. any *dangerous* and *unlawful* act *or*
   2. any *lawful act* in an extremely *careless* or negligent manner.

FOR DISCUSSION

1. Under the laws of Joyce Ann Miller's state, what is the major difference between the crimes of murder and manslaughter?

2. What is malice aforethought? What is premeditation? (If necessary, review materials in "Murder" on pages 12–13.)

3. Reread section 274 of the state code. What is the major difference between first and second-degree murder?

4. Reread section 298 of the state code. What is the major difference between voluntary and involuntary manslaughter?

Is It Murder?

In this activity, students examine hypothetical situations and determine which form of homicide should be charged in each.

1. Form pairs.
2. Each pair should read the descriptions, below, of other killings in Joyce Ann Miller's state. For each one, decide which form of criminal homicide should be charged, based on the elements from the state criminal code. For additional help, refer to "Degrees of Homicide" on pages 12-13.
   a. Mr. Jones poisoned his wife's coffee over a period of several weeks, resulting in her death.
   b. David, not aiming at anyone, fired his rifle into a passing bus, killing the driver.
   c. Mary, furious because Joan hit her with an umbrella, stabbed and killed Joan.
   d. Jim threw apples onto the highway from an overpass, causing a car to swerve off the road and crash. The driver died from his injuries. (A state law makes throwing anything off an overpass a misdemeanor.)
   e. Donna, a scuba diver, pulled her friend's mouthpiece regulator out when they were 50 feet underwater as a joke. Her friend drowned.
3. When everyone finishes, discuss each situation with the whole class.

Case Notes: In the Defense of Thomas Evans

After his arrest, Thomas Evans exercised his *Miranda* rights and remained silent. He called his parents, who hired a private attorney, Susan Jaffee, to represent him. Many defendants cannot afford an attorney and must wait for the court to appoint a public defender or free private attorney to represent them. To qualify for such an appointment, defendants must show that they cannot afford to pay an attorney.

The first thing Evans' attorney did was go to the police station to interview her client. Jaffee asked Evans to explain what happened. Evans told his side of the story, and she took notes.

Evans' Story

"Last Monday night I went to a party at my girlfriend Gail's house. We drank some beer and had a good time. Then sometime around 3 a.m. a bunch of guys started to fight. I don't even know why it started. All I know is that I got hit on the head with a beer bottle. It split my scalp, and I was all bloody. I had to go to the hospital. It took five stitches to stop the bleeding.

"While we were driving to the hospital, I was mad, and I wanted to know who hit me. When one of the guys mentioned that Oscar Hanks could have done it, I knew he was right. Oscar and I got into a fight about a month ago, and he knifed me in the leg.

"The day after Gail's party, I decided to get back at Oscar. I know it was dumb, but I decided to take my Dad's shotgun and blast a bunch of holes in Oscar's truck. He really loves that truck, you know. Well, this is when I got into trouble. I got the shotgun, and even asked Joel Robertson how to work it. He's a hunter and has a couple of his own. Then I went over to Gail's to get her to drive me around Oscar's neighborhood. I spotted his truck and was going to blast it. Before I had a chance, the car swerved or something, and the gun went off. I didn't even think I hit anything. I didn't see anybody. Still, it was real scary! I told Gail to get us out of there fast.

"Look, I know I'm in big trouble. But believe me, I didn't mean to fire the gun or shoot that little girl. I didn't even know she was there! I swear, it was an accident."

How It Looks to Evans' Attorney

Susan Jaffee finished jotting down her notes and then gave Evans an overview of her thoughts on the case.

"Tom, I hope you are telling me the truth. But even if you are, it's still going to be a tough case to defend. For one thing, the shooting death of a 4-year-old girl is going to stir up a lot of emotion in this community. The newspapers and TV news have been running stories for weeks on youth violence and gangs, and your case will get a lot of coverage. At this point, the police are talking about first-degree murder, and with all this publicity the prosecutor could stick to those charges. We'll just have to wait until they review the evidence and decide what charges to file. They might decide to charge you with something less serious. Meanwhile, I'll start checking out the witnesses. A lot can happen between now and the trial.

"To begin with, we have to get through your first court appearance. I'll need to ask you some questions. This information might help get you out on bail. It will be difficult, but if your family can raise the money, I'll try.

"Next, we have to face a probable cause hearing where the judge will decide whether you have to stand trial on whatever the prosecution charges you with. In the meantime, we have the right to discovery. This means we will find out exactly what evidence the prosecution is relying on. The probable cause hearing will give us a chance to test some of their witnesses.

"If there is a finding of probable cause, you will have to appear at an arraignment. There, depending on what happens, you'll have to plead to the charges and a trial will be scheduled. At that stage, I might be able to do something about the publicity problem. At the very least, we'll do our best to make sure the jurors are not influenced too much by media reports.

"While we are waiting to hear from the prosecutors, I want you to think about some things. I want you to think over everything you have told me today. If you have forgotten anything, I want to know. If you did not give me the whole story, I want to know. Right now, I'm the best friend you've got. No surprises, OK?"

Back in her office, Jaffee reviewed the information Evans had given her about his background. She knew that the probation department would be compiling a similar report for the judge to consider in deciding on the issue of Evans' pretrial release. A summary of her notes follows.

File: Thomas Evans/Background

Prior Arrests/Convictions

No prior convictions. One arrest for disturbing the peace. The charges were subsequently dropped. At the age of 17, Evans was cited for reckless driving and his driver's license was suspended for six months.

Employment

Employed full time as an assistant manager of the parts department of a local auto dealership. He has held his present position for nearly six months after having worked there part time during high school. His current income is $26,000 a year.

School Record

Evans was an average student throughout high school. Because of poor attendance, however, he completed some credits for graduation at a continuation high school. He was suspended twice, once for fighting, once for truancy. Recently, he completed a special three-week course offered by Ford Motor Company in parts management before qualifying for his present job.

Residence

Evans' dad died when he was 5. He lives at home with his mother, sister, and younger cousin. He makes monthly contributions for rent, utilities, food, and maintenance.

CHAPTER 12
PRETRIAL

The American pretrial criminal system is the outgrowth of institutions that originated on the Continent and in England and were adapted to suit the peculiar needs of a mobile frontier society. The pretrial process reflects a profound awareness of the need to protect an individual from arbitrary government prosecution.
– Lewis Katz, *Justice Is the Crime* (1972)

FIRST APPEARANCE BEFORE A JUDGE | THE QUESTION OF BAIL | PROSECUTORIAL REVIEW
PLEA BARGAINING | PROBABLE CAUSE HEARING | EVANS' PROBABLE CAUSE HEARING
ARRAIGNMENT | PRETRIAL MOTIONS | A PRETRIAL MOTION

Key Step: First Appearance Before a Judge

Purpose

To ensure that criminal suspects know their rights and are not mistreated by authorities, most jurisdictions require that the police bring an arrested person before a judge. Some states require that this first appearance take place within a specified period — for example, within 24 or 48 hours after arrest. Other jurisdictions simply say that it must take place without unnecessary delay.

Typical Procedures

The judge:
- **Informs the person arrested of the charges.**
- **Informs the person arrested of the right to counsel.** If the person cannot afford to hire an attorney, the judge will appoint one. (These court-appointed lawyers for criminal defendants are often government employees, known as public defenders. In some cases, the judge appoints private attorneys to represent criminal defendants.)
- **Determines bail.** Generally, state laws or court rules set bail schedules for misdemeanor offenses. Thus, if a person is accused of committing a misdemeanor, the judge simply refers to the predetermined bail list to set bail. In felony cases, a judge has three choices:
  1. Fix the amount of bail (often with reference to state-imposed standards).
  2. Release the arrested person without bail (on the person's own recognizance).
  3. In limited instances, deny bail altogether.

Case Notes: The Question of Bail

Excessive bail shall not be required . . . .
–Eighth Amendment to the U.S. Constitution (1791)

As outlined in the Key Step, there are two ways for criminal defendants to be released from jail pending trial. First, a judge might set bail: The judge will require defendants to deposit a certain amount of money with the court as security that they will come back for trial. Some defendants have enough money to pay for bail themselves. Others rely on private bail bond companies to post the necessary amount for a fee — usually between 10 and 20 percent of the amount. If defendants post bail and show up for trial, they (or the bail bond company) get the bail money back. Defendants who fail to appear in court lose all their bail money.

The second method of pretrial release is release on one's own recognizance. This means that a judge releases a criminal suspect after the suspect promises to return for trial. No bail is required. This method is usually available only to persons accused of non-violent and relatively minor crimes. As in bail cases, the judge must be convinced that the defendant will not leave town or try to intimidate witnesses before the trial.

In certain cases, a judge may refuse to release a defendant prior to trial. Many state criminal codes define particular crimes as non-bailable offenses. Typically, these are crimes punishable by death or by life imprisonment without the possibility of parole. In some states, defendants who have stalked their victims, who are members of criminal organizations, or who pose a high risk of running away may also be denied bail. These defendants present a much greater danger to society or a higher risk of the defendant fleeing to avoid prosecution.

Judicial Criteria for Setting Bail

Under the criminal laws of the state where Joyce Ann Miller was killed, the offense in this particular case is bailable. As for being released on his own recognizance, Evans would have almost no chance in this or any other state. Therefore the criminal court judge must determine an appropriate amount of bail for Thomas Wade Evans.

The criteria that a judge must take into consideration in setting bail include among other things:
- The crime.
- The past record of the accused.
- The likelihood that the defendant will remain in the state and appear in court.

CLASS ACTIVITY

Bail Hearing

In this activity, students role play the bail hearing in the Evans case. In preparation for this, you might invite a criminal lawyer into the class to take part in the activity and debriefing.

1. Form three groups. Students in the first group role play prosecuting attorneys, those in the second role play defense attorneys, and those in the third role play judges. Assume that $100,000 is the minimum bail set by law and that the maximum would be $500,000. Each group should meet separately and follow the instructions (below) for its group.
2. After the groups have prepared, form small groups consisting of one prosecutor, one defense attorney, and one judge. The judge in each group should conduct the bail hearing.
3. After both sides have presented their arguments, the judges should write down their decisions on Thomas Evans' bail and their reasoning.
4. Reconvene as a class, and each judge should announce the bail set for Thomas Evans and discuss the facts and arguments that influenced the decision. If a criminal lawyer has taken part in the activity, he or she should be asked to discuss the likely outcome of the bail hearing if this had been a real case.
5. Conclude the activity by holding a discussion using the debriefing questions on page 181.

Attorney Instructions

Prosecutors: To make sure Thomas Evans appears for trial, you believe that a high bail is necessary. Work with a partner from within your own group to develop arguments to support your position. Refer to the **Police Crime Investigation Report** on pages 174–176. List five or more facts you think are the most important to support your position. Keep in mind the criteria (mentioned above in **The Question of Bail**) that the judge will apply in deciding. Once you have developed your arguments and have listed the facts to back them up, share your ideas with the other members of the prosecution group. What are the three best arguments in favor of a higher bail for the accused in this case? What facts do you have to support your arguments?

Defense attorneys: You will be trying to persuade the judge to set as low a bail as possible for your client, Thomas Evans. Work with a partner from within your group to develop arguments in favor of your position. You believe he will appear for trial and you want to minimize his financial burden. Evans' mom has told you that at most she can raise $15,000. Since a bond requires 10 percent up front, this means the maximum bail the family can meet is $150,000. Refer

(Continued on next page.)

to the **Police Crime Investigation Report** on pages 174–176 and **In the Defense of Thomas Evans** on pages 177–178. List five or more facts you think are the most important to support your position. Keep in mind the criteria (mentioned above in **The Question of Bail**) that the judge will apply in deciding. Once you have developed your arguments and have listed the facts to back them up, share your ideas with the other members of the defense group. What are the three best arguments in favor of a low bail for the accused in this case? What facts do you have to support your arguments?

Judge Instructions

Your job will be to run the hearing, listen to the lawyers' arguments, and determine what bail should be set for Thomas Evans. Work with a partner from within your group to develop questions to ask the attorneys. List five or more questions you think are important. Keep in mind the criteria (mentioned above in **The Question of Bail**) that you, the judges, will apply in deciding. Once you have developed your questions, share your ideas with the other members of the judge group.

At the bail hearing, let the attorney for the defendant speak first, then the prosecutor. You may interrupt the attorneys to ask questions. After hearing both sides, make your decision on what Thomas Evans' bail should be. Be sure to base your decision on the criteria. Do not announce your decision to the attorneys. Instead write it on a piece of paper. Be prepared to discuss the facts and arguments that influenced your decision.

Debriefing Questions

1. Do you agree that bail should sometimes be denied and an accused person held in custody? Explain your answer. If you agree, under what circumstances should judges be allowed to deny bail? Why?
2. The American criminal trial system is based on the notion that a person is presumed to be innocent until proven guilty. Do you think that the system of bail runs contrary to this concept? Why or why not?

Case Notes: Prosecutorial Review

The prosecutor in a criminal case shall: (a) refrain from prosecuting a charge that the prosecutor knows is not supported by probable cause. . . .
– From Rule 3.8 of the American Bar Association's Model Rules of Professional Conduct (2010)

After the police make a felony arrest, the prosecutor reviews the case to decide what crimes should be charged and what strategies might be used in handling the case. The prosecutor exercises what is called **prosecutorial discretion** in choosing how to approach the case. Depending on the jurisdiction, the review can be made by an individual prosecutor or by a special team of prosecutors working closely with the police in evaluating cases after arrest. After the review, the case may be assigned to another prosecutor.

During the initial review, prosecutors must first decide if they have enough evidence to file formal charges against the person arrested. To do this, they must go over the possible charges. Then they must review each element of these crimes and decide if they have enough evidence to prove it. For example, the crime of larceny usually has the following four elements:
(1) The taking and carrying away
(2) of personal property
(3) that belongs to another person
(4) with the intent to *permanently deprive the owner* of possession of the property.

In addition, many states distinguish between the crime of grand larceny (a felony) and petty larceny (a misdemeanor) depending on the value of the property taken. (In many states, for example, taking property valued at $500 or more is a felony; taking property of a lesser value is a misdemeanor.)

Analyzing a Case

Imagine that prosecutors have to decide whether to file formal court charges for grand larceny in a state with the theft laws described above. They have the following evidence drawn from the police investigation and report:

John Witness saw Mary Defendant reach into a car, remove a watch from the dashboard, and walk away with it. John summoned the police. They caught Mary several blocks away while she was trying to sell the watch to a passerby. Other evidence includes a statement by the owner identifying the watch as her property.

Basis for Declination of Prosecution by U.S. Attorneys	
Basis	**Percentage**
Insufficient evidence (case-related problems)	48.2%
Prosecution by others	21%
Agency request	10.0%
Other	9.2%
Lack of resources	5.7%
Interest of justice	3.2%
Suspect-related problems	2.6%

Source: *Compendium of Federal Justice Statistics, 2004,* Bureau of Justice Statistics (2006)

Should Mary be charged with grand larceny? To find out, it is necessary to match the evidence with each element of the crime.

In this case, John Witness' testimony establishes a taking and carrying away of the watch. The location of the property (on the dashboard) and the owner's statement establish another person's ownership. The law defines a watch as personal property. The testimony of the police officer and passerby establishes the necessary intent element. (By trying to sell the watch to another, Mary has demonstrated an intent to permanently deprive the owner of the property.)

So far it looks as if the prosecutors have enough evidence to prove a case of larceny beyond a reasonable doubt. But should they file a felony or misdemeanor complaint? The answer to this question depends on the value of the watch. The prosecutor can have an investigator find evidence of the watch's value. If it turns out the watch was worth more than $500, a felony charge can be made. If the evidence does not support such a high value, a charge for the lesser crime of petty larceny can be filed.

As you can see, evaluating a case can be quite complex. Many related issues may come into play. Was all the important evidence legally obtained? Are the witnesses reliable and believable? What evidence might the defense produce that counters the prosecutor's case?

Factors in Exercising Discretion

In general, the prosecutors should prosecute if, after a thorough investigation, they find that:

(1) a crime has been committed,

(2) they can identify the person or persons who committed it, and

(3) they have evidence that supports a guilty verdict.

But as has been mentioned, the prosecutor does have discretion in deciding what charges, if any, to bring. To decide, a prosecutor might consider many factors, for example:

- Is there reasonable doubt that the defendant is guilty?
- Was the harm caused by the offense inconsequential?
- Is the probable punishment out of proportion to the offense or the offender?
- Is the crime itself rarely enforced (to the extent that the community no longer considers it a crime)?
- Is the offender extremely young or old?
- Is the crime not a high priority of the prosecutor's office (e.g., violent crimes tend to have high priority; so-called victimless crimes may not)?
- Is the case too old to find witnesses or physical evidence?

What Should the Charge Be?

In the following scene, three prosecuting attorneys — Martin, Stein, and Kawahara — have been assigned to review the Evans case. They are going over the crimes that they might bring against Evans.

Martin: Let's start with the most serious offense. First-degree murder requires *malice aforethought* and *premeditation*. The decision to kill someone had to have been weighed and reflected upon after the intent to kill was formed. Now, in Evans' case we have evidence that he had more than 12 hours to consider killing Oscar Hanks . . .

Stein: Just one problem — he didn't kill Oscar Hanks.

Kawahara: I don't see any big problem there. If we can show that Evans did form the intent to kill Hanks, we might be able to invoke the **transferred intent doctrine**. It holds that the elements of first-degree murder can be satisfied even if the killer gets someone other than his intended victim. Also, Evans may have thought that the little girl was Hanks' sister or maybe a relative. Or maybe he formed a whole new intent to kill the little girl and premeditated before pulling the trigger.

Martin: Maybe, but it doesn't seem likely. What about second-degree murder? Remember malice aforethought can be established by an intent to do any act posing an obvious risk that death or great bodily harm may result. Here we have a guy who stated a desire to get Hanks. He loaded a shotgun, got into a car, and started blasting away. I don't care if he was trying to hit the little girl, the house, or the truck. People were on the street. He didn't care about their safety, and he should have known that he was endangering them. Also, just firing at the truck is a felony. Any killings that take place while attempting to commit a felony are murder under the **felony murder rule**.

Stein: Let's not be too hasty. What if Evans didn't "start blasting away," as you put it? What if the gun just went off accidentally?

Martin: You would consider a charge of involuntary manslaughter?

Stein: Sure. Such careless handling of a loaded shotgun in a residential area amounts to criminal negligence in my book.

Kawahara: At the very least.

Martin: I suppose voluntary manslaughter is also a possibility.

Stein: Be serious, Martin. After 12 hours? Even if he was seriously provoked by Hanks, he had plenty of time to cool off.

Martin: Maybe so. Anyway, we've got plenty to think about and we've got to decide. The newspapers are showing a lot of interest in this case. The boss told me that she has a personal interest in this case — top priority and all that. We've got to charge Evans with something. But what?

ASK AN EXPERT

Invite a criminal attorney to your class. Ask how prosecutorial review and discretion work in your area. What factors does the prosecutor use to decide which crimes to charge? Invite the attorney to join you in the activity **The Prosecutor Decides** and lead the final discussion.

FOR DISCUSSION

1. In your own words, what is prosecutorial discretion? What are its advantages and disadvantages?
2. Review the factors in exercising prosecutorial discretion on page 182. Which do you think are valid? Which, if any, don't you think should be used? Why?
3. Review **What Should the Charge Be?** on page 182. Then answer the following questions:
   - What is the doctrine of transferred intent? How does it apply to the Evans case? (Try drawing a diagram on the board using the characters from the case.)
   - Why might Prosecutor Stein think that the facts do not support premeditation or transferred intent?
   - Why did Prosecutor Stein argue against a charge of voluntary manslaughter?
   - What additional evidence, if any, do the prosecutors need to make a decision?

The Prosecutor Decides

In this activity, students role play prosecutors deciding which charges to file in the Thomas Evans case.

1. Form small groups. Each group is made up of prosecutors working with Martin, Stein, and Kawahara on the Thomas Evans case.
2. Each group should:
   a. Review the following materials:
      (1) **Police Crime Investigation Report**, pages 174–176.
      (2) **State Criminal Code Sections**, page 176.
      (3) **What Should the Charge Be?**, pages 182–183.
      (You may also wish to consult **Murder** on pages 12–13 for additional background information.)
   b. Answer the questions below under **Possible Charges**. One person should record the group's answers on a sheet of paper. Be prepared to discuss your answers with the class.
3. Considering all relevant factors, what crime would you charge Thomas Evans with? (Be prepared to present and discuss your final recommendation with the class.)
4. Have groups report and hold a class discussion on the appropriate charge.

Possible Charges

First-Degree Murder. Is there evidence that . . .
- Thomas Evans formed an intent to kill Oscar Hanks? Explain.
- Thomas Evans premeditated the crime? Explain.
- Thomas Evans' intent was transferred to the killing of Joyce Ann Miller (using the doctrine of transferred intent)? Explain.

or
- Thomas Evans formed an intent to kill and premeditated the killing of Joyce Ann Miller? Explain.

Second-Degree Murder. Is there evidence that . . .
- Thomas Evans formed an intent to kill Joyce Ann Miller? Explain.

or
- Thomas Evans had the intent to do an act where there was an obvious risk that death or great bodily harm would result? Explain.

Voluntary Manslaughter. Is there evidence that . . .
- Thomas Evans formed an intent to kill Oscar Hanks? Explain.
- Oscar Hanks seriously provoked the actions of Thomas Evans? Explain.
- Thomas Evans did not have sufficient time to calm down after being provoked? Explain.

Involuntary Manslaughter. Is there evidence that . . .
- Thomas Evans committed an act in a criminally negligent manner? Explain.

or
- Thomas Evans committed a dangerous and unlawful act? Explain.

Plea Bargaining

For many centuries, Anglo-American courts did not encourage guilty pleas but actively discouraged them.
– Albert Alschuler, law professor, *University of Chicago Law Review* (1983)

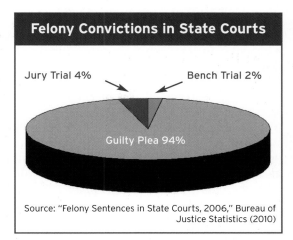

Felony Convictions in State Courts

Jury Trial 4%   Bench Trial 2%

Guilty Plea 94%

Source: "Felony Sentences in State Courts, 2006," Bureau of Justice Statistics (2010)

This unit takes us completely through the criminal case process. It begins with an arrest and ends with a trial and verdict. Most criminal cases do not go this far. In about 90 percent of all criminal convictions, the defendant pleads guilty. Often the defendant decides to plead guilty because of a plea agreement made with the prosecutor. In return for a reduction in charges or a lighter sentence, the defendant agrees to plead guilty. This is known as plea bargaining.

A plea agreement can occur at almost any stage in a criminal case. An agreement is sometimes reached before the preliminary hearing or shortly after. The prosecution and defense can agree to a plea before trial, during trial, and even just before the jury returns with its verdict. In fact, the two sides sometimes carry on plea negotiations throughout all the stages of the case process. The negotiations may not simply cover what charges or sentence each side will accept. Often each side tries to convince the other of what facts can be proven in court. Once they agree to the facts, then they can agree to a plea.

In some jurisdictions, the judge plays an active role in plea bargaining. In most states, however, the judge takes no part in the negotiations. This means that prosecutors can make no promises about sentencing. The most prosecutors can offer is to make sentencing recommendations, which judges often accept. But a judge may impose a stiffer sentence than the one the prosecutor recommends. The judge may even refuse to accept the guilty plea if the judge believes the facts do not warrant it. (This, however, rarely happens.)

Critics have objected to plea bargaining for many different reasons. Some explain that the trial process is carefully designed to protect the defendant's rights, guarantee a fair trial, and ensure that only the guilty get convicted. They argue that plea bargaining subverts all of these. In a plea bargain, a court does not examine whether the defendant's rights were violated, a trial does not take place, and worst of all, they say, an innocent person may go to prison. They point out that a prosecutor with a weak case and a defendant facing a long sentence may not want to gamble with a trial. In this situation, they say, a defendant may plead guilty to get a light sentence even if the defendant is totally innocent.

Some critics emphasize that plea bargaining tarnishes the dignity of the justice system. According to them, it turns the important process of dispensing justice into a game of "let's make a deal." They say it even punishes defendants who refuse to go along with the game and go to trial. These defendants, they say, receive harsher sentences than those who agree to a plea.

Other critics use this last point to complain that plea bargains result in defendants serving less time than they should. Plea bargaining, they say, lets defendants off the hook too often.

Supporters of plea bargaining offer several reasons in favor of it. They point out that the courts couldn't possibly handle the load if every case went to trial. Millions of dollars would have to be spent on new courtrooms, judges, prosecutors, and defense attorneys. Plea bargaining, they say, saves money and time. It gives prosecutors time to pursue more important cases and keeps more police on the streets instead of spending hours in courtrooms. In addition, it saves victims of crimes from the emotional trauma of testifying, and it gives them the satisfaction of seeing the defendant confess to the crime in court. This admission of guilt, they add, is the first step in rehabilitating a criminal. Moreover, supporters point out that more criminals go to prison because of plea bargains. They note that anything can happen at trial. A jury may find that the prosecution has not proven guilt beyond a reasonable doubt and set the defendant free. Plea bargaining, they say, gives the prosecution and defense a chance to agree on a fair disposition of the case. It can even help alleviate harsh mandatory sentences that some first-time defendants face.

The Supreme Court has dealt with issues surrounding plea bargaining. The court has upheld plea bargains as long as the defendant has not been coerced and both sides comply with the deal. In 1971 in *Santobello v. New York*, Chief Justice Warren Burger stated that " 'plea bargaining' . . . is an essential component of the administration of justice. Properly administered, it is to be encouraged." The previous year in *North Carolina v. Alford*, the court even refused to overturn a plea agreement when the defendant claimed he did not commit the crime but was just pleading guilty to avoid the death penalty. The court upheld the guilty plea because the record showed strong evidence of the defendant's guilt and the defendant recognized that he would probably be found guilty of first-degree murder at a jury trial.

In recent years, the court has decided a series of cases ruling that defendants are entitled to effective counsel in plea bargains. In *Padilla v. Kentucky* (2010), the defense attorney had erroneously told the defendant that his agreeing to a guilty plea would not cause his deportation. In *Missouri v. Frye* (2012), the defendant pleaded guilty to driving without a license and was sentenced to three years, but his attorney had not informed him of an earlier plea offer of 90 days in jail. In *Lafler v. Cooper* (2012), the defense attorney misinformed the defendant that he could not be convicted of assault with intent to murder because all four shots he had fired had hit the victim below the waist. Based on this advice, the defendant rejected a plea offer of four to seven years in prison. Instead, he went to trial, was convicted, and was sentenced to 15 to 30 years behind bars. The Supreme Court ruled in each case that the defendant had received ineffective counsel during the plea bargain. Writing for the court in *Lafler*, Justice Anthony Kennedy stated:

> [C]riminal justice today is for the most part a system of pleas, not a system of trials. . . . [T]he right to adequate assistance of counsel cannot be defined or enforced without taking account of the central role plea bargaining plays in securing convictions and determining sentences.

Some states have attempted to eliminate plea bargains. Alaska in 1975 did away with them. The courts were not overwhelmed with trials. The same percentage of defendants continued to plead guilty. Skeptics think they kept pleading guilty because informal agreements were still made despite the ban. In 1982, California voters approved Proposition 8. Among other things, it banned plea bargains for defendants formally charged with serious felonies or driving under the influence. Several years later, a study found that prosecutors and defense attorneys started making their plea agreements before charges were formally filed.

In recent years, the stakes for plea bargains have risen. Many states have adopted three-strikes laws, which impose harsher penalties and even life sentences on certain repeat offenders. Some defendants resist pleading to a charge if it will count as a strike, especially a third strike. They are more willing to opt for a trial, and the process of reaching a plea agreement has become more complex.

FOR DISCUSSION

1. What are the advantages of plea bargains? What are the disadvantages? Do you think they should be banned? Explain?

2. Assuming that plea bargaining exists, do you think courts should be allowed to take *Alford* pleas? Why or why not?

3. Justice Antonin Scalia dissented in all three cases extending the right of effective counsel to plea bargains. Below are comments he made about each case:

   - *Padilla v. Kentucky*: "The Sixth Amendment guarantees the accused a lawyer 'for his defense' against a 'criminal prosecutio[n]' — not for sound advice about the collateral consequences of conviction."

   - *Missouri v. Frye*: "Counsel's mistake did not deprive Frye of any substantive or procedural right; only of the opportunity to accept a plea bargain to which he had no entitlement in the first place."

   - *Lafler v. Cooper*: "The defendant has been fairly tried, lawfully convicted, and properly sentenced, and any 'remedy' provided for this will do nothing but undo the just results of a fair adversarial process."

What points is he making in each case? How do you think the justices in the majority would respond? Do you agree with the majority opinion in each of these cases or the dissent? Explain.

CLASS ACTIVITY

Plea Bargain

In this activity, students role play a plea bargain in the Evans case.

1. Form pairs. One person in each pair should assume the role of prosecutor and the other of defense attorney.
2. Imagine that the prosecution has charged Thomas Evans with first-degree murder. Spend a few minutes and try to reach a plea agreement that satisfies both of you.
3. Each pair should report to the class on the results of its plea negotiations.
4. Hold a class discussion using the debriefing questions.

Debriefing Questions

1. How many groups reached an agreement? What did you agree to? Do you think the agreement was fair? Do you think the defendant would accept it?
2. What problems did you have in negotiating? Do you think you had enough time? Enough information? If not, what additional time or information would you need?
3. Defense attorneys sometimes accuse prosecutors of overcharging (charging the defendant with crimes that he or she could never be convicted of) to help them in plea bargaining. Do you think this might be a danger? Do you think your agreement would have been different if the prosecution had started with second-degree murder instead of first-degree?

Key Step: Probable Cause Hearing

Purpose

Before a felony case can go to trial, a court must find that there is *probable cause* to believe that a crime was committed and the person arrested committed it. The purpose of the probable cause hearing is to keep charges with insufficient evidence from being brought to trial. The hearing thus protects both the accused and the state from spending time and money unnecessarily.

Types of Hearings

Preliminary Hearing. Some states use preliminary hearings or examinations to determine if the person arrested should be brought to trial. Other states use them to determine if the accused should be bound over for a grand jury hearing. At the preliminary hearing, the prosecution presents evidence to a judge to prove that there is probable cause. The defense may cross-examine the prosecutor's witnesses. In many states, however, crime victims do not have to testify in person. Their statements can be read to the court, so the defense cannot cross-examine them.

If the judge finds that there is probable cause, the prosecution is authorized to file a document called an **information** with the court, and preparations for the trial begin.

Grand Jury. In some states and in all federal felony cases, grand juries determine probable cause. A grand jury is made up of citizens — usually 23 people — from the county where the crime occurred. It meets in closed session, and the prosecutor calls witnesses. The defense attorney does not get to cross-examine these witnesses or participate in the hearing. After the prosecution presents its case, the grand jury votes on whether probable cause exists. If a certain number of the 23 grand jurors — often 12 or 14 — find probable cause, then an **indictment** is issued. Like an information, an indictment is a document accusing the defendant of committing a crime. Following an indictment, preparation for trial begins.

In many states, the prosecutor has the option of using a grand jury or a preliminary hearing. Since the accused has no right to

counsel or to cross-examine the state's witnesses in grand jury hearings, a prosecutor might be more likely to seek a grand jury indictment when cross-examination would be traumatic to a witness (e.g., for sex crimes or for very young or frail witnesses). Most felony cases, however, use a preliminary hearing and information.

Complaint — for misdemeanors only. In misdemeanor cases, no separate hearing is held to establish probable cause after the accused has been arrested. A written complaint against the person arrested serves as the formal accusation to begin the prosecution of misdemeanor cases. (The defendant can ask for a copy of the complaint with copies of the police report attached.)

Case Notes: Evans' Probable Cause Hearing

When Tom Evans heard Susan Jaffee's voice on the phone, he felt nervous. What she said did not calm him down.

"I've got some news for you, Tom. The prosecutor decided to take your case to the grand jury instead of holding a preliminary hearing."

Tom remembered her saying that the next step would be the probable cause hearing. He asked, "Is it worse to have a grand jury instead of a preliminary hearing?"

"It's worse in that I won't get to cross-examine any of the witnesses. But sometimes prosecutors take their weaker cases to grand juries, because the prosecutors are more in control at grand jury hearings than preliminary hearings. So maybe it's not such bad news."

"So what do we do now?" asked Tom.

"We wait. You might be called to testify before the grand jury. If you are, I cannot go in with you. But you will just refuse to testify. You will take the Fifth Amendment."

Tom heard nothing about the grand jury for two weeks. Finally, Susan Jaffee called. "The grand jury returned an indictment today — second-degree murder."

The words stunned Tom. "Murder?" he stammered.

"Second degree."

"How did the grand jury decide that?" Tom asked.

"I don't know, Tom. We'll get a copy of the grand jury's transcript. We'll read what the witnesses had to say. Then we'll be ready for our next step — your arraignment."

🔍 Key Step: Arraignment

Purpose

After an information, indictment, or complaint has been filed, the defendant is called into court to **plead to the charges**. This court appearance is known as the arraignment. (In most misdemeanor cases, this step takes place at the defendant's first and only pretrial hearing.) Aside from various insanity pleas, the defendant has three basic choices of pleas:

- **Not guilty.**
- **Guilty.**
- **Nolo Contendere.** (No contest. This has the same effect as a guilty plea, except it does not serve as an admission of guilt if the defendant is sued in a civil case.)

In some cases, a defendant may plead guilty and receive a **deferred entry of judgment**. This means that if the defendant successfully completes agreed-on actions (such as going through a drug treatment program or taking an anger management class), then the record of the defendant's arrest and guilty plea will be erased. (The record is not erased for all purposes. It may be brought up, for example, in immigration cases, and a person may be deported or denied naturalized citizenship based on the guilty plea.)

Typical Procedure

The judge:

- Informs the defendant of various constitutional rights.
- Reads the information or indictment and usually gives the defendant a copy.
- Asks the defendant to plead to the charges.
- Asks whether the defendant wants a jury trial or a court trial (decided by the judge without a jury).

The defendant may make pretrial motions (e.g., to suppress illegally obtained evidence or to transfer the case to a different judge).

Pretrial Motions

Rolla, Mo. — As his client's scheduled trial date gets closer, the attorney representing murder suspect Frank Colvin, 34, of Rolla, has filed several motions with the court, including one asking a judge to suppress evidence against Colvin.
– News article from *Rolla Daily News* (2012)

Before a case goes to trial, both the prosecution and defense can present pretrial motions to the judge. Pretrial motions ask the court to take specific action. For example, the defense may make a motion to dismiss the case. Or, the prosecution may make a motion to add charges against the defendant. The judge at the arraignment or soon afterward will set a deadline for parties to make pretrial motions.

The party making a motion is called the moving party. When making a pretrial motion, the moving parties are usually required to submit their motions in writing. They must state the grounds for the motion and may support the motion with written legal arguments and affidavits, sworn statements. The opposing party is given a chance to respond in writing.

The judge may then schedule a motion hearing. At this hearing, the parties will make oral arguments and plead their case, and the judge will ask questions. Sometimes, the parties may even call witnesses to testify. The judge will either rule on the motion at the end of the pretrial hearing or take a few days before ruling.

Motions play an important role in the appeals process. An appellate court can normally only rule on legal issues that were raised at trial or pretrial. For example, if the defense wants to appeal that a piece of evidence should not have been introduced at trial, it can only do so if the defense made a motion to exclude the evidence or objected at the trial. If the defense failed to make a motion or object to the evidence, it cannot later appeal that the evidence was introduced.

Below are some examples of pretrial motions.

Suppression of Evidence

One of the most common pretrial motions is to suppress evidence. Under the exclusionary rule, illegally obtained evidence may not be used at trial. Thus if the police gained evidence through an illegal search of the defendant's house or through an improper interrogation of the defendant, this evidence may be excluded

at the defendant's trial. But it is not automatically excluded. The defense must make a motion to suppress the evidence.

Pretrial Publicity

Several different motions address the problem of pretrial publicity. The Sixth Amendment guarantees every criminal defendant the right to a trial before an impartial jury. A problem arises in high profile cases that generate a great deal of publicity. The publicity may infect the jury pool and make jurors incapable of judging the case solely on the evidence presented in court. The court can do little to control the publicity because the First Amendment guarantees freedom of speech and the press. But a prosecutor or defense attorney can make the following motions to help ensure an impartial jury:

- **Motion for change of venue.** This motion asks to move the case to a different location. For example, in 2009, a transit police officer in Oakland, California, shot an unarmed suspect in the back. Several onlookers caught the shooting on video. News outlets throughout the San Francisco area repeatedly broadcast the videos. (Oakland is across the bay from San Francisco.) The court granted the defense's motion for a change of venue, and the trial was moved to Los Angeles.
- **Motion for a continuance.** A continuance is a delay in the trial. A court may grant a motion to wait for publicity about the case to die down.
- **Motion for a gag order.** Because of the First Amendment, a judge cannot order the news media not to cover a case. But a judge

can order trial participants — prosecutors, police, defense counsel, and witnesses — not to talk to the press. This is known as a gag order.

- **Motion to sequester the jury.** After the jury is chosen, jury members may still hear news about the trial. To minimize the chance of their hearing prejudicial news stories, a judge may grant a motion to sequester the jury. This means that the jurors will not return home every day, but rather live together in court-arranged housing for the duration of the trial. For example, in 2011 in the highly publicized Florida trial of Casey Anthony, who was accused of murdering her daughter, the jury was sequestered for the seven-week trial. Jurors were lodged in a hotel, ate all their meals together, and were denied access to radio and television broadcasts. They could watch selected DVDs and read one heavily censored newspaper. On Sundays, they were allowed family visits. Deputies ran errands for them or accompanied them whenever they went out.

The news media commonly cover crimes. A court will not grant one of these motions just because a case has been in the news. It will do so only when the publicity is so overpowering that it could prevent a fair trial.

Dismissal

The defense may move to dismiss the charges against the defendant. The defense may make such a motion on different grounds, such as:

- **Defendant's right to a speedy trial has been denied.** If the prosecution has delayed bringing the case to trial, the defense may move to dismiss. But the delay must not have been caused by the defense.
- **The prosecution does not have enough evidence to go to trial.**
- **The statute is unconstitutional.** If the defendant is charged with breaking a new statute, the defense may ask to dismiss on the grounds that the statute violates the U.S. or state constitution. A trial judge is likely to deny such a motion, because this issue is something that appeals courts normally decide. But the defense cannot appeal the constitutionality of the law unless it has raised this issue during the trial or pretrial.

Sever or Join

The prosecution may want to try defendants together in one trial. It can make a motion to join them if the defendants participated in the same offenses. It is more efficient for the courts to try the defendants together if the same evidence can be used against all the defendants.

A defendant, however, may not want to be tried with other defendants, especially if the defendant played a minor role in committing the crime. Such a defendant may make a motion of severance and move for a separate trial. Courts will grant severance only if it appears that the defendant's right to a fair trial will be impaired.

Mental Capacity to Stand Trial

In rare instances, the defense may make a motion that the defendant is not mentally capable of standing trial. This occurred in a recent high-profile case.

In January 2011, U.S. Representative Gabrielle Giffords was meeting with constituents at a Tucson, Arizona, supermarket. Suddenly, a gunman began firing a semi-automatic pistol. Giffords was gravely injured, and six others were killed, including a U.S. district judge.

A young man named Jared Loughner was subdued and arrested at the scene. He faces a 49-count indictment. His lawyer has entered a plea of not guilty. The prosecution's investigators indicated Loughner has had a history of behaving strangely and making bizarre statements. He was unable to hold down a job, and his local community college had requested he not return until he got a mental health clearance.

In May 2011, a hearing was held to determine whether Loughner had the mental capacity to stand trial. Almost every defendant is mentally capable of standing trial, even those who later are found not guilty by reason of insanity. Defendants simply have to pass a two-part test:

1. They must be coherent enough to provide their attorney with information needed for the case.
2. They must understand the significance of the trial and their relation to it.

In Loughner's case, the judge and prosecution each selected psychologists to examine the defendant. The experts interviewed Loughner many times, found that he suffered from schizophrenia, and reported that he did not understand the proceedings. Acting on their reports, the judge suspended the proceedings against Loughner and ordered him held in a prison mental facility. Like other defendants judged incapable of standing trial, he will be treated, with anti-psychotic drugs if necessary and appropriate. If he recovers sufficiently, he will be brought back to stand trial. Until then, he cannot be tried and has not been convicted of the prosecution's charges.

FOR DISCUSSION

1. What are pretrial motions? Why are they important?
2. What threat does pretrial publicity pose to a fair trial? Which of the pretrial motions, if granted, do you think could offer the best protection against the harmful effects of publicity? Why?
3. Imagine that a prosecutor has indicted 20 people as part of a drug conspiracy case. If you were the attorney defending a person accused of being a messenger in the conspiracy, what pretrial motion or motions would you make? Why?
4. Why do you think courts require that defendants be mentally capable of standing trial? Do you agree? Explain. What is the test to determine whether a defendant is mentally capable of standing trial? Do you think anything else should be added to the test? Explain. What is the difference between the tests for a defendant being mentally incapable of standing trial and for a defendant being legally insane?

Case Notes:
A Pretrial Motion

Joyce Ann Miller's death shocked the residents of the community. Many citizens and community leaders condemned what they called "this latest example of youth violence." Newspapers covered the case extensively. Neighbors of the Miller family told TV reporters that they wanted the death penalty for Evans. A police officer was quoted in a local newspaper as saying that he thought Joyce Ann's death must have been a "joy killing." A representative of the district attorney's office announced at a press conference that he believed "drugs were involved." One newspaper headline read, "Child Killer Says It Was 'An Accident!'" Thomas Evans' attorney, Susan Jaffee, also received several anonymous phone calls threatening to harm her if she did not drop out of the case.

A Problem for the Defense

All of this deeply concerned Jaffee. She feared that the publicity would hurt her client's chances of getting a fair trial. Finding jurors who

had not already formed an opinion about the case would be difficult. Even if such jurors were found, they could still be influenced by publicity and public opinion during the trial itself.

After the grand jury found that Evans would have to stand trial, his attorney decided to act. At the arraignment he would plead not guilty and ask for a jury trial. Then she would make a motion for a gag order.

Motion for a Gag Order

Judges may issue **gag orders** to help ensure that criminal defendants receive a fair trial. These orders prohibit trial participants and government officials from making statements to the press. By preventing these statements, gag orders make it less likely that pretrial publicity will influence the fact finder — the judge or jury.

It is crucial that the judge or jury be impartial. When judges act as the fact finder, it is assumed they will be able to ignore outside influences and decide the facts solely from the trial evidence. Jurors, who have little or no experience with the law, might be more easily swayed by outside influences, including opinions of friends, statements by public officials, and newspaper or TV accounts of the crime. For example, what might happen if a juror were to read about a piece of evidence legally excluded from consideration at trial that pointed to the defendant's guilt? Knowing this fact might influence that juror's opinion and if he or she shared it with other jurors, it could sway the whole jury. Gag orders are designed to prevent such interference. Those who disobey gag orders can be held in contempt of court and punished.

At the close of her argument for her motion, Ms. Jaffee made the following statement:

Public reaction to the death of Joyce Ann Miller has almost reached hysteria. Public officials, including the police and representatives of the district attorney's office, have made prejudicial and unfounded statements about the case. The news media is behaving irresponsibly by suggesting that Thomas Evans is already guilty. If these incidents continue, it will be impossible to conduct a fair trial, if indeed it is even possible now. Under these circumstances, a gag order is essential, your honor.

The prosecutor argued against issuing a gag order. He reminded the judge that public attention to such a case was natural. Under the U.S. Constitution's First Amendment, the news media have a right to keep the public informed. If denied access to participants in the trial, reporters might print or broadcast misinformation. Furthermore, he argued that a gag order should only be used in exceptional circumstances and that normal procedures such as cautioning the jury not to discuss or read about the case would probably be sufficient.

The judge thanked the attorneys and said that she would consider the matter and announce her decision the next day.

CLASS ACTIVITY

Ruling on the Motion

Imagine that you are the judge who must rule on the defense's motion for a gag order in this case. To prepare your ruling, complete the following steps:

1. Review **A Pretrial Motion**, pages 192–193, and the "Pretrial Publicity" section of **Pretrial Motions**, pages 190–191.
2. In coming to a decision, consider these questions:
   - What is the purpose of a gag order?
   - What are some arguments in favor of issuing a gag order in this case?
   - What are some arguments against issuing a gag order? What rights and interests would be affected?
   - Are the alternatives to a gag order mentioned by the prosecutor sufficient to preserve a fair trial in this case
   - Should a gag order be issued in the Evans case? Why or why not?
3. Write a one-page decision stating your reasons for it. Be prepared to present it to the rest of the class for discussion.

CHAPTER 13
TRIAL

In all criminal prosecutions, the accused shall enjoy the right to a speedy and public trial, by an impartial jury of the State and district wherein the crime shall have been committed, which district shall have been previously ascertained by law, and to be informed of the nature and cause of the accusation; to be confronted with the witnesses against him; to have compulsory process for obtaining witnesses in his favor, and to have the Assistance of Counsel for his defence.
– Sixth Amendment to the U.S. Constitution (1791)

TRIAL PROCEDURES | CAST OF CHARACTERS | THE TRIAL OF THOMAS EVANS | JURY SELECTION
TRIAL STRATEGY | OPENING STATEMENTS | DIRECT AND CIRCUMSTANTIAL EVIDENCE
RULES OF EVIDENCE | CLOSING STATEMENTS | INSTRUCTING THE JURY

🔑 Key Step:
Trial Procedures

Strict rules ensure that each side in a trial will have an equal chance to present its case. A judge must make sure that each side follows these rules closely. The major procedures observed in a criminal court trial are outlined below.

1. Jury Selection

In all criminal jury trials, the first step is to impanel, or select, a jury. Prosecution and defense attorneys pose questions to prospective jurors. The judge may also take an active role in the process.

2. Opening Statements

After calling the court to order, the judge will ask for the trial to begin with opening statements from the prosecution and defense. The opening statement outlines the evidence each side intends to present during the trial. The prosecution delivers its opening statement first. The defense attorney usually follows immediately with a statement, but may delay it until after the prosecution presents all its evidence.

3. Presenting Evidence

The prosecution presents its side of the case first. This is called the prosecution's **case-in-chief.** It usually consists of introducing material objects called exhibits (e.g., a gun) as well as questioning prosecution witnesses. After the prosecution has finished presenting its side, the defense may introduce its exhibits and witnesses. Both exhibits and witnesses' testimony are trial evidence. Strict rules of evidence must be followed, however, before either is allowed into the trial.

Attorneys conduct **direct examination** when they question their own witnesses. After direct examination, opposing attorneys **cross-examine** the witnesses. Lawyers conduct cross-examination to test and find weaknesses in the testimony of their opponents' witnesses. They may also try to put doubts into the minds of the jurors about the credibility, or believability, of these witnesses.

4. Closing Arguments

After each side has presented all its evidence, each side makes a closing statement to the jury. In these closing arguments, attorneys summarize what has been established or not established during the trial. The closing argument presents attorneys with their last chance to persuade the jury. The defense delivers the first closing argument to the jury. The closing argument of the prosecution ends the evidence phase of the trial. (In many jurisdictions, three closing arguments are made: The prosecution goes first, the defense follows, and the prosecution is given the final word.)

5. Instructions to the Jurors

Following the closing arguments, the judge gives instructions to the jury. These instructions state the law that applies to the case. The judge reminds the jurors to base their verdict solely on the evidence admitted during the trial. Since the prosecution has the burden of proof, the judge instructs the jurors to find a verdict of guilty only if they believe the prosecution has proven its case beyond a reasonable doubt.

6. Jury Deliberations

After hearing the judge's instructions, the jury leaves the courtroom and meets in a jury room to decide on a verdict. Jury members first select a foreperson who will lead their discussions. The jury then reviews the evidence and votes on a verdict. Although the U.S. Supreme Court has ruled that unanimous verdicts of guilty or not guilty are not mandatory in all criminal cases, most states still require unanimity.

Several votes may be necessary before the jurors arrive at a unanimous verdict. If after a reasonable time, the jurors cannot reach a unanimous verdict, they become a "hung jury." The foreperson will report this fact to the judge. If the judge believes that further jury deliberations are futile, the judge will declare a mistrial. The prosecutor will then have to either request another trial with a new jury or drop the charges against the defendant. If the jury returns a unanimous verdict of not guilty, the defendant goes free. If the jury unanimously finds the defendant guilty, the judge will set a date for a sentencing hearing.

Case Notes: Cast of Characters

The atmosphere of the Criminal Court of Cook County was ominously businesslike on the morning of June 21, 1886. Save for the group of women gathered about the judge behind the judicial desk, no one in the huge, barnlike court-room seemed to be in attendance from mere idle curiosity, and everyone, from the judge upon the bench to the bailiffs guarding the doors, looked unmistakably grave.

– Frederick Trevor Hill, "The Chicago Anarchists' Case" in *Harper's Magazine* (1907)

A criminal courtroom in session is filled with people. Some are spectators. Some are friends and family of the victim or accused. Others take an active part in the trial itself. The following descriptions will give you an idea about the major participants. (Some you have already met, but review them again carefully.) As the trial of Thomas Evans progresses, you will be asked at times to take on their roles.

The **judge** presides over the trial. He or she rules on all motions made by the attorneys, on the admissibility of testimony or items in evidence, and on the procedures to be followed during the trial. At the end of the trial, the judge instructs the jury about the applicable rules of law. In a criminal trial, if the jury reaches a verdict of guilty, the judge then determines the sentence to be given the convicted person. (In almost all states, the jury determines the punishment in death-penalty cases.) If the jury reaches a verdict of not guilty, the judge discharges the defendant.

The **bailiff** is usually a deputy sheriff, marshal, or some other law-enforcement officer. The bailiff:
- keeps order in the courtroom.
- protects the jury from outside influence.
- assists the court clerk in ceremonial duties, such as asking all to rise when the judge enters the court.

The **court clerk** is the main administrative assistant to the judge. The clerk:
- keeps track of courtroom proceedings.
- catalogs and takes custody of exhibits and other items of evidence.
- prepares all written orders of the court (summons and warrants, for example) as directed by the judge.
- administers oaths to witnesses.
- calls the jurors for selection.

The **court reporter** records by machine or shorthand everything said in the trial. The court reporter prepares a typewritten transcript of these records.

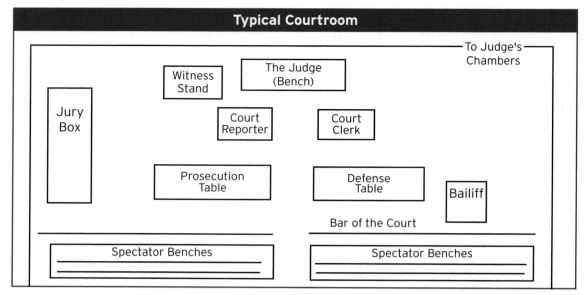

Typical Courtroom

The **prosecution lawyers** are members of the city attorney's office, district attorney's office, state attorney general's office, or U.S. attorney's office. They represent the people of the city, county, state, or United States. They must prove that the accused is guilty of a particular crime beyond a reasonable doubt.

The **defense lawyers** are private attorneys or members of publicly supported organizations, such as the public defender's office. They must defend the accused by showing that the government does not have enough evidence to convict the defendant. All lawyers — both prosecution and defense — are officers of the court. They must therefore observe all rules of law and ethics so that a fair trial will take place.

The **defendant** is the person accused of a crime. The defendant assists the defense

lawyers in presenting the case and accepts or appeals the results of the trial.

Police officers investigate crimes, and when they uncover enough facts to establish probable cause, they arrest suspects. The rest of the criminal case process tests these facts. Their job does not end with arrest, however. They also help prosecutors prepare for trial and frequently testify as witnesses.

Witnesses are persons asked to tell under oath what they know about the case. Most may only testify about what they actually saw and heard. But **expert witnesses** may testify about their knowledge and give opinions. They are persons with special knowledge, such as doctors, psychologists, and scientists.

The **jury** is a panel of adult citizens (usually 12) from the community. It must decide questions

THE COURTROOM SETTING

As with all dramas, a criminal trial has a setting: It is the courtroom. In it the judge presides, the jury is impaneled, witnesses are sworn in and examined, and a verdict is rendered. On this stage, the fates of individuals are debated and decided, and the aims of justice are pursued. Some courtrooms are ornately carved in dark woods and rich furnishings. Others are designed with an eye toward efficiency and practicality. Some are old and threadbare. Others are new and starkly modern. All serve the same purpose.

Above is a diagram of a typical courtroom. When conducting the activities in the trial of Thomas Evans, arrange your classroom similarly.

For Discussion

1. In most courtrooms, the judge's bench is on a raised platform. Why do you think this is so?
2. In all courtrooms, the witness stand is on the side of the judge's bench closest to the jury box. Why do you think this is so?
3. The partition between the spectators and the active courtroom participants has traditionally been called the bar. Why do you think it is there? Who may pass the bar?

of fact from the evidence presented in the court-room and reach a verdict based on those facts. Alternative jurors, usually two or four, also sit on juries in case one or more of the regular jurors are removed or cannot continue on the jury. Alternative jurors listen to all the trial proceedings, but do not participate in the jury deliberations or verdict unless they are placed on the regular jury.

FOR DISCUSSION
1. What are the main functions of the defense and prosecuting attorneys?
2. At trial, whose role is it to decide issues of law? Whose role is charged with deciding issues about facts?

ACTIVITY

In the Halls of Justice

There is perhaps no better way to understand the criminal court process than to observe it in person. To do this, you must visit a courthouse.

As a class or in small groups, make arrangements to visit a criminal courthouse. Many court-houses have tour programs or will accommodate groups. Contact the court's clerk of services or the clerk of the criminal docket for information. The clerk can suggest an appropriate time for the visit and help you plan an itinerary. Try to include a visit to (1) a preliminary hearing, (2) an arraignment, (3) a jury selection, and (4) a criminal trial.

When you arrive at the courthouse, observe appropriate dress and decorum. Be especially quiet when entering or leaving courtrooms. Use the following information guide and questions to help arrange your visit and for reporting your experience to the class.

Information You Will Need: (1) name of the courthouse, (2) its address, (3) the telephone number, (4) the reporting time, (5) the contact person (if any).

Questions for Field Experience Report
1. Describe the general environment of the courthouse. Are the court facilities crowded and noisy, or calm and businesslike?
2. Describe the security arrangements in the court building and in the courtrooms.
3. In the arraignment court, *describe what is going on.*
4. In a preliminary hearing, *describe what is going on.*
5. At a criminal jury trial:
   - What is the case about?
   - Is it a felony or misdemeanor prosecution?
   - Who is the prosecutor — a deputy district attorney, deputy city attorney, a federal prosecutor?
   - *What do you observe* the prosecutor doing during the trial?
   - Who is the defense attorney — a deputy public defender or a private attorney?
   - *What do you observe* the defense attorney doing during the trial?
   - *What do you observe* the judge doing during the trial?
   - *Describe* the questioning of one witness in the trial.
   - Do the jurors seem to be attentive? Describe them.
   - What is your overall impression of the courthouse visit? Were you confused by anything you saw or heard?
6. If the opportunity arises or can be arranged, interview an officer of the court (e.g., court clerk, judge, or attorney). Select questions from the following list or make up your own.
   - Does the court have a large backlog of cases? If so, why?
   - Does plea bargaining take place? How? What is your opinion of it?
   - What percentage of the cases before the court are disposed of by plea bargaining?
   - How long does it take a criminal case to come to trial in this court?
   - What percentage of defendants at trial are represented by public defenders?
   - In what percentage of trials is the defendant found guilty?
   - What percentage of those convicted by the court are locked up in a correctional institution? Put on probation?
   - What percentage of accused persons remain in jail awaiting their trials?

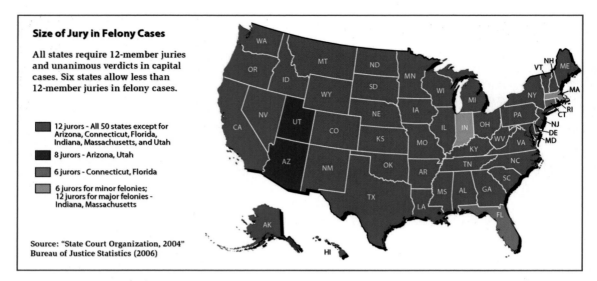

Size of Jury in Felony Cases

All states require 12-member juries and unanimous verdicts in capital cases. Six states allow less than 12-member juries in felony cases.

- 12 jurors - All 50 states except for Arizona, Connecticut, Florida, Indiana, Massachusetts, and Utah
- 8 jurors - Arizona, Utah
- 6 jurors - Connecticut, Florida
- 6 jurors for minor felonies; 12 jurors for major felonies - Indiana, Massachusetts

Source: "State Court Organization, 2004" Bureau of Justice Statistics (2006)

Case Notes: The Trial of Thomas Evans

Thomas Evans felt mixed feelings of dread and relief as he climbed the wide steps leading to the massive courthouse door. In the weeks since the shooting, he had thought of little else. His mind played the events over and over again. Often, he hoped for the trial to start — only when it was over could his life begin again. There had been delays. Motions were made and extensions of time granted. Though he had complete trust in his lawyer, he wished she could move things along faster. Now at last his trial would begin. Today was the day.

Inside the main lobby of the courthouse, Tom looked at a blur of moving figures. The footsteps of people going about court business echoed off the cold marble walls. The drone of a hundred conversations filled his ears, yet he and his parents barely spoke at all. They were too occupied with trying to find the right courtroom by the appointed hour, 9 a.m.

At last they found it, Department D, Criminal Trials Division. Tom breathed a sigh of relief when he saw Ms. Jaffee leaning against the court rail. She smiled as he approached and directed his parents to seats in the spectator gallery directly behind the defense table.

Although she had already prepared Tom for what would take place at his trial, she briefly explained it all again. He listened carefully, vaguely comforted by the confidence in her voice, until she repeated what the charge would be: "Second-degree murder." No matter how she said it, it sent a chill through his body. Ms. Jaffee reached across and patted his arm. "It's a serious thing, Tom," she smiled, "but they haven't proven anything yet."

Just then the clerk stood up and said in a loud voice: "All rise and come to order. The Superior Court is now open and in session. The Honorable Judge Coghlan presiding."

Tom looked up just in time to see a black-robed figure enter from a door behind the bench and sit down. She softly tapped her gavel several times and said, "The case of *People v. Evans*. Is the state ready?"

The prosecutor said, "The state is ready to proceed, your honor."

Turning to Ms. Jaffee, the judge repeated the question, "Is the defendant ready?"

Ms. Jaffee spoke in a loud firm voice, "Yes, your honor."

The trial of Thomas Evans had begun.

FOR DISCUSSION
1. What is the charge in the Thomas Evans case? What are its elements?
2. Review **Key Step: Trial Procedures** on pages 194–195. What will happen next in Thomas Evans' trial?

Key Step: Jury Selection

Selected at random, people on juries come from the defendant's community. Their names may be gathered from voter registration lists and driver's license lists, depending on the state. These citizens are then called to jury duty. Before a trial starts, a group of up to 40 from the jury pool go to the courtroom where the trial will take place. The court clerk draws the names of 12 of them — called prospective jurors — and asks them to sit in the jury box. Prospective jurors then take an oath promising to answer truthfully the questions put to them by the judge and lawyers.

Next comes **voir dire** — questioning of the prospective jurors by the judge and attorneys for both sides. The judge starts the voir dire by telling the jurors the charge(s) against the defendant and by asking them their name, age, address, occupation, and previous jury experience. The judge might also inquire if there is any reason why they should not be jurors in this particular case. (For example, a person who had been a victim of a similar crime might not be able to be a truly impartial juror.) The judge will excuse prospective jurors from a case if their answers indicate a bias or prejudice toward one side. Prospective jurors may also be excused if they would suffer economically due to the length of the trial. The excused jurors, however, may have to serve in another case.

If the judge finds no reason to excuse a prospective juror, the attorneys for both sides normally get an opportunity to question the juror in greater depth. In most states, the attorneys themselves question the jurors. In others, the attorneys submit questions to the judge, who conducts the questioning. Based on the answers jurors give, attorneys get jurors excused from the case by challenging them.

There are two types of challenges. A **challenge for cause** occurs when a lawyer claims the prospective juror does not meet the government's legal requirements or is biased and could probably not reach an impartial verdict. After the attorney explains the reasons for challenging for cause, the judge must decide whether to excuse or accept the prospective juror. Usually there is no limit on challenges for cause.

A **peremptory challenge** needs no explanation from the attorney. When a lawyer makes a peremptory challenge, the prospective

All jurors take an oath to base their verdicts solely on the evidence presented in court.

juror being questioned is automatically excused. Each side, however, has only a limited number of these challenges. According to U.S. Supreme Court rulings, neither the prosecution nor defense may make a peremptory challenge on the basis of a juror's race or gender (*Batson v. Kentucky*, 1986; *Georgia v. McCollum*, 1992; *J.E.B. v. Alabama ex rel. T.B.*, 1994; *Miller-El v. Dretke*, 2005).

The voir dire continues until 12 jurors and alternates (usually two or four) have been chosen. (Some jurisdictions allow juries of six, seven, or eight persons.) In some cases, especially those that have been highly publicized, lawyers challenge many prospective jurors before a full jury is selected. This process may take anywhere from a few hours to many days to complete. Once the jury has been chosen, it is **impaneled**, or made official, by taking another oath. Jurors swear that they will try to reach a fair and impartial verdict based solely on the evidence presented during the trial.

FOR DISCUSSION

1. Why do you think there is no limit on the number of challenges for cause and a limit on peremptory challenges?
2. Should the Supreme Court ban peremptory challenges based on religion or disability? Why or why not?
3. The goals of the judge, prosecution, and defense in criminal trials are often quite different. What differences might they have about jury selection?

CLASS ACTIVITY

Choosing a Jury

In this activity, students simulate the jury selection for the Thomas Evans trial. In advance, you might invite an attorney to attend your simulation and play the role of the judge.

1. Class members should have the following roles: 2–4 prosecuting attorneys; 2–4 defense attorneys; 14 prospective jurors; 1 court clerk; observers (remainder of class).
2. Students should read their appropriate role descriptions below. In addition, observers and lawyers should read the materials on **How to Ask Effective Questions**, below, and **Sample Questions for Lawyers in a Criminal Case** (pages 200–201).
3. The court clerk should:
   - Swear in the prospective jurors before the voir dire begins.
   - Call the first prospective juror (by name) to the jury box.
4. The judge should tell all of the prospective jurors the charge against Thomas Evans and then ask the first prospective juror some introductory questions.
5. Prosecutors, and then defense attorneys, question the first prospective juror and either accept or challenge the juror. If a challenge for cause is raised, the judge should rule on it. Each side is allowed only one peremptory challenge.
6. Repeat steps 4 and 5 above until all prospective jurors have been questioned. Observers should watch the proceedings carefully and then complete the **Observer Evaluation Form** (page 202).

Lawyers for Both Sides

Lawyers will question each prospective juror searching for persons to accept or to challenge for cause. Before the simulation begins, lawyers should prepare a list of questions to ask prospective jurors.

How to Ask Effective Questions

The following list should be used by the attorney role players in preparing effective questions. In addition, observers should use this list for evaluating the questions asked by the attorney role players.

1. Plan most of your questions ahead of time. Make sure that they are precisely worded.
2. Begin with basic questions about the juror's background. Then ask more advanced questions on the juror's feelings about the case.
3. Always keep the question's purpose in mind when you are formulating it.
4. Individualize your questions. Reword any long or complex question if an individual juror does not understand it.
5. Develop questions that call for short responses. Don't include too many things in one question.
6. Avoid questions that require a single "yes" or "no" answer. You do not want to limit jurors' responses. Prepare questions that allow jurors to express their feelings in their own words. For example, the question, "Do you have any prejudices against insurance companies?" might be changed to "What is your opinion of insurance companies?"
7. Explore incomplete answers. If a juror claims not to know an answer, you should ask questions to find out why.
8. Unless it is crucial to your case, try to avoid questions already addressed to a juror by another attorney. You usually do not need to go over the same ground twice.

Sample Questions for Lawyers in a Criminal Case

1. Are you married? Do you have any children? If so, what are their ages?
2. What type of work do you do?
3. What is your educational background?
4. Have you ever had any jury experience before?

(Continued on next page.)

5. Have you ever been a victim of a crime?
6. Have you ever been convicted of a crime?
7. Would any of the criminal cases you heard in previous jury duty limit your ability to sit on future cases?
8. Was there anything about your previous jury experience that would lead you to feel that you may have some prejudices either for or against the prosecution? For or against the defendant?
9. Do you have an opinion on this case?
10. Is there anything about what you have seen since you came for jury duty that would lead you to feel that you have an opinion on this case?
11. Have you heard about this case in the media (television, radio, Internet, etc.)? If so, was there anything that leads you to believe the defendant is guilty or not guilty?
12. Do you believe that the defendant is innocent until proven guilty?
13. Would you tend to believe the police officers in their testimony more readily than you would a person who was not a police officer?
14. Were you ever connected with any type of law enforcement?
15. Do you have any relatives who would have any interest in seeing the jury reach a verdict either for or against the defendant in this case?
16. If you are chosen as a juror, will you stand on your own individual analysis of the evidence and not be swayed by the emotions of other jurors?

Court Clerk

Before voir dire begins, the court clerk will ask all prospective jurors to raise their right hands and state: "I solemnly swear I will answer all questions truthfully and to the best of my ability." The court clerk will call each prospective juror, in turn, to the witness stand for voir-dire questioning.

Prospective Jurors

Each student should assume the role of one of the prospective jurors described in the biographies below and answer the judge's and attorneys' questions accordingly.

1. **Michael:** Anglo, 38 years old, a high school dropout. He is a third cousin to Tom Evans, but has never met him. He is a mechanic, married with five children and is a non-drinker. He has no prior jury duty.
2. **Ralph:** Latino, 61 years old, married with two children, college education. Ralph is an officer in his United Auto Workers local. He has no prior jury duty.
3. **Judy:** Of Greek descent, 22 years old, and single. She attends law school and wants to become a criminal defense lawyer. She lives with her parents, does not work, and has no prior jury duty.
4. **Bob:** Asian, 69 years old, single. High school graduate. Bob is a retired construction worker and has no prior jury duty.
5. **Richard:** Anglo, 38 years old. He is married with six children and is an attorney at law. He has no prior jury duty.
6. **Rosa:** Latina, 62 years old, married with two children and three grandchildren. She finished high school, has been married for 30 years, and is a supervisor at the post office. Her niece was once wounded in a drive-by shooting by a youth gang. She has served on one prior jury, which heard a criminal prosecution for being drunk in a public place. She voted to convict.
7. **Bernice:** African American, 39 years old, married with one child. College graduate with a B.A. in English. Bernice is a counselor at Freedom High School, where she has worked for the past 13 years. She has no prior jury duty.
8. **Russell:** Anglo, 57 years old, college graduate. He has been a vice president in charge of a large business corporation for 10 years. He is married with two children and is a former alcoholic. No prior jury duty.

(Continued on next page.)

9. **Carol:** African American, 32 years old, divorced three years ago, with one child. Protestant. A college graduate, she is a marketing analyst, but is currently unemployed and is receiving unemployment benefits. She is active in the Black Community Action Council. She has no prior jury duty.

10. **James:** Of Irish descent, 58 years old, high school education. James is a produce manager in a supermarket, is married and has one child. As a young man, he was once convicted for a misdemeanor — disturbing the peace. No prior jury duty.

11. **Maria:** Latina, 54 years old, high school education. She is a widow with three children who live with her. Maria has worked as an insurance agent for more than 35 years. She has managed to pay off the mortgage on her modest home and send her oldest child to college. She has no prior jury duty.

12. **Larry:** African American, 38 years old, married with four children. A college graduate, he is a computer programmer. No prior jury duty.

13. **Priscilla:** Asian, 62 years old, widow, ex-college professor. She derives her income from her pension. She has had two prior jury duties. Both cases involved grand theft auto, and she voted to acquit both times.

14. **Janis:** Anglo, 70 years old, single. She works as a secretary for a small accounting firm. She has no prior jury duty.

Observers

As part of the courtroom audience, you can observe all the role players. Your job is to evaluate the simulation. The observer evaluation form should help you focus on the key issues. Copy the form onto a sheet of paper leaving enough room for you to answer the questions. You will present and discuss your impressions with the entire group at the end of the simulation.

Debriefing Questions

1. Have the observers read their evaluations to the class. Discuss the answers.
2. Ask your visiting attorney:
    *   How did this simulation compare with real voir dire in your local courts?
    *   How fair and effective is voir dire?

OBSERVER EVALUATION FORM

Copy this form on a sheet of paper.

1. Put a (+) next to the most realistic role players. Put a (-) next to the least realistic groups.
    * Prospective jurors
    * Lawyers
    * Judge

2. The jurors who most realistically portrayed their roles were:

3. Based on the jury that was finally selected, who do you think will win this case? Why?

4. An effective question asked by the defense attorney was:

5. An effective question asked by the prosecuting attorney was:

6. A good question not asked of the prospective jurors is:

Case Notes: Trial Strategy

In his trial, Thomas Evans faces two charges — second-degree murder and the lesser included offense of manslaughter.

A lesser included offense is one that shares most, but not all of the elements of the greater crime. Manslaughter is a lesser included offense of murder, theft is a lesser included offense of robbery, and criminal trespass is a lesser included offense of burglary. A defendant cannot be convicted of both the greater offense and the lesser included offense. But if the prosecution fails to prove the greater offense, the defendant could still be convicted of the lesser included offense. Thus, in the Evans case, both sides must prepare for the two charges.

Before a trial begins, attorneys must analyze the case and prepare their trial strategies, beginning with a careful review of the charges. To properly defend or prosecute a case, attorneys must understand all potential arguments, both for and against their interests. By completing this analysis *before* the trial begins, every decision and presentation the attorneys make will be informed and will support the outcome they seek.

One way to analyze a case thoroughly is to use a chart identifying all of the elements of the charges, as well as the corresponding evidence that could be used to prove or disprove each of

those elements. Below is the outline for a chart based on the charge of second-degree murder. It lists the two elements for second-degree murder — (1) a killing and (2) with malice aforethought. An attorney would fill out a chart for each witness. Then the attorney could better understand what needed to be proved or disproved at trial.

Chart for Trial Strategy in *People v. Evans*	
Section 274—Second-Degree Murder. A killing with malice aforethought. **Witness:**	
Supporting Facts for the Prosecution	**Supporting Facts for the Defense**
element of crime — "a killing"	
element of crime—"with malice aforethought"	

Preparing for Trial

In this activity, students complete charts that will help prepare trial strategy.

1. Form two groups of lawyers — one representing the prosecution and one representing the defense. Within the groups, form six attorney teams (pairs or triads).

2. Each team should:
   a. Be responsible for one witness statement. (The witness statements are on pages 212–214.)
   b. Review the statutory language of second-degree murder. (The charges are on page 217.)
   c. Carefully read the assigned statements and identify supporting facts for **both** the prosecution and defense cases. This information should be recorded onto a chart, similar to the one on page 203.
   d. Make a second chart for involuntary manslaughter by repeating steps b and c.

3. After students complete the charts, the teams should regroup with all the members of their law offices and present their findings.

4. Students should make copies of the charts so they have a complete view of what the prosecution and defense need to prove. The charts will help them throughout the trial.

Case Notes: Opening Statements

Praised be he who can state a cause in a clear, simple and succinct manner, and then stop.
– Justice Harry H. Belt, Oregon Supreme Court, *Jungwirth v. Jungwirth* (1925)

Once the jury has been impaneled, the attorneys for both sides deliver an **opening statement** about the case to the jury. Opening statements outline the facts that the attorneys expect to prove during the trial. An opening statement should present the jury with an orderly and easy-to-understand version of the case from the attorney's perspective. It should be persuasive but without emotion.

In criminal trials, the prosecuting attorney goes first. Usually, the defense gives its opening statement immediately afterward. The defense may, however, choose to wait until the prosecution has called all its witnesses and the defense is ready to present its case-in-chief.

Writing an Opening Statement

To prepare an opening statement, attorneys must organize and outline the entire case they intend to prove at trial. A good opening statement should:

- Explain what the attorney plans to prove and how the attorney will do it.
- Present the events of the case in a clear, orderly sequence.
- Suggest a motive or emphasize a lack of motive for the crime.

Attorneys usually begin their statement with a formal introduction:

"Your honor, ladies and gentlemen of the jury, opposing counsel, my name is [full name], representing the [people of (name of the state) — or — defendant Thomas Evans] in this action."

The attorneys then turn to the jury and begin their statements.

Opening statements often include such phrases as:
- The evidence will show that . . .
- The facts will prove that . . .
- Witness [name] will be called to testify that . . .

CLASS ACTIVITY

Writing an Opening Statement

In this activity, students take the roles of defense attorneys or prosecutors and write an opening statement for the Thomas Evans trial. They may find it useful to use the charts they prepared in **Class Activity: Preparing for Trial**.

1. The class should divide in half: one half to take the role of lawyers for the state, the other for the defense.
2. As homework, each student should:
   a. List the most important facts of the Thomas Evans case *from his or her assigned point of view* (prosecution or defense).
   b. Write a one- or two-page opening statement from his or her assigned point of view.
3. In class, students should meet in groups of four, deliver their opening statements to each other, and choose the best one.
4. Then groups should join together to form new groups of eight and the two students chosen should deliver their statements and have the group decide which is best.
5. The finalists from each group should stand and deliver their opening statements to the whole class.
6. The class should select the best opening statement given for each side on the basis of: (a) use of facts, (b) clarity, and (c) presentation.

Case Notes: Direct and Circumstantial Evidence

If a man go into the London Docks sober without means of getting drunk, and comes out of one of the cellars very drunk wherein are a million gallons of wine, I think that would be reasonable evidence that he had stolen some of the wine in that cellar, though you could not prove that any wine was stolen, or any wine was missed.

– Sir William Henry Maule, English judge, *Reg. v. Burton* (1854)

Evidence proves or disproves facts in a trial. The trier of fact — judge or jury — must base its verdict solely on the evidence admitted at the trial. Testimony of witnesses, documents, drawings, and physical objects, such as weapons, drugs, clothing, and other items — these are all forms of evidence that the fact finder considers and weighs in reaching a verdict.

There are two basic kinds of evidence: direct and circumstantial. In a criminal case, **direct evidence** is evidence of one or more of the elements of a given crime. For example:
- Will sees Maria point a gun at Marsha and pull the trigger. In a trial for murder or manslaughter, Will's testimony about what he saw Maria do would be *direct evidence* against her.
- Miguel hears Warren scream at his neighbor, "I'm going to take this bat and kill you, old man!" In a trial for assault, Miguel's and the old man's testimony would be *direct evidence* against Warren.

Circumstantial evidence in criminal cases *indirectly* supports one or more elements of a crime. Circumstantial evidence requires the fact finder to make an inference that something happened. For example:
- Will sees Maria with a smoking gun in her hand standing over Marsha's dead body. In a trial for murder or manslauhter, this would be *circumstantial evidence* that she shot Marsha.
- Miguel sees Warren running away from the old man's house with a bat in his hand. In a trial for assault, this would be *circumstantial* evidence.

It is possible for the same evidence to be both direct and circumstantial. It all depends on how it is used. Imagine that Brad's fingerprints are found on a murder weapon. The fingerprints are direct evidence that Brad had possession of the weapon. It is circumstantial evidence that Brad had used it in a murder.

The distinction between direct and circumstantial evidence may make little difference. Both are important if the fact finder believes them to be convincing or credible in a particular case. In fact, many criminal suspects are tried and convicted only with compelling circumstantial evidence.

CLASS ACTIVITY

Direct or Circumstantial

In this activity, students analyze samples of evidence to determine whether they are direct or circumstantial evidence.

Each student should:
1. Down the side of a sheet of paper, write the letters "a" through "e."
2. Read the items below. For each item, write on the paper whether the evidence described is *direct* or *circumstantial*. Explain each answer.
   a. Suzanne is charged with resisting arrest. Officer Monroe testifies that the defendant hit him with her briefcase after he had stopped her on the highway for speeding.
   b. Charles is on trial for vandalism. An expert testifies that the color and composition of the paint found on the school building is identical to that of a can of paint found in Charles' book bag.
   c. Jennifer is on trial for the burglary of a local record shop. Mrs. Ramirez testifies that she saw Jennifer's car parked outside the record shop at the time the burglary is believed to have taken place.
   d. Jeff is charged with the sale of marijuana. An undercover narcotics agent testifies that Jeff handed him a large bag of marijuana and took $2,000 in cash from him.
   e. Danny is on trial for kidnaping a 2-year-old girl. Ms. Joseph, Danny's landlady, testifies that she saw Danny loading an unusually large bundle covered with a sheet into his car just minutes after the crime was reported by the victim's parents.

Case Notes: Rules of Evidence

It is for ordinary minds, and not for psychoanalysts, that our rules of evidence are framed. They have their source very often in considerations of administrative convenience, of practical expediency, and not in rules of logic.
– U.S. Supreme Court Justice Benjamin Cardozo, *Shepard v. U.S.* (1933)

Many rules dictate when and how evidence may be presented in court. Known as rules of evidence, they help ensure that trials will be fair, orderly, and more likely to discover the truth. They do this, for example, by excluding from court any evidence that is unreliable or unreasonably prejudicial or inflammatory. Also, in some instances, the rules require that attorneys in a trial take certain steps before they can introduce evidence.

Sometimes judges make their own objections to an attorney's questions or a witness's answer. But in most situations, all evidence will be admitted into a trial unless an attorney objects that it violates one of the rules of evidence. So lawyers must know the rules of evidence well. Such knowledge helps them prove their case, because they can present evidence important to their case and keep out an opponent's improper evidence, which could hurt their case.

The rules of evidence in state and federal courts are complex and often differ. On the next few pages, you will find an explanation of some basic rules of evidence followed in all American courts.

1. Relevance

First and foremost, evidence must be **relevant** to an issue in the case. It must help prove the defendant's guilt or innocence. This rule prevents the fact finder from confusing essential facts of the case with extraneous details.

Suppose that a prosecutor is trying to prove that Bob robbed a bank. Evidence offered to prove that Bob speaks several languages is probably not relevant. The defendant's skills in foreign languages are not at issue.

But what if a witness has testified that the robber spoke French? Evidence offered to prove that Bob speaks French would, in this case, be relevant.

But what is relevant to prove that fact? Evidence that Bob owns a French poodle would not be relevant, because it has no value in proving he speaks French. But evidence that Bob has a master's degree in French would be relevant.

Even relevant evidence may not be admissible if its value in deciding an issue — its **probative value** — is *outweighed* by other considerations. Thus a judge may disallow relevant evidence if it is unfairly prejudicial, confusing to the jury, or a waste of time.

In fact, prior criminal convictions of the defendant are not normally allowed into evidence. For example, if Jay is accused of burglary, the prosecutions may not usually introduce evidence that he has committed other crimes. But the prior criminal convictions can be introduced to prove the defendant used the same method of committing the crime before. Imagine that the evidence in Jay's case proves the burglar broke a bedroom window, entered the house, stole jewelry, and left a typewritten note saying "thanks for the stuff." If Jay had been previously convicted of committing a burglary in the same way, evidence of this prior conviction could be admitted.

How to Object:
- "Objection, your honor. This evidence is not relevant to the issues of this trial."
- "Objection, your honor. Counsel's question calls for irrelevant testimony."
- If the objection is made *after* the witness answers: "Objection, your honor. The testimony is not relevant to the facts of this case. I ask that it be stricken from the record."

If the judge thinks an objection is invalid, the judge will say, "Objection overruled." But if the judge agrees with the objection, the judge will say, "Objection sustained."

2. Foundation

To establish the relevance of evidence, attorneys may need to **lay a proper foundation**. Laying a foundation means that before a witness can testify to certain facts, it must be shown that the witness was in a position to know about these facts. For example, if a prosecutor asks a witness if he saw Bob leave the scene of the bank robbery, the defense attorney may object for a lack of foundation.

After the court sustains — or upholds — this objection, the prosecutor would have to ask the witness if he was near the bank on the day of the robbery. This lays the foundation

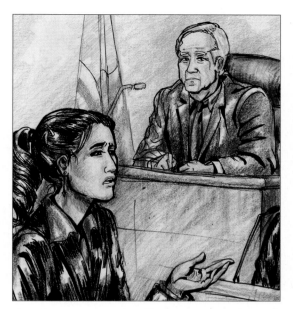

that the witness is legally competent to testify to the underlying fact.

Sometimes when an attorney is laying a foundation, the opposing attorney may object that the testimony is irrelevant. The questioning attorney then has to explain how the testimony relates to the case.

How to Object:
- "Objection, your honor. There is a lack of foundation."

3. Personal Knowledge

Witnesses in a trial must have personal knowledge of what they testify about. Jessica could not, for example, testify that Isaac is a bad driver if she had never seen Isaac drive.

How to Object:
- "Objection, your honor. The witness has no personal knowledge to answer the question."
- If the objection is made *after the witness answers*: "Objection, your honor. I ask that the witness's testimony be stricken from the record because the witness has no personal knowledge of the matter."

4. Hearsay

In general, witnesses must have personal knowledge of the facts they testify about. Evidence is more trustworthy if a witness observed something directly ("I saw Bill steal the wallet") rather than heard something second-hand ("Mary told me Bill stole the wallet"). Second-hand statements are normally regarded as hearsay evidence.

Consider some examples:

- Sam, a witness in Marty's murder trial, tells the court that he overheard a friend of Marty's say, "Marty killed Joe because he had to."
- The prosecution attempts to introduce a letter written by Marty's sister, which states: "Marty needed the money so he killed him."

Both of these are examples of hearsay evidence. It is unlikely that either of them would be admissible as evidence in a trial. **Hearsay evidence is any out-of-court statement — oral or written — offered to prove the truth of that statement.** (Think about the word "hearsay." It is something "heard" out of court and "said" in court to prove that what was asserted is true.)

Consider another example from Marty's trial:
- Sam testifies, "I heard Joe yell to Marty, 'Get out of the way.' "

Is this hearsay? It's an out-of-court statement. But it's not offered to prove the truth of the statement. Instead, it is being introduced to show that Joe had warned Marty by shouting. So it is not hearsay, and a court would admit this testimony into evidence. Hearsay is a tricky subject.

It grows even more complicated because there are various exceptions to the rule that hearsay is not admissible. Below are a few of the most common exceptions:

a. **Admissions against interest.** When parties to a case make statements that go against their legal interest, these statements are usually admissible evidence. If, for example, Sam testified, "Marty told me that he wanted to kill Joe," this statement would be admissible because it was made by Marty (the defendant and thus a party to the case) and it goes against his legal interest (i.e., it hurts his case).

b. **Excited utterance.** Any statement made by a person in an excited state is usually admissible.

c. **State of mind.** Any statement that shows the speaker's state of mind is usually admissible. For example, if before the murder Joe told Sam, "I'm really scared." This statement would be admissible in testimony by Sam.

d. **Official records and writings by public employees.**

e. **Records made in the regular course of doing business.**

How to Object:
- "Objection, your honor. Counsel's question calls for hearsay."
- If the objection is raised *after the witness answers*: "Objection, your honor. This testimony is hearsay. I ask that it be stricken from the record."

5. Opinion Testimony

With a few limited exceptions, only experts with special knowledge and qualifications can give their opinions in a trial. An attorney who calls an expert to testify must first qualify the individual as an expert. In other words, an attorney must lay a foundation that the person qualifies as an expert. The attorney does this by asking a series of questions about the person's professional training and experience in a particular field. The attorney then asks the court to acknowledge the witness's specific expertise.

All witnesses, even non-experts, may give their opinions about things like color, size, weight, drunkenness, speed of a moving object — anything within the realm of a person's ordinary, everyday experience or perception.

How to Object:
- "Objection, your honor. Counsel is asking the witness to give an opinion."
- If the objection is made *after the witness answers*: "Objection, your honor. This witness was not qualified as an expert. I ask that the witness's opinion be stricken from the record."

6. Argumentative Questions

Witnesses may ordinarily only be asked questions to get facts from them. Questions that challenge witnesses to reconcile differing parts of their testimony may be objected to as being argumentative. For example, an attorney asks, "How can you expect the court to believe that you were at Main Street that day when you previously testified you were out of town?" This question may be objected to as argumentative.

How to Object
- "Objection, your honor. Counsel is being argumentative."
- "Objection, your honor. Counsel is badgering the witness."

7. Special Rules for Direct Examination

Direct examination takes place when lawyers call their own witnesses to the stand and ask them questions.

a. Form of Questions

Generally, attorneys must ask questions that evoke a short narrative answer from the witness, but not an answer that is too long or rambling. In direct examination, attorneys usually may not ask leading questions. A leading question is one that suggests the desired answer. It usually elicits a "yes" or "no" answer. Often, leading questions are really statements with something like, "isn't that right?", "isn't that so?", or "didn't you?" tacked on the end.

For example, this question would be proper on direct examination (assuming that the fact was in issue): "Mr. Stevens, when did you and your wife adopt Charles?"

This one would be improper: "You and your wife adopted Charles two years ago, didn't you, Mr. Stevens?"

How to Object:
- "Objection, your honor. Counsel is leading the witness."

b. Character

Unless a person's character is at issue in a case, witnesses generally cannot testify about a person's character. But a witness's honesty is one aspect of character always at issue. In addition, the defense may introduce evidence of the defendant's good character and, if relevant, show the bad character of an important prosecution witness. Once the defense introduces character evidence, the prosecution can try to refute it.

Consider these examples:
- The prosecutor calls the owner of the defendant's apartment to testify. She testifies that the defendant often stumbled in drunk at all hours of the night. This character evidence would *not* be admissible unless the defendant had already introduced evidence of good character. Even then, a judge might disallow it because its prejudicial nature would probably outweigh its probative value.
- The defendant's minister testifies that the defendant attends church every week and has a reputation in the community as a law-abiding person. This would be admissible.

How to Object:
- "Objection, your honor. The witness's character is not at issue in this case."
- "Objection, your honor. The question calls for inadmissible character evidence."

c. Refreshing Recollections

Imagine that you are a witness of a hit-and-run accident. Two years later, the driver of the car comes to trial. The prosecutor calls you to the stand and asks you to describe what you saw. You give as many details as you can, but when the attorney asks you what the license plate number was on the car, you draw a blank. "I know I saw it and I know I told you when you talked to me after the accident," you answer, "but it's been so long — I just can't remember the number."

Since cases often take time before coming to trial, witnesses often may have a hard time recalling specific details of events occurring months or years earlier. In addition, witnesses may be so nervous that their memories fail them. The rules of evidence deal with this problem by allowing attorneys to help their witnesses remember. This is called "refreshing the witness's recollection." In the example above, the attorney could take a typed copy of a statement you made near the time of the accident, mark it as an "exhibit," have you read it, and then take the statement away. She could then ask you the question about the license plate number again. "*Now* I remember," you answer. "The number was XOJ 489."

8. Special Rules for Cross-Examination

After direct examination, the lawyer for the opposing side cross-examines each witness. Cross-examination has two purposes. It is designed to:
1. Clarify the witness's testimony from the other side's point of view.
2. Give the opposing side an opportunity to **impeach** the witness — that is, to attack the witness's credibility.

a. Form of Questions

While leading questions (e.g., "You drank like a fish that night, didn't you, Mr. Saski?") are usually not permitted during direct examination, they are allowed during cross-examination.

b. Scope of Cross-Examination

Cross-examination questions are limited to matters that were brought out on direct examination. In other words, cross-examination may not go beyond the scope of the direct examination. Most judges, however, broadly interpret this rule.

How to Object:

- "Objection, your honor. Counsel's question is going beyond the scope of direct examination."

c. Impeachment

Impeaching a witness on cross-examination is designed to reduce the importance that the fact finder gives a witness's story. An attorney can impeach a witness by asking about:

- **Bias or prejudice** the witness has toward the issues or parties in the case.
- The **accuracy** of what the witness saw, heard, smelled, etc.
- **Prior statements** that the witness made that are **inconsistent** with the witness's testimony in court.
- **Prior criminal convictions** of the witness, but only if they relate directly to truth-telling ability.
- **Prior acts of misconduct**, but only if they relate directly to the witness's ability to tell the truth. (Such questions may only be asked if the attorney conducting the cross-examination has information showing that the bad conduct actually happened. The attorney may not base the question on some rumor or just ask the question to make the witness look bad.)

If the witness's credibility is attacked on cross-examination, the attorney whose witness has been impeached may ask more questions to try to limit the damage done and restore the witness's credibility. This is done on **redirect examination** by the lawyer who put the witness on the stand in the first place.

FOR DISCUSSION

1. Why is eyewitness testimony ("I saw Bill steal the wallet") more trustworthy than something heard secondhand ("Mary told me she saw Bill steal the wallet")? How can the first statement be tested in court? How can the second statement?
2. When are leading questions permitted and prohibited? Why do you think this difference exists?
3. Can you think of examples of relevant testimony that would not be allowed in evidence?

CLASS ACTIVITY

Objection

In this activity, students decide whether to make objections in trial situations based on the Thomas Evans case.

Each student should write the letters "a" through "l" down the side of a sheet of paper. Each should (1) next to each letter write "yes" or "no" to indicate whether an objection should be made in each situation and (2) give a reason for each answer.

a. Karen Miller testifies: "I am convinced my little girl was intentionally killed by the Evans boy."

b. Joel Robertson testifies: "A friend of mine said he saw Oscar hit Tom over the head with a beer bottle."

c. The prosecutor asks Gail Duran: "What kind of potato chips did you serve at your party?"

d. Karen Miller testifies: "I told the police officer that I thought whoever shot Joyce was on drugs."

e. On cross-examination, the attorney asks Gail Duran: "You didn't stop the car when you heard the explosion behind you, did you?"

f. Karen Miller testifies: "Joyce was shot with a 12-gauge shotgun."

g. Joel Robertson testifies: "Oscar Hanks always parks his truck across the street from his house. It must have been there that day when Joyce Miller was shot."

h. Lt. Tony Jackson of the police department testifies: "We know that Tom Evans had connections with drug dealers in the area."

i. One of the guests from Gail Duran's party testifies: "Tom Evans told me after the fight that he was going to fix Oscar Hanks once and for all."

j. A neighbor of Karen Miller states that a car with a gun sticking out of the back window drove by at about 15 miles per hour.

k. On direct examination, Evans' attorney asks him: "You never intended to shoot anyone, did you?"

l. Joel Robertson testifies: "If you ask me, a shotgun is effective up to about 20 yards."

Cross Fire

Now that you've had a chance to test your understanding of some basic rules of evidence, take the role of attorneys and prepare to examine witnesses in the case of Thomas Evans.

It is recommended that you invite a lawyer or law student into class to work with the attorney groups and act as judge during the direct and cross-examination of witnesses. (If none is available, the teacher should take the role of judge.)

1. Form the following groups: Six teams of prosecutors (numbered 1–6) consisting of 2–3 students each; six teams of defense attorneys (numbered 1–6) consisting of 2–3 students each; and six witnesses.
2. Students should prepare by following the instructions for their appropriate group (witnesses or attorneys) described below.
3. After all of the teams have developed their questions, role play the examination of the witnesses. The team assigned to cross-examine a particular witness should be primarily responsible for raising objections to the direct examination, although *all* students on the opposing team may do so. Likewise, a team assigned to direct examination of a particular witness should be primarily responsible for raising objections to the cross-examination of its witness. The visiting attorney or law student should rule on the objections and help debrief the activity.
4. After all witnesses have been examined and cross-examined, discuss the debriefing questions on page 214.

Witness Instructions

Select one of the six witness statements on pages 212–214 and study it carefully. For this activity, try to become the character described. Be prepared to answer questions that both the prosecuting and defense attorneys might ask you. When you are on the stand, it will be your job to recall the events leading up to Joyce Miller's killing. Do not add anything to the facts contained in your witness statement.

Attorney Instructions

One of the six prosecution teams should be responsible for each of these tasks:
1. Direct examination of Joel Robertson
2. Direct examination of Gail Duran
3. Direct examination of Lt. Tony Jackson
4. Direct examination of Karen Miller
5. Cross-examination of Thomas Evans
6. Cross-examination of Lillian Sweet

One of the six defense teams should be responsible for each of these tasks:
1. Direct examination of Thomas Evans
2. Direct examination of Lillian Sweet
3. Cross-examination of Joel Robertson
4. Cross-examination of Gail Duran
5. Cross-examination of Lt. Tony Jackson
6. Cross-examination of Karen Miller

To prepare to examine witnesses, carefully review:
1. **The Rules of Evidence**, pages 206–210, so that you can raise or counter objections.
2. The statement of the witness you are assigned, pages 212–214.

Your team should **develop questions** for the witness you are assigned to. Keep in mind the rules of evidence and your team's overall strategy for the case.

The prosecution must prove Thomas Evans guilty of murder beyond a reasonable doubt.

(Continued on next page.)

It must bring up evidence in its favor and anticipate and attempt to dilute the impact of evidence against it. The defense must raise every reasonable doubt it can about Evans' guilt.

In most states, a defendant charged with murder could be found guilty of manslaughter instead. Since Evans has no alibi and doesn't deny being in the car with the shotgun in his hand, the case will boil down to the issue of Evans' *intent*. The prosecution will try to prove that Evans knew exactly what he was doing and that he intended to shoot the gun. The defense, on the other hand, will try to show that Evans didn't really mean to hurt anyone and that the gun went off accidentally.

Since you can only cross-examine witnesses about what they testified about on direct examination, cross-examination questions can be difficult to write in advance. But the witnesses' statements should give you an idea of what witnesses are likely to be asked on direct, and you can write cross-examination questions accordingly. You should then be alert during direct examination so you can get rid of any inappropriate cross questions you have developed.

Also, be prepared to object to any statements you believe violate the rules of evidence.

Statement of Karen Miller

My name is Karen Miller. I am 25 years old and divorced.

I was home on the evening of July 6. Around 7 p.m., Joyce was playing in the front yard. I asked her to close the front gate and come inside the house, since it was her bath time. As I watched her go to the gate, a black car slowly drove down the block. I think it was a late model Camaro, but I'm not really sure. Suddenly, the barrel of a rifle or shotgun was pointing from the car window right at Joyce. Before I could say or do anything, there was an explosion, and the car took off quickly.

At that instant, I looked at Joyce and saw her fall to the ground. Horrified, I ran to her and saw blood all over her face and body.

I can't describe the occupants of the black Camaro. Still, I think the driver was a young woman.

A red Toyota truck was parked in front of my house that evening. I believe it belonged to a teenager named Oscar who lives across the street.

Statement of Joel Robertson

I am Joel Robertson and I am 21 years old. I have known Tom for a few years, but we're not close friends.

On the evening of July 5, I attended a party at Gail Duran's house. I and most of the others at the party drank beer for several hours. Around 3:30 a.m., a fight broke out. I was not involved in the fight, but I saw Tom Evans get hit over the head with a beer bottle. I did not know who did it. I and some of the others at the party took Tom Evans to the hospital for emergency treatment. On the way to the hospital, Evans kept asking who hit him with the bottle. He was really angry. The people in the car suggested several names, including Oscar Hanks.

The next day about 5 p.m., Tom Evans came over to my apartment. Evans was still very angry about what had happened the night before. I know from past experience that Evans is the type of guy to carry a grudge. He's a real hothead. He was always getting into fights with guys at school and in our neighborhood. Evans told me that he thought he knew the guy who split open his scalp. He said he thought the guy was Oscar Hanks. Evans told me, "I'm going to put a scare into that guy that he won't forget."

We watched a video for a while and had a soft drink. Evans was really nervous. A little later, Evans started asking me about my gun collection. I am a hunter and collect rifles and shotguns. Evans was especially interested in one of my shotguns. He asked me to show him how to work it. He also asked me how far a shotgun would shoot. I responded that a shotgun would be effective up to about 20 yards. About 6 p.m., Evans left my apartment.

(Continued on next page.)

Statement of Gail Duran

My name is Gail Duran. I am 17. I have been dating Tom Evans for about a year.

On the evening of July 5, I had a party for about 50 of my friends while my parents were on vacation. During the party a lot of people got drunk on beer. Sometime around 3 a.m., a fight broke out among about a dozen guys. Tom was hit on the head with a beer bottle. There was blood all over the place. I asked Joel Robertson and some others to take Tom to the hospital while I tried to get everybody out of the house before the police came.

The next day Tom called me to say he was all right and would be over to see me later on. Around 6:30 p.m., Tom arrived at my place. He was very upset about getting hit the night before. He said he thought he knew who had hit him with the bottle. He said it was Oscar Hanks. Tom then asked me to go for a ride with him. I agreed to go with him.

Tom asked me to drive his car while he sat in the back. Tom owns a Chevrolet Camaro. He told me he wanted to look for Oscar Hanks. He gave me directions to drive to Fourth Street. While driving down Fourth Street Tom said, "Hey, that's his truck. Slow down, Gail." As I slowed down, I noticed for the first time that Tom had a shotgun in the back of the car with him.

At this point, I really got scared and began to swerve down the street. I had never seen Tom act this way before. Then there was a loud bang, and Tom yelled to me, "Get us out of here, fast!" I managed to drive out of the neighborhood. I stopped on a quiet street. Tom got into the driver's seat and took me home.

On the way home, Tom told me that the shotgun just went off by itself, but he did not think he had hit anything. I did not actually see the shotgun discharge, but I believe that the swerving motion of the car must have caused Tom to accidentally pull the trigger. Tom would never intentionally shoot anyone. He's always been a sensitive and gentle guy. Sure, he had a few fist fights when we were in high school, but he didn't mean anything by it. He's basically a great guy.

Statement of Thomas Wade Evans

My name is Thomas Wade Evans, age 18. I have recently graduated from high school. I work at an auto parts store.

I was totally shocked when I was arrested for shooting a little girl. I have never been in serious trouble before. I was suspended from high school once or twice because of problems with other guys, but they always started the fights, not me.

Gail Duran is my girlfriend. She and I have been going together for about a year. I went to her party on July 5 and had a good time drinking beer with my friends until I got in a fight with a dozen other guys around 3 a.m. During the fight, I was struck in the back of the head with a beer bottle. Joel Robertson and some others at the party took me to the hospital. It took five stitches to close the wound on my scalp.

The next day (July 6), I called Gail and told her I was all right and that I would be dropping by later in the day.

I was angry at Oscar and wanted to pay him back some way. So I decided to take my father's shotgun and scare him a little.

After picking up the shotgun, I stopped by Joel Robertson's apartment around 5 p.m. I knew he was a hunter. I got him to tell me how to work a shotgun so I could make Oscar think I was serious. But I never knew the gun was loaded, and I never meant to hurt him. I just wanted to teach him a lesson.

From Joel's place, I went over to see Gail. I asked her to go with me for a drive. I had her drive my car while I sat in the back seat looking for Oscar's house. I knew he lived somewhere on Fourth Street. I also knew he drove a red Toyota truck. Finally, I spotted his truck parked along the street. But the car suddenly lurched, and the next thing I knew, the shotgun went off accidentally. I panicked. I didn't know it was loaded! I told Gail to get out of the neighborhood fast. I did not see anybody in the yard where Joyce Ann Miller was killed and certainly did not aim the shotgun at her. It was an accident.

(Continued on next page.)

Statement of Lillian Sweet

My name is Lillian Sweet. I am a retired school principal. I have a Ph.D. in educational administration from the University of Illinois. I was a history teacher and a school guidance counselor before I became a principal.

I have known Tom Evans since he was a little boy. I've lived down the street from the Evans family for almost 20 years, and I was the principal of the high school that Tom attended.

I did have to suspend him for brawling with other boys once or twice. But kids will be kids. I think Tom was just following the lead of his friends in those days. As a principal, I was not very seriously concerned about Tom's behavior. I knew he'd grow up to be the fine young man he is today.

Tom has always been a joy to have in the neighborhood. He is kind to old people and children. He helps his mother with grocery shopping. Sometimes he even drives me to my doctor appointments if the weather is bad or he has a free afternoon.

In my opinion, Tom could never have done what he is accused of doing. He's a very stable and responsible young man. He's just not capable of murder.

Statement of Lt. Tony Jackson

NOTE : For Lt. Jackson's statement, see the **Police Crime Investigation Report** on pages 174–176.

Debriefing Questions

1. Which witnesses were most important to the prosecution and defense? Why?
2. Which questions were most effective during the direct examinations? During the cross-examinations?
3. Which objections were raised most often? Why do you think this happened?
4. What characteristics do you think tend to make a witness seem believable? What characteristics detract from a witness's credibility?
5. What qualities would a person need to be a successful trial lawyer? Explain.

Case Notes: Closing Statements

Be brief, be pointed; let your matter stand
Lucid in order, solid, and at hand;
Spend not your words on trifles, but condense;
Strike with the mass of thought, not drops of
sense;Press to the close with vigor, once begun,
And leave, (how hard the task!) leave off,
when done.
. . . Victory in law is gain'd, as battles fought,
Not by the numbers, but the forces brought.

– Joseph Story, U.S. Supreme Court justice, "Advice to a Young Lawyer" (1831)

After the defense's case-in-chief, the opposing counsels make closing arguments. These arguments give the attorneys a chance to summarize their cases, review the testimony of witnesses, and make a last appeal to the judge or jury.

Guidelines for an Effective Closing Statement

An effective closing statement should:
1. Be emotionally charged and strongly appealing (unlike the calm, rational opening statement).
2. Only refer to evidence admitted during the trial.
3. Emphasize facts that support the claims of your side.
4. Note weaknesses or inconsistencies in the opposing side's case.
5. Summarize the favorable testimony.
6. Attempt to reconcile inconsistencies that might hurt your side.
7. Be presented so that notes are barely necessary.
8. Be well-organized (starting and ending with your strongest point helps to structure the presentation and give you a good introduction and conclusion).
9. Focus on reasonable doubt. The prosecution should emphasize that the state has proven the elements of the crime beyond a reasonable doubt. The defense should raise questions suggesting that reasonable doubt exists.

Proper phrasing includes:
- The evidence has clearly shown that . . .
- Based on this testimony, there can be no doubt that . . .
- The prosecution has failed to prove that . . .
- The defense would have you believe . . .

10. Conclude with an appeal to convict or acquit the defendant.

CLASS ACTIVITY

The Defense Rests . . .

In this activity, students take the role of attorneys developing closing arguments in the case of *People v. Evans*.
1. Each student should:
   - Choose to represent either the prosecution or defense.
   - Review the witness statements on pages 212–214 and consider the main points brought out in witnesses' testimony in the previous activity.
   - Develop a three-minute closing argument for presentation to the class. (Be sure to follow the above **Guidelines for an Effective Closing Statement**.)
2. Twelve members should be chosen to act as a jury. They will judge the quality of the presentations. To do this, each must take a blank piece of paper and make a rating sheet as follows: Write each presenter's name and role (prosecutor or defense attorney). Under each presenter's name, write the numbers one through 10 in a column. Each of the numbers corresponds to one of the **Guidelines for an Effective Closing Statement**. At the close of each presentation, place a check mark next to the item if the presenter's statement met the criterion.
3. Three prosecutors and three defense attorneys should make closing arguments. (Alternate defense attorneys and prosecutors with the defense going first.) After all have presented, poll the jury to find out which prosecutor and defense attorney made the best presentation. Jurors should explain their choices based on the listed criteria.

Case Notes: Instructing the Jury

The jury injects a democratic element into the law. This element is vital to the effective administration of criminal justice, not only in safeguarding the rights of the accused, but in encouraging popular acceptance of the laws and the necessary general acquiescence in their application. It can hardly be denied that trial by jury removes a great burden from the shoulders of the judiciary. Martyrdom does not come easily to a man who has been found guilty as charged by twelve of his neighbors and fellow citizens.
— U.S. Supreme Court Justice Hugo Black, dissenting in *Green v. U.S.* (1958)

After closing arguments in a criminal trial, the judge gives the jury instructions it must consider when arriving at a verdict. This process is sometimes called **charging the jury**. These instructions serve to explain the law, point out the elements of a crime that must be proved, and show the relationship of the evidence to the issues on trial. In some states, judges may develop their own instructions with input from the opposing attorneys. But judges must be careful, because inaccurate or misleading instructions to the jury are the most common reason for verdicts being overturned on appeal. In many states, judges base their instructions on models adopted by the legislature. In recent years, some states have developed new jury instructions that are supposed to be easier for jurors to understand. They have tried to eliminate unnecessary legal terms and to more clearly explain the law.

Imagine you are in the jury box. The court clerk in the case of *People v. Evans* rises and announces: "The court will now charge the jury. No one may leave or enter the room during the charge." Judge Coghlan then gives the following instructions:

Ladies and gentlemen of the jury:

It is my duty to instruct you in the law that applies to this case. You must follow the law as I state it to you.

1. Duties of the Judge and Jury

In determining whether the defendant is guilty or not guilty, you — as jurors — must base your decision entirely on the evidence presented during this trial and on the law as explained by me. You must not be governed by sympathy, guesswork, emotion, prejudice, or public opinion. You must not be influenced by the mere fact that the defendant has been arrested, charged, and brought to trial.

2. Evidence

If the evidence equally supports two reasonable versions of the truth, one of which points to the defendant's guilt and the other to the defendant's innocence, it is your duty to adopt the version pointing to the defendant's innocence.

3. Credibility of Witnesses

Every person who testifies under oath is a witness. You are the sole judges of the credibility of the witnesses who have testified in this case.

Discrepancies or differences that occur in a witness's testimony, or between one witness and another, do not necessarily mean that a witness is lying. Failure to recollect facts is a common human experience. In addition, two persons witnessing the same incident will often see or hear it differently. You may simply have to decide which version of the facts is more believable.

4. Statements of Counsel and Evidence Stricken From the Record

Any testimony or other evidence rejected or stricken from the record is to be treated as if you had never heard it.

Also, if an objection to a question was sustained, you must disregard the question. This means that you must not speculate about what witnesses might have said if they had been allowed to answer. Neither may you speculate about why an objection was made to a question.

5. Presumption of Innocence – Reasonable Doubt – Burden of Proof

A defendant in a criminal action is presumed to be innocent until proven guilty. This presumption places upon the prosecution the burden of proving the defendant guilty beyond a reasonable doubt. This does not mean that no possible doubt must exist, because doubt will always exist. A reasonable doubt is based upon reason and common sense, not just on speculation. It may arise from a careful and impartial consideration of all the evidence, or from lack of evidence. Beyond a reasonable doubt means that after hearing all the evidence, a juror is firmly convinced that the defendant is guilty.

6. The Charges in This Case

Thomas Wade Evans has been charged with two crimes: Second-degree murder and involuntary manslaughter.

Second-Degree Murder

Second-degree murder is the unlawful killing of a human being with malice aforethought.

Malice aforethought may be either express or implied. It is express when a person intends unlawfully to kill a human being. It is implied when the killing results from an intentional act that:
(1) is dangerous to human life, *and*
(2) was deliberately performed with knowledge of the danger and with conscious disregard for human life.

Malice does not necessarily require any ill will or hatred of the person killed.

Aforethought does not imply deliberation or the lapse of considerable time. It only means that the required mental state must come before rather than follow the act.

If you find beyond a reasonable doubt by the evidence presented in this trial that Thomas Wade Evans intended to kill Joyce Ann Miller, then you shall return a verdict of second-degree murder.

OR

If you find beyond a reasonable doubt by the evidence presented in this trial that Thomas Wade Evans intended to fire the shotgun that killed Joyce Ann Miller, and that the act involved a high degree of probability that death would result, and that it was done with conscious disregard for human life, you shall return a verdict of second-degree murder.

Lesser Charge: Involuntary Manslaughter

Involuntary manslaughter is the unlawful killing of a human being without malice aforethought and without intent to kill. If you are satisfied beyond a reasonable doubt that the killing was unintentional and the direct result of a very dangerous or unlawful act, you shall return a verdict of involuntary manslaughter.

7. Doubt Whether Murder or Manslaughter

If you are satisfied beyond a reasonable doubt that the killing was unlawful, but you have a reasonable doubt whether the crime is murder or manslaughter, you must give the defendant the benefit of this doubt and find it to be manslaughter rather than murder.

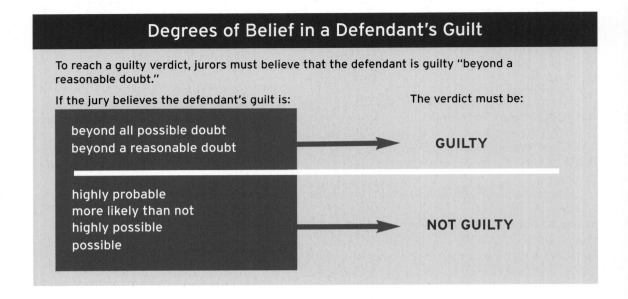

Degrees of Belief in a Defendant's Guilt

To reach a guilty verdict, jurors must believe that the defendant is guilty "beyond a reasonable doubt."

If the jury believes the defendant's guilt is:

beyond all possible doubt
beyond a reasonable doubt

→ **GUILTY**

highly probable
more likely than not
highly possible
possible

→ **NOT GUILTY**

The verdict must be:

8. Unanimous Agreement as to Offense: Second-Degree Murder or Manslaughter

Before you may return a verdict in this case, you must agree unanimously. If you return a verdict of not guilty, it must be agreed on unanimously. If you return a guilty verdict, you must unanimously find him guilty of manslaughter or of murder in the second degree.

9. Each Juror Must Make an Independent Decision

Each of you must decide the case for yourself, but you should also do so only after discussing the evidence and these instructions with the other jurors.

You should not hesitate to change your opinion if you are convinced it is wrong. You should not, however, be influenced one way or the other because the majority of jurors favor a certain verdict.

10. Concluding Instructions

You shall now retire and select one of your number to act as foreperson. The foreperson will preside over your deliberations. To reach a verdict, all jurors must agree to the decision. As soon as all of you have agreed upon a verdict, you shall have it dated and signed by your foreperson, and then you shall return to announce it to the court.

FOR DISCUSSION

1. What things *should* be considered and discussed by the jurors? What things *should not* enter into the jury's deliberations?
2. Review the definition of "beyond a reasonable doubt" in instruction #5. According to this definition, which one of the following statements would be true?
   a. A juror should vote to convict *only* if 100 percent sure that the defendant is guilty.
   b. A juror should vote to acquit if the juror believes there is any possible chance that the defendant is not guilty.
   c. A juror should vote to convict if the juror believes that a very high degree of probability exists that the defendant is guilty.
3. Review the second-degree murder charge against Thomas Wade Evans in instruction #6. According to the prosecution, how was Joyce Ann Miller killed? According to the defense, how was Joyce Ann Miller killed?

We, the Jury

In this activity, students take the role of jury members charged with rendering a final verdict in the case of *People v. Evans*. To complete this activity, follow these procedures:

1. Form two or three juries of 12 students each. (Remaining students may form a smaller jury.)
2. Each jury should:
   a. Appoint a foreperson who will help lead discussions, collect signatures on the verdict, date it, and deliver it to the court.
   b. Refer to the judge's instructions on pages 216–218 during the deliberations.
   c. Let the foreperson take one or more polls to determine if the jury has reached a consensus. (Remember the verdict must be unanimous.)
   d. First determine the verdict on the charge of second-degree murder. If the jury finds Evans not guilty or it deadlocks on this issue, then it should determine the verdict for involuntary manslaughter. If it finds Evans guilty of second-degree murder, it does not need to consider the lesser charge of involuntary manslaughter.
3. After about 15 minutes, the teacher, acting as judge, will ask the juries if they have reached a verdict.
   • A jury that cannot reach a unanimous verdict will be considered a hung jury.
   • The forepersons of juries reaching a unanimous verdict will deliver it to the court along with the 12 signatures attesting to it.
4. In either case, the judge may poll individual jurors and ask them to explain the reasons for their decision. (In a real case, a judge polling individual jurors may not ask for the reasons behind a decision.)

Debriefing Questions

1. Sometimes juries are unable to reach a verdict and become what is known as hung juries. How is it possible for people who have heard the same evidence to reach different conclusions?
2. How does this jury activity compare to what you know about real jury deliberations? For example, were some students unable to be objective after having taken the role of the defense or prosecution? Did the jurors know too much about the case?
3. Which witnesses did you find most believable? Least credible? What makes a witness credible?
4. Which roles were the most difficult to play? Why?
5. What did you learn about the job of the judge, attorneys, witnesses, and jurors?

CLASS ACTIVITY

Verdict

As a concluding activity, write an essay explaining your personal verdict in the Thomas Evans case.

Sources for Unit 3

ABA, " Model Rules of Professional Conduct." 2010. URL: www.americanbar.org · ABA, "Standards Relating to the Prosecutor Function." 1979. · *America's Problem-Solving Courts*. Nat. Assoc. of Criminal Defense Lawyers, 2009. URL: www.nacdl.org · "Back on Track," BJA, 2009, FS 000316. · *Calif. Commission on the Fair Administration of Justice, Final Report*. State of Calif.,. 2008. · Castille, R. "A Special Court for Veterans," *NY Times*, 11/10/2010. · Clark, T. *et al. Fair Trial/Free Press*. Benziger Bruce & Glencoe, Inc., 1977. Some material in this chapter was adapted from this book with permission. · "County-Based & Local Public Defender Offices, 2007," BJS, 2010, NCJ 231175. · "Drug Courts," BJA, NIJ, OJJDP, 2011, NCJ 236074. · *Drug Courts & State Mandated Drug Treatment Programs*, NIJ-Sp., 2008, NCJ 223975. · "Drug Courts," ONDCP, 2010, FS 000346. · "Drug Courts," NIJ, 2006, NCJ 211081. · *Exploring the Key Components of Drug Courts*, NIJ-Sp., 2008, NCJ 223853. · Federal Criminal Case Processing Statistics, BJS, 2012, URL: http://bjs.ojp.usdoj.gov/fjsrc · *Felony Defendants in Large Urban Counties, 2006."* BJS, 2010. NCJ 228944. · "Felony Sentences in State Courts, 2006." BJS, 2009. NCJ 226846. · *A Guide to the Role of Crime Victims in Mental Health Courts*, OVC-Sp., 2008, NCJ 223344. · Hayden, P. "Reconsidering the Litigator's Absolute Privilege to Defame," 54 *Ohio State Law J.*, vol. 54, 1993. · Hayes, B., "Voters & Judges," *Bill of Rights in Action*, Spring, 1998. · Henning P. "Prosecutorial Misconduct & Constitutional Remedies," *Washington U. Law Q.*, vol. 77, 1999. · *Impact & Cost-Benefit Analysis of the Anchorage Wellness Court*, NIJ-Sp., 2008, NCJ 227605. · *Impact of a Mature Drug Court Over 10 Years of Operation*, NIJ-Sp., 2007, NCJ 219225. · Indigent Defense Systems, BJS, 2012, URL: http://bjs.ojp.usdoj.gov · Kelley, E. "Inconsistent Prosecutorial Theories Revisited," *The Champion*, 12/2005. · "Killing Time," NIJ-Sp., 2007, NCJ 220985. · King, R. *et al.* "Drug Courts," Sentencing Project, 2009. URL: www.sentencingproject.org · "Leave No Veteran Behind," *The Economist*, 6/2/2011. · Lithwick, D. "Why veterans deserve special courts," *Newsweek*, 2/10/2010. · "Making the Drug Problem Smaller, 2001–2008," ONDCP, 2009, NCJ 226159. · McMichael W. "Special courts help vets regain discipline," *Army Times*, 2/20/2011. · *Mental Health Courts*, BJA-Sp., 2009, NCJ 228274. · Minsker, N. "Prosecutorial Misconduct in Death Penalty Cases," *Calif. Western Law Rev.*, vol. 45, 2009. · Mor, J."The Anonymous Accused," *Boston College Law Rev.*, Vol. 44, No. 3, 2003. · *National Drug Control Strategy 2012*, ONDCP, 2012. · *Painting the Current Picture*, BJA-Sp., 2011, NCJ 235776. · Prosecution, BJS, 2012, URL: http://bjs.ojp.usdoj.gov · "Prosecutors in State Courts, 2007." BJS, 2011. NCJ 213799. · "Public Defender Offices, 2007 — Statistical Tables," BJS, 2009, NCJ 228538. · "Public Defense Reform Since Gideon," BJA, 2010, NCJ 230794. · *Report to the Nation on Crime & Justice*, Washington, D.C.: BJS, 1988. · Ridolfi, K. *et al.* "Preventable Error," Northern Calif. Innocence Project, Santa Clara U. School of Law, 2010. · Saltzburg, S. "Lawyers, Clients & the Adversary System," *Mercer Law Rev.*, vol. 37, 1986. · Simon, W. "The Ethics of Criminal Defense," *Mich. Law Rev.*, vol. 91, 1993. · State Court Organization, BJS, 2012, URL: www.ojp.usdoj.gov · "State Court Organization, 1987–2004," BJS, 2007, NCJ 217996. · "State Public Defender Programs, 2007," BJS, 2010, NCJ 228229. · "Statewide Coordination of Problem-Solving Courts," BJA-Sp., 2011, NCJ 236476. · Subin, H. "Is This Lie Necessary?, *Georgetown J. of Legal Ethics*, 1988. · "Tale of Three Cities," BJA-Sp., 2010, NCJ 232872. · *Transferability of the Anchorage Wellness Court Model*, NIJ-Sp., 2008, NCJ 227606.

Unit 4
CORRECTIONS

Jay is 19 years old. He was convicted of stealing a car. Today, he will appear before a judge to be sentenced. He is about to enter **corrections** – the part of our criminal justice system that deals with convicted offenders. Though Jay has never been in trouble with the law before, he has a lot to worry about. Will the judge send him to prison? Or, because he has no prior record, will he be given some alternative to prison – probation or some kind of community service?

If you asked Jay's victim, you might hear a demand that he go to prison. If you asked someone familiar with the prison system, however, you might get a different opinion. Some might even argue that Jay should be given a second chance. Many experts believe that contact with hardened criminals only locks someone into a life of crime.

In many parts of the country, Jay could be sentenced to a special program in a group home, where he would work under the supervision of a staff of trained specialists. In that setting, he could receive psychological counseling and job training. Or he could be sent to a boot camp program that tries to instill self-discipline in young offenders.

This chapter explores how sentencing decisions are made and what the alternatives are – prison, probation, community service, and several innovative programs, which may be promising alternatives to existing programs. We will also explore how prisons developed, the problems they currently face, and some experimental corrections programs that are under way. Finally, you will take a look at what is perhaps the most hotly debated of all corrections issues – the death penalty.

CHAPTER 14
SENTENCING

If a man put out the eye of another man, his eye shall be put out.
– Code of Hammurabi (c. 1780 B.C.)

THE PURPOSE OF PUNISHMENT | A BRIEF HISTORY OF PUNISHMENT IN THE U.S. | SENTENCING LAWS
THE SHAKY STATUS OF SENTENCING GUIDELINES | DO SENTENCES HAVE TO BE PROPORTIONATE?
FEDERAL SENTENCING: CRACK VERSUS COCAINE

The Purpose of Punishment

Will the punishment of the thief bring back the stolen money? No more so than the hanging of a murderer restores his victim to life.
– Abraham Lincoln (1809-1865), U.S. president

All societies have maintained the right to punish people who break their rules. But what is the purpose of punishment? What is it supposed to accomplish? This is a difficult question to answer. Experts and lay people alike often disagree. Over the years, theories have been advanced about different ways of handling wrongdoers — from ducking stools to imprisonment to psychotherapy.

People advocating one approach have often condemned all others as brutal, or unjust, or ineffective. Some scholars, however, have tried to bring some order to the debate by developing an inclusive theory of punishment. This theory holds that one approach might work best in one situation while another would be better in a different situation.

The following are brief descriptions of each of the major reasons for punishing a lawbreaker:

Rehabilitation seeks to treat and reform the lawbreaker. Advocates of this theory believe that prison or release programs should try to turn the wrongdoer into a productive member of society. To implement this theory, the prison system has to provide job training, psychological counseling, and educational programs. And these programs should be tailored to the best interests of the individual prisoner. Critics of the rehabilitation theory admit that it may be a noble idea, but they argue that it just doesn't work in practice.

Restitution seeks repayment. The offender repays the victim or community in money or services. Critics say money and services cannot repay for the harm caused by violent crimes.

Incapacitation seeks to isolate a criminal from society to protect ordinary citizens. Confinement in a secure prison makes it impossible for a criminal to commit further crimes in the surrounding society. Critics of this theory point out that most criminals have fixed prison terms, and they will be released sooner or later. If nothing is done to reform them, the protection is only temporary.

Deterrence seeks to prevent further crimes. This can operate in two ways. One way, called *specific* deterrence, targets the criminal in question, hoping that the memory of punishment will deter that criminal from any further crime. *General* deterrence targets other potential criminals. Others will see the punishment and be discouraged from committing the same crime. Critics argue that few criminals expect to be caught, and deterrence is only powerful when criminals fear they will be caught and punished.

Retribution seeks revenge. This is perhaps the oldest theory of punishment, based on the idea that society has to retaliate against a person who commits a crime. This idea dates back to the ancient "eye for an eye" philosophies of Mesopotamian and Judeo-Christian traditions. Advocates say that by imposing punishment we in some way get even with criminals. Some critics of retribution say it is too cruel for a modern society, and others claim that it does nothing to address serious issues like reforming criminals or protecting the innocent.

FOR DISCUSSION

1. Which of the five reasons for punishment do you agree with? Disagree with? Why?
2. If someone broke into your house and stole your television, what do you think would be an appropriate punishment? Which of the reasons for punishment did you base the punishment on?
3. In recent years, two theories of punishment have been advanced. Do you think each of the following is a new theory or does it fit under one or more of the theories described in the article?
   a. **Just deserts.** A person should be punished according to the seriousness of the crime. The more serious the crime, the harsher the punishment should be. In words, offenders should get the punishment they deserve.
   b. **Restorative justice.** It seeks to meet the needs of the victim, the wrongdoer, and the community. It tries to get the wrongdoer to admit the wrongdoing to the victim and to work to make the victim and community whole.

CLASS ACTIVITY

The Student Court

In this activity, students act as members of a student court, assigning penalties to those who break school rules. Wrongdoers may be sentenced to detention, hours of school service, loss of student body privileges, or other penalties the court thinks appropriate.

1. Form student courts of five students each.
2. Each court should:
   a. Appoint a chief judge to lead the discussion and to assign one of the cases below to each student. That student is responsible for taking notes and reporting the penalty in that case to the whole class.
   b. Review the cases below, which have come before the court. After discussion, the court should set an appropriate and specific penalty for each wrongdoer.
3. Reconvene as a class. Put headings on the board using the names of the five rule breakers. The appropriate member of each court should report its recommended penalty and write it under the appropriate heading.
4. For each sentence described, discuss and decide whether it best meets the purposes of (a) rehabilitation, (b) restitution, (c) incapacitation, (d) deterrence, (e) retribution, or (f) some combination. Conclude with a class discussion using the debriefing questions.

Cases

1. **Chris Hodges** was caught smoking in the restroom. This is his second offense.
2. **Terry Rodriguez** was cited for littering the campus quad area during lunch period.
3. **Kelly Janus**, a candidate for student body treasurer, was caught tearing down other candidates' campaign posters.
4. **Linden Sommerville** started a food fight in the cafeteria by smashing an overripe banana in her friend's hair.
5. **Jan Turner** defaced several library books.

Debriefing Questions

1. Which of the sentences recommended by the student courts do you think are fair? Which are not fair? Why?
2. Which of the five theories of punishment comes closest to your idea of what is just? Why?

A Brief History of Punishment in the U.S.

The history of correction is a graveyard of abandoned fads.

– Robert Martinson, criminologist, *Rehabilitation, Recidivism, and Research* (1976)

Since 1970, most states have cracked down on crime and sent many criminals to prison. America today has more than 2 million people behind bars, about seven times the number of people in prison and jail in 1970. America has a far higher percentage of its citizens in prison than any other country in the world.

This drastic change is not unique. America's attitudes on crime and punishment have changed dramatically many times in its history. Looking back on this history, we can gain some insight into the problems we face today.

Punishment in Colonial America

Before the American Revolution, all the colonies punished even minor offenses harshly. For petty offenses, public humiliation was used. A lawbreaker might have to stand in a public square, hands locked up in a device called a pillory or sit with feet locked in stocks. In many towns, offenders were tied to ducking stools and dunked into the icy water of a river or pond. Some lawbreakers were forced to wear a symbol of their crime, such as the large red "A" for adultery that was sewn to the dress of the character Hester Prynne in Nathaniel Hawthorne's novel *The Scarlet Letter*.

More serious lawbreakers might receive lashings at a public whipping post. Others, particularly runaway slaves in the Southern colonies, might be branded with a hot iron or mutilated by cutting off their toes. In Northern colonies, thieves might have their ears cut off or the letter "T" branded on their necks or faces. This was not only a punishment, but a warning to other thieves. For many serious crimes, the penalty was death by public hanging.

Some colonies had jails to house the accused while they awaited trial. Jailkeepers often ran these institutions for profit, and inmates had to pay for their own food and blankets. Some poor inmates starved to death before their trials began. Many inmates were hired out to work as laborers building roads and working farms, and the profits went to the jailkeepers. One observer noted seeing inmates weighed down by "iron collars and chains, to which bombshells were attached, to be dragged along while they performed their degrading service."

Regret and Remorse: The Penitentiary

After the American Revolution, concerned citizens of the new American republic objected to the brutal treatment of criminals. In Pennsylvania, the Quakers, an influential religious group opposed to war and violence, worked for reform. They introduced the idea of changing criminals' behavior by locking them up behind high thick walls. This reform movement led to the first prisons as we know them today. In 1790, Philadelphia built a block of cells. Each cell was six by eight feet wide and nine feet high. The Quakers hoped that solitary confinement would give criminals the opportunity to think about their deeds and become penitent, or sorry, for what they had done. Early prisons, therefore, came to be called **penitentiaries**. The Quakers also sponsored other reforms, including separating prisoners by sex, keeping children out of adult jails, and providing food and clothing to inmates at government expense.

The Pennsylvania System, as these reforms were called, represented a change in the philosophy of how to deal with criminals. Its purpose was not just to punish, but also to *correct* the behavior of lawbreakers. This new idea of correcting, or reforming, criminal behavior soon spread throughout the United States and Europe.

Unfortunately, the system of corrections sponsored by the Quakers seldom accomplished its purpose. Prisoners locked up in solitary confinement frequently became sick, went insane, or died. In 1842, Charles Dickens, the famous English novelist and social reformer, visited the Pennsylvania penitentiaries and reported:

> I believe it, in its effects, to be cruel and wrong. In its intention, I am well convinced that it is kind, humane, and meant for reformation, but I am persuaded that those who devised this system of prison discipline . . . do not know what it is they are doing. I believe that very few men are capable of estimating the immense amount of torture and agony which this dreadful punishment . . . inflicts upon the sufferers . . . . I hold this slow and daily tampering with the mysteries of the brain to be immensely worse than any torture of the body.

Leading a Useful Life: The Work System

The failure of solitary confinement led prison officials to try a new system that emphasized work instead of isolation. Under this system, prisoners were locked up in cells at night. But during the day, they worked together in prison shops and ate in a common dining

The youth reformatory in Elmira, N.Y., started a rehabilitation program in 1877.

area. At first, rules banned talking among prisoners. Later reforms allowed conversation.

The work system became widely used, and it still influences prison philosophy today. In many prisons, inmates learned to operate simple machines to manufacture items such as furniture for government offices. In some places, prisoners performed services such as growing food or cleaning laundry.

Treating Criminal Behavior: Rehabilitation

Following the Civil War, a new group of prison reformers questioned the work system. These reformers argued that criminal behavior was like a disease and that prisons should try to cure the disease with some form of treatment. Prisoners should be **rehabilitated** and ready to take up a normal life in society when they were released.

A rehabilitation program was first tried in 1877 in a youth reformatory at Elmira, New York. Elmira offered its young offenders school classes, vocational training, health care, and counseling. When inmates demonstrated that they were ready for release, they could leave. Many other youth reformatories soon took up this new system.

Adult prisons also adopted parts of the Elmira system. By 1918, doctors, psychologists, and social workers were being brought into the prison to help rehabilitate prisoners. In addition, many states set up separate prison facilities for dangerous prisoners, low-risk prisoners, women, drug addicts, and the criminally insane. Rehabilitation became the model for American prisons.

Getting Them Off the Streets: Incapacitation

As crime rates soared in the 1960s and 1970s, however, many began to question whether rehabilitation worked. They pointed to high **recidivism** rates — the rate that those released from prison go on to commit further crimes. About half of those released from prison were arrested again within three years. As the crime rate grew, the public supported more "get tough on crime measures." Officials turned away from the model of rehabilitation to one of incapacitation, getting criminals off the street so they cannot harm anyone. This has resulted in the staggering number of people behind bars in America today. But the debate over how to treat criminals hasn't stopped. Every generation of Americans has carried on this debate. It continues today.

FOR DISCUSSION
1. Why did prisons develop?
2. Discuss this statement: "The history of corrections has been one of good intentions and bad results." What does it mean? Do you agree with it? Why or why not?

CLASS ACTIVITY

Pros and Cons of Punishment

In this activity, students evaluate different types of punishment.
1. Form pairs. Assign each pair to examine one of the eight punishments below. Each pair should list the advantages and disadvantages of the punishment.
   a. Solitary confinement
   b. Hard physical labor
   c. Public humiliation
   d. Physical punishment
   e. Therapy
   f. Fines
   g. Probation
   h. Community service
2. The pairs assigned each punishment should report to the class. Hold a class discussion on each punishment by asking the following questions:
   a. Is this kind of punishment still in use today? If not, why not?
   b. What types of criminals or crimes might this punishment fit? Why?
3. Debrief the activity by asking: What other types of punishment can you think of? What are their advantages and disadvantages?

Sentencing Laws

It is obviously repugnant to one's sense of justice that the judgment meted out . . . should depend in large part on a purely fortuitous circumstance; namely the personality of the particular judge before whom the case happens to come for disposition.
– Then-Attorney General Robert H. Jackson, in a statement to Congress (1940)

William Smith, a banker, has been convicted of fraud. He secretly altered his bank's computer system to steal one dollar a year from every customer. He has no previous record, and no one was badly hurt by the crime.

Jennie Blaine has been found guilty of manslaughter. She hit and killed an 8-year-old girl while driving drunk. Blaine is the sole support for her own three children, and she just lost her job. She has no previous record.

Andy Travers, a heroin addict, has been found guilty of beating an 80-year-old woman to death during a burglary. He has several previous drug convictions.

Should they all go to prison? Would it be better for society if some criminals are given fines, or probation, or community service, or other alternatives?

The decisions are made at sentencing hearings held shortly after the defendant is found guilty. Most jurisdictions provide that a sentence must be imposed "without unreasonable delay." Many provide an actual time limit such as 14 or 21 days after conviction.

Juries make sentencing recommendations in death-penalty cases. Judges typically make all other sentencing decisions. It's a heavy responsibility. Defendants may be losing years of their freedom. Every defendant is entitled to careful consideration. And, of course, judges must consider the innocent citizens in the community.

One dangerous criminal turned loose can harm many people. Judges must try to be fair, objective, and impartial — all of this while burdened by heavy caseloads and busy schedules.

Before the hearing, the judge is usually provided with a pre-sentencing report, usually prepared by the probation department. It includes information about the defendant's family background, previous convictions, character, and attitudes. This report helps the judge understand the defendant and decide whether efforts at rehabilitation might be effective. Many jurisdictions also require a pre-sentencing court conference with the offender and sometimes a psychological examination.

The U.S. Supreme Court has ruled that the defendant is entitled to have an attorney participate at the sentencing hearing (*Mempa v. Rhay*, 1967). The prosecution and defense may present information to the court and make sentencing recommendations. In many states, the crime victim and victim's family may make a statement about how the crime has impacted their lives. The defendant, in most states, also has the right to **allocute**, to make a statement to the court before sentence is passed.

Unless restricted by law, the judge may consider many **factors in sentencing**, such as:

- **The crime.** Was the harm caused by the crime great or small?
- **The offender's actions.** Were the offender's actions brutal, dangerous, and callous, or were they unintentional and restrained?
- **The victim.** Was the victim an aggressor or was the victim particularly vulnerable due to age or reduced mental or physical capacity?
- **Weapon.** Did the offender use a dangerous weapon or was the offender unarmed?
- **Offender's participation.** Did the offender plan and promote the crime or simply aid and follow others?

Corrections Population

Almost 7 million adults in the United States were under correctional supervision in 2010.

In Prison	1,518,104
In Jail	748,728
On Probation	4,055,514
On Parole	840,676

Source: *Correctional Population in the United States, 2010*, Bureau of Justice Statistics (2011)

- **Criminal record.** Has the offender committed previous crimes? How serious were they?
- **Psychological state.** Was the offender deliberate and calculating? Or was the offender provoked or under some sort of stress?
- **Age.** Is the offender either very young and inexperienced or old and infirm?
- **Offender's attitude.** Is the offender hostile and defiant? Or does the offender admit guilt and show remorse?
- **Public's attitude.** How will the public and law enforcement react to the sentence?
- **Other factors.** These might include the offender's reputation, position in the community, general character, and prior contributions to society.

In sentencing, the judge must follow the state penal code, which sets out the punishments for crimes. Misdemeanors are generally punished in increments of days or months — up to *one year* — in a county or city jail. Felonies are generally punished in increments of years in state prison. Sentencing structures vary, depending on the state, and include indeterminate sentences, determinate sentences, mandatory sentences, sentencing guidelines, or some combination.

Indeterminate Sentences. As prison reformers at the turn of the 20th century focused on rehabilitation, they felt that flexible sentencing could better meet the needs of individual convicts. A criminal who reformed sooner could be released sooner, and one who did not reform, could be kept a longer time. As long as the corrections system stressed rehabilitation, flexible sentences became the norm. These flexible prison terms became known as **indeterminate** sentences, because there was no pre-determined time to serve. Usually, the sentence was stated as a range of years. For example, forgery might carry a penalty of one to five years in prison; burglary, five to 10 years; manslaughter, five to 20. The judge decided the range of the sentence. How much time the prisoner actually served was left to the state **parole board**, which determined when a prisoner should be released.

States with indeterminate sentencing vary on how much discretion they give judges. Many states give judges the power to suspend or give alternative sentences. In some states, the judge

Most states today have fixed sentencing laws, mandating specific terms for convicts.

decides on both the maximum and the minimum sentences within statutory limits. In other states, the judge sets only the maximum. In still others, the statutes spell out the limits, and the judge has no choice but to apply them.

In recent years, indeterminate sentencing has come under attack from several directions. Some critics say that flexibility has allowed lenient parole boards to let dangerous criminals out too soon. Other critics claim that indeterminate sentencing produces arbitrary and unjust prison terms. One car thief might serve two years in prison, another five, and another seven.

Determinate Sentencing. Since the 1970s, many states have introduced **determinate**, or **fixed-term**, sentencing, which actually was the norm during the 19th century. In this system, parole boards do not decide when to release prisoners. Instead, judges sentence defendants to a specific time of imprisonment, based on the severity of the crime. For example, a robbery might be punished by a year in prison, but an armed robbery could bring a five-year sentence. Prisoners would know at the time of sentencing when their prison terms would end. In most parts of the country, there is a trend back to fixed-term sentencing.

In states with determinate sentencing, judges often have discretion to give alternative sentences. These alternatives include suspended sentences, time in a local jail, time

SENTENCING GUIDELINES GRID
Presumptive Sentence Lengths in Months

Italicized numbers within the grid denote the range within which a judge may sentence without the sentence being deemed a departure. Offenders with nonimprisonment felony sentences are subject to jail time according to law.

CRIMINAL HISTORY SCORE

SEVERITY LEVEL OF CONVICTION OFFENSE (Common offenses)		0	1	2	3	4	5	6 or more
Murder, 2nd Degree	XI	306 *261-367*	326 *278-391*	346 *295-415*	366 *312-439*	386 *329-463*	406 *346-480*	426 *363-480*
Murder, 3rd Degree	X	150 *128-180*	165 *141-198*	180 *153-216*	195 *166-234*	210 *179-252*	225 *192-270*	240 *204-288*
Aggravated Assault	IX	86 *74-103*	98 *84-117*	110 *94-132*	122 *104-146*	134 *114-160*	146 *125-175*	158 *135-189*
Involuntary Manslaughter	VIII	48 *41-57*	58 *50-69*	68 *58-81*	78 *67-93*	88 *75-105*	98 *84-117*	108 *92-129*
Felony DWI	VII	36	42	48	54 *46-64*	60 *51-72*	66 *57-79*	72 *62-84*
Burglary	VI	21	27	33	39 *34-46*	45 *39-54*	51 *44-61*	57 *49-68*
Perjury	V	18	23	28	33 *29-39*	38 *33-45*	43 *37-51*	48 *41-57*
Receiving Stolen Property	IV	12	15	18	21	24 *21-28*	27 *23-32*	30 *26-36*
Theft Crimes (Over $5,000)	III	12	13	15	17	19 *17-22*	21 *18-25*	23 *20-27*
Theft Crimes ($5,000 or less)	II	12	12	13	15	17	19	21 *18-25*
Tampering with a Fire Alarm	I	12	12	12	13	15	17	19 *17-22*

Presumptive commitment to state imprisonment. First-degree murder is excluded from the guidelines by law and continues to have a mandatory life sentence.

Presumptive stayed sentence; at the discretion of the judge, up to a year in jail and/or other non-jail sanctions can be imposed as conditions of probation.

Source: Adapted from *Minnesota Sentencing Guidelines & Commentary* (2011)

served on weekends, community service, working to pay restitution to a victim, time in halfway houses, or being released under the supervision of a probation officer. But if judges choose to give a prison term, statutes set the term.

Mandatory sentencing laws. These take away the option of alternative sentences. They require judges to sentence offenders to prison terms. Almost every state has passed mandatory sentencing laws for certain situations, such as use-a-gun, go-to-jail laws and repeat-offender laws like three-strike laws. Usually, a judge has no option but to impose the mandatory sentence and cannot shorten it, suspend it, or give an alternative sentence. The federal Anti-Drug-Abuse Act of 1986 sets many mandatory-minimum sentences for drug offenses. It allows no exceptions for first offenses or other factors.

Sentencing guidelines. These are a more elaborate attempt to curtail discretion in sentencing. They provide formulas for judges to use in all sentencing decisions. For example, in 1980 Minnesota enacted a grid formula, which reflects two sentencing factors — the crime's severity and the offender's criminal history. The judge does little more than work out where a particular criminal falls on the grid, and the sentence is automatically defined. If the judge wishes to modify the grid sentence, reasons for any variance must be given in writing. On the left is a simplified version of Minnesota's grid. More than half the states and the federal government have enacted sentencing guidelines.

FOR DISCUSSION

1. Review the list of sentencing factors on pages 226–227. Which do you think are the most important? Least important? Explain.
2. Are there any additional factors you think judges should consider? What factors should they not consider? Explain.
3. What is the difference between fixed and indeterminate sentencing? What are some arguments for fixed sentences? What are some arguments for indeterminate sentences? Which do you think is more just? Why?
4. What are mandatory sentences? What do you think are the pluses and minuses of these sentences? Do you think they are a good idea? Explain.
5. What role do you think each of the following groups should have in sentencing: judges, juries, parole boards, and legislatures? Explain.

ASK AN EXPERT

Invite a criminal attorney or criminal court judge to take part in and help debrief the activity **The Sentencing of Thomas Evans.**

CLASS ACTIVITY

The Sentencing of Thomas Evans

In this activity, students sentence Thomas Evans, the defendant in the previous unit. If a jury had found Evans guilty, it could have convicted him of one of two crimes — second-degree murder or involuntary manslaughter. For this activity, half of the groups will assume that Evans was convicted of involuntary manslaughter and the other half, second-degree murder. Students will role play judges imposing an appropriate sentence based on three different statutes: Determinate-Sentencing Statute, Indeterminate-Sentencing Statute, and Sentencing Guideline Statute. Each type of statute allows judges to choose within a range of sentences.

1. As a class, review and briefly discuss each of the three statutes below.
2. Form pairs, each pair acting as judges. Each pair should be designated either A or B. All the A pairs assume that Evans received a second-degree murder verdict. All B pairs assume an involuntary-manslaughter verdict.
3. Each pair should:
   a. Review each of the sentencing factors on pages 226–227 and discuss how these factors affect the Evans case. Refer to information contained in the **Pre-Sentencing Report** on page 231.
   b. Discuss the following questions:
      (1) Which circumstances in Evans' situation point to a harsh sentence? Make a list.
      (2) Which circumstances in Evans' situation point to leniency and the probability of his reform? Make a list.
   c. Decide on three sentences, based on the three sentencing statutes:
      (1) For the determinate statute, specify the exact number of years.
      (2) For the indeterminate statute, specify both a minimum *and* a maximum number of years.
      (3) For the sentencing guideline statute, specify the exact number of months. Then figure out the term in years and months for reporting to the class.
   d. Assume that your jurisdiction allows you to suspend the sentence under the sentencing statute and to impose an alternative sentence. Discuss and decide whether Evans

(Continued on next page.)

should serve the statutory prison term or should have his sentence suspended. Prepare a brief written statement justifying your choice. A suspended sentence would take the following form:

> Thomas Evans' prison sentence is hereby suspended. Evans will serve one year in a county jail. For a *certain number* of years following county jail, he will be closely supervised by a probation officer and have to meet *certain probation conditions*. Should Evans violate any terms of probation, he will be returned to prison to serve his prison term.

If you choose to suspend the sentence, decide how long his probation should last and the probation conditions. For a list of possible probation conditions, see page 267.

4. Each pair should report to the class on the sentences imposed. The sentences reported by each pair should be written on the board.
5. After discussing the sentences submitted, take a class vote on the choices recorded on the board.
6. Debrief the activity with the questions on page 231.

§575. Determinate-Sentencing Statute

For all determinate sentences, three prison terms are listed — a lesser term, a standard term, and a greater term. The standard term is the second one listed. It should be imposed unless the judge decides that aggravating factors or mitigating factors dictate the greater or the lesser sentence.

(a) Involuntary manslaughter is punishable by imprisonment in the state prison for two, three, or four years.

(b) Second-degree murder is punishable by imprisonment in the state prison for 10, 20, or 30 years.

§606. Indeterminate Sentencing Statute

The court shall impose both a minimum term and a maximum term as follows:

(a) Minimum term of sentence. The minimum term of an indeterminate sentence shall be at least one year and the term shall be fixed as follows:

   (1) For involuntary manslaughter, the minimum term shall be fixed by the court and shall not be less than one year nor more than five years.

   (2) For second-degree murder, the minimum term shall be fixed by the court and shall not be less than 15 years nor more than 25 years.

(b) Maximum term of sentence. The maximum term of an indeterminate sentence shall be at least three years and the term shall be fixed as follows:

   (1) For involuntary manslaughter, the term shall be fixed by the court and shall not exceed 15 years.

   (2) For second-degree murder, the term shall be fixed by the court and shall not exceed 50 years.

§898. Sentencing-Guideline Statute

a. All convicted persons shall be sentenced according to the sentencing guideline grid (on page 228).

b. If a judge wants to depart from the sentencing guideline, the reason must be compelling and the judge must explain the sentence in writing.

c. Instructions for using the sentencing guideline grid:

   1. Determine the severity level of the crime.

   2. Calculate the criminal history score. Juvenile convictions score zero points except for felony convictions, which count one point each. Adult convictions score one point for each misdemeanor and two points for each felony.

   3. Find the box where the severity level of the crime and the criminal history score intersect. This box tells the sentence in months.

      (a) If the box is shaded, the judge should suspend the sentence and put the offender on probation. At the discretion of the judge, up to a year in jail and other non-jail sanctions can be imposed as conditions of probation.

      (b) If the box is not shaded, then the judge should impose a sentence within the range given.

(Continued on the next page.)

Debriefing Questions

1. Which group of statutes — determinate, indeterminate, sentencing guideline — had the greatest range of sentences? The smallest range? Why?
2. Which sentences seemed the fairest? The most unfair? Why?
3. Which type of sentencing statute would you support in your state? Why?
4. Would you favor judges having the discretion to give alternative sentences instead of prison terms? Why or why not?
5. In most states, mandatory sentencing laws would force a prison term on Tom Evans because he used a gun. Do you think mandatory sentences are a good idea? Why or why not?
6. There is a great difference in punishment between second-degree murder and involuntary manslaughter. Do you think a jury should be told of the difference before it decides a verdict of guilty or not guilty? Why or why not?

Pre-Sentencing Report

Below is a pre-sentencing report submitted by the probation department:

Background Report on Thomas Wade Evans

Age: 18

Social background: Thomas Wade Evans is the oldest of five children. As the oldest child, he was pressured to excel in sports and school as his father had done. Around age 12, Evans rebelled against his parents and school. He ran away from home two times. At school, he received failing grades and got into numerous fistfights. He was suspended from middle school once for fighting and from high school once for carrying a knife. His teachers and friends report that Evans had a quick temper and would carry a grudge for a long time. At age 17, Evans was transferred to a continuation high school because of poor attendance and lack of credits at his regular high school. He attended the continuation school and earned enough credits to get a high school diploma. Evans worked for short periods as a fast food cook, gas station attendant, and car wash worker.

Prior Record: Evans, Thomas Wade

Age	Arrest Record	Action by Juvenile Authorities
10	Runaway	Counseled and released to parents by police
12	Runaway	Counseled and released to parents by police
13	Curfew	Counseled and released to parents by police
17	Reckless Driving (misdemeanor)	Formal probation (six months)

Age	Arrest Record	Action by Adult Authorities
18	Disturbing the peace (bar fighting) (misdemeanor)	Conviction; $200 fine

Current Background: Evans now lives in his mother's home with his sister and younger cousin. His parents were divorced when he was 16. He contributes $700 per month out of his salary to household expenses. Evans is currently employed as an assistant parts department manager at a local auto dealer. His income is $26,000 per year. His immediate supervisor, Hans Spencer, reports that Evans has performed well in his current position and is effective in dealing with customers. Neighbors report that except for some loud parties and squealing tires, Evans seems to have settled down since high school. A number of his neighbors and friends have offered to vouch for his character.

Police informants indicate that Evans and Oscar Hanks have had a long-standing feud going back to high school. One month before Evans was arrested for the Joyce Ann Miller shooting, he and Oscar Hanks were arrested for disturbing the peace at a local bar. According to witnesses, Hanks knifed Evans in the leg during the fight at the bar. Evans, however, refused to cooperate with the district attorney in the prosecution of Hanks for assault with a deadly weapon.

The Shaky Status of Sentencing Guidelines

What I have feared most has now come to pass: Over 20 years of sentencing reform are all but lost, and tens of thousands of criminal judgments are in jeopardy.
– Supreme Court Justice Sandra Day O'Connor, dissenting in *Blakely v. Washington* (2004)

In recent years, the U.S. Supreme Court has decided several cases that have clouded the future of sentencing guidelines.

In 2000, the Supreme Court decided the case of *Apprendi v. New Jersey*. The defendant, Charles Apprendi, had fired several shots into the New Jersey home of an African-American family. In a plea agreement, he pleaded guilty to possessing a firearm for an unlawful purpose. The crime under New Jersey law carried a penalty of between five and 10 years. Under a New Jersey hate-crime sentencing law, a trial judge could extend a term if the judge found *by a preponderance of the evidence* that the defendant committed the crime "with a purpose to intimidate an individual or group of individuals because of race, color, gender, handicap, religion, sexual orientation or ethnicity." The trial judge in *Apprendi* held a hearing, found that Apprendi had violated the hate-crime law, and sentenced him to 12 years in prison.

Apprendi appealed, claiming that the judge had violated the Sixth and 14th amendments by enhancing his sentence under the hate-crime law. The Sixth Amendment declares: "In all criminal prosecutions, the accused shall enjoy the right to a speedy and public trial, by an impartial jury . . . ." The 14th Amendment says that no "State shall deprive any person of life, liberty, or property, without due process of law . . . ."

The Supreme Court in a 5–4 decision agreed with Apprendi. The court noted that the Sixth Amendment gives a criminal defendant the right to a jury trial. It further noted that "due process of law" means, among other things, that the state must prove a criminal defendant guilty beyond a reasonable doubt. Writing for the court majority, Justice John Paul Stevens said: "Taken together, these rights indisputably entitle a criminal defendant to 'a jury determination that [he] is guilty of every element of the crime with which he is charged, beyond a reasonable doubt.' " The court ruled that the judge only had discretion to sentence Apprendi to between five and 10 years. The court held that the "Constitution requires that any fact that increases the penalty for a crime beyond the prescribed statutory maximum, other than the fact of a prior conviction, must be submitted to a jury and proved beyond a reasonable doubt."

Writing in dissent, Justice Steven Breyer accused the court majority of ignoring tradition and prior cases. He said that judges have always weighed various factors to enhance or decrease a sentence. He stated:

> The factor at issue here — motive — is such a factor. Whether a robber takes money to finance other crimes or to feed a starving family can matter, and long has mattered, when the length of a sentence is at issue. The State of New Jersey has determined that one motive — racial hatred — is particularly bad and ought to make a difference in respect to punishment for a crime. That determination is reasonable. The procedures mandated are consistent with traditional sentencing practice.

Blakely v. Washington (2004)

In 2004, the Supreme Court decided *Blakely v. Washington*, a case involving the state of Washington's sentencing guidelines. Blakely, the defendant, kidnapped his estranged wife in Washington, bound her with duct tape, and put her in the trunk of his car. He waited for his 13-year-old son to come home from school and ordered him to follow Blakely in a second car. He threatened to kill the boy's mother with a shotgun if the boy did not obey. The two cars drove to Montana.

Caught and returned to Washington, Blakely pleaded guilty to kidnapping, which carried a sentence under the guidelines of 49 to 53 months. At the sentencing hearing, however, the judge heard testimony from the estranged wife. He found that the defendant had acted with "deliberate cruelty" and sentenced Blakely to a term of 90 months, 37 months longer than the maximum term. The sentencing guidelines set "deliberate cruelty" as one of the grounds for a judge to increase a sentence beyond the maximum term. When the defense objected to the sentence, the judge held a three-day hearing. The defendant testified as did his estranged wife, a police officer, and medical experts. After the testimony, the judge again found "deliberate cruelty" and sentenced Blakely to 90 months.

Blakely appealed, challenging the authority of the judge to extend the sentence beyond the

The justices of the U.S. Supreme Court in 2012, from left to right: Clarence Thomas, Sonia Sotomayor, Antonin Scalia, Stephen Breyer, Chief Justice John Roberts, Samuel Alito, Anthony Kennedy, Elena Kagan, and Ruth Bader Ginsburg.

maximum term. Washington's Court of Appeals affirmed the judgment, declaring the judge had followed Washington law. The Supreme Court of Washington refused to hear the case. The U.S. Supreme Court, however, granted certiorari.

The U.S. Supreme Court, by the same 5–4 majority as in *Apprendi*, held that Blakely's exceptional sentence violated the Sixth Amendment. This time Justice Antonin Scalia wrote the majority opinion. He cited the rule in *Apprendi*: "Other than the fact of a prior conviction, any fact that increases the penalty for a crime beyond the prescribed statutory maximum must be submitted to a jury, and proved beyond a reasonable doubt." In this case, the judge based the extended sentence on a finding of "deliberate cruelty." Since this fact was neither found by a jury nor admitted by the defendant as part of a guilty plea, the judge's sentence violated the Sixth Amendment.

Following this decision, many states began redrafting their sentencing guidelines. Many federal judges postponed sentencing until the Supreme Court ruled on Federal Sentencing Guidelines.

To establish sentencing guidelines, Congress had set up the U.S. Sentencing Commission in 1984. Congress set a broad range of punishments for each criminal act. The role of the Sentencing Commission was to set specific guidelines for sentencing, which federal judges were mandated to follow.

U.S. v. Booker (2005)

Two cases challenging Federal Sentencing Guidelines were rushed to the Supreme Court.

In *U.S. v. Booker*, the Supreme Court considered both cases together.

In one of the cases, defendant Freddie Booker was charged with possession with intent to distribute at least 50 grams of crack cocaine. Hearing evidence that Booker possessed about 90 grams of crack, the jury convicted him. Federal law set a minimum sentence of 10 years and a maximum of life imprisonment for this crime. Given Booker's criminal record and the amount of crack the jury found he had, the Sentencing Guidelines set the sentence at 210 to 262 months (about 17 to 22 years). At the sentencing hearing, the judge heard evidence that Booker possessed far more than 90 grams of crack and that he had lied on the witness stand. The judge concluded that the state had proved these facts by a preponderance of the evidence. These findings mandated a higher sentence under the Sentencing Guidelines. The judge therefore sentenced Booker to 360 months (30 years) in prison. Booker appealed the sentence.

In the other case, defendant Duncan Fanfan was charged with conspiracy to distribute at least 500 grams of cocaine. A jury convicted him after finding that he possessed 500 or more grams of cocaine. Under the guidelines, the maximum sentence was 78 months (6½ years). The judge held a sentencing hearing and found several facts by a preponderance of the evidence that justified a sentence of 188 to 235 months (about 15 to 19 years). The facts were that Fanfan carried crack and much greater amounts of cocaine than the jury knew about, and he was a leader of the conspiracy. But noting the *Blakely* case, which had just been decided, the judge refused to impose the greater sentence. The prosecution appealed the sentence.

The cases posed two questions for the U.S. Supreme Court:

1. Does the rule in *Apprendi* and *Blakely* apply to the Federal Sentencing Guidelines?
2. If so, can the guidelines remain in effect?

As to the first question, the same 5–4 court majority in *Apprendi* and *Blakely* answered that the rule applies to the Federal Sentencing Guidelines. Writing for the majority, Justice Stevens emphasized that "any fact that increases the penalty for a crime beyond the prescribed statutory maximum must be submitted to a jury." In Booker's case, the jury returned a verdict that had a maximum sentence of 262 months under the sentencing guidelines. Then the judge found additional facts that mandated a greater sentence. These new facts, said Stevens, must be found by a jury.

On the second question, a different 5–4 majority decided the fate of the sentencing guidelines. Writing for the majority, Justice Breyer found that the sentencing guidelines can no longer be mandatory. Judges can look to them for advice, but they do not have to follow them. For example, in Booker's case, federal law sets a range of 10 years to life for his crime. A judge can sentence a defendant to any sentence within that range. The sentence can be appealed if it is "unreasonable," given the circumstances. To help judges determine what is reasonable, they can look at the sentencing guidelines. But they are no longer bound by them. Breyer stressed Congress could come up with a different solution: "Ours, of course, is not the last word: The ball now lies in Congress' court."

The dissenters on the second question argued that it was up to Congress to decide what to do about the sentencing guidelines. Congress had made them mandatory. The court had ruled that the mandatory guidelines violated the Sixth Amendment. The court should not make them advisory. This is up to Congress.

This case was unusual because it had two majority opinions — one for each of the two questions. The reason for the two opinions was Justice Ruth Bader Ginsburg. She had voted with the majority in *Apprendi* and *Blakely* and on the first question in *Booker*. But on the second question, she switched sides and joined the four justices who had dissented in *Apprendi* and *Booker*.

The effect of the *Booker* decision made no difference to the two defendants in the case. Following the decision, Booker and Fanfan went back for re-sentencing. Booker's judge handed down the same 30-year sentence. Fanfan received a 210-month sentence (17½ years).

Reasonable Sentences

After *Booker*, the prosecution and defense could appeal if the sentences were unreasonable.

---

18 U.S. CODE § 3553. IMPOSITION OF A SENTENCE

(a) Factors To Be Considered in Imposing a Sentence.

. . . The court, in determining the particular sentence to be imposed, shall consider —

(1) the nature and circumstances of the offense and the history and characteristics of the defendant;

(2) the need for the sentence imposed —

    (A) to reflect the seriousness of the offense, to promote respect for the law, and to provide just punishment for the offense;

    (B) to afford adequate deterrence to criminal conduct;

    (C) to protect the public from further crimes of the defendant; and

    (D) to provide the defendant with needed educational or vocational training, medical care, or other correctional treatment in the most effective manner;

(3) the kinds of sentences available;

(4) the kinds of sentence and the sentencing range established for —

    (A) the applicable category of offense committed by the applicable category of defendant as set forth in the guidelines. . . .

(5) any pertinent policy statement . . . issued by the Sentencing Commission . . . .

(6) the need to avoid unwarranted sentence disparities among defendants with similar records who have been found guilty of similar conduct; and

(7) the need to provide restitution to any victims of the offense.

In later cases, the Supreme Court looked at what unreasonable meant. It decided that appeals courts should presume that any sentence within the guidelines is reasonable (*Rita v. U.S.*, 2007). When a sentence departs from the guidelines, however, the appeals courts may not presume the sentence is unreasonable. The guidelines are merely one factor to consider. (See the factors set out in the U.S. Code on page 234.)

Thus, in *Gall v. U.S.* (2007), the Supreme Court upheld the sentence of three years probation in a drug case that the Federal Sentencing Guidelines called for three years in prison. The defendant, Brian Gall, had worked for drug dealers distributing ecstacy when he was a student at the University of Iowa. After a few months, however, he stopped using drugs and stopped working for the dealers. When he graduated, he moved out of state, and built a new life free of drugs and crime. Three years later, he was arrested along with the dealers. Gall pleaded guilty. The trial judge concluded that in Gall's case, "a sentence of imprisonment may work to promote not respect, but derision, of the law if the law is viewed as merely a means to dispense harsh punishment without taking into account the real conduct and circumstances involved in sentencing." The prosecution appealed the sentence, and the Court of Appeals reversed it as an abuse of discretion. The defense appealed to the U.S. Supreme Court. The Supreme Court ruled that the judge's sentence had addressed all the factors required in the U.S. Code and his sentence was reasonable.

Cunningham v. California (2007)

In 2007, the Supreme Court heard a challenge to California's determinate sentencing law. That law sets three possible sentences for each offense: a lower, middle, and higher sentence. For example, the California Penal Code says: "Carjacking is punishable by imprisonment in the state prison for a term of three, five, or nine years." A judge must sentence a convicted defendant to the middle sentence unless the judge at a sentencing hearing decides, by a preponderance of the evidence, that mitigating or aggravating factors exist. If they do, then the judge may impose the lower or higher sentence.

John Cunningham was convicted of continuous sexual abuse of a child under 14. The middle term was 12 years, but at his sentencing hearing, the judge found aggravating factors and sentenced Cunningham to the higher term, 16 years. Cunningham appealed his sentence.

When the appeal reached the U.S. Supreme Court, the court ruled that California's determinate sentencing law violated the Sixth Amendment. It noted that:

> This Court has repeatedly held that, under the Sixth Amendment, any fact that exposes a defendant to a greater potential sentence must be found by a jury, not a judge, and established beyond a reasonable doubt, not merely by a preponderance of the evidence.

Effect of These Cases on Sentencing

On the states, the effect of these Supreme Court decisions will depend on the jurisdiction. Some states do not mandate greater punishment for crimes committed under certain circumstances. These states are not affected by the decisions. Other states do mandate greater punishments. They must make sure that their laws require that juries find the facts necessary for the mandated punishment. Many states are rewriting their sentencing statutes to comply with the decisions.

At the federal level, Congress faces a choice. The Supreme Court has made the sentencing guidelines advisory. Some people think that Congress should wait and see what happens with this approach.

Others believe that Congress should follow the states and make juries the finders of all facts related to sentencing. This could be done at a separate sentencing hearing following a guilty verdict.

Still others believe that Congress should impose sentences with a higher range and let judges sentence. The higher ranges would prevent judges from being too lenient in their decisions.

FOR DISCUSSION

1. What were the decisions in the *Apprendi* and *Blakely* cases? Do you agree with them? Explain.

2. What were the two questions in *Booker*? How did the court decide these questions? Do you agree with them? Explain.

3. Aside from number four (the sentencing guidelines), which of the seven "Factors To Be Considered in Imposing a Sentence" in the U.S. Code do you think are most important? Why?

4. If you had been the trial judge in Gall's case, what sentence would you have imposed? Why? Do you think the sentence the judge imposed was reasonable? Explain.

5. Do you think the *Cunningham* case was correctly decided? Explain.

6. The above Section 3553 of the U.S. Code's Title 18 sets the factors a judge may consider in imposing a sentence. Section 3582 says that a judge may only use these factors and must recognize "that imprisonment is not an appropriate means of promoting correction and rehabilitation." In *U.S. v. Kubeczko* (2011), a federal appeals court imagined two different sentencing statements by a judge:

   (a) "I'm not worried that you'll commit more crimes if I gave you a shorter sentence; I am giving you a long sentence to enable you to obtain psychiatric assistance that will bring about your complete rehabilitation."

   (b) "I am going to sentence you to a sentence long enough to enable you to obtain psychiatric assistance, because until then you will continue to be a danger to the public because you can't control your violent impulses."

   Which, if any, of these sentencing statements is legal under the U.S. Code?

7. What are the choices that Congress faces regarding Sentencing Guidelines?

CLASS ACTIVITY

What Should Congress Do?

The Supreme Court decision in *Booker* has left Congress with choices on what to do about sentencing guidelines. In this activity, students role play the Judiciary Committee deciding what to do about sentencing guidelines.

1. Form groups of four to five students. Each group will be a Judiciary Committee. Each group should:
   a. Review and discuss the choices facing Congress.
   b. Decide what is the best choice and why.
   c. Prepare to report back their choices and reasons.
2. Reconvene as a class.
   a. Each group should report back.
   b. Hold a class discussion on what Congress should do.
   c. Vote on the options.

Do Sentences Have to Be Proportionate?

Excessive bail shall not be required, nor excessive fines imposed, nor cruel and unusual punishments inflicted.
– Eighth Amendment to the U.S. Constitution (1791)

Does the Eighth Amendment prohibit excessive or inappropriate punishment? For example, would a prison sentence of 25 years to life for stealing a slice of pizza be thrown out as a violation of the Eighth Amendment? More specifically, would it matter that the sentence was part of a repeat-offender law?

In 1983, the U.S. Supreme Court ruled that an overly harsh sentence was unconstitutional. A South Dakota court had sentenced a man to life in prison for passing a $100 bad check. The sentence followed a state repeat-offender law that allowed a life sentence without possibility of parole for anyone convicted of a fourth felony. A 5–4 majority of the Supreme Court in *Solem v. Helm* (1983) struck down the life sentence. It ruled "as a matter of principle, that a criminal sentence must be proportionate to the crime for which the defendant has been convicted."

The court pointed out three objective factors to decide whether a sentence is proportionate to the crime. These include comparing (1) the seriousness of the crime to the severity of the penalty, (2) the kinds of sentences other criminals were given for the same crime, and (3) the kinds of sentences given in other jurisdictions.

In 1991 in *Harmelin v. Michigan*, however, the Supreme Court seemed to back away from its ruling in *Solem*. Harmelin, an Air Force veteran with no prior record, was convicted of possessing 672 grams of cocaine. Under a Michigan mandatory-sentencing law, he received a sentence of life in prison with no possibility of parole. This is the same sentence that a person convicted of first-degree murder would receive in Michigan. In neighboring Ohio, Harmelin would have received a sentence of from five to 15 years.

A 5–4 majority of the court upheld the sentence. The decision was a plurality decision. Although five justices agreed with the majority decision, they could not agree on the reasons for it. Three of the justices ruled that the sentence was not "grossly disproportionate" to the crime.

Two other justices in majority, Scalia and Rehnquist, declared that *Solem* was "simply wrong." They said that the Eighth Amendment to the Constitution does not require felony sentences to be proportionate to the crime except in death-penalty cases. The Eighth Amendment's prohibition against "cruel and unusual punishment," they said, only banned types of punishment such as torture, beheading, and burning at the stake. It did not apply to the length of prison terms. They argued that a "proportionality principle" would be simply an invitation for the court to impose its subjective opinion over that of a legislative body. They noted that courts could weigh the proportionality of a death sentence because it "differs from all other forms of criminal punishment, not in degree but in kind. It is unique in its total irrevocability."

The four dissenters believed the sentence failed to pass the proportionality test stated in *Solem*. They rejected Justices Rehnquist and Scalia's argument that the Eighth Amendment only required proportionality in capital cases. They argued it was required in all punishments.

In 2003, the Supreme Court decided two cases challenging California's three-strikes law: *Ewing v. California* and *Lockyer v. Andrade*. Under California's law, any person convicted of two serious or violent felonies shall be sentenced to 25 years to life when convicted of a third felony. The third felony does not have to be serious or violent. The law denies parole for the first 25 years of the sentence.

In *Ewing*, defendant Gary Ewing went to a golf shop, stuck three golf clubs down his pant legs, and walked out of the store. Caught in the parking lot, he was charged and convicted of grand theft (the value of the golf clubs totaled more than $1,000). Ewing had a long criminal history of drug, burglary, and robbery convictions. The court sentenced him to 25 years to life under the three-strikes law.

In *Andrade*, defendant Leandro Andrade walked into a K-Mart, took five videotapes, walked out without paying, and was caught. Two weeks later, he tried to steal four videotapes from another K-Mart and was caught again. The total value of the nine tapes was about $150. He was tried and convicted of two counts of petty theft with a prior conviction, a felony under California law. Like Ewing, Andrade had a long criminal history — theft, burglary, and drug convictions. He was sentenced

Does the Eighth Amendment require that sentences fit the crime?

to two consecutive terms of 25 years to life under the three-strikes law.

The U.S. Supreme Court by a 5–4 vote upheld the sentences in both cases. The majority in *Ewing* was divided as it was in *Harmelin*. Three justices decided that the penalty was not grossly disproportionate to the crime. Writing for these justices, Justice Sandra Day O'Connor said that state legislatures have vast authority to make sentencing laws. The Supreme Court, she noted, should not act as a "superlegislature" to decide whether a state's sentencing laws are wise. It only decides whether they are constitutional.

She said that the Constitution does not mandate states to adopt any one theory of punishment. "A sentence can have a variety of justifications, such as incapacitation, deterrence, retribution, or rehabilitation." She pointed out that in enacting its three-strikes law, California wanted to keep repeat offenders off the street. She then went on to determine whether the punishment was grossly disproportionate to the crime. She noted that the crime of grand theft was serious in itself. But she said the court should not just look at this crime, but at Ewing's whole criminal history. She concluded: "Ewing's sentence is justified by the State's public-safety interest in incapacitating and deterring recidivist felons, and amply supported by his own long, serious criminal record."

Two other justices in majority once again agreed with the judgment, but disagreed with the reasons. Writing a concurring opinion, Justice Scalia echoing his opinion in *Harmelin* stated that the court should not look into whether a sentence was disproportionate to the crime.

The four dissenters again applied the three tests in *Solem* and found the sentence grossly disproportionate to the crime. They noted that before the three-strikes law, the maximum sentence for grand theft was 10 years and enhancements for repeat offenses could have added four years. The federal government under U.S. Sentencing Guidelines would have added a maximum of 18 months to his sentence.

FOR DISCUSSION

1. Do you think that the decisions in *Solem* and *Harmelin* are compatible? Explain.
2. What theory of punishment is California's three-strikes law based on?
3. In *Ewing*, Justice O'Connor stated that the Supreme Court is not a "superlegislature." What did she mean? Do you agree? Explain.
4. Do you think the Eighth Amendment requires sentences be proportional to the crime? Why or why not?
5. There were three opinions in *Ewing*: the majority, concurring, and dissenting opinions. What did each say?

CLASS ACTIVITY

Cruel and Unusual

In this activity, students take part in a role play of the *Ewing* decision on the constitutionality of California's three-strikes law.

1. Form small groups.
2. Imagine that your group is the court deciding the *Ewing* case. Do the following:
   a. Review the facts of the *Ewing* case.
   b. Examine and discuss the majority, concurring, and dissenting opinions in the case.
   c. Decide how your group would decide the case.
   d. Prepare to present your decision and the reasons for it to the rest of the class.
3. Each group should report back. Debrief by asking what were the strongest arguments on each side.

Federal Sentencing: Crack Versus Cocaine

Crack cocaine first appeared in New York City neighborhoods in 1985 as an inexpensive cocaine product that was ingested by smoking.
– Fagan & Chin, "Initiation Into Crack and Cocaine," *Contemporary Drug Problems* (1989)

In 1980, federal prisons held only 24,000 people. By 2009, the federal prison population had soared to more than 200,000. This increase was due mainly to the war on drugs. In 1980, drug offenders accounted for only a quarter of all federal prisoners. By 2009, almost 50 percent were drug offenders.

Many of the drug offenders put in federal prison were African Americans. Blacks make up about 12 percent of the general population and about the same percentage of drug users. Yet the percentage of African Americans, mostly drug offenders, in federal prisons jumped from 30 percent in 1987 to almost 40 percent in 2009. One reason for the increase was a change in federal sentencing laws.

In the 1980s, crack cocaine hit the streets. Crack is made by cooking a mixture of water, baking soda, and powder cocaine. When the concoction dries, it becomes hard. "Rocks" can be broken off and sold in small amounts to users. Unlike powder cocaine, which is usually snorted, crack is smoked and quickly produces an intense high. (Powder cocaine can do the same if it is injected.)

Offering a cheap high, crack quickly grew popular in inner-city neighborhoods where it was sold on the streets. Soon rival gangs started fighting over who controlled the crack trade on different streets. Neighborhoods became terrorized by these turf wars. The media filled with stories of drive-by shootings and "crack babies" born addicted to cocaine. The 1986 drug-related death of University of Maryland star basketball player Len Bias drew further national attention to the cocaine problem.

Congress responded by passing the Anti-Drug Abuse Acts of 1986 and 1988. The acts created the Office of National Drug Control Policy. Its director, commonly called the "drug czar," plans the nation's strategy in the drug war.

Among other things, the acts also set harsh penalties for dealers in cocaine. The law mandated a mandatory minimum 10-year sentence without parole for those dealing 5,000 grams

(11 pounds) or more of powder cocaine. Those dealing 500 grams (1.1 pounds) or more receive a mandatory five-year minimum.

Congress also set a similar two-tiered structure for crack sentences. But Congress believed crack cocaine to be more addictive, more linked to violent crime, and more likely to be dealt in small quantities than powder cocaine. It therefore set the minimum amounts of crack drastically lower than powder cocaine. A person dealing 50 grams (1.8 ounces) of crack receives the same 10-year-minimum sentence as a person with 5,000 grams of powder cocaine. A person possessing 5 grams (0.2 ounces) of crack gets the same five-year-minimum sentence as a person possessing 500 grams of powder cocaine. In other words, Congress set a 100:1 ratio between powder and crack cocaine. (Most state drug laws also set a ratio between the two drugs, but none as large as 100:1.)

When Congress passed these laws, no one objected that they would affect blacks more than other groups. Because of its price, crack was favored by inner-city, predominantly black, drug users and dealers. Police concentrated on inner-city neighborhoods where crack was dealt on the street or in "crack houses" known to neighbors and police. It was more difficult to track down white dealers of crack and powder-cocaine who usually met indoors in various neighborhoods. As a result, more African-American dealers were arrested and more than 80 percent of the crack dealers sentenced in federal courts were black. In the early 1980s, the sentences and time served in federal prison for blacks and whites averaged about the same length. By 1995, blacks were serving federal sentences 40 percent longer than whites.

Pros and Cons

This disparity has provoked debate over the fairness of the sentencing laws. Critics have questioned the wisdom of punishing crack and powder cocaine differently. They point out that both are cocaine and that powder cocaine can quite easily be made into crack. Criminologist Jerome Skolnick stated: "The law is equivalent, if eggs were illegal, to punishing the possession of omelets 100 times more severely than the possession of raw eggs."

Critics also have argued that the law makes small-time crack dealers suffer the same punishment as higher-level cocaine dealers. Five

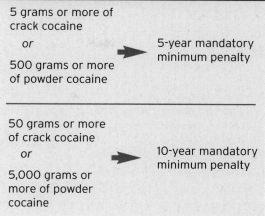

The 100–1 Ratio in Federal Crack and Powder Cocaine Sentences

5 grams or more of crack cocaine

or

500 grams or more of powder cocaine

→ 5-year mandatory minimum penalty

50 grams or more of crack cocaine

or

5,000 grams or more of powder cocaine

→ 10-year mandatory minimum penalty

hundred grams of powder cocaine produces 2,500 to 5,000 doses and has a street value of from $32,500 to $50,000. This compares to 5 grams of crack, which produces 10 to 50 doses and is worth between $225 and $750.

Critics have also questioned the association of crack and violence. Crack users, they argue, are no more prone to violence than powder cocaine users. The violence associated with crack, they explain, comes from the drug trade. Violence of this sort, they argue, could be linked to any illegal drug. They point out that Miami in the 1980s had the nation's worst rate of violence, and it was linked to trafficking powder cocaine. When crack first appeared, violence erupted over territorial disputes among crack dealers. This violence, say the critics, has since died down.

Finally, some critics think the laws are racist. Whites commit the most drug crimes. Yet blacks get the most punishment.

Supporters of the laws believe they make sense. Crack, they argue, devastated inner-city neighborhoods. Because it was sold openly, it threatened these areas. Drive-by shootings and gang wars erupted over control of the crack business. Unlike crack, cocaine was usually sold behind closed doors and therefore did much less harm to communities.

Supporters also argue that crack is far more addictive than powder cocaine (as the two drugs are usually administered). Crack addicts, they say, pose special problems. Many commit crimes to support their habits. Pregnant addicts give birth to "crack babies," born addicted and damaged. Supporters say that crack's relatively

Prisoner Profile

Location
87% in state prisons
13% in federal prisons

Gender
93%   male
7%   female

Race or Ethnicity
38%   black
36%   white
22%   Hispanic
4%   other

Age

17 or younger	0.2%
18-19	1.4%
20-29	28.2%
30-39	30.2%
40-54	32.0%
55 or older	8.1%

Most Serious Offense

State inmates

Violent	53%
Property	19%
Drug	18%
Public-order	9%
Other	1.0%

Federal inmates

Violent	7.8%
Property	5.9%
Drug	51%
Public-order	8.2%
Weapon	11.2%
Immigration	15.1%

Detail may not add to 100% due to rounding.

Source: "Prisoners in 2010," Bureau of Justice Statistics (2011)

low cost and greater addictiveness makes it more likely to spread and a greater threat to society than powder cocaine.

Further, even some who think the laws are misguided do not think they are racist. Randall Kennedy, a black Harvard law professor, believes they are not racist because they weren't passed with racist intent. He has stated that "there's a difference between something being mistaken and counterproductive and something being racist. . . . [T]he war on drugs may very well be counterproductive, but no, I don't think it's racist."

Court Challenges

Defendants have challenged the 100:1 ratio in federal appeals courts, but the courts have refused to overturn the sentencing laws. The Supreme Court has declined to hear any of these cases. The challenges have been mainly based on three legal grounds.

The first is that the 100:1 ratio, in practice, discriminates against African Americans and denies them equal protection of the law. (The 14th Amendment prevents states from denying anyone equal protection. The courts have held that the Fifth Amendment's due process clause requires the same of the federal government.) The courts have found, however, that neither the laws nor lawmakers had a discriminatory purpose. Therefore the courts have held that the laws must simply pass a "rational basis" test. Courts have ruled that the laws pass this test, because Congress had a legitimate purpose in protecting the public against a cheap, addictive drug and it believed that the 100:1 ratio would help do this.

One state court struck down its sentencing law as violating the state's guarantee of equal protection. Minnesota law had a 100:30 powder-to-crack ratio. The court noted that the ratio affected mainly African American drug users and therefore violated the state's guarantee of equal protection. (*Minnesota v. Russell*, 1991). The Minnesota legislature rewrote the law and made sentencing the same for 30 grams of cocaine as it was for 30 grams of crack.

The second legal argument is that the laws violate due process because there are different punishments for the same drug — crack and powder cocaine. Some courts have rejected this argument stating that the two drugs are different. Other courts have stated that even if they are the same drug, they differ in usage and effect on the user.

The final legal argument is that the laws violate the Eighth Amendment's ban on cruel and unusual punishment. The Supreme Court in *Solem v. Helm* ruled that criminal punishments cannot be disproportionate to the crime. The Third Circuit in *U.S. v. Frazier*, however, found that:

> There are reasonable grounds for imposing a greater punishment for offenses involving a particular weight of [crack] than for comparable offenses involving the same weight of cocaine. These grounds include differences in . . . the method of use, the effect on the user, and the collateral social effects of the traffic in the drug.

The Supreme Court has never heard a case on the constitutionality of the disparity between crack and powder cocaine sentences. But it has decided a case that charged prosecutors with singling out African Americans for prosecution under federal crack laws. Four defendants moved to have their case dismissed because all 24 crack cases prosecuted in 1991 by one office had black defendants. The trial judge ordered prosecutors to provide a list of all crack cases and the race of the defendants for the previous three years. Prosecutors refused and appealed all the way to the Supreme Court. In 1996 in *U.S. v. Armstrong*, the court in an 8–1 decision reversed the trial judge's order. The court ruled that to prove a selective prosecution case, defendants must show that prosecutors are refusing to prosecute other cases involving white defendants. The statistics shown by the defendants in this case, said the court, proved nothing, because "people of *all* races" do not "commit *all* types of crimes." The court pointed out that statistics showed that more than 90 percent of all convicted LSD dealers, prostitutes, and pornographers were white.

Congressional Action

In 1995, the U.S. Sentencing Commission recommended that the 100:1 ratio be equalized to 1:1. To address the problem of violence, it recommended that sentences be enhanced if guns or violence are involved in the crime. The commission is an independent, permanent agency set up by Congress. It develops sentencing guidelines for federal crimes. Congress rejected the recommendation.

For more than a decade, proposals were made to change the ratio, but Congress refused to act. Finally, in 2010, Congress passed the Fair Sentencing Act. This act lowered the ratio to 18:1. (Under the law, 28 grams of crack will result in a five-year mandatory sentence and 280 grams will trigger a mandatory 10-year sentence. The sentences for powder cocaine remain the same.) The act also did away with the mandatory five-year term for first-time possession of crack.

The debate over sentencing for crack and powder cocaine will continue. Supporters of the 1:1 ratio believe the new law is a step in the right direction but still call for a 1:1 ratio. Opponents of the new law fear it will reignite the crack violence of the 1980s and call for a return to the 100:1 ratio.

In 2011, the U.S. Sentencing Commission voted to make the 18:1 ratio retroactive. That means an estimated 12,000 prisoners will receive reductions in their sentences.

FOR DISCUSSION

1. What is the 100:1 ratio?
2. Do you agree with the new 18:1 ratio? If Congress were to equalize the crack-powder ratio at 1:1, what might be some reasons for and against either lowering the amount of powder, raising the amount of crack, or moving both? Explain.
3. Since the 2005 U.S. Supreme Court decision in *U.S. v. Booker*, the U.S. Sentencing Guidelines have become advisory only and not mandatory. If you were a federal judge, would you follow the new guidelines that reflect the 18:1 ratio? Explain.
4. Do you think the federal sentencing laws on crack cocaine discriminate against African Americans? Explain.

CLASS ACTIVITY

The Ratio

In this activity, students role play a congressional committee deciding whether to recommend changing the 18:1 ratio.
1. Form small groups. Each is a congressional committee considering changing the 18:1 ratio. Each group should:
   a. Make a list of the pros and cons of the 18:1 ratio.
   b. Decide whether or not to recommend changing the ratio.
   c. If the committee decides to change the ratio, it should decide what the new ratio should be and whether to lower the amount of powder, raise the amount of crack, or move both.
   d. Prepare to report back its recommendations and the reasons for them.
2. The groups should report back and the class should hold a discussion. Conclude the activity by taking a vote on whether or not to change the ratio.

CHAPTER 15
PRISON

The vilest deeds like poison weeds
Bloom well in prison air:
It is only what is good in man
That wastes and withers there. . . .
– Oscar Wilde, from *The Ballad of Reading Gaol* (1898)

TYPES OF PRISONS | OVERCROWDING IN PRISONS | PRISON REVOLTS | POLICIES BEHIND THE RISE IN INCARCERATION | ARE TOO MANY PEOPLE BEHIND BARS? | PAROLE | STAYING OUT OF PRISON

Types of Prisons

A prison is a house of care,
A place where none can thrive,
A touchstone true to try a friend,
A grave for one alive.
Sometimes a place of right,
Sometimes a place of wrong,
Sometimes a place of rogues and thieves,
And honest men among.
– Inscription on Scotland's Edinburgh Tolbooth prison (torn down in 1817)

Today in the United States, more than 2 million people are behind bars. The more than 1,000 state and federal prisons hold about two-thirds of them. More than 3,000 county and municipal jails hold the other third. Prisons may be well-designed, progressive institutions, but some are overcrowded, filthy, and brutal. Some have become notorious for extortion, violence, homosexual rape, and vicious racial gangs — a virtual hell of fear and savagery.

At their best, our prisons can provide well-planned opportunities for education and vocational training, but at their worst, they offer little more than a few hours a day out of the cell to stand around in a crowded prison yard. More than half of all prison inmates are idle for most of the day. The former head of the Federal Bureau of Prisons has said, "Idleness is the most serious problem in virtually every penal institution."

Security Levels

Prisons typically fall into three security levels. Maximum-security prisons are usually large institutions holding several thousand prisoners. High fences (sometimes electrified), thick walls, and guard towers separate the prisoners from society. Inside, armed guards watch over prisoners. A group of cells make up a cell block, which can be locked down from other cell blocks. In large prisons, several cell blocks make up a prison wing, which also can be shut down separately. The prisoners wear drab uniforms, and each is assigned a number. Prisoners are given little opportunity to associate with one another. Tighter security exists for prisoners awaiting capital punishment on death row, a separate cell block of a maximum-security prison. About 40 percent of all prisoners reside in maximum-security prisons.

Medium-security prisons are typically smaller versions of maximum-security prisons. They do, however, allow prisoners a greater degree of freedom. They are permitted, for example, to use the library, exercise yard, and showers with fewer restrictions. They must, however, at specific times each day be in their cell or assigned place for the day's headcount, which can take place up to four times a day. About 40 percent of all prisoners are in medium-security prisons.

Minimum-security prisons can be far different. They usually allow prisoners to roam within the confines of the prison. Some have dormitory rooms and others have private rooms instead of cells. Prisoners usually wear uniforms, but some prisons allow inmates the freedom to choose their own wardrobe.

In the federal prison system, the three levels of prisons carry different names. High-security prisons are U.S. Penitentiaries. Medium-security prisons are known as Federal Correctional Institutions. Minimum-security prisons are called Federal Prison Camps.

Super-Maximum-Security Prisons

Super-maximum-security prisons are designed to hold the most dangerous prisoners. These prisoners have been disruptive or violent while imprisoned and need to be separated from other prisoners.

Super-maximum-security prisons date back to 1934, when the federal government

started Alcatraz. Known as the Rock, the penitentiary was located on a small island in San Francisco Bay. The treacherous ocean currents made escape all but impossible. A small prison, Alcatraz housed in single cells about 300 of the most hardened federal prisoners. No one is known to have escaped and survived. Of the 14 escape attempts made, prison officials captured all except five inmates who remain missing and presumed drowned.

When Alcatraz closed in 1963, a new U.S. Penitentiary opened near Marion, Illinois. At first, prison officials did not use this prison to replace Alcatraz. Within a few years, however, officials started transferring the worst federal prisoners to Marion and turned it into a super-maximum-security facility. Prisoners were kept in individual cells. During the few hours each week that they left their cells, they wore handcuffs and sometimes leg shackles.

In 1994, the federal government opened a new super-maximum-security prison in Florence, Colorado. It holds about 500 prisoners, each in a separate cell and isolated from other prisoners. Every cell has a bed, stool, toilet, sink, and shower. A small black-and-white television in each cell can deliver orders from guards. The only view outside the cell is through a tiny window showing the sky. The plumbing is flood-proof; the bedding, fireproof. The furniture is made of cement and cannot be moved. Prisoners get their meals through a slot in the door. They leave their cells a couple times a week to exercise alone in wire cages. Guards watch the prisoners through almost 200 video cameras and can control 1,400 gates electronically. Escape is almost impossible.

Many states have started building super-maximum-security prisons or adding them as wings to other prisons. California's Pelican Bay State Prison, located near the Oregon border, is an example. One wing holds 2,000 in maximum-security. Another wing houses 1,500 prisoners in super-maximum-security. Prisoners in the super-maximum-security wing live alone in windowless cells that they seldom leave. Outside the walls of the prison is another facility for about 300 minium-security prisoners.

Because they lock up the most dangerous offenders, super-maximum security prisons enjoy widespread support from the public. But several human rights groups have lodged complaints against them. Jenni Gainsborough, public policy coordinator for the National Prison Project of the ACLU, has stated: "There is tremendous potential for abuse in these places — the isolation, the weapons, the lack of any clear independent oversight. And the mental effect on people, particularly those who come in with mental problems, can be horrifying." In 1994, several prisoners brought a successful class-action suit against the super-maximum-security wing at Pelican Bay. A federal trial judge in *Madrid v. Gomez* upheld allegations that penitentiary guards used excessive force, and he also ruled the prison could not hold inmates with mental illnesses in isolation.

Under the new policy, an inmate can be placed in OSP when first entering the prison system if the inmate is convicted of particular crimes (such as organized crime). Or the inmate can be placed there later due to misconduct (such as leading a prison gang). To place an inmate in OSP, a prison official fills out a form detailing "matters such as the inmate's recent violence, escape attempts, gang affiliation, underlying offense," etc. A panel reviews the form and holds a hearing. The inmate may go to the hearing and offer written statements, but may not call witnesses. If the panel recommends placing the inmate in OSP, it must provide the reasons in writing and the decision is reviewed twice more. Once in OSP, an inmate gets another review in 30 days and another every year.

The prisoners argued that Ohio officials should spell out exactly what conduct merited being placed in OSP. They also contended that prisoners should be allowed to call witnesses at the hearings and have their status reviewed twice a year. Without these procedures, they argued, Ohio was violating their rights under the 14th Amendment. This amendment protects against deprivations of "life, liberty, or property, without due process of law." The prisoners argued that being placed in OSP was a violation of prisoners' liberty and demanded due process.

In response, the state of Ohio argued two positions:
1. Prisoners have no rights of liberty, and therefore the 14th Amendment does not protect them from deprivations of liberty.
2. Even if they have a right to liberty, Ohio's procedures meet due process.

In 2005, the Supreme Court decided this case in *Wilkinson v. Austin*. Writing for a unanimous court, Justice Anthony Kennedy noted that an ordinary part of prison life consists of lockdowns and periods of temporary solitary confinement. But he pointed out that confinement in OSP was not temporary and placement in OSP disqualified a prisoner from being considered for parole. He said that taken together these factors "impose an atypical and significant hardship within the correctional context. It follows that [prisoners] have a liberty interest in avoiding assignment to OSP."

Although the court ruled that prisoners are being deprived of liberty when placed in OSP, the court went on to say that Ohio's procedures met due process standards. It provided prisoners with notice of the reasons they were being moved, opportunities to reply, and multiple levels of review.

Private Prisons

Since the 1980s, some states and the federal government have turned to private industry to help reduce prison overcrowding. Private security firms have gone into the prison business, in some cases contracting to operate existing prisons and jails, and in others, building new prisons. In several cases, private operators have built prisons hoping to get a contract to hold prisoners.

Private prisons currently hold about 130,000 inmates. One-fourth of them are in the federal system. More than 30 states have private facilities. The state with the most inmates in private prisons is Texas, with more than 19,000 prisoners, about 11 percent of its prison population. Five Western states and Vermont — all with small prison populations — have more than one-fourth of their inmates in private prisons. Some experts estimate that more than 25 percent of all prison beds may eventually be in private hands, mostly in minimum-security institutions.

The idea of privatizing prisons has drawn criticism. Ira P. Robbins, a professor at the American University Law School in Washington, D.C., says, "It's privatization run amok." The American Civil Liberties Union has expressed fears that private companies will be less accountable than the state and may even try to prolong prison sentences to keep earning their per-day fees. Neighbors often wonder if private companies will maintain the same standards for security. Over the long term, some also a fear that putting a large number of prison beds in private hands will create a permanent lobby in favor of long prison sentences. They think the drive to increase profits may well hold back the move to community corrections and alternative sentencing.

Supporters of private prisons dismiss these claims. They argue that private prisons are newer, better managed, and less costly than government-run institutions. As for security, they argue that most private prisons take only minimum-security prisoners anyway. Finally, they maintain that it is unlikely private-prison companies would lobby for longer prison terms because there is such an excess of prisoners already.

FOR DISCUSSION
1. Do you think super-maximum-security prisons are a good idea? Explain.
2. Do you think that prisoners should be able to challenge being placed in a super-max? Why or why not?
3. Why do you think states and the federal government are turning to private facilities?
4. Do you think privatizing prisons is a good idea? Why or why not?

Overcrowding in Prisons

The degree of civilization in a society can be judged by entering its prisons.
– Fyodor Dostoevsky, Russian writer, *The House of the Dead* (1861)

As the U.S. prison population has increased, one of the biggest prison problems is overcrowding. In fact, the federal prison system and more than half of all state prisons are running over capacity. In some cases as many as 11 prisoners are held in cells designed for four. Overcrowding can lead to discipline problems, unrest, unhealthy conditions, and far too often, violence.

The following prison conditions were described in the 1978 Supreme Court decision of *Hutto v. Finney*:

The ordinary Arkansas convict had to endure . . . "a dark and evil world completely alien to the free world . . . ." Confinement in punitive isolation was for an indeterminate period of time. An average of four, and sometimes as many as 10 or 11, prisoners were crowded into windowless 8'x 10' cells containing no furniture other than a source of water and a toilet that could only be flushed from outside the cell . . . . At night the prisoners were given mattresses to spread on the floor. Although some prisoners suffered from infectious diseases, such as hepatitis and venereal disease, mattresses were removed and jumbled together each morning, then returned to the cells at random in the evening. Prisoners in isolation received fewer than 1,000 calories a day; their meals consisted primarily of four-inch squares of "grue," a substance created by mashing meat, potatoes, oleo, syrup, vegetables, eggs and seasoning into a paste and baking the mixture in a pan.

Beginning in the late 1970s, the federal judiciary began ordering states to upgrade their prisons and reduce overcrowding. Cases brought by public-interest lawyers charged that inmates in the most dangerous and overcrowded prisons were being subjected to "cruel and unusual punishment" as forbidden by the Eighth Amendment of the U.S. Constitution.

In several cases, the Supreme Court agreed. It held that the Eighth Amendment prohibits penalties that "transgress today's broad and idealistic concepts of dignity, civilized standards, humanity and decency." (*Estelle v. Gamble*, 1976)

PRISONERS IN U.S. PRISONS

	Prisoners	Imprisonment Rate*
U.S. Total	1,605,127	502
Federal	209,771	61
State	1,395,356	442
Alabama	31,764	650
Alaska	5,597	357
Arizona	40,130	580
Arkansas	16,204	522
California	165,062	458
Colorado	22,815	450
Connecticut	19,321	382
Delaware	6,598	447
Florida	104,306	559
Georgia	49,164	526
Hawaii	5,912	317
Idaho	7,431	476
Illinois	48,418	349
Indiana	28,028	447
Iowa	9,455	292
Kansas	9,051	305
Kentucky	20,544	478
Louisiana	39,445	881
Maine	2,154	150
Maryland	22,645	382
Massachusetts	11,312	213
Michigan	44,113	457
Minnesota	9,796	189
Mississippi	21,067	702
Missouri	30,623	509
Montana	3,716	368
Nebraska	4,587	243
Nevada	12,653	470
New Hampshire	2,761	206
New Jersey	25,007	291
New Mexico	6,659	316
New York	56,656	298
North Carolina	40,116	369
North Dakota	1,487	228
Ohio	51,712	446
Oklahoma	26,252	657
Oregon	14,014	373
Pennsylvania	51,264	406
Rhode Island	3,357	211
South Carolina	23,578	512
South Dakota	3,434	420
Tennessee	27,451	426
Texas	173,649	648
Utah	6,807	232
Vermont	2,079	277
Virginia	37,410	480
Washington	18,235	271
West Virginia	6,681	346
Wisconsin	22,724	369
Wyoming	2,112	377

*Imprisonment rate is the number of prisoners sentenced to more than 1 year per 100,000 U.S. residents.

Source: *Prisoners in 2010*, Bureau of Justice Statistics (2011)

Some federal courts imposed rigid deadlines to end overcrowding. These deadlines had short-term and long-term effects. In Alabama, for instance, some 200 prisoners were released well before the end of their sentences to satisfy a federal court order. Texas was repeatedly forced to halt new prison admissions to satisfy the courts, and a federal judge threatened the state with fines of $800,000 a day until it alleviated overcrowding. Some Texas legislators even proposed turning barges, unused oil-drilling rigs, and foreclosed buildings into makeshift prisons.

In most states, the 1980s saw a surge of new prison construction to try to keep pace with the increasing number of prisoners. Building prisons became a $17 billion a year industry. A new prison averaged more than $50,000 per cell to build, and annual costs rose to about $20,000 to guard and house each prisoner. Some prison authorities were pleased by the court actions since the judicial orders forced reluctant state legislatures to appropriate funds.

In 1981, however, the U.S. Supreme Court seemed to back away from further prison reform. The court decided the case of *Rhodes v. Chapman*, which had raised the issue of whether confining two prisoners in a cell built for one violated the Eighth Amendment. The court ruled that it did not. Voting 8–1, the justices held that overcrowding does not in itself violate the Eighth Amendment, if overall prison conditions meet contemporary standards of decency. Justice O'Connor wrote for the majority that "harsh conditions" are the price of crime and the Constitution does not require comfortable prisons.

Federal courts, however, still can demand changes to prisons when overcrowding causes dangerous, unfit conditions. A federal court may still even order a state to limit its prison population.

But Congress in 1995 passed the Prison Litigation Reform Act, with the purpose of making court-mandated prison caps "a remedy of last resort." The act set up a process that courts must follow. First, a federal trial court must issue an order to improve the dangerous conditions and give the state a reasonable time to comply with the order. If the state fails to improve the dangerous conditions, then the trial court can set up a special three-judge panel. Before it can order a state to limit its prison population, the panel must find that (1) "crowding is the primary cause of the violation of a Federal right" and (2) no other action "will remedy the violation of the

Federal right." It also requires that the panel give "substantial weight" to "public safety" and make sure that the remedy "extends no further than necessary to correct the violation of the Federal right." Such a process can take years.

When a three-judge panel recently ordered a massive reduction in prisoners in California, the order was appealed. The U.S. Supreme Court had to decide whether to let the order stand.

With 173,000 in its prisons, California held more prisoners than any other state. (Texas was a close second.) In fact, one of every 10 prisoners in the United States is in a California prison cell. For more than a decade, California prisons have operated at about double their 80,000 prisoner capacity. The court described California prison conditions:

> Prisoners are crammed into spaces neither designed nor intended to house inmates. As many as 200 prisoners may live in a gymnasium, monitored by as few as two or three correctional officers. . . . As many as 54 prisoners may share a single toilet. . . . The consequences of overcrowding identified by the Governor include " 'increased, substantial risk for transmission of infectious illness' " and a suicide rate " 'approaching an average of one per week.' "

The three-judge panel had consolidated two cases. One case challenged medical care and the other, mental health care in California prisons. Both cases had been in the courts for a long time, one for more than 20 years. Although California had made attempts, the panel found that medical and mental health care were deteriorating and overcrowding was the cause. Since no remedy other than reducing the number of California prisoners would work, the panel ordered California within two years to reduce its prison population to 137 percent of capacity (down from its current 200 percent). This meant that California had about 37,000 prisoners above that limit. It could increase prison capacity by building new prisons for them, place them in jails, send them out of state, release them on parole, or some combination of these options. California asked the Supreme Court to overturn this order.

In 2011 in *Brown v. Plata*, the U.S. Supreme Court, in a 5–4 decision, upheld the order from the three-judge panel. The court majority noted a long litany of horrible conditions in mental and medical care.

> Prisoners in California with serious mental illness do not receive minimal, adequate

Since the *Brown v. Plata* decision in 2011, California has lowered its prison population.

care. Because of a shortage of treatment beds, suicidal inmates may be held for prolonged periods in telephone-booth sized cages without toilets. . . . A psychiatric expert reported observing an inmate who had been held in such a cage for nearly 24 hours, standing in a pool of his own urine, unresponsive and nearly catatonic. Prison officials explained they had " 'no place to put him.' " . . . . Wait times for mental health care range as high as 12 months. . . . In 2006, the suicide rate in California's prisons was nearly 80% higher than the national average for prison populations . . . .

Prisoners suffering from physical illness also receive severely deficient care. . . . A correctional officer testified that, in one prison, up to 50 sick inmates may be held together in a 12-by 20-foot cage for up to five hours awaiting treatment. . . . The number of staff is inadequate, and prisoners face significant delays in access to care. A prisoner with severe abdominal pain died after a 5-week delay in referral to a specialist; a prisoner with "constant and extreme" chest pain died after an 8-hour delay in evaluation by a doctor; and a prisoner died of testicular cancer after a "failure of MDs to work up for cancer in a young man with 17 months of testicular pain." . . . . Doctor Ronald Shansky, former medical director of the Illinois state prison system, surveyed death reviews for California prisoners. He concluded that extreme departures from the standard of care were "widespread," . . . and that the proportion of "possibly preventable or preventable" deaths was "extremely high."

The court majority cited evidence showing that overcrowding was the primary cause. "Numerous experts testified that crowding is the primary cause of the constitutional violations." For example, Dr. Shansky testified that "even if the prisons were able to fill all of their vacant health care positions, which they have not been able to do to date, . . . the prisons would still be unable to handle the level of need given the current overcrowding." The evidence also revealed that the prisons did not have enough space to house additional needed staff.

The court majority also found that no other remedy was available. In dire fiscal straits, California was not planning on building more prisons. Nor was the state, after years of trying, able to find health care providers willing to work in its prisons.

Finally, the court majority addressed the issue of public safety. It noted: "Expert witnesses produced statistical evidence that prison populations had been lowered without adversely affecting public safety in a number of jurisdictions." It stated that California could release non-violent offenders who had earned good time credits, stop imprisoning parolees who only commit technical parole violations, and divert "low-risk offenders to community programs such as drug treatment, day reporting centers, and electronic monitoring."

The dissenters wrote two separate dissenting opinions. The dissents presented a number of different arguments. In Justice Antonin Scalia's dissent, he argued that probably only a small percentage of prisoners could allege violations in their Eighth Amendment protection against cruel and unusual punishment due to inadequate medical or mental health care. Yet the court was ordering California to release prisoners not shown to have suffered from inadequate care. Scalia contended that the court order extended further than necessary to correct the problem, and thus violated the Prison Litigation Reform Act.

In my view, a court may not order a prisoner's release unless it determines that the prisoner is suffering from a violation of his constitutional rights, and that his release, and no other relief, will remedy that violation. Thus, if the court determines that a particular prisoner is being denied constitutionally required medical treatment, and the release of that prisoner (and no other remedy) would enable him to obtain medical treatment, then the court can order his release; but a court may not order the release of prisoners who have suffered no violations of their constitutional rights, merely to make it less likely that that will happen to them in the future.

Justice Samuel Alito's dissent also argued that the three-court panel's order failed to meet the requirements of the Prison Litigation Reform Act. First, he did not believe it met the requirement that no action other than ordering a reduction in the number of prisoners "will remedy the violation of the Federal right."

Is it plausible that none of these deficiencies can be remedied without releasing [thousands of] prisoners? Without taking that radical and dangerous step, exam tables and counter tops cannot properly be disinfected? None of the system's dilapidated facilities can be repaired? Needed medications and equipment cannot be purchased and used? Staff vacancies cannot be filled? The qualifications of prison physicians cannot be improved? A better records management system cannot be developed and implemented?

I do not dispute that general overcrowding *contributes* to many of the California system's healthcare problems. But it by no means follows that reducing overcrowding is the only or the best or even a particularly good way to alleviate those problems.

Second, argued Alito, the three-judge panel did not give "substantial weight" to "public safety," as required under the law. In creating this law,

. . . Congress was well aware of the impact of previous prisoner release orders. The prisoner release program carried out a few years earlier in Philadelphia is illustrative. In the early 1990's, federal courts enforced a cap on the number of inmates in the Philadelphia prison system, and thousands of inmates were set free. Although efforts were made to release only those prisoners who were least likely to commit violent crimes, that attempt was spectacularly unsuccessful. During an 18-month period, the Philadelphia police rearrested thousands of these prisoners for committing 9,732 new crimes. Those defendants were charged with 79 murders, 90 rapes, 1,113 assaults, 959 robberies, 701 burglaries, and 2,748 thefts, not to mention thousands of drug offenses. Members of Congress were well aware of this experience.

. . .

Before putting public safety at risk, every reasonable precaution should be taken. The decision below should be reversed . . . . I fear that today's decision, like prior prisoner release orders, will lead to a grim roster of victims. I hope that I am wrong. In a few years, we will see.

FOR DISCUSSION

1. What problems can prison overcrowding cause?
2. Do you agree with the U.S. Supreme Court decision in *Rhodes v. Chapman*? Why or why not?
3. What is the purpose of the Prison Litigation Reform Act? What are its requirements? Could Congress pass a law that denied prisoners their constitutional rights? Explain.
4. What were the facts of the case of *Brown v. Plata*? What was the issue? What were the holding and reasoning of the court? What did the dissenters say? Do you agree with the decision? Explain.

CLASS ACTIVITY

Brown v. Plata

Opinion pieces appear many places — on the radio, on television, in newspapers and magazines, and in blogs. In this activity, you are going to get the opportunity to voice your opinion.

Did the U.S. Supreme Court make the right decision in *Brown v. Plata*? This decision provoked much controversy. Write a persuasive article stating your opinion on the case.

In your opinion piece, do the following:
a. Explain the case.
b. State your opinion on the decision.
c. Back your opinion with persuasive arguments defending or attacking the decision.
d. Be sure to counter arguments put forward by the other side.
e. End with a strong conclusion.

Before you turn it in, be sure to read it aloud to see if it reads well and proofread and correct it.

Prison Revolts

Groups of angry prisoners holding 33 guards as hostages at the Attica State Correctional Facility continued negotiations into this morning with State Correction Commissioner Russell G. Oswald.

— Report from the *New York Times* (Sept. 11, 1971)

Prison revolts help focus public attention on conditions inside American prisons. In 2011, for example, the media reported that two prisoners suffered multiple stab wounds in a prison riot at California's maximum security prison in Sacramento. Since the 1950s, at least one major prison riot has erupted each year. The two most famous revolts took place in 1971 and 1980.

In September 1971, more than 1,200 prisoners at New York's Attica State Prison seized Cell Block D and took 33 guards hostage to protest what they called oppressive prison conditions. Influenced by the political movements of the 1960s, particularly radical African-American organizations, the prisoners immediately organized themselves, setting up a sick bay, clean-up details, an elected negotiating committee, and a security force to guard and protect the hostages. One guard who had been seriously injured was sent out to the hospital and 10 other hostages needing medical aid were released. The prisoners' first statement said, "We are men. We are not beasts, and do not intend to be beaten or driven."

The prisoners met with a mediating team that eventually included the New York director of prisons, lawyers, journalists, and local political leaders. Their demands were mostly for humane treatment: better prison conditions, freedom of religion to allow Muslim worship, meaningful job training, the right to hold political meetings, and an amnesty for the takeover. Most of the demands, except the amnesty, were granted. But this omission became crucial when the injured guard died in the hospital. Still, by the third day, most of the mediators felt they were near a deal if Governor Nelson Rockefeller would come to Attica to give any agreement credibility. Rockefeller thought it would be unwise and stayed away.

On Monday, the fourth day of the revolt, guards and state police assaulted Cell Block D with helicopters and nausea gas. More than 500 men firing rifles and shotguns poured into

Attica State Prison was the site of a major prison riot in 1971.

the yard. The gunfire killed 33 inmates and nine hostages and seriously wounded more than 100 other prisoners. In the aftermath, prisoners were stripped and beaten, and forced to run gantlets of angry guards. Some observers charged that a few of those killed died hours after the prison had been retaken. More than 20 years later, a civil court awarded prisoners millions of dollars in damages for violations of their civil rights after the assault.

Life at Attica

Almost everyone, including the head of New York prisons, agreed that the uprising had been sparked by terrible prison conditions. Every inmate entered Attica in shackles and leg-irons. He was issued gray prison clothes and then placed in an isolation cell where he stayed for two days. After four to eight weeks of lockup for about 20 hours a day, he was assigned a job and transferred to a cell block.

Each prisoner at Attica had a cell about the size of a walk-in closet, six feet by nine feet. The nearest window was across the corridor. He had a bed, a metal stool, a small table, a two-drawer metal cabinet, an open toilet, a cold-water sink, and one 60-watt bulb. For the rest of his imprisonment, he spent 14 to 16 hours a day alone in this cell.

Five hours a day were for work or school, one hour or so for recreation, and about half an hour for each meal. Each man could shower once a week. During weekdays, the daily routine began at 5:50 a.m. and the men were locked in for the night at 6:30 p.m. They could talk between cells until 8 p.m. after which time silence was required. The lights went out at 11 p.m.

Vocational training was mostly work in a huge laundry at 30 cents a day or being assigned with 15 other men to a one-man machine tool in a shop that never dropped below 100 degrees F. Little education was available, the meals were often inedible, and there were hundreds of prison rules. Prison officials read all mail. In addition, more than 75 percent of the prisoners at Attica were black or Puerto Rican, and all 383 guards were white. Charges of racial discrimination were common.

The revolt spurred four separate investigations of conditions at Attica, and many of the more serious abuses were eventually corrected.

New Mexico State Prison

The revolt at New Mexico State Prison nine years later could hardly have been more different from the one at Attica. In February 1980, prisoners at the New Mexico prison broke into the

THE STANFORD PRISON EXPERIMENT

The 1971 Stanford Prison Experiment was a famous psychological study conducted by Philip G. Zimbardo, a psychology professor at Stanford University. The experiment sought to examine people's response to captivity and the psychological effects of a prison setting.

Male college student volunteers were randomly divided into two groups: prisoners and guards. Playing the role of prison superintendent, Zimbardo told the guards they could use any means except violence to maintain control of the prison, but he offered them no other training.

The experiment began with police arresting "prisoners" at their homes. Blindfolded and taken in police cars to a makeshift prison in a university basement, they were searched, stripped naked, given identification numbers to be used instead of names, and issued smocks as uniforms and chains to wear around their ankles. Then they were placed in small cells, each barely large enough for three cots. The intention was to give the prisoners a sense of powerlessness.

Many times throughout the day, the guards ordered the prisoners to count off and give their ID numbers. They even woke them several times for counts late at night. If prisoners didn't cooperate, guards ordered them to do push-ups.

By the second day, the prisoners had had enough. They barricaded themselves in their cells and taunted the guards. The guards responded by breaking into the cells, stripping the prisoners, and taking out the cots. The guards decided to use psychological tactics to break the relationships the prisoners had formed. They created a "privileged" cell for the prisoners least involved in the rebellion. These prisoners were given their uniforms and beds back, allowed to clean themselves, and allowed to eat while prisoners in the other cells lost these privileges. After half a day, to confuse the prisoners, the guards changed who was in the "privileged" cell and "bad" cells. The prisoners grew suspicious of each other, thinking others were leaking information to the guards. As solidarity among the prisoners broke down, the guards focused on maintaining control. The guards decided when prisoners could go to the bathroom and set up an isolation cell for troublemakers.

Zimbardo terminated the study early because he felt the experiment was getting out of hand and could harm those involved. He concluded that his study demonstrated that a situation giving one group power over another could influence the average person's behavior and sense of morality, thus changing ordinary people into tyrants.

Many have heralded Zimbardo's study, but it also has drawn critics, who call his findings subjective and unscientific. Some criticize the experiment's lack of a control group and independent variables. Others have said that Zimbardo's direct interaction with participants as prison superintendent potentially influenced the study. Other scholars have found his group of volunteers not to be a random sample representative of the population. His group of volunteers was all male, all college students, and tested to make sure no one was mentally ill. Also, critics say the study involved too few people to make sweeping conclusions about the population.

control room, seized the guards, and opened all the cells. The political movements of the 1960s had passed, and no one at New Mexico thought of trying to organize or control the revolt. Some prisoners went to the sick bay and started a drug orgy. Others went on a rampage smashing furniture and setting fires. One group broke into an isolation area where prison informers were held. Thirty-three prisoners were hacked to death or tortured to death with blowtorches. Prison officials tried to negotiate, but they found no one in charge to negotiate with.

As the violence died down, most of the prisoners came out one-by-one to surrender peacefully. Those who didn't come out offered no resistance when police and National Guardsmen stormed the prison 36 hours later. At Attica, all the deaths, except the one guard injured in the takeover, had come at the hands of the police. In New Mexico, the inmates themselves had done all the killing.

Despite the differences, post-riot commissions found many of the same abuses in New Mexico. In fact, some conditions were probably worse. In New Mexico, prisoners did not have individual cells, and homosexual rape was widespread. Also, drugs had become much more common by 1980, and many of the prisoners were intoxicated during the riot. The following is one convict's letter, detailing some of his complaints:

> We seldom see any kind of exercise, the heat is turned on high in some of the dorms whether it is a warm day or not, the food is bad, the mail is lost or comes late, the lighting in most dorms is bad, and all around we face harassment by the guards.

Attica and New Mexico by no means represented the worst prisons in the United States. They were just unlucky enough to have the necessary conditions come together to set off riots.

Gangs

Some conditions at Attica and New Mexico have improved since the uprisings, but these prisons are still subject to the overcrowding and other problems that plague most of our maximum- and medium-security institutions. Perhaps the biggest new prison problem has been the growth of violent, race- and ethnic-based gangs. Beginning in the 1970s, as dramatized in Edward James Olmos' film *American Me*, these gangs were organized almost exclusively along racial or ethnic lines.

They have spread to almost every American prison. The best known are the Black Guerrilla Family for African Americans, two competing families of what is popularly called the Mexican Mafia for Hispanics, and the Aryan White Brotherhood.

These groups demand obedience and provide a sense of protection and community for their members. Because of their racial and ethnic makeup, many of the gangs make heavy use of racist slogans and symbols, and they glory in violent acts against other races and ethnic groups.

Conflicts among the gangs have grown so intense that some institutions have segregated prisoners by race. California, for example, segregates prisoners by race for the first 60 days they enter an institution. California prison authorities say they are reluctant to give official sanction to racial separation, but they say they have little choice if they want to protect the lives of the prisoners. In 2005, the U.S. Supreme Court decided a case challenging this practice, *Johnson v. California*. The court did not make a final decision on the practice. Instead, it decided that the practice must be looked at with "strict scrutiny," the most rigorous test of any policy. To pass strict scrutiny, the practice must serve a "compelling governmental interest" and be the least restrictive means of achieving that interest. The case was sent back to the trial court, which applying the strict scrutiny test, decided that the practice passed the test. Once again, Johnson appealed. When the case reached the U.S. Supreme Court, which chooses which cases it will take, the court decided not to hear it. Thus, the California practice remains in place.

FOR DISCUSSION

1. How did the revolts at Attica and New Mexico prisons differ? Why? Give several reasons.
2. What, if anything, do you think can be done to prevent future prison revolts? Explain.
3. How might conditions in a maximum-security prison affect a first-time offender?
4. Do you think California's policy of dividing prisoners by race for 60 days makes sense? Do you think it passes strict scrutiny? Explain.
5. How do you think the racial divisions in the prisons can be resolved?

Policies Behind the Rise in Incarceration

Increases sentences for defendants convicted of any felony who have prior convictions for violent or serious felonies such as rape, robbery or burglary. . . . Convicted felons with two or more such prior convictions would receive a life sentence with a minimum term three times the normal sentence or 25 years, whichever is greater.
– Ballot language for California's Proposition 184, "Three Strikes" (1984)

As crime rates started soaring in the 1960s and 1970s, the public demanded that officials do something about crime. Politicians started promising to "get tough on crime." They adopted new policies designed to put more criminals behind bars.

Get-Tough Policies

Three major get-tough policies have greatly increased the number of people behind bars and the length of their sentences.

Mandatory sentencing. Mandatory sentencing laws require judges to sentence offenders to prison terms. Since the 1980s, almost every state has passed mandatory sentencing laws for certain situations, such as repeat-offender laws and use-a-gun, go-to-jail laws. Usually, a judge has no option but to impose the mandatory sentence and cannot shorten it, suspend it, or give an alternative sentence.

In 1973, New York passed harsh mandatory minimum sentences for drug offenses. In the 1980s, the federal government and many other states followed New York's lead. Soon a quarter of all prison inmates were offenders who only committed low-level, non-violent drug offenses.

By 2010, more than a half of all federal prisoners were drug offenders. About a quarter of all state prisoners were behind bars for drug offenses.

Three strikes and you're out. This is a more recent form of mandatory sentence for repeat offenders. It mandates a lengthy, or even a life prison term, for certain third felony convictions. The federal government and many states have adopted versions of the three-strikes law. The three-strikes provision in federal law requires that the three convictions must be for violent felonies. In some states, like California, only the first two convictions must be for

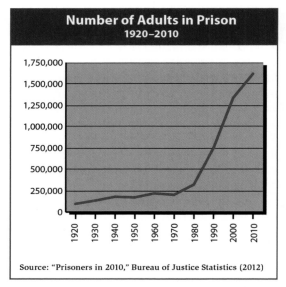

Number of Adults in Prison
1920–2010

Source: "Prisoners in 2010," Bureau of Justice Statistics (2012)

violent or other specified felonies. The third can be for any felony.

Truth in Sentencing. These laws attempt to reduce or eliminate parole. Before the end of a sentence, most convicts are released into the community on parole under the supervision of a parole officer. In some cases, they are put on parole after serving less than half their sentence. Some prisoners are released by state parole boards. Others are released early because they have earned credits, called **good time**, against their full term. They can earn good-time credits by behaving well and participating in special programs. Some jurisdictions allow prisoners to earn as much as one day of good time for every two days served. Prison authorities say they need good-time programs to keep order.

Truth in sentencing laws, however, force convicts to serve close to their full sentences. Since 1987, the federal government has adopted truth in sentencing. All federal convicts must serve at least 85 percent of their sentence. The 1994 and 1995 federal crime bills offered prison construction aid to states that adopt truth-in-sentencing laws for violent offenders. Most states have passed such laws. One state, Wisconsin, even requires all felony offenders to serve 100 percent of their sentence.

* * *

For most of this century, our nation's prison and jail population had remained stable — at or below 300,000 prisoners. Beginning in the 1970s, the get-tough policies began being enacted, and states and the federal government started locking up more prisoners. By 1990, they had put 1 million prisoners behind bars. One decade later, the total had reached 2 million prisoners, and by 2009, 2.2 million. An additional 5 million convicts are currently on probation and parole. The rate of incarceration in America is the highest in the world. The rate is five to 11 times higher than most other industrialized countries.

For Discussion

1. What are mandatory sentences? What do you think might be some arguments in favor of them? Against them?
2. What are the different types of three-strikes laws?
3. What are truth-in-sentencing laws? What do you think might be some arguments in favor of them? Against them?
4. Today, due to budgetary problems, states are trying to lower the number of prisoners they hold. If you were an adviser to a governor trying to lower incarceration in the state, what changes in get-tough policies would you recommend? Why?

CLASS ACTIVITY

Three Strikes

In this activity, students role play advisers to a state legislator who is considering introducing three-strikes legislation.

1. Form small groups. Each is a group of advisers to a state legislator who is considering introducing three-strikes legislation. Each group should:
   a. Make a list of the pros and cons of three strikes.
   b. Consider whether any felony or only violent felonies should count as strikes.
   c. Decide whether or not to recommend three-strikes legislation.
   d. Prepare to report back its recommendation and the reasons for it.
2. The groups should report back and the class should hold a discussion.
3. Students should conclude the activity by voting on two different three-strikes proposals — one with all felonies counting as strikes and one with only violent felonies counting.

Are Too Many People Behind Bars?

The United States has 756 people in jail per 100,000 people. No other country has more than 700, and only two are over 600 Russia (629) and Rwanda (604).
– Ta-Nehisi Coates, "Hoodlums" in *The Atlantic* (2010)

The Bureau of Justice Statistics estimates the average cost is about $22,000 per year to house a prisoner. (This ranges from more than $40,000 in California to about $13,000 in Louisiana.) It also costs billions of dollars to build prisons and jails. With 2.2 million in prison or jail, it costs taxpayers about $74 billion each year to build prisons and house the prisoners. Is it worth it?

For years, many advocates thought it was. In 1994, the American Legislative Exchange Council (ALEC), a non-profit bipartisan membership organization for conservative state legislators published its *Report Card on Crime and Punishment*. In the foreword, former U.S. Attorney General William P. Barr emphasized that "*getting tough works.*" He said that "increasing prison capacity is the single most effective strategy for controlling crime."

The ALEC report showed that the violent crime rate in 1992 was almost five times higher than that of 1960. The report blamed this increase on the failure of states to lock up greater numbers of violent criminals. It noted that until 1975, despite increasing violent crime, the actual number of inmates in state prisons fell. The report said that, responding to public demands, state legislatures in the 1970s started adopting mandatory sentencing laws. These laws required judges to sentence certain offenders to prison. By 1975, the number of prisoners started climbing and has been climbing steadily ever since.

Because of this new trend in incarceration, said the report, some progress had been made in reducing violent crime. The report attributed the falls in violent crime in the early 1980s and 1990s to the rise in incarceration. In the words of former Attorney General Barr, "the eighties worked and the sixties didn't. It doesn't take a rocket scientist to decide which path to follow."

Following this report, the incarceration rate continued to climb and the crime rate started dropping. Supporters of get-tough policies believe greater incarceration caused the decline in crime. Others disagree.

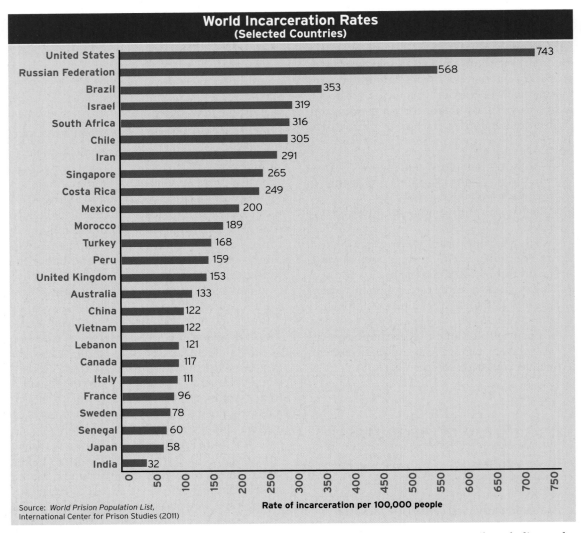

World Incarceration Rates
(Selected Countries)

Country	Rate
United States	743
Russian Federation	568
Brazil	353
Israel	319
South Africa	316
Chile	305
Iran	291
Singapore	265
Costa Rica	249
Mexico	200
Morocco	189
Turkey	168
Peru	159
United Kingdom	153
Australia	133
China	122
Vietnam	122
Lebanon	121
Canada	117
Italy	111
France	96
Sweden	78
Senegal	60
Japan	58
India	32

Rate of incarceration per 100,000 people

Source: *World Prision Population List,*
International Center for Prison Studies (2011)

Pros and Cons

The supporters give two reasons why increased incarceration works. First, it deters others from committing violent acts. When people realize that they will go to prison for a long time, they think twice about committing a violent crime. But even staunch advocates of get-tough policies admit that deterrence is difficult to document. So most cite the second reason: Locking criminals up keeps them from committing crimes. This is known as incapacitation. By some estimates, the average violent street offender commits 12 crimes a year. If the offender is in prison, this saves the public from 12 violent crimes. Moreover, studies indicate that a small percentage of offenders commit many crimes. (See **Studies Show That a Few Criminals Account for Much Crime** on page 255.) If these habitual offenders were imprisoned, the nation would experience a significant drop in serious crime.

Criminologist James Q. Wilson believes the "tough-on-crime laws endorsed by the public had an important effect on reducing the crime rate."

In much of Europe, national political leaders rejected the use of prison, and as a result the rate of many crimes rose when American crime rates were falling. In 1976, for example, England had a robbery rate lower than did the United States, but by 1996 England's rate was one-quarter higher, its auto theft rate one-third higher, and its burglary and assault rates twice as high as in this country.

Some critics of massive incarceration doubt that it affects crime rates. They cite the strong economy, better policing, the end of the crack epidemic, and other factors as causing the drop in crime rates that began in the 1990s. They point out that incarceration rates have been climbing since 1975 and during much of that time, crime rates increased. Supporters of increased incarceration counter that crime would have been much worse during that period without the increased incarceration. A Bureau of Justice Statistics study in 1991 supported that view. But a study published in *Crime and Delinquency* in 1992 comparing two states with far different incarceration rates found that the rates didn't affect the rates of violent crime.

Criminologist Franklin Zimring has compared the experience of New York City, which has greatly reduced crime, to the rest of the nation.

> Over the period from 1990 to 2009, the rate of imprisonment in the United States, outside of New York City, went up by 65 percent. Even though there was a general crime decline, we kept throwing people in prison. In New York City, the rate of imprisonment and jailing didn't go up at all, it went down 28 percent. So what you have is that the one American city that did best in the crime control sweepstakes of the 1990s and the 21st century actually had less use of incarceration than everyplace else. . . . This is a country that had only one answer to its crime problems for 45 years. This is a country that increased the number of people it locked up by sixfold over the 40 years after 1970. So in essence what New York has done was demonstrate that the major investment we were making in controlling crime was simultaneously inefficient and unnecessary.

Many critics focus on the inefficiency of locking up so many people. They claim the get-tough policies result in **collective incapacitation** — long sentences given to all felons. Non-dangerous prisoners serve along with the dangerous, and prisoners serve time long after they reach an age where they pose no danger. These critics advocate **selective incapacitation** — targeting the small percentage of career criminals who commit most crimes and targeting other offenders during their most crime-prone years (usually between the ages of 18 and 30). This, they say, would reduce crime without requiring so many in prison. The only practical way to do this, however, would be to allow judges and parole boards more discretion in sentencing. Those who favor getting tough on crime oppose this, because they believe judges and parole boards are frequently too lenient on criminals.

Critics also point to the high number of drug offenders in prison. Criminologist Alfred Blumstein thinks long sentences for these offenders are ineffective.

> In the case of drug dealing . . . , the market is resilient in responding to the demand, and recruits replacements for those sent to prison. . . . This replacement effect largely nullifies any incapacitation effect of incarcerating drug dealers. Indeed, it has been the case that the replacements, usually young men, were far more dangerous than the older and more restrained men they replaced.

Criminologist Mark Kleiman believes we should limit prison to three types of offenders:

> There are people who do such appalling stuff that we want to make an example of them — say, Bernie Madoff. There are people who are violent criminals and whose rate of crime is high enough that it's worth $40,000 a year not to have them in our hair. And then there are people who won't behave on the outside. You put an ankle bracelet on him, he takes the ankle bracelet off; he's picked himself a prison cell. Everybody else we can adequately punish and control in the community. [See pages 58–60 for information on Madoff.]

STUDIES SHOW THAT A FEW CRIMINALS ACCOUNT FOR MUCH CRIME

A long-term study by criminologist Marvin Wolfgang followed the arrest records of all males born in the years 1945 and 1958 in Philadelphia. A mere 7 percent of the males were responsible for more than half the crime stemming from the group. Those in the 7-percent group had been arrested at least five times each by age 18. They committed two-thirds of all the violent crime and about three-fourths of all rapes, robberies, and murders.

A study by the RAND Corporation found that each year the most active robbers averaged almost 90 crimes and the most active burglars averaged more than 200 offenses. A review of habitual offender studies by criminologist Alfred Blumstein showed that the most active 10 percent of criminals committed about 100 crimes in a year.

WHAT ABOUT REHABILITATION?

Many feel that massive incarceration has caused the nation's correctional systems to turn away from rehabilitating prisoners. According to those who hold this view, with so many inmates in custody, the best that most prison systems can do is warehouse them. Supporters of massive incarceration say that rehabilitation never worked and incapacitation works. They point to a review of more than 200 studies of correctional programs by criminologist Robert Martinson in 1974. His review found that no program reduced the rate of **recidivism** (the rate of those released from prison who go on to commit new crimes). Since "nothing works," it's pointless and wasteful, they argue, to try to rehabilitate prisoners. Martinson's review is one of the most influential and often cited studies in criminology. Follow-up studies supported Martinson.

In the intervening decades, however, hundreds of new studies have looked at the effect of rehabilitation programs on recidivism rates. These studies have cast doubt on Martinson's conclusion that nothing works. In 2007, researchers Mark Lipsey and Francis Cullen did a major review of these studies. They concluded that "rehabilitation works."

[R]ehabilitation treatment is capable of reducing the reoffense rates of convicted offenders . . . . The volume of research and the consistency of the findings of the systematic reviews make this a sufficiently sound general conclusion, bordering on beyond a reasonable doubt, to provide a basis for correctional practice and policy.

The researchers called for more research on which rehabilitation programs are most effective for particular offenders. They also pointed out that the "increased punitive emphasis of recent decades has led to less rehabilitation programming, resulting in many offenders not being exposed to any significant treatment at all." More than 600,000 convicts are released into society every year, most of them without going through any rehabilitation program.

Many critics of massive incarceration cite its cost. With local, state, and federal governments spending a combined total of about $74 billion each year on corrections, critics argue that corrections budgets are crowding out other worthwhile items. California, for example, now spends more on its prison system than on its University of California system. Critics say crime prevention programs and even police are feeling the squeeze. A 2011 study by the Bureau of Justice Statistics reported that from 1982 to 2007 spending on police increased 125 percent. In the same period, spending on corrections increased more than 250 percent.

But the question is whether incarceration is worth its price. In 1987, Edwin Zedlewski, an economist for the National Institute of Justice, did a cost-benefit analysis of incarceration. He figured the annual cost of housing an inmate as $25,000. He estimated that each criminal committed an average of 187 crimes each year and that the average cost of each crime was $2,300. Based on these figures, he calculated that the benefits outweighed the costs by 17 to 1.

Critics pointed out that only the most active criminals would commit so many crimes. Zedlewski stood by his estimates, but limited them to the prison population remaining in the 300,000 to 600,000 range (which is now far surpassed). Above that range, the law of diminishing returns may set in, as most high-rate offenders may already be in prison.

But still experts differ. Criminologist John DiIulio strongly supports three-strike laws as highly effective at targeting high-rate offenders. Critics of three strikes cite a study by the RAND Corporation. It found that less than $1 billion of crime-prevention spending would have the same impact on crime as California's three-strikes law, which costs an estimated $5.5 billion a year.

Both DiIulio and another RAND study agree that mandatory minimums for drug offenses should be repealed because they are not cost effective. Jay Apperson, a federal prosecutor, disagrees. He thinks they are necessary to convict high-level drug dealers. He states: "Our experience is that without tough mandatory minimum sentences, defendants facing a few years time are generally willing to serve it, rather than finger violent suppliers and big-time traffickers."

One critic of massive incarceration has warned that it would be difficult to change course. He claims that a "prison-industrial complex" has developed, consisting of prison guard unions, politicians using the fear of crime to win votes, rural areas whose economies depend on a nearby prison, and private companies who look on the large prison budgets as opportunities for profit.

But this "complex" is not invincible. In recent years, as the crime rate has gone down, voters in some states have turned down bond issues for new prisons, and cash-strapped states cannot spend more money on their prison systems.

The two states with the most prisoners — California and Texas — have begun looking for alternatives to imprisonment. California voters overwhelmingly approved an initiative to send most non-violent drug possession offenders into treatment instead of prison. Since 2007, Texas has sent many low-risk offenders into treatment programs for drug, mental-health, and alcohol problems instead of sending them to prison.

FOR DISCUSSION

1. The United States has the highest rate of incarceration of any country in the world. What dangers might too many people in prison pose to a democratic society? What dangers might come from having too few in prison?
2. Do you think prisons should have more rehabilitation programs for prisoners? Explain.
3. Studies show that a few offenders commit the vast majority of crimes. If this is true, what effect should it have on incarceration policy?
4. What are the main arguments in favor of imprisoning so many people? What are the main arguments against it? Do you think it is a good idea to have so many people locked up? Why or why not?

ACTIVITY

Prison Sentences

Write a brief essay, either supporting or opposing the following proposition: *America should continue to put more people convicted of crimes behind bars.*

Parole

The number of felons released on parole will continue to grow, because ever more convicts are being sent to prison and because crowded prisons are being forced to release some of those convicts early in order to meet budget limits and population caps. The condition of those ex-prisoners after return to civilian life will be, on average, terrible. Many of them will be homeless . . . . Most of them will have untreated physical illnesses, mental diseases, addiction disorders, or a combination of these. Two-thirds of them will be back behind bars within three years.
– Kleiman and Hawken, "Fixing the Parole System" in *Science and Technology* (2008)

The word **parole** comes from the French for "to speak," or "to give your word." Parole is a process of returning prisoners to society if they have displayed good behavior in prison and if they give their word to avoid further crime. Near the end of their prison terms, prisoners come before a parole board where their behavior and attitudes are examined. Those who are judged rehabilitated or ready for release are granted parole. The parolee is then supervised for a specified time after release to make sure the promise is kept. A parole officer sees to it that the conditions of parole are met and that the parolee makes a successful transition to life on the outside.

Some critics believe that the extensive use of parole is a mistake and too lenient on prisoners. They argue that hardened criminals come to think of tricking the parole board as a game. Others take the view that parole offers a stepping stone back into the real world, and the time of release should be tailored to the individual prisoner.

Today the trend is toward fixed sentences and a reduced role for the parole board. At least 16 states have abolished parole. But in other states, most prisoners are still eventually released on parole. Even in states with fixed sentences, prisoners can be released on parole by earning good-time credits against their sentences.

Nationwide, about two-thirds more people are on parole than are locked up in prison. Yet the public hears little about this part of the corrections system. When the public does hear something about parole, it is usually about one of its failures or mistakes.

Parole works best when combined with effective supervision. Today, however, the

number of people to be supervised is growing rapidly while the number of supervisors is staying the same or even shrinking. Although county or state officials may oversee probation, a state parole board runs parole in many states. Both systems in most states have suffered badly from limited budgets.

The Parole Process

The parole system is generally defined by state statutes, or in the case of federal prisoners, by federal law. Most states have independent parole boards. The boards function as hearing panels to determine whether prisoners eligible for parole deserve it. Parole board members are often political appointees who have professional staff members and case workers to advise them.

The case workers compile reports on prisoners eligible for parole. They gather information about an individual's behavior while in prison and what awaits the prisoner in the community. They find out about the prisoner's family, opportunities for employment, access to friends, availability of housing, and the general climate that awaits the parolee in the community. An offer of employment is often key to winning parole board approval. A prisoner's success is much more likely if a stable job is available.

If released on parole, offenders must meet regularly with a parole officer and show that they are living up to the conditions of their re-

lease. Most often, these conditions forbid the use of alcohol and controlled substances, possession of firearms, or association with other ex-convicts. Offenders must ask permission to change their residence, to travel from one area to another, to marry, or even to buy a car.

The parole officer has two, sometimes conflicting, roles. The first is as a social worker, trying to help the parolee make a successful transition from prison to the community. The second is as a corrections officer, watching for any criminal tendencies. If necessary, the parole officer may have the individual jailed pending an investigation of parole violations or new criminal acts.

Ideal caseloads are considered to be roughly 35 per officer, or as few as 20 for serious offenders. In some jurisdictions, however, budget problems have pushed case loads up as high as 250 parolees per case worker. That's less than 10 minutes per week per case, which is rarely adequate to check up on a parolee, let alone offer help or advice.

Notorious Cases

Notorious cases pose special problems. One problem is whether publicity denies some prisoners equal treatment. The case of **Sirhan Bishara Sirhan** illustrates this problem. In June 1968, Sirhan shot and killed U.S. Senator Robert F. Kennedy, who had just won the presidential primary in California. Convicted of murder, Sirhan was sent to the maximum-security Soledad prison in California. A tentative parole date was set for 1982, but a public debate erupted over whether Sirhan should ever be paroled. Many people thought that the killer of a presidential candidate should never walk free. Nearly 4,000 letters flooded the parole board, as well as a petition bearing over 8,000 signatures — all opposing parole.

Sirhan's attorney claimed that his client had a nearly spotless prison record, that his 13 years in prison were already twice as much time behind bars as most murderers served in California, and that there was no solid evidence that he was any longer a threat to anyone.

The Los Angeles District Attorney presented new evidence that Sirhan was a continuing danger. The D.A. said Sirhan had written two threatening letters in the early 1970s. One corrections department psychiatrist did not feel this was unusual considering the stress that Sirhan had been under. Others were not so sure. The D.A. also cited testimony from fellow prisoners that Sirhan had threatened to kill others. But questions were raised about the accuracy of this testimony.

In its reconsideration of the release date, the board finally denied Sirhan parole. In all subsequent hearings, it has denied him parole. Many people believe the board has based its decisions on the nature of the original crime and worries about Sirhan's continuing danger to others. Some people believe the parole board has yielded to public pressure and will never release Sirhan.

A second problem arises when notorious offenders do get released. Parolees normally must return to the counties they lived in before their conviction. But communities often object to the return of notorious criminals, particularly child molesters and murderers. **Lawrence Singleton** offers an extreme example. In the late 1970s, Singleton picked up a 15-year-old hitchhiker, brutally raped her, chopped off her forearms, and left her in the California desert to die. Somehow she lived. Convicted for the crime, Singleton was sentenced to 12 years in prison, the maximum then possible under California law. A model prisoner, he earned enough good time to be released in 1987 after only eight years. His crime had aroused so much attention that parole authorities did not know where to place him. They tried convincing other states to take him, but none would.

Characteristics of Adults on Parole

Gender
12%	Female
88%	Male

Race or Ethnicity
42%	White
39%	Black
18%	Hispanic
1%	Other

Type of Offense
27%	Violent
24%	Property
35%	Drug
15%	Other

Status of Supervision
82%	Active
7%	Inactive
6%	Absconded
4%	Supervised out of state
2%	Other

Adults Entering Parole
28%	Discretionary parole*
51%	Mandatory parole**
9%	Reinstatement
9%	Supervised release
3%	Other

Adults leaving parole
35%	Successful completion	
22%	Returned to incarceration	
	6%	With new sentence
	16%	Other
6%	Absconder	
1%	Other unsatisfactory exits	
1%	Transferred	
1%	Death	
1%	Other	

* Discretionary parole means a prisoner was put on parole by a parole board.

**Mandatory parole means a prisoner was released because of good-time credits or a sentencing statute.

Detail may not sum to total because of rounding.

Source: "Prisoners in 2010," Bureau of Justice Statistics (2011)

They even talked of housing him on prison grounds. Finally, amid much outcry and media coverage, they placed him in his original community in Northern California. But citizen protests proved so intense that Singleton could not remain. Encountering protests wherever he went, he moved from community to community in Northern California. When his parole ended, he moved to Florida. In 1997, he murdered a prostitute and was sentenced to death. He died of natural causes in prison in 2001.

FOR DISCUSSION

1. What problems do parole officers face?
2. Why do parole boards have less power in states with fixed sentencing laws?
3. Infamous convicts, such as Charles Manson and Mark David Chapman (the murderer of John Lennon), have been repeatedly denied parole. Do you think public opinion or pressure about such cases should influence parole board decisions? Why or why not?
4. Where should notorious offenders be placed if their community does not want them back? Explain your answer.

CLASS ACTIVITY

Parole Board

In this activity, students role play members of a parole board deciding whether to grant parole to convicts.

1. Form groups of three to five students. Each group will role play a parole board and should:
   a. Read each of the cases below.
   b. Decide whether to grant or deny parole in each case.
   c. Prepare to present its decisions and reasons for them to the class.
2. The groups should report on their decisions and reasons for them. Discuss what purpose further imprisonment would serve in each case. (Refer to the purpose of punishment discussed on pages 222–223.)
3. Conclude the activity by holding a class vote on whether to grant or deny parole in each case.

Case 1: Sirhan Bishara Sirhan. See details on this case in the article above.

Case 2: Leonard Smith. Smith is one of the oldest prisoners held in your state. Fifty years ago when he was 18, he took part in a bank robbery. He held a knife to a teller's throat. When she did something that displeased him, he slit her throat. Smith has been a model prisoner, has earned a college degree, and is deeply remorseful for his criminal act. He is serving an indeterminate sentence of one to 75 years.

Case 3: Helen Campbell. Five years ago Campbell was convicted of second-degree murder and sentenced to a fixed term of 15 years. Campbell murdered her husband in his sleep. Campbell testified (and witnesses supported her testimony) that her husband had beaten her for 10 years. Campbell has been a model prisoner. This is her first parole hearing.

Case 4: David Garcia. Garcia was convicted of burglary and sentenced to an indeterminate term of from two to 10 years. He has served seven years, twice as long as most for his crime. Prison officials consider him dangerous and potentially violent.

Staying Out of Prison

One of the most profound challenges facing American society is the reintegration of more than 600,000 adults — about 1,600 a day — who leave state and federal prisons and return home each year.

– Joan Petersilia, law professor, *When Prisoners Come Home* (2009)

Two convicts study in a prison library.

Many ex-convicts have difficulty staying out of trouble — and out of prison — once they are released. Ex-convicts have special needs that the parole program alone often cannot address. Several special programs, however, have been developed to help them. One such program, the 7th Step Foundation, uses ex-offenders as counselors to help juveniles, parolees, and those who are soon to be released.

Case Study of an Ex-Offender

The following case study is based on an interview with a 7th Step counselor.

"One of the inmates who had a life sentence without parole organized a group of the most dangerous criminals in the prison. I joined the group. We got together to help keep juvenile delinquents from turning to crime. Every Saturday these kids would be brought into the prison. We would talk to them and show them around. We showed them death row and the electric chair. It really shook them up. That program helped those kids, and it also helped me get turned around.

"When I left prison I felt totally helpless and frightened. I didn't know how to talk to a lady, how to take a lady out, or how to dress. Fitting into society is a real problem. You have a feeling you want to make up for lost time — and it's hard to sit still even for five minutes.

"As far as adjusting to society, I don't know how long it will take. For me, getting in my car and coming to work is a thrill. To go to the icebox and get a drink is a great feeling for me. I've only been out four months. That's a small amount of time compared to 21 years in an institution. The adjustment period is not over, and I don't have any more chances. Next time I'll be sent away for the rest of my life.

"I've been a thief all my life, and I've been a pretty good thief. For me, it is easy to be bad and it's a struggle to be good. I could go out and get money just like that. It's my profession — the only thing I am good at — so far.

"How do you tell someone you've been in prison for 21 years — how do you tell them? How do you tell them you've been arrested for murder? How do you tell them these things and then expect them to give you a job?"

CLASS ACTIVITY

Staying Out

Imagine that you are reporter doing a story on the struggles and challenges of prisoners just paroled and trying to stay out of prison. Make up a fictional parolee or parolees, and write a report on their experiences in the first few weeks after release. Include the following incidents and give an account about how the parolee dealt with them.

- Finding a place to live.
- Relating to family and loved ones.
- Searching for a job and going to a job interview.
- Running into an old friend from criminal days, one who the parolee is forbidden to associate with.
- The parolee's reflection on the maximum-security prison.

When everyone finishes, students (who want to) should read their stories aloud in class and discuss them.

CHAPTER 16
ALTERNATIVES TO PRISON

In the past two decades, states and the federal government have developed and implemented new correctional options in an attempt to reduce correctional crowding and costs, better manage higher-risk offenders in the community, reduce crime, and achieve greater fairness and effectiveness in criminal sanctions for adults.

– Gail A. Caputo, criminologist, *Intermediate Sanctions in Corrections* (2004)

THE NEED FOR ALTERNATIVES | FINES | PROBATION | REVOKING PROBATION
COMMUNITY SERVICE | COMMUNITY CORRECTIONS

The Need for Alternatives

[W]hat if the prisons could be turned inside out, with convicts released into society under constant electronic surveillance? Radical though it may seem, early experiments suggest that such a science-fiction scenario might cut crime, reduce costs, and even prove more just.

– Graeme Wood, "Prison Without Walls" in *The Atlantic* (2010)

Since the 1970s, the public has grown increasingly impatient with America's crime problem. This has led to an increased demand for strict punishment, tough sentencing, and long prison terms. More and more offenders are imprisoned each year. Prisons and jails have filled and suffer severe overcrowding. Because of the overcrowding, each year federal and state governments spend billions of dollars building and staffing prisons. During the 1990s, space for about 1 million new prisoners was built. Yet prisons and jails remain overcrowded, and more prisons are needed to hold prisoners.

Costs of housing prisoners have become so staggering that many legislators are looking at less costly, but effective, sentencing alternatives. Many corrections specialists insist that community-based correctional alternatives, which are far cheaper, can be more effective than prison sentences. These alternatives may be better at helping a criminal learn how to function effectively in society. Some common alternatives are fines, probation, community-service programs, and supervision in a halfway house.

Fines

Fines should be imposed on a wide range of criminal offenses, including lesser felonies. The goal is to reduce corrections populations, especially prison and jail populations. . . . Combining fines with suspended sentences or community service will minimize the drain on system resources.

– Edwin W. Zedlewski, "Alternatives to Custodial Supervision," NIJ (2010)

Imposed in about three-fourths of all cases, fines are the most common punishment inflicted on convicted offenders. They can be imposed along with other punishments, such as probation or prison, or as the sole punishment. If a fine is the only punishment, the offender can continue living at home without supervision, and the government will get some additional money. As such, fines offer clear cost savings over imprisonment.

But judges seldom impose fines as the sole punishment for serious offenders, because the offenders would remain in the community with no one keeping tabs on them. So usually only low-risk offenses, such as traffic infractions, many misdemeanors, and some non-violent felonies, are punished by fines alone.

Fines raise two problems. The first is purely a practical problem. Since most criminals are poor, does it make sense to punish them with fines? A fine might push an offender into committing new crimes simply to pay for the old one.

The second problem is one of fairness. If two criminals, one rich and the other poor, are fined $500 for the same offense, have they received equal punishment? A $500 fine could create hardship on the poor criminal, but mean little to the rich one.

Prison Spending

States spent about $39.5 billion on prisons in fiscal year 2003.
The average annual operating expenditure per inmate was $22,650.

Operating expenditures	$36.9 billion	94%
Salaries, wages, benefits	22.9	62
Other	14.0	38
Capital expenditures	$2.3 billion	6%
Construction	1.8	4.5
Equipment	0.4	1.0
Land	0.1	.5
Total	39.2 billion	100%

Detail may not add to total due to rounding.

Source: "Justice Expenditures and Employment in the U.S., 2003," Bureau of Justice Statistics (2006)

To balance the equation, some jurisdictions are experimenting with **day fines**, which are calculated on how much a person earns each day. The penalty for drunk driving, for example, might be 30 day fines. This would mean that a person earning $300 per day would pay 30 times $300, or $9,000. A person earning $40 per day would pay 30 times $20, or $1,200. But this method also raises questions of fairness: Why should two people who commit the same act be fined such different amounts?

The Supreme Court has made one important ruling on the fairness of fines. Judges commonly used to issue alternative sentences, such as 30 days in jail or $300 in fines. In the 1971 case of *Tate v. Short*, a unanimous Supreme Court ruled these alternative sentences unconstitutional. The court stated these sentences violated the equal protection clause of the 14th Amendment, because they forced the poor into jail while permitting the rich to pay their way out.

FOR DISCUSSION

1. In what circumstances do you think fines are appropriate punishment? When would they be inappropriate? Explain.
2. Do you think fines could substitute for imprisonment in some cases? Why or why not?
3. What are day fines? What problem do they address? Do you think they are a good idea? Why or why not?
4. Do you agree with the Supreme Court's decision in *Tate v. Short*? Why or why not?

CLASS ACTIVITY

One Fine Day

Some criminal justice experts recommend using day fines for most non-violent offenses. In this activity, students role play advisers to a governor considering instituting a comprehensive day-fine program.

1. Form small groups. Each is a group of advisers to the governor who is considering introducing legislation making day fines the only punishment for first and second offenses of non-violent crimes. Each group should:
   a. Make a list of the pros and cons of such a proposal.
   b. Decide whether or not to recommend the proposal.
   c. Prepare to report back its recommendation and the reasons for it.
2. The groups should report back, and the class should hold a discussion. Conclude the activity by taking a vote on whether or not the class favors the proposal.

Probation

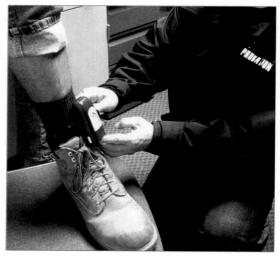

Ankle bracelets allow officials to keep track of the movements of probationers.

No one really knows what a probation officer does . . . . Sometimes you're a cop, sometimes a social worker. . . . There's a fine balance. I may have one offender who screwed up one time, and he's trying to get a new direction in his life, and fifteen minutes later I may be with a guy who's a career criminal.
– Chris Stanton quoted in "Sure Beats Work" in *The New Yorker* (2005)

Probation comes from the Latin word *to prove*. Offenders sentenced to probation are allowed to return to the community, but must regularly prove that they meet conditions set by the court. The court retains the authority to cancel probation and imprison the offender if the conditions are violated.

Probation was developed in the mid-1800s as a humanitarian measure to keep petty offenders away from the corrupting influence of prisons. By 1925, every state offered probation for juveniles, but it was 1956 before every state offered it for adults.

Today, many convicts, especially first-time offenders, are placed on probation. More than twice as many U.S. convicts are on probation than are serving sentences in prisons and jails.

Probation offers many benefits. Its costs are low, about $1,000 per year for each person on probation (**probationer**) versus $20,000–$60,000 per year for each prisoner. Probationers can stay employed, take care of their families, and pay taxes. Since probationers remain in the community, they do not have the re-entry problems that prison inmates have when their sentences end.

Like parole, probation only works well if it is combined with effective supervision. Offenders must report on a regular basis to a probation officer to make sure they meet all the conditions set by the court. Originally the probation officer was a judge or a citizen volunteer. Early in the 20th century, however, supervising probation became a career in itself.

Individuals interested in becoming probation officers often take college degrees in social work, with special classes in criminology and corrections. Some probation officers also take classes in psychology and therapy to help offenders with their emotional problems.

Recent probation theory emphasizes the need to establish strong links between the offender and the community. Family, school, business, and church connections help an offender feel part of a community. These ties make a return to criminal behavior much less likely. Unfortunately, many probation departments, like other government agencies, lack sufficient resources and personnel. As a result, many probation officers must handle high caseloads making adequate supervision difficult.

High-Tech House Arrest

In recent years as technology has progressed, more courts are using house arrest for criminals. Offenders are required to wear a tamper-resistant ankle bracelet to monitor their location, usually to make sure they remain at home when they are not at work.

In some systems, the device broadcasts continuously to a second unit on the telephone, and this unit tells the probation department immediately if the offender leaves home. In other systems, the offender is telephoned at random times and must verify being home with a tone from the device. In newer systems, the unit has GPS that tracks the offender at all times. If the offender strays from where he is supposed to be, a computer alerts the probation department. Some GPS units even include a cell phone to contact the offender.

Electronic house arrest costs vary. The older systems cost about $2 a day. The GPS system costs about $9 per day to monitor each device, compared to about $100 a day for jail time. In addition, the offender is usually required to pay some of the cost of electronic monitoring.

Because it is cheaper than jail time and relieves jail crowding, many jurisdictions are adopting electronic monitoring. The advantages for the prisoner are obvious — staying at home, avoiding the humiliations and dangers of jail, and sometimes even being able to continue in a job. This form of monitoring can also be combined with community service or other forms of community-based corrections. The devices can also be used to monitor those on parole and those awaiting trial.

Florida has used electronic monitoring for more than 25 years. In 2010, a study funded by the U.S. Justice Department compared Florida convicts on electronic monitoring with those on other forms of community supervision. The study found that those on electronic monitoring had a 31 percent lower failure rate. Although all types of offenders did well on electronic monitoring, it worked less well with violent offenders than with those convicted of sex, property, drug, and other crimes. Also, the GPS system had better results than the older systems.

Who Should Be Placed on Probation?

There is general agreement about the criteria that should be used in deciding whether an offender should be placed on probation. The following is a list of factors that might be used by a judge to help identify likely candidates for probation:

a. The defendant did not cause or threaten serious harm.
b. The defendant did not intend to cause or threaten serious harm.
c. The defendant acted under a strong provocation.

d. Some factors tend to excuse or justify the criminal conduct (e.g., the defendant was an accomplice and did not participate that much in the crime, the defendant mistakenly believed the conduct was legal).
e. The victim contributed in some way to the commission of the crime.
f. The defendant has agreed to compensate the victim.
g. The defendant has no recent history of prior delinquency or criminal activity.
h. The criminal conduct was the result of circumstances unlikely to occur again.
i. The defendant's character and attitudes show that he or she is unlikely to commit another crime.
j. The defendant is likely to benefit from probationary treatment.
k. The imprisonment of the defendant would cause excessive hardship to the defendant or his or her dependents.

FOR DISCUSSION

1. How are probation and parole alike? How are they different?
2. What are some advantages in granting probation to an offender? What are some possible disadvantages?
3. What are some qualities that it would be helpful for a probation officer to have?
4. Do you think high-tech house arrest should be used more commonly? Why or why not? If you agree that it should be used, for what crimes is it best suited?
5. Which of the factors for identifying likely candidates for probation do you think are most important? Least important? Why?

ASK AN EXPERT

Interview a probation officer in your community. To find one, consult the governmental listings in your phone book or contact your local court. Find out about your jurisdiction's probation procedures and administration. For example, you might ask:

• How are probation services organized in your jurisdiction?
• What is the average caseload of a probation officer?
• What percentage of offenders successfully complete their probation? How does this compare to other jurisdictions?
• What is the typical day of a probation officer like?
• What conditions are most important for successful probation?
• What are the biggest challenges to successful probation?

Who Gets Probation?

In this activity, students decide whether convicted offenders should be placed on probation.

1. Form small groups. Each group should:
   a. Review the list of factors for identifying likely candidates for probation.
   b. Assign two or three of the factors to each person.
   c. Discuss the cases below, one by one. For each case, have each person in the group say whether his or her assigned factors apply to that case. Then discuss whether the factors apply or not.
   d. For each case, decide whether the offender should be placed on probation and explain the reasons behind each decision.
2. Regroup as a class and groups should report their answers and the reasons for them. Students should compare their decisions with those from other groups.

Cases

a. **Art Lewis**, while setting off fireworks in a wilderness area, started a fire that burned down a U.S. Forest Service utility shed and destroyed a bulldozer. He has no prior criminal record.

b. **Barbara Keane** was convicted of pickpocketing. She has one prior conviction for prostitution. She has paid back the money she took and has become actively involved in church charitable work.

c. **Carol Doepel** was convicted of the attempted murder of a co-worker. Though she has no prior criminal record, she has been fired from three jobs for assaulting employees. She is currently undergoing therapy.

d. **David Perkins** was convicted of embezzling $20,000 from his employer. Twenty years ago, he served one year in prison for forgery. Since that time, he has raised a family and has been active in community-service work.

Revoking Probation

On any given day, a large number of the admissions to America's prisons come from individuals who have failed to comply with the conditions of their parole or probation supervision. For years, the revocation and incarceration rate of probationers and parolees has had a significant impact on the growth of the prison population.
– Gail Hughes, "The Violation Population" in *Corrections Today* (2007)

When an offender is convicted and placed on probation, the judge almost always sets a number of probation conditions. These conditions limit the offender's behavior, and they are often related to the offender's crime or criminal inclination. For example, a convicted forger might be forbidden to possess blank checks, but this condition would not apply to a convicted drunk driver. (See **Possible Probation Conditions**.)

A probation officer is an agent of the court who monitors the activities of **probationers** — offenders on probation. For probation to be effective, probation officers must carefully supervise offenders. Unfortunately, budget constraints often require probation officers to take on heavy caseloads. Officers usually require probationers to report regularly and they sometimes make surprise spot checks of probationers' condition, activities, and whereabouts.

If a probationer violates the terms set by the court, the probation officer has two choices. The officer may issue a warning, or if the violation is serious enough, the officer may order the probationer back to court for a probation revocation hearing.

At a revocation hearing, the judge decides whether to continue probation or revoke it. If probation is revoked, the probationer is usually fined or imprisoned. Sometimes, a judge will continue probation but add new, stricter conditions.

The Large Number of Probationers

Along with the huge increase in incarceration in recent decades, the number of probationers has also exploded. In 1980, about 1 million people were on parole in the United States. By 2009, that number had grown to 4.2 million probationers.

The large number of probationers has put a strain on the caseloads of probation officers. It has also made it difficult to deal with probation violations. An estimated 40 percent of probationers violate their conditions of probation. This poses a problem. All of them cannot be sent to prison for these violations. Our prison systems are already operating far above capacity. Yet probation violations should be taken seriously.

Hawaii's HOPE Probation

Hawaii's HOPE Probation is an innovative program for dealing with probation violators. (HOPE stands for Hawaii's Opportunity Probation and Enforcement.) It began in 2004 in the court of Hawaii state trial judge Steven Alm. His docket was full of probation revocation hearings. Probation officers were recommending probationers be sent to prison because of multiple probation violations. It was common practice for probation officers to issue warnings for violations before they finally grew frustrated and asked the court to intervene. Thus probationers missed appointments and even failed drug tests without any consequences. Only after multiple probation violations did officers ask the court to revoke probation and send the violator to prison.

Judge Alm recognized that sending a probationer to prison for a single violation may be too harsh (depending on the violation). But he also thought that ignoring violations sent the wrong message, leading probationers to believe they could do as they pleased.

The judge set a new policy (which came to be known as HOPE Probation). He told probationers and probation officers that the court would punish every probation violation. When a probationer missed an appointment or failed a drug test, the probationer would be arrested and stay in jail until appearing back in court (usually within a couple of days). The judge would not revoke the probation, but would send the probationer to jail for a few days as punishment. The idea was that people respond

POSSIBLE PROBATION CONDITIONS

This is a list of the kinds of probation conditions a criminal court judge might set depending on the crime.
1. Spend a short time in the county jail before probation begins.
2. Pay a specified fine, plus a penalty assessment.
3. Make restitution of a specified amount to the victim through the probation officer.
4. Do not drink alcoholic beverages and stay out of bars.
5. Do not use or possess narcotics or associated paraphernalia, and stay away from places where drug users congregate.
6. Do not associate with persons known by the defendant to be drug users or sellers.
7. Submit to periodic drug testing.
8. Possess no blank checks, write no checks, and have no checking account.
9. Do not gamble, engage in bookmaking, or possess gambling paraphernalia, and do not be present in places where gambling or bookmaking goes on.
10. Do not associate with certain named persons.
11. Cooperate with the probation officer in a defined plan of behavior.
12. Support dependents.
13. Seek and enroll in schooling or job training as approved by the probation officer.
14. Maintain a steady job.
15. Stay at a residence approved by the probation officer.
16. Perform a certain amount of community service each month.
17. Submit to a 10 p.m. curfew.
18. Surrender any driver's license to the court clerk to be returned to the Department of Motor Vehicles.
19. Do not drive a motor vehicle unless lawfully licensed and insured.
20. Do not own, use, or possess any dangerous weapon.
21. Submit to search at any time of day or night by any law-enforcement officer with or without a warrant.
22. Obey all laws, orders, rules, and regulations of the Probation Department and of the court.

to the threat of immediate punishment: The severity of the penalty is not as important as its swiftness and certainty.

The judge also set up frequent random drug tests. For the first two months of HOPE Probation, probationers are tested at least twice a week. If they pass the tests, the tests become less frequent as probation continues.

Judge Alm also decided that new probationers would not be put in drug treatment unless they requested it. The judge recognized that not every drug user was an addict. Drug treatment would be reserved for those who kept failing the drug tests. These probationers were put in residential treatment, which would have been too expensive if everyone had been required to go into treatment. Those sent to drug treatment understood that their probation would be revoked if they failed to complete the treatment.

Many worried that Judge Alm's court would be flooded with probation violators. But it did not happen. When probationers saw that they would be punished for violating probation, most of them stopped violating their conditions of probation.

With its success, HOPE Probation has expanded to all felony probationers in Hawaii. Research studies have shown that missed appointments and positive drug tests are down about 90 percent. Arrest rates for HOPE probationers are three times lower than for other probationers. And probation is revoked for 9 percent of HOPE probationers, compared to 30 percent of other probationers. Two other states have begun their own versions of the program, and others are considering adopting it.

FOR DISCUSSION

1. Which of the **Possible Probation Conditions** (on page 267) would you recommend for every probationer? Why?
2. What is a probation revocation hearing?
3. What problems do large numbers of probationers pose?
4. What are the elements of HOPE Probation?
5. When asked for the reason behind HOPE Probation's success, one criminologist said that when our children misbehave, we don't say, "You have a 50–50 chance nine months from now of being grounded." What do you think he meant? Do you agree with his point? Explain.

CLASS ACTIVITY

Probation Revocation Hearing

In this activity, members of the class role play a probation revocation hearing. At the conclusion of the role play, the class will decide whether probation should be revoked in the case presented.

1. If possible, invite a probation officer, criminal lawyer, or judge to help you conduct and debrief this activity. Ask the guest to compare the procedures in this activity with those followed in your jurisdiction.
2. Form groups of four. Each group should:
   a. Assign students the following roles: judge, probationer (named Lee Miller), probation officer, and public defender. Assign any remaining students as additional probation officers.
   b. Read and study the description of the roles and the probation report that follows the role descriptions. (As an option, students can prepare for their role by meeting with those in other groups who are playing the same role.)
   c. When ready, conduct the probation revocation hearing with members of the group, using the **Procedures for Revocation Hearing**, below.
3. When you are finished with the simulation, regroup as a class. Judges from each group should announce their decisions and the reasoning behind them. Ask any guests how these simulated decisions compare to actual decisions. Debrief the activity with the questions on page 269.

Procedures for Revocation Hearing

1. The judge opens the hearing and asks if all parties are present and ready.
2. The judge asks the public defender to present the probationer's case.
3. The public defender may cross-examine the probation officer.
4. The public defender may call Lee Miller to testify. If this happens, the judge may also ask questions.

(Continued on next page.)

5. The judge may ask the probation officer questions at any time.
6. The public defender should close by summarizing the arguments against revoking Lee Miller's probation.
7. The judge should then ask the probation officer to summarize the arguments in favor of revoking probation. If there is more than one probation officer, both should participate.
8. Finally, the judge decides whether to revoke Lee Miller's probation. Refer to the alternatives listed in the judge's role description in the next section.

Role Descriptions

Probationer Lee Miller. You feel that circumstances forced you to violate the conditions of your probation. Consequently, you feel your probation should not be revoked. Talk with the public defender who is representing you and discuss the strategy you should follow at your hearing. Decide with the public defender whether you should take the witness stand and testify on your own behalf, but remember that this will subject you to cross-examination by the judge. You have the right to remain silent if you wish.

Public Defender. You represent Lee Miller at the probation revocation hearing. Discuss with your client the strategy to follow in attempting to convince the judge not to revoke probation. Decide whether to call the probation officer to the witness stand in order to cross-examine the officer's recommendations about revoking probation. Also, decide whether your client should take the witness stand to testify. Your client has the right to remain silent, but if the client does testify, the judge may also ask questions.

Probation Officer. You are Lee Miller's probation officer. You have written the probation report that follows. This will be the focus of this hearing. If you are called to testify, you should defend your recommendation that Miller's probation be revoked and that the one-year suspended jail sentence be imposed.

Judge. You were the trial judge at Lee Miller's trial. After the conviction, you sentenced Miller to a one-year county jail term. Then you suspended the sentence and placed Miller on probation. Today, you must decide what to do in view of the probation violations. Your alternatives are as follows:
1. Continue the probation under the existing conditions.
2. Continue probation with additional conditions that you will impose.
3. Revoke probation and impose the one-year sentence.

Debriefing Questions

1. Did some judges decide differently from others? If so, how do you account for these differences?
2. Assume that there was a great deal of publicity surrounding Lee Miller's original trial and that many people in the community were angry because Miller was placed on probation rather than being sent to jail. Do you think the judge's decision should be affected by community feelings of this sort? Why or why not?
3. How is the probation revocation hearing different from a trial? How is it similar?
4. In your opinion, is the probation revocation hearing a fair way to decide whether a probation should be revoked? Why or why not?

PROBATION REPORT

Name of Probationer: **Lee Miller**   **Age:** **38**   **Marital Status:** **Divorced**

Occupation: **Assembly line worker**   **Employer:** **United Radio Company**

Current Conviction

1. Probationer Lee Miller was convicted two months ago of driving under the influence of alcohol.
2. Sentence: One year in county jail (suspended), $1,000 fine, placed on two-year formal probation.
3. Conditions of probation:
   a. Probationer must pay the fine within six months.
   b. Probationer must not drink any alcoholic beverages and must stay out of places where they are the chief items of sale.
   c. Probationer must cooperate with the probation officer in a plan for commuting without the use of a motor vehicle.
   d. Probationer must maintain employment with United Radio Company.
   e. Probationer must maintain residence at current address, as directed by the probation officer.
   f. Probationer must surrender driver's license to the clerk of the court to be returned to the Department of Motor Vehicles.
   g. Probationer must obey all laws, orders, rules, and regulations of the probation department and of the court.
   h. **Special condition:** Probationer is not to drive any motor vehicle during the period of probation.

Probation Violation Report

1. Two weeks ago at 7:55 a.m., probationer Miller was stopped for speeding and driving erratically by a highway patrol officer. The officer administered several field tests for drunk driving and concluded that probationer Miller may have been driving under the influence of alcohol. Probationer Miller was arrested and taken to a local highway patrol station where a chemical test for alcohol consumption was administered. The result of this test showed no indication of alcohol. Probationer Miller was cited for speeding and driving without a license, then released. Probationer reported the violation and admitted that he had a couple of beers the night before with a friend.
2. Probation Violations:
   a. Probationer Miller drank an alcoholic beverage.
   b. Probationer Miller drove an automobile without a license, and violated the speed law.
   c. **Special condition:** Probationer Miller drove a motor vehicle during the period of probation.

Statement of Probationer

I admit that I drove an automobile and was speeding in violation of my probation. But I reported these violations myself to my probation officer within 24 hours of the incident.

I admit that I had a couple of beers the night before, but only in my own apartment. A friend had come over to spend the evening and brought some beer. But I was asleep by midnight.

I overslept the next morning and had to get to work in half an hour. I have been taking the bus to work, but this takes an hour. I decided to ask a neighbor if I could borrow his car so that I could get to work on time. He said it was OK to take the car.

I already had been late to work two times this month. So I was speeding and moving in and out of lanes to get to work on time. I was afraid that if I lost my job I would not be able to make support payments for my daughter and pay off my fine to the court. Both are conditions of my probation.

As it turned out, I was half a day late for work, but my boss listened to my story and decided to give me one more chance. I believe that I have learned my lesson from this, and I promise to strictly follow my conditions of probation in the future.

Recommendations of Probation Officer

Probationer Miller seems to mean well but also appears weak-willed. I recommend that the probation be revoked and the suspended one-year county jail sentence be imposed.

Community Service

Community Service Orders are uncontroversially recognized as punishments. We can, however, best understand their meaning and point by seeing them as public forms of . . . reparation . . . . This meaning is most obvious when . . . the work that the offender is required to undertake has some obvious relation to the nature of her offense — as when a vandal's Order requires her to work at repairing the effects, if not of her own vandalism, then of others' vandalism, or in other ways improving the local environment.
— R.A. Duff, *Punishment, Communication, and Community* (2001)

Community service is a common sentence for those who commit non-violent misdemeanors.

Probation is only one possible alternative to imprisonment. Another increasingly common alternative is community service. Community service can benefit both the offender and society as a whole, as demonstrated by the following examples.

Chris Lester, 18, was convicted of destruction of public property after he vandalized his school. Because this was his first offense, the judge did not think that a jail sentence was necessary. Instead, the judge fined him $1,000 and required him to clean graffiti off the walls of public buildings.

Albert and Miriam Johnson, a husband and wife, were convicted of criminal child neglect. Because of their religious beliefs, the couple kept their son away from medical care when he was ill. As a result, the boy nearly died. The judge sentenced the couple to do volunteer work at a nearby state hospital.

The community-service approach to sentencing is generally limited to people who have committed non-violent crimes. These can include traffic offenses, public drunkenness, drug abuse, and white-collar offenses. Often, the assigned work, such as cleaning up graffiti, is directly related to the kind of crime committed.

The Los Angeles County System

Los Angeles County has developed a broad system for referring offenders convicted of misdemeanors to community-service agencies. This system, called the **Court Referral Community Service Program**, involves the cooperation of three groups:

1. **Superior Court judges** who agree to refer some misdemeanor offenders to community service instead of imprisonment or other punishment.

2. **Community agencies** that need volunteer help. These agencies include hospitals, the YMCA and YWCA, the Red Cross, suicide and rape-crisis centers, teenage hot lines, alcohol and drug-abuse clinics, and many other community-based agencies that depend heavily on volunteers.

3. **Volunteer Centers (VCs)**. A countywide system of these centers was in existence before the court referral program. The VCs act as clearinghouses for anyone wishing to do volunteer work. They regularly contact community agencies to create lists of volunteer positions that need to be filled. The courts asked the VCs to begin placing referrals from the court system alongside their regular volunteers. The VCs help find useful jobs in many community agencies for non-violent offenders.

The Case of Cory Baker

Cory Baker, age 40, was speeding in a school zone. He struck a car and injured a child. Just before the accident, Cory had lost his job as a carpenter on a construction project. In Superior Court, Cory was convicted of speeding and reckless driving.

Instead of sentencing Cory to jail, or requiring him to pay a large fine, the judge instructed him to do 40 hours of work for a community-service agency. The court referred Cory to a nearby Volunteer Center for placement with a community agency.

Within a week, Cory had made an appointment for an interview at a local VC office. He was asked about his skills and interests, and about his willingness to do volunteer work. Cory said that he was happy to become a court-referral volunteer.

The VC interviewer showed Cory a list of volunteer jobs near his home. Cory noticed that several agencies needed skilled workers, including carpenters. He chose the George Henry Home for Boys, a private group home for delinquent boys.

Next, Cory scheduled an interview with the George Henry Home. The director of the home was satisfied with Cory and promptly put him to work.

Cory worked at the George Henry Home for about five hours a week for two months. During this time, he got to know many of the boys, and he showed some of them how to do basic carpentry. Cory's work impressed the director and staff at the home. After he had put in his 40 hours of referral volunteer work, Cory was asked to continue at the home as a paid worker. Cory accepted and was hired to set up a carpentry shop for the boys.

Does It Work?

Not all court-referral volunteers are as fortunate as Cory Baker. Nevertheless, most do have a positive experience. As one Los Angeles judge noted:

Community service . . . can work wonders. That's the beauty of it. Oftentimes, personal stress is the reason the people are here in the first place. If the man gets involved in helping others, he is helping himself as well.

Some critics of community-service sentences say that it is too soft. They call for stronger punishments such as prison terms. In response to such criticism, a federal judge said, "We have to examine the overall public interest. 'Warehousing' criminals in prison has not been successful. It just spawns more criminals."

FOR DISCUSSION
1. Do you approve or disapprove of community-service sentencing? Why or why not?
2. Should community-service sentencing be available to convicted adult felons? To juvenile criminal offenders? Why or why not?
3. What might be some problems in expanding community-service sentencing to those convicted of violent crimes?

Community Corrections

Community-based corrections is the most promising means of accomplishing the changes in offender behavior that the public expects — and now demands — of corrections.
– National Advisory Commission on Criminal Justice Standards and Goals (1973)

Community-service referrals provide one alternative to prison that can help offenders develop roots in their communities rather than pushing them away or locking them out. There are several other programs such as halfway houses and treatment centers that can offer similar benefits. These are often called **community correctional programs**, and they can help offenders such as the following:

Rudy was lonely, bored, and 19. At a friend's urging, he helped steal a late-model Mercedes-Benz from a shopping-mall parking lot. Caught only a few blocks away, he is now awaiting sentencing for grand theft auto.

Anna has completed more than two years of a three-year sentence in prison for passing bad checks. This was her second offense. She wants to get out, but she is a little frightened. She wonders what might happen if she can't make it. Without support, will she be tempted to pass bad checks again? She worries whenever she thinks about going out on her own.

Both Rudy and Anna might benefit from a community correctional program. Rudy is not a hardened criminal, and he may only need help learning how to funnel his energies into positive activities. Anna, too, wants to make a go of her life. To make the transition out of prison, she needs to live in a structured environment for a time to give her direction and support.

What is a Community Correctional Program?

Community correctional programs are based in local facilities such as halfway houses, community treatment centers, residential care facilities, and group homes. Local centers offer individualized care and supervision for those who would benefit from such a program. This approach can involve the community more directly in dealing with problems of crime.

Most prisons are run by state and federal agencies. And most jails, though they are locally run, are largely intended to hold people who are awaiting trial or have been given fairly

Halfway houses can help prisoners transition back into society.

short jail terms for misdemeanors. They offer few opportunities for counseling, rehabilitation, or job training. Advocates of community corrections argue that most of our criminal justice system is already locally based — the police, courts, prosecutors, and public defenders — so there should be local responsibility and control in the correctional system as well.

The community-corrections approach began in the early 1970s. Since then, some states have tried to divert a large percentage of state and county prisoners into correctional programs located closer to their home communities. Community facilities can provide a supervised environment for troubled juveniles, non-violent offenders, and some prison inmates who are ready to start taking steps back into society.

Pre-Release Programs

Some of the first programs developed by the community-corrections movement were halfway houses. These serve as way stations in helping prison inmates back into society. The Federal Bureau of Prisons and most state correctional systems offer pre-release programs. They are mainly for prisoners, like Anna (from

our example above), in the last few months of their term who are judged a low risk of returning to crime.

Some pre-release programs operate businesses, providing both income and work experience for the residents. Others simply provide a home and supervision, and the residents are allowed out during work hours to go to jobs in the outside community. As residents demonstrate more responsibility, they are granted more privileges and independence. Gradually, offenders assume complete responsibility for their everyday activities and are ready to reenter the community.

Beyond Pre-Release Programs

In 1974, Minnesota put into practice a Community Corrections Act. This act extended the state's community corrections beyond pre-release halfway houses. Minnesota's goal was to divert all but the most serious offenders into programs in their home communities. The state set up an extensive community system that accepts many of its offenders into programs *immediately* after sentencing. Those offenders never see the inside of a prison.

Community correctional facilities can provide education, drug treatment, counseling, job training, and other help for offenders to improve their lives.

Goals of Community-based Corrections

The overriding goal of any community corrections program is to guide ex-offenders back into the community and help them develop positive, law-abiding lifestyles. This process works best under the supervision of professional counselors who can offer support and guidance.

Many offenders may need family, child, and marriage counseling. Others need legal counseling. Ex-alcohol and drug abusers often face severe temptation and require counseling and supervision. Offenders who want to go back to school can discuss their plans with educational counselors. Some may choose job training. Others simply need a therapist or support group to discuss their problems.

Group support can be important. Many offenders identify best with people who have similar backgrounds and with people who have themselves overcome criminal attitudes and behavior.

The community facilities often look a lot like ordinary neighborhood homes and apartment buildings. They blend in rather than stand out. Residents have their own bedrooms. Some have roommates. They share cooking and cleaning responsibilities, much like a large family. Residents are encouraged to develop a closeness that offers emotional support, companionship, and shared responsibility.

Obstacles to Community Corrections

Community-based correctional programs face obstacles such as funding, habitual and violent criminals, and community attitudes. Many of these obstacles are deep-rooted in the community itself and prevent state, county, and federal correctional administrators from transferring all eligible prisoners into community programs.

Funding

Our nation's corrections systems currently cost about $74 billion a year to operate, involving tens of thousands of administrators and correctional officers. To divert a large percentage of the nation's prisoners into community correctional programs would require a tremendous restructuring and rechanneling of funds. This

ASK AN EXPERT

Many communities have ex-convict self-help groups. If there is such a group in your community, ask if it would provide speakers to your class. Questions to ask the visitor might include:

- What are conditions like in prison? What was the hardest part of prison life?
- Did your experiences help you adjust to life after you were released? If so, how? If not, why not?
- What was the hardest aspect about your adjustment to freedom once you were released from prison?
- Do you know about pre-release or halfway house programs? Did you participate in one? If so, what were your experiences?
- Do you think that a community corrections program is helpful to the offender or community? Why or why not?
- How do you feel society should deal with the criminal offender?

would require a fundamental and wrenching re-form of a correctional system that is over 100 years old. Many people in the correctional system would resist such sweeping changes.

Habitual and Violent Criminals

Certain types of criminals pose further problems. Halfway houses require cooperation and social behavior. Habitual lawbreakers often cannot meet that standard. They have always lived in a criminal culture, and they commonly reject opportunities to explore and develop new community contacts.

In addition, many fear that offenders with records of violent behavior will not change. Violent offenders might harm innocent community members while staying in a halfway house. Some programs simply refuse to admit criminals with histories of violence.

Community Attitudes

When an old home or apartment building is converted into a halfway house, nearby residents often fear a wave of crime will sweep their neighborhood or that property values will decline. Residents predict that homes will be burglarized, women raped, automobiles stolen, and eventually, property values lowered — all because convicts live in the neighborhood and come and go as they please. Fear drastically multiplies if a halfway house resident does in fact commit a crime in the neighborhood. These fears are often reinforced by feelings that halfway houses are soft on criminals and don't punish their residents enough.

These are serious problems. To work properly, community-based corrections need to win the support of the community. And the facilities need to be highly structured, supportive environments with frequent counseling and training and effective supervision. For all their good intentions, community facilities must not endanger their neighborhoods.

FOR DISCUSSION

1. What are some of the advantages of community-based corrections programs? What are some disadvantages?
2. What types of offenders do you think community-based corrections are appropriate for? Inappropriate for? Why?

CLASS ACTIVITY

Halfway House

If a halfway house were proposed for your neighborhood, would you support it? Would your neighbors? In this activity, students role play a city council hearing determining whether to grant a zoning variance that would allow a halfway house to be placed in a particular residential neighborhood.

Imagine that a non-profit group has opened a halfway house that treats drug offenders referred to it by the courts. Neighbors learning of the halfway house objected to its presence and went to a lawyer. The lawyer learned that zoning regulations for the neighborhood allow only five unrelated persons in a single dwelling. The purpose of these regulations is to preserve parts of the city for family homes. The non-profit has requested that the city council grant a zoning variance (an exception to the regulation).

1. Form three groups: city council (seven members), residents opposing the halfway house (half of the remaining students) and people from the non-profit and other parts of the community who favor the halfway house (the other half of the students).
2. The three groups should meet separately. Those favoring and opposing the variance should develop arguments supporting their position. They should each pick three people to speak at the city council hearing. The city council should develop questions to ask the opposing sides. It should also select a person to chair the hearing and one member to represent the neighborhood (the other six members represent other parts of the city).
3. When the hearing begins, the chairperson should state the issue to be decided and call alternately one person in favor and one person opposed to the variance. After all six people have spoken and been questioned by the council, the council should vote.
4. Debrief the activity by discussing how realistic were the fears expressed by the residents in the role play.

CHAPTER 17

CAPITAL PUNISHMENT

For after all, death cases are indeed different in kind from all other litigation. The penalty, once imposed, is irrevocable.

– U.S. Supreme Court Justice John Paul Stevens, concurring in *Coleman v. Balkom* (1981)

A SHORT HISTORY OF THE DEATH PENALTY IN AMERICA | PUBLIC OPINION ON THE DEATH PENALTY
RECENT LEGAL HISTORY OF THE DEATH PENALTY | THE EXECUTION OF KARLA FAYE TUCKER
ARE WE EXECUTING INNOCENT PEOPLE? | DOES THE DEATH PENALTY DETER MURDERS?

A Short History of the Death Penalty in America

CARSON CITY, Nev., Feb. 8 (Associated Press) — Lethal gas as a form of capital punishment was used for the first time here today when Gee Jon, . . . convicted of killing a rival tong man, was put to death.

– News article (1924)

"Capital punishment" is another expression for the "death penalty," the legal execution of a criminal. The word *capital* comes from the Latin word for head. In ancient times, capital punishment was often carried out by beheading. This method has never been used in America. But criminals have been put to death by shooting, hanging, electrocution, poison gas, and lethal injection. Today, all states with the death penalty use lethal injection. Some states, however, allow one of these other methods as an option.

Once a person is sentenced to death in America, most states follow a similar procedure. The sentenced criminal is normally held in a maximum-security prison's special section known as death row. Usually, prisoners on death row have little contact with other prisoners. Each occupies a small cell alone, and each takes meals and exercises alone. This life may continue for years during appeals of the sentence. An appeal hearing for a death sentence is automatic in every state except Arkansas.

In the American colonies, legal executions took place as early as 1630. As in England, the death penalty was imposed for many crimes, even minor ones such as picking pockets or stealing a loaf of bread. During the 1800s in England, for example, 270 crimes were capital offenses, or crimes punishable by death. Thousands of people sometimes attended public hangings. Gradually,

however, England and America reduced the number of capital offenses, until the main focus was on first-degree murder — murders showing deliberation, willfulness, and premeditation. They also moved executions within the walls of prisons to eliminate the spectacle of public executions.

In the 1800s, many people in America and Europe began to oppose the death penalty. Michigan abolished it in 1845 and Wisconsin entered the Union in 1848 without a death penalty in its statutes. The movement against the death penalty grew stronger after World War II, especially in Europe, where many were weary of so much killing during the war. One by one all the Western European nations and Canada did away with capital punishment, until the United States was the last Western democracy that still executed criminals.

Seventeen American states, mainly clustered in the Midwest and Northeast, have banned executions. New York, which had banned the death penalty 30 years before, reinstated it in 1995. But the New York Court of Appeals struck down the law in 2004, and the state legislature has refused to pass a new death-penalty law. New Jersey (2007), New Mexico (2009), Illinois (2011), and Connecticut (2012) recently joined the ranks of states without capital punishment. And in 2011, the governor of Oregon announced a moratorium on the death penalty in that state while he remained in office.

FOR DISCUSSION

1. Why do you think prisons separate those sentenced to death from other prisoners?
2. Which, if any, of the methods of execution seems most humane? Why?
3. Do you think it matters that the United States is the only Western democracy that executes criminals? Explain.

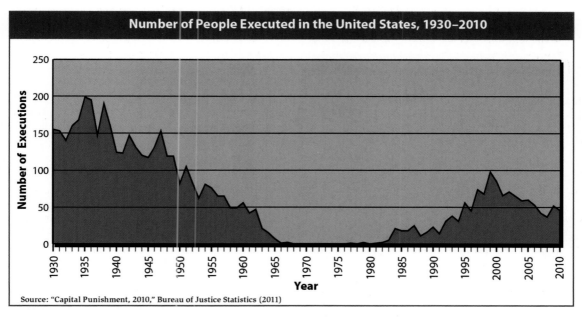

Number of People Executed in the United States, 1930–2010

Source: "Capital Punishment, 2010," Bureau of Justice Statistics (2011)

Public Opinion on the Death Penalty

Ambivalence about the death penalty is an American tradition. When the Republic was founded, all the states, following English law, imposed capital punishment. But the humanistic impulses that favored democracy led to questions about whether the state should have the right to kill the citizens upon whose consent government was erected.

– Scott Turow, attorney and author, "To Kill or Not to Kill" in *The New Yorker* (2003)

Public opinion on the death penalty has shifted over time. In the 1930s, opinion polls showed strong support for capital punishment. From that time, support gradually declined. By the mid-1960s, it had fallen to less than 50 percent. But then support started to rise again. By the 1990s, following decades of widespread anxiety over crime and violence, some states such as California were showing almost 80 percent of the population in favor of executing criminals. Other polls showed that 62 percent of the population felt that the death penalty deterred crime, and 51 percent said they would support it even if it did not deter crime. But polls also show that the strength of this support depends on how you ask the question. Note the differences between the two questions asked by Gallup polls on pages 277–278.

In 1991, researcher Robert M. Bohm did an analysis of 21 different polls on the death penalty. He found that certain factors — people's religion, age, occupation, or size of the city they lived in — showed little relation to their attitude on capital punishment. But other factors did. Men were more likely to favor it than women. Whites supported it more than

WHAT DO YOU THINK SHOULD BE THE PENALTY FOR MURDER:
THE DEATH PENALTY OR LIFE IMPRISOMENT WITH ABSOLUTELY NO POSSIBILITY OF PAROLE?

	Death Penalty %	Life Imprisonment %	No Opinion %
2010	49	46	6
2007	47	48	5
2004	50	46	6
2003	53	44	3
2002	52	43	5
2001	52	42	4
2000	52	37	11
1999	56	38	6
1997	61	29	10
1994	50	32	18
1993	59	29	12
1992	50	37	13
1991	53	35	11
1986	55	35	10
1985	56	34	10

Source: Gallup Poll

ARE YOU IN FAVOR OF THE DEATH PENALTY FOR A PERSON CONVICTED OF MURDER?

	For	Against	No Opinion
	%	%	%
2011	61	35	4
2010	64	29	6
2009	65	31	5
2008	64	30	5
2007	69	27	4
2006	65	28	7
2005	64	30	6
2004	71	26	3
2003	70	28	2
2002	72	25	3
2001	65	27	8
2000	66	26	8
1999	71	22	7
1995	77	13	10
1994	80	16	4
1991	76	18	6
1988	79	16	5
1986	70	22	8
1985	72	20	8
1981	66	25	9
1978	62	27	11
1976	66	26	8
1972	57	32	11
1971	49	40	11
1969	51	40	9
1967	54	38	8
1966	42	47	11
1965	45	43	12
1960	53	36	11
1957	47	34	18
1956	53	34	13
1953	68	25	7
1937	60	33	7

Source: Gallup Poll

blacks. Republicans endorsed it more than Democrats. The wealthy approved it more than the poor. Most surprisingly, people from the South were more likely to oppose the death penalty than people from other regions.

Over the years, the Gallup Poll has tracked the public's attitude toward capital punishment. On pages 277 and 278 are two polls asking questions often cited in debates over the death penalty.

FOR DISCUSSION
1. What do you think accounts for the shift in public opinion favoring the death penalty?
2. What do you think accounts for the different responses to the two questions? Which question do you think is better? Why?

ACTIVITY

Death Penalty Poll

In this activity, students conduct a poll on the death penalty.
1. Decide who you are going to poll. It can be the community, the school, or just one grade level.
2. Decide on how to get a random sample of the group you are polling. Determine how large a sample you will take.
3. Divide the class in two. One group should ask the first question; the other group, the second question.
4. Tabulate the results.

Debriefing Questions
1. How do your results compare with the official poll results?
2. How do you account for the similarities or differences?

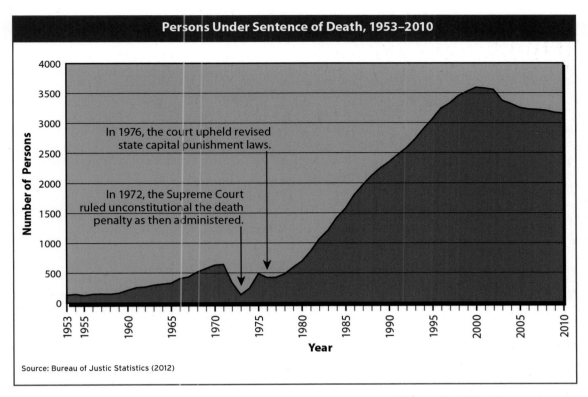

Persons Under Sentence of Death, 1953–2010

In 1976, the court upheld revised state capital punishment laws.

In 1972, the Supreme Court ruled unconstitutional the death penalty as then administered.

Number of Persons

Year

Source: Bureau of Justic Statistics (2012)

Recent Legal History of the Death Penalty

These death sentences are cruel and unusual in the same way that being struck by lightning is cruel and unusual.
– U.S. Supreme Court Justice Potter Stewart concurring in *Furman v. Georgia* (1972)

The 1950s and 1960s saw public protests over capital punishment, and the number of executions in America gradually declined. In 1967, there were only two, and the following year saw the beginning of an unofficial moratorium on executions. States waited to see how the Supreme Court would rule on the constitutionality of capital punishment. No executions took place in the United States from 1968 through 1976.

In the 1972 case of *Furman v. Georgia*, the Supreme Court declared capital punishment unconstitutional as it was then applied. The court said the death penalty was a violation of the Eighth Amendment prohibition against cruel and unusual punishment because of the inconsistency in who was given a death sentence and who was not. The court suggested that new laws might be acceptable, if they provided clear standards for imposing death sentences.

Between 1972 and 1976, 35 states wrote new capital punishment laws to try to meet the Supreme Court's suggestions. These new laws fell into two broad groups. One group, represented by laws in Georgia, Texas, and Florida, clearly described which capital crimes could be punished by death. These laws also set up a weighing system for deciding when the death penalty should be applied. In a separate penalty trial after a conviction for first-degree murder, a jury would consider **mitigating** circumstances, which tended to excuse the crime or the criminal's behavior, and **aggravating** circumstances, which made the crime seem worse. The court could only sentence someone to death if the aggravating circumstances outweighed any mitigating circumstances.

A second group of laws, represented by statutes from North Carolina and Louisiana, sought to overcome the Supreme Court's objections in another way. These laws simply made the death penalty mandatory for anyone convicted of a capital crime.

In 1976, the Supreme Court in *Gregg v. Georgia* ruled that the first type of law, based on the act of balancing mitigating and aggravating circumstances, was constitutional. This upheld the Georgia, Texas, and Florida death penalties. The court, however, struck down the second type. It declared unconstitutional North Carolina's and Louisiana's mandatory death sentences. The court said a mandatory sentence was unduly harsh and rigid and made no allowance for the particular circumstances of each case.

Executions began again in 1977, though many states still waited for a ruling on one further major issue: whether the death penalty was being applied equally. From 1977 through 1985, only 50 executions took place, though almost 2,000 prisoners waited on death rows.

The test case came with the Georgia case of *McCleskey v. Kemp* (1987). In it, lawyers for the condemned man submitted a careful study of how the death penalty had been applied in Georgia during the 1970s.

The study, by University of Iowa Professor David Baldus, showed that blacks who had killed whites had been sentenced to die seven times more often than whites who had killed blacks. Even after accounting for other variables, such as the viciousness of the crime, blacks had been sentenced to die more than four times as often as whites.

In its decision, the U.S. Supreme Court acknowledged that there seemed to be some *statistical* racial discrimination in Georgia's application of the death penalty. But the justices ruled by a 5–4 vote that a mere statistical variation was not enough to invalidate the death penalty. To do that, the defendant would have to show that the state had somehow encouraged the result or that there was actual discrimination in a particular case. Since the defendant had offered no such proof, which would be difficult to acquire, the court upheld the death penalty.

In the decade after *McCleskey*, the court tended to support the prosecution and made appealing a death sentence more difficult. The justices ruled that:

- Death-row inmates have no right to free legal assistance after an initial round of appeals. *Murray v. Giarratano* (1989)
- Inmates may lose their right to appeal if they make procedural errors. *Coleman v. Thompson* (1991)
- Inmates can't take advantage of any rule changes or precedents set *after* they have exhausted their appeals. *Teague v. Lane* (1989), *Butler v. McKellar* (1990), and *Saffle v. Parks* (1990)
- The prosecution may introduce victim-impact statements in penalty hearings. These statements may detail the pain and suffering of the victim. This decision overturned several earlier rulings banning such statements because they tend to inflame juries against convicted murderers. *Payne v. Tennessee* (1991)
- Death-row inmates cannot get a federal hearing on new-found evidence showing innocence unless that evidence overwhelmingly proves their innocence. *Herrera v. Collins* (1993)

In 1996, Congress passed the Anti-Terrorism and Effective Death Penalty Act. Part of this act limited state prisoners' habeas corpus appeals in federal court. The writ of habeas corpus is guaranteed by the U.S. Constitution. The writ is an order to bring a prisoner before a court to determine if the prisoner is legally held. Many death-penalty appeals are petitions of habeas corpus. Supporters of the act say many prisoners are simply buying time by filing frivolous habeas corpus petitions. Opponents of the law argued that capital cases should be carefully reviewed and that the act prevents this. In *Felker v. Turpin* in 1996, the Supreme Court upheld this part of the act.

But beginning in 2000, the Supreme Court decided a series of cases that upheld prisoners' rights to appeal and limited the death penalty. In 2000, it overturned two federal court decisions that had rejected state habeas corpus appeals because of the 1996 act. The Supreme Court said that the 1996 act only banned unreasonable appeals. When "clearly established" constitutional rights have been violated, the federal courts may intervene. The two Virginia cases involved defendants with the same last name, but the defendants were not related.

In *Terry Williams v. Taylor*, the court ruled 6–3 that the defendant had been deprived of his right to effective counsel. The defense attorney failed to mention at the sentencing hearing that the defendant was borderline mentally retarded, he had been fed whiskey as a child, and his parents had been jailed for child abuse and neglect.

In *Michael Wayne Williams v. Taylor*, a unanimous court ruled that the defendant did not receive a fair trial. The jury forewoman failed to disclose that she was the ex-wife of the sheriff and a former client of the prosecutor.

In 1989, the Supreme Court had ruled that mentally retarded criminals could be executed

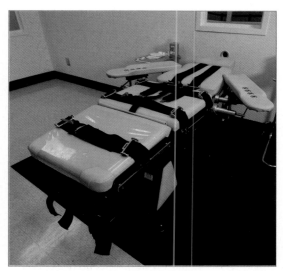
Today every state with the death penalty uses lethal injection.

(*Penry v. Lynaugh*). In 2002, the court overruled this opinion in the case of *Atkins v. Virginia*. In a 6–3 decision, the court declared that it was cruel and unusual punishment to execute the mentally retarded. The court noted that since its decision in *Penry*, the number of states outlawing such executions had grown from two to 18 and that in other states the practice is rare. The court majority found that a consensus had grown in the United States against executing mentally retarded persons.

In 2005 in *Roper v. Simmons*, the Supreme Court overruled a previous decision on executing murderers who were under 18 when committing the crime. The court declared such executions violated the Eighth Amendment. The 5–4 court majority pointed out that only two nations in the world allowed such executions — the United States and Somalia. It also noted that although 19 states permitted these executions, only three states had carried them out in the last decade.

In 2006 in *House v. Bell*, the Supreme Court held that federal courts could hear a habeas corpus appeal when "in light of new evidence, 'it is more likely than not that no reasonable juror would have found [the defendant] guilty beyond a reasonable doubt.' " In his 1985 trial, Paul House had been found guilty of murdering a woman. The prosecution had argued that House had attempted to rape the woman, and the prosecution had showed that semen consistent with House's was on the victim's clothing. DNA testing later showed that the semen

belonged to the woman's husband. Other witnesses later came forward saying that the husband had admitted to the crime. The Supreme Court ruled that this new evidence was sufficient to have the case reopened.

The Supreme Court has also struck down the death penalty for crimes against individuals that do not result in death. In 1977, the court ruled unconstitutional a law that imposed the death penalty for the crime of raping an adult woman (*Coker v. Georgia*). In 2008 in *Kennedy v. Louisiana*, the court struck down the death penalty for the crime of raping a child. The court has left open the question of whether capital punishment can be applied to crimes *against the state* that do not result in death — treason, espionage, and drug kingpin activity (all of which are capital offenses under federal law).

In recent years, about 50 prisoners have been executed each year. More than 3,000 inmates wait on death rows in prisons across America. Much of this backlog is caused by appeals. Even though some rulings have made it harder to appeal, it still takes an average of 14 years from a sentence of death to execution.

Death-penalty cases cost states much more than non-capital murder cases. The trials are longer, the appeals are lengthier, and it costs more to provide prisoners special housing on death row. The California Commission on the Fair Administration of Justice concluded that California spends $137.7 million every year maintaining the death penalty. It estimated it would cost California only $11.5 million per year if California eliminated capital punishment and imposed sentences of life without the possibility of parole. Two states, New Jersey and New Mexico, that recently did away with the death penalty cited its enormous cost.

As for the appeals themselves, two studies by a Columbia Law School professor, published in 2000 and 2002, found that most death-row appeals succeed. Surveying the almost 5,000 capital cases appealed in state and federal courts between 1973 and 1995, the first study revealed that appeals courts found errors serious enough to overturn convictions in almost 70 percent of the cases. Three-fourths of those with overturned convictions got a sentence less than death when the case was retried or plea bargained. The second study found: "The higher the rate at which a state or county imposes death verdicts, the greater the probability that *each* death verdict will have to be reversed because of serious error."

Opponents of the death penalty argue that these statistics expose a deeply flawed system. Supporters of the death penalty counter that the studies reveal how carefully the system reviews each case to make sure only those deserving the death penalty receive it.

FOR DISCUSSION

1. What reason did the Supreme Court give in *Furman* for saying that death penalty statutes were unconstitutional? How did states change their statutes to make them constitutional? Do you agree with the court that these statutes are constitutional? Why or why not?

2. What did the court decide in the *McCleskey* case? Do you agree with its decision? Why or why not?

3. Which of the decisions after *McCleskey* do you agree with? Disagree with? Why?

4. Some have argued that capital punishment is just too expensive. Do you agree? Explain.

CLASS ACTIVITY

Life or Death

In this activity, students role play sentencing juries in capital cases using a capital punishment statute. The defendant in each case has already been convicted of first-degree murder. Each jury must determine the penalty. The only two choices available are life imprisonment or death.

1. Form four juries. Review the **Capital Punishment Statute**, below. Each jury should decide one of the four cases on page 282–283.

2. Members of each jury should:
   a. Make a list of the *mitigating circumstances*, those that seem to call for mercy.
   b. Make a list of *aggravating circumstances*, or those that make the crime seem especially violent or repulsive.
   c. Weigh the *mitigating* and the *aggravating* circumstances against each other. If they feel the case calls for leniency, they should recommend life imprisonment. If they think the case is particularly barbarous or savage, they should recommend death. The recommendation does not have to be unanimous. Only a majority is required for a sentencing recommendation.
   d. Prepare to report to the class. One student in each group should report the mitigating circumstances the group considered. Another student should report the aggravating circumstances. A third student should report the sentence and the number of students who voted each way.

Capital Punishment Statute. After finding a defendant guilty of murder in the first degree, the jury shall look at the circumstances of the crime and at the character of the individual defendant. If it finds the aggravating circumstances of the crime and the defendant outweigh the mitigating circumstances, it shall return a recommendation of the death penalty. Otherwise, it shall recommend life imprisonment.

Case 1: Luby Waxton   **Age: 22**   **Sex: Male**

Luby has been in and out of jail ever since he was a teenager. He was convicted of shoplifting, burglary, and assault with a deadly weapon. He received a light sentence for each, because he has the mental capacity of an 8 year old.

On June 3 of this year, Waxton began drinking in the morning. He decided to rob a local grocery store to get some money. That afternoon, Waxton bought a small handgun.

When he got to the market, he entered the store, bought some cigarettes, and then announced a holdup. Waxton went behind the counter and emptied the cash register. He put his gun to the sales clerk's head and pulled the trigger. The clerk, an old woman, died instantly.

Waxton was convicted of armed robbery and murder in the first degree.

(Continued on next page.)

Case 2: James Woodson   Age: 24   Sex: Male

Woodson has no prior record of being arrested.

Woodson has been active in the anti-abortion movement. He believes that abortion is murder. After taking part in picketing an abortion clinic, Woodson became frustrated that the clinic remained open. He believed that much stronger action was necessary, but knew his fellow picketers would not go along with him.

So late on the night of July 17, he broke into the clinic. He poured gasoline throughout the first floor and put a match to it. The clinic burned to the ground. Unknown to Woodson, a security guard was on the third floor. The guard died in the fire.

Woodson was convicted of arson and first-degree murder.

Case 3: Phong Tran   Age: 18   Sex: Male

Tran has a series of prior juvenile arrests for petty theft and assault. He has been involved in gang activity for the past five years.

His family immigrated to the United States when he was 7 years old. His father abandoned the family shortly afterward, and his mother could not handle three children by herself. Placed in a foster home at age 13, he ran away and took to the streets.

He found a new family in a local gang, headed by Tony Chin, age 35. Chin provided boys in the gang free housing, meals, movies, and video games. In return, they ran errands, protected Chin's businesses, and helped Chin's criminal enterprises. Tran looked on Chin as his father.

On January 7 of this year, Chin handed Tran a gun and told him that a "customer" needed a new Mercedes. Tran went to a mini-mall and waited in the parking lot. When Sally Kim drove up in a new Mercedes, Tran ran up, pointed a gun at her, and demanded she get out. The car lurched and Tran shot Kim, killing her.

Phong Tran was convicted of first-degree murder.

Case 4: Sonia Williams   Age: 27   Sex: Female

Williams has no prior record.

On September 10 of this year, Williams called the police and reported that she had been raped by a man named Greg. She was taken to a hospital where a doctor examined her. He said he could find no evidence of rape.

The police investigated her report and told Williams they could not arrest Greg. It was dark, they said, and so she could have been mistaken about the identity of the attacker. Besides, they said, Greg had a perfect alibi for the night in question.

Williams decided to take matters into her own hands. She bought a gun and waited around the corner where he allegedly first attacked her. When Greg and a friend approached, she told Greg she had been looking for him and was glad to see him. She invited the two men to go somewhere for a drink. They got into her car and drove to a secluded spot, where she shot and killed both men.

Sonia Williams was convicted of first-degree murder.

Debriefing Questions

1. Do you think different juries would weigh the aggravating and mitigating circumstances differently? If so, is this fair? Why or why not?
2. If you were called to jury duty in a capital case, could you vote for the death penalty if circumstances warranted it? Why or why not?
3. Assume for the moment that you approve of the death penalty. What crimes should it apply to? Why?

The Execution of Karla Faye Tucker

Her final legal battles exhausted, the double killer smiled and said: "I love you all" before receiving a lethal injection.
– Report in *The Mirror* on Karla Faye Tucker's execution (1998)

Karla Faye Tucker was the first woman executed in Texas since 1863.

At the end of 2010, 3,158 prisoners were on death rows in the United States. California held the most (683), followed by Florida (390), Texas (330), and Pennsylvania (218). Despite these numbers, only about 50 convicts are executed each year. Part of this can be explained by the long appeals process. But there also appears to be a social reluctance to begin executing massive numbers of prisoners. Between 1977 and 2009, 1,187 executions took place, most of them in the South. In fact, the state of Texas by itself accounted for more than a third of them.

Most of the executions have provoked little protest within the United States. Overseas, many of the executions have drawn widespread attention and some massive protests. One execution hotly debated in America was that of Karla Faye Tucker, the first woman to be executed in Texas since 1863.

Tucker had been a heroin addict since the age of 10. By 13, she was traveling with a rock band. For many years, she worked as a prostitute. In 1983 at age 23, she and her 37-year-old boyfriend broke into a biker's apartment. Intoxicated on drugs and alcohol, they intended to steal money that the biker owed them. Her boyfriend attacked the biker with a hammer as he lay in bed. As the man lay unconscious, he moaned. Tucker later testified she found the moaning annoying and started striking him with a pickax. Her 28 blows killed him. Then she discovered that the biker had not been alone in bed. A woman crouched in the corner. Tucker and her boyfriend killed the woman.

Awaiting trial for the brutal murders, Tucker started reading the Bible. She said she soon realized the enormity of her crime. "At the time, I didn't understand how the Holy Spirit works," she said. "I just remember the whole weight of everything I had done suddenly became a reality. Two precious lives were gone because of me." She agreed to testify against her boyfriend with no promise of leniency. She thought she deserved the death penalty.

Both she and her boyfriend were convicted and sentenced to death. During the 14 years she waited on death row, she became a born-again Christian. In 1993, she married a prison minister. She spent her days acting as a minister and anti-drug counselor to prisoners. She also changed her mind about the death penalty. "I can't take back the lives I took, but I can help save lives now," said Tucker. "I can be a part of the solution."

She drew supporters from unlikely quarters. The Rev. Jerry Falwell, a strong supporter of the death penalty, argued she should be spared. The detective who arrested her and the prosecutor in the case believed her change was genuine and hoped her sentence would be commuted to life. Even the brother of the woman she killed urged authorities not to execute her. A poll of Texans, who overwhelming support the death penalty, found less than half favored carrying out her death sentence. In the two months before the execution, about 25,000 letters, faxes, and phone calls reached the governor's office. They ran about 5 to 1 against killing her.

The governor only had power to commute her sentence to life if state Board of Pardons and Paroles recommended it. The board voted unanimously against her, as it had in 17 straight cases. On February 3, 1998, she was executed.

One reason Tucker's case drew so much attention was that few women are executed. About one of every 10 people arrested for murder is a woman. But only one out of 50 people sentenced to death is a woman. Since 1977, only one other had been executed before Tucker. (As of 2011, 12 women have been executed since 1977.)

But Tucker's supporters argued that they didn't champion her cause because she was a woman. Another woman was put to death in Florida a few weeks after Tucker with little protest. They wanted Tucker saved because she felt genuine remorse and had changed into a new person.

Some who thought she should be executed did not believe she had really changed. Others, however, did believe her. But they didn't think this should make a difference. She had committed a brutal crime, they argued, and she deserved to pay for it with her life. "She's had her mercy," said Dianne Clements, president of Justice for All, a Houston-based criminal justice reform organization. "She's had 14 years to put herself right by God."

FOR DISCUSSION

1. At the start of this unit, five purposes of punishment were discussed. What were they?
2. For those who favored the execution of Tucker, what purpose(s) of punishment do you think they believed it served?
3. Again looking at the purposes of punishment, what do you think those opposing her execution would argue?
4. Do you think Karla Faye Tucker should have been executed? Explain.

Are We Executing Innocent People?

Not long after Willingham's arrest, authorities received a message from a prison inmate named Johnny Webb, who was in the same jail as Willingham. Webb alleged that Willingham had confessed to him that he took "some kind of lighter fluid, squirting [it] around the walls and the floor, and set a fire." The case against Willingham was considered airtight.
– David Grann, "Trial by Fire: Did Texas Execute an Innocent Man?" in *The New Yorker* (2009)

Karla Tucker never claimed to be innocent. But many on death row do. In fact, according to the Death Penalty Information Center, an anti-capital punishment group, 138 prisoners since 1973 have been released from death row because they were innocent. Some were exonerated due to the efforts of the Innocence Project. Led by Cardozo Law School professors Peter Neufeld and Barry Scheck, the Innocence Project provides free legal assistance to inmates who want to prove their innocence through DNA tests. The project is run by volunteers and inmates must pay for the DNA testing themselves. Because of budget constraints, the project can only offer its services to a select number of prisoners. Scheck has argued that all states should authorize DNA testing when the tests could prove a person's innocence.

One of the first states to allow DNA testing was Illinois. In this state, 12 inmates on death row have been executed since capital punishment resumed in 1977. But 13 have been released because they were innocent. One of the 13 was two days away from being executed before his execution was stayed.

Serious due process issues can also raise doubts about a death-penalty conviction. In November 1999, the *Chicago Tribune* ran a series of investigative articles analyzing all 285 death-penalty cases in Illinois since 1977. The *Tribune* found that 40 percent of these cases had at least one of the following elements:

- The defendant had an attorney who had been disbarred or suspended, penalties reserved for lawyers who are unethical or incompetent.
- The prosecution's case relied on a jailhouse informant, who received lenient treatment for naming the defendant. Many consider this type of evidence highly unreliable.

- The prosecution's case relied on testimony from a crime lab technician who made a visual comparison of hairs. This is an outmoded practice that some states bar from being used in court.
- The defendant was black and the jury was all white.

In 2000, Illinois Republican Governor George H. Ryan, a supporter of capital punishment, took the extraordinary step of placing a moratorium on all executions in the state. He said he had "grave concerns about . . . [the] state's shameful record of convicting innocent people and putting them on death row." He called for an investigation of the state's death-penalty procedures.

Three years later, just days before he was to leave office in January 2003, Ryan announced that he was commuting the sentences of all 156 prisoners on Illinois' death row. The prisoners will serve life sentences without the possibility of parole. Ryan said that three years of study had shown deep-seated problems with capital trials, sentencing, and appeals. He stated: "Because the Illinois death penalty system is arbitrary and capricious and therefore immoral, I no longer shall tinker with the machinery of death."

The moratorium caused an outcry of protest, but it remained in place for eight years. Finally, in 2011, Democratic Governor Pat Quinn signed a bill abolishing capital punishment in Illinois.

In 2004, Congress passed the Innocence Protection Act. Among other things, it gives federal prisoners the right to ask a court for DNA tests to prove their innocence. It also provides grants to states that adopt measures that allow prisoners easier access to DNA tests, preserve biological evidence used for DNA testing, and issue minimum standards for court-appointed defense attorneys.

Scheck of the Innocence Project supports this new law. He believes many innocent people are on death row. Although he strongly advocates DNA testing, he says that it cannot solve all the problems in the criminal justice system, because biological evidence is only available in about 60 percent of all violent crimes, primarily in rapes and murders.

Supporters of the death penalty respond that no innocent person has been put to death since capital punishment was reformed in 1977 (and probably since 1900). They point out that all death-penalty cases are carefully reviewed, much more carefully than other cases. Dudley Sharp, a death-penalty expert, says that because of all the due process protections, it is far more likely that an innocent person "sentenced to a life term will die . . . in prison, than it is that an innocent will be executed."

The Execution of Willingham

Opponents of the death penalty have listed several executed people who may have been innocent. The innocence of each is deeply disputed. One of the most publicized cases is that of Cameron Willingham, executed in Texas in 2004. His case was the subject of a long investigative article in the *New Yorker* magazine and a 2011 documentary film, *Incendiary: The Willingham Case.*

In 1991, Willingham's three young daughters were killed when a fire destroyed their house in Corsicana, a small city in east central Texas. Willingham had escaped from the house and had to be restrained, even handcuffed, to prevent him from running back into the house. His wife was away at the time.

Later, fire investigators saw arson as the cause of the fire. "V" patterns of soot charred walls in three different parts of the wooden house, indicating that the fire had three separate sources. The floor had "pour patterns," indicating that a liquid accelerant (such as lighter fluid) had been poured on it. A chemical found in lighter fluid was recovered from samples taken near the front door. Glass from the house's broken windows had web-like cracks, caused by a hot fire, another sign of an accelerant. When investigators learned that Willingham had run from the house barefoot without burning his feet, they were sure he had set the fire. The hot floor would have burned him, they reasoned, unless he had set the fires while leaving the house.

Willingham was 23 years old, a high school dropout, out of work, and without money. He had had run-ins with the law, and he had sometimes hit his wife. His wife, at first, did not believe he had killed their daughters, because although he mistreated her, he spoiled them. She much later decided he must have done it.

Willingham was arrested and charged with murder. The prosecutor offered Willingham life imprisonment in return for a guilty plea. His defense attorneys urged him to accept the offer, but Willingham refused, claiming his innocence. At his trial, in addition to the testimony of the arson investigators, a jailhouse informant testified Willingham had confessed to him. (Later, the informant recanted his testimony and then recanted his recantation.) The prosecution also presented testimony from two experts that Willingham was a sociopath, a person without a conscience. Willingham was convicted and sentenced to death.

Early in 2004, as Willingham was on death row, a leading fire expert reviewed the evidence compiled by the arson investigators. He found no evidence of arson and said the arson investigators' conclusions were based on "junk science."

His report explained that "pour" and "V patterns" are common in fires that reach flashover, the point when everything in a room catches on fire. Flashover can occur quickly, even without an accelerant. The only way to tell whether an accelerant was used is to find traces of the chemical. The only trace was found near the front door. When the expert viewed a picture of the house taken before the fire, he saw that the family kept a grill and lighter fluid near the front door. That was the most likely source of the chemical found near the front door. The web patterns in the broken glass were caused by rapid cooling (when water from the fire hoses hit the glass), not from heat. The expert reasoned that Willingham was able to run barefoot from the house without getting burned because he left before that part of the house had reached flashover. The expert concluded the fire was an accident, probably caused by wiring or a space heater.

Willingham's lawyer rushed the expert's report and a petition for clemency to the Texas Board of Pardons and Parole. The board denied the petition, and the governor turned down a request to stay the execution. Willingham was executed in February 2004.

The following year, the Texas Forensic Science Commission hired Craig Beyler, a noted fire scientist, to investigate the Willingham case. His report found the findings of arson baseless: They "are nothing more than a collection of personal beliefs that have nothing to do with science-based fire investigation."

The *Chicago Tribune* did a series of investigative articles on the case. In 2009, it concluded:

Number of Persons Executed, by Jurisdiction, 1930-2010

Jurisdiction	Number Executed	
	Since 1930	Since 1977
Texas	610	464
Georgia	400	48
New York	329	0
California	302	13
North Carolina	293	43
Florida	227	69
South Carolina	190	42
Virginia	181	108
Ohio	180	41
Alabama	163	49
Louisiana	160	28
Mississippi	160	13
Pennsylvania	155	3
Arkansas	143	27
Oklahoma	129	94
Missouri	123	67
Kentucky	105	3
Illinois	102	12
Tennessee	94	6
New Jersey	74	0
Maryland	71	5
Arizona	60	24
Indiana	52	20
Washington	51	5
Colorado	48	1
District of Columbia	40	0
West Virginia	40	0
Nevada	38	12
Federal system	36	3
Massachusetts	27	0
Delaware	25	14
Oregon	21	2
Connecticut	21	1
Utah	19	7
Iowa	18	0
Kansas	15	0
New Mexico	9	1
Montana	8	3
Wyoming	8	1
Nebraska	7	3
Idaho	4	1
Vermont	4	0
New Hampshire	1	0
South Dakota	1	0
U.S. total	**4,744**	**1,234**

Source: "Capital Punishment, 2010," Bureau of Justice Statistics (2011)

Over the past five years, the Willingham case has been reviewed by nine of the nation's top fire scientists — first for the *Tribune*, then for the Innocence Project, and now for the commission. All concluded that the original investigators relied on outdated theories and folklore to justify the determination of arson. The only other evidence of significance against Willingham was twice-recanted testimony by another inmate who testified that Willingham had confessed to him. Jailhouse snitches are viewed with skepticism in the justice system, so much so that some jurisdictions have restrictions against their use.

Despite the conclusions of the fire scientists, two attorneys at his trial remain convinced Willingham was guilty. The prosecutor admits the fire investigation was "flawed," but said other evidence was presented. He said, "Willingham was a serial wife abuser, both physically and emotionally. His violent nature was further established by evidence of his vicious attacks on animals which is common to violent sociopaths." One of his defense attorneys agreed. He said of Willingham, "He had no conscience. Why do monsters kill? They like killing."

FOR DISCUSSION

1. Do you think Illinois Governor George H. Ryan was correct in suspending all executions in the state? Was he correct in commuting all the sentences? Do you favor a moratorium across the United States? Explain.

2. Do you think the federal Innocence Protection Act is needed? Explain.

3. What was the Willingham case about? Do you think he should have been executed? Explain.

4. If it could be proven that a number of innocent people have been executed, would that make you more likely to oppose the death penalty? Explain.

Does the Death Penalty Deter Murders?

Punishment is not inflicted by a rational man for the sake of the crime that has been committed — after all one cannot undo what is past — but for the sake of the future, to prevent either the same man or, by the spectacle of his punishment, someone else, from doing wrong again.
– Plato (429-347 B.C.), Greek philosopher, *Protagoras*

Since 1995, more than a dozen studies have claimed that executions and sentences of death reduce the murder rate. The studies have analyzed state and county death-penalty data over the past several decades.

One study found that each execution on average resulted in 18 fewer murders. Another study set the average lower — at five fewer murders — and yet another at three fewer murders.

One study looked at the types of murders deterred and found that executions even deterred murders by intimates and those done in the heat of passion. It also looked at the waiting time on death row. It found that for every 2.75 years the wait time before execution is reduced, "one extra murder is deterred."

Another study looked at the effect of the brief ban on capital punishment from 1972 to 1976 caused by the Supreme Court decision in *Furman v. Georgia*. The study found that the murder rate went up in 91 percent of the states when the ban went into effect. The murder rate dropped in 67 percent of the states when the death penalty was reinstated.

Still another study looked at differences state by state. It found that capital punishment in only six states deterred murders. The other 21 states with capital punishment did not deter murders. The difference was that the six states executed more convicts. They executed at least nine persons between the years 1977 and 1996. The study concluded that for deterrence to work, a state must execute a certain number of prisoners. Once states pass this threshold, the study found, the deterrent effect is strong.

An author of one of the studies stated, "I personally am opposed to the death penalty. But my research shows that there is a deterrent effect."

The Critics

All these studies have provoked great controversy and come under attack. Richard Berk, a UCLA professor of statistics and sociology, analyzed the studies in a 2005 paper titled "New Claims about Executions and General Deterrence: Déjà Vu All Over Again?" After reviewing the studies, he concluded that "credible evidence for deterrence is lacking." Jeffrey Fagan, a professor at Columbia Law School, testified on the studies to a committee of the New York State Assembly in 2005. He noted that older studies had made claims similar to the recent ones. In fact, one was mentioned in the Supreme Court decision in *Gregg v. Georgia*. The older studies have been discredited.

Fagan concluded that the new studies were no better. He said that it would be extremely difficult to prove executions caused a decline in the murder rate. These studies, he argued, fell far short. He pointed out that all the studies except one failed to distinguish between different types of murder. The one that did found that executions deterred murders by intimates and those done in the heat of passion, "a claim that flies in the face of six decades of theory, research and facts on homicide." He went on to say that the studies produced erratic results, failed to account for trends, ignored missing data, did not examine whether murderers knew about executions in their state, did not look at the deterrence effect of life without parole sentences, and failed to look at alternative causes of changes in the murder rate. He thought the studies were so shoddy that he called them "junk science."

Another critical study in 2005 examined all the studies to date. It found no evidence to support the claim that capital punishment deters murder:

> [T]he death penalty . . . is applied so rarely that the number of homicides it can plausibly have caused or deterred cannot be reliably disentangled from the large year-to-year changes in the homicide rate caused by other factors.

The critics have themselves drawn critics, and new studies have arisen finding that the death penalty deters. One study in 2009 limited itself to Texas. It found that between .5 and 2.5 murders were deterred in the months after an execution.

In 2012, a special committee of the National Academies of Science weighed in. The committee investigated numerous studies and found them all flawed.

Convicts sentenced to death live on death row, separated from other prisoners.

The committee concludes that research to date on the effect of capital punishment on homicide is not informative about whether capital punishment decreases, increases, or has no effect on homicide rates. Therefore, the committee recommends that these studies not be used to inform deliberations requiring judgments about the effect of the death penalty on homicide.

The committee made recommendations on how to conduct future studies on deterrence, but recognized that the studies will not "come quickly or easily."

In short, the field awaits a definitive study on whether the death penalty deters.

The Moral Debate

If it is found that capital punishment deters murders, that will be a strong argument in favor of capital punishment. In fact, in a *Stanford Law Review* article, two law professors argue that if deterrence is proven, it would be morally wrong for a state not to have the death penalty. If a state refused to impose capital punishment, they argue, it would

> effectively condemn numerous innocent people to death. States that choose life imprisonment, when they might choose capital punishment, are ensuring the deaths of a large number of innocent people.

Another law professor in the same issue of the *Stanford Law Review* argued against their position:

> Their argument is unable to explain why we might not, under conceivable circumstances, be morally obligated to adopt punishments far more brutal and extreme even than execution, or to inflict similarly brutal and extreme harms on innocent members of an offender's family (as punishment of the offender, not of the innocent), or to extend the use of capital punishment to contexts in which many deaths result from behavior far less culpable than murder, such as highway fatalities due to drunkenness or negligence.

FOR DISCUSSION

1. What do the deterrence studies show? What do you think is the strongest criticism of the studies? Do you think the studies are valid? Explain.
2. What moral argument did two professors make in the *Stanford Law Review*? Do you agree with their argument? Why?
3. If it were proven that every execution deterred a certain number of murders, would you be more likely to favor the death penalty? Explain.

CLASS ACTIVITY

Should the Death Penalty Be Outlawed?

In this activity, students literally take a stand on capital punishment and discuss their stand with others.

1. Students should read and familiarize themselves with **Death Penalty Arguments** on page 291.
2. Students should take a moment to think about how they feel about this question: **Should the Death Penalty Be Outlawed?**
3. According to how each student feels about the question, students should form a single line in the room. Make one end of the room mark the spot for those who absolutely favor the death penalty. The other end marks the spot for those who absolutely oppose the death penalty. The stronger that people feel one way or the other, the closer they should be to the ends of the line. Those unsure of their opinion belong in the middle. In a class of 26 students, for example, the line could look like this:

   absolutely wrong   absolutely right
   A B C D E F G H I J K L M N O P Q R S T U V W X Y Z

4. While they are standing in line, students should pair up with a person next to them in line and share three reasons for their opinions.
5. As indicated by the diagram below, divide the line in half and students in one half of the line should move so that they face students in the other half of the line. In this manner, students with strong positions (A B C, X Y Z) should be facing students with moderate positions (K L M, N O P).

   A B C D E F G H I J K L M
   N O P Q R S T U V W X Y Z

6. With the lines parallel, each student now faces a partner with a vastly different opinion, e.g., A–N. Partners should exchange opinions with each other. One partner should start speaking. When the first one finishes, the other partner must paraphrase what the speaker said. If the paraphrase is not right, then the speaker should explain again until the partner gets it right. Then the other partner may speak. The partners can go back and forth, but each time they must correctly paraphrase what the other said.

Debriefing Questions

1. Did you find it difficult to paraphrase the other person's opinions? Why or why not?
2. Which reasons did you find most persuasive? Least persuasive? Why?

DEATH PENALTY ARGUMENTS

Pro

1. Capital cases are carefully reviewed. Mistakes are discovered. It has been more than 50 years since an innocent person has been executed.

2. Capital punishment keeps people from committing murders. Recent studies have shown that executions deter murders.

3. If a person takes a life, that person should pay by giving a life. "An eye for an eye and a tooth for a tooth." This is in accordance with the *punishment* purpose of the criminal justice system.

4. To receive capital punishment, a person must be convicted of committing a horrible crime. The jury is carefully instructed and appellate courts scrutinize the case. If a defendant has been discriminated against, the appellate court will overturn the conviction. The procedure meets all "due process of law" standards.

5. Some criminals are so dangerous that they must never be allowed to live in society. They cannot be rehabilitated. If allowed to live, they may escape or kill a guard or another prisoner. They should be executed to make sure they never harm anyone again.

6. Capital punishment is specifically allowed by the language of the Bill of Rights. The Fifth Amendment says that no person shall be deprived "of *life*, liberty or property without due process of law." [Italics added.]

7. The public wants the death penalty. Polls in some states run as high as 80 percent in favor.

8. Capital punishment would be less expensive if frivolous appeals were eliminated. But even if it is more expensive, it's worth it.

Con

1. Many innocent people have been released from death rows. Many undoubtedly remain. Are we willing to risk executing innocent people?

2. There is no evidence that capital punishment has a deterrent effect. In states that have abolished the death penalty, murder rates have declined or remained the same. Most murderers do not think of the consequences, while many others *want* to be punished. These people will not be deterred.

3. Killing a criminal is an evil on top of an evil. All the Western democracies have abolished it, many religions oppose it, and it is an embarrassment to most civilized people.

4. It is almost impossible to apply capital punishment fairly. Evidence shows that African-Americans and other minorities are sentenced to death far out of proportion to others, especially when a white victim is killed. Chance and arbitrary decision making can affect the sentence in many ways – prosecutorial decisions, plea bargains, the jury's feeling toward the defendant and the crime, and the lawyer's competence. Chance should not be a factor in a life-or-death decision.

5. Life imprisonment without the possibility of parole is punishment enough, and it keeps criminals off the streets just as well as executing them.

6. Customs and conditions have changed since the Constitution was written. Just as slavery is no longer acceptable, the death penalty should be considered cruel and unusual punishment.

7. Public opinion has gone up and down on the death penalty. No other Western democracy executes criminals. We should join the ranks of these countries.

8. Capital punishment costs more than life imprisonment. At current costs, the appeals and hearings for a single death-penalty case cost the government between $2 and $3 million.

Sources for Unit 4

ALI Model Penal Code, Sec. 7.01 [2]. Factors that identify likely candidates for probation adapted from this section. · Alter, J. "The Death Penalty on Trial." *Newsweek*, 6/12/2000. · "The Day Fine," NIJ-Sp., 2010, NCJ 230401. · *Assessing Consistency & Fairness in Sentencing*, NIJ-Sp., 2008, NCJ 223854. · "Justice Expenditure & Employment in the U.S. — 1982–2007," BJS, 2011. NCJ 236218. · Berk, R., "New Claims about Executions & General Deterrence." 3/11/2005. URL: http://preprints.stat.ucla.edu · "Beyond the Prison Bubble," NIJ, 2011, NCJ 235893. · Bohm, R. *The Death Penalty in America*. Cincinnati, Ohio: Anderson Pub., 1991. · Bonczar, T. "Prevalence of Imprisonment in the U.S. Population, 1974–2001." Wash., DC: BJS, 2003. · *Building an Offender Reentry Program*, BJA, 2007, NCJ 219079. · *Calif. Commission on the Fair Administration of Justice, Final Report*. State of Calif., 2008. · Caulkins, J. *et al. Mandatory Minimum Drug Sentences*. Santa Monica: RAND, 1997. · "Census of Jail Facilities, 2006," BJS, 2011, NCJ 230188. · "Census of State & Federal Correctional Facilities, 2005," BJS, 2008, NCJ 222182. · Chaiken, M. *et al. Redefining the Career Criminal*. Wash., DC: NIJ, 1990. · "Characteristics of State Parole Supervising Agencies, 2006," BJS, 2008, NCJ 222180. · Connors, E. *et al. Convicted by Juries, Exonerated by Science*. Wash., DC: NIJ, 1996. · "Capital Punishment, 2010," BJS, 2011, NCJ 236510. · *Correctional Populations in the U.S., 2010*, BJS, 2011, NCJ 236319. · Corrections, BJS, 2012, URL: http://bjs.ojp.usdoj.gov · "Corrections Today...& Tomorrow," NIJ, 2008, NCJ 221166. · "Cost, Performance Studies Look at Prison Privatization," NIJ, 2008, NCJ 221507. · *Developing Data Driven Supervision Protocols for Positive Parole Outcomes*, NIJ-Sp., 2009, NCJ 228855. · Ditton, P. *et al.* "Truth in Sentencing in State Prisons." Wash., DC: BJS, 1999. · *Doing Death in Texas*, NIJ-Sp., 2011, NCJ 236354. · "Felony Sentences in State Courts, 2006." BJS, 2009. NCJ 226846. · *Effectiveness of Prisoner Reentry Services as Crime-Control*, NIJ-Sp., 2008, NCJ 225369. · *Effect of Criminal Justice Involvement in the Transition to Adulthood*, NIJ-Sp., 2009, NCJ 228380. · Ehlers, S. *et al. Still Striking Out*. Wash., DC: Public Policy Institute, 2004. · Ekland-Olson, S. *et al.* "Crime & Incarceration." *Crime & Delinquency*, Vol. 38 No. 3, 7/1992. · "Electronic Monitoring Reduces Recidivism," NIJ, 2011, NCJ 234460. · *Examining The Impact of Ohio's Progressive Sanction Grid*, NIJ-Sp., 2008, NCJ 224317. · Fagan, J. "Deterrence & the Death Penalty." Test. to NY State Assembly, 1/21/2005. · *Federal Criminal Justice Statistics, 2009*, BJS, 2011, NCJ 234184. · *Federal Justice Statistics, 2009 — Statistical Tables*, BJS, 2011, NCJ 233464. · "Felony Sentences in State Courts, 2006 — Statistical Tables," BJS, 2009, NCJ 226846. · Fialkoff, D. "Standardizing Parole Violation Sanctions," *NIJ Journal* No. 263, 2010. · Flanders, S., *Capital Punishment*. Rev. Ed., NY: Facts on File, 2000. · "Friends of Hope." URL: www.hopeprobation.org · Greenwood, P. *et al. Selective Incapacitation*. Santa Monica.: RAND, 1982. · Greenwood, P. *et al.*, "An Assessment of the Effects of Calif.'s Three Strikes Law." Greenwood & Assoc., 2002. · Greenwood, P. *et al. Diverting Children from a Life of Crime*. Santa Monica: RAND, 1996. · Dezhbakhsh, H. *et al.* "Does Capital Punishment Have a Deterrent Effect?" *American Law Econ. Rev.* 5 (2), 2003. · "The Impact of Incarceration on Crime," Pew Center on the States, 2008. · *Impact of Incarceration on Young Offenders*, NIJ-Sp., 2009, NCJ 227403. · "Hawaii Hope," NIJ, 2010, NCJ 230416. · "Incarceration & Crime," Sentencing Project, 2005. · *Increasing Public Safety Through Successful Offender Reentry*, BJA-Sp., 2007, NCJ 222306. · International Justice Statistics, BJS, 2012, URL: http://bjs.ojp.usdoj.gov · "Inmate Behavior Management," NIC, August 2009, NCJ 228272. · *Investigating Prisoner Reentry*, NIJ-Sp., 2009, NCJ 228584. · *Jail Administrator's Toolkit for Reentry*, BJA, 2008, NCJ 222041. · *Jail Information Model*, COPS, 2006, NCJ 216619. · "Jail Inmates at Midyear 2010," BJS, 2011, NCJ 233431. · "Profile of Jail Inmates, 2002." BJS, 2004. NCJ 201932. · *Justice Delayed? Time Consumption in Capital Appeals*, NIJ-Sp., 2007, NCJ 217555. · "Justice Expenditures & Employment, 1982–2007," BJS, 2011, NCJ 236218. · Kerr, P. "The Detoxing of Prisoner 88A0802." *NY Times Mag.* 6/27/1993. · Landry, T. " 'Punishment' & the Eighth Amendment," *Ohio Law J.*, vol. 57, 1996. · Langan, P., "America's Soaring Prison Population," *Science*, 3/29/1991. · Liebman, J. *et al.* "A Broken System: Part I." Columbia Law School, 2000. · ___. "A Broken System: Part II." Columbia Law School, 2002. · *Life After Lockup*, BJA, 2008, NCJ 220095. · Lippke, R. "Crime Reduction & the Length of Prison Sentences." *Law & Policy*, Vol. 24, 1/2002. · Lippman, J. "How One State Reduced Both Crime & Incarceration," *Hofstra Law Rev.*, vol. 38, Summer 2010. · Lipton, D. *et al. The Effectiveness of Correctional Treatment*. NY: Praeger P, 1974. · Lynch, J. *et al.* "Did Getting Tough on Crime Pay?" Urban Institute, 1997. URL: www.urban.org · *Maintaining Prison Order*, NIJ-Sp., 2008, NCJ 226458. · *Managing Drug Involved Probationers with Swift & Certain Sanctions*, NIJ-Sp., 2009, NCJ 229023. · McDonald D. *et al.*, ed. *Day Fines in American Courts*. NIJ, 1992. · "Medical Problems of Prisoners," BJS, 2008, NCJ 221740. · *Minnesota Sentencing Guidelines & Commentary*. St. Paul: Minn. Sentencing Guideline Commission, 2011. · "Mortality in Local Jails, 2000–07," BJS, 2010, NCJ 222988. · Nagin, D. *et al.*, ed. *Deterrence and the Death Penalty*. Wash., DC: Nat. Academies P, 2012. · *Parole Violations & Revocations in Calif.* NIJ-Sp., October 2008, NCJ 224521. · Piehl, A. *et al. Right-Sizing Justice*. NY: Manhattan Inst., Civic Report No. 8. 9/1999. URL: www.manhattan-institute.org/pdf/cr_08.pdf · *Planning & Assessing a Law Enforcement Reentry Strategy*, COPS, 2008, NCJ 223915. · *Prisoner Reentry Experiences of Adult Males*, NIJ-Sp., 2009, NCJ 230419. · *Probation & Parole in the U.S., 2010*, BJS, 2011, NCJ 236019. · "Prison & Jail Deaths in Custody, 2000–2009," BJS, 2011, NCJ 236219. · "Prisoners in 2010," BJS, 2011, NCJ 236096. · *Quantitative & Qualitative Assessment of Electronic Monitoring*, NIJ-Sp., 2010, NCJ 230530. · *Race & the Decision to Seek the Death Penalty in Federal Cases*, NIJ-Sp., 2006, NCJ 214730. · "Reducing Crime & Incarceration," Pew Charitable Trusts, 2008. · "Reentry Courts," BJA-Sp., 2011, NCJ 234087. · Reentry Trends in the U.S., BJS, 2005, URL: http://bjs.ojp.usdoj.gov · "Reevaluating the Deterrent Effect of Capital Punishment," NIJ-Sp., 2006, NCJ 216548. · Rogers, D. "The Mythical Relationship Between Incarceration & Crime Rates, *Justice Matters*, Fall 2007. · Rosich, K. *et al.* "Truth in Sentencing & State Sentencing Practices." *NIJ Journal*, July 2005. · Stemen, D. "Reconsidering Incarceration," Vera Inst. of Justice, 2007. · Prison Expenditures. BJS, 2012. URL: http://bjs.ojp.usdoj.gov · Sunstein, C. *et al. Is Capital Punishment Morally Required?*. AEI-Brookings Joint Center for Regulatory Studies, 3/2005. URL: http://papers.ssrn.com · Tracy, P. *et al. Delinquency in Two Birth Cohorts*. U.S. Dept. of Justice, 1985. · Travis, J. "But They All Come Back." Wash., DC: NIJ, 2000. · Useem, B. *et al.* "Resolution of Prison Riots." Wash., DC: NIJ, 1995. · Useem, B. *et al. Crime-Control Effect of Incarceration*. Wash., DC: NIJ, 2001. · Henningfeld, A., ed., *The Death Penalty*. St. Paul: Greenhaven P, 2006. · Wilson, James Q. "Does Incarceration Reduce Crime Rates?" *LA Times*, 3/30/2008. · ___. "Do the Time, Lower the Crime," AEI Online, 4/8/2008. URL: www.aei.org · ___. "Thinking About Crime, *The Atlantic*, 9/1983. · Visher, C. "Major Study Examines Prisoners & Their Reentry Needs," *NIJ Journal* No. 258, October 2007. · Wolfgang, M. *et al. Delinquency in a Birth Cohort*. Chicago: U. of Chicago P, 1972. · Zedlewski, E., "New Mathematics of Imprisonment," 35 *Crime & Delinquency*, 1/1989. · ___. "Making Confinement Decisions." Wash., DC: NIJ, 1987.

Unit 5
JUVENILE JUSTICE

In January 1690, Nicholas Carter of London, England, was accused of stealing a beaver hat off the head of Mr. William Cummins as he walked down Brumley Street. Carter was caught and confessed his crime. After hearing the confession, a judge found Carter guilty as charged and sentenced him to death. A week later, he was hanged. Nicholas Carter was born in 1675. He was 14 years old.

What if Nicholas had been an American born in 1900, 1950, or 1990? What would happen to the 14-year-old Nicholas Carter today?

For one thing, he wouldn't be tried in an adult court. He'd have a hearing in a court reserved for juveniles. His family history, school records, and other personal information would be closely examined. Even if the juvenile court judge decided that Nicholas had stolen the hat, the judge would try to put Nicholas in a program designed to rehabilitate him.

Why are children treated so differently today? Nineteenth and early 20th century reforms produced two separate systems of justice in America, based on almost opposite philosophies. The adult criminal justice system applies to supposedly mature, responsible persons who have lived, depending on the state, at least 16 or 18 years. Those younger than the specified age fall under the jurisdiction of the juvenile justice system.

This dual system has its critics. Many Americans believe that all persons in trouble with the law, no matter what their age, should have the benefit of the greater due-process protections found in the adult system. Others argue that some juveniles should be processed according to the rules of the adult system not for their protection, but for society's protection. They feel that the juvenile justice system, with its emphasis on rehabilitation, puts too many young, hard-core criminals back on the streets. The fact that these criminals are only 14 or 15 doesn't prevent them from committing crimes and ruining other people's lives. Others have yet another perspective: Whether or not the theory behind our current juvenile system is correct, it just isn't working. Changes must be made for the benefit of troubled young people and for the good of society.

After exploring the history and philosophy of the juvenile justice system, this unit examines issues raised by its critics and supporters. Who ought to be there? What rights should young people have as protection against the system? Should the system focus on rehabilitation or punishment?

Finally, statistics show that people under 18 account for more than 10 percent of all arrests. Many criminals start their life of crime as juveniles. To find solutions to our crime problem, we must examine how the law currently treats juveniles and how that treatment can be improved.

CHAPTER 18

FROM CRIMINAL TO DELINQUENT

We ought to have a "children's court" in Chicago, and we ought to have a "children's judge," who should attend to no other business.
– Frederick Wines, member of the Illinois State Board of Charities, in a speech (1898)

CHILDREN AND THE LAW: A HISTORY | FROM CRIMINAL TO DELINQUENT
DIFFERENT WORLDS: THE TWO SYSTEMS

Children and the Law: A History

When children appear, we justify all our weaknesses, compromises, snobberies, by saying: "It's for the children's sake."
– Anton Chekhov (1860-1904), Russian author

In the Middle Ages, children took part in adult activities as soon as they could walk and talk. They were working by the age of 5 or 6. Most families needed every available pair of hands to grow enough food or weave enough cloth to survive. Shorter life expectancy also forced people into early adulthood. The average life span was only 40 years. No one had time for a leisurely childhood, much less an adolescence.

Children were expected to work hard, and they were also expected to obey adult laws. Anyone old enough to commit a crime was thought old enough to be punished for it. Painful forms of trial, like ordeal and combat, and harsh punishments, like being hanged or burned at the stake, fell on all criminals, no matter what their ages.

In the 16th and 17th centuries, medieval attitudes began to soften. Though children were still thrust into adulthood at the age of 4 or 5, most of Europe began to think of them as needing adult protection and guidance. In England, the common law reflected this change in attitude. The king or queen became the *parens patriae* — the parent of the country. Representing the monarch, English courts acted as *parens patriae* to manage orphans' estates, protect children's property from wasteful parents, and provide for abandoned young people.

The Age of Reason

About this time, another important concept worked its way into English common law: the idea of intent. To commit a crime, a person not only had to perform a forbidden action, the person also had to intend to commit that act.

The concept of intent changed how children were treated under English common law. Society now believed that children were naive and innocent. Though they might accidentally cause harm, children did not know enough about right and wrong, or about the effects of their actions, to form criminal intent. Since they couldn't form intent, children couldn't commit crimes.

At what age could they form the intent necessary for committing crimes? The 18th century's answer to this question was based on traditional Christian beliefs, which held that 7 was the "age of reason." After age 7, according to the church, children knew the difference between right and wrong and became responsible for their actions and moral decisions.

By the late 18th century, English common law had taken this rationale one step further. English judges usually dismissed cases against defendants under age 7. In recognition of society's changing view about the length of childhood, they also dismissed cases against persons aged 7 to 14 unless the prosecution could prove that the child was capable of forming criminal intent.

The English criminal justice system treated everyone over 14 years old — and everyone between 7 and 14 proven capable of forming criminal intent — exactly alike. Officially, all were tried in the same courts by the same rules. If convicted, all were locked up in the same jails and subject to the same harsh penalties. In actual practice, however, the system showed children and adolescents leniency. For example, although English courts sentenced 103 persons age 8 and under to death between 1801 and 1836, not one of these executions actually took place. Even so, the law allowed people of a very young age to be executed or imprisoned.

Young people hang out on a street corner known for gangs in Springfield, Mass., around the turn of the 20th century.

Colonists transplanted the English common law, complete with the concepts of *parens patriae*, criminal intent, and the age of reason, to North American soil. The religious beliefs of many of these settlers emphasized training children for obedient, religious, and productive adult lives.

Save the Children

By the 19th century, America was rapidly changing. Factories sprang up across the Northeast, and the nation's urban population was growing faster than its rural population. In 1820, 7 percent of America's people lived in cities. That proportion had risen to 15 percent by 1850 and 35 percent by 1890.

Many of the new city residents were immigrants. Others were country people looking for greater opportunity and an escape from the exhausting routines of rural life. Survival in the city, however, was a full-time occupation. Crowded into small rooms with their struggling family, urban children often escaped to the streets. Other children were abandoned by their parents and turned to picking pockets, shoplifting, begging, and looting for survival.

Often, young people banded together. As early as 1791, children's gangs were noted on the streets of Philadelphia scaring horses with firecrackers. During the 19th century, gangs turned from pranks to serious crime. By the Civil War, youth gangs took part in arson and mob violence and regularly fought battles with the police.

Citizens' groups in every American city expressed concern about these wayward youngsters, but people were unsure of what to do about them. If caught in a crime, children over 7 and under 14 faced prosecution in the adult criminal justice system and often ended up in adult prisons. Many people questioned the wisdom of this result. Through contact with older criminals, children learned to perfect their skills at robbery, mayhem, and murder. Also, then as now, adults in prison regularly abused younger and weaker inmates.

House of Refuge

Early in the 19th century, American cities began to provide alternatives to adult prisons for children. In 1824, using *parens patriae* as its rationale, the New York City government established the New York House of Refuge for abandoned, deprived, and criminal children. Other state and local governments soon followed suit. These institutions, which came to be known as reform schools, opened in almost every large urban center.

The reform schools tried to break youngsters' bad habits by a combination of religion, education, and hard work. Run by private organizations, many schools, however, began to operate not for reform, but for profit. They glossed over moral and practical education. As headmasters pressed for greater productivity, children spent more time in workshops and less in classrooms.

As living conditions deteriorated, many young people rebelled. In 1859, 15-year-old Dan Crean set fire to the Massachusetts Reform School. Two years later, in another part of the state, angry girls burned their school to the ground. Reform schools, like prisons before them, came to be known as "universities of crime."

Stuck in the System

Once in these schools, students could not easily get out. In 1838, for example, a court committed Mary Ann Crouse to the Philadelphia House of Refuge because her mother complained about her behavior. By the time her father found out, Mary Ann was already locked up. When the House of Refuge refused to release her to his custody, Mr. Crouse began a legal battle to get his daughter back.

His battle eventually took him to the Supreme Court of Pennsylvania. He argued that the House of Refuge had violated his daughter's constitutional rights. Mary Ann had been locked up without a jury trial, a right guaranteed to all Americans.

After lengthy deliberation, the court ruled in favor of the House of Refuge. The court stated that the right to a trial by jury did not apply to juveniles taken to the House of Refuge. It only applied to people accused of crimes. Since Mary Ann was not accused of any crime, she had no right to a jury trial.

According to the court, Mary Ann was institutionalized not because of criminal guilt, but because her mother no longer wanted to take responsibility for her upbringing. Citing the doctrine of *parens patriae*, the court declared that the state, in this instance represented by the House of Refuge, had every right to assume the parental role. As the court concluded, Mary Ann "had been snatched from a course which must have ended in confirmed depravity, and not only is the restraint of her person lawful, but it would be an act of cruelty to release her from it." (*Ex Parte Crouse*, 1838)

FOR DISCUSSION

1. What is the doctrine of *parens patriae*? Do you think it has validity today? Why or why not?
2. At what age do you think children should be held criminally responsible for their actions?
3. What were the negative effects of placing juveniles in the adult criminal system?
4. What arguments can you think of against keeping Mary Ann in the House of Refuge?

From Criminal to Delinquent

The problem for determination by the judge is not, Has this boy or girl committed a specific wrong, but What is he, how has he become what he is, and what had best be done in his interest and in the interest of the state to save him from a downward career.
– Julian W. Mack (1886-1943), judge in Chicago's first juvenile court and later a federal judge

American cities didn't rely entirely on reform schools to cope with young people in trouble. During the latter half of the 19th century, other innovative ideas developed as well.

Since contact between juveniles and adult criminals was seen as a major problem, many states began setting aside special times for juvenile trials, keeping juvenile records separate from adults, and sentencing juveniles to age-segregated prisons.

Massachusetts began experimenting with probation as an alternative to imprisonment. But probation presented problems when applied to young urban criminals. Sending them back to their communities usually meant returning them to an environment that was the root of their problems. If a juvenile's family couldn't provide a good home, the courts sometimes tried to identify a relative or family friend to take responsibility for the child's probation.

This led to the development of another innovation: the foster family. Recognizing that reform schools or problem families could cause more harm than good, government officials compiled lists of trustworthy families and individuals who could provide temporary care for children in trouble. Abandoned or neglected children were also placed in foster homes.

Though each of the experiments in juvenile reform was successful to some degree, by the 1890s, a reform movement was pushing for more inventive methods.

The situation in Chicago was especially bad. Vice and crime plagued the Chicago Reform School. Judges preferred to send all but the most hardened juvenile offenders to the adult jail. They felt the jail was safer. The school's reputation was so bad that when it burned down in 1871, the government refused to provide money to rebuild it. This left Chicago, one of the nation's largest cities, with no system for handling neglected or criminal young people.

The Chicago Women's Club stepped in to fill the gap. It set up a school for young people

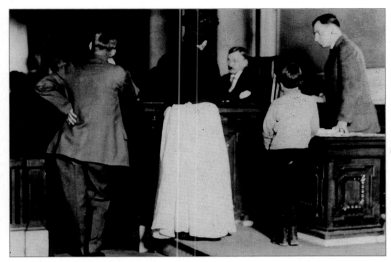

An 8 year old stood charged with stealing a bicycle in juvenile court in St. Louis, May 1910.

serving time in the city's jails. It opened a city police station for women and children arrestees so they wouldn't have to mingle with hardened male criminals.

Working with juveniles made club members come to some radical conclusions. Members felt that placing juveniles in the adult criminal justice system made matters worse. Why not start over and build a separate justice system, just for juveniles, based on principles related to the needs and problems of children?

In the first place, club members believed that no rational adult could hold children responsible for their actions. Wayward, disobedient, and criminal behaviors, they believed, were diseases caused by poverty and neglect, circumstances over which a child had no control. One might as logically blame children for catching the measles as blame them for running away from troubles at home or following bad examples set by friends.

Second, the concept of crime — specific prohibited acts — was too limited to help children. Certainly, young people must be prevented from robbing, raping, and murdering. But they also must be protected from other, less well-defined actions, like associating with immoral people, staying out too late at night, or disobeying authority. These actions greatly damaged young people by encouraging bad habits and leading to more destructive behavior.

Furthermore, it was unfair to label children as criminals. A new word for wrongdoers was needed. The word **delinquent** seemed much more appropriate. The Women's Club also decided that children convicted of crimes should not be punished. Instead, young persons who

committed delinquent acts should be re-educated and rehabilitated so they would not repeat their offenses.

Moreover, young persons should not necessarily undergo the same rehabilitation programs. Some children would best benefit from the harsh life of reform school. Others would do better in the gentler care of foster parents. Still others could be returned to their families on probation. Each child should receive **individualized treatment**.

Finally, since no one was being punished, the carefully regulated trial process of the adult courtroom was not needed. That process tended to intimidate children and might hinder rather than help, the Women's Club reasoned. To consider each child's best interests and deliver the personalized justice demanded by this new system, a judge needed more freedom than adult procedures permitted. Judges hearing juvenile cases should work in informal rooms, more like counseling offices than courtrooms. Questioning and decision making should also be flexible and informal. Only in such a non-adversarial atmosphere could judges determine appropriate ways to help young people in trouble.

When the Women's Club first raised these ideas in 1892, its own lawyers argued that the system was unconstitutional. Not only did it reverse or suspend the basic principles of American justice, it stripped the accused young persons of their rights. Club members retorted that children needed help, not rights.

In spite of the initial negative response, the Women's Club proposal was widely discussed. In 1898, the Illinois State Board of Charities asked the Chicago Bar Association to draft legislation based on the club's plan. After hearings, the Illinois legislature passed the Juvenile Court Act. The nation's first juvenile court officially opened its doors on July 1, 1899.

Other states responded enthusiastically to this new system. Within 25 years, all but Maine and Wyoming had passed laws based on the Illinois model. Over the years, court decisions and administrative policies have modified the juvenile justice system. But the current juvenile justice systems throughout the United States owe their roots to that first Chicago experiment.

FOR DISCUSSION

1. Do you agree with the reasoning advanced by reformers in the Chicago Women's Club? Why or why not?
2. Are young people incapable of forming criminal intent? Should they be treated rather than punished when they harm others?
3. Should young people who commit crimes be treated differently from adults? Explain.

CLASS ACTIVITY

Same or Different?

Should juveniles be treated the same as adults? In this activity, students evaluate situations to determine whether the juvenile and adult in each case should be treated the same or differently.

1. Form small groups. Each group should:
   a. Examine each of the four pairs of cases listed below. In each, after considering the individuals' intent and responsibility, decide whether the juvenile and adult should receive the same treatment or punishment.
   b. Be prepared to explain the reasons for each decision.
2. After the groups decide all the cases, they should present their findings to the class and compare their decisions with those made by other groups. Conclude the activity with a discussion using the debriefing questions, below.

Case 1
- Jerry, 27, lives in an adult apartment complex. One of his neighbors regularly holds loud parties lasting long into the night. After a frustrating confrontation late one evening, Jerry picks up a rock and throws it through his neighbor's window.
- A neighbor chases Harold, 10, and his friends from her yard and warns them not to play baseball on her property. In retaliation, Harold throws a rock through her window.

Case 2
- Cynthia, 35, finds out that her husband is leaving her. At the height of an argument, she kills him.
- Mike, 8, is furious with his 4-year-old sister for ruining his favorite toy. He picks up his father's shotgun and kills her.

Case 3
- When the store clerk's back is turned, Connie, 23, slides an expensive scarf into her purse and walks out of the store. Apprehended by store detectives on the sidewalk, she complains that she was tired of paying exorbitant prices for everything.
- Nancy, 14, steals a digital watch from a department store display. Her only excuse, when she's caught, is that her friends dared her to do it.

Case 4
- Jim, 39, makes obscene phone calls to women in his neighborhood. He enjoys their confused and helpless reaction and likes to give them a good scare.
- Andy, 15, makes an obscene phone call to one of his teachers. He wants to see how she will react.

Debriefing Questions

1. Which cases were the most difficult to decide? Why?
2. Do you think the criminal justice system should treat children differently from adults? If so, at what age should they be treated the same as adults?

Different Worlds:
The Two Systems

It is a hallmark of our juvenile justice system in the United States that virtually from its inception at the end of the last century its proceedings have been conducted outside of the public's full gaze and the youths brought before our juvenile courts have been shielded from publicity.
– Justice William Rehnquist (later chief justice), *Smith v. Daily Mail Publishing Co.* (1979)

Under current law, the treatment of juveniles differs from that of adults. Though the specifics of treatment vary from state to state, the chart on the next page notes many differences between the juvenile and adult systems.

One main difference is that the juvenile system is based on rehabilitating juvenile offenders: It is not based on punishment. Another major difference is that criminal cases are matters of public record. The hearings and trials are open to the public. In the juvenile system, the hearings are private.

There has, however, been a tendency in recent years, to eliminate some differences between adult and juvenile court. One difference that is slowly being eroded is an insistence on confidentiality. Many states now allow media access to the identity, and sometimes the physical images, of some juveniles involved in delinquency proceedings.

Another change in some states involves expunging (destroying) records. In the past, most state laws provided for automatic expungement of juvenile court records. Today, expungement in some states is limited to only minor offenses. In other states, it occurs only after a motion to the court, and the judge must decide whether the records should be destroyed. More than half the states now have laws providing that certain records cannot be destroyed.

As a result of these and other changes, a finding of delinquency may now have so called "collateral consequences." An adjudication of delinquency may disqualify a juvenile's right to possess firearms when he becomes an adult. A juvenile adjudicated for certain offenses may be disqualified from enlisting in the armed forces. And in many states, if a youth is convicted of a crime when he becomes an adult, the fact that he had been tried as a juvenile and found to be delinquent, may result in a harsher sentence.

The goal of the juvenile court system is still rehabilitation, not punishment. But because of the changes in the law, a finding of delinquency can now have a negative effect on the life of an ex-offender.

COMPARISON OF THE TWO SYSTEMS

Adult System	Juvenile System
Persons can be legally arrested if they are suspected of committing a **crime**.	Juveniles can be **taken into custody** if they are suspected of committing a **delinquent act**.
The state files formal criminal charges in the form of an **indictment, information, or complaint.**	The state files a **petition** with the juvenile court.
Persons may be released on **bail** or **on their own recognizance** or **may be held in jail** until trial.	Juveniles may be released into **custody of their parents, held in custody** until an official hearing, or placed on **probation** without an official hearing.
Decisions are made by **judges** and **juries**.	Decisions are made by **hearing officers, commissioners,** and **juvenile court judges**.
A **trial** determines whether or not an accused person is guilty beyond reasonable doubt of a specific crime.	An **adjudicatory hearing** determines the truth or falsity of the petition beyond a reasonable doubt.
After a **verdict of guilty**, a **sentencing hearing** is held to determine the sentence.	After a **finding of delinquency**, a **dispositional hearing** determines if the juvenile is in need of state supervision or care.
A convicted person may be placed on **probation, fined,** or sentenced to a specified length of confinement in a **jail** or **prison**.	Juveniles judged in need of care are made **wards of the court**. They may be placed on **probation**, placed in a group or individual **foster home**, **fined**, or committed to an unspecified length of confinement in a **reform school, state institution,** or **camp**.
Before the end of a prison term, a prisoner may be released and put on **parole**.	After release from confinement, juveniles may be supervised in a program of **aftercare**.
Proceedings and records are **public**.	Proceedings and records are kept **private**.
The main goal is **punishment**.	The main goal is **rehabilitation**.

FOR DISCUSSION

1. Looking at the chart on this page, which differences seem to be merely words? If some differences are just words, does it make any sense to use different words? Why or why not?

2. What are the major differences between the two systems? Try to explain some of these important differences in light of the early 20th-century reforms. In your opinion are these differences justified? Explain.

3. Do you think all juvenile records should be automatically expunged? Explain.

4. What are some "collateral consequences" of a delinquency offense? Do you think these consequences should exist? Explain.

CHAPTER 19
THE PROBLEM OF DELINQUENCY

The Legislative Assembly declares that in delinquency cases, the purposes of the Oregon juvenile justice system from apprehension forward are to protect the public and reduce juvenile delinquency and to provide fair and impartial procedures for the initiation, adjudication and disposition of allegations of delinquent conduct.

– Section 419C.001, *Oregon Juvenile Code: Delinquency* (2009)

WHAT IS DELINQUENCY? | A TOUR OF THE SYSTEM | INITIAL DETENTION OF JUVENILES

What Is Delinquency?

Gee, Officer Krupke
We're very upset
We never had the love
That every child oughta get
We ain't no delinquents
We're misunderstood
Deep down inside us there is good

– Stephen Sondheim, "Gee, Officer Krupke" in *West Side Story* (1957)

Young people get brought into the juvenile justice system for committing specific acts. These acts fall into two categories:

(1) Those that would be considered criminal if committed by an adult. These are called **delinquent acts**.

(2) Those that are thought harmful to young people because they might be dangerous or lead to criminal behavior. These are called **status offenses** because they only apply to those who have the status of juveniles.

Status offenses cover a wide variety of behaviors — running away from home, drinking alcohol, skipping school, disobeying parents, violating curfews, etc. Some states classify youth who exhibit these behaviors as "wayward" or "incorrigible." Others term status offenders as CHINS, PINS, or MINS — children, persons, or minors in need of supervision.

Since states must define status offenses, the laws can be quite broad and even vague. California's old section 601 of its Welfare and Institutions Code was a good example:

Any person under the age of 18 years who persistently or habitually refuses to obey the reasonable and proper orders or directions of his parents . . . or school authorities, . . . or who is habitually truant . . . *or who . . . is in danger of leading an idle, dissolute, lewd, or immoral life*, is within the jurisdiction of the juvenile court which may adjudge such person to be a ward of the court. (Emphasis added.)

California's code no longer contains the emphasized words.

FOR DISCUSSION
1. What is delinquency?
2. What are status offenses? Do you think they should be classified as delinquent behavior?
3. Why do you think California removed the words *"who . . . is in danger of leading an idle, dissolute, lewd, or immoral life"* from its code?

Are You Now or Have You Ever Been?

Who should be processed through the juvenile justice system? In this activity, students clarify their opinions on this issue.

1. Form small groups. Each group should:
   a. Carefully read the list **Should It Be Classified as a Delinquent Act or Status Offense?** In many states, juvenile courts may intervene when a person under 18 commits any of the actions described on this list.
   b. Discuss the items on the list using these questions:
      - Which are actually crimes?
      - Of the remainder, which do you think are harmful to young people? Why?
      - Which of the actions on the list should not, in your opinion, be classified as delinquent or status offenses? Why?
2. The groups should report back their answers. Hold a class discussion. Conclude by discussing the debriefing questions.

Should It Be Classified as a Delinquent Act or Status Offense?

a. Taking a car without the owner's permission
b. Disobeying your parents
c. Cutting school
d. Going into a building you aren't supposed to be in
e. Running away from home
f. Taking something from a store without paying for it
g. Driving recklessly
h. Buying or drinking alcoholic beverages
i. Using or selling marijuana or drugs
j. Smoking cigarettes at school or in public
k. Hitting a teacher
l. Having sexual relations
m. Deliberately damaging school property
n. Getting in a fight
o. Taking something that does not belong to you
p. Staying out past midnight

Debriefing Questions

1. Which of these behaviors did most groups think were delinquent acts? Status offenses? Neither?
2. How would you define a juvenile delinquent?

A Tour of the System

It is important to remember that the United States has at least 51 different juvenile justice systems, not one. Each state and the District of Columbia has its own laws that govern its juvenile justice system. How juvenile courts operate may vary from county to county and municipality to municipality within a state.
– National Research Council, *Juvenile Crime, Juvenile Justice* (2001)

Recent statistics indicate that almost 2 million American youth pass through the juvenile justice system each year. The statistics overlook the many juveniles who never enter the system, but who are referred to social welfare agencies because of abuse, neglect, or status offenses. Although the system still takes status offenders in extreme cases, it handles at least 10 times as many delinquency cases. The chart on page 303 shows what happens to those brought into the system for delinquency.

Police bring most juveniles into the system. But 17 percent are brought in by parents, school officials, probation officers, and social welfare agencies.

About a quarter of those brought in are accused of violent crimes — murder, rape, robbery, or assault. Over one-third are detained for property crimes — theft, burglary, vandalism, receiving stolen property, and arson. Another quarter or so are taken into custody for public-order offenses, such as obstruction of justice, disorderly conduct, weapons charges, and public intoxication. The remaining juveniles — just over 10 percent — are accused of drug offenses.

At the juvenile court, an intake worker, usually a probation officer or a social worker, must decide what to do with these juveniles. The worker typically looks at the offense, the strength of the case, and the juvenile's history and needs. After consulting with a prosecutor, the worker may choose to file a petition against the juvenile. This will lead to a hearing in juvenile court.

But more than 40 percent of the juveniles are not petitioned. Of these juveniles, many are simply let go. The remainder are informally processed in the system. They agree to specific conditions, such as repaying the victim, attending school, and meeting a curfew, and they must check in with a probation

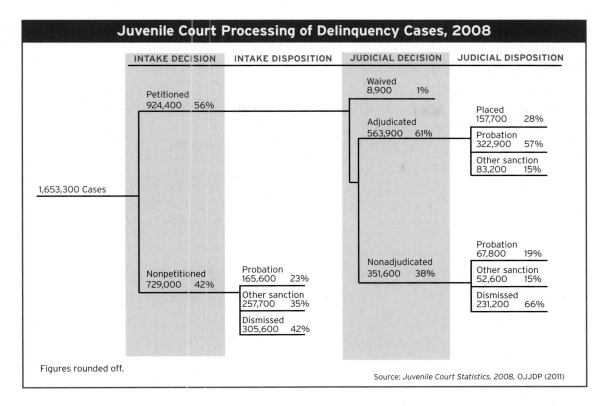

Juvenile Court Processing of Delinquency Cases, 2008

INTAKE DECISION	INTAKE DISPOSITION	JUDICIAL DECISION	JUDICIAL DISPOSITION

1,653,300 Cases

Petitioned 924,400 56%

Waived 8,900 1%

Adjudicated 563,900 61%

Placed 157,700 28%
Probation 322,900 57%
Other sanction 83,200 15%

Nonpetitioned 729,000 42%

Probation 165,600 23%
Other sanction 257,700 35%
Dismissed 305,600 42%

Nonadjudicated 351,600 38%

Probation 67,800 19%
Other sanction 52,600 15%
Dismissed 231,200 66%

Figures rounded off.

Source: *Juvenile Court Statistics, 2008*, OJJDP (2011)

officer. If they break the agreement, a formal petition will be filed.

Those petitioned must appear at initial hearings. At these hearings, juvenile court judges examine the petitions. A tiny percentage of cases are waived to adult court. These cases represent the most serious offenders.

The remainder of cases are sent to adjudicatory hearings. At about 40 percent of the hearings, the juvenile is found not delinquent. Most of these juveniles are released. The rest are handled informally. About one-fifth are put on probation. And most others are referred to social agencies.

Finally, what happens to the about 60 percent adjudicated delinquent? Most receive probation. About one-sixth are ordered to pay a fine, pay restitution to the victim, perform community service, or sent to a treatment or counseling program. About one-fourth are placed out of their homes into foster homes, group homes, or secure facilities.

As you can see on the chart, many juveniles are put outside the system, or diverted, at each stage. Of the original juveniles taken into custody, fewer than 10 percent wind up placed outside their homes. The juvenile court system relies on decision makers at

each stage to act "in the best interests of the child." Each of these decision makers — from the police officer to the intake worker to the juvenile court judge — is given wide discretion in resolving delinquency problems. The system encourages these decision makers to resolve the problems informally, if possible, instead of sending a juvenile deeper into the system.

FOR DISCUSSION

1. How do police officers, intake workers, and juvenile court judges exercise discretion in the juvenile justice system? Give some examples. What are some advantages and disadvantages of this discretion? Explain.

2. Why do you think juvenile justice officials prefer to resolve delinquency problems informally? What are the advantages and disadvantages?

3. Look at the chart. At what stage do juveniles have the best chance of getting their cases dismissed? At what stage do they have the worst chance? How do you account for this?

CLASS ACTIVITY

Who Should Be in the System?

Who belongs in the juvenile justice system? In this activity, students evaluate which, if any, government agency should be responsible for juveniles in different situations.

1. Form pairs. Each pair should:
   a. Discuss each of the situations below.
   b. Decide which, if any, government agency should be responsible for **juveniles** in the situations described below. (Do **not** answer what agency should deal with the adults in these situations.) Decide whether the juvenile in each situation should be sent to:
      • state or local service agencies
      • juvenile courts
      • adult criminal courts
      • no government institution (the matter should be handled privately)
   c. Write the conclusions on a sheet of paper.
2. Regroup as a class and students should compare their answers.
3. Debrief the activity using the questions below.

Situations

a. **Abuse or neglect.** Children are poorly fed or clothed, beaten, sexually molested, or denied vital medical treatment by their parents.
b. **Criminal influence.** Children are exposed to or taught illegal behavior (e.g., drug abuse, criminal acts) by their parents.
c. **Economic hardship.** Children have parents who cannot afford to take care of them.
d. **Unconventional homes.** Children have parents who live according to moral standards different from those of the general community (e.g., households with polygamous living arrangements, those with unusual religious beliefs).
e. **Ungovernability.** Children cannot be controlled by their parents.
f. **Runaways.** Children habitually run away from home.
g. **Status offenses.** Children commit status offenses, such as curfew violations or truancy.
h. **Abuse of intoxicating substances.** Children use drugs or alcohol.
i. **Misdemeanors.** Children loiter, joy-ride, make obscene phone calls, etc.
j. **Victimless crimes.** Children commit victimless crimes such as prostitution.
k. **Shoplifting.**
l. **Major theft or other property crimes.**
m. **Violent crimes.**

Debriefing Questions

1. Which actions should be handled privately? Why?
2. Which actions deserve court involvement? Why? How do you determine whether juvenile or adult criminal courts should handle the matters?
3. Which actions should be handled by social service agencies? Why?
4. Which situations do most people agree about? Which cause the most disagreement? Why?

Initial Detention of Juveniles

While some youth may need to be detained to protect the public, two-thirds of those detained are held for non-violent crimes.
– Annie E. Casey Foundation, *Detention Reform Brief* (2007)

When first taken into custody, juveniles go to a detention center, often called juvenile hall. Unlike adults, juveniles may be held in custody until their hearings without any chance of bail. At the option of a probation officer, they may be released into their parents' custody before the hearing. If the probation officer decides to keep a juvenile in custody, a judge reviews this decision, usually within 48 hours.

In some jurisdictions, most juveniles spend at least one day in custody. Most are released within five days. Many of these juveniles are accused of non-violent offenses or even status offenses.

Aside from worsening overcrowding, such detention creates several other problems. First of all, it's expensive. It may cost more than $100 to house one juvenile per night, which amounts to more than $40,000 per year.

Second, it crowds together juveniles who shouldn't be together. Juvenile hall may hold those awaiting their hearings along with juveniles who have already had their hearings and are either waiting to be placed elsewhere or serving their time in juvenile hall itself. Serious offenders stay alongside lesser ones.

Finally, pre-hearing detention creates risks to inmate safety. Not only do violent offenders present a threat to others, but troubled youth in detention pose a high risk of suicide.

Sacramento County, Calif., decided to do something about pre-hearing detention. Obviously, it could not just release all the juveniles. Some posed a threat to the community. Others might not show up for their hearings. The county had to find a solution that would satisfy the need for public safety. It needed a way to identify youth in custody who could be safely released.

It came up with a risk-assessment checklist for each juvenile. A copy is on page 306. Probation officers score each juvenile according to this checklist. The officers check off each factor that applies to the juvenile, and next to the factor is a point score. For example, if the juvenile previously committed another offense while waiting for a hearing, that is worth 3 points. For aggravating and mitigating factors, the officers are

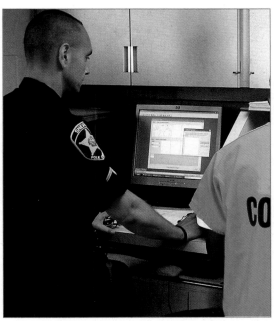

Before any hearing, an intake officer at juvenile hall decides whether to hold a juvenile or release the juvenile into a parent's custody.

given a range of points from 1 to 3 and must decide the score. After filling out the checklist, officers total the scores. Those juveniles scoring 10 points or more are detained. Those scoring under 10 go home or to a shelter. But probation officers have the right to override the score. So whether a juvenile scores over or under 10 points, a probation officer still makes the final decision on whether to detain or release the juvenile.

The checklist has thus far proved successful. In 1994, 54 percent of juveniles brought to juvenile hall in Sacramento remained in detention. By 1997, the percentage had dropped to 41 percent. In 1994, 22 percent of the juveniles released were rearrested for committing another offense. By 1997, this percentage had declined to 15 percent. So even though a greater percentage were released in 1997, a smaller percentage were rearrested.

Sacramento has continued using its risk assessment. Data collected during 2011 showed that less than 2 percent of the juveniles released based on the risk assessment failed to show up for court. Thus the procedure is achieving its intended results. It allows less serious offenders who do not pose a significant public safety risk to go home instead of being locked up with more serious offenders. And it reduces the county's costs.

FOR DISCUSSION

1. What are the pros and cons of locking up all juveniles brought to juvenile hall until their hearing dates?

2. Authorities in Sacramento, and most experts, believe that there are only two reasons to detain juveniles before a hearing: (1) They pose a threat to society or (2) they may not show up for the hearing. Do you think there are other valid reasons? Explain.

Sacramento County Pretrial Juvenile Detention Risk Assessment

Name of Minor: _____ Screened By:_____

Date: _____

Instructions: Score each factor below and enter scores in the right-hand column. Select only one score for each of the nine factors.

FACTOR			SCORE
1. MOST SERIOUS INSTANT OFFENSE . . . . _____			
( ) ANY 707(b) offense (see page 307)	10	( ) Other felony offenses except drugs	5
( ) Felony crimes of violence	8	( ) Sale of drugs or possession for sale of drugs	5
( ) Felony sexual offenses	7	( ) Possession of drugs	3
( ) Series of three or more separate felony offenses	7	( ) Misdemeanors involving violence (3	3/2
( ) Felony high-speed chase (driver only)	7	points); other misdemeanors (2 points)	
		( ) Probation violations	1
2. WEAPONS ENHANCEMENT . . . . _____			
( ) Possession of firearm and ammunition	2	( ) Possession of firearm (no ammunition) or other weapon	1
3. WARRANTS . . . . _____			
( ) Surrendered	2	( ) Apprehended	3
4. LEGAL STATUS (Check only one) . . . . _____			
( ) Currently on Home Supervision Program	7	( ) Ward: last offense more than 1 year	2
( ) Pending Court:	6	( ) Ward: last sustained offense within 3 months	4
( ) No current status, but prior probation status or 2+ referrals by law enforcement:	1	( ) Ward: last offense 3 months to 1 year	3
		( ) None	0

5. RISK OF FAILURE TO APPEAR . . . . _____
( ) # of Previous Court FTAs ____ : 1 to 3 points

6. RISK OF NEW OFFENSE . . . . _____
( ) Previously sustained new offense while pending court: 3

7. MITIGATING FACTORS (Can decrease by a total of 1-3 points–specify points) . . . . _____

( ) Stable & supportive family or caretaker	____	( ) Stability in school and/or employment ____
( ) First offense at 16 or older	____	( ) No arrests within the last year ____
( ) Successful completion of furlough, home supervision, or electronic monitoring	____	( ) Other (specify):_____ ____

8. AGGRAVATING FACTORS (Can increase by a total of 1-3 points–specify points) . . . . _____

( ) Witness intimidation	____	( ) Gang membership ____
( ) Runaway behavior from home	____	( ) Recalcitrant behavior/curfew ____
( ) Victim threats	____	( ) Misdemeanor high-speed chase ____
( ) Poor or no attendance at school	____	( ) Other (specify):_____ ____

9. MANDATORY DETENTION CASES (Add "M" along with total score) . . . . _____

( ) Escape from county institution	( ) Abscond from placement	( ) Placement failure
( ) Electronic monitoring arrest	( ) Home supervision arrest	( ) Furlough failure
( ) Weapons–personal use of firearm in commission of felony offense		

DETENTION DECISION (check):   TOTAL SCORE _____

( ) Detain (10 or more points)   ( ) Release without restriction (0-5 points)
( ) Release to non-secure detention (6-9 points)
_____ Home Supervision _____ Shelter _____ Other

OVERRIDE DECISION (specify reason):
( ) Parent/guardian refusal to pick up   ( ) Threat to public safety   ( ) Likely to flee
( ) Unable to reach parent/guardian   ( ) Victim threats or victim resides in home   ( ) Safety of minor
( ) Other (specify):_____

Explain decision on back.

Adapted from Sacramento County Pretrial Juvenile Detention Risk Assessment

---

Detain or Release

In this activity, students role play juvenile probation officers in charge of intake at a juvenile facility in a large city.

1. Form pairs. Each pair will determine whether juveniles remain in detention or are released to their parents. Each pair should:
   a. Use the **Sacramento Pre-Trial Juvenile Detention Risk Assessment** to help make the decisions. But regardless of the score, you make the final decision to release or detain the juvenile.
   b. Review the **Six Sample Cases** on pages 308–309.
   c. Score each case on a sheet of paper.
   d. Make a recommendation to release or detain. If your recommendation goes against the Risk Assessment's recommendation, write an explanation for your decision. If the two of you cannot agree on a case, write down both your decisions.
2. Students should explain their decisions to the whole class.
3. Debrief the activity using the questions below.

Debriefing Questions

1. On which cases did most people agree with the Risk Assessment recommendation? Were there some cases that most people disagreed with its recommendation? Why?
2. Are there other criteria that you believe should be added? Some that should be changed? Why?
3. What sorts of juveniles, if any, should be held in custody before their hearings? Why?

WIC 707(b) Offenses for Risk Assessment

Murder
Arson of an inhabited building
Armed robbery
Rape
Kidnapping
Assault with a deadly weapon
Aggravated assault
Discharging a firearm in an inhabited building

CASE #1

Name: Tom Sugino   **Age: 16**   **Charge: Motor vehicle theft** (felony)

Circumstances: Late one Thursday night, Sugino and a 19-year-old friend hot-wired an expensive sports car parked in the garage of an apartment complex where both worked as maintenance workers. They drove the car 120 miles to an ocean-side resort. The theft was discovered approximately 48 hours later when the two young men were arrested for disorderly conduct.

Previous Record: Three recorded detentions by police, all within the last 12 months, two for curfew violations, one for underage drinking. Released on summary probation, without formal adjudication, in all three instances.

Personal Background: Junior in high school — an average student with an average attendance record. Only child, father deceased, lives with mother who works nights as a waitress and with his elderly grandmother. Part-time work since age 14, fired from current job because of this incident. One psychologist's report indicates normal profile. Another suggests serious emotional disturbance as a result of father's death.

CASE #2

Name: Linda Dubrensky   **Age: 15**   **Charge: Selling narcotics** (felony)

Circumstances: Dubrensky's arrest came from police undercover work at a local community college where Dubrensky, a high school junior, was not enrolled. After selling small amounts of heroin to police agents posing as students, Dubrensky volunteered to set up a major purchase for agents. In the middle of this $100,000 transaction, both Dubrensky and her 35-year-old supplier were arrested.

Previous Record: Two recorded police contacts (one for curfew violation) in the last year. One prior juvenile adjudication for possession of heroin about eight months ago. Served one month in the County Home for Girls; six months participation in a diversion program for drug abusers.

Personal Background: School records indicate a moderate rate of truancy, a bright student who does not work up to potential. No work record. Medical report indicates that Dubrensky is addicted to heroin. Family of two children, mother, stepfather. Mother works as a tax accountant, stepfather is a currently unemployed aerospace engineer; both are members of Alcoholics Anonymous.

CASE #3

Name: Martin Robinson   **Age: 16**   **Charge: Armed robbery,**
                                                      first-degree murder (felonies)

Circumstances: Robinson and three other juveniles, two armed with handguns, robbed a local market. One owner pulled a gun and in the following shootout, the owner, a 66-year-old woman, was killed. Robinson was not armed and did not shoot the woman, but he did most of the talking during the robbery. Robinson and two others, both 14, were apprehended shortly after the incident. The fourth suspect, a 15-year-old, is still at large.

Previous Record: None

Personal Background: School records indicate a high rate of truancy. Minimal work record, no steady job at time of arrest. Psychiatric report indicates severe emotional disturbance. Family of three children, mother, grandmother. The mother works as a store clerk.

(Continued on next page.)

CASE #4

Name: Patricia Ann Warner   **Age: 15**   **Charge: Breaking and entering, burglary** (felony)

Circumstances: Warner and her 20-year-old boyfriend broke through the back windows of a local electronics shop after neutralizing the alarm. Police on patrol detected the crime in progress. Warner was apprehended carrying a flat-screen television to the car. Her boyfriend was picked up several blocks away attempting to escape. In the car, police found a home computer, tablet computers, and other equipment with an estimated total value of more than $9,000.

Previous Record: Two prior detentions for questioning by police. One resulted when Warner and a 32-year-old female companion were picked up for selling dinnerware from the back of a van. Neither female had a bill of sale for the merchandise. Because of her youth, Warner was released without charge. Her companion was cited for peddling without a license, a misdemeanor. One juvenile adjudication for marijuana possession about nine months ago. Spent 10 weeks enrolled in a diversion program.

Personal Background: School records indicate a high rate of truancy; poor scholastic achievement probably caused by a minor learning disability. No work record. Psychological reports indicate emotional instability and suggest the possibility of child abuse in the Warner home. She is the oldest of four children; both parents presently are employed at blue-collar jobs.

CASE #5

Name: Tom Kennedy   **Age: 16**   **Charge: Possession of a concealed weapon** (misdemeanor)

Circumstances: Kennedy, not a gang member, has to contend with two rival neighborhood gangs. Although he knows members of both and has been approached to join, he has resisted. Three days ago, a rumor circulated around the school that one gang was out to kill him. Fearing for his life, Tom took his father's unloaded revolver to school the next day. He let word out through his friends that he had a gun and that "nobody had better mess with me." Hearing about Tom's threat, a security guard stopped Tom, frisked him, and called the police.

Previous Record: None.

Personal Background: School records indicate a poor student, but teachers consider him bright. No work record. Family of four children, three younger sisters. Both parents present in home. Father unemployed and has drinking problem. Mother supports family as a cashier in a supermarket.

CASE #6

Name: Roger Duncan   **Age: 16**   **Charge: Arson** (felony)

Circumstances: Roger and a 20-year-old friend set fire to an apartment building under construction in their neighborhood. Roger's mother had been served with an eviction notice earlier in the week. The landlord also owned the burned building. A neighbor saw the two boys fleeing the scene. They were taken into custody the following day.

Previous Record: Three prior detentions in the last year. One month ago was put on probation for shoplifting.

Personal Background: School records indicate a moderate rate of truancy and low scholastic achievement. No work record. Family of five children, two of whom are in jail. Mother present in home. Father's whereabouts unknown.

CHAPTER 20
CHILDREN &
THE CONSTITUTION

From the inception of the juvenile court system, wide differences have been tolerated — indeed insisted upon — between the procedural rights accorded to adults and those of juveniles. In practically all jurisdictions, there are rights granted to adults which are withheld from juveniles.
– Supreme Court Justice Abe Fortas, *In re Gault* (1967)

THE RIGHTS OF JUVENILES | SCHOOL SEARCHES | SCHOOL DRUG TESTING

The Rights of Juveniles

The powers of the Star Chamber were a trifle in comparison with those of our juvenile courts.
– Roscoe Pound, legal scholar and dean of Harvard Law School from 1916 to 1936

Parens patriae, "individualized treatment," and "the best interests of the child" are the cornerstones of the juvenile justice system. Children are delinquents, not criminals; they are not imprisoned; they are detained. This special treatment is often necessary and beneficial. It can also raise serious constitutional questions. What provisions of the Constitution and Bill of Rights apply to juveniles? Which do not? The Supreme Court has faced these problems many times. Consider the following landmark case.

The Phone Call

On the evening of June 8, 1964, Mr. and Mrs. Gault of Maricopa County, Arizona, returned from work and couldn't find their 15-year-old son, Gerry. He wasn't at school. He wasn't with any of his friends. After a frantic search, they finally found out police had taken their son to the Children's Detention Home. Gerry had been arrested that afternoon for allegedly making an obscene phone call to a neighbor.

The Gaults rushed to get their son, but the Detention Home would not release him. Instead, the family was told a hearing would be held about Gerry's case the next day. On June 9, an Arizona probation officer filed a petition with the juvenile court. It stated that Gerry was a delinquent minor, but it contained no details about his alleged crime. Gerry and his parents were not told he could consult an attorney or refuse to answer questions. The offended neighbor wasn't even present at the hearing.

After it was over, Gerry was sent back to the Detention Home.

When Gerry was released a few days later, his mother received a notice of another hearing on June 15. Again, the neighbor was absent. Again, no records were kept. When it was over, the juvenile court judge committed Gerald Gault, a juvenile delinquent, to the Arizona State Industrial School until he reached age 21. In other words, Gerry received a six-year sentence. The maximum adult punishment for his alleged crime was a $50 fine and two months in jail.

The Gaults immediately filed a petition of habeas corpus on Gerry's behalf, arguing that their son had been denied his due process rights. The Arizona state courts, however, denied the petition. Because the adult and juvenile systems had different aims, explained the Arizona Supreme Court, they required different definitions of due process. If the state applied strict adult regulations to juvenile cases, it could not provide the individualized justice that was the heart of the juvenile system. Though Gerry's treatment did not meet adult due process requirements, the boy had not been treated differently from other juveniles. Arizona agencies had followed their normal procedures, and the decision to confine the boy was therefore upheld.

Unconvinced, the Gaults appealed to the U.S. Supreme Court. In 1967, the high court responded, shaking the foundation of the American juvenile justice system. A majority of five justices reversed the Arizona ruling and granted the Gaults' habeas corpus petition.

In *Re Gault* (1967)

Prior to *Gault*, U.S. courts had upheld the idea that young people had a right "not to liberty, but to custody." In other words, their right

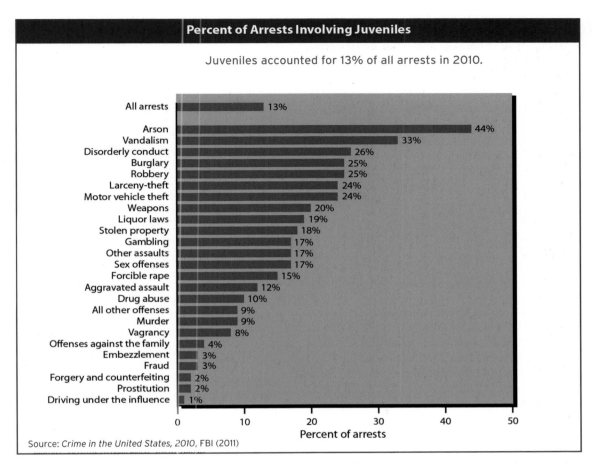

Percent of Arrests Involving Juveniles

Juveniles accounted for 13% of all arrests in 2010.

Category	Percent of arrests
All arrests	13%
Arson	44%
Vandalism	33%
Disorderly conduct	26%
Burglary	25%
Robbery	25%
Larceny-theft	24%
Motor vehicle theft	24%
Weapons	20%
Liquor laws	19%
Stolen property	18%
Gambling	17%
Other assaults	17%
Sex offenses	17%
Forcible rape	15%
Aggravated assault	12%
Drug abuse	10%
All other offenses	9%
Murder	9%
Vagrancy	8%
Offenses against the family	4%
Embezzlement	3%
Fraud	3%
Forgery and counterfeiting	2%
Prostitution	2%
Driving under the influence	1%

Percent of arrests

Source: *Crime in the United States, 2010,* FBI (2011)

to protection outweighed their right to independence. In the *Gault* decision, the Supreme Court held that juveniles, just like adults, have a vested interest in not getting locked up. It makes no difference whether the jail is called a reform school, a detention home, or a prison. Any juvenile proceeding that could lead to confinement must follow minimum standards of fairness and due process.

The majority opinion explicitly stated what some of these standards were.

1. **Defendants must be informed of the charges against them.** Notice of the charges is an essential element of a fair trial. Until he found himself in a hearing room, neither Gerry nor his parents knew the charges against him. The official petition, which the Gaults did not see prior to the hearing, said only that Gerry was "in need of protection of this Honorable Court." The Supreme Court was not satisfied with this general charge. Detained juveniles and their parents must be told specifically what conduct is under question and why a hearing is being held. Moreover, this information must be provided well

in advance of the hearing so the accused can prepare a response.

2. **All young people subject to confinement have a right to an attorney and must be informed of this right.** The state must provide attorneys for those too poor to afford legal fees. In theory, the hearing and probation officers were supposed to be looking out for young people's best interest. But since confinement is so much like punishment, the court decided that young people needed legal counsel. Attorneys would also help young people better understand what was happening to them in the juvenile justice process.

3. **Before questioning at hearings, juvenile court judges must inform young persons of their right to remain silent.** In addition, if a young person refuses to answer questions, that refusal cannot be used as an indication of guilt. Under oath during the habeas corpus proceedings, Gerry's hearing officer testified that at both hearings the boy had confessed to making the offensive phone call. Also under oath, Gerry's mother, who was present at both hearings,

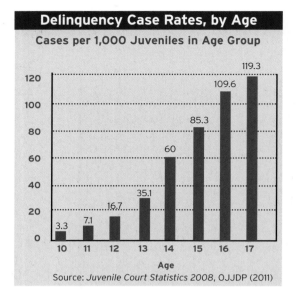

Delinquency Case Rates, by Age

Cases per 1,000 Juveniles in Age Group

Age	10	11	12	13	14	15	16	17
	3.3	7.1	16.7	35.1	60	85.3	109.6	119.3

Source: *Juvenile Court Statistics 2008*, OJJDP (2011)

denied this claim. She asserted that her son only confessed to dialing the phone, but that another boy had done all the talking. The Supreme Court announced that the conflicting testimony was irrelevant because neither Gerry nor his family had been informed of the boy's right to remain silent. The Constitution protected juveniles as well as adults from self-incrimination.

4. **Juveniles have the right to cross-examine their accusers.** The neighbor who accused Gerry Gault never appeared at a hearing to confirm her accusation or explain why she blamed Gerry for the phone call. The Supreme Court decided that was not fair. Confronting and questioning witnesses is an important part of determining the validity of evidence.

Though it marked the first big step in asserting juveniles' rights, the *Gault* decision was also significant because of the rights it did not guarantee. The court refused to apply its due process requirements to cases where the detained juvenile was sent to a foster home or in other ways "set free." Nor did it insist that juveniles receive all the constitutional protections available to adults. *Gault* left questions about whether other constitutional issues (such as the exclusionary rule, *Miranda* warnings, and the rights to speedy, public, and jury trials) applied to juveniles.

In a series of cases in the 1970s, the Supreme Court ruled on some of these constitutional issues. But in 1984 in *Schall v. Martin*, the Supreme Court reaffirmed the basic principle of the juvenile justice system — *parens patriae*. In

that case, New York authorities had charged Gregory Martin with robbery, assault, and possession of a weapon. They held him in custody until his adjudicatory hearing under the New York Family Court Act. The act allowed detaining for 17 days juveniles who might commit further crimes before their hearing.

Martin challenged in federal court his detention and that of other juveniles under the act. The District Court and Court of Appeals ruled that his detention violated due process. They pointed out that the "vast majority of juvenile detained" under the act "either have their petitions dismissed" or are released after a hearing. They concluded that the act "is utilized principally, not for preventive purposes, but to impose punishment for unadjudicated criminal acts."

The case was appealed to the Supreme Court, which voted 6–3 to uphold the act. The court recognized that juveniles have an interest in liberty. "But," stated the court, "that interest must be qualified by the recognition that juveniles, unlike adults, are always in some form of custody. . . . They are assumed to be subject to the control of their parents, and if parental control falters, the State must play its part as *parens patriae*." In this role, the state was locking Martin up prior to his hearing to protect him and the community from further wrongdoing. This, said the court, was a legitimate state interest. In fact, the court noted that every state has laws allowing for preventive detention of juveniles accused of crime. It found that New York provided procedures to prevent "erroneous and unnecessary deprivations of liberty." Juveniles were given a hearing, and judges had to state their reasons in writing if they decided to detain a juvenile.

FOR DISCUSSION

1. Why do you think Gerry Gault's hearing officer decided that the 15 year old was delinquent and in need of the state's protection? Do you think Gerry could be defined as delinquent? Why or why not?

2. What rights did the Supreme Court guarantee juveniles in the *Gault* decision? What rights were not guaranteed?

3. It has been said that *In Re Gault* "shook the American juvenile justice system to its foundations." How did it contradict the philosophy behind our juvenile justice system?

4. Do you agree with the court's decision in *Schall*? Why or why not?

The Court Decides

In the years since Gerry Gault's release, the Supreme Court has been asked to answer some of the questions raised by the *Gault* decision. The facts and arguments of five of these important cases are noted below. In this activity, students role play Supreme Court justices and decide these cases.

1. Form courts consisting of an odd number of students (three or five is preferable).
2. Each court should decide one of the **Five Important Juvenile Justice Cases** (pages 313–317). Be sure that each case is heard by at least one court.
3. Each court should:
   a. Appoint one member as court chief justice to lead the discussions.
   b. Read and discuss the facts and arguments of its case.
   c. Have the chief justice poll the justices one at a time to express an opinion on the issues of the case (majority wins).
   d. Have one representative report its decision and the reasons behind it to the class as a whole. If some members of the group disagree with the decision, have a second representative report the minority opinion.
4. Debrief the activity using the questions below.

Debriefing Questions

1. What decision did each student court reach? Compare your decisions with those made by the U.S. Supreme Court, noted in the teacher's guide.
2. What are some of the advantages of applying the reasonable-doubt standard of proof in juvenile cases? What are some of the disadvantages?
3. How might making juvenile hearings public help society? Help accused individuals? Why might this be harmful to society?
4. If you were accused of an unlawful act, would you prefer a jury trial or a delinquency hearing? Why? Would you want proceedings at your trial made public? Explain.
5. If juveniles were given jury trials, who should serve on the jury? The juvenile's peers? Adults? A mixture of both groups? Why?
6. Do you think double jeopardy protection should attach to juvenile hearings? Why or why not?

Five Important Juvenile Justice Cases

CASE #1: A Standard of Proof

In Re Winship (1970)

Adults can be convicted of crimes only if their guilt is proved beyond a reasonable doubt. In non-criminal cases, the standard of proof is different. To win a civil suit, parties normally only have to have the greater amount of evidence — the "preponderance of evidence," as it is known. Since New York considered juvenile proceedings to be civil, its legislature passed a law stating that delinquency did not have to be proved beyond a reasonable doubt. Juvenile courts could declare a young person delinquent based on a preponderance of the evidence.

Samuel Winship was 12 years old when brought before a New York juvenile court for allegedly stealing $112 from a woman's purse. Based on a preponderance of the evidence, the judge found Samuel delinquent and committed him to a training school until he reached age 18. After state courts upheld the commitment, Samuel appealed his case to the Supreme Court.

On appeal, Samuel's attorneys argued that:
- Winship's commitment was, in effect, punishment for stealing the $112.
- Winship was being punished unfairly because his guilt had not been proved beyond a reasonable doubt.
- The reasonable-doubt standard is an integral part of due process guaranteed by the 14th Amendment.

(Continued on next page.)

Attorneys for the state on appeal claimed that:

- Winship's commitment was not punishment. The court made no determination about his guilt. Juvenile courts do not determine guilt because it does not fit the purpose of the juvenile justice system.
- If forced to apply the stricter reasonable-doubt standard, juvenile courts would lose their informality and personalized justice, which are why these courts exist.
- The reasonable-doubt standard comes from English common law. It is not expressly required by the Constitution or the 14th Amendment.
- Each state legislature has the right to determine the standard of proof most appropriate to its own citizens.

Issue for Decision:

Does due process, as guaranteed by the Constitution and its 14th Amendment, require that juvenile courts apply the reasonable-doubt standard?

CASE #2: Public Trial
In Re Burrus (1971)

Barbara and her friends experienced precisely the kind of treatment the Sixth Amendment guarantee of a public trial was meant to prohibit. The young people were convicted and sentenced for activities that were at heart political. Had the case been heard in public, this abuse of the judicial power probably would not have occurred.

Attorneys for the young people requested that their juvenile hearings be opened to the general public.

The hearing officer denied the request and excluded the general public from the hearings. After the hearings, he declared the young people juvenile delinquents and committed them to an institution until they reached the age of majority. He then suspended all these commitments and placed all the offenders on probation.

An appeal to the North Carolina Supreme Court successfully reversed the commitments, but that court upheld the delinquency findings and ruled that a juvenile was not guaranteed a public trial under the Constitution. Lawyers for Burrus and her friends appealed the case to the U.S. Supreme Court.

On appeal, Burrus' attorneys argued that:

- The findings of delinquency were, in effect, convictions.
- The Sixth Amendment guarantees Americans a public trial by jury prior to conviction of a criminal offense.
- Barbara and her friends experienced precisely the kind of treatment the Sixth Amendment guarantee of a public trial was meant to prohibit. The young people were convicted and sentenced for activities that were at heart political. Had the case been heard in public, this abuse of the judicial power probably would not have occurred.

Opposing attorneys on appeal argued that:

- The findings of delinquency were not convictions and that the young people were never accused of crimes. Such accusations do not fit the spirit of juvenile justice.
- The Sixth Amendment mandates a public trial only in criminal prosecutions. A public trial was not therefore required by the Constitution.
- Privacy in juvenile proceedings protects the reputations of the young people involved.
- The issue of whether to give people public trials should be decided by the individual states.

Issue for Decision:

Under the Sixth Amendment of the Constitution, are juveniles entitled to a public trial in juvenile court?

(Continued on next page.)

CASE #3: Trial by Jury

McKeiver v. Pennsylvania (1971)

McKeiver, 15, had never been in trouble before. He joined a group of about 25 young friends as they chased three younger teenagers down the street. When the group caught up with their victims, they threatened the youngsters and took 25 cents from one boy. McKeiver and a 16-year-old friend were caught and charged with theft and assault. Both boys requested to have their cases tried by a jury, and in each instance, the request was denied. At their juvenile hearings, both teenagers were found to be delinquent. McKeiver was put on probation. His friend was committed to an institution. Ultimately, the case was appealed to the Supreme Court.

On appeal, McKeiver's attorneys claimed that:
- The State of Pennsylvania had interfered with both defendants' rights under the Sixth and 14th amendments by denying them trials by jury.
- Juvenile court proceedings are so similar to criminal trials that defendants' due process rights must be protected.
- Trial by jury is one of the most fundamental of all American due process rights.
- If accused of McKeiver's alleged offense, an adult would have been given a jury trial. It was unfair to discriminate against McKeiver and his friend merely on the basis of their ages.

Attorneys for the state of Pennsylvania on appeal argued that:
- The Constitution only mandates trials by jury in criminal cases.
- No matter how many similar features the two processes share, a juvenile proceeding is not a criminal prosecution. A juvenile hearing differs both in philosophy and in practice from a criminal prosecution.
- A judge or hearing officer is just as competent to determine facts as a jury would be.
- Giving juveniles jury trials would destroy the system's design as a protective mechanism for handling young people in trouble. Government studies have recommended against using jury trials for juveniles.
- Each state should be allowed to decide whether it wishes to extend the right to a jury trial to young people in its own jurisdiction.

Issue for Decision:

Under the Sixth and 14th amendments to the Constitution, are juveniles entitled to a jury trial in juvenile court?

CASE #4: Protection Against Double Jeopardy

Breed v. Jones (1975)

The Fifth Amendment states that no person shall "be subject for the same offense to be twice put in jeopardy . . . ." Simply put, this means that no person can be tried twice for the same crime.

But there are instances where defendants are put on trial twice, which are not considered double jeopardy. Consider the following examples:
- A jury is unable to reach a verdict in George's murder trial. The judge declares a mistrial. George may be tried again.
- George is found guilty of murder. On appeal, an appellate court overturns his conviction because the prosecution introduced illegally obtained evidence at the trial. George may be retried without the illegal evidence.

But the following are clear examples of double jeopardy:

(Continued on next page.)

- State X tries George for murder. A jury finds him not guilty. State X may not try George again for the same murder.
- State X tries George for murder. A jury finds him guilty and sentences him to 20 years in prison. State X may not try George again for the same murder when he gets out of prison.

Jones, 17, allegedly committed an armed robbery. Taken to Los Angeles County Juvenile Court, he was detained until a petition against him was heard. At the adjudicatory hearing, two prosecution witnesses testified, and Jones testified in his own defense. The juvenile court judge found him delinquent. At the dispositional hearing two weeks later, the juvenile court judge found that Jones did not belong in the juvenile system. The judge ruled that Jones should be tried as an adult. Over objections by the defense attorney that Jones had already been tried, Jones was transferred for trial. In adult court, he was tried, convicted, and sentenced for armed robbery.

On appeal, Jones' attorneys claimed that:
- Because Jones had already been tried in juvenile court for armed robbery, his trial in adult court violated his right against double jeopardy guaranteed by the Fifth Amendment.
- Juvenile court hearings are essentially criminal hearings. They determine whether the juvenile committed an offense and they may take away the juvenile's liberty.
- Applying double-jeopardy protection to juvenile court proceedings will help adjudicatory hearings. Juveniles will be more cooperative if they know what they say will not be held against them in adult court.
- If juveniles are to be transferred to adult court, this must be done before any adjudication in juvenile court.

Attorneys for the state of California on appeal argued that:
- The Constitution only protects against double jeopardy in criminal prosecutions.
- Juvenile court hearings are not criminal proceedings. The juvenile system tries to rehabilitate delinquents. All the court did was determine that Jones did not belong in the juvenile system.
- Even if double jeopardy applies to juvenile proceedings, the adult court proceedings were merely part of the same process as the juvenile court proceedings. Jones was only going to be punished once for his offense. Therefore his trial in adult court did not amount to double jeopardy.
- Juvenile court proceedings are informal and need to be flexible to best treat juveniles' interests.

Issue for Decision:

Under the Fifth and 14th amendments to the Constitution, does an adjudicatory hearing in juvenile court and a subsequent trial in adult court for the same offense amount to double jeopardy?

(Continued on next page.)

CASE #5: *Miranda* **Rules for Juveniles**

J.D.B. v. North Carolina **(2011)**

A seventh grader, J.D.B. was called out of class by a uniformed police officer and taken to a school conference room. Behind closed doors, police questioned him about two home break-ins and thefts. Another police officer and two school administrators were also in the conference room. Questioned for more than half an hour and advised by the vice principal to "do the right thing," J.D.B. finally confessed that he and a friend had committed the break-ins. J.D.B. was never read the *Miranda* warnings nor was he advised that he was free to leave the conference room. When the school bell rang at the end of the day, J.D.B. was allowed to go home.

A petition was filed in juvenile court against J.D.B. At an adjudicatory hearing, J.D.B.'s confession was admitted into evidence over the objections of his defense attorney. The court found J.D.B. delinquent.

On appeal, J.D.B.'s attorneys argued that the court should have ruled his confession inadmissible. His attorneys claimed:

- When J.D.B. was questioned, he was in custody and therefore he should have received *Miranda* warnings.
- To determine whether someone is in custody, courts look at the objective circumstances. Age should be considered as one of the objective circumstances.
- J.D.B., age 13, was surrounded by authority figures, in a strange room, behind closed doors. He had no reason to believe he could get up and leave the room. Studies have shown that juveniles under 16 are more likely to obey adult authority in a legal setting.

Attorneys for the state of North Carolina argued:

- When J.D.B. was questioned, he was not in custody, and therefore no *Miranda* warnings were required.
- The test of whether someone is in custody is an objective test. It is not a test of whether someone *felt* he was in custody. Age has never been considered as part of the objective test.
- To add age as a factor introduces subjectivity and makes it difficult for a police officer to determine whether someone is in custody. It would open the door to other subjective factors such as intelligence, maturity, and prior involvement with the law.

Issue for Decision:

Must police consider a juvenile's age when determining whether he is custody for *Miranda* purposes?

School Searches

In carrying out searches and other disciplinary functions pursuant to such policies, school officials act as representatives of the State, not merely as surrogates for the parents, and they cannot claim the parents' immunity from the strictures of the Fourth Amendment.

– Supreme Court Justice Byron White, *New Jersey v. T.L.O.* (1985)

Since its *Gault* decision, the Supreme Court has ruled several times on the rights of juveniles. It has held that the Fourth Amendment applies to juveniles as well as adults. But does it apply to students in school? Does it restrict searches by school officials? Or are these officials merely filling a parental role and, acting as parents, can they conduct searches without restrictions from the Fourth Amendment? The Supreme Court has made two important rulings on searches by school officials.

New Jersey v. T.L.O. (1985)

In 1985 in *New Jersey v. T.L.O.*, the court decided how the Fourth Amendment applied to high school students. In this case, a high school teacher caught T.L.O. smoking in the girl's bathroom. (The court used the student's initials to avoid disclosing her identity, which is New Jersey's policy for juveniles.) When taken to the vice principal, T.L.O. denied smoking and said she had never smoked. The vice principal took T.L.O.'s purse and searched it. Finding cigarettes

and rolling papers, he kept searching. He found marijuana, plastic bags, a roll of dollar bills, and a customer list. So he called the police.

Charged with possession of marijuana with intent to sell, T.L.O. was found delinquent by a juvenile court. T.L.O. appealed the finding, arguing that the search of her purse violated her Fourth Amendment rights. The case ultimately went to the U.S. Supreme Court.

The state of New Jersey argued that the Fourth Amendment only applied to police searches, not to searches by school officials. The Supreme Court rejected this argument. The amendment covered searches by all government officials.

The court similarly rejected New Jersey's claim that because school officials must closely supervise students, students have no reasonable expectation of privacy "in articles of personal property 'unnecessarily' carried into a school." The court stated that students routinely bring legitimate personal items to school — keys, money, pictures, diaries — and there is no reason to deny students an expectation of privacy in these items.

But the court also recognized that schools need to maintain discipline. To determine whether the search was reasonable and constitutional, the court balanced the student's expectation of privacy against the school's need for discipline. In doing so, it made two important decisions about school searches:

- **School officials do not need warrants.** Requiring warrants would disrupt the informal discipline procedures necessary to run a school. All the members of the court agreed with this conclusion.
- **School officials do not need probable cause.** All searches, whether with or without a warrant, traditionally require probable cause. Probable cause means that the facts leading up to the search must be strong enough that an independent, cautious person would have good reason to believe that the person committed a crime (or school infraction). Again, because of the school setting, the court felt school officials needed a lesser standard. The court settled on "reasonableness" as the new standard for school searches. Two justices dissented from the court's decision to abandon the traditional, well-defined probable cause standard.

Since T.L.O. denied smoking, the court found it reasonable for the vice principal to investigate the teacher's accusation by searching T.L.O.'s purse for cigarettes. Once he found the rolling papers, the court believed it was reasonable for him to continue searching the purse. So the court found the search constitutional.

All the justices agreed that school officials do not need search warrants. The dissenters, however, believed that the standard for a school search should be probable cause, the standard set in the Fourth Amendment. The principal had probable cause to search the purse for cigarettes, but once finding them, had no probable cause to continue rummaging through her purse.

Safford Union School Dist. #1 v. Redding (2009)

Safford Middle School in Safford, Arizona, had a policy against students' bringing any drugs on campus, including prescription and over-the-counter drugs. In October 2003, a student told administrators that students were bringing drugs and weapons to school and that he had gotten sick from taking pills another student had given him. A week later, the boy handed the vice principal a prescription-strength ibuprofen pill. He said he had gotten the pill from Marissa Glines and that students were planning on taking pills at lunch. The vice principal called Glines into his office. Her teacher had given the vice principal a day planner, which the teacher had found near Glines in the classroom. Inside the day planner were knives, lighters, and a cigarette. He asked Glines to turn out her pockets and open her wallet. He discovered several ibuprofen and one naproxen (these are anti-inflammatory and pain pills). He sent Glines to the nurse's office, where she was asked to disrobe to her underwear and to pull out her bra to the side and shake it and to pull the elastic open on her panties. No more pills were found.

Glines had told the vice principal that she had gotten the pills from her friend Savana Redding, a 13 year old. When Redding was called into his office, he asked her about the day planner. She admitted it was hers, but said she had lent it to Glines days ago and knew nothing about the things found in it. She also denied knowing anything about the pills. She consented to the vice principal's search of her backpack, which turned up nothing. Then he sent her to the nurse for a search of her clothing and a strip search. Nothing was found.

When Redding's mother learned of the search, she filed suit against the school district for violating her daughter's Fourth Amendment rights. The District Court dismissed the lawsuit, and the case was appealed, and it finally reached the Supreme Court.

By an 8–1 vote, the Supreme Court ruled that the strip search violated Redding's Fourth Amendment rights. The court found that the vice principal had reasonable suspicion to search Redding's backpack and outer clothing, but he went too far in asking the nurse to conduct a strip search.

> In sum, what was missing from the suspected facts that pointed to Savana was any indication of danger to the students from the power of the drugs or their quantity, and any reason to suppose that Savana was carrying pills in her underwear. We think that the combination of these deficiencies was fatal to finding the search reasonable.

On other grounds, however, the court ruled that the lawsuit could not go forward.

FOR DISCUSSION

1. What two rulings on school searches did the Supreme Court make in *T.L.O.*? Do you agree with the rulings? Explain.
2. Do you agree with the ruling in the *Safford* case? Explain. If you do agree, can you think of a situation when a strip search would be reasonable? Explain.

Applying T.L.O.

The federal courts have heard various challenges to school searches following the T.L.O. decision. In this activity, students role play federal appeals courts and decide cases on schools and the Fourth Amendment.

1. Divide into small groups. Each group will role play a federal appeals court and decide three cases. The issue in each is: Did this search violate the Fourth Amendment?
2. Each group should do the following:
   a. Read and discuss each case below.
   b. Decide in light of the *T.L.O.* decision whether the search in each case is reasonable.
   c. Be prepared to report to the class on the decision in each case and the reasons for the decision.
3. Regroup and have one group report on Case #1. Hold a class discussion on the case. Repeat this process for each case.

CASE #1: *Bridgman v. New Trier High School* (1997). Caught smoking twice, Andrew Bridgman, a freshman at New Trier Township High School in Illinois, was sent to an after-school stop-smoking program. At the program, Bridgman was giggling, and in the opinion of the program coordinator, acting unruly and distracted. She noticed that Bridgman's eyes were bloodshot, his pupils dilated, his handwriting erratic, and some of his answers were "flippant." She took Bridgman into another room and asked him if he was on drugs. Bridgman said no. She took him to the nurse's office, and the nurse took his blood pressure and pulse rate, which were elevated. The nurse did not conclude from these tests that Bridgman was on drugs. The nurse saw that Bridgman's pupils were dilated, but did not think his eyes were bloodshot or that he was acting strangely. The coordinator told Bridgman to take off his shirt and hat and empty his pockets. When Bridgman sarcastically asked whether she wanted him to remove his shoes and socks, she said yes. Bridgman kept on his undershirt and pants. Following this, Bridgman's mother arrived and took him home. The next day, she took him to a doctor, who gave him a drug test, which showed Bridgman was not on drugs. Bridgman sued, claiming the search violated the Fourth Amendment.

CASE #2: *DesRoches v. Caprio* (1998). At Granby High School, a public high school in Norfolk, Virginia, a student left a pair of girls' tennis shoes on her desk during lunch. The class met both before and after lunch. When she returned, the shoes were missing. The teacher had been in the classroom for most of the lunch period, but the door was unlocked, and students from the class had been in and out. Students also reported seeing one unidentified student not from the class enter the room. After a search around the classroom, the teacher reported the incident to the dean of students. A ring had gone missing from the same class the day before. The dean decided to search the belongings of all 19 students in the class. When he asked if anyone objected, James DesRoches and another student raised their hands. The dean informed them that school policy authorized a 10-day suspension for any student who refused to consent. The other student changed his mind and consented, but DesRoches still refused. The dean searched the bags and backpacks of the other students and found nothing. The dean took DesRoches to the principal's office, DesRoches still refused, and he was suspended for 10 days. DesRoches sued in federal court, claiming the search demanded of him was unconstitutional.

CASE #3: *Brannum v. Overton School Board* (2008). As a security measure, the school board had video surveillance cameras installed at Livingston Middle School in Tennessee. Cameras were placed throughout the school, including in the boys' and girls' locker rooms. The recorded images were sent to the vice principal's computer and stored on its hard drive. Shortly after the cameras were installed, the vice principal reported to the principal that the cameras were recording students dressing for sports. The principal left the cameras as they were. The recordings were accessible via the Internet, but a user would have to know the default user name and password (which were never changed). The cameras operated for about a year and a half until a visiting girls' basketball team complained about them. When the director of schools was notified, he viewed the pictures via the Internet and ordered the cameras removed from the locker rooms. Thirty-four students sued the district, claiming their Fourth Amendment rights were violated.

School Drug Testing

Traditionally at common law, and still today, unemancipated minors lack some of the most fundamental rights of self-determination — including even the right of liberty in its narrow sense, i.e., the right to come and go at will. They are subject, even as to their physical freedom, to the control of their parents or guardians.
– Supreme Court Justice Antonin Scalia, *Vernonia School District v. Acton* (1995)

Drugs are a problem in America, and they pose a particular problem in schools. To quell drug use among students, some school districts have instituted random drug testing for students involved in particular activities. In other words, students must take a drug test regardless of whether school officials have any suspicion that the student takes drugs. The question is whether these searches can meet the reasonableness standard set in *T.L.O.*

In the *T.L.O.* case, the school suspected T.L.O. of wrongdoing. But the court explicitly said: "We do not decide whether individualized suspicion is an essential element of the reasonableness standard we adopt for searches by school authorities." Are random drug tests at schools reasonable and therefore constitutional? The Supreme Court has ruled twice on this question.

Vernonia School District v. Acton (1995)

In the late 1980s in the small logging community of Vernonia, Oregon, teachers reported an increase in drug use in the school district and a decline in school discipline. When the district discovered that student athletes were the leaders of the drug culture, the district, with parental approval, began a program of random drug testing for all student athletes. To participate in sports, students and their parents had to sign a permission slip giving their consent to random drug tests. All student athletes had to agree to provide urine samples in the presence of an adult monitor of the same sex. Samples were taken from everyone at the beginning of the sports season and then randomly throughout the season. Anyone who tested positive had to provide another sample. If that tested positive, then the student was given a choice of attending an assistance program with weekly drug tests or being suspended from the team for the remainder of the current season and next season. If caught a second time, students were automatically suspended for two seasons.

In 1991, seventh grader James Acton wanted to play football. But he and his parents refused to sign a permission slip for drug testing, and so school authorities refused to allow him to play. The Actons sued in federal court, claiming the school district had violated James' Fourth Amendment rights.

The case was eventually appealed to the U.S. Supreme Court. In *Vernonia School District v. Acton*, the Supreme Court in a 6–3 decision upheld the program. Writing for the majority, Justice Antonin Scalia cited three major factors in the decision. The first, and most important, factor was that a public school district serves "as guardian and tutor of children entrusted to its care." Students possess a lower expectation of privacy than adults. "Traditionally at common law, and still today . . . minors lack some of the most fundamental rights of self-determination — including even the right of liberty in its narrow sense, i.e., the right to come and go at will." The court said that athletes have an even lesser expectation of privacy than students in general. "Somewhat like adults who choose to participate in a 'closely regulated industry,' students who voluntarily participate in school athletics have reason to expect intrusions upon normal rights and privileges, including privacy."

The second factor was the minimal type of intrusion in this case. The court noted that during the testing, "male students produce

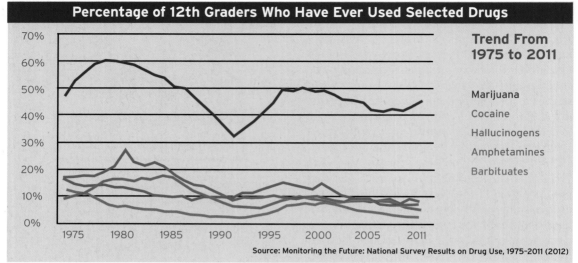

Percentage of 12th Graders Who Have Ever Used Selected Drugs

Trend From
1975 to 2011

Marijuana
Cocaine
Hallucinogens
Amphetamines
Barbituates

Source: Monitoring the Future: National Survey Results on Drug Use, 1975-2011 (2012)

samples at a urinal along a wall. They remain fully clothed and are only observed from behind, if at all. Female students produce samples in an enclosed stall, with a female monitor standing outside listening only for sounds of tampering." The court pointed out that the experience was similar to anyone using a public restroom. In addition, the court pointed out that a negative result on a drug test resulted only in a student not playing sports. The student was not disciplined further. Nor was the negative result turned over to the police for criminal charges.

The third factor was the state's compelling interest in the drug testing program. The district court found that the school was experiencing an epidemic of drug use and that the student body was in a "state of rebellion." The court also noted the studies showing increased risks of harm from drug addiction at younger ages and a specific increase in the likelihood of physical harm to athletes whose reaction times are slowed and whose ability to sense fatigue and pain is reduced.

Writing for the three dissenters, Justice Sandra Day O'Connor focused on the lack of any individualized suspicion in the program. The dissenters pointed out that the Fourth Amendment was written to prevent writs of assistance, which were used by the British in colonial times. These writs gave British officials the right to conduct blanket searches of people's homes without any suspicion of wrongdoing.

The dissenters argued that blanket searches constitute a great threat to liberty because they can affect many people. Under a blanket search,

authorities search everyone to find out if anyone is doing something wrong. This is different from individualized suspicion, when the authorities search someone they have reason to suspect of wrongdoing. This type of search affects only one person at a time.

The dissenters argued that blanket screening should be allowed only in special situations, when an individualized suspicion requirement would not work. They believed that *Vernonia* was not such a case. "The great irony of this case is that most (though not all) of the evidence the District introduced to justify its suspicionless drug-testing program consisted of first- or second-hand stories of particular, identifiable students acting in ways that plainly gave rise to reasonable suspicion of in-school drug use — and thus that would have justified a drug-related search under our *T.L.O.* decision." The dissenters would have required that evidence of individual disciplinary problems be used in support of individual searches.

The dissenters also rejected the court majority's belief that the searches were not intrusive. They noted that the testing of urine was more intrusive than other types of searches that triggered Fourth Amendment protection.

Board of Education v. Earls (2002)

Tecumseh, Oklahoma, is a rural community about 40 miles south of Oklahoma City. In 1998, the school board for Tecumseh adopted a new drug-testing policy. The policy was almost identical to that of the Vernonia School District except that it included all students involved in extracurricular activities. That meant, for example, that the middle and high schools tested members of the Academic Team, Future Farmers of America, Future Homemakers of America, band, choir, pompom squad, and cheerleaders as well as those on sports teams.

Unlike Vernonia, the Tecumseh school district was not experiencing an epidemic of drug abuse. But teachers had reported seeing students who appeared under the influence of drugs and overhearing students talking about using drugs. A drug-sniffing dog had found marijuana cigarettes near a school parking lot. Police had once found drugs in the car of a member of the Future Farmers of America. And community members had called the school district to complain about the drug problem.

In response to the new drug-testing policy, parents of two students filed suit in federal court. They claimed that the drug-testing policy violated their students' Fourth Amendment rights. The trial court rejected the suit. But the Court of Appeals reversed the trial court, finding the policy in violation of the Fourth Amendment. The court stated that the school board had failed to show any need for the policy. It held that to justify the policy, the board needed to "demonstrate that there is some identifiable drug abuse problem among a sufficient number of those subject to the testing" so that "testing that group of students will actually redress its drug problem."

The school board appealed to the U.S. Supreme Court. In a 5–4 decision *Board of Education v. Earls*, the court upheld the testing program, relying heavily on its analysis in *Vernonia*. Justice Clarence Thomas, writing for the majority, explained that "Fourth Amendment rights . . . are different in public schools . . . ." To determine whether the drug testing is reasonable, said Thomas, the court must balance the intrusion against the governmental interest in drug testing. The court majority found the intrusion to be the same as in *Vernonia*. The court went on to determine that the government interest in drug testing was strong. Thomas explained that the particular circumstances of the school's drug problem were irrelevant to the determination:

> Given the nationwide epidemic of drug use, and the evidence of increased drug use in Tecumseh schools, it was entirely reasonable for the School District to enact this particular drug testing policy. . . . Indeed, it would make little sense to require a school district to wait for a substantial portion of its students to begin using drugs before it was allowed to institute a drug testing program designed to deter drug use.

Justice Ruth Bader Ginsburg penned the dissent. She had voted with the majority in *Vernonia*. Her dissent stated that the majority opinion had abandoned a large part of the rationale in *Vernonia*, which hinged on the dangers particular to student athletes. The dissent pointed to the two reasons behind the majority's opinion in *Earls*: (1) the need to combat a nationwide drug epidemic and (2) the non-intrusive nature of urinalysis. She said these reasons would support drug testing for all students. "Had the *Vernonia* Court agreed that public school attendance, in and of itself, permitted the State to test each student's blood or urine for drugs, the opinion in *Vernonia* could have saved many words."

The dissent also noted that prior to the adoption of the policy, the school district had reported to the federal government that drugs and alcohol were not significant problems. The dissenters further suggested that the testing program might have the opposite effect intended and that drug users would simply withdraw from extracurricular activities.

FOR DISCUSSION

1. How was the *Vernonia* case different from *T.L.O.* and *Safford*? What was the school board's policy in this case? What did the court decide? Do you think it was the right decision? Explain.

2. How did the *Earls* decision extend the *Vernonia* decision? Do you agree with the majority or the dissenters in *Earls*? Why?

ASK AN EXPERT

You have read about the major U.S. Supreme Court decisions on the rights of juveniles in the justice system. The U.S. Constitution sets the minimum limits on what states may do. Many states have enacted laws expanding the rights of juveniles. For example, in some states, a trial by jury is required in juvenile cases. Ask a juvenile court judge or a lawyer who specializes in juvenile cases to find out what the law is in your state regarding interrogation of juveniles, school searches, and hearings in juvenile court.

Universal School Testing

Imagine that Temple Unified School District operates four high schools, nine middle schools, and 27 elementary schools. In the last year, an epidemic of drug use has hit the middle and high schools. Reacting to community and parental concern, the district has enacted the following policy:

All students will be required to take a drug test at the beginning of the year. Students have a choice of taking a urine or blood test. Students taking the urine test will be able to go to a private stall to provide the urine sample with an adult monitor of the same sex listening outside the stall. The blood test will be taken by the school nurse. During the school year, additional tests will be taken from names drawn at random. Anyone who tests positive must take another test. If that test is positive, then the student will be required to attend special anti-drug classes after school and be tested twice more during the year. Anyone in the special class who tests positive will be transferred to a special middle or high school. Anyone at that school who tests positive will be removed to a special part of the campus to take even more intensive anti-drug classes. No student failing a drug test will be turned over to the police, and all test results will remain confidential.

Parents of two students have challenged this policy as violating the students' Fourth Amendment rights.

In this activity, students role play attorneys and Supreme Court justices involved in this challenge.

The court will decide this issue: **Does the school board policy mandating drug tests for all middle and high school students in the district violate the Fourth Amendment?**

1. Form triads. A person in each group should take one of these roles: attorney for the school district, attorney for the two students, or justice of the Supreme Court.
2. Regroup so that all school district attorneys are together, attorneys for the two students are together, and justices of the Supreme Court are together. All students should discuss the cases in the article. The attorneys should develop arguments for their side, and the justices should create questions to ask both sides.
3. Return to the original triads. The justice in each group should allow each side to speak and can ask questions of each side.
4. When the courts are done, the justices should meet in the front of the room and discuss the case. Finally, each justice should vote and explain his or her reasons.

CHAPTER 21
JUVENILE CORRECTIONS

I've been struck by the upside-down priorities of the juvenile justice system. We are willing to spend the least amount of money to keep a kid at home, more to put him in a foster home, and the most to institutionalize him.
– Marian Wright-Edelman (1939–), president and founder of the Children's Defense Fund

OPTIONS FOR PLACING JUVENILES OFFENDERS | WHAT ARE THE BEST OPTIONS? | PROBLEMS WITH LOCKING UP JUVENILES | AT HOME PLUS | THE QUESTION OF WAIVER | CHRISTOPHER SIMMONS AND THE DEATH PENALTY | IMPORTANT CASES ON SENTENCING JUVENILES | CURRENT TRENDS AND CONTROVERSIES

Options for Placing Juvenile Offenders

We've just got to have a better youth released than the one that came into the criminal justice system.
– Texas state Senator John Whitmire, quoted in *Correctional News* (2012)

After finding juveniles delinquent, juvenile court judges must decide what to do with the young offenders. In the juvenile system, this is called making a disposition. As with adult court judges, they have a number of options. Judges try to choose the option that has the best chance of rehabilitating the particular delinquent youth. Depending on the jurisdiction, judges must choose among:

- **Juvenile detention centers.** These are facilities where juveniles are first brought. Many await their hearing here. Others await placement following disposition. But juveniles may also be confined in these centers, usually for short terms, following a finding of delinquency.

- **Training camps, or training schools.** Often located in rural settings, these large, state-run institutions typically hold from 100 to 1,000 juveniles. They are meant for the most serious offenders.

- **Small, secure residential facilities.** Holding only 10 to 15 juveniles and an equal number of staff, these facilities confine serious, violent offenders. They may be run by the state, but often small non-profit groups operate them.

- **Camps and ranches.** Located in rural areas, these secure facilities normally accommodate about 100 juveniles. They emphasize discipline and school work. Most offer counseling.

- **Boot camps.** Run like Army basic training, these camps subject juveniles to shaven heads, physical training, and strict discipline. Known as shock incarceration, boot camps take juveniles for short terms and try to shock them into changing their behavior.

- **Wilderness programs.** In rigorous outdoor settings, these programs try to build self-esteem and teamwork in troubled youth.

A crew from California's Pine Grove Youth Conservation Camp prepares to train in fire suppression.

Group homes. Often called halfway houses, these facilities typically house about 20 young people. Juveniles living in these homes often attend school, hold jobs, and move about the community. But they must obey house rules. Most group homes also provide counseling.

• **Substance-abuse treatment centers.** These residences focus on treating drug and alcohol abuse. Like halfway houses, they normally hold about 20 juveniles. But these facilities often limit residents' contact with the community during treatment.

• **Foster homes.** Screened by the state, families take juveniles into their homes. States set standards about food, clothing, and other treatment, and they limit the number of children a foster family may care for. In return, foster families receive a certain amount of money for each child's upkeep.

YOUTH COURT: AN ALTERNATIVE FOR OFFENDERS

Youth courts, also known as peer or teen courts, are a recent innovation in juvenile sentencing. Run by young volunteers, the courts hear cases and sentence their peers for non-violent offenses or problem behaviors. In most courts, young people take the roles of judge, prosecutor, defense attorney, and jurors.

Profile of Youth Court

Most Common Offenses:

1. Theft or shoplifting
2. Vandalism
3. Alcohol possession or use
4. Disorderly conduct
5. Minor assault

Most Common Sanctions:

1. Community service
2. Apology to victim
3. Written essay
4. Educational workshop
5. Jury duty on a youth court

Source: Facts and Stats, National Association of Youth Courts, www.youthcourt.net

Usually the courts do not determine whether the defendants are guilty. Instead, youthful offenders, often called *respondents*, must first admit their wrongdoing to be eligible for youth court. In all youth courts, a parent or guardian and the respondent must agree to participate.

Youth courts often handle cases that would otherwise be prosecuted in juvenile court, traffic court, or the school's disciplinary process. Most youth courts operate around partnerships among school, local government, and community organizations. Many youth courts work closely with local juvenile justice officials such as parole officers or juvenile counselors. Respondents who successfully complete a sentence handed down by a youth court generally avoid establishing a criminal record.

The courts are based on the theory that if peer pressure gets some young people in trouble, peer pressure might also serve to get them out of trouble. They teach young offenders that there are penalties to pay for misbehavior, and that these penalties can be fairly administered by their peers.

A study released by the Urban Institute compared recidivism rates of youth court defendants with those of similar defendants tried by the regular juvenile justice system. Using statistics from four well-established youth courts, the study found that after six months, youth court respondents had an 8 percent rate of recidivism as compared to an 18 percent recidivism rate of the defendants processed through the juvenile justice system.

FOR DISCUSSION
1. What are youth courts? What purposes do they serve?
2. Do you think youth courts are a good idea? Why or why not?

- **In-home placement.** Under this disposition, juveniles return to their homes.

When judges choose in-home placement or foster homes, they may have several more options to choose from

- **Diversion to day treatment programs.** These programs differ greatly. Some are all day, every day. Others meet after school or on weekends. Some replace school. Others teach about the legal system or the effects of substance abuse. Others provide supervised recreational activities. Juveniles diverted to these programs must attend for a specific length of time.
- **Intensive or highly intensive probation.** Working with few juveniles, probation officers meet often with them. In intensive probation, they meet every day. In highly intensive probation, they meet several times a day.
- **Probation.** Juveniles are released under fairly strict conditions. They may, for example, be required to:
  - report regularly to a probation officer,
  - stop associating with certain friends,
  - submit to home or body searches on request, and
  - take a weekly urine test (if they have been detained on a drug charge).

Juveniles who break the terms of their probation can be returned to court for an alternative disposition.
- **Summary probation.** After assuring the authorities that they will not misbehave, juveniles are released under parental or adult supervision. If they break their promise, the juveniles return to court for stricter treatment and supervision.

FOR DISCUSSION

1. The article lists many placement options. Which sounds least effective for juvenile offenders? The most effective? Why?
2. Are any of the options better suited to particular problems? Explain.

What Are the Best Options?

A judge in one county has many options to craft appropriate orders for young offenders. In the next county over, especially if it is an urban county, a judge may have very few options between probation and incarceration. That's like choosing between aspirin or a lobotomy for a migraine.
– Christine Todd Whitman (1946-), former governor of New Jersey

In most jurisdictions, judges do not have a vast array of options for placing juveniles. Thus they frequently either place juveniles on probation or send them to secure facilities, usually juvenile detention centers or training schools. Community placements and intensive probation are sometimes not available.

Their unavailability is ironic. The juvenile justice system has always encouraged community-based treatments for young people in trouble. Such programs can often more easily adapt to the needs of individual juveniles than institutional programs. But in the late 1970s, a public backlash against community programs arose after juvenile court judges began assigning violent offenders to programs designed for nonviolent offenders. In the 1980s and 1990s, opinions were mixed about both the safety and the effectiveness of rehabilitating delinquents in non-institutional settings.

States reacted with different programs to treat juvenile offenders. In some states the urge to get tough on young lawbreakers took control and laws were passed curbing judges' discretion in sentencing and mandating long periods of detention. Those states turned away from the traditional model of rehabilitation to one of punishment.

By 2000, however, the tide turned again. Juvenile rights groups brought lawsuits to close down large detention centers, and new laws were passed providing monetary incentives for community-based programs. Research results showed that community programs were more effective in preventing crime (and cost less) than lockups in training camps. And more attention has been given to the fact that a majority of youth in the juvenile detention centers suffer from problems with mental illness and drug abuse. Many states and counties now think that one of the most effective roads to rehabilitation is to keep offenders at home and to provide special mental health services to both the youth and to their parents.

Locking Up Youth in California

California was one of many states that adopted a tough-on-crime policy for juveniles in the 1980s and 1990s. The state built more secure facilities and sent juveniles to them for longer periods. Serious youth offenders were typically sent to training schools, often in remote locations, run by the state's Division of Juvenile Justice (before 2005, it was called the California Youth Authority). The state-run facilities were enormous structures, surrounded by guard towers, spotlights and barbed wire. In many of the facilities, youths were housed in solitary cells which were 8½ by 11 feet. Most had concrete beds, a sink, and a toilet, but no windows. In many cases, youths were confined to their rooms for 23 hours a day, and in some cases were not even released for the one hour required for "large muscle exercise."

In the late 1990s, things began to change. Legislators and the public became increasingly aware of abusive conditions in the state facilities. The *Los Angeles Times* and *San Jose Mercury News* began publishing reports of violence between inmates and between staff and inmates. They reported on inmate deaths from homicide and suicide. The state Senate held public hearings about allegations of abuse, and the Office of the Inspector General conducted a series of investigations further documenting institutional abuse. It became increasingly clear that conditions in the state's juvenile prisons were unacceptable and that the training schools should be improved or closed.

In 2007 the state passed a "realignment" law for youthful offenders. Under the new law, only the most violent offenders and sex offenders could be sent to state facilities. All other juvenile offenders had to be kept in county facilities. Within a decade, five major state juvenile facilities were shut down (as well as four forestry camps). The number of youths in the state's juvenile prisons declined by 80 percent. In 1996, more than 10,000 youths had been incarcerated in state facilities. By the end of 2009, that number had fallen to 1,499. Serious offenders are still being sent to state facilities, and California is still working to implement reforms and follow the best practices that have been implemented in other states.

Small Is Beautiful in Missouri

Missouri began developing a new approach for incarcerating serious juvenile offenders in the early 1980s. It closed down its two large prison-like facilities and in their place, the Department of Youth Services (DYS) set up about 30 small local centers, with no more than 30–36 youths per center. The centers are housed around the state, and DYS attempts to assign offenders to a facility within 50 miles of their home. The state believes that family connections are crucial. If necessary, the government will send a van to enable parents to visit.

Each center has dorm rooms with 10–12 beds. All the rooms have a dresser and closet space for each person. The youth are allowed to dress in their own clothes and to keep personal mementos on their dresser. Connected to each dorm is a living room with couches and coffee tables as well as a classroom and a common room where the dorm members meet every evening to talk about their personal histories and their future goals. There is a home-like atmosphere: beanbag chairs, potted plants, and pictures on the walls, mostly created by the youths themselves. And there are live pets — dogs and cats and even live chickens. In one facility, the youth work with rescue dogs, training them for adoption by local residents.

Missouri's focus is on rehabilitation, rather than punishment. The facilities are staffed by teachers and counselors, not prison guards. The teenagers in the facilities are assigned to 10-member teams with two counselors, and they study, eat, sleep, and exercise together. During the day, team members gather several times to share concerns and complaints. After school, they gather in group treatment rooms.

California Juvenile Correction Facilities

Facility	Location	Population
H. G. Stark	Chino	*Closed in 2010*
N. A. Chaderjian	Stockton	339
Pine Grove	Pine Grove	77
Preston	Ione	*Closed in 2011*
DeWitt Nelson	Stockton	*Closed in 2008*
O.H. Close	Stockton	228
Paso Robles	Paso Robles	*Closed in 2008*
Reception Center	Norwalk	*Closed in 2011*
Ventura	Ventura	354
Total		**998**

Source: *Monthly Facility Population*, California Department of Corrections & Rehabilitation, Division of Juvenile Justice (2012)

Sitting on pillows on the floor they discuss difficult times and their lives and try to understand why they ended up where they are.

The Missouri model has proved very successful. There is almost no violence in the facilities. At one maximum-security center in Kansas City, teenagers recalled only three scuffles in the prior year, none of them serious. There is no record of staff assaults, and no inmate has committed suicide in the past 20 years. Recidivism rates are also very low. Of the 1,120 teens released from a DYS facility in 2005 only about a quarter of those released were reincarcerated for a new offense or rule violation within 3 years — a dramatically lower rate than in most other states.

Many former inmates have testified to the success of Missouri's emphasis on rehabilitation. Brian Laoruangroch spoke before the Missouri legislature about how the juvenile system had changed his life. Brian had struggled for years with drugs and other troubles. When he testified, he had recently been elected student body president at the University of Missouri.

Dealing With the Mentally Ill

Many children who suffer from mental illness end up in the juvenile delinquency system. A federally funded study found that between 50 and 75 percent of teenagers in the juvenile justice system nationwide had a diagnosable mental disorder. Twenty percent of juveniles in custody have a mental health problem that significantly impairs their ability to function. Many of these children can suffer devastating consequences from being locked up in detention facilities without the specialized treatment and support that they need.

In an effort to address this problem, Santa Clara County, Calif., designed the first juvenile mental health court in 2001. More than 40 counties around the country now have such courts. The common goal of these courts is to identify the children who have mental disorders as early as possible, to develop alternatives to incarceration, and to provide services in the community that help address the underlying cause of each youth's offenses. The courts typically work with representatives from other agencies, including district attorneys, probation departments, mental health agencies, the school district, and the public defenders' office. With support from these agencies, mental health courts designate a

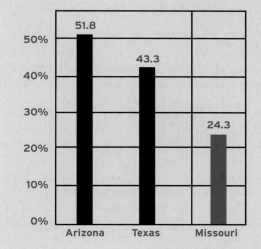

Juvenile Re-incarceration

Percentage of Youth Re-incarcerated in Juvenile or Adult Correctional Facilities for Either New Offenses or Rule Violations within 3 Years of Release from a Juvenile Facility

Source: *The Missouri Model*, Annie E. Casey Foundation (2010)

team that designs an individualized treatment plan for children diagnosed with a mental disorder and assigns a probation officer to monitor the child's progress.

When Santa Clara first established a mental health court, Pablo D. had already been incarcerated in a detention facility, the Ranch, for almost a year. He had run away from the Ranch several times and assaulted another juvenile when he was mocked for being "psycho." After each escape, the judge sent him back to the Ranch. But after the mental health court was established and Pablo was assessed by a multi-disciplinary team including mental health professionals, he was diagnosed with bipolar disorder. After reading the team's assessment, the judge understood that more detention would not work. So Pablo was sent home and went to therapists who helped him work on managing his emotions and provided him with appropriate medication. He worked with his probation officer and a school counselor, enrolled in high school, and tried out for the football team.

A pilot program is also underway in Washington state to serve juvenile offenders with mental illness and chemical dependency who have already been incarcerated. The Family Integrated Transition (FIT) program admits juveniles under 17½ years old who suffer from both mental illness and a chemical dependency. It provides intensive family therapy to help youth re-enter the community after they finish detention. A recent case involved B.L., who had been sent away for two years. When B.L. was scheduled for release, the FIT coach assigned to work with B.L. learned that most of his family — including his parents — were addicted to methamphetamine and heroin and couldn't be located. So the coach contacted B.L.'s grandparents, went to the facility, and drove B.L. to his grandparents' home. The coach went with B.L. to a local treatment program and helped him learn how to negotiate with his grandmother. When B.L. was found watching a pay per view program at night, the coach helped him write an apology letter and took away the cord so B.L. couldn't watch after he went to bed. With the coach's help B.L. finished high school and was accepted into an aerospace technology program with a scholarship. He will be the first in his family to have a college education.

Research on What Works

Many states, like California, have decided that their top priority should be to keep youths out of high-security lockup facilities. Texas, like California, experienced problems of abuse in its state facilities. In response, Texas adopted reforms allowing only youths charged with felony offenses to go to lockups. As a result, the number of youths in state secure facilities fell from about 5,000 in 2007 to about 1,200 in 2011. The state is now following the Missouri model and working to develop programs to keep youths closer to home.

The Missouri model has been hailed as a "guiding light" for reform in juvenile justice, and a great deal of data supports the conclusion that the Missouri system works. Different states measure recidivism in different ways: e.g., the percentage of youth sentenced to adult prison within three years of release (Arizona, Indiana, Maryland), the percent re-incarcerated in a juvenile facility for a new offense or sentenced to an adult prison within two years of release (New Jersey), the percent either recommitted to a juvenile facility for a new offense or sentenced to adult prison or probation within one year of release (Florida). By any of these measurements, Missouri's outcomes are better. Data on safety comparing 97 "above-average"

facilities showed that assaults are four-and-a-half times more frequent in these facilities than in Missouri's facilities. And Missouri has had significant success in helping young offenders succeed in school. Three-fourths of the youths in the Missouri facilities advance at least as fast as a typical student in public school, and 90 percent earn high school credits. In 2008 one-fourth of all youth exiting a Missouri facility after their 16th birthday had completed their high school education.

Research is also being done to measure the success of programs designed to identify mentally ill offenders and provide them with special treatment. In Washington state, data has been gathered comparing the outcomes of mentally ill children in counties with mental health courts and with FIT pilot programs to counties that do not yet have those programs. The FIT program data show a significantly lower rate of felony re-arrests. Where there is less crime, taxpayers spend less money on the criminal justice system. And fewer crimes mean fewer crime victims. Factoring in these costs, the FIT program has been shown to cost $8,968 per offender, and to save the taxpayers and crime victims $28,215, an overall net gain of $19,247 per youth. Like the Missouri model, the goal of the FIT program in Washington state is rehabilitation, not punishment. And like the Missouri model, data indicate it works.

FOR DISCUSSION

1. Why do you think many states turned toward locking up many juvenile offenders? Why is the trend today away from locking them up?
2. What do you think is the best way of dealing with young mentally ill offenders? Why?
3. What are the benefits and costs of Missouri's approach to juvenile offenders? Do you agree with its approach? Explain.

Problems With Locking Up Juveniles

[N]o juvenile shall be detained or confined in any jail or lockup for adults . . . .
– Juvenile Justice and Delinquency Prevention Act (1974)

In May 1982, Christopher Peterman, 17, found himself in the juvenile section of the Ada County Jail in Boise, Idaho. He had been picked up because he had failed to pay $73 in traffic tickets. Instead of sending him to the juvenile detention center, authorities sent him to the jail to teach him a lesson. Housed with him were other juveniles sent over from the center because they were too violent or difficult to handle. Five of these juveniles attacked Christopher in his cell. For four-and-one-half hours, they took turns burning, gouging, and kicking him. Christopher died from his injuries.

Christopher's case is a horror story about what can happen when violent and non-violent juveniles are locked up together. Not surprisingly, the results of incarcerating non-violent juveniles with violent adults can be equally as tragic. Rape is a common occurrence. The suicide rate of young people in adult jail is *seven times* greater than those incarcerated with other juveniles. In adult institutions, young people can receive the same rough treatment meted out to adult inmates. Even if the juveniles survive physically, they are likely to carry psychological scars.

In the mid-1970s, almost 500,000 juveniles were locked up in adult jails. In 1974, Congress passed the Juvenile Justice and Delinquency Prevention Act. This law declared that no state could receive federal grants unless it separated adults from juveniles in jails. Congress amended the act in 1980 mandating that adults and juveniles be kept in completely separate facilities.

By 2010, only about 7,500 remained in adult jails. Most of them were allowed to be held under exceptions created by federal regulations to the act. Regulations permit jail confinement of juveniles convicted or awaiting trials as adult offenders. About three-fourths of the 7,500 fit this category. The remainder fell under regulations allowing adult jails to hold alleged delinquents for six hours before and after initial court appearances until other arrangements can be made.

The 1974 act also ordered states to remove status offenders from locked facilities. In 1975, status offenders made up about 40 percent of those held in secure juvenile facilities. By 2008, fewer than 8 percent remained. Regulations to the act allow accused status offenders to be locked up for a maximum of 24 hours following their first contact with police or juvenile court. Most of the status offenders locked up probably fall under this exception.

Juveniles Held in Residential Facilities	
Custody Rate per 100,000 Juveniles	
National Average	**279**
10 Highest	
District of Columbia	588
South Dakota	513
Wyoming	443
Delaware	401
Alaska	383
Indiana	382
Kansas	370
Nebraska	359
Nevada	348
Pennsylvania	344
Ohio	341
10 Lowest	
Vermont	69
Hawaii	101
New Hampshire	125
Mississippi	131
North Carolina	144
Connecticut	148
Maryland	149
Maine	150
New Mexico	170
New Jersey	176

Source: "Juveniles in Residential Placement, 2008," OJJDP

FOR DISCUSSION

1. What does the 1974 Juvenile Justice and Delinquency Prevention Act compel states to do? How is the act enforced?
2. Do you agree with the purposes of the act? Why or why not?
3. The article mentions three regulations to the act. What are they? Do you agree with them? Explain.

At Home Plus

Community-based programs are cost-effective solutions for a large number of delinquent youth. These alternatives to secure detention and confinement are intended to reduce crowding, cut the costs of operating juvenile detention centers, shield offenders from the stigma of institutionalization, help offenders avoid associating with youth who have more serious delinquent histories, and maintain positive ties between the juvenile and his or her family and community.
– James Austin, Kelly Dedel Johnson, and Ronald Weitzer, "Alternatives to the Secure Detention and Confinement of Juvenile Offenders" (2005)

Sending juvenile offenders back home has serious risks. The juveniles will likely act as they always have. Why should they change if nothing in their environment has changed? Many juveniles got in trouble in the first place because of problems with family, friends, or school. Sending them back to these settings risks further problems. Yet sending juveniles back to their homes can help juveniles deal with their problems head on. But the young people are going to need help. The following are descriptions of four innovative programs designed for young offenders at home or in foster homes.

Intensive Case Management

Twenty years ago, the Center on Criminal and Juvenile Justice, a non-profit organization in San Francisco, began a program to target very high-risk youth in the juvenile justice system and offer them a community-based alternative to detention. The Detention Diversion Advocacy Program (DDAP) gets referrals from defense attorneys, probation officers, district attorneys, parents, and courts. DDAP staff members meet with potential clients and develop a case plan to present to the court. The case plan describes specific conditions and outcomes that the youth promises to meet in exchange for the judge deciding to release the juvenile from custody.

The key to DDAP is intensive oversight. While probation officers typically have caseloads of more than 70 young people, DDAP staff members never have caseloads of more than 12, and they have face-to-face visits anywhere from three times a day (during the first week after referral) to three times a week (in the second and third months) and work to connect their clients to an individualized range of community-based services.

Some staff members have backgrounds similar to their clients, which helps build trusting relationships. Victor's case is one of many where a close and continuing relationship changed the client's life. After being arrested for involvement in a shooting between rival gang members, Victor was referred to DDAP. He was 16 years old and lived in a single-parent household with an ailing mom who spoke little English. After interviewing Victor and his mother, his case manager got Victor into an alternative school, an after-school program, tutoring, and a part-time job with a small stipend. He also got Victor and his mom involved in activities outside their neighborhood — in places where they had never been. His manager helped Victor remove tattoos from his face and arms, officially denouncing his gang, and helped him enroll in a local city college where Victor is studying to be a mechanic.

DDAP has had significant success in working with serious offenders like Victor. A study by the Office of Juvenile Justice in the U.S. Department of Justice compared 271 youth referred to DDAP with a group of 271 youth who remained in the juvenile court system. The study found the overall recidivism rate of the DDAP group to be 34 percent compared to 60 percent for the comparison group. The recidivism rate for major felonies was 24 percent for the DDAP group compared to 46 percent for the comparison group. Not surprisingly, DDAP is being replicated in many cities around the country.

Day Treatment Program: AMIkids

Based in Florida, this privately operated organization runs more than 50 programs in nine states. Its day treatment programs focus on improving juveniles' self-esteem and respect for others by building teamwork and academic skills. Focusing on hands-on, experiential learning, juveniles are actively engaged in academics. Each student receives an individual performance plan for counseling, behavior, and academics. Students earn points, which allow them greater privileges and advancement in the programs. Limited to fewer than 50 juveniles at any time, programs last six to nine months with students returning home each night. Staff can give individuals a lot of attention as there is one staff member for every 10 juveniles. The juveniles in the programs range in age from 14 to 18 and include moderate to habitual offenders, most with eight to 12 offenses. Most students are far below grade level in school on entering the programs. A remarkably low 24 percent of those completing the programs commit offenses again. Compared to residential care programs, these programs cost very little.

Juvenile Alternative Work Service

At dispositional hearings, Los Angeles County judges sentence juveniles who have broken probation to short juvenile-hall time, normally about 20 days. But this disposition may be put on hold if a juvenile agrees to take part in JAWS, a program run by the Probation Department. Instead of spending the 20 days in juvenile hall, the juvenile works for 20 Saturdays or Sundays on JAWS work crews. Los Angeles sends out about 10 of these crews each weekend.

With seven to 10 members each, the crews do manual, outdoor labor, usually cleaning and yard maintenance. If the juvenile fails to show up or is disruptive at the work site, the court may impose the original sentence for juvenile hall. The majority of juvenile participants complete their requirements for probation and avoid going to juvenile hall. The Probation Department also benefits because it receives money from cities and school districts that contract to have the work done. The revenue pays for part of the cost of the program, making it far less expensive than sending juveniles to juvenile hall.

COPE

Research shows that mentally ill youth involved in the juvenile justice system do better when their special needs are met with community-based services that keep them at home. The Texas legislature recently cut back funding for secure juvenile facilities and reallocated the money to county juvenile probation departments. Many of those probation departments have used the money to develop programs for the mentally ill.

One of those counties is Travis County, Texas, which has a deferred prosecution program called COPE (Collaborative Opportunities for Positive Experiences). The goal of COPE is to intervene with mentally ill offenders early in the court process, and where possible, to prevent detention. In Travis County, each case ac-

A teacher helps a student in a youth facility.

cepted for "deferred prosecution" is reviewed by a team that includes a judge, a casework manager, an assistant district attorney, a psychologist, and a director of special services. The team accepts young offenders into COPE if they have a diagnosis such as depression, bipolar disorder, or schizophrenia and if the youth and his family agree to participate. After being accepted, the youth along with the family and team work to develop a plan that includes therapy for youth and families, work with an anger management group, and educational assistance and special services advocacy. The plan also includes incentives to encourage the youth to follow the plan. The program typically lasts from six months to a year, and after successful completion, the youth's charge is dismissed and juvenile record cleared. In 2009, 82 percent of the 92 youth in the program graduated successfully, and 65 percent have not committed another offense.

FOR DISCUSSION

1. What are the main benefits of all these programs?
2. Which program do you think would be most effective in preventing juveniles from committing another offense? Least effective? Why? Does the program you consider least effective have any value?

Individual Treatment Plan

In this activity, students prepare individual treatment plans for juvenile offenders.

1. Form groups of three. Members of each group role play case workers assigned six cases (the **Six Sample Cases** on pages 308–309) for which they must develop individual treatment plans. Each case has been found delinquent. Members of each group should:
   a. Divide the cases equally among the group. (If the group has three members, then each member is responsible for two cases.)
   b. Write a treatment plan for each case using what they have learned about various dispositional options for juveniles. The treatment plan should include various placements, the length of stay in each, and what behavior would allow the juvenile to progress from one placement to another.
   c. When finished with the plans, discuss the cases with the other members and explain the reasoning behind your decisions.
2. Students should report back. Go over each case and compare the different approaches that members of the class proposed. Debrief the activity using the questions below.

Debriefing Questions

1. Which cases were the easiest to decide? The most difficult? Why?
2. Did you choose relatively costly or inexpensive treatment plans?
3. Which of the options you chose are available for juveniles in your area?

The Question of Waiver

In Michigan, as in many states, prosecutors can try defendants older than fourteen in adult court without a hearing, a statement of reasons, or an investigation into the adolescent's background. The decision cannot be reviewed or appealed. This allows prosecutors to bypass the juvenile justice system.
– Rachel Aviv, "No Remorse" in *The New Yorker* (2012)

- John S., 15, has been charged with murder while attempting to rob a gas station.
- Mary B., 16, has been charged with prostitution, her fifth arrest on this charge. Living by herself on and off since she was 14, she has run away from two foster homes and one halfway house.

What do these two offenders have in common? Both may be subject to waiver — transfer to the adult criminal courts. In certain cases, a motion may be filed in juvenile court asking that it waive its jurisdiction and transfer the matter to a regular adult court. If this motion is granted, the juvenile is treated just as an adult offender would be. The issue of waiving juvenile jurisdiction with certain types of young offenders has been hotly debated in recent years.

Legal Standards for Waiver

In 1966, a year before *Gault*, the U.S. Supreme Court in *Kent v. U.S.* made a significant ruling on waiving jurisdiction to adult courts. In this case, a juvenile had confessed to serious crimes. His attorney, fearing the juvenile would be transferred to adult court, filed a motion requesting a hearing on this issue. The juvenile court judge did not rule on the motion, but simply waived jurisdiction to adult court, stating he had made a "full investigation" of the case. The Supreme Court ruled that this did not meet due process standards. The court held that juvenile courts waiving jurisdiction must hold a special hearing — often called a fitness hearing. At that hearing, the accused juvenile must be represented by an attorney who has access to all relevant court files. In addition, the hearing officer must state the reasons for the decision in writing so that the decision can be reviewed.

The Supreme Court also issued guidelines for making waiver decisions. Before sending a young person through the adult courts, a hearing officer should consider:

1. How serious was the crime? Does the community need to be protected from the offender?
2. Was the crime committed in a violent or aggressive manner? Was it premeditated?
3. Was it a crime against persons or against property?
4. Will the adult court prosecute the case?
5. Are the co-defendants, if any, adult? If so, should all the defendants be tried together?
6. How sophisticated and mature is the juvenile? (This is to be determined by examining the youth's home life, emotional stability, and lifestyle.)
7. What is the juvenile's prior court record and history of contact with law enforcement?
8. Can the juvenile be rehabilitated through normal juvenile procedures? If so, can the public be protected during the juvenile's treatment?

Every state now has a method for treating minors as adults in certain cases. In fact, states may have a combination of methods, depending on the crime charged and the age of the juvenile. The methods fall into three categories:

Judicial Waiver. The judge, at a fitness hearing, decides whether the juvenile should be tried in adult court. For example, Illinois, Mississippi, and Wyoming allow judges to waive juveniles to adult court for any offense at age 13. North Dakota sets the age at 16 for most offenses and at 14 for some serious crimes. Under judicial waiver, the judge must comply with the standards set forth in *Kent* and appeals courts may review the decision. Almost every state uses judicial waiver for certain crimes.

Prosecutorial Discretion, or Direct File. The prosecutor decides whether to file the case in juvenile or adult court. For example, Vermont allows prosecutors to file cases in adult court for any offense at age 16. Florida allows it at age 16 for any crime and at age 14 for murder and a few other serious crimes. Unlike judicial waiver, the prosecutor has complete discretion and the decision cannot be overturned on appeal. More than a dozen states allow prosecutorial discretion in some cases.

Legislative Exclusion. In more than half the states, the legislature mandates that certain crimes be prosecuted in adult court. For example, Arizona excludes juveniles over 14 from

Trends in Judicial Waiver

The year with the most juvenile cases judicially waived to adult court was 1994.

Offense/demographic	1985	1994	2008
Total cases waived	7,200	13,700	8,900
Most serious offense			
Person	33%	42%	50%
Property	53	37	29
Drugs	5	12	12
Public order	9	9	10
Gender			
Male	95%	94%	91%
Female	5	6	9
Age at referral			
15 or younger	7%	15%	13%
16 or older	93	85	87
Race/ethnicity			
White	59%	54%	55%
Black	40	42	42
Other	2	3	4

Note: Detail may not add to 100% because of rounding.

Source: "Delinquency Cases Waived to Criminal Court, 2008," OJJDP (2011)

being tried in juvenile court if they are charged with murder, specified felonies, or any felony if they have previously been charged with a felony.

Kansas, Indiana, and Vermont allow juveniles to be tried as adults at the youngest age — 10 (but in Indiana and Vermont, only for certain crimes). More than 20 states set no minimum age. Ten states set the minimum age at 14. Moreover, most states have adopted the rule of "once an adult, always an adult." This means that if convicted as an adult, a juvenile will be tried as an adult for any subsequent offense.

Those who favor treating more juveniles as adults believe that juveniles who commit horrible crimes must pay for them. They also think the policy serves two other purposes — incapacitation and deterrence. The young people, they point out, will be locked up far longer in adult prisons than in juvenile facilities. (The California Division of Juvenile Justice, for example, may only hold juvenile offenders until age 25.) They emphasize that those locked up will not be committing crimes. Furthermore, they believe that getting tough will deter other juveniles from committing crimes.

Many juvenile justice experts doubt that treating more juveniles as adults will reduce the crime problem. They think that putting juveniles in adult prisons means we are giving up on them. They explain that adult prisons have abandoned rehabilitation. When these inmates get out, they argue, they will be hardened criminals. Others point out that we are not just sending away violent predators. Many waiver provisions allow non-violent offenders as well as violent offenders to be tried as adults.

FOR DISCUSSION

1. Do you think waiving jurisdiction of some juvenile offenders is a good idea? Why or why not?
2. If you think waiver is a good idea, what offenders should be transferred to adult courts? Should it be done through judicial waiver, prosecutorial discretion, or legislative exclusion? Explain.
3. Would you add any additional guidelines for determining judicial waiver? Describe them.

CLASS ACTIVITY

A Waiver Hearing

In this activity, students role play juvenile judges in a waiver hearing. Form groups of three. Each group should:

1. Take the role of a juvenile court judge in a state allowing waiver of jurisdiction when the juvenile is over 14 and accused of a felony.
2. Apply the eight general guidelines on page 335 to the **Six Sample Cases** beginning on page 308. Discuss each case.
3. Decide which (if any) of the young people should be tried as juveniles and which (if any) should be tried as adults.
4. In accordance with the Supreme Court ruling, write a statement of the reasons for their decisions.

Debriefing Questions

1. Compare your decisions with those of your classmates. Is there a general agreement about the reasons for these decisions?
2. Based on their alleged crimes, which juveniles represent the clearest threat to the community? Which are least harmful?
3. Based on prior records and personal backgrounds, which juveniles are most potentially harmful?
4. Of these two factors, crime and background, which was most important to your decisions?
5. Which of these juveniles do you think should be punished? Which could be rehabilitated? Which seem most, and least, likely to be rehabilitated by the juvenile justice system?
6. In adult court, these cases will be tried by juries unless the defendants waive their rights to a jury trial. Do you think any of these juveniles would benefit by a jury trial? Why or why not?
7. What do you think should be the youngest age that juveniles should be waived from juvenile court jurisdiction? Why?
8. Are there any circumstances under which juvenile courts should not be allowed to waive jurisdiction?

Christopher Simmons and the Death Penalty

It is by now beyond serious dispute that the Eighth Amendment's prohibition of "cruel and unusual punishments" is not a static command. Its mandate would be little more than a dead letter today if it barred only those sanctions — like the execution of children under the age of seven — that civilized society had already repudiated in 1791.

– U.S. Supreme Court Justice Sandra Day O'Connor, dissenting in *Roper v. Simmons* (2005)

Christopher Simmons was convicted of a brutal murder he committed at age 17.

Christopher Simmons was 17 years old and a junior in high school when he decided that he wanted to commit a murder. He discussed his idea with two friends, Charles and John, who were 15 and 16. Christopher's plan was to commit a burglary, tie up the victim, and throw the person off a bridge.

At 2 a.m. one night, the friends met to carry out the plan (though John decided to drop out). Christopher and Charles broke into the home of Shirley Crook. They entered her bedroom and covered her mouth and eyes with duct tape. They carried her to her minivan and drove to a railway bridge across the Meramac River (near St. Louis, Missouri). After tying her hands and feet with electrical wire, they threw her off the bridge, and she drowned.

Simmons bragged about the killing to his friends, saying that he had killed a woman "because the bitch seen my face." He was arrested at school the next day and taken to the police station. The police read him his *Miranda* rights. Simmons waived his rights and agreed to answer questions. After two hours, he confessed to the brutal murder. He also agreed to reenact the murder at the crime scene.

Simmons was tried as an adult and found guilty of murder. The state sought the death penalty. In instructing the jury, the judge said that age should be considered as a mitigating factor. The defense argued that Simmons' age should make a huge difference, pointing out that 17 year olds can't drink, serve on juries, vote, or even see certain movies, because "legislatures have wisely decided that individuals of a certain age aren't responsible enough." The prosecutor responded, "Age, he says. Think about age. Seventeen years old. Isn't that scary? Doesn't that scare you? Mitigating? Quite the contrary I submit. Quite the contrary."

After Simmons was found guilty and sentenced to death, his lawyers filed two motions for post-conviction relief. The Missouri Supreme Court denied the first motion, but granted the second, based on a recent Supreme Court ruling concerning the Eighth Amendment. The state then appealed to the U.S. Supreme Court.

FOR DISCUSSION

1. At the time of Simmons' sentence, 12 states did not allow the death penalty at all. Of the remaining 38 states, 20 allowed the execution of juveniles and 18 set the minimum age for capital punishment at 18. Do you think these statistics are relevant in determining whether the death penalty for juveniles is cruel and unusual punishment? Why or why not?

2. The judge instructed the jury to consider Simmons' young age as a mitigating factor. Simmons' lawyer reminded the jurors that juveniles of Simmons' age cannot drink, serve on juries, or marry without a parent's consent because "the legislatures have wisely decided that individuals of a certain age aren't responsible enough." Do you think that the limits for drinking or serving on a jury should be the same as the limits for capital punishment? Explain.

3. Do you think that executing juveniles under 18 is cruel and unusual punishment? Explain.

Important Cases on Sentencing Juveniles

The issue before the Court is whether the Constitution permits a juvenile offender to be sentenced to life in prison without parole for a nonhomicide crime.
– U.S. Supreme Court Justice Anthony Kennedy, *Graham v. Florida* (2010)

In 2005, the U.S. Supreme Court decided *Roper v. Simmons*. The court voted 5 to 4 that the Eighth Amendment prohibits the death penalty for crimes committed by an offender under 18. The court looked at how state legislatures and juries had ruled on the death penalty. Because a majority of states (30) prohibit the death penalty for juveniles, and because juries rarely sentence juveniles to death even in states where it is allowed, the court held that there is a "national consensus" against executing juveniles.

The court also found that juveniles are different from adults, because they are less mature and less responsible, more susceptible to outside influences, and more likely to make "impetuous and ill considered" decisions. The Eighth Amendment requires that the death penalty be reserved for the worst crimes and the worst offenders. Because of their immaturity, the court held that juveniles, as a group, are less culpable than adults. The court acknowledged that in a rare case, a juvenile might be sufficiently mature — and have acted with sufficient depravity — to merit the sentence of death. But there is also the possibility, and even likelihood, that in the case of a brutal crime, the jury might overlook the mitigating factors of immaturity and vulnerability. Therefore, the court concluded, "a line must be drawn." It chose to draw that line at 18, which is the same point that society draws between childhood and adulthood for many other purposes.

The court also noted that the United States is the only country in the world that gives official sanction to the juvenile death penalty. Writing for the majority, Justice Anthony Kennedy said that the opinion of the world community "while not controlling our outcome, does provide respected and significant confirmation for our own conclusions."

The four dissenters strongly disagreed. Justice Sandra Day O'Connor wrote that some

U.S. Supreme Court Justice Anthony Kennedy was appointed to the court by President Reagan.

murderers under 18 are sufficiently mature to deserve the death penalty, and juries should be free to make that assessment. In a separate dissenting opinion, Justice Antonin Scalia said that the majority opinion had made "a mockery" of constitutional precedent. Scalia said that little had changed since 1988, when the Supreme Court had ruled in *Stanford v. Kentucky* that the Eighth Amendment did not ban executing offenders who were 16 and 17. And he strongly disagreed with the conclusion that juries cannot be trusted to make decisions about the defendant's culpability, taking into account age and other mitigating and aggravating factors. This "startling" conclusion, he said, "undermines the very foundations of our capital sentencing system." And he expressed strong disapproval of the court making reference to the views of other countries in the world. "Acknowledgment of foreign approval," he said, "has no place in the legal opinion of this Court."

Graham v. Florida (2010)

Five years later, the U.S. Supreme Court heard another important case on sentencing juveniles. At age 16, Terrance Jamar Graham and three other juveniles tried to rob a barbecue restaurant in Florida. A friend who worked at the restaurant left the back door unlocked for them at closing time. Wearing masks, Graham and one accomplice entered the restaurant through the unlocked door. His accomplice struck the manager twice with a metal bar, the manager screamed, and the two fled with no money to the awaiting car with the third accomplice.

Graham was arrested, and the prosecutor decided to charge him as an adult. Graham pleaded guilty to armed burglary with assault or battery and to attempted armed robbery. Since it was his first offense, he was sentenced to probation.

Six months later, Graham was arrested for taking part in a home invasion robbery. His probation officer filed a petition saying that Graham had violated his probation. At a series of hearings, the court determined he had violated his probation by possessing a firearm, violating the law (the home invasion robbery), and associating with criminals. The judge sentenced him on the original charges of armed burglary and robbery to life imprisonment. Since Florida had abolished parole, he was sentenced, in effect, to life without possibility of parole.

Graham appealed the sentence. His attorneys argued that in a non-homicide case, sentencing a juvenile to life without parole violated the Eighth Amendment. A Florida court of appeal affirmed the sentence, and the Florida Supreme Court refused to hear the case.

The U.S. Supreme Court agreed to hear the case. By a 6–3 vote, the court overturned the decisions of the Florida courts. A court majority ruled that in a non-homicide case, sentencing a juvenile to life without parole is cruel and unusual punishment and therefore banned by the Eighth Amendment.

Writing the majority opinion, Justice Anthony Kennedy made the following arguments:

- The Eighth Amendment requires that a sentence not be grossly disproportionate to the offense. One way to determine whether a sentence is grossly disproportionate is to look at what other states are doing. Each year, about 350,000 juveniles commit violent crimes. Yet across the U.S., only 129 juveniles are serving life sentences for non-homicide offenses, and this number includes offenders who committed their crimes years ago. Of the 129 juveniles, 77 are in Florida prisons. Only 10

other states and the federal government house the remaining 52 juveniles. A clear consensus exists among the states against these sentences.

- *Roper v. Simmons* is based on the principle that because juvenile offenders have lower culpability and a greater capacity for change, they do not deserve the severest punishments. Life without possibility of parole is the second harshest punishment a state may impose. It is even harsher on a juvenile because a juvenile will spend more time behind bars. A person given this sentence is denied the chance to prove he has changed and been rehabilitated. Most juveniles can change, and no psychologist (let alone a judge) can identify which can and cannot.

- This sentence cannot be justified by any of the four main purposes of punishment. Retribution does not justify imposing the second harshest punishment on the less culpable juvenile offender. Studies have shown that juveniles are less susceptible to deterrence. To justify incapacitation, it must be assumed that the offender will pose a danger to society for the rest of his life, but this cannot be known. And finally, the sentence rules out the purpose of rehabilitation. "A sentence lacking any legitimate penological justification is by its nature disproportionate to the offense."

- No other nation in the world imposes life sentences without parole for juveniles for non-homicide offenses. In fact, the U.N. Convention on the Rights of the Child (1990), an agreement ratified by every nation except Somalia and the U.S., bans "life imprisonment without possibility of release . . . for offences committed by persons below eighteen years of age."

Chief Justice John Roberts was one of the six justices who voted to overturn Graham's sentence of life without parole. But he did not join the majority opinion. He saw no reason for a categorical rule against such sentences for juveniles. He believed that each case should be examined to see whether the punishment is grossly disproportionate to the crime, taking into account the age of the offender. He noted that "Graham's sentence was far more severe than" similar cases in Florida and other states. He concluded his concurring opinion:

In my view, Graham's age — together with the nature of his criminal activity and the unusual severity of his sentence — tips the constitutional balance. I thus concur in the Court's judgment that Graham's sentence of life without parole violated the Eighth Amendment.

Justice Clarence Thomas wrote the opinion for the three dissenting justices. He argued that it does not violate the Eighth Amendment to impose a life-without-parole sentence on a juvenile non-homicide offender.

- Graham's sentence is not grossly disproportionate to his offense. The court has affirmed sentences for mandatory life sentences for non-violent offenses. For example in *Harmelin v. Michigan*, the court upheld a life sentence without the possibility of parole for a person convicted of possessing 672 grams of cocaine. Graham's crime was a violent crime. Furthermore, 37 states plus the federal government and District of Columbia permit life sentences without parole for juveniles committing certain non-homicide crimes. Thus, no consensus exists among the states against these sentences.

- International law is not relevant. The U.S. has not ratified the U.N. Convention on the Rights of the Child, so it does not apply to the United States. Given that most states permit life without possibility of parole sentences for juveniles in non-homicide cases, international law does not indicate a trend in the United States.

- The *Roper v. Simmons* decision did not eliminate harsh prison sentences for juveniles. It is a death penalty case, and the court has repeatedly stressed that capital punishment is different from other punishments, requires special procedures and rules, and is reserved for the worst offenders. Life sentences have never been reserved for the worst offenders. If states are not allowed to sentence juveniles to life without parole, does not the same logic require that they not sentence them to long prison terms?

- Every state takes into account the age of the convict when making a sentencing decision. The Florida legislature, like many legislatures across the country, has decided that some juveniles need harsher sentences.

States have the right and obligation to decide the punishments for crimes and whether these punishments deter, incapacitate, or exact retribution on juveniles. The court in Florida recognized that Graham was a juvenile and gave him a second chance with probation. When he violated his probation, the court decided a harsher sentence was merited. This was in accord with the system that Florida created.

The *Jackson* and *Miller* Cases (2012)

In 2012, the U.S. Supreme Court heard two new cases, each involving 14-year-old offenders sentenced to life without parole for committing homicide.

In *Jackson v. Hobbs*, Kuntrell Jackson stood as a lookout outside an Arkansas liquor store while his 14- and 15-year-old partners entered, one of them armed with a sawed-off shotgun, and attempted to rob the store. After the clerk repeatedly denied having any money, she was shot dead. The three fled, but were arrested later.

In *Miller v. Alabama*, Evan Miller lived with his mother in a trailer park. One night around midnight, Cole Cannon, their 52-year-old neighbor, knocked on the door and asked for some food. While his mom prepared the food, Miller and a 16-year-old friend sneaked into Cannon's trailer, looking for drugs. They found none, but stole some baseball cards. They returned to the Miller trailer and planned to steal money from Cannon's wallet. They returned with Cannon to his trailer, smoked marijuana, and played a drinking game with him. Soon Cannon, very drunk, passed out. Miller took the wallet from Cannon's pocket and removed about $300. But when he attempted to put the empty wallet back in Cannon's pocket, Cannon woke up and grabbed Miller's throat. Miller's friend struck Cannon with a baseball bat. Miller jumped on Cannon and began beating him with his fists and then with the bat. When they left the trailer, Cannon was alive, but unable to move. A few minutes later, they returned, set several fires in the trailer, and left Cannon to die. Miller was later arrested.

In both the *Jackson* and *Miller* cases, the 14-year-old defendants were tried as adults, convicted of murder, and sentenced to life in prison without the possibility of parole. The U.S. Supreme Court agreed to hear both cases.

FOR DISCUSSION

1. Do you agree with the Supreme Court's decision in the Christopher Simmons case? Why or why not?
2. Do you agree with the Supreme Court's decision in the Terrance Graham case? Explain.
3. The majority in both *Simmons* and *Graham* decided to make categorical rules. What is a categorical rule? Do you think they were appropriate in each case? Explain.
4. Do you think that international opinion on juvenile sentences should be considered in deciding cases like *Simmons* and *Graham*?
5. Neither Christopher Simmons nor Terrance Graham was set free by the Supreme Court's decisions in their cases. Simmons' new sentence is life without the possibility of parole (which may change depending on the outcome of the *Jackson* and *Miller* cases). Graham's sentence was changed to 25 years (without the possibility of parole). Imagine that the trial court had changed Graham's sentence to 70 years behind bars. Do you think the Supreme Court would find that sentence cruel and unusual? Explain.

CLASS ACTIVITY

The *Jackson* and *Miller* Cases

In this activity, students role play Supreme Court justices and decide the two cases.

The court will decide this issue: **In a murder case, is sentencing a juvenile to life without the possibility of parole cruel and unusual punishment and therefore banned by the Eighth Amendment?**

1. Form groups of five or seven. Each group will be a Supreme Court.
2. Each group should do the following:
   a. Select a chief justice to lead the discussion.
   b. Reread and discuss the parts on the article on the *Roper* and *Graham* decisions.
   c. Read and discuss **Juveniles Under 15**, below.
   d. Compare these decisions to the two new cases of *Jackson* and *Miller*.
   e. Discuss and decide each of the cases: *Jackson* and *Miller*. The group has these options for decisions:
      (1) Rule that *in this particular case* the sentence of life without parole violates the Eighth Amendment.
      (2) Rule that *in this particular case* the sentence of life without parole does not violate the Eighth Amendment.
      (3) Rule that *in every case*, a sentence of life without parole for juveniles convicted of murder does not violate the Eighth Amendment.
      (4) Rule that *in every case*, the sentence of life without parole for juveniles violates the Eighth Amendment. (Or, the court could narrow its decision to juveniles under 15, as both Jackson and Miller were under 15.)
   f. Be prepared to report its decisions on each case and its reasons for each decision.
3. Each group should report its decisions and reasons for them.
4. Hold a class discussion on the two cases.

Juveniles Under 15

Consider these two facts when deciding the *Miller* and *Jackson* cases:
- 38 of the 50 states plus the federal government allow sentences of life without parole for 14 year olds convicted of murder.
- 79 juveniles under 15 are serving sentences of life without parole in prisons across the nation.

Current Trends and Controversies

The majority of detained youth are not the older violent offenders that the public assumes are under lock and key. Many detained youth are quite young. . . . Nearly 70% are held for non-violent offenses.
– National Center for Juvenile Justice (1999)

Over the years, reformers have focused on different issues in the juvenile justice system. During the 1960s and early 1970s, advocates pushed for due-process rights for juveniles. The U.S. Supreme Court responded with its *Gault* decision, which declared juveniles did have these rights. Subsequent court decisions and much state legislation further defined juveniles' rights.

Beginning in the mid-1970s, reformers turned their focus on detention issues, particularly on restricting who could be in secure lockups. The Juvenile Justice and Delinquency Act of 1974 and its subsequent amendments achieved two major reforms of detention. It outlawed placing status offenders in secure detention, and it mandated separate facilities for adults and juveniles.

From the late 1970s to the present, the public in many states has called for getting tough on juvenile offenders. Many states locked up juveniles in record numbers. Even in periods when the juvenile arrest rate for violent crimes dropped, the incarceration rate climbed. In the wake of highly publicized, violent juvenile crimes, many have called for even more harsh sentences on juveniles. Princeton Professor John Dilluio once warned of a "rising wave of superpredators," caused by the growing teen population. Shay Bilchik, former head of the Office of Juvenile Justice and Delinquency Prevention, dismissed the idea of a growing number of superpredators. "For starters, only about one-half of 1 percent of juveniles ages 10 to 17 were arrested for a violent crime last year, and of all juvenile offenders, just 6 to 8 percent are serious, violent, or chronic offenders. So to talk of a generation of superpredators is not only false but unfair." Bilchik and others believe that getting tough has not and will not prevent violent crimes. They urge a return to the traditional model of rehabilitation for juvenile offenders.

Today, due to the economic crisis of 2008, the huge cost of locking up so many juveniles, and calls for reform, the number in custody is dropping. It has fallen to about 100,000 juveniles across the nation in custody, down from a high of 120,000 in 1997. This is still an enormous number. In comparison, the United Kingdom, which has one-fifth the population of the U.S., has just 3,000 juveniles in custody.

The high detention rates have given rise to another controversy. Today, the overwhelming majority of juveniles in detention are minorities. Although African Americans constitute only 15 percent of juveniles aged 10–17, they make up about a third of the juveniles in custody. Blacks do not commit more crimes than whites. The number of whites arrested far surpasses the number of blacks arrested. But as they make their way through the juvenile justice system, blacks tend to stay in the system and end up in custody. Whites tend to get out of the system and not be placed in custody.

So the controversy arises: Does the juvenile justice system unfairly discriminate against minorities, particularly African-American youths?

Many experts believe that racial discrimination does not cause black youth to remain longer in the system. They point to two separate studies which have shown that black judges are more likely than white judges to keep a black juvenile in custody. They believe that social class rather than race explains why blacks stay in the system. Most of the blacks caught in the system come from poor inner-city neighborhoods. Most of the whites come from a middle-class background. If a middle-class white juvenile gets into trouble, the parents may get a lawyer and a psychologist to help. They will come to court with a plan of action. On the other hand, an inner-city juvenile may only have an overworked public defender, who probably will meet the juvenile just before the hearing. This juvenile has limited access to social services, community agencies, or psychologists. And the juvenile's neighborhood may be filled with gangs and drug traffickers. What is the best interest of each child? Given each juvenile's resources, a judge might find it better to let the middle-class juvenile stay at home and better to send the inner-city offender to a detention facility that has social services. So social class rather than race may explain the different treatment of whites and blacks.

Other experts disagree. They say that while class may account for some of the disparity,

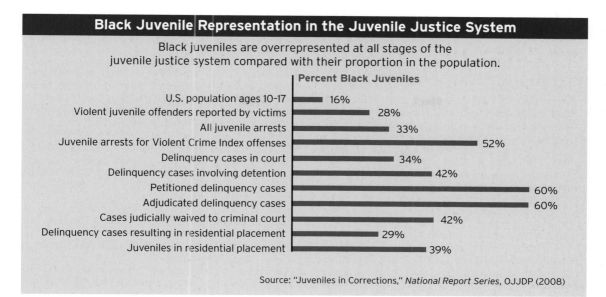

Black Juvenile Representation in the Juvenile Justice System

Black juveniles are overrepresented at all stages of the juvenile justice system compared with their proportion in the population.

Percent Black Juveniles

U.S. population ages 10-17	16%
Violent juvenile offenders reported by victims	28%
All juvenile arrests	33%
Juvenile arrests for Violent Crime Index offenses	52%
Delinquency cases in court	34%
Delinquency cases involving detention	42%
Petitioned delinquency cases	60%
Adjudicated delinquency cases	60%
Cases judicially waived to criminal court	42%
Delinquency cases resulting in residential placement	29%
Juveniles in residential placement	39%

Source: "Juveniles in Corrections," *National Report Series*, OJJDP (2008)

racism also plays a role. The juvenile justice system allows decision makers wide discretion at every stage of the juvenile justice process. Racism, they argue, can easily creep into such a system.

The Office of Juvenile Justice and Delinquency Prevention commissioned a project to examine all the existing research about race in the juvenile justice system. In 1992, the project issued a report concluding that "there is substantial support for the statement that there are race effects in operation within the juvenile justice system, both direct and indirect in nature." By "race effects," the project meant that race explains why blacks remain in the system.

In 1989, Congress amended the Juvenile Justice and Delinquency Act. It required states to examine why so many minorities were in their lockups. States must justify any over-representation of minorities at every stage of their juvenile justice systems. In 1992, Congress further amended the act tying funding to compliance. Since then, about 40 states have started intervention and prevention programs aimed at helping youth who are at risk of engaging in crime.

One final controversy should be mentioned. It's one that has plagued the system from its beginning: What should be done with status offenders (such as truants or those who run away from home)? Although status offenders have been removed from locked facilities, some still pass through the juvenile justice system along with more serious offenders. Current debate arises over whether status offenders belong in the juvenile justice system at all. Many experts believe status offenders should be treated as cases of abuse or neglect — not as offenders. They argue that the court should turn its control of status offenders over to welfare agencies, private charities, and counseling centers.

FOR DISCUSSION

1. Do you think the juvenile justice system should focus on rehabilitation or punishment? Why?
2. How do you account for the great number of minority youth in detention? What do you think can be done about it? Explain.
3. Should status offenders be treated as offenders or as cases of abuse and neglect? Why?

CLASS ACTIVITY

What Should Be Done?

Write a brief essay either supporting or opposing the following statement: *Instead of trying to rehabilitate serious offenders, the juvenile justice system should impose longer sentences to keep them off the streets.*

Sources for Unit 5

"Alternatives to the Secure Detention & Confinement of Juvenile Offenders," OJJDP, 2005. · Anderson, C. *et al.* "Calif. Youth Authority Warehouses." Books Not Bars, Center on Juvenile & Criminal Justice, SF, 2005. URL: http://nicic.org/Library/020386 · "Characteristics of Juvenile Suicide in Confinement," OJJDP, 2009, NCJ 214434. · "Conditions of Confinement," OJJDP, 2010, NCJ 227729. · "Crime in Calif. 2010," Calif. Dept. of Justice, URL: http://oag.ca.gov/crime · *Delays in Youth Justice*, NIJ-Sp., 2009, NCJ 228493. · "Delinquency Cases in Juvenile Court, 2008," OJJDP, 2011, NCJ 236479. · "Delinquency Cases Waived to Criminal Court, 2008," OJJDP, 2011, NCJ 236481. · "Disproportionate Minority Contact," OJJDP, 2009, NCJ 228306. · *Disproportionate Minority Contact in the Juvenile Justice System*, OJJDP-Sp., 2007, NCJ 219743. · *Economic Eval. of the Serious & Violent Offender Reentry Initiative*, NIJ-Sp., 2009, NCJ 230422. · *Effect of Criminal Justice Involvement in the Transition to Adulthood*, NIJ-Sp., 2009, NCJ 228380. · *Exploring the Impact of Inst. Placement on the Recidivism of Delinquent Youth*, NIJ-Sp., 2006, NCJ 217590. · "Five Year Outcomes in a Randomized Trial of a Community-Based Multi-Agency Intensive Supervision Juvenile Probation Program," NIJ-Sp., 2010, NCJ 232621. · Gatti, U. *et al.* "Iatrogenic Effect of Juvenile Justice," *J. of Child Psychology & Psychiatry*, Vol. 50, No. 8, 2009. · "Girls Study Group," OJJDP, 2008, NCJ 223434. · Greenwood, P. *et al. One More Chance*, Santa Monica: RAND, 5/1985. · Greenwood, P. "Correctional Programs for Chronic Juvenile Offenders." Santa Monica: RAND, 1988. · Griffin, P. *et al. Trying Juveniles as Adults in Criminal Court*, Wash., DC: OJJDP, 1998. · Harms, P. *et al.* "Trends in the Murder of Juveniles: 1980–2000." Wash., DC: OJJDP, 2004. · Harris, R., "Kids in Custody." *LA Times*. Series from 8/22 to 8/25/1993. · Hjalmarsson, R. "Criminal Justice Involvement & High School Completion," *J. of Urban Econ.*, Vol. 63, No. 2, 2008. · Holman, B. *et al.* "The Dangers of Detention,"Justice Policy Inst., 2007. · "Hot Spots of Juvenile Crime," OJJDP, 2011, NCJ 231575. · *Impact of Incarceration on Young Offenders*, NIJ-Sp., 2009, NCJ 227403. · "JDAI Annual Results Report: 2009," Annie E. Casey Found., 2010. · "Juvenile Arrests 2009," OJJDP, 2011, NCJ 236477. · "Juvenile Delinquency Probation Caseload, 2008," OJJDP, 2011, NCJ 236478. · *Juvenile Crime, Juvenile Justice.* Nat. Academies P, 2001. · *Juvenile Justice Reform.* Little Hoover Commission, 2008. · "Juvenile Residential Facility Census, 2008," OJJDP, 2011, NCJ 231683. · *Juvenile Runaways*, COPS, 2006, NCJ 213594. · "Juveniles in Residential Placement: 1997–2008," OJJDP, 2010, NCJ 229379. · *Juvenile Suicide in Confinement*, OJJDP, 2008, NCJ 213691. · "Juvenile Transfer Laws" OJJDP, 2010, NCJ 220595. · Keely, J., "Will Adjudicated Youth Return to School After Residential Placement?" *J. of Correctional Ed.*, Vol. 57, No. 1, 2006. · Kelly, J. "Psych Meds in Jails," *Youth Today*, 10/2010. · Krisberg, B. *et al.* "Juvenile Intensive Supervision Programs," *NCCD Focus*, 2/1991. · Lipsey, M., "The Primary Factors that Characterize Effective Interventions with Juvenile Offenders," *Victims & Offenders*, Vol. 4, No. 2, 2009. · Loughran, T. *et al.* "Estimating a Dose-Response Relationship Between Length of Stay & Future Recidivism in Serious Juvenile Offenders," *Criminology*, Vol. 47, No. 3, 2009. · Males, M. "Statistical Bigotry." *Youth Today*, 4/2005. · Males, M. *et al.* "The Calif. Miracle," Center on Juvenile & Criminal Justice, July 2010. · ___. "Crime Rates & Youth Incarceration in Texas & Calif. Compared" Center on Juvenile & Criminal Justice, 6/2007. · McCurley, C. *et al.* "Victims of Violent Juvenile Crime." Wash., DC: OJJDP, 2004. · Mendel, R. *The Missouri Model*, Annie E. Casey Found., 2010. · *Multilevel Analysis of Juvenile Court Processes.* NIJ-Sp., 2008, NCJ 223465. · Nat. Center for Juvenile Justice. URL: www.ncjj.org · "Nat. Center for Youth in Custody," OJJDP, 2011, NCJ 235770. · "Nat. Juvenile Custody Trends 1978–1989," Wash., DC: OJJDP, 1992. · *Pathways from Dependency & Neglect to Delinquency: Part Two*, NIJ-Sp., 2007, NCJ 220288. · "Person Offense Cases in Juvenile Court, 2008," OJJDP, 2011, NCJ 236480. · Pierce, R. *et al. Juvenile Justice Reform.* Wash., DC: Nat. Conf. of State Legis., 1989. · Pope, C. *et al.* "Race as a Factor in Juvenile Arrests." Wash., DC: OJJDP, 2003. · ___. *Minorities & the Juvenile Justice System* Wash., DC: OJJDP, 1992. · "Psychiatric Disorders of Youth in Detention," OJJDP, 2006, NCJ 210331. · Puzzanchera, C. *et al. Juvenile Court Statistics 2008*, Nat. Center for Juvenile Justice, 2011. · "Reducing Disproportionate Minority Contact," OJJDP, 2009, NCJ 218861. · *Reentry Experiences of Confined Juvenile Offenders*, NIJ-Sp., 2009, NCJ 230423. · "Report to Congress on Juvenile Violence Research," Wash., DC: OJJDP, 1999. · Rust, B. "Juvenile Jailhouse Rocked." *Advocasey* Fall/Winter 1999. URL: www.aecf.org · Sanders, W., ed. *Juvenile Offenders for a Thousand Years*. Chapel Hill: U. of N. Carolina P, 1970. · *Self-Reported Law-Violating Behavior from Adolescence to Early Adulthood in a Modern Cohort*, NIJ-Sp., 2006, NCJ 217588. · Shepherd, R. "Collateral Consequences of Juvenile Proceedings: Part I." *Criminal Justice Mag.*, Vol. 15, No. 2, Summer 2000. · ___. "Collateral Consequences of Juvenile Proceedings: Part II." *Criminal Justice Mag.*, Vol. 15, No. 3, Fall 2000. · ___. "The Juvenile Court at 100 Years," *Juvenile Justice*, Vol. VI, No. 2, 12/1999. · Sickmund, M. "Juvenile Offenders in Residential Placement." Wash., DC: OJJDP, 2002. · ___. "Juveniles in Corrections." Wash., DC: OJJDP, 2004. · Snyder, H. *et al. Juvenile Offenders & Victims.* Wash., DC: OJJDP, 1999. · Stahl, A. "Offenders in Juvenile Court, 1997," Wash., DC: OJJDP, 2000. · Statistical Briefing Book, OJJDP, 2012, URL: www.ojjdp.gov/ojstatbb · Steinhart, D. *Juvenile Detention Risk Assessment.* Annie E. Casey Found., 2006. · "Survey of Youth in Residential Placement," OJJDP-Sp., 2010, NCJ 227660. · Vito, G. *et al. Juvenile Justice Today.* NY: Prentice Hall, 2003. · Wasserman, G. *et al.* "Prevention of Serious & Violent Juvenile Offending," Wash., DC: OJJDP, 2000. · "Youth Courts," OJJDP-Sp., 2008, NCJ 222592. · "Youth's Characteristics & Backgrounds," OJJDP, 2010, NCJ 227730. · "Youth's Needs & Services," OJJDP, 2010, NCJ 227728.

Unit 6
SOLUTIONS

Crime affects all of us. Even if we aren't touched directly, we pay extra for insurance, we worry about the safety of our family and friends, and we worry about where we can walk safely. Americans regularly list crime as one of their top concerns. Billions of dollars are lost every year to criminals, and billions more are spent in the fight against crime.

One major problem in finding solutions to crime comes from basic disagreements over its causes. Sociologists, criminologists, politicians, and ordinary citizens often debate the issue. We begin this unit with an examination of some of the debates about the causes of crime.

We then turn to an examination of the role government plays in combating crime. You have already seen examples of the direct role played by the police, prosecutors, courts, and correctional systems in dealing with criminals. We will examine our government's crucial role in determining policies to reduce crime. We will take a look at the executive, legislative, and judicial branches throughout our federal system. In our examination, we will also discuss the debate over whether our criminal justice system, in its battle against crime, discriminates against minority groups.

Finally, we will address the role ordinary citizens can play in fighting crime. We will explore both negative and positive actions citizens have taken to guard their communities – from vigilante action to neighborhood watch groups. Then you will get a chance to form a citizen task force and make practical proposals for reducing crime.

The problem of crime is complex. Every theory and every proposed solution raises fundamental ethical, political, and economic questions. These questions must be squarely faced if America is to make any progress in its battle against crime.

CHAPTER 22
THE CAUSES OF CRIME

Many writers claim that nearly all crime is caused by economic conditions, or in other words that poverty is practically the whole cause of crime. Endless statistics have been gathered on this subject which seem to show conclusively that property crimes are largely the result of the unequal distribution of wealth. But crime of any class cannot be safely ascribed to a single cause. Life is too complex, heredity is too variant and imperfect, too many separate things contribute to human behavior, to make it possible to trace all actions to a single cause.

– Clarence Darrow (1857-1938), defense attorney, *Crime: Its Cause and Treatment*

THEORIES AND APPROACHES | SOCIAL AND CULTURAL FACTORS
INDIVIDUAL AND SITUATIONAL FACTORS

Theories and Approaches

Violence is a serious public health problem in the United States.
– Web site of the Centers for Disease Control and Prevention (2012)

America has a serious crime problem. The rates of property crimes, such as theft and burglary, are actually on levels similar to or even below other countries. But the rate of violent crime is another matter. Statistics show that the U.S.'s rate of violent crime far surpasses that of any Western democracy. The city of New York during the 1990s cut its number of murders in half. But the city, with a population about 9 million, still had half as many murders each year as the entire nation of Italy, population 58 million. Homicide is the second leading cause of death for Americans age 15 to 24 and the leading cause of death for African Americans age 15 to 34.

Looking at these statistics, doctors at the U.S. Centers for Disease Control have called violent crime an epidemic in the United States. Along with many others, they seek measures to deal with this problem. By examining the causes of crime and violence, they believe individuals, communities, and the nation can take action to stem the tide of violence in our society.

What then are the causes of crime? There is no easy answer. Some people have argued that all crime comes from inborn traits. Others have insisted that it comes from poverty, discrimination, lack of hope, or the breakdown of family values. Still others have contended that crime comes from personalities warped by drugs, disease, or childhood abuse. The list of possible causes can go on and on.

While few people today would argue crime has but one cause, people still emphasize one factor over another. And they debate whether one factor is a cause or effect of another. The diagram below charts some of the most commonly cited causes of crime. For convenience, we have put them into two groups — (1) social and cultural factors and (2) individual and situational factors.

Social & Cultural	Individual & Situational
• POVERTY	• BIOLOGY
• UNEMPLOYMENT	• RATIONAL CHOICE
• RACIAL DISCRIMINATION	• GUNS
• CHILD ABUSE	• ALCOHOL
• AMERICAN VALUES	• DRUGS
• VIOLENCE IN THE MEDIA	

Social and Cultural Factors

Poverty is the parent of revolution and crime.
– Aristotle (384-322 B.C.), Greek philosopher, *Politics*

Social problems — such as poverty, unemployment, racial discrimination, and child abuse — and cultural influences — such as American values and violence on television — are often mentioned as causes of crime. They do not cause crime in any direct sense. The vast majority of poor people, for example, remain law-abiding all their lives. But these factors may make it more likely that some people turn to crime.

Poverty, Unemployment, and Racial Discrimination

Many people believe that poverty contributes to the crime rate. Statistics do show much higher rates of crime in poor communities. You only have to drive through a high-poverty area and look at the barred windows and security doors to know that the people who live there worry about crime.

A study using data from Columbus, Ohio, showed that neighborhoods with the most poverty had the highest rates of crime. Neighborhoods with poverty rates above 40 percent had crime rates three times higher than neighborhoods with poverty rates under 20 percent.

Poverty and unemployment are highest in minority communities, particularly among African Americans and Latinos. About a fourth of all blacks and Latinos live below the poverty line, compared to about 10 percent of whites. Despair and hopelessness may also give rise to crime in these communities. Inner-city residents, mostly minorities, get arrested and jailed at high rates. Homicide is the leading cause of death of black males between the ages 15 and 34, and the second leading cause of Hispanic males in the same age group. White males of the same age are far less likely to die of homicide.

One of the great causes of poverty, of course, is lack of jobs. In 1992, the crime rate was high and so was unemployment. Throughout the rest of the 1990s, unemployment dropped rapidly and so did the crime rate. This decline in crime went against expectations because more people in the 18–30 age group entered the population. This is the most crime-prone age and many experts had predicted rising crime rates. Some experts attribute the fall in crime to the booming economy. They argue that unlike the 1960s when the economy also boomed, this economy provided more jobs for the poor.

Some social scientists have found a direct relationship between joblessness and crime and other social problems. A detailed long-term study by Dr. Harvey Brenner of Johns Hopkins University found that for every 1 percent increase in the unemployment rate, the United States sees:

650 extra homicides
3,300 extra state prison admissions
920 extra suicides
500 extra deaths from alcoholism.

Other studies have been less conclusive. A review of 30 studies on whether joblessness leads to crime found insufficient evidence proving or disproving the connection. Others point out that unemployment began to rise from 2001 to 2003, dropped slightly in 2004 and 2005, and rose sharply beginning in 2008. During this period and through 2011, the crime rate has continued to fall.

Child Abuse and Neglect

The family is usually the greatest single influence on a person's life. In a family, we learn how to behave, how to treat other people, and how to view ourselves. Children who experience cruelty or lack of affection can develop anti-social habits or serious mental problems. Some problems may show up much later, as the child grows. Many sociologists believe that parents who abuse their children start a cycle of abuse from generation to generation. Abused children often grow up to abuse their children.

In a study reported in *Science* magazine, sociologists found that neglected children were one and one-half more times as likely to commit violent crimes later in life than non-neglected children. Abused children were twice as likely to become violent criminals. Abused children are also six times as likely to abuse their own children. The study concluded that the abusive family was one place where society should try to break the continuing cycle of violence. Neglect and abuse within a family can lay the roots for a life of violent crime.

Almost 3 million children are reported as victims of abuse or neglect every year. Many cases of abuse undoubtedly never get reported.

A National Institute of Justice study found that "childhood abuse increased the odds of future delinquency and adult criminality overall by 40 percent." Some social scientists insist that almost all career criminals, particularly those involved in crimes of violence, were abused as children.

Values That Make Crime More Acceptable

Many people believe that Americans hold certain values or beliefs that may encourage criminal conduct. One such value might be our **love of material goods**. Judging by our mass media, our society seems to place a high value on owning new things. The cumulative message of much advertising is that happiness comes from having things. Wealth and material possessions translate into status or position in society. Thus people often want things they cannot afford to buy, and some people may steal and rob to get what they want.

Another value or belief that some claim affects America's crime rate is the idea that **violence is acceptable** and even admirable. Part of American folklore is the hero who fights criminals. Our movies and television programs often show sheriffs, police officers, and cowboys using guns and violence to combat the violence of criminals. Similarly, such programs may show people committing violent acts. This does not mean that individual Americans favor the use of violence. Rather, it means that Americans may view violence as a normal part of life. Some people believe that this idea may encourage criminal behavior.

Finally, some people have connected our crime problem to the **decline of traditional family values**. They argue that many of our social problems, including crime, stem from a decline in values such as being religious, valuing education, getting married, and working hard to get ahead. The loss of these values and a greater acceptance of non-traditional attitudes and behaviors, some believe, can lead to greater poverty, social breakdown, and even crime.

The Media

The American Psychological Association notes that by the seventh grade, the average American will have watched on television 8,000 murders, plus another 100,000 acts of violence. Does watching this much violence make Americans more prone to violence? In 1972, the U.S. surgeon general, the highest medical officer in the federal government, an-

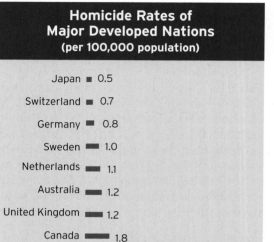

Homicide Rates of Major Developed Nations
(per 100,000 population)

Japan	0.5
Switzerland	0.7
Germany	0.8
Sweden	1.0
Netherlands	1.1
Australia	1.2
United Kingdom	1.2
Canada	1.8
United States	5.0

Source: "Global Study on Homicide," UNODC (2011)

nounced that "televised violence, indeed, does have an adverse effect on certain members of our society."

In the years that followed, the National Institute of Mental Health, the Department of Justice, the American Academy of Pediatrics, and numerous scientific studies have backed up the words of the surgeon general. Many social scientists have concluded that televised violence can contribute to antisocial behavior in children. This is particularly true when the children come from violent homes or neighborhoods. It adds to the culture of violence surrounding them. After a five-year study, the American Psychological Association reported in February 1992 that "TV violence can cause aggressive behavior and can cultivate values favoring the use of aggression to resolve conflicts."

Critics complain that violence has crept into all the media — network television, cable television, movies, videos, music lyrics, the Internet, and video games. They believe the media are creating a culture of violence. As an example, they point to "Grand Theft Auto," a highly popular, ultra-violent series of video games in which users steal cars, run over people, and kill police. Critics call it a "murder simulator" that trains young people to kill.

Gerard Jones, author of *Men of Tomorrow: Geeks, Gangsters and the Birth of the Comic Book*, thinks that violent video games do not cause violent crime. He points out that since these games first went on the market in 1997, the violent crime rate has dropped dramatically. He contends that new types of entertainment favored by young people have historically and wrongly come under fire for causing violence in young people. In the 1950s, it was comic books; in the 1930s, gangster movies.

Defenders of the media believe that it is far too simple-minded to blame violence on the media. Millions of people, they point out, view violence in the media. Only a few commit acts of violence. According to them, the reasons some people commit violence are complex and rooted in various social problems, such as increasing poverty and unemployment. Violence in entertainment, as they see it, is being made a scapegoat for society's problems. They contend that television simply reflects the level of violence in society. It does nothing to cause the violence.

A study published in *Pediatrics* lent some support to this viewpoint. The study, by Mark Singer of Case Western Reserve University in Cleveland, examined more than 2,000 third to eighth grade students. It found "disturbingly high" levels of violence among the students. But the study found only a small link between this violence and watching heavy doses of television violence. Instead, the study mainly linked the violence to students witnessing or being a victim of real-life violence at home, in the community, or at school.

The question of violence in the arts has now become a battleground between those who insist on First Amendment free-speech rights and those who insist the question is really one of corporate responsibility.

FOR DISCUSSION

1. Which do you think are the most important cultural or social factors that contribute to crime? Which are the least important? Why?
2. Which factors are most difficult to change? Which are the easiest?
3. If all murderers drank milk as children, does this prove drinking milk leads to murder? Explain.

Individual and Situational Factors

Opportunity makes the thief.
– English proverb

Another approach to studying crime is to focus on the individual and on situational factors. Crimes, after all, are committed by particular individuals in particular situations. Are some individuals more likely to commit crimes? Do crimes arise more often in certain situations? Scientists looking at individuals have looked at many possible causes of crime, including such diverse causes as biology and rational choice. Other scientists looking for situational factors in crime have studied guns, alcohol, and drugs.

Biology

Some modern researchers believe that **biological traits** may predispose some people to crime. Professors Richard J. Herrnstein and James Q. Wilson in *Crime and Human Nature* cite various studies. Studies of twins show that identical twins are much more likely than fraternal twins to have the same criminal records. Unlike fraternal twins, identical twins share the same genetic makeup. So these studies seem to indicate biology plays a role in criminality.

Even more startling is a study comparing two groups of adopted boys. The first group contained boys raised by non-criminal adopted parents but whose natural parents were criminals. The second group had boys raised by criminal adopted parents but whose natural parents were not criminals. Most people would think that the boys in the second group — raised by criminal parents — would be more likely to commit crimes. But the studies found otherwise. The boys in the first group were more likely to have criminal records.

Herrnstein and Wilson point out several biological traits that predispose a person to crime. The first is simply being male. In all known societies, young males account for almost all violent crimes. Experiments have shown male sex hormones increase aggression. Young males often have trouble adjusting to the hormones. Many engage in rowdy behavior. Some commit crimes.

A second biological trait, according to Herrnstein and Wilson, is intelligence. Studies have shown that criminals generally score low

Sixteen Techniques of Situational Crime Prevention

INCREASE THE EFFORT	INCREASE THE RISKS	REDUCE THE REWARDS	REMOVE THE EXCUSES
Harden targets steering locks anti-robbery screens tamper-proof seals	**Screen entrances/exits** electronic merchandise tags baggage screening ticket gates	**Remove targets** removable car radios women's refuges phone cards	**Set rules** hotel registration customs declaration codes of conduct
Control access entry phones PIN numbers fenced yards	**Formal surveillance** security cameras security guards burglar alarms	**Identify property** vehicle licensing property marking car-parts marking	**Alert conscience** roadside speedometers "idiots drink-and-drive" signs "shoplifting is stealing" signs
Deflect offenders street closings separation of rival fans bus stop placement	**Surveillance by employees** park attendants concierges CCTV systems	**Reduce temptation** rapid repair of vandalism off-street parking gender-neutral listings	**Control disinhibitors** drinking-age laws car ignition breathalyser V-chip in TV
Control facilitators credit card photos caller ID gun controls	**Natural surveillance** street lighting low hedges defensible space	**Deny benefits** ink merchandise tags PIN for car radios graffiti cleaning	**Assist compliance** litter bins public lavatories easy library check-out

Source: Clarke, Ronald. V. (Ed.). *Situational Crime Prevention: Successful Case Studies,* Second Edition. Albany, NY: Harrow & Heston (1997)

on intelligence tests. It isn't really known why low intelligence and crime are related. One theory is that people with low intelligence may get frustrated with school, grow angry and resentful, and start committing delinquent acts.

Another biological trait, according to Herrnstein and Wilson, is temperament. They point out that high-rate offenders typically are impulsive, rebellious thrill-seekers. To some extent, these characteristics may be inherited.

These studies provoke much controversy. Critics cast doubt on the twin and adoption studies. They criticize classifying intelligence and temperament as biological traits. But the critics are far less harsh on Herrnstein and Wilson's prescription for change:

> We know that a very small fraction of all young males commit so large a fraction of serious street crime that we can properly blame these chronic offenders for most such crime. We also know that chronic

offenders typically begin their misconduct at an early age. Early family and preschool programs may be far better repositories for the crime-prevention dollar than rehabilitation programs aimed — usually futilely — at the 19-or 20-year-old veteran offender.

Drugs and Alcohol

More than 30 percent of state prison inmates report they were under the influence of drugs when they committed their crimes. Over half admit to using drugs during the month prior to their offense. But drugs are not the only substance linked to crime. Almost 40 percent of state inmates convicted of violent crimes had been drinking before they committed their crimes.

The connection between crime and alcohol has long been noted. What to do about it is another question. Reformers at the beginning of the 20th century managed to pass the

18th Amendment to the U.S. Constitution. Effective in January 1920, it banned the sale and distribution of alcohol. But this amendment and laws supporting it were vastly unpopular. People flaunted the law and continued drinking. Gangsters grew rich smuggling and distributing alcohol. In 1933, the 21st Amendment repealed the ill-fated 18th, and alcohol has remained legal in most of the country ever since.

Guns

About 40 percent of those convicted of murder and robbery reported carrying a firearm when they committed the crime. Some criminologists tie the easy access to guns, particularly handguns, to America's high rate of violent crime.

Guns and gun ownership are common in the United States — far more so than in other democracies, which have stricter gun laws. Historically, Americans needed guns to survive on the frontier. In more recent years, incidents of violent crime, especially in urban areas, have caused millions of Americans to doubt that they can rely on police protection alone. Experts claim that 13,500 of every 100,000 Americans own handguns. As a comparison, the rate per 100,000 in Canada is 3,000 and in England, under 500. (In England, even the police do not normally carry guns.)

In 1998, the U.S. Centers for Disease Control conducted a survey of 36 developed countries. It found that the United States had the highest rate of gun-inflicted homicides. The U.S. rate of 12.95 gun homicides per 100,000 contrasted sharply with England's rate of 0.41 and South Korea's rate of 0.12. Other studies in the United States have linked the availability of handguns in a community to its rate of gun injury and homicide.

Several studies have questioned the link between guns and violent crime. Although many criminals use guns, these studies have found no evidence that decreasing the availability of guns would lower homicide rates.

This debate on the link between guns and violence often arises over the issue of gun control. This is one of the most hotly debated topics in America. One side argues that "guns don't kill people; people kill people." People on this side believe that to stop violent crime, we must focus on criminals, not guns. The other side argues that "people with guns kill people." Those on this side believe violent crime can be lowered by making guns less available in society. Recent

An officer tags guns seized at crime scenes.

U.S. Supreme Court decisions, however, have ruled that individuals have a constitutional right to own guns for self-defense.

Rational Choice

Many people believe crime involves rational choice on the part of criminals. This theory takes various forms.

In its simplest form, this theory means that people choose to become criminals. People make some sort of cost-benefit analysis before committing crimes. They calculate the benefits — these could be economic gain, the thrill of committing the crime, or any pleasure they could derive from the crime. They weigh the benefits against the costs. These could be the risk of getting caught, the harshness of punishment, pangs of conscience, or any pain they could receive from the criminal act. If the benefits outweigh the costs, then they will commit the crime.

After making a cost-benefit analysis, certain people would be more likely to choose to commit crimes. Poor people would have more to gain than rich people. People without consciences (known as psychopaths or sociopaths) would feel freer to commit crimes than most people.

Another form of rational-choice theory does not attempt to explain why people become criminals. It simply notes that criminals act rationally in one sense at least: *Most do not want to get caught.* This means that criminals will most often take the easiest path to commit a crime and may be deterred if something stands in their way. Thus car thieves prefer an unlocked car to a locked car, a car without an alarm to one with an alarm, and an empty car to one with a person in it. This logic applies to many crimes. Robbers, for example, seem to prefer lone victims as the risk of being robbed increases when a person is alone.

According to this theory, the way to cut crime is to make it more difficult, more risky, and less rewarding for the criminal. This can be done in many ways — stronger locks, increased police patrols, fewer people carrying cash, etc. The chart on page 350 lists quite a few techniques.

The question is: Do these techniques reduce crime or do they merely displace it? What happens, for example, if we make cars difficult to steal by equipping them with anti-theft devices? Will car thieves, frustrated with not being able to break into cars, turn to the violent crime of carjacking — stealing cars at gunpoint? Or, will they turn to a different kind of stealing, such as committing daytime burglaries? Or, will they stop committing crimes? Researchers have not conclusively answered these questions.

FOR DISCUSSION
1. Which do you think are the most important individual or situational factors that contribute to crime? Which are the least important? Why?
2. Which factors are most difficult to change? Which are the easiest?
3. Which of all the theories discussed do you think is most important? Which is least important? Why?
4. What additional factors do you think contribute to crime?
5. White-collar crimes are often committed by employed, well-educated people from good family backgrounds. If they don't need money, why would such people commit fraud or embezzlement?

CLASS ACTIVITY

The Causes of Crime
In this activity, students develop solutions to the problem of crime.
1. Form groups of four members each. Each group should:
   a. Discuss the various causes of crime and select the one cause it considers most important.
   b. Brainstorm solutions to crime, based on the cause it has chosen.
   c. Discuss the solutions it comes up with and choose its best solution.
   d. Discuss the costs and benefits of this solution.
   e. Prepare a brief presentation for the class on the solution.
2. Reconvene as a class. Each group should make a brief presentation supporting its solution. List the solutions on the board. Hold a debriefing discussion. Conclude by taking a class vote on which solution it believes is best.

Debriefing Questions
1. Which causes seemed easier to find solutions for? Why?
2. Which solutions would be easiest to put into effect? Why?
3. Which solutions do you think would work best? Why?

CHAPTER 23
CRIME AND THE GOVERNMENT

We the People of the United States, in Order to form a more perfect Union, establish Justice, insure domestic Tranquility, provide for the common defence, promote the general Welfare, and secure the Blessings of Liberty to ourselves and our Posterity, do ordain and establish this Constitution for the United States of America.
– Preamble to the U.S. Constitution (1787)

THE ROLE OF GOVERNMENT | CRIME AND THE FEDERAL GOVERNMENT
FEDERAL POLICY: THE PATRIOT ACT | POLICIES ON GUNS | AN ATTACK ON CRIME: THE STATE LEVEL
STATE SUPREME COURTS AND STATE CONSTITUTIONS | THE COLOR OF JUSTICE

The Role of Government

The true administration of justice is the firmest pillar of good government.
– Saying engraved on face of the New York City Criminal Courts Building

Americans often look to government to solve problems, and the problem of crime is no exception. What *can* government do to help solve America's crime problems?

To address crime problems, government makes laws, it enforces the law, and it adjudicates cases and punishes the guilty.

Legislators and members of the executive branch push for and debate the merits of laws. Some laws define new crimes. Others create programs to deal with problems such as drug addiction. Those on different sides of issues gather data and collect research to fight political battles over how best to address crime problems.

The government enforces the criminal law. Local police and county sheriffs handle most crime, but state and federal agencies are also active in enforcing the law. Law-enforcement officers at every level are guided and limited by legislation, court orders, and codes of conduct.

Courts adjudicate criminal cases, deciding whether criminal defendants are guilty or not guilty. Prosecutors work for the government and bring cases against defendants. Judges decide what laws and procedures apply, leaving juries of private citizens to decide what the facts are in each case.

Finally, a system of corrections handles those people convicted of crimes. Jails and prisons house offenders. Parole and probation officers keep track of offenders who have been released into the community.

The entire justice system is run by the government. Politicians — presidents, governors, mayors — are elected, evaluated, and replaced often on the basis of how well they meet our expectations regarding criminal law and policy.

Crime and the Federal Government

If men were angels, no government would be necessary.
– James Madison, U.S. president and "father" of the Constitution, *Federalist No. 51* (1788)

The U.S. Constitution divides the power of government into three distinct branches — the executive, legislative, and judicial. The Constitution lays out the responsibilities and powers of each branch. All three branches have responsibilities in addressing the crime problem.

The Executive Branch

As head of the executive branch, the president is responsible for enforcing federal laws. Article II,

Federal Agencies With Arrest and Firearm Authority

Agency	Number of full-time officers
U.S. Customs and Border Protection	36,863
Federal Bureau of Prisons	16,835
Federal Bureau of Investigation	12,760
U.S. Immigration and Customs Enforcement	12,446
U.S. Secret Service	5,213
Administrative Office of the U.S. Courts*	4,696
Drug Enforcement Administration	4,308
U.S. Marshals Service	3,313
Veterans Health Administration	3,128
Internal Revenue Service, Criminal Investigation	2,636
Bureau of Alcohol, Tobacco, Firearms and Explosives	2,541
U.S. Postal Inspection Service	2,288
U.S. Capitol Police	1,637
National Park Service - Rangers	1,404
Bureau of Diplomatic Security	1,049
Pentagon Force Protection Agency	725
U.S. Forest Service	644
U.S. Fish and Wildlife Service	598
National Park Service- U.S. Park Police	547
National Nuclear Security Administration	363
U.S. Mint Police	316
Amtrak Police	305
Bureau of Indian Affairs	277
Bureau of Land Management	255

*Limited to federal probation officers employed in federal judicial districts that allow officers to carry firearms.

Agencies with less than 250 officers not listed.

Source: *Census of Federal Law Enforcement Officers, 2008,* Bureau of Justice Statistics (2012)

Section 3, of the Constitution holds that the president "shall take care that the laws be faithfully executed." One way that the president exercises this power is by supervising executive agencies and departments, particularly the departments of Justice, Treasury, and Homeland Security.

Six main agencies handle most federal investigations:

The Federal Bureau of Investigation
The Drug Enforcement Administration
The Secret Service
The Postal Inspection Service
The Bureau of Alcohol, Tobacco, Firearms and Explosives
Immigration and Customs Enforcement

In addition to the big six, many other federal agencies conduct investigations: the Department of Veterans Affairs, Environmental Protection Agency, Federal Trade Commission, Fish and Wildlife Service, Food and Drug Administration, Health and Human Services, Internal Revenue Service, Securities and Exchange Commission, and U.S. Marshals Service. Most of these agencies can investigate lawbreaking, collect evidence, make arrests, and present cases to federal prosecutors.

Federal cases are prosecuted by the Department of Justice and by its U.S. attorneys throughout the country. U.S. attorneys are appointed by the president. The attorney general heads the Department of Justice.

The Legislative Branch

The Constitution outlines the powers of the U.S. Congress. In the area of criminal justice, Congress makes laws that define federal crimes and set punishments. It has made some of these laws to meet the specific requirements of Section 8 of the Constitution, which says that Congress must control America's postal services, mints, revenues, and taxes. To carry out these responsibilities, Congress has passed laws against tampering with the mail, counterfeiting coins, and smuggling. Congress has also passed statutes that outlaw spying and espionage against the United States. And Congress has used its powers over commerce to make laws against carrying stolen goods across state lines or kidnapping. These are all federal crimes.

Congress also makes laws for those parts of the country that do not fall under the jurisdiction of a state government. For example, federal law governs the District of Columbia, federal forests, military bases, post offices, federal courts, and ships at sea or airplanes in the air. In most areas, however, state and local lawmakers make the bulk of criminal laws, because the framers of the Constitution did not want all lawmaking power centralized.

Whether a specific act falls under federal or state law depends on the act and on where it is committed. For example, if John Deadly shoots and kills a man on a street in Wichita, he has committed murder and would be tried under the Kansas State Penal Code. On the other hand, if John Deadly kills a letter carrier who is out delivering mail in Wichita, he has not only committed a murder, punishable by the state of Kansas, he has also committed the federal crime of assaulting a federal employee. If he's caught, John can be tried under state law for the murder and under federal law for the assault.

But the situation is different if John Deadly shoots and kills the letter carrier *inside* the post office. Even though it is in Kansas, the post office is considered federal territory. If John is caught, he can be tried according to federal murder statutes.

Congress does not merely define crimes. It also passes legislation and creates agencies to study and reduce crime. The Office of Juvenile Justice and Delinquency Prevention (OJJDP) is an example of such an agency. Under congressional mandate to "improve the quality of juvenile justice in the United States," OJJDP allocates federal funds and coordinates programs to reduce juvenile delinquency and exploitation of children.

The Judicial Branch

The Constitution places the power of the judicial branch in the hands of "one Supreme Court and in such inferior courts the Congress may from time to time ordain and establish." Today, the federal court system consists of three basic levels — the U.S. district courts, which handle trials; U.S. courts of appeals; and the U.S. Supreme Court.

Courts at all levels, state and federal, must interpret the meaning of laws. Consider this section of the U.S. Code, which makes it against the law "for any person . . . who has been convicted *in any court*, of a crime punishable by imprisonment for a term exceeding one year . . . to . . . possess . . . any firearm."

What does "in any court" mean? Does it include a person convicted in a court in Japan? Or is it limited to U.S. courts?

In 1994, Gary Small was convicted in Japan of attempting to smuggle guns. He served five years in a Japanese prison, and when he was released, he returned home to the United States. After he bought a gun in Pennsylvania, federal prosecutors charged him under the section of the U.S. Code cited above. He argued that "in any court" meant "in any U.S. court." The trial judge disagreed. The U.S. Court of Appeals affirmed the trial court. Small appealed to the U.S. Supreme Court.

In 2005 in *Small v. U.S.*, the Supreme by a 5–3 vote ruled that "in any court" meant "in any U.S. court." The court majority stated that the context of the phrase is important. It pointed out that "Congress generally legislates with domestic concerns in mind," and probably did not mean foreign courts, which have different laws from the United States. The three dissenters argued that "any court" meant "any court" and should be interpreted this way.

The Supreme Court's decision does much more than resolve this one case. It sets a **precedent** — or a general rule to follow. The next time someone is charged under a statute that says "any court," an attorney can refer to the *Small* decision and ask that the statute be decided according to the precedent.

FOR DISCUSSION

1. For what part of the American criminal legal process is the legislative branch of the federal government responsible? The executive branch? The judicial branch?

2. Describe a crime that falls under the jurisdiction of federal rather than state law.

3. How do courts set precedents? How can precedents change the law? Do you think courts should follow precedents? Why or why not?

4. How might the *Small* decision affect the way laws are written?

What Does It Mean?

Written laws can sometimes be difficult to interpret. In this activity, students will role play courts deciding actual cases on the meaning of words in statutes.

1. Form small groups. Each group will role play the appellate court mentioned in each case.
2. Assign each group one of the **Cases**, below.
3. Each group should:
   a. Discuss and decide the question about its assigned case.
   b. Be prepared to report its answer and reasons for it to the class. If the group does not agree, a majority and minority report should be made.
   c. If time permits, read and discuss the other cases so group members can weigh in on the discussion of them.
4. Have the groups assigned to each case report on their decisions and hold a class discussion on each case.

Case 1: *Watson v. U.S.* (2007). Wanting a gun, Watson traded OxyContin, a narcotic, for a semiautomatic pistol. His exchange was with an undercover police officer. He was later arrested and convicted of drug charges. He was given a mandatory sentence based on a section of the U.S. Code. It set a mandatory minimum sentence to anyone who "during and in relation to any crime of violence or drug trafficking crime[,] . . . uses . . . a firearm." Watson appealed his sentence, claiming he was not "using" a firearm. His appeal eventually reached the U.S. Supreme Court.

Question for the U.S. Supreme Court: Did Watson use a firearm?

Case 2: *New Mexico v. Ogden* (1994). Ogden was charged with first-degree murder for shooting and killing a uniformed Community Service Officer. The prosecution filed a death-penalty case, because the New Mexico Code makes it an aggravating circumstance if "the victim was a peace officer who was acting in the lawful discharge of an official duty when he was murdered." Ogden made a pretrial objection that a Community Service Officer is not a "peace officer." The trial judge agreed, and the prosecution appealed all the way to the New Mexico Supreme Court.

The code does not define the term "peace officer." Community Service Officers are paid to lighten the workload of city police by doing traffic control, patrolling the city, investigating non-injury accidents, issuing parking citations, helping stranded motorists, and investigating misdemeanor crimes such as bicycle theft and shoplifting. They are not trained by the police academy and are not authorized to make arrests. They do not carry guns, but do carry a chemical spray, wear bullet-proof vests, and are trained in self-defense. They also carry two-way radios and drive marked patrol cars.

Question for the New Mexico Supreme Court: Is a Community Service Officer a peace officer?

Case 3: *Tune v. Texas Dept. of Public Safety* (2000). In 1972, Tune pleaded guilty to a felony and was sentenced to two years of probation. After Tune completed his probation, the court ordered his conviction set aside, dismissed the indictment, and discharged him from probation. In 1999, Tune applied for a permit to carry a concealed handgun. The Texas Department of Public Safety turned him down because the law says no permit shall be issued to anyone who has "been convicted of a felony." He appealed the department's decision because his conviction had been set aside. A lower court agreed with him, the Texas court of appeals reversed the lower court, and Tune appealed to the Texas Supreme Court.

Question for the Texas Supreme Court: Should we consider Tune "convicted of a felony"?

Case 4: *Maddox v. Florida* (2006). Pulled over for making an illegal lane change, Maddox had no proof of insurance and no driver's license. He gave a false name and signed the ticket with the false name. His identity was discovered, and he was charged with, among other things, forgery. The ticket was the main evidence against him on the forgery charge. Maddox was tried and convicted. He appealed, arguing that the Florida Code bans the ticket from being used as evidence in court.

As in other states, signing a ticket in Florida is not an admission of guilt. But Florida law is worded: "Such citations shall not be admissible evidence in any trial."

Question for the Florida Supreme Court: Should the ticket have been allowed in as evidence at Maddox's trial for forgery?

A little more than a month after the September 11, 2001, terrorist attacks, President George W. Bush signed the Patriot Act into law.

Federal Policy: The Patriot Act

Those who would give up essential liberty to purchase a little temporary safety deserve neither liberty nor safety.
– Benjamin Franklin (1706-1790)

[The] Bill of Rights [is not] a suicide pact.
– Robert H. Jackson, Supreme Court justice, dissenting in *Terminiello v. Chicago* (1949)

Terrorists struck America on September 11, 2001. Highjacking four planes, they flew two of them into the World Trade Center towers in New York and another into the Pentagon in Washington. The fourth plane crashed in Pennsylvania before it reached its target in Washington. Within two hours, both of the massive 110-story twin towers had collapsed. A wing of the Pentagon was severely damaged. More than 3,000 people died in the attacks. Two days later, the White House identified the culprits as members of Al Qaeda, an Islamist terrorist group based in Afghanistan, but with terrorist cells throughout the world. The hijackers had worked out of Al Qaeda terrorist cells operating in the United States. No one knew whether more terrorist attacks were coming.

Soon after September 11, then-U.S. Attorney General John Ashcroft brought before Congress a list of recommended changes in the law to combat terrorism. Some of these measures had long been opposed by members of Congress as infringing on the rights of Americans.

But September 11 had swept away all previous objections. The U.S. Senate quickly passed the USA PATRIOT Act. (Its title is a 10-letter acronym standing for Uniting and Strengthening America by Providing Appropriate Tools Required to Intercept and Obstruct Terrorism.) Only one senator, Russell Feingold (D-Wis.), voted against it.

The next day, the House of Representatives passed the bill 357–66. The final bill was 342 pages long and changed more than 15 existing laws. Most of the Justice Department's recommendations were incorporated into it, but several provisions were set to expire in 2005.

On October 26, President George W. Bush signed the Patriot Act into law. He praised the "new tools to fight the present danger . . . a threat like no other our Nation has ever faced." He also asserted that the Patriot Act "upholds and respects the civil liberties guaranteed by our Constitution."

The Patriot Act defines "domestic terrorism" as

activities within the United States that . . . involve acts dangerous to human life that . . . appear to be intended —
(i) to intimidate or coerce a civilian population;
(ii) to influence the policy of a government by intimidation or coercion; or
(iii) to affect the conduct of a government by mass destruction, assassination, or kidnapping. . . .

The Patriot Act and Privacy

Some of the most controversial parts of the Patriot Act surround issues of privacy and government surveillance. The Fourth Amendment to the U.S. Constitution protects the "right of the people to be secure in their persons, houses, papers, and effects, against unreasonable searches and seizures . . . ." It requires law-enforcement officers to obtain warrants before making most searches. To get a warrant, officers must make sworn statements before a

The Patriot Act expanded the powers of law enforcement to conduct surveillance and make searches.

judge "particularly describing the place to be searched, and the persons or things to be seized." The judge may issue a search warrant only if officers show "probable cause" that the person is engaged in criminal activity. Federal law requires that officers report to the court on the results of the search.

Surveillance, such as wiretaps and physical searches, requires officers to prove "probable cause" of criminality. Even before the Patriot Act, there were exceptions under federal law.

One was for so-called "pen-trap" orders. Telephone companies use a pen-trap device to record the numbers dialed to and from a particular telephone. To obtain these numbers from a telephone company, officers must get a pen-trap order from a judge. They do not need to show probable cause, but must certify that the information is needed for an ongoing criminal investigation. The reason for the lesser standard is that these records are far less intrusive than wiretaps and physical searches.

Another major exception was for matters before the Federal Intelligence Surveillance Court. In 1978, Congress passed the Federal Intelligence Surveillance Act (FISA), which created the court, following scandals revealing that U.S. intelligence agencies had spied on hundreds of thousands of American citizens, most notably the Reverend Martin Luther King Jr.

FISA was a compromise between those who wanted to leave U.S. intelligence agencies free from restrictions and those who wanted intelligence agencies to apply for search warrants like other law-enforcement agencies. Congress required U.S. intelligence agencies (the FBI and National Security Agency) to apply for warrants for wiretaps and other surveillance on foreign governments and suspected foreign agents. But because the agencies are not investigating domestic crime, they do not have to meet the probable-cause standard. They only have to certify that the purpose of the investigation is to track a foreign government or agent. They do not have to report to the court on the results of the surveillance. The court meets in secret with only government representatives present and has never denied an intelligence agency's application for a search warrant.

The Patriot Act expands all these exceptions to the probable-cause requirement. Section 215 of the act permits the FBI to go before the Foreign Intelligence Surveillance Court for an order to search for "any tangible things" connected to a terrorism suspect. The order would be granted as long as the FBI certifies that the search is "to protect against international terrorism or clandestine intelligence activities [spying]." But the FBI would not need to meet the stronger standard of probable cause.

The Patriot Act now authorizes this court to issue search orders directed at any U.S. citizen whom the FBI believes may be involved in terrorist activities. Such activities may, in part, even involve First Amendment protected acts such as participating in non-violent public protests.

In Section 215, "any tangible things" may include almost any kind of property — such as books, documents, and computers. The FBI may also monitor or seize personal records held by public libraries, bookstores, medical offices, Internet providers, churches, political groups, universities, and other businesses and institutions. The Patriot Act prohibits third parties served with Section 215 orders such as Internet providers and public librarians to inform anyone that the FBI has conducted a search of their records.

Section 216 of the Patriot Act extends pen-trap orders to include e-mail and web browsing. The FBI can ask Internet service providers to turn over a log of the web sites a person visits and the addresses of e-mail coming to and from the person's computer.

Section 213 authorizes so-called "sneak-and-peek" searches for all federal criminal investigations. When applying for a search warrant, officers may show that there is "reasonable cause to believe that providing immediate notification . . . may have an adverse result." If the judge approves, then the FBI can delay notifying a citizen about the search for a "reasonable period." In 2005, the period was changed to 30 days unless the facts justify a longer delay. Thus, the FBI may search a citizen's home or business in secret. The FBI says these searches may be necessary to prevent the destruction of evidence or to keep from jeopardizing an ongoing secret investigation.

FISA required that the purpose of any search or electronic surveillance must be to obtain foreign intelligence information. The courts interpreted purpose to mean "primary purpose." Section 218 of the Patriot Act modified it to be a "significant purpose."

Court Challenges

A number of court cases have challenged the Patriot Act. One of the most publicized cases involved the 2004 terrorist attack in Spain. Bombs exploded on commuter trains in Madrid, killing 191 people and injuring more than a thousand others. The Spanish National Police found a fingerprint on a plastic bag containing detonators. Spain sent copies of the print to police around the world. The FBI believed the print matched Brandon Mayfield, a 38-year-old American born in Oregon and former U.S. Army officer. Mayfield worked as an attorney and lived with his wife and three children in a suburb of Portland. He was also a practicing Muslim. He had never been in trouble with the law. Since 1994, Mayfield had never left the United States.

After getting approval from the Federal Intelligence Surveillance Court, the FBI placed electronic listening devices and conducted sneak-and-peak searches in Mayfield's home and law office. The Mayfields detected that someone had entered their home, but believed it was burglars. The FBI sent Mayfield's fingerprints to the Spanish police, who examined them and concluded they did not match the print on the plastic bag. Nevertheless, the FBI applied for a search warrant in federal District Court, claiming the print on the plastic bag was a "100% positive identification" of Mayfield. The court issued a search warrant, and the FBI seized Mayfield's computer and many papers. Mayfield later was arrested and imprisoned for two weeks, as the news media around the world reported on the arrest. When the Spanish police announced that they had matched the fingerprint and arrested a suspect, Mayfield was released.

Mayfield sued the U.S. government for false arrest, unlawful imprisonment, and conducting illegal searches and seizures. The case was settled out of court. Mayfield received $2 million, an apology, and a promise that everything seized would be returned to him. In return, Mayfield promised not to sue the government except for seeking declaratory relief on the constitutionality of parts of the Patriot Act.

In declaratory relief, parties ask a court to make a judgment of their rights under the law. In Mayfield's declaratory relief hearing in District Court, a trial court, the judge ruled parts of the Patriot Act unconstitutional. The judge noted that FISA could avoid requiring probable cause because it dealt with foreign intelligence, not with crimes. But the Patriot Act allowed searches and electronic surveillance if a "significant purpose" was foreign intelligence. If the government asserts this purpose, it can now "obtain surveillance orders . . . even if the government's primary purpose is to gather evidence of domestic criminal activity."

Since the adoption of the Bill of Rights in 1791, the government has been prohibited from gathering evidence for use in a prosecution against an American citizen in a courtroom unless the government could prove the existence of probable cause that a crime has been committed. The hard won legislative compromise previously embodied in FISA reduced the probable cause requirement only for national security intelligence gathering. The Patriot Act effectively eliminates that compromise by allowing the Executive Branch to bypass the Fourth Amendment in gathering evidence for a criminal prosecution.

The government appealed the ruling, and the Ninth Circuit Court of Appeals in 2010 in *Mayfield v. U.S.* reversed the trial court's ruling. The appeals court did not base its decision on the constitutionality of the Patriot Act. Instead, it ruled that Mayfield lacked standing to bring the case. Standing means that a party has a personal stake in the outcome of a case. A person cannot challenge the constitutionality of a law unless the person can show that he will be immediately harmed by the law. Mayfield argued he had standing because the government had not returned all his papers. The appeals court ruled he did not have standing because even if he won the declaratory judgment, the court could not order his papers returned to him. Mayfield in his settlement had agreed not to pursue such an order.

Mayfield appealed to the U.S. Supreme Court, but the court decided not to hear the case. In fact, the court has so far only decided to hear one case on the Patriot Act. The court upheld a part of the Patriot Act that bans giving material support to terrorist organizations.

The Debate Over the Patriot Act

According to the Bill of Rights Defense Committee, eight states (Alaska, California, Colorado, Hawaii, Idaho, Maine, Montana and Vermont) and 406 cities, towns and counties have passed resolutions protesting provisions of the Patriot Act.

In a report called "Unpatriotic Acts," the American Civil Liberties Union warned that American freedom was endangered by the Patriot Act: "Section 215 is likely to chill lawful dissent. If people think that their conversations, their emails, and their reading habits are being monitored, people will feel less comfort-able saying what they think — especially if they disagree with government policies."

In a *Washington Post* opinion piece, Heather MacDonald, a writer at the Manhattan Institute, defended the Patriot Act. She countered the ACLU by stressing that Section 215 requires a court order. She said there was no reason for anyone to feel "afraid to read books" or "terrified into silence. . . . Were that ever the case, it would be thanks to the misinformation spread by advocates and politicians, not because of any real threat posed by" the Patriot Act.

Despite criticism of the act, Congress has voted twice to reauthorize it — in 2005 and again in 2011 (a stop-gap measure was passed in 2010). During the latest reauthorization debate, Senator Ron Wyden of Oregon, a member of the Senate Intelligence committee charged that the government has classified how it interprets Section 215. He said, "When the American people find out how their government has secretly interpreted the Patriot Act, they will be stunned and they will be angry." The Justice Department responded: "Section 215 is not a secret law, nor has it been implemented under secret legal opinions by the Justice Department."

Congress will continue to monitor and debate the Patriot Act, and the Supreme Court may rule on additional challenges to it. The basic question that the Congress and court will have to answer is: What is the proper balance between national security and protecting individual rights?

FOR DISCUSSION

1. How does the Patriot Act define "domestic terrorism"? Do you think participants in public protests could ever be accused of "domestic terrorism" under this definition? Why or why not?

2. The Justice Department has proposed that the government should be able to ask a court to revoke the citizenship of any American who provides "material support" to terrorists. Do you support the proposal? Why or why not?

3. Explain the District Court's and Ninth Circuit's opinions in *Mayfield v. U.S.* Which do you think is right? Why?

4. At the beginning of the article are two famous quotations. What do they mean? Which, if any, do you agree with? Explain.

National Security and Freedom

In this activity, students discuss sections of the Patriot Act and decide whether they favor or oppose them.

1. Form small groups.
2. Members of each group should discuss and then decide whether to support or oppose the following parts of the Patriot Act:
   a. Section 213 "sneak-and-peek" searches of a person's property.
   b. Section 215 orders by the Foreign Intelligence Surveillance Court for searches of a citizen's "tangible things" based on FBI certification rather than probable cause.
   c. Section 215 searches of a citizen's public library records.
   d. Section 215 requirement that third parties like librarians are prohibited from informing anyone an FBI search has taken place.
3. The whole class should next discuss the Patriot Act provisions one at a time. At the beginning of each discussion, group members should report their decision along with their reasons for it. The students should then try to persuade each other to support or oppose the provision. At the end of the discussion on each provision, the class should vote to support or oppose it.
4. Using information and arguments from the article and class discussion, the students should write an essay on this question:

   What is the proper balance between national security and the protection of individual rights?

Policies on Guns

A well regulated Militia, being necessary to the security of a free State, the right of the people to keep and bear Arms, shall not be infringed.
– Second Amendment to the U.S. Constitution (1791)

Americans possess more than 200 million firearms. Each year about 640,000 violent crimes, including 16,000 murders are committed with guns, mostly handguns. Some people believe gun-control laws, which restrict gun ownership, can reduce the bloodshed. Others believe that guns help protect Americans and gun laws should be less strict.

Americans have highly conflicting views on gun laws. According to a 2011 Gallup Poll, the public splits 44 percent in favor of stricter gun laws, 43 percent in favor of keeping gun laws as they are now, and 11 percent in favor of making our gun laws less strict. This is a record low favoring stricter gun laws. Twenty years earlier, the same poll found almost 80 percent of Americans favoring stricter gun laws.

Gun control faces stiff opposition in the United States. Millions of Americans point out that gun ownership is a right and that guns serve a legitimate purpose in society. They argue that guns are not the problem. Rather than penalizing law-abiding gun owners, they favor punishing more harshly those who use guns to commit crimes.

The opposition is led by the National Rifle Association (NRA) and the gun industry. The NRA represents almost 4-million hunters and gun enthusiasts. The gun industry, made up of manufacturers and retailers, earns billions of dollars annually. Together they form a powerful opposition to legislation imposing control on guns.

Over the years, however, the federal government has enacted five major nationwide gun laws. In 1934, it prohibited the possession of machine guns, sawed-off shotguns, and silencers. The Gun Control Act of 1968 limited the importation and sale of cheap handguns, known as Saturday Night Specials, and prohibited the interstate sale of handguns. The Brady Act, passed in 1993, requires a five-day waiting period for all handgun purchases. The 1994 crime bill banned the import and manufacture of certain military assault weapons. A 1996 law banned anyone convicted of a domestic violence offense from owning or using a gun.

The 1994 assault-weapon ban expired in September 2004. President George W. Bush stated that he favored extending the ban, but Congress refused to extend it. Supporters of the ban say that assault weapons pose tremendous dangers to the public, and there is no good reason for private citizens to possess them. Opponents say that few crimes are committed with assault weapons (and those are by criminals who can easily get around the ban) and the ban violates the Second Amendment.

The Second Amendment in the Courts

The Second Amendment grants the right to "keep and bear Arms." The extent of this right was debated until recently as the U.S. Constitution Supreme Court made only one ruling on the Second Amendment in the 20th century. In 1939 in *U.S. v. Miller*, a defendant was convicted of transporting a sawed-off shotgun in violation of the federal government's 1934 gun law. The defendant appealed his conviction saying the law violated the Second Amendment. A unanimous court rejected this argument. The court noted that the "obvious purpose" of the Second Amendment was "to assure the continuation and render possible the effectiveness of" militias. "It must be interpreted and applied with that end in view." The court concluded: "In the absence of any evidence tending to show that possession or use of a . . . [saw-off shotgun] . . . has some reasonable relationship to the preservation or efficiency of a well regulated militia, we cannot say that the Second Amendment guarantees the right to keep and bear such an instrument."

In the wake of the *Miller* decision, federal appeals courts upheld gun-control laws when they were challenged on Second Amendment grounds. In 2008, however, in *D.C. v. Heller*, the U.S. Supreme Court in a 5–4 vote struck down a D.C. law that essentially banned handguns and ruled that the Second Amendment secures "an individual right to keep and bear arms." It held that government could not ban "handguns held and used for self-defense in the home." Two years later, in *McDonald v. Chicago*, the court ruled that this right applied to state governments under the 14th Amendment, because "the right to keep and bear arms" is "among those fundamental rights necessary to our system of ordered liberty."

The effect of these decisions on gun-control laws is not clear. The decision in *Heller* stated:

Like most rights, the right secured by the Second Amendment is not unlimited. From Blackstone through the 19th-century cases, commentators and courts routinely explained that the right was not a right to keep and carry any weapon whatsoever in any manner whatsoever and for whatever purpose. . . . For example, the majority of the 19th-century courts to consider the question held that prohibitions on carrying concealed weapons were lawful under the Second Amendment or state analogues. . . . [N]othing in our opinion should be taken to cast doubt on longstanding prohibitions on the possession of firearms by felons and the mentally ill, or laws forbidding the carrying of firearms in sensitive places such as schools and government buildings, or laws imposing conditions and qualifications on the commercial sale of arms.

Thus far, following the *Heller* decision, federal courts have continued to uphold gun-control laws. The debate has moved from whether the Second Amendment confers an individual right to whether a particular law is a reasonable regulation under the Second Amendment.

Measures Favored by Gun Enthusiasts

For many years, gun enthusiasts and proponents of gun control have been fighting over gun measures, those currently in existence and proposed measures. Below are a few measures favored by gun enthusiasts.

Right to Carry Laws. Over the last 30 years, gun enthusiasts have been successful in getting many states to pass laws allowing more people to carry concealed handguns. Currently, four states have no restrictions on people carrying such weapons: Alaska, Arizona, Vermont, and Wyoming. Thirty-eight states have "shall-issue" laws. These laws provide that if a person meets certain requirements, the authorities shall issue a concealed gun permit. The conditions typically include being a resident, being over 18, passing a criminal background check, attending a handgun-safety class, and paying a fee.

The remaining states have laws that gun enthusiasts would like to change. Ten states have "may issue" laws, meaning that the authorities may issue a permit if the person meets certain requirements, but they don't have to issue it and often do not. One state, Illinois, does not allow anyone to carry a concealed handgun.

Extension of Places Where Weapons May Be Carried. Many gun enthusiasts believe law-abiding people should be able to carry their guns almost anywhere, and they are seeking to break down legal barriers preventing them from carrying their guns.

For almost 100 years, guns were banned in National Parks, where hunting is not allowed. A new federal law was passed in 2010, making it legal for people to carry guns into National Parks if they are complying with federal law and the gun laws of the state the park is in. Thus, today a person with a state concealed weapon permit may carry a concealed hand-gun in almost all national parks.

Many states outlaw carrying loaded guns (even with a permit) into bars and other places that serve alcohol. Recently, four states — Tennessee, Arizona, Georgia and Virginia — have passed laws allowing people to enter such establishments with weapons as long as they are otherwise complying with state law. Eighteen other states permit guns in restaurants serving alcohol.

Gun enthusiasts support right to carry laws and extending places where guns may be carried because they believe law-abiding citizens should be allowed to protect themselves and others and that criminals will carry guns regardless of what the law says. Opponents of these laws assert that more guns will put more people in danger and result in more gunshot wounds and deaths.

Gun-Control Measures

In addition to renewing the assault weapons ban, supporters of gun control favor a number of proposed gun-control laws, each of them opposed by gun enthusiasts.

Requiring gun owners to register firearms and to have a state firearms license. Supporters say that just as the state registers cars and licenses to people who drive, the state should also license gun owners and register guns. They think such a system would help keep guns out of the wrong hands. Opponents believe this is the first step to outlawing guns, which will only keep guns away from law-abiding people. They also say the car comparison is faulty. Cars, they say, cause many more deaths than guns and, unlike gun ownership, car ownership is a privilege, not a right.

Compel gun manufacturers to install safety devices. Proposals include requiring built-in

Workers destroy weapons confiscated by police.

locks and eventually "smart guns," which can be operated only by the lawful owner. Supporters believe these will prevent others from using the gun. Opponents believe these devices increase the costs, may cause the weapons to misfire, and may be unconstitutional.

Make bullet manufacturers put serial numbers on every bullet. The serial number would also be on the box of ammunition and sellers would record who bought each box. Supporters say bullets are often recovered at a crime scene and having serial numbers would help solve crimes. Opponents respond that criminals would remove serial numbers and the high cost to manufacturers would be passed on to everyone buying bullets.

Limit gun purchases to one a month per person. Much of the illegal gun trade is carried on by middlemen who buy guns from dealers in bulk and sell them to juveniles and criminals. Supporters say this law will stop the middlemen from buying guns. Opponents

ARGUMENTS ON HANDGUN CONTROL

Against Handgun Control	For Handgun Control
Gun control impinges on a basic right of all Americans – the right to protect themselves. This right is so important that the Second Amendment to the Constitution guarantees the right to bear arms.	The Second Amendment is not an unlimited right. Most gun-control laws are reasonable restrictions on this right.
With our society's high rate of violence and lack of adequate policing, guns offer citizens protection.	Guns are far more likely to harm members of the owner's household than offer protection against criminals.
"Guns don't kill people. People kill people." Switzerland, which has a low rate of murder, requires most adult males to keep automatic weapons at home for the army.	Guns make bad situations worse. Our murder rate is higher than other countries because handguns are so readily available.
"When guns are outlawed, only outlaws will have guns." Criminals will always find ways of getting guns or other weapons. Washington, D.C., and other jurisdictions with strong gun-control laws have the worst murder rates in the country.	Most of the crimes committed with guns in Washington, D.C., are committed with guns bought in nearby states with lax gun laws.
Instead of penalizing ordinary citizens, the proper way to keep criminals from using guns is to impose harsher penalties on criminals who use them.	We already impose mandatory sentences on criminals using guns.
Our country has too many guns in circulation for gun-control laws to be effective.	Canada had similar laws to ours until the 1920s. Gun control has worked there.
Even if gun-control laws did reduce the use of handguns, criminals would simply shift to other weapons.	Guns are more lethal than other weapons. A person shot with a gun is five times more likely to die than a person stabbed with a knife.

think criminals can easily get around this law by using groups of people to buy guns. Again, they say, only the law-abiding will be prevented from buying guns.

Ban large-capacity ammunition clips. Under this proposal, it would be against the law to possess or sell ammunition clips that contain more than 10 rounds of ammunition. Supporters point out that these clips are not necessary for hunting or self-defense, but have been used in several recent mass slayings. Opponents argue that these clips do promote self-defense, particularly if a person is attacked by a mob.

Supporters and opponents have long debated the merits of gun control. (See **Arguments on Handgun Control** for some of the most common arguments.)

Supporters of gun control point to other Western democracies, such as Canada, which have strict gun-control laws and far lower rates of violent crime. They cite a 1988 study in the *New England Journal of Medicine* comparing a Canadian city, Vancouver, with an American city, Seattle, which are about 100 miles apart. The risk of being murdered by a handgun was about five times higher in Seattle. And a person assaulted in Seattle was twice as likely to die as a person assaulted in Vancouver. Supporters of gun control argue that strict gun-control laws will reduce violent crime in America.

Opponents of gun control question the link between guns and violent crime. They cite countries, such as Switzerland and Israel, which mandate that citizen-soldiers keep guns at home and yet have low murder rates. Opponents say that gun-control laws have no effect on criminals. They point to Washington, D.C. Until recently, it in effect banned handguns, and yet it still had one of the worst murder rates in the country. Gun-control laws, they say, only make it more difficult for law-abiding citizens to buy firearms, which is a citizen's right under the Constitution.

FOR DISCUSSION

1. Do you agree with the *Heller* and *McDonald* decisions? Explain.
2. Do you think gun control can reduce violent crime? Why or why not?
3. Which of the gun-control policies mentioned seem the best? The worst? Why?

An Attack on Crime: The State Level

We must bear in mind that under our federal system of government, the states have primary authority for dealing with most crimes committed within their border, and that includes the vast majority of violent crimes.
– William French Smith (1917–1990), U.S. attorney general

Like the federal government, state governments are divided into three branches — executive, legislative, and judicial. State legislatures define crimes and pass other crime bills, which the governor signs into law. State codes define all felony offenses and many lesser offenses, but local governments enact some misdemeanors and local ordinances.

In turn, state, county, and municipal police departments enforce these laws. The most visible of the state police agencies is usually the state police or highway patrol, but the state also has narcotics, investigative, and other units. Almost every county has a sheriff's department run by an elected sheriff. By far the largest law-enforcement agencies are the local police, which account for more three-fourths of all those employed as law-enforcement officers.

People accused of violating state or local crimes appear before state criminal trial courts. If convicted, they serve sentences in municipal jails or state prisons. They may also appeal their convictions in appellate courts. The highest appellate court in the state is usually called the state supreme court. It has the final word in interpreting state law and the state constitution.

Defendants can appeal to the U.S. Supreme Court only on issues of U.S. constitutional law.

FOR DISCUSSION

1. Why do you think controlling violent crime is primarily the responsibility of the states?
2. Under what circumstances could the U.S. Supreme Court overturn a state law? Explain.

Rate of Violent Crime in Each State

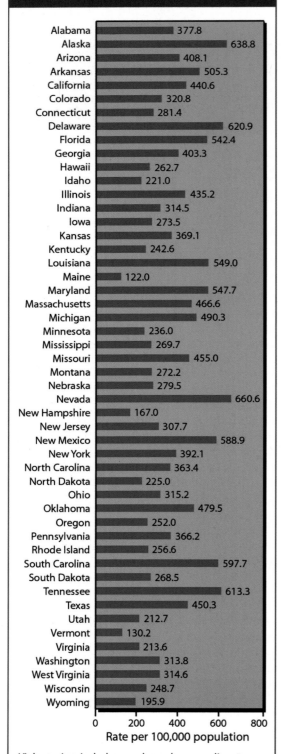

State	Rate
Alabama	377.8
Alaska	638.8
Arizona	408.1
Arkansas	505.3
California	440.6
Colorado	320.8
Connecticut	281.4
Delaware	620.9
Florida	542.4
Georgia	403.3
Hawaii	262.7
Idaho	221.0
Illinois	435.2
Indiana	314.5
Iowa	273.5
Kansas	369.1
Kentucky	242.6
Louisiana	549.0
Maine	122.0
Maryland	547.7
Massachusetts	466.6
Michigan	490.3
Minnesota	236.0
Mississippi	269.7
Missouri	455.0
Montana	272.2
Nebraska	279.5
Nevada	660.6
New Hampshire	167.0
New Jersey	307.7
New Mexico	588.9
New York	392.1
North Carolina	363.4
North Dakota	225.0
Ohio	315.2
Oklahoma	479.5
Oregon	252.0
Pennsylvania	366.2
Rhode Island	256.6
South Carolina	597.7
South Dakota	268.5
Tennessee	613.3
Texas	450.3
Utah	212.7
Vermont	130.2
Virginia	213.6
Washington	313.8
West Virginia	314.6
Wisconsin	248.7
Wyoming	195.9

Rate per 100,000 population

Violent crime includes murder and non-negligent manslaughter, forcible rape, robbery, and aggravated assault.

Source: Sourcebook of Criminal Justice Statistics Online (2010)

CLASS ACTIVITY

A State Senate Committee

Passing anti-crime legislation is not as simple as learning the facts and holding a debate. In this activity, students learn some of the ins and outs of state legislation. They take part in a role play based on a fictional state's attack on its crime problem. In the role play, students serve on a state senate committee discussing proposed Senate Bill 1715, an anti-crime bill.

1. As a class, read the background information on **The Fictional State of Columbia,** plus the description of the anti-crime bill (**Senate Bill 1715**) and the **Description of the State Districts**. In the role play, each student represents one of the districts described.

2. Hold a discussion using the discussion questions on page 369.

3. Form committees of five or 10 students each. (If the committee has 10 members, the chairperson should be non-voting so that there are an uneven number of members.) Each committee should:

   a. Count off and assign either one or two persons (depending on the number of people on the committee) to represent one of the five districts.

   b. Select a chairperson.

   c. Have each person reread his or her district's description.

4. Before beginning committee deliberations, students should meet in district caucuses for preliminary discussions. This means all the members representing a particular district, such as district 1, should meet in one group to discuss the district's reaction toward the three provisions of the bill. Go over which sections the district favors, which it opposes, and discuss changes the district would like in the bill.

5. The students should next return to their senate committee. The committees should carefully review all three provisions of SB 1715, discuss, and vote on the measure by following these steps:

   Step 1. Committee chairperson or a designated member reads aloud the text of the first provision of SB 1715.

(Continued on next page.)

Step 2. Chairperson calls on members to discuss this provision and how their districts feel about it.

Step 3. Chairperson calls for amendments. Committee members can propose amendments to the provision. Members discuss any amendments and vote on them.

Step 4. Chairperson has the committee vote on the provision, including any amendments the committee has added. There are three possible votes:

Pass, which will send the bill to the full senate with a recommendation to pass it.

Defeat, which will send the bill to the full senate with a recommendation to defeat it.

Table, which will tie the bill up in committee indefinitely.

Step 5. The committee repeats the steps for all three provisions of the bill and then writes a brief report on the committee's recommendations. (Break up the report so that different people on the committee work on different parts of the report.)

6. Reconvene as a class playing the full senate. Each committee should read its report. The whole class will then vote on any amendments offered and will then vote whether to pass or defeat the bill.

The Fictional State of Columbia

Columbia is a picturesque mountain and prairie state in the middle of the country far away from the coasts. It has almost 4 million residents, about half of whom live in rural areas on farms or in small towns. Columbia has many dairy farms and egg ranches. It also has a few large agricultural corporations that raise hogs, cattle, corn, and wheat.

Two million Columbians live in cities, almost a million in the biggest city, Athena. Industries in the Athena area mainly make textiles, clothing, and computer hardware. There is one auto assembly plant. A particularly rugged mountain range passes through the western part of the state, and tourists flock to the mountains in the summer and winter. Tourists also come to see Gold Canyon near the mountains, which is the site of the White Water mining district with many ghost towns and abandoned mines. Many Europeans come to see the mining areas and stay in one of the spas in the foothills. Tourism has become an important addition to a weak economy.

Although crime has fallen slightly in recent years, Columbia still has a major crime problem. It got national publicity last year when the daughter of the Danish ambassador was accidentally killed in a mini-market holdup. The crime problem grew serious in Athena when drugs were first imported by a West Coast gang 30 years ago. Since then, the problem has spread to most of the smaller cities in the state.

Senate Bill 1715

State Senator Alan Parsons introduced a bill designed to solve Columbia's crime problem. He incorporated many sweeping changes into his bill, which was assigned the number SB 1715, which stands for Senate Bill 1715. This is the bill:

Preamble: We, the people of Columbia, declare that it is our inalienable right to live in a society free from the fear and threat of criminal attack upon our property and persons. We declare that the men and women who commit crimes are the enemies of our state, our society, and our general welfare. For this reason, we amend the Columbia Constitution and Penal Code to include the following provisions:

Provision 1: Any person who has already been convicted of two felonies shall, upon conviction of a third and separate felony, be sentenced to serve 25 years in state prison. This penalty is mandatory for all felons upon their third conviction and is to be served without possibility of parole.

Provision 2: Any citizen who wounds, disables, or apprehends a person committing or attempting to commit a robbery or burglary within the jurisdiction of this state shall be entitled to $5,000 upon the capture and conviction of said felon. In the event of the death of said felon, an award of $5,000 shall be made upon a finding of justifiable homicide by a duly constituted coroner's jury.

(Continued on next page.)

Provision 3: The legislature hereby appropriates $50 million from the general fund for use by county, municipal, or township governments for either of the following purposes:

a. The hiring, training, and maintenance of additional police officers.

b. The renovation of jails or the construction of additional cells in existing jails. This fund shall be administered and distributed by the state attorney general's office upon application by local governments.

Description of the State Districts

In the role play that follows, you will represent one of the following districts in the state of Columbia. It will help you in the role play to be familiar with all the districts.

District 1

Most of the district is made up of the richer suburbs of Athena. There are two large modern malls to serve them and the state's only theme park, Prairieland. A lot of the residents are newly wealthy and have moved here to escape the troubles of the inner city. The state capital buildings in Athena are just across the district line, and many of the higher level state administrators live here.

The areas of District 1 nearest the city are often targeted for burglaries, and several brutal muggings and rapes have occurred on local streets. Recently, there has been a number of carjackings, with new models taken from their owners at gunpoint.

The people in District 1 want someone to take action against crime immediately. Many of them, however, are against taxation, and they are worried about the budget impact of new anticrime measures. Also, several important people in District 1 have expressed concerns about the first provision of the bill. They do not want the bill to cover "victimless" crimes, such as drug use or gambling, and they don't want attention given to white-collar crime, such as embezzlement or corporate fraud.

District 2

District 2 is on the opposite side of Athena from District 1, and it includes most of the blue-collar suburbs and the industries. It is mostly white, though some African Americans and Latinos have moved into the edge of the district. A recent recession and the closing of two electronics plants have hit District 2 hard. Almost 10 percent of the work force is unemployed. Even the auto assembly plant has cut production and laid off a quarter of its employees.

In the past, the main problems in the district were juvenile delinquency and fights outside several notorious bars. Now, however, the number of muggings and street robberies is rising. Also, the biggest industries report a number of suspicious fires and acts of sabotage. Gang graffiti has begun to appear on walls everywhere.

People in District 2 are angry, but they are not sure what to do. Many of them talk about getting tougher on the criminals, and they blame the police. They feel that richer areas like District 1 get much better policing than they do.

District 3

District 3 is in the northwest part of the state. It includes Gold Canyon and was once the Whitewater Mining district. The minerals were played out long ago, and it is now mainly a picturesque tourist area in the foothills. The district features many resorts and spas. The biggest town is College Park, which contains Columbia State University, and most of the faculty and students live here.

Crime has decreased most in this district. The campus police have the university area under control, and a few extra units of the state police have managed to stop victimization of tourists.

People in the Whitewater area are worried that publicity about crime will scare off tourists. They want a well-publicized anti-crime campaign that will reassure potential tourists. Many other voters in the district, however, are opposed to what they see as repressive legislation like SB 1715.

(Continued on next page.)

The people near the university are largely opposed to handguns. They passed a local ordinance to require a long waiting period before purchasing any firearm. They would strongly oppose any state law that would encourage people to buy handguns.

District 4

This district is in the center of the state and largely agricultural. The largest town, Lone Pine, has just over 1,000 people and serves the surrounding farms. Three very large agricultural corporations employ hundreds of field hands and some administrators. People in the smaller towns run cafes and gas stations that depend on tourists passing through to the mountains in the west.

A few years ago, little crime took place in District 4, except an occasional gas station holdup and a rare murder. Recently, gangs from the cities have made raids on the larger farms or on businesses on payroll day. There have even been a few midnight assaults and rapes in the small towns.

Many district residents blame Athena for the crime, and they feel no one in the big city takes them seriously. Some are talking about taking the law into their own hands and forming vigilante posses.

District 5

District 5 includes all of the central city of Athena. The residents are mostly poor, and many work minimum-wage jobs in service industries in the city core. Those who do have jobs in the industries in the suburbs have to commute long distances. African Americans are about a third of the population, Latinos are another third, and the rest is made up of relatively new Asian immigrants and poor whites.

Crime rates have traditionally been higher in District 5, but over the last decade they have actually dropped. Many people feel this is because of an active neighborhood-watch program and a well-funded federal jobs program for city youth.

Most urban residents oppose SB 1715. There have been many state cutbacks on welfare programs, and Athenians feel that the extra money proposed in the bill would be better spent combating poverty. They feel that is the way to fight crime.

Urban residents feel their neighborhood-watch and jobs programs are working, and they would like to see these expanded and reproduced in other population centers in the state. They want more money devoted to social welfare and anti-poverty programs. They also feel the second provision of the bill would just increase the level of violence and encourage dangerous vigilante action.

For Discussion

1. The preamble to SB 1715 declares that criminals are "enemies of the state." Are all criminals enemies of the state? What might be some problems with such an attitude?
2. Reread the provisions of SB 1715 one at a time. Answer the following questions for each:
   * What are some possible consequences if this proposition were enacted into law? Explain.
   * Which of these would have a positive impact on society? Which would have a negative impact? Explain.

Debriefing Questions

1. How does Columbia differ from your state? Which district described is closest to the one you live in? Why?
2. Would the people of your state support such a crime bill? Why or why not?
3. Do you think this exercise was a realistic representation of how your state senate would deal with a crime bill? Why or why not?

The Florida Supreme Court building in Tallahassee.

State Supreme Courts and State Constitutions

Despite the similarity between the text of article I, paragraph 7 of the New Jersey Constitution and the text of the Fourth Amendment, we have found on several occasions that the former "affords our citizens greater protection against unreasonable searches and seizures than does the Fourth Amendment."

– Robert L. Clifford, justice of the New Jersey Supreme Court, *New Jersey v. Hempele* (1990)

As the Supreme Court in recent years has restricted the rights of criminal defendants, defendants have increasingly looked to state supreme courts to protect their rights.

How can a state court offer more protection than the U.S. Supreme Court? The U.S. Supreme Court, after all, makes the final decision on matters of U.S. constitutional law. It decides whether the Constitution guarantees certain rights and what the extent of these rights is. A state supreme court could not, for example, declare that the *U.S.* Constitution gives people a right to privacy in the items they put out for trash collection, because the U.S. Supreme Court in *California v. Greenwood* (1988) has already ruled the U.S. Constitution grants no such right. The U.S. Supreme Court would reverse any contrary decision by a state court.

But a state supreme court could declare that its *state* constitution granted that right. Several state supreme courts have done this. [See *New Jersey v. Hempele* (1990), *Washington v. Boland* (1990), *Hawaii v. Lopez* (1995), *Vermont v. Morris* (1996), and *New Hampshire v. Goss* (2003).]

In each of these cases, the state supreme court ruled that under its state's constitution, residents have a right to privacy in items put in the trash. This right is protected independently by the state constitution. The U.S. Supreme Court cannot overrule these decisions, because state supreme courts are the final judges of the meaning of their constitutions.

These constitutions can grant *more* rights than the U.S. Constitution. Thus criminal defendants appealing their convictions often ask state courts to find their rights have been violated under the state constitution. In many cases in the last 30 years, state supreme courts have ruled that their constitutions granted more protections than the U.S. Constitution. If the U.S. Supreme Court continues to restrict the rights of criminal defendants, more defendants will look to their state constitutions for protection. At least two states, however, have restricted this practice. In 1982, the voters of California passed the Victims' Bill of Rights, which limited the rights of criminal defendants under the California Constitution to those granted under the U.S. Constitution. That same year, Florida voters approved a measure that made the Florida Constitution's protection against unreasonable searches the same as that provided by the U.S. Constitution's Fourth Amendment.

FOR DISCUSSION

1. On what basis can state courts grant greater protections for criminal defendants than those guaranteed by the U.S. Constitution?
2. Do you think state courts should do this? Why or why not?
3. Could a state court restrict or deny rights guaranteed by the U.S. Constitution? Explain.

The Color of Justice

A justice system which tolerates injustice is doomed to collapse.
– Leonard Noisette, quoted in *Reducing Racial Disparities in the Criminal Justice System* (2000)

In 1991 in Los Angeles, a bystander video-taped police officers beating Rodney King, a black man, after a car chase. People in the African-American community had long complained of cases of police brutality. At long last, they had clear evidence — a videotape. But at the trial in state court, the jury acquitted the four officers of using excessive force. A major riot erupted in Los Angeles following the verdict.

Although two of the officers were subsequently convicted in federal court, many in the African-American and in other minority communities argue that this case shows how difficult it is for people of color to get justice from the criminal justice system. Racial discrimination, they say, permeates the system.

Critics who claim that racism taints the system have cited its treatment of African-American and Hispanic males. For example, a Bureau of Justice Statistics analysis showed that if current incarceration rates remain unchanged, 32 percent of black males and 17 percent of male Latinos born in 2001 can expect to spend time in prison during their lifetime. This compares to only 6 percent of white males who will go to prison. African Americans make up 12 percent of the U.S. population, but today compose 40 percent of all prison inmates and 42 percent of those sentenced to death.

The question remains whether these statistics come from racism in the criminal justice system or from other causes. Social scientists and politicians have argued about this question for decades.

In a controversial 1975 article, titled "White Racism, Black Crime, and American Justice," criminologist Robert Staples argued that discrimination pervades the justice system. He said the legal system was made by white men to protect white interests and keep blacks down. Staples charged that the system was characterized by second-rate legal help for black defendants, biased jurors, and judges who discriminate in sentencing.

A dozen years later, sociologist William Wilbanks rejected the discrimination argument. In his book, *The Myth of a Racist Criminal Justice System*, Wilbanks reviewed scores

Is the criminal justice system plagued with racism?

of studies that showed statistical inequalities between whites and blacks in arrest rates, imprisonment, and other areas of criminal justice. He found that the inequalities came from factors other than racial discrimination, such as poverty and the defendant's prior record.

Other sociologists, too, have suggested that the apparent inequalities have more to do with poverty than race. Street crimes such as robbery and assault, prominent in the statistics, are usually committed by people from poor backgrounds. Today, about one quarter of all African Americans and Latinos live below the official poverty line. This compares to about 10 percent of all whites.

The connection between poverty and crime has long been noted. During the 1930s, a much larger part of the white population was poor, and whites committed a greater percentage of street crime. Whites then accounted for nearly 80 percent of those in prisons and jails compared to 36 percent today. The question of poverty alone may well account for many of the apparent inequalities in the system.

A RAND Corporation study, however, unearthed some disturbing data. RAND compared the treatment of whites and blacks at key decision points in the criminal justice system. The researchers found that black defendants seemed to be treated more harshly at key points such as sentencing. But the researchers did not identify a cause for these inequalities. Later studies have provided more insight into this data.

Arrest

African Americans accounted for more than a third of the arrests in 2010 for violent crimes. This far surpasses their numbers in the population. Does this disparity come from racial discrimination? Those who say "no" point out that this percentage corresponds to reports from the National Crime Victimization Survey. This survey interviews thousands of victims of crime each year. The percentage of victims who say their perpetrator was black closely matches the percentage of African Americans arrested. A survey of arrest studies concluded, however, that "police are involved in at least some discrimination against members of racial and ethnic minorities."

African Americans also have a disproportionately high arrest rate for drug possession and trafficking. Blacks are only 12 percent of the population and 13 percent of drug users, but they constituted almost a third of those arrested in 2010. This may be due in part to the use of "racial profiling." In many parts of the country, it is alleged that police use drug-courier profiles to stop black males for alleged driving violations. A study in New Jersey documenting traffic stops in 1989–91 found that 72 percent of drivers stopped and arrested were African American, while only 14 percent of cars had a black driver or occupant. State data for the same period showed that blacks and whites had the same rate of traffic violations. A study in Maryland a few years later showed similar results: 17 percent of traffic-code violators were black, but 72 percent of those stopped and searched were black. These types of law-enforcement policies may result in blacks acquiring a criminal record more rapidly than whites.

In many jurisdictions, more blacks than whites are released after arrest. This is particularly true for less serious offenses such as prostitution, gambling, and public drunkenness. What this means is unclear. Some say it means that police and prosecutors are more likely to treat African Americans leniently. Others say it means that blacks are more likely to be arrested on insufficient evidence or harassed by police.

The release rate also varies according to neighborhood. If blacks are arrested in largely minority neighborhoods, they are more likely to be released than whites. But there is no difference in integrated neighborhoods.

Plea Bargaining

More than 90 percent of all criminal cases never go to trial. The defendant pleads guilty, often after the prosecutor and defense attorney negotiate. A 1990 study of about 1,000 cases by the U.S. Sentencing Commission found that whites did better in plea bargains. Twenty-five percent of whites, 18 percent of blacks, and 12 percent of Latinos got their sentences reduced through bargaining. The reason for the disparity was not determined.

The *San Jose Mercury News* conducted a massive study of 700,000 California legal cases over a 10-year period. The paper reported in December 1991 that a third of the white adults who were arrested, but had no prior record, were able to get felony charges against them reduced. Only a quarter of the African-Americans and Latinos with no prior records were as successful in plea bargaining.

The *Mercury News* study did not blame intentional racism for these inequalities. It did, however, suggest that subtle cultural fears and insensitivity contributed to the problem. The study noted that more than 80 percent of all California prosecutors and judges are white, while more than 60 percent of those arrested are non-white.

Jury Verdicts

In 1985, Cornell law professor Sheri Lynn Johnson reviewed a dozen mock-jury studies. She concluded that the "race of the defendant significantly and directly affects the determination of guilt." In these studies, identical trials were simulated, sometimes with white defendants and sometimes with African Americans. Professor Johnson discovered that white jurors were more likely to find a black defendant guilty than a white defendant, even though the mock trials were based on the same crime and the same evidence.

Professor Johnson also found that black jurors behaved with the reverse bias. They found

More than 60 percent of all those in federal or state prisons are black or Latino.

white defendants guilty more often than black defendants. Furthermore, the race of the **victim** in the case affected both groups. If the victim was black, white jurors tended to find a white defendant less blameworthy. In the same way, if the victim was white, black jurors found black defendants less blameworthy.

According to these mock-jury experiments, both white and black jurors seem to discriminate. Professor Johnson did not, however, think the juror bias was intentional. "Because the process of attributing guilt on the basis of race appears to be subconscious," Johnson says, "jurors are unlikely either to be aware of or to be able to control that process."

The mock trials did have one encouraging result. When white and black mock jurors met together, as many real juries do, the effect of race tended to disappear. This result seems to indicate that the best way to eliminate racial bias in verdicts is to select racially mixed juries.

A study published in the *Quarterly Journal of Economics* in 2012 seemed to confirm much of Johnson's research. It examined data from felony jury trials in Florida from 2000 to 2010. The researchers found that

(i) juries formed from all-white jury pools convict black defendants significantly . . . more often than white defendants, and (ii) this gap in conviction rates is entirely eliminated when the jury pool includes at least one black member.

The U.S. Supreme Court has moved to promote racially mixed juries by prohibiting prosecutors and defense lawyers from using peremptory challenges to remove potential jurors based on race. (See *Batson v. Kentucky*, 1986, and *Georgia v. McCollum*, 1992.) Justice Thurgood Marshall went even further and called for ending the use of peremptory challenges altogether. Only by banning peremptory challenges, Justice Marshall said, can racial discrimination in jury selection be ended (*Batson v. Kentucky*).

More than 20 years later, there is growing evidence that the rulings in *Batson* and *McCollum* are difficult to enforce. Studies of cases in many states show that both prosecutors and defense lawyers often continue to rely on race-based stereotypes in selecting juries. In 2005 in *Miller-El v. Dretke*, the Supreme Court reviewed a case involving a black Texas death-row inmate. Miller-El was tried in 1986 for the death of a clerk during a robbery at a Holiday Inn in Dallas. At the trial, the prosecutors had used peremptory challenges to remove 10 of 11 potential black jurors. The Supreme Court found clear evidence that the prosecutors' decision was the result of racial bias and overturned the conviction. The majority stated that allowing discrimination in jury selection "invites cynicism respecting the jury's neutrality" and undermines public confidence in the courts. In a concurring opinion, Justice Stephen Breyer echoed Justice Marshall and suggested that the whole system of peremptory challenges should be reconsidered.

Sentencing

The RAND Corporation study found that convicted African Americans were more likely than whites to go to prison. And their sentences were longer. "This disparity," the study concluded, "suggests that probation officers, judges, and parole boards are exercising discretion in sentencing or release decisions in ways that result in de facto discrimination against blacks." **De facto** means the discrimination exists in fact, but without legal authority. It may not be intentional.

Unintended discrimination can occur at many points in the legal process. Probation officers often prepare pre-sentencing reports for a judge. The judge uses the reports to help make sentencing decisions. Reports include information on the criminal's prior record, family background, education, marital status, and employment history. Many African Americans convicted of crimes come from deprived backgrounds. They may have things in their record — unemployment, trouble in school, family problems — that judges, who largely come from middle-class backgrounds, cannot relate to. This may sway some judges to treat them more harshly in sentencing.

In a 1999 survey of studies on discrimination in the justice system, researcher Christopher Stone found that much of the disparity in sentencing could be traced to differences in arrest charges and prior records of those convicted. He concluded: "There is no evidence of disparity that stretches across the justice system as a whole . . . . But studies of individual jurisdictions and specific parts of the court process do find some evidence of race bias in a significant number of cases."

Stone considered drug offences separately. Some federal mandatory sentences have come under fire for discriminating against minorities. Critics point to different sentences mandated for crack cocaine, a drug popular in poor minority communities, and powder cocaine, a drug used in wealthier communities. Under federal law, dealing 28 grams of crack gets a first-time offender a mandatory minimum sentence of five years. To receive a similar mandatory minimum sentence for trafficking in powder cocaine, an offender must possess 500 grams. Stone stated: "Whatever one believes about the rationality of the decision to create special, harsher penalties for crack cocaine, the concentration of these sentences on black defendants is striking." (See pages 238–241 for details on crack and powder cocaine sentencing.)

States often have similar disparities in drug sentencing laws. In a 1996 study of California drug sentencing laws, researchers found that possession of crack cocaine and heroin, more commonly used by minorities, carried stiffer penalties than possession of methamphetamines, more commonly used by whites.

Death Penalty

University of Iowa law professor David Baldus studied 2,000 murder cases prosecuted by the state of Georgia during the 1970s. The Baldus study showed that defendants convicted of killing whites were more than four times more likely to receive the death penalty than those convicted of murdering blacks. The study also revealed that black defendants who murdered whites had by far the greatest chance of being sentenced to death.

A Georgia black man who had been sentenced to death in 1978 for killing a white police officer used this study in his appeal to the U.S. Supreme Court. He claimed that the Baldus study proved that Georgia's jurors and judges discriminated against African-American defendants. In a 5–4 decision, the Supreme Court accepted the results of the study, but ruled that it did not prove discrimination. Writing for the majority, Justice Lewis F. Powell concluded that the study failed to "demonstrate a constitutionally significant risk of racial bias affecting the Georgia capital sentencing process." (*McCleskey v. Kemp*, 1987)

While the Baldus study showed a big disparity in death-penalty verdicts depending on the race of the victim, it found that black defendants were only 1.1 times more likely to receive the death penalty than white defendants. A Government Accounting Office report in 1990 also found no clear statistical data showing that the race of a defendant affected the determination of a death sentence. (The report did find, however, that the defendant was much more likely to be sentenced to death if the victim was white than if the victim was non-white.)

A more recent study, however, showed that race-of-defendant bias seems to plague the federal system. A Department of Justice study of the federal system between 1995 and 2000 found that of 159 cases that federal attorneys approved for death-penalty prosecution, 72 percent involved minority defendants. The study also found that many more white defendants received pretrial waivers for the death penalty in a plea agreement than did blacks and Latinos. An earlier congressional report reviewed cases involving people convicted under a drug kingpin law between 1988 and 1994. That report found that while only 24 percent of those convicted under the law were black, the prosecutors chose to pursue the death penalty much more frequently against blacks than whites (78 percent of death-penalty defendants were black, and only 11 percent were white and 11 percent Latino).

While racial disparities continue to exist in the American criminal justice system, commentators differ over the cause. Supreme Court decisions since 1960 have rooted out many overtly racist practices, such as in jury selection, but it is more difficult to address unintentional racist factors. Because these factors come from subtle assumptions and fears deeply ingrained in the wider society, only when society changes will they disappear.

Critics of the system, however, insist that inequalities, regardless of their basis, should not be swept under the rug. They must be paid attention to and any discrimination found must be eliminated. Policies that lead to discriminatory results must be re-examined. Many critics believe that the disparities in the system would be easier to accept as unbiased if more decision makers — police, prosecutors, judges, and juries — were people of color.

FOR DISCUSSION

1. Describe the disparities between white and black defendants at each of the following key decision points: arrest, plea bargaining, jury verdicts, sentencing, and death penalty.
2. What do you think accounts for these disparities? Explain.
3. According to Andrew Hacker, author of *Two Nations, Black and White, Separate, Hostile, Unequal*, "The feeling persists that a black man who rapes or robs a white person has inflicted more harm than black or white criminals who prey on victims of their own race." Do you agree with this statement? Why or why not?

CLASS ACTIVITY

Toward a Colorblind Justice System

Various proposals have been put forward to prevent discrimination in arrests, plea bargaining, jury verdicts, sentencing, and the death penalty. In this activity, students evaluate a few of these and come up with suggestions of their own.

1. Form small groups. Each group should focus on one of the five policy areas below and should:
    a. Read its policy, evaluate it, and report back to the class.
    b. To evaluate the policy, answer the following questions:
        (1) What problem is the policy designed to address? Does it address the problem? Why or why not?
        (2) Who might support the policy? Who might oppose it? Why?
        (3) What benefits might come from the policy?
        (4) What costs might result from the policy?
        (5) What other policies might address the problem? Are they better? Why?
        (6) What policy should be adopted? Why?
2. The groups should report back. Conclude the activity with a discussion using the debriefing questions on page 376.

I. Arrests

Policy: Police should collect data on the race and release records of every person they arrest.

Pros: This will enable departments to track officers who arrest minorities without sufficient cause.

Cons: Police have too much paperwork already and the statistics collected will be meaningless.

(Continued on next page.)

II. Plea Bargaining

Policy: Plea bargaining should be abolished.

Pros: It will do away with an informal process subject to abuse because the courts do not review it. It will ensure that all defendants have their day in court.

Cons: Doing away with plea bargaining will clog the courts with cases awaiting trial, resulting in increased court costs.

III. Jury Verdicts

Policy: Peremptory challenges should be abolished. (Peremptory challenges allow attorneys to exclude a limited number of prospective jurors for any reason except race and gender.)

Pros: Even though they are not supposed to, attorneys still use peremptory challenges to exclude jurors on account of race. This will end the practice.

Cons: It is already illegal to exclude jurors on account of race. Doing away with peremptory challenges is too extreme. These challenges help both the prosecution and defense exclude jurors who they feel might not be impartial.

IV. Sentencing

Policy: Federal law should not make first-time drug offenders face mandatory sentences. Judges should be allowed more discretion in sentencing these drug offenders.

Pros: Mandatory minimum sentences cause first-time offenders, mostly minorities, to go into an already overcrowded prison system.

Cons: Mandatory minimum sentences are needed to show we are serious in our war on drugs.

V. Death Penalty

Policy: Congress should reverse the decision in *McCleskey*. If statistical studies show racial disparities in a state's imposition of the death penalty, then minority defendants should not be sentenced to death in that state.

Pros: Race should play no role in whether or not a person receives the death penalty. The death penalty should be limited to aggravated cases where whites and blacks receive the same treatment.

Cons: Mere discrepancies in statistics should not invalidate the death penalty. A defendant should have to show discrimination in the particular case or that the state intended to discriminate.

Debriefing Questions

1. Which policies garnered the most support? The least support? Why?
2. What other policies did you think of that could prevent racial discrimination in the criminal justice system? Do you think they would work? Why or why not?
3. Why is it important that the criminal justice system not be perceived as racially biased?

CHAPTER 24

CRIME AND THE CITIZEN

If the criminal justice system [is] to work, the participation of citizens [is] essential, with some form of a partnership between the police and the community being highly desirable.
– Dennis Jay Kenney, *Crime, Fear, and the New York City Subways* (1987)

GETTING INVOLVED IN FIGHTING CRIME | VIGILANTES IN AMERICAN HISTORY | CRIME IN SCHOOLS
BURGLARY PREVENTION | A CONCLUSION ON CRIME

Getting Involved in Fighting Crime

[I]n Japan, you can walk into a park at midnight and sit on a bench and nothing will happen to you. You're completely safe, day or night. You can go anywhere. You won't be robbed or beaten or killed. You're not always looking behind you, not always worrying. You don't need walls or body-guards. . . . You're free. It's a wonderful feeling. Here, everybody has to lock themselves up. Lock the door. Lock the car. People who spend their whole lives locked up are in prison.
– Michael Crichton, *Rising Sun* (1992)

Americans fear crime. The crime rate has fallen steadily since the early 1990s. Yet almost every year for the last 20 years, a majority of Americans have responded "more" to the Gallup Poll's question, "Is there more crime in your area than there was a year ago, or less?"

The fear of crime has spurred people into taking individual action against crime. They have built walls, bought guns, and installed security systems. A whole new security industry has blossomed. There are now more private security guards than police in the United States. But today and throughout our history ordinary citizens have banded together to fight crime — sometimes legally and other times illegally.

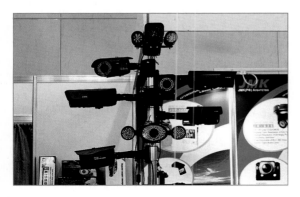

Vigilantes in American History

As they controlled the press, they wrote their own history, and the world generally gives them the credit of having purged San Francisco of rowdies and roughs; but their success has given great stimulus to a dangerous principle, that would at any time justify the mob in seizing all the power of government; and who is to say that the Vigilance Committee may not be composed of the worst, instead of the best, elements of a community?
– William Tecumseh Sherman, *Memoirs of General William T. Sherman* (1876)

Violence and crime have been a major part of American history from the beginning. Vigilantes have been with us almost as long. Repeatedly, groups of citizens have banded together to take the law into their own hands and punish suspected criminals. These groups were usually well organized and had leaders and rules. Before illegally punishing their suspects, they often held some sort of trial. But the suspects usually had little chance to defend themselves or be acquitted.

Before 1900, vigilantism was relatively common in the United States. Episodes of vigilante justice occurred all over the country. Historians know of well over 300 vigilante movements in American history. Their size varied from small groups of about a dozen people to large organizations including thousands of citizens. Most numbered several hundred. Vigilante groups went by various names, including *regulators*, *slickers*, *stranglers*, *committees of safety*, and *vigilance committees*.

People usually formed vigilante organizations for a specific purpose. Once the job was done, the vigilantes disbanded. Most operated for less than a year.

In the early years of our country, vigilantes ordinarily whipped, beat, or tarred and feathered those they believed guilty. But by the 1850s, hanging had become widespread. Those not hanged were usually forced to leave the area. Few escaped punishment.

Most vigilante groups were composed of normally law-abiding merchants, ranchers, and other prominent citizens. Their leaders were usually the wealthiest and most important people in the area. Why did these kinds of people resort to an illegal and often violent method of handling criminals? There were several reasons.

The most important reason was that the frontier lacked police, courts, and jails. Until 1900, many people lived in isolated frontier settlements far from established law and order. Faced with doing nothing about rampaging outlaws or taking the law into their own hands, respectable people chose the vigilante solution. Frontier Americans were used to relying on themselves to solve problems.

In some cases, the reason for vigilance committees was simply to keep taxes low. It was much cheaper to take care of criminals by hauling them before a group of vigilantes than paying sheriffs, judges, prosecutors, and jailers to do the job.

The Earliest Vigilantes

The first vigilante movement in America was formed in the South Carolina backwoods in the 1760s. A newly settled frontier area, it had just undergone a costly Indian war with the Cherokees. Orphaned and homeless young people drifted into outlaw bands. These bands stole horses, kidnapped, raped, and robbed.

Since the area had no sheriffs or courts, a group known as the Regulators was organized in 1767. Composed of up to 6,000 normally law-abiding settlers, the Regulators attacked and broke up the outlaw gangs. The lawbreakers were given trials, whipped, driven out of the area, or forced to work on farms. Sixteen were killed.

The Regulators disbanded in 1769 when courts and sheriffs were established. But this group of vigilantes provided a model that many other vigilance movements throughout the country would later copy.

Vigilante movements were set up again and again before the Civil War to deal with horse thieves, counterfeiters, gamblers, and bands of robbers. Vigilantes were particularly active in Alabama, Mississippi, Louisiana, Iowa, Indiana, and Illinois.

Vigilantes from the West

Vigilante groups were more numerous and generally more deadly in the West. Between 1850 and 1900, about 200 vigilante movements occurred. Vigilantes executed more than 500 accused horse and cattle thieves, murderers, robbers, and others. Texas holds the record for the most vigilante killings with 140. But one Montana vigilante group in 1884 carried out 35 executions. Theodore Roosevelt, working as a cowboy in Montana at this time, wanted to join the vigilantes but never got the chance.

Some historians have attempted to classify vigilante movements as *constructive* and *destructive*. According to this viewpoint, constructive vigilante groups got rid of the criminal element quickly, restored order, and disbanded. These groups usually had widespread public support. Destructive vigilante movements were often divided from within and frequently led to chaos and violence.

A good example of a destructive type of vigilante movement was the Regulator-Moderator War of Shelby County, Texas. In 1840, when Texas was an independent country, a group of Regulators formed to get rid of a corrupt ring of county officials. The county had attracted thieves, counterfeiters, and murderers.

The Regulator leader was killed and replaced by a man who took his role so seriously that he wore a military uniform. Soon an opposing group of vigilantes calling themselves the Moderators banded together. But criminals infiltrated both groups. Violence, revenge, and feuds erupted. The original reason for the formation of the vigilante movement was forgotten. An all-out battle broke out between the Regulators and Moderators in 1844 involving hundreds of men. Sam Houston and the Lone Star Republic militia finally stopped the violence.

The Johnson County Invasion in Wyoming is an example of what has been called constructive vigilantism. Some big cattle ranchers, used to grazing their large herds on open range land, took exception when homesteaders began to fence off land. At first, the cattle barons accused the homesteaders of rustling. A few homesteaders were murdered, but no one was ever convicted of the killings. In April 1892, the large cattle ranchers brought in a trainload of heavily armed gunfighters supposedly to go after rustlers. In reality, they were hired to force out the homesteaders. The gunmen quickly went to work and killed two set-

Sharpshooters of San Francisco's 1856 Committee of Vigilance.

tlers. Enraged, the homesteaders formed a vigilante group, rounded up the invaders, and held them until federal troops arrived. Unfortunately, after being bailed out of jail by the cattle barons, the gunslingers disappeared and were never put on trial.

The San Francisco Vigilance Committees

Two of the most famous examples of vigilantism in American history occurred in San Francisco in 1851 and 1856.

In 1851, with the Gold Rush at its peak, San Francisco was wide open, rough, and dangerous. Its police could do little to stop a wave of crimes. A Committee of Vigilance was formed, composed of more than 500 leading citizens. William T. Coleman, a young merchant, led the committee.

The Committee of Vigilance announced that "no thief, burglar, incendiary, or assassin shall escape punishment, either by the quibbles of the law, the insecurity of prisons, the carelessness or corruption of the police, or a laxity of those who pretend to administer justice." Clearly, these San Francisco vigilantes had a low opinion of those responsible for law and order in the city.

Before the year ended, the committee had whipped one accused criminal, hanged four others, forced 15 to leave the city, and handed over another 15 to legal authorities. After cleaning up the city, the committee disbanded.

Five years later, however, San Francisco was in worse shape than before. Murders and other crimes were rampant. Even more frightening to San Francisco business leaders was the corrupt political machine that ran the city government. David C. Broderick, the Democratic Party leader of San Francisco, controlled the city. Kept in power by the votes of Irish-Catholic workers, Broderick stuffed his pockets and those of his friends with public funds. Businessmen resented that their tax dollars financed Broderick and his friends. By 1856, San Francisco was facing bankruptcy. Businessmen in the city, who depended on credit from Eastern banks, were worried.

James King, editor of the *San Francisco Daily Evening Bulletin*, wrote editorials attacking the crime problem and the corruption of the Broderick political machine. King, who had been a vigilante in 1851, also began to revive talk of vigilante justice. On May 14, 1856, he was shot to death on a San Francisco street.

The following day, William T. Coleman, leader of the vigilantes in 1851, formed a new vigilance committee. Within a few days, the vigilance committee arrested, tried, and hanged one of Broderick's political flunkies for the shooting.

During the next few months, perhaps as many as 8,000 San Franciscans joined the vigilantes. Most were merchants and skilled workers. Few were Irish. Coleman held almost dictatorial powers. With an executive committee of businessmen, he drew up a list of suspects. People were arrested and tried at vigilante headquarters, which was called Fort Gunnybags because it was protected with sandbags. In all, the committee executed four accused criminals. It put Broderick's henchmen on ships headed for Eastern and foreign ports and told them never to come back to the city. It called Broderick himself before the vigilance committee. When he was released, he left town.

In operation only three months, the vigilance committee disbanded on August 18 with a parade through the city. But the vigilance committee formed a political organization, the People's Party, that controlled San Francisco's city government for the next 10 years.

Was Vigilantism Ever Justified?

Vigilantism has repeatedly surfaced in American history. Was vigilante justice ever warranted? One former Colorado vigilante thought vigilante justice worked better than legal procedures. "There were no appeals in those days," he said, "no writs of errors, no attorney's fees, no pardon in six months. Punishment was swift, sure, and certain." On the other hand, a New York City newspaper editorial criticizing the San Francisco vigilance committee of 1856 stated: "Better to endure the evil of escape of criminals than to inaugurate a reign of terror which today may punish one guilty head, and tomorrow wreak its mistaken vengeance on many innocent lives."

FOR DISCUSSION

1. Why did normally law-abiding and well-to-do citizens turn to illegal vigilante methods? Do you think that people today could turn to vigilantism? Explain.

2. How are vigilante groups and lynch mobs different? How are they similar?

3. Do you think vigilantism was ever justified in American history? Do you think it would ever be justified today? Why or why not?

Crime in Schools

Our nation's schools should be safe havens for teaching and learning, free of crime and violence. Any instance of crime or violence at school not only affects the individuals involved, but also may disrupt the educational process and affect bystanders, the school itself, and the surrounding community.
– *Indicators of School Crime and Safety,* Bureau of Justice Statistics and the National Center for Education Statistics (2010)

Crime and violence in schools are far greater today than the 1950s. A teacher from that decade would be astonished to enter some of our urban schools today and find police in the halls and metal detectors at the doors to keep out guns and knives. But the problems do not just belong to urban schools. The worst school shootings in recent years have taken place at rural and suburban schools.

The National Center for Education Statistics reports about 1.2 million crimes a year on public school grounds. About 100,000 of these crimes are serious violent crimes (rape, sexual assault, robbery, and aggravated assault). Eight percent of high school students reported being threatened or injured with a weapon in the last year. And each year about 8 percent of all teachers report being threatened with injury by a student.

Schools have not always been so hazardous. From the 1950s through the middle 1960s, the main school problems were pranks, some ethnic rivalry, isolated fistfights, and occasional vandalism. By the early 1970s, much more serious problems were occurring. Schools started to experience crimes of violence, drug offenses, rape, and even shootings.

Schools and Gangs

Schools, of course, reflect the communities they serve. In the early 1980s, crack cocaine and heavily armed drug-dealing gangs overran many urban communities. Gang members and gang "wanna-bes" adopted symbols such as colored head scarves and football team jackets. In some places, drug dealing and gang rivalries spilled over into the schools. Increased levels of violence in society as a whole affected the schools. Personal feuds over a girlfriend or an insult that would once have ended in a fistfight could sometimes turn into a gun battle. In New York City schools during the 1992 school year alone, five teachers, one policeman, two parents, and 16 students were shot.

Beginning in the 1990s, crime began to decrease in American society and in schools as well. In 1992, there were almost 150 crimes at school per 1,000 students. By 1997, this rate had dropped to 100 and by 2008 to 47. Serious violent crimes had decreased as well, falling from 10 per 1,000 in 1992 to 4 per 1,000 in 2008.

Reports of gangs at school have also declined in recent years. In 1989, about 15 percent of students reported gangs at their school. By 1995, this percentage had risen to almost 30 percent. But in 2007, the percentage fell to 23 percent. Gangs are often linked to school violence.

Bullying in School

Schoolyard behavior like teasing is often considered to be a normal part of growing up. Everyone seems to have experienced it or witnessed it. When it threatens the safety and well-being of students, however, it crosses the line into bullying.

Basically, bullying is harassment, usually systematic and ongoing, of someone weaker or more vulnerable. It can be physical, verbal, or emotional. In 2007, a third of all sixth through 12th graders reported being bullied at school. (More than 40 percent of sixth graders said they were bullied, and reports of bullying declined in each higher grade, with about a quarter of 12th graders reporting being bullied.) Reported incidents consisted of being made fun of (21 percent); being threatened with harm (5 percent); being the subject of rumors (18 percent); being pushed, shoved, tripped, or spit on (11 percent); and having property destroyed (4 percent).

A new and growing form of bullying is cyberbullying. With the Internet providing anonymity, cyberbullies feel less inhibited to hurl insults and heap ridicule on their victims. Researchers call this the "disinhibition effect."

Bullies may post video clips or publish personal information about their victims. They also might attempt to assume the identity of their victim, publishing embarrassing information that can lead to ridicule or abuse by others.

In 2010, Phoebe Prince, a 15-year-old living in Massachusetts, committed suicide after being bullied by other students. She suffered both face-to-face bullying and cyberbullying, including derogatory comments on Internet social networks. After the suicide, five students

As crime has dropped in the U.S., it has also fallen in schools.

involved in the bullying were convicted of criminal charges.

The Phoebe Prince story shows how victims are at great risk of depression. Victims may also experience anxiety, loss of self-esteem, and relationship problems with parents and friends. They may suffer physical pain and gastrointestinal problems due to stress. Bullying can have negative effects on victims' academic performance and other activities.

Bullying also affects the bully. Students who bully are more likely to get into fights, vandalize property, and drop out of school. Bullies are more likely to be convicted of crimes. It is common for bullies to actually be "bully-victims," or victims who turn around and bully others.

Many existing laws already allow criminal prosecution for threats, stalking, identity theft, and many forms of harassment. In recent years, 47 states have passed anti-bullying laws. For example, in the wake of the Phoebe Prince case, Massachusetts adopted a wide-ranging anti-bullying and cyberbullying law. Each school must have an anti-bullying plan, an anti-bullying teaching program, a counseling program for victims and bullies, and procedures for reporting bullying. It also made certain bullying a felony under its stalking and harassment laws (see **Massachusetts' Criminal Laws on Bullying**, below).

Shootings in Suburban and Rural Areas

Since the 1990s, a number of shootings have taken place at non-urban schools. Out of the way places, such as Moses Lake, Washington; Bethel, Alaska; Pearl, Mississippi; Springfield, Oregon; West Paducah, Kentucky; Red Lion, Pennsylvania; Cold Springs and Red Lake, Minnesota; and Chardon, Ohio, have experienced school shootings and killings.

In two instances, boys planned their shootings together. In 1998, two students opened fire on students gathered outside because of a false fire alarm at a middle school in Jonesboro, Arkansas, killing four girls and a teacher. In 1999 in Littleton, Colorado, two students went on a rampage killing 13 others and themselves at a high school.

These shootings shocked the nation. It seemed to many that if shootings could take place in these schools, they could happen anywhere. One parent summed up the fears of many: "It scares me to death that I'm sending my child to a school . . . and in light of getting an education, I may end up burying her."

Some commentators think these fears are overblown. They point out that lightning kills twice as many people each year as are killed in schools. They see no growing trend in school killings. They explain that school killings account for a small percentage of the homicides involving juveniles.

Even so, parents and students want schools as safe and orderly as possible. Schools in crisis cannot educate effectively. Disruptions and a sense of fear distract students and teachers from education.

Safety Measures

Educators and schools across the nation are trying various measures to improve school safety. Although the goal of each school is the same, the problem varies from school to school. Some schools are safe and want to remain so. Others are plagued with problems and need to restore order. Different strategies are being tried. These include:

Increasing school security. Most schools now require visitors to sign in before entering the school, and 90 percent monitor access to their buildings. Two-thirds of all schools maintain "closed campuses," barring students from leaving for lunch. About half of all schools have security cameras. Three out of four have telephones in classrooms. About seven out of 10 high schools have police or security guards stationed on the campus. About 20 percent report

MASSACHUSETTS' CRIMINAL LAWS ON BULLYING

Stalking: Section 43. (a) Whoever (1) willfully and maliciously engages in a knowing pattern of conduct or series of acts over a period of time directed at a specific person which seriously alarms or annoys that person and would cause a reasonable person to suffer substantial emotional distress, and (2) makes a threat with the intent to place the person in imminent fear of death or bodily injury, shall be guilty of the crime of stalking and shall be punished by imprisonment in the state prison for not more than five years or by a fine of not more than one thousand dollars, or imprisonment in the house of correction for not more than two and one-half years or both. Such conduct, acts or threats described in this paragraph shall include . . . conduct, acts or threats conducted by mail or by use of a telephonic or telecommunication device including . . . electronic mail, internet communications and facsimile communications.

Harassment: Section 43A. (a) Whoever willfully and maliciously engages in a knowing pattern of conduct or series of acts over a period of time directed at a specific person, which seriously alarms that person and would cause a reasonable person to suffer substantial emotional distress, shall be guilty of the crime of criminal harassment and shall be punished by imprisonment in a house of correction for not more than two and one-half years or by a fine of not more than $1,000, or by both such fine and imprisonment. Such conduct or acts described in this paragraph shall include . . . conduct or acts conducted by mail or by use of a telephonic or telecommunication device including . . . electronic mail, internet communications or facsimile communications.

WHAT DO WE KNOW ABOUT SCHOOL ATTACKERS?

A study by the U.S. Secret Service and the U.S. Department of Education examined 37 incidents of targeted school violence in the United States. Here is what researchers learned about the attackers in those incidents:

Developed idea to harm target before attack	95 percent
Behaved in a way pre-incident that caused others concern or indicated a need for help	93 percent
Told friend, schoolmate or sibling about idea before incident	81 percent
Felt bullied, threatened, attacked by others	71 percent
Obtained gun used in attack from own (or relative's) home	68 percent
Had a known history of weapon use	63 percent
Had a known history of drug/alcohol abuse	24 percent
Previous diagnosis of mental health or behavior disorder	17 percent
Academic performance	Ranged from excellent to failing

Source: "Preventing, Preparing for Critical Incidents in Schools," *National Institute of Justice Journal*, No. 262 (2009)

running drug sweeps. A few schools have resorted to metal detectors, but only 1 percent use them daily. Some schools have removed lockers to eliminate hiding places for guns or drugs. A few have done away with teachers' bathrooms, so that teachers have to visit the students' bathrooms regularly to discourage illegal activities.

Adopting "zero tolerance" policies. These policies mandate tough action, from suspension to expulsion, for certain offenses. The Gun-Free Schools Act ordered that each state receiving federal education funds enact a law requiring that any student at school who brings a gun or possesses a gun be expelled for at least one year. In the 2007–2008 school year, about 3 percent of all schools reported expelling a student for having a gun. About four-fifths of all schools also have zero-tolerance policies for alcohol, drugs, violence, and tobacco.

Running violence-prevention programs. More than three-fourths of all schools operate some type of violence-prevention or anti-bullying program. Most of these programs are ongoing, but about a tenth of all schools have one-day programs only. The programs vary. Some offer conflict and peer mediation. Others are part of classroom instruction. Service learning links classroom learning to activities in the community. Law-related education helps students understand the legal system and social issues through interactive classroom lessons. Character education teaches basic values.

Mandating school uniforms. This policy aims to deter property crimes prompted when students wear designer clothing and expensive sneakers. It also prevents gang members from wearing gang colors and insignia and helps school officials recognize intruders on the campus. Although the policy has received a lot of press, only 17.5 percent of all schools have adopted uniforms — only about 9 percent at the high school level.

Making schools less impersonal. Many large schools are trying to break down their cold, impersonal atmosphere by creating "schools within schools." Some are hiring more teachers to minimize school violence associated with classroom overcrowding. Some schools are offering specialized vocational training, which young people can recognize as important. The National School Safety Center encourages schools to set up student committees to study school safety and even hold court on violators.

Schools across the country have set up committees to work on improving school safety. They are considering proposals such as these and others.

1. Describe how school conditions differed in each of the following periods: 1950–1969, 1970–1992, and 1993–present.
2. Does your school look different from a school of the 1950s? What is different and why?
3. Does your school have a crime problem? If so, what do you think are the primary causes of crime in your school? Explain. What do you think can be done about the problem?

CLASS ACTIVITY

A School Plan

In this activity, students examine problems and develop solutions to potential crime problems at their school.
1. Divide into small groups.
2. Each group should do the following:
   a. Discuss what types of crime problems or potential problems the school has. Does it have problems with violence, gangs, theft, graffiti, bullying?
   b. Decide on one main problem that you think is important.
   c. Discuss possible solutions to the problem (be sure to also consider solutions mentioned in the article).
   d. Decide on a solution.
   e. Be prepared to present to the class the problem and how to address it.
3. When the groups report, consider inviting an administrator to discuss the crime problems at school, the students' suggestions, and what is currently being done about them.

ACTIVITY

What Are Communities Doing About Crime in Schools?

At your school or community library or on the Internet, research about crime in schools. Choose one of the following problem areas: vandalism, burglaries, robberies, assaults on teachers and students, confiscations of weapons, rapes, or murders. Research to find the following:
1. What schools across the country are doing to attack the problem?
2. What are the latest statistics on this problem in schools?

Report your findings to the class.

Burglary Prevention

A Neighborhood Watch program is a group of people living in the same area who want to make their neighborhood safer by working together and in conjunction with local law enforcement to reduce crime and improve their quality of life.
– National Sheriffs' Association, *Neighborhood Watch Manual* (2005)

A **burglary** is an unlawful entry into a building or car with the intent to commit a crime, usually theft. It is the most common major felony in America. More than 2 million burglaries are reported every year, and law-enforcement experts believe an amount equal to that go unreported. That works out to more than 10,000 burglaries every day. The reported losses amount to $4.6 billion. To get an idea of how much money that is, imagine earning $1,000 a day. At that rate, it would take you more than 12,000 years to earn $4.6 billion. Only about 12 percent of these burglaries are ever cleared up by the police.

Burglary is a crime of opportunity. In about a third of all burglaries, force isn't used and nothing is broken. Many people fail to lock their doors or windows, and many others use inadequate locks. This makes the burglar's job easier. In many cases, it is no harder for a burglar to pick a lock than for a normal person to open a door and walk in.

Perhaps more than anything else, burglars benefit when neighbors do not know each other. A neighbor is literally someone who lives nearby, but the word has come to suggest much more in our culture. Neighbors are supposed to be friendly and helpful. In the 19th century, neighbors traditionally banded together to help each other build houses and barns, sow and harvest crops, and protect their communities. But in our modern society, such tasks are taken care of by professionals, and people move so often that neighborly communities rarely develop. Because of the growing crime problem, many residents are afraid of talking to strangers — including their own neighbors.

These circumstances have made the burglars' task much easier. A stranger can often enter a community without being noticed and can go right up to a house without neighbors becoming suspicious.

Neighborhoods have responded in several ways to prevent burglaries. Some wealthier

communities have hired private security companies to patrol their neighborhoods continuously. Others have turned themselves into gated communities, behind high walls and drive-in gates with 24-hour security guards.

One interesting experiment, modeled on the "Broken Windows" theory, was tried out in the 1980s in Virginia. In a high-burglary area, the community carted away trash and abandoned cars, filled in potholes, swept the streets, and painted out graffiti. The burglary rate dropped immediately by 35 percent. The people who ran the experiment argued that broken windows and other signs of urban decay "create fear in citizens and attract predators." They showed that simple attention to the look of an area can dramatically reduce crime.

Another response to the burglary problem has been the development of **Neighborhood Watch** groups or **block associations**. Police have often urged citizens to create Neighborhood Watch groups, especially in cities where community-policing programs are being set up. Neighborhood Watch groups try to re-establish a sense of community. Members meet to discuss ways to make their area safer. They get to know one another, watch over one another's homes, and sometimes even clean up unsightly areas.

Neighborhood Watch programs have proven successful in reducing crime, according to careful studies conducted in Seattle, San Diego, and Detroit. In one Detroit neighborhood,

burglaries were reduced by 62 percent. The idea of neighborhood associations has even moved to the suburbs.

The Tierra Bonita Neighborhood Association

Tierra Bonita is an upper-middle-class hillside suburb on the West Coast. Because its houses are set back from the road, isolated by shrubbery and trees, burglars were attracted to the area. In particular, burglars were breaking into homes when the residents went away on vacation. The police did what they could to increase patrolling, but only three officers were available at any one time to cover the whole area. The problem only got worse.

In desperation, a few energetic residents took the lead and called a meeting. More than 1,600 residents formed the Tierra Bonita Association of Neighborhoods. The association took on many tasks, but its top priority was an anti-burglary program. It formed an anti-burglary committee and invited the police to a public meeting to discuss the problem.

The police opened the meeting with a video that showed how burglars break in. It recommended simple steps residents could take to safeguard their homes. The residents then set up a neighborhood-watch plan. Each block elected a coordinator, who was to be the primary contact with the police department. Block coordinators collected names and addresses so they knew who lived in their neighborhood. If anything suspicious happened, people could report it to the coordinator. And if someone went away on vacation, the coordinator could arrange to check the house periodically.

The association posted signs at every road leading into the area saying, "Tierra Bonita is a Neighborhood Watch Community." It set up a buddy system, so neighbors could watch one another's homes. Buddies also helped each other upgrade their locks and window latches. If one family in a buddy group went on vacation, the

ASK AN EXPERT

You can make a difference in fighting burglary in your own community. Most police departments have burglary-prevention units. Invite an officer from one of these units to come to your class and discuss the burglary problem in your community and practical steps for burglary prevention.

other could bring in the newspaper, open and close the drapes, and make the house look lived in. Finally, the association agreed to hold regular meetings to keep community spirit alive and to introduce new residents to the program.

In the first full year of operation, the burglary rate in Tierra Bonita dropped 54 percent.

FOR DISCUSSION

1. Why do you think it's so difficult for the police to catch burglars without help from citizens?
2. What are some easy ways to reduce burglary rates? What can individual homeowners do?
3. How much responsibility should neighbors have for each other? Could neighborhood watches lead to an invasion of people's privacy? How could such problems be avoided?
4. Have you ever seen someone suspicious hanging around a neighbor's home? Did you call the police? Would you if it happened again? Why?
5. Is there a neighborhood-watch plan in your area? How is it working?

ACTIVITY

A Home Security Check

Walk through your own home and check how secure it is. While the following precautions will not guarantee protection from burglary, they will help deter it.

Door locks. A standard door lock has a slanted tongue only about a half inch long. It can be forced open easily by most burglars. The best protection for a door is a deadbolt. The bolt should extend at least an inch from the door, and it should have a hardened steel insert. Deadbolts with twist handles should not be within easy reach of a glass window.

Doors. A lock does little good if the door can be broken down easily. All outside doors should be at least 1¾ inches thick and made of metal or solid hardwood. The frames should be equally strong and fit the doors snugly.

Sliding glass doors. Burglars often enter houses through one of these doors. They simply lift the door out of its track. To prevent this, bolts or pins should be fitted into holes drilled through the track into the door frame. The bolt or pin can be easily removed from the inside when you want to use the door. A broomstick lying in the track provides some protection, but is much less effective.

Sash windows. For wooden sash windows, a bolt or pin should secure the two sashes to each other. For aluminum sash windows, buy a track lock that prevents the window from opening.

Sliding windows. Sliding windows can be secured in a way similar to sliding glass doors. A pin mechanism can be attached to the sliding window so it slides into a hole in the frame. Track locks are available, but many of these can be pushed aside with enough force on the window. If you use a track lock or a stick in the track, you should also fit a device on top of the window to prevent it being lifted out of its track.

Louvered windows. There are no easy ways to make louvered windows completely secure. Burglars can often slide the glass panes right out of their frames. On most louvered windows, the operating lever provides some locking protection if it is closed all the way. Make sure you cannot rotate the panes by hand when the lever is closed.

Window bars and grilles. If the house has window grilles, make sure they can be opened from inside in case of fire.

Shrubbery and lights outside. Shrubbery outside the windows should be trimmed so it does not give burglars a place to hide while they are trying to break in. Night lights should illuminate any dark areas where a burglar might lurk.

Valuables. You should have a list (or photos) of all the valuable items in the house and their serial numbers. Keep the list in a safe place, so it could be used later to help reclaim any stolen items or to catch a burglar or a dealer in stolen goods. As additional protection, you can engrave your name on all valuable items and then post a notice prominently in a window that all valuable items in the house are marked. Most police departments will lend an engraving tool to local residents.

Alarm system. If your home has an alarm system, test it to make sure it works. Test the window sensors or motion detectors to make sure they all work.

A Citizen Task Force

In this simulation, students take the role of citizens of Athena, a city plagued by an upsurge in crime. The city has just received special federal funds to help solve its crime problem. A decision must be made about how the funds are to be used. The city council has created a special fund in the mayor's budget and made the mayor responsible for distribution. The mayor has created a citizen task force to make recommendations on how the money should be spent. Many community members and organizations have a great interest in the task force's decision and ideas on what should be recommended.

The simulation has two parts. In part 1, members of community organizations attend a reception and try to persuade task force members to fund their programs. In part 2, the task force members decide how the funds should be allocated in a public meeting.

1. As a class, read and discuss **The Mayor's Speech**, below.
2. Form seven groups. One group will be the task force and should have six to 10 members. The remaining students will be members of six community organizations: Athena Police Department, Athena Chamber of Commerce, Urban Youth Association, Athena Police Protective League, Citizens for Public Safety, and Channel 14 Television. Students should join one of these organizations so that each has about the same number of members.
3. Each group should:
   a. Appoint a chairperson.
   b. Review **The Mayor's Speech** briefly and then read the six proposals for 108F grants.
   c. Rank the six proposals in order of which would be the most effective. Which proposal do you think would really help stop Athena's crime problem? Write a list with the most effective on top and the least effective on the bottom.
   d. Rank the six proposals again, this time in order of which would be the most effective *for the least amount of money.*
   e. Read and follow its group's instructions (See **Task Force Instructions, Part 1**, or **Community Organization Instructions**, below.)
4. Hold the reception.
5. After the reception, the task force should meet in front of the whole class to discuss the proposals and make its recommendation to the mayor. The task force should read and follow **Task Force Instructions, Part 2**, below.
6. When the task force has reached a decision on the allocation of the funds, discuss the decision as a class using the debriefing questions on page 391.

The Mayor's Speech

A few days ago, Athena's mayor made the following remarks at a meeting of the Chamber of Commerce. The remarks were printed in their entirety in the *Athena Daily News*. The speech has aroused a great deal of discussion, particularly about how the funds should be spent. The text of the mayor's speech follows. Read it and think about recommendations you might make.

* * *

Good afternoon. I'm pleased to report today that Athena is bustling. Our population is growing, our standard of living is increasing, and in the last year alone three major new industries relocated here. These are high-tech corporations, and they brought in new jobs and created business for local suppliers. While I would like to take full credit for these developments, I know many of you have also worked hard to revitalize Athena. All of us here today deserve a warm round of applause for what we have done for our city.

But let's remember that Athena still faces many challenges. One problem in particular stands out. Because of this problem, we have faced deeply personal losses, even deaths of loved ones. Some of us can no longer afford insurance for our businesses or homes. Some of us have given up going out in the evening.

(Continued on next page.)

I am speaking, of course, of the recent increase in certain crimes here in Athena. Before I address this issue, I want to make one thing perfectly clear. We do not believe the crime problem has been caused by weak laws, lenient courts, or poor police work. We have the best criminal justice system in the world. It is not my intention here today to try to fix blame for our problems or find a scapegoat. Our task is to find solutions.

Athena is not alone. In spite of an overall drop in crime, crime is still a problem for many cities across the nation. The need to find solutions has been noted in the press and in numerous government studies. The federal government has money available to help. It has a pilot anti-crime program that will make some funds available to the cities. These funds are to be used at our discretion in attacking the crime problem. Under section 108F of the program, we are entitled to $300,000 a year. At today's costs, that is not a very large amount, but it is a start, and we must use it well.

Because of previous commitments to our Victim's Assistance Program, $120,000 of this money must be earmarked for crime victims. It will be used to cover the medical bills of victims, funeral expenses for their families, and to provide psychological counseling to those left disturbed and frightened. These are the forgotten men, women, and children who have suffered most from the rise in crime. It is altogether fitting that a share of the 108F funds be committed to them.

For the remaining $180,000, the money is to be spent at our discretion as long as it is targeting crime control. Today, I would like to solicit your opinions and suggestions for the use of these 108F funds. How should this money be spent? What programs would you like to see put into effect? To help make these decisions, I am going to appoint a citizens' task force. The task force will be made up of Athenans from all walks of life. It will review suggestions that have already been made by various city departments and citizens' groups, and members of the task force will make their recommendations to me. I remind you that Athenans have solved many problems in the past by working together. If we stick together and share our wisdom with one another, we can take a major stride toward licking this problem, too.

* * *

Several weeks before the mayor's speech, news of funds for Athena spread throughout the city. Community groups that thought they had a chance to obtain some of the funds began preparing proposals for programs to be funded. As soon as the mayor let it be known that proposals were requested, several organizations were ready to deliver them. Within a few days, six proposals arrived at the mayor's office.

Not every proposal could be fully funded. Either all would be funded for less than requested, or some would not be funded at all. Consequently, representatives of each sponsoring group were eager to influence those who would make the final decision.

This evening, the mayor is holding a reception in honor of the Anti-Crime Task Force. The mayor, staff, and the members of the task force as well as representatives of community organizations will be there.

Those attending the reception understand that this social event is an important opportunity for exchanging views informally, off the record. Both the members of the committee and the representatives of various community organizations know that the decision on who will receive the funds could be influenced by talking to the right people.

For Discussion
1. What is Athena's current problem? Why has the task force been called together?
2. What is the mayor's plan for $120,000 of the 108F funding? Do you agree with this commitment of part of the funds?

(Continued on next page.)

Task Force Instructions, Part 1

As a member of this task force, your job is to consider the issues carefully and help the mayor decide on the best way to allocate the 108F funds. The mayor wants the task force to develop a consensus on its views before making its recommendations.

You know that citizen activists will be at the reception and that they will want to talk to you about the funding recommendations you will soon make. So at the reception, be sure to:

Give feedback. Inform citizens of your concerns about their proposals. Ask them to respond to these concerns by giving you arguments to take to the meeting. How they respond can help give you information to make a decision.

Speak to people from as many groups as possible. Those vying for your attention may resent your spending too much time with any one person or group.

Remember your political role. Be polite, listen carefully, but don't make any promises you can't keep. If you back out of a commitment, the committee and the mayor will look foolish.

Instructions for Community Organizations

You want to ensure that your organization's proposal is fully understood by as many members of the task force as possible. Your goal at the reception is to convince them that your proposal should be fully funded. When talking with task force members, review the list of proposals and concentrate on the proposal for your organization.

Present your best arguments.

Stress the strengths of your organization.

Explain why the proposal is a good idea for solving the crime problem in Athena.

Keep your presentation brief and to the point.

Ask for a firm commitment in support of your proposal.

Plan your strategy. Time at the reception is limited. Before it begins, consider the following:

Should you concentrate on presenting the reasons why your proposal is best? Or on pointing out weaknesses in the other approaches and proposals? You may want to make use of your rankings of all the proposals.

Should members of the group talk with as many committee members as they can? Or should each group member focus on a different person? Should you try to convince other groups to join with your group?

Write a slogan for your group.

Remember, this is a social occasion. Inappropriate behavior may prejudice members of the committee against you. Avoid arguing or interrupting conversations. See how subtle you can be.

Proposals for 108F Grants

PROPOSAL 1: Police Aides

Sponsor: Athena Police Department

Cost: $108,000

This is a six-month program to provide each of the 14 two-officer patrols in the downtown area with one half-time aide. These aides would be students studying police science or public administration. They would take over clerical duties and allow officers to spend more time on patrol. The budget would pay for 14 aides, at $15 an hour, for 20 hours per week. The program would last six months, providing an additional 7,000 hours of police patrol time.

(Continued on next page.)

PROPOSAL 2: Force One Security Patrol

Sponsor: Athena Chamber of Commerce

Cost: $144,000

This six-month program would provide a two-person private security patrol for the downtown area, during non-business hours. The patrol would function from 5 p.m. to 8 a.m. weekdays and round the clock on weekends. The private agency would hire, train, and equip the patrol. The budget covers salaries, expenses, and transportation costs for six months.

PROPOSAL 3: Self-Defense Classes

Sponsor: Urban Youth Association

Cost: $45,000

This year-round program would cover the fees for basic self-defense classes for up to a total of 500 Athenans. The basic course lasts four days a week for three weeks. Columbia Self-Defense normally charges $450 for this course, but by offering it for a large group, they will be charging the city only $81 per person. The Urban Youth Association has agreed to publicize the course and help select participants. Priority will go to low-income and elderly persons.

PROPOSAL 4: Crime Prevention Seminars

Sponsor: Athena Police Department

Cost: $67,500

This is a year-round program that would provide four two-hour discussion seminars a week for one year. The seminars would be taught by police officers and would focus on ways private citizens and neighborhood-watch groups can help prevent crime. The budget would cover officer salaries, publicity expenses, and money for preparing pamphlets and visual aids for the seminars.

PROPOSAL 5: Citizenswatch Patrols

Sponsor: Citizens for Public Safety

Cost: $33,000

This year-round program would help fund Citizenswatch patrols by business people and others. The patrols would cover the downtown and high-income residential areas. The patrol group is already formed and has made 46 citizen's arrests over the last six months. Unfortunately, only half those caught were brought to trial. In many cases, the untrained patrollers collected evidence incorrectly or violated the rights of those they detained. The budget will buy 40 citizen-band car radios and 20 hand-held walkie-talkies to improve communications with the police. Leaders of the group hope getting officers to the scene sooner will improve the conviction rate.

PROPOSAL 6: Crimescope Hotline

Sponsor: Channel 14 Television

Cost: $75,000

This year-round program would provide a 24-hour telephone line, plus $75,000 in reward money to secret witnesses. Channel 14 has offered to raise half the reward money from private sources. Informants would be given code numbers, and their information would be passed on to the police. If the information resulted in a conviction, the informant would be paid a reward.

(Continued on next page.)

Task Force Instructions, Part 2

These are the instructions for the task force to use after the reception. The task force should meet in front of the whole class to discuss the proposals and make its recommendation to the mayor. The committee should review and modify, if necessary, its previous rankings. The committee must now decide on how to spend the $180,000.

Before convening their meeting, committee members should think about the following questions:

Should the committee fund one or two of the programs it feels is most effective?

Should it partially fund several programs?

Should it fund the least expensive programs? Will the proposals rated highly serve a broad range of community interests?

Will the proposals you fund serve more than one segment of the population?

The chairperson should run the meeting. This is an open meeting. The entire class will observe your deliberations. Write the following information on the board. Remember the committee cannot spend more than $180,000.

	Request	Award
1. Police Aides	$108,000	
2. Force One Security Patrol	$144,000	
3. Self-Defense Classes	$ 45,000	
4. Crime Prevention Seminars	$ 67,500	
5. Citizenswatch Patrols	$ 33,000	
6. Crimescope Hotline	$ 75,000	
TOTAL	$ 472,500	$180,000

Discuss each of the proposals and then decide how much to spend on each.

Debriefing Questions

1. Which proposals seemed weakest? Which seemed strongest? Why?
2. After hearing the task force's discussion, did you change your mind on any of the proposals? Why?
3. What seemed to make some groups more successful in persuading the task force?
4. What additional proposals can you think of that would help solve Athena's crime problems? Describe and summarize them on the board. What are the strengths of each? What are the weaknesses? Would any of these be better than those proposed to the mayor? Why?

To conclude the discussion, you may wish to conduct a class vote to find out which proposal discussed the class thinks would be the most effective.

A Conclusion on Crime

Crime or the relative absence of crime is very much city-, community- and neighborhood-specific. Different neighborhoods today are having very different experiences.
– Christopher Stone, chair of Harvard's Criminal Justice Policy and Management Program (2008)

The units in this book have covered crime, police, the criminal case, corrections, juvenile justice, and solutions. The book has revealed many debates over issues, but a few things are clear. America still has a significant crime problem. It also has a sophisticated criminal justice system.

Other things aren't quite so clear. Just how serious is America's crime problem? Is America's criminal justice system working and, if so, how well? What should be preserved? What should be changed? Americans — experts and non-experts alike — are divided on the answers to these questions. Differences of opinion on the exclusionary rule, tougher criminal laws, harsher sentencing, the death penalty, handguns, and the causes of crime often reflect and fuel the debates.

Public Perceptions

One thing seems more clear. Scientifically conducted polls indicate that people often believe the problem of crime is getting worse, even in times when the crime rate is dropping. Public attitudes also tend to favor harsher punishment for criminals, less judicial discretion in sentencing, and the death penalty as methods for reducing crime.

The news and entertainment media may be contributing to the perception that crime is out of control. Crime makes a good story. Newspapers and news broadcasts, especially local newscasts, devote significant coverage to crime and criminal-justice issues. Much of the coverage is balanced and factual. Other times it borders on the sensational.

Many movie and television dramas also focus on crimes and criminals for their stories. Several television "reality shows" follow real police officers on their patrols. The average viewer sees several murders a week on screen, plus dozens of other acts of violence.

Although the media seem to feed the public's fear of crime, much of that fear is based on reality. Despite declines in crime since the 1990s, America's rate of violent crime has remained higher than the rates in other developed countries. In certain poor neighborhoods, violent crime rates have not declined. Almost everyone has some direct experience of crime — as a victim, friend of a victim, or even as someone who just has to pay high insurance rates. Under such conditions, what should be done? For many years, the debate has centered around two answers: getting tough on crime versus attacking the root causes of crime.

Hardline Answers

Much of the public seems to favor getting tougher on criminals. Responding to this public demand, politicians over the years have made various proposals, such as:

Build more prisons.
Make prison sentences longer.
Institute and carry out the death penalty.
Restrict bail for dangerous suspects and for convicted persons waiting on appeals.
Abolish parole.
Give judges less discretion in sentencing.
Make prison sentences mandatory for many crimes.
Restrict the use of the insanity defense.
Transfer more juveniles to adult courts.
Hire more police.

States and the federal government have already enacted many of these get-tough proposals. Some people believe that their implementation has caused the crime rate to drop. They think that crime would drop even further if more states adopted them all.

Although many Americans favor get-tough measures, others disagree. Critics of the get-tough approach claim it doesn't work, it costs too much, and it is not sustainable. They argue that crime began dropping in the 1990s because the economy boomed and the crack cocaine epidemic ended — not because of the get-tough measures. Critics also note that each year half a million prisoners go back into society. They worry that we may find our streets dominated by masses of hardened criminals as more and more prisoners are released.

Attacking Root Causes

The critics say that get-tough policies offer only a short-term answer to violent crime. In fact, many critics see the entire criminal justice system — police, courts, prisons — as incapable of affecting violent crime in the long run. The criminal justice system, they explain, reacts to violent crime after it has occurred. Locking up prisoners may prevent them from committing more crimes while they are imprisoned. But according to critics, it would be far better to prevent violent crime from occurring in the first place. One researcher has compared the criminal justice system to "operating an expensive ambulance service at the bottom of a cliff." In his view, it would be far more effective and cheaper to prevent people from falling in the first place.

This is not a new idea. Many experts have long believed the solution to violent crime is to attack its roots — poverty, racial discrimination, unemployment, lack of education, troubled families, and other social problems.

Searching for an answer to the violent crime of the 1960s, President Lyndon B. Johnson established the National Commission on the Causes and Prevention of Violence. In its final report in 1969, the commission stated that "the way in which we can make the greatest progress toward reducing violence in America is by taking the actions necessary to improve the conditions of family and community life for all who live in our cities, and especially the poor who are concentrated in the ghetto slums."

In 1990, the Milton S. Eisenhower Foundation, a non-profit group created to follow up on the commission's work on violence, issued a report. It called for the federal government to spend $10 billion a year to provide more early childhood education, reform inner-city schooling, create a youth investment corporation to assist inner-city youth, reform school-to-work programs, help repair urban areas, provide jobs for high-risk youth, and change the focus of the drug war to prevention and treatment.

Social programs have fallen out of favor. Opponents tar them as "1960s programs" and "budget busters." Many argue that it's impossible to identify who will be a violent criminal or who won't. According to them, this means that prevention programs must target large segments of the population, wasting money on programs for people who don't need them.

Further, critics say that violence prevention programs do not work. Assuming we could identify future violent criminals, they argue, violence prevention programs cannot guarantee success. People can go through them and still commit violent acts. They conclude that the community cannot gamble its safety on violence prevention programs.

New Deterrence Strategies

In recent years, alternatives to the traditional get-tough and root-cause approaches have emerged. Supporters of these alternatives view the traditional approaches as too costly and not terribly effective at reducing crime.

They believe the get-tough approach has devastated poor minority communities, sentencing drug offenders to long prison terms and making them unemployable when they get out of prison. They think we can reduce violent crime and recidivism without sending so many people to prison.

Similarly, they think root-cause programs to improve education and job skills might be worthwhile, but not for reducing violent crime. Even if the programs were effective, it would take years before they would take effect. David Kennedy, currently the director of John Jay College's Center for Crime Prevention and Control, says: "When fall comes and it gets cold, you put on a sweater, build a fire, build a house. You don't go to work on the root causes of winter."

The alternative strategies focus on deterrence. Deterrence theory is fairly simple. If someone knows he will be punished for doing something wrong, he will avoid doing it. For deterrence to work, however, the punishment must be swift and certain.

One deterrence strategy, Operation Ceasefire, focuses on reducing gang violence, which accounts for much of the worst violence in the U.S. Gangs and other groups also commit large numbers of lesser crimes. Operation Ceasefire relies on the fact that most members of violent gangs have already gotten in trouble with the law, and many are on probation, on parole, or wanted by the police. When a shooting occurs, the police crack down on the gang responsible for it, taking advantage of all legal "levers" against members of the gang. The Operation Ceasefire team informs members of other gangs that the next shooting attributed to their gang will cause a similar crackdown on their gang. This threat, which can and will be backed up, deters further shootings. This strategy has been successful in a number of cities across the nation. (For more detail on Operation Ceasefire and the Drug Market Intervention, another related deterrence strategy, see pages 87–90.)

Another deterrence strategy addresses the problem of probation and parole. While we have 2 million people behind bars, we have 5 million people on probation or parole. Most new entries to prison are not people who have committed new crimes; instead they are people who have violated their probation or parole. Many of them are returned to prison for minor or technical violations, such as not showing up to an appointment or failing a drug test. Probation and parole officers, with huge caseloads, typically ignore violations or issue warnings until they get fed up and ask a court to revoke the probation or parole. Under a new program called HOPE Probation, the judge explains to new probationers that they will be brought back to court for every violation. When violations occur, the court, in a quick proceeding, punishes violators not by revoking their probation and sending them to prison (unless it is a serious violation) but by sentencing them to a few days in jail. Since probationers know that any violation will get them jail time, they avoid violating their probation. HOPE Probation has been tremendously successful in reducing the number of probation revocations. This program shows great promise and could be implemented with parolees. It has the potential to greatly reduce the number of prisoners without threatening public safety. (For more detail on HOPE Probation, see pages 267–268.)

These new deterrence strategies also have critics. Hardline supporters consider them risky and untested "hug-a-thug" strategies. Root-cause supporters believe only improving economic and social conditions can affect crime in the long run.

FOR DISCUSSION

1. After studying the issues, has your opinion about America's crime problem changed? If so, how?
2. What do you think should be done about crime in the United States? Explain.

CLASS ACTIVITY

What Should Be Done?

Pretend you are a researcher drafting a study on crime in America. Prepare the concluding section of the report, **Recommendations on the Crime Problem**. Use what you have learned from this book, class discussions, outside resources, and your own research. State your own ideas, opinions, and reasons. Prepare a presentation of your conclusion for the class.

Sources for Unit 6

"Adolescents, Neighborhoods, & Violence," NIJ, 9/2007, NCJ 217397. · "Alcohol & Crime," NCADD, 2012, URL: www.ncadd.org · "Alcohol & Crime: Data From 2002 to 2008," BJS, 2010, NCJ 231685. · *Alcohol Outlets as Attractors of Violence & Disorder*, NIJ-Sp., 2008, NCJ 227646. · *America's Children*, OJJDP, 2011, NCJ 235151. · Anwar, Shamena *et al.* "The Impact of Jury Race in Criminal Trials," *Quarterly J. of Econ.*, 4/17/2012. · "Background Checks for Firearms Transfers," BJS, 2010, NCJ 231679. · Ballantine, A. "Racial Differences in the War on Drugs," 4/20/2011, URL: www.vrdc.cornell.edu · Barnes, C. *et al.* "Race, Drug, & Criminal Sentencing," *J. of Criminal Justice* 24 (1), 1996. · Beeson, A. *et al.* "Unpatriotic Acts." ACLU. 7/2003. URL: www.aclu.org · Bellair, P. *et al.* "Community, Inequality, & Crime." *Sociological Focus* 32:1–5, 1999. · "Blueprints for Violence Prevention," Center for the Study of Violence Prevention, 2012, URL: www.colorado.edu/cspv · Bonczar, T. "Prevalence of Imprisonment in the U.S. Population, 1974–2001." Wash., DC: BJS, 2003. · Bazelon, E. "Bullies Beware," *Slate*, 5/30/2010, URL: www.slate.com · "Bringing Geography to the Practice of Analyzing Crime Through Technology," NIJ-Sp., 2010, NCJ 230757. · "Bruised Inside: What Our Children Say About Youth Violence, What Causes It, & What We Need to Do About It," Wash., DC: Nat. Assoc. of Attorneys General, 2000. · *Bullying in Schools*, COPS, 2009, NCJ 227422. · "Bullying in Schools," OJJDP, 2011, NCJ 234205. · Chandler, K. "Students' Reports of School Crime: 1989 & 1995." Wash., DC: U.S. Dept. of Ed. & Justice, 1998. · "Child Abuse & Neglect Research," Dept. of Health & Human Services, 2011. URL: www.acf.hhs.gov · "Children's Exposure to Violence," OJJDP, 2009, NCJ 227744. · Clarke, R. *Improving Street Lighting to Reduce Crime in Residential Areas*, COPS, 2008, NCJ 226359. · ___, ed. *Situational Crime Prevention: Successful Case Studies*, 2nd Ed. Albany, NY: Harrow & Heston,1997. · ___. *Understanding Risky Facilities*, COPS, 2007, NCJ 218075. · *Community Organizations & Crime*, NIJ-Sp., 2009, NCJ 227645. · *Contingencies in the Long-Term Impact of Work on Crime Among Youth*, NIJ-Sp., 2010, NCJ 232222. · *Crime Gun Risk Factors*, NIJ-Sp., 2007, NCJ 221074. · *Crime in the U.S., 2010.* Wash., D.C.: FBI, 2011. · "Does Neighborhood Watch Reduce Crime?," COPS, 2008, NCJ 223916. · Croddy, M. *et al. The Challenge of Violence*, L.A.: CRF, 1997. · Deaths: Final Data for 2008. CDC, 2011. URL: www.cdc.gov · Deaths: Leading Causes for 2008. CDC, 2011. URL: www.cdc.gov · Bluestone, B. *et al. Deindustrialization of America*. NY: Basic Books, 1982. · "Enforcement of the Brady Act, 2009," BJS-Sp., April 2011, NCJ 234173. · *Evaluation of Bullyproofing Your School*, NIJ-Sp., 2007, NCJ 221078. · Felson, M. *et al. Opportunity Makes the Thief*. London: Research Development Statistics, 1998. · Firearms & Crime Statistics, BJS, 2012, URL: http://bjs.ojp.usdoj.gov/content/guns.cfm · *Gender, Mental Illness, & Crime*, NIJ-Sp., September 2008, NCJ 224028. · *Probation & Parole in the U.S., 2010*, BJS, 2011, NCJ 236019. · Good, C. "Rand Paul vs. the PATRIOT Act," Atlantic Blog, 2/15/11, URL: www.theatlantic.com · ___. "With Deal to Renew PATRIOT Act, Reformers Will Have to Wait," Atlantic Blog, 5/19/11, URL: www.theatlantic.com · Gottfredson, G. *et al.* "Toward Safe & Orderly Schools," Wash., DC: NIJ, 2004. · Greenfeld, L. *Alcohol & Crime*, BJS, 1998. · *Guide for Preventing & Responding to School Violence, 2nd Edition*, BJA-Sp., 2009, NCJ 228960. · "Prisoners in 2010," BJS, 2011, NCJ 236096. · Hawkins, D. "Controlling Crime Before It Happens," *NIJ Journal*, 8/1995. · Hofstadter, R. *et al.*, ed. *American Violence*, NY: Knopf, 1970. · Homicide trends in the U.S., BJS, 2012, URL: http://bjs.ojp.usdoj.gov · *Impact Evaluation of Youth Crime Watch Programs*, NIJ-Sp., 2008, NCJ 226356. · *Impulsivity, Offending, & the Neighborhood: Investigating the Person-Context Nexus*, NIJ-Sp., 2007, NCJ 226781. · *Intersection of Genes, the Environment, & Crime & Delinquency*, NIJ-Sp., 2006, NCJ 231609. · *Investigation & Prosecution of Homicide Cases in the U.S.* NIJ-Sp., 2006, NCJ 214753. · *Justice on Trial*, Leadership Conference on Civil Rights, 2000. URL: http://nicic.org · Kellam, S. *et al.* "Preventing School Violence," Wash., DC: NIJ, 2000. · Lichtblau, E., "Senate Makes Permanent Nearly All Provisions of Patriot Act, With a Few Restrictions." *NY Times*, 7/30/2005. · Lithwick, D. *et al.* "A Guide to the Patriot Act," *Slate*, 9/2003, URL: www.slate.com · Martz, C., "The Patriot Act," *Bill of Rights in Action*, Fall 2003. · ___. "Does the Criminal Justice System Discriminate Against African Americans?"*Bill of Rights in Action*, Winter 1992. · Mauer, M. "The Crisis of the Young African American Male & the Criminal Justice System." Prepared for the U.S. Commission on Civil Rights, 1999. · ___. "Americans Behind Bars" Wash., DC: The Sentencing Project. 1992. · Mediati, N. "Secure Your Life in 12 Steps," *PC World*, June 2011. · "Nat. Child Abuse Statistics," Childhelp, 2012, URL: www.childhelp.org · "Neighborhood Watch Manual," BJA-Sp., 2010, NCJ 231132. · "Nexus Between Economics & Family Violence," NIJ-Sp., 2010, NCJ 229913. · *Pathways from Dependency & Neglect to Delinquency: Part Two*, NIJ-Sp., 2007, NCJ 220288. · *Policymaker's Guide to Building Our Way Out of Crime*, COPS, 2009, NCJ 227421. · "Predicting a Criminal's Journey to Crime," NIJ, 2006, NCJ 212264. · *Preventing Crime, Saving Children: Monitoring, Mentoring, & Ministering*. Second Report of the Council on Crime in America. NY: The Manhattan Inst., 1997. · Pristin, T. "Soul-Searching on Violence by the Industry." *LA Times*. 5/18/1992. · *Reducing Racial Disparity in the Criminal Justice System*. Sentencing Project, 2008. · *Report of the Nat. Summit on Justice Reinvestment & Public Safety Council of State Governments*, BJA-Sp., 2011, NCJ 233019. · Robers, S. *et al. Indicators of School Crime & Safety: 2011*. U.S. Dept. of Ed. & Justice. NCES 2012002, 2011. · *School-Based Programs to Reduce Bullying & Victimization*, NIJ-Sp., 2009, NCJ 229377. · "School-Based Partnerships," COPS, 2006, NCJ 216230. · School Crime, NIJ, 2012. URL: http://www.nij.gov · Schuster, B. "Preventing, Preparing for Critical Incidents in Schools," *NIJ Journal* No. 262, 3/2009. · "Seven Deadly Days." *Time*. 7/17/1989. · Sheley, J., "Controlling Violence," *Preventing School Violence*, Wash., DC: NIJ, 2000. · Sherman, L. *et al.* "Preventing Crime: What Works, What Doesn't, What's Promising," Wash., DC: NIJ, 1998. · Singer, M. *et al.* "Contributors to Violent Behavior Among Elementary & Middle School Children," *Pediatrics* v. 104, 1999. · *Situational Crime Prevention at Specific Locations in Community Context: Place & Neighborhood Effects*, NIJ-Sp., 2009, NCJ 229364. · Sloan, J. *et al.* "Handgun Regulations, Crime, Assaults, Homicide." *New England J.of Medicine.* 11/10/1988. · *Social Norms Approach to Community-Based Crime Prevention*, NIJ-Sp., 2009, NCJ 226821. · *Solutions for Safer Communities*, BJA, 2010, NCJ 225799. · *Spreading the Wealth*, NIJ-Sp., 2010, NCJ 232084. · Drugs & Crime, BJS, 2012, URL: http://bjs.ojp.usdoj.gov · Steinberg, J. *et al.*, ed. *Urban America: Policy Choices for L.A. & the Nation*, Santa Monica: RAND, 1992. · Stone, C. "Race, Crime, & the Administration of Justice," *NIJ Journal*, April 1999. · "Students' Reports of School Crime: 1989 & 1995" Wash., DC: BJS & Nat. Center for Education Statistics, 1998. · "Trends for Background Checks for Firearm Transfers, 1999–2008," BJS-Sp., 7/2010, NCJ 231187. · *Video Surveillance of Public Places*, COPS, 2006, NCJ 213593. · Weitzer, R. "Racial Discrimination in the Criminal Justice System," *J. of Criminal Justice* 24 (4). 1996. · Widom, C. "The Cycle of Violence," *Science*, 14 April 1989. · Wikipedia articles on "Patriot Act," "Phoebe Prince," URL: http://en.wikipedia.org · Wilson, J. *et al. Crime & Human Nature*. NY: Simon & Schuster, 1985. · Wilson, R. *et al.* "Preventing Neighborhood Crime," *NIJ Journal* No. 263, 6/2009. · "Your Security," *Consumer Reports*, 6/2011. · Zimring, F. *et al. The Citizen's Guide to Gun Control*. NY: Macmillan Pub., 1987.

EXCERPTS FROM THE U.S. CONSTITUTION

Selected Sections of the U.S. Constitution, Ratified 1788

Preamble

We, the People of the United States, in Order to form a more perfect Union, establish Justice, insure domestic Tranquility, provide for the common defence, promote the general Welfare, and secure the Blessings of Liberty to ourselves and our Posterity, do ordain and establish this Constitution for the United States of America.

Article I

Section 1. All legislative Powers herein granted shall be vested in a Congress of the United States, which shall consist of a Senate and House of Representatives.

Section 8. The Congress shall have Power . . . To provide for the Punishment of counterfeiting the Securities and Coin of the United States . . . . To constitute tribunals inferior to the supreme Court; To define and punish Piracies and Felonies committed on the high Seas, and Offenses against the Law of Nations . . . To make all Laws which shall be necessary and proper for carrying into Execution the foregoing Powers, and all other Powers vested by this Constitution in the Government of the United States . . . .

Section 9. . . . . The Privilege of the Writ of Habeas Corpus shall not be suspended, unless when in cases of Rebellion or Invasion the public safety may require it.

No Bill of Attainder or ex post facto Law shall be passed.

Section 10. No state shall . . . pass any bill of attainder, ex post facto law . . . .

Article II

Section 1. The executive Power shall be vested in a President of the United States of America. He shall hold his Office during the Term of four Years, and, together with the Vice President, chosen for the same Term, be elected as follows . . . .

Section 2. The President shall be Commander in Chief of the Army and Navy of the United States, and of the Militia of the several States, when called into the actual Service of the United States; he may require the Opinion, in writing, of the principal Officer in each of the executive Departments, upon any Subject relating to the Duties of their respective Offices, and he shall have Power to grant Reprieves and Pardons for Offences against the United States, except in Cases of Impeachment.

He shall have Power, by and with the Advice and Consent of the Senate to make Treaties, provided two-thirds of the Senators present concur; and he shall nominate and by and with the Advice and Consent of the Senate, shall appoint Ambassadors, other public Ministers and Consuls, Judges of the supreme Court, and all other Officers of the United States, whose Appointments are not herein otherwise provided for, and which shall be established by Law: but the Congress may by Law vest the Appointment of such inferior Officers, as they think proper, in the President alone, in the Courts of Law, or in the Heads of Departments.

Section 3. . . . . He shall take Care that the Laws be faithfully executed . . . .

Section 4. The President, Vice-President and all Civil Officers of the United States, shall be removed from Office on Impeachment for, and Conviction of, Treason, Bribery, or other high Crimes and Misdemeanors.

Article III

Section 1. The judicial Power of the United States, shall be vested in one supreme Court, and in such inferior Courts as the Congress may from time to time ordain and establish. The Judges, both of the supreme and inferior Courts, shall hold their Offices during good Behaviour, and shall, at stated Times, receive for their Services, a Compensation, which shall not be diminished during their Continuance in Office.

Section 2. The judicial Power shall extend to all Cases, in Law and Equity, arising under this Constitution, the Laws of the United States, and Treaties made, or which shall be made under their Authority; — to all Cases affecting Ambassadors, other public Ministers and Consuls; — to all Cases of admiralty and maritime Jurisdiction; — to Controversies to which the United States shall be a Party; — to Controversies between two or more States; — between a State and Citizens of another State; — between Citizens of different States; — between Citizens of the same State claiming Lands under Grants of different States, and between a State, or the Citizens thereof, and foreign States, Citizens or Subjects.

In all Cases affecting Ambassadors, other public Ministers and Consuls, and those in which a State shall be Party; the supreme Court shall have original Jurisdiction. In all the other Cases before mentioned, the supreme Court shall have appellate Jurisdiction, both as to Law and Fact, with such Exceptions, and under such Regulations as the Congress shall make.

The Trial of all Crimes, except in Cases of Impeachment, shall be by Jury; and such Trial shall be held in the State where the said Crimes shall have been committed; but when not committed within any State, the Trial shall be at such Place or Places as the Congress may by Law have directed.

Section 3. Treason against the United States shall consist only in levying War against them, or in adhering to their Enemies, giving them Aid and Comfort. No Person shall be convicted of Treason unless on the Testimony of two Witnesses to the same overt Act, or on Confession in open Court.

The Congress shall have Power to declare the Punishment of Treason, but no Attainder of Treason shall work Corruption of Blood, or Forfeiture except during the Life of the Person attainted.

Article IV

Section 1. Full faith and Credit shall be given in each State to the public Acts, Records, and judicial Proceedings of every other State. And the Congress may by general Laws prescribe the Manner in which such Acts, Records and Proceedings shall be proved, and the Effect thereof.

Section 2. The Citizens of each State shall be entitled to all Privileges and Immunities of Citizens in the several States.

A Person charged in any State with Treason, Felony or other Crime, who shall flee from Justice, and be found in another State, shall, on Demand of the executive Authority of the State from which he fled, be delivered up, to be removed to the State having Jurisdiction of the Crime. . . .

Section 4. The United States shall guarantee to every State in this Union a Republican Form of Government, and shall protect each of them against Invasion; and on Application of the Legislature, or of the Executive (when the Legislature cannot be convened) against domestic Violence.

Article VI

This Constitution, and the Laws of the United States which shall be made in Pursuance thereof; and all Treaties made, or which shall be made, under the Authority of the United States, shall be the supreme Law of the Land; and the Judges in every State shall be bound thereby, any Thing in the Constitution or Laws of any State to the Contrary notwithstanding. . . .

Selected Amendments from the Bill of Rights, Ratified 1791

First Amendment. Congress shall make no law respecting an establishment of religion, or prohibiting the free exercise thereof; or abridging the freedom of speech, or of the press; or the right of the people peaceably to assemble, and to petition the Government for a redress of grievances.

Second Amendment. A well regulated Militia, being necessary to the security of a free State, the right of the people to keep and bear Arms, shall not be infringed.

Fourth Amendment. The right of the people to be secure in their persons, houses, papers, and effects, against unreasonable searches and seizures, shall not be violated, and no Warrants shall issue, but upon probable cause, supported by Oath or affirmation, and particularly describing the place to be searched, and the persons or things to be seized.

Fifth Amendment. No person shall be held to answer for a capital, or otherwise infamous crime, unless on a presentment or indictment of a Grand Jury, except in cases arising in the land or naval forces, or in the Militia, when in actual service in time of War or public danger; nor shall any person be subject of the same offence to be twice put in jeopardy of life or limb; nor shall be compelled in any criminal case to be a witness against himself, nor be deprived of life, liberty, or property, without due process of law; nor shall private property be taken for public use, without just compensation.

Sixth Amendment. In all criminal prosecutions, the accused shall enjoy the right to a speedy and public trial, by an impartial jury of the State and district wherein the crime shall have been committed, which district shall have been previously ascertained by law, and to be informed of the nature and cause of the accusation; to be confronted with the witnesses against him to have compulsory process for obtaining witnesses in his favor, and to have the Assistance of Counsel for his defence.

Seventh Amendment. In Suits at common law, where the value in controversy shall exceed twenty dollars, the right of trial by jury shall be preserved, and no fact tried by a jury, shall be otherwise re-examined in any Court of the United States, than according to the rules of the common law.

Eighth Amendment. Excessive bail shall not be required, nor excessive fines imposed, nor cruel and unusual punishments inflicted.

Ninth Amendment. The enumeration in the Constitution, of certain rights, shall not be construed to deny or disparage others retained by the people.

10th Amendment. The powers not delegated to the United States by the Constitution, nor prohibited by it to the States, are reserved to the States respectively, or to the people.

Selected Later Amendments

13th Amendment, Ratified 1865. Neither slavery nor involuntary servitude, except as a punishment for crime whereof the party shall have been duly convicted, shall exist within the United States, or any place subject to their jurisdiction.

14th Amendment, Ratified 1868. All persons born or naturalized in the United States, and subject to the jurisdiction thereof, are citizens of the United States and of the State wherein they reside. No State shall make or enforce any law which shall abridge the privileges or immunities of citizens of the United States; nor shall any State deprive any person of life, liberty, of property, without due process of the law; nor deny to any person within its jurisdiction the equal protection of the laws.

GLOSSARY

accessory after the fact The crime of helping a felon avoid getting caught after the felony has been committed. It is considered an **inchoate crime**.

accomplice Someone who aids another in committing a crime, either before or during the crime.

acquit To find not guilty.

adjudicatory hearing A fact-finding hearing in the juvenile justice system to determine whether a juvenile is delinquent. The equivalent to a trial in the adult system.

affidavit A written statement made under oath.

affirmative defense A defense such as insanity, self-defense, and entrapment. If proved by the defendant, it makes the defendant not guilty of the crime even if the prosecution can prove the elements of the crime.

age of majority The age a person is considered an adult for legal purposes.

aggravated assault According to the UCR, an unlawful attack by one person upon another for the purpose of inflicting severe or aggravated bodily injury. Normally committed with a weapon.

alibi The defense that the person was elsewhere when the crime was committed and therefore could not have committed the crime.

anthropologists Scientists who study human customs and cultures.

appeal A request that an appellate court review a decision of a lower court.

appellate court A court that hears appeals; not a trial court; an appeals court.

attorney A lawyer; legal counsel. A person authorized to practice law.

attorney at law See **attorney**.

arraignment A court hearing in which the defendant must enter a plea, such as guilty or not guilty.

arrest To take a person into custody for the purpose of charging the person with a crime.

arrestee The person arrested.

arson According to the UCR, any willful or malicious burning of another's property.

assault Technically, the immediate threat of attacking someone, but usually it means a physical attack on another person. See **battery**.

assault with a deadly weapon The crime of attacking someone with a weapon that could cause fatal injuries. See **aggravated assault**.

attempt The crime of taking substantial steps toward committing a crime, but not actually committing it. Attempt is considered an **inchoate crime**.

bail A pretrial procedure permitting an arrested person to stay out of jail by depositing a set amount of money as security that the person will show up for trial.

bailiff A police officer assigned to the courtroom to keep order.

battery The illegal touching of another person, usually an attack. When used in the phrase assault and battery, the assault is the threat of the attack and the battery the physical attack itself.

bench The judge's desk in the courtroom.

bench trial A trial held before a judge alone without a jury.

bill of attainder A legislative enactment that punishes a person in place of a trial. Banned by the U.S. Constitution.

Bill of Rights The first 10 amendments to the U.S. Constitution, which describe the rights and protections guaranteed to each citizen.

booking The official process of recording the arrest. A booking officer records the accused's name and address, the charges, and time and place of arrest, and may take fingerprints and photographs of the accused.

bribery The crime of offering public officials money or something of value to influence their decisions. Public officials who accept such gifts are also guilty of the crime.

bunco A con game; a swindle.

burden of proof The responsibility of proving facts in a case. In a criminal trial, the prosecution has the burden of proving its case beyond a reasonable doubt.

Bureau of Justice Statistics An agency of the Department of Justice that collects crime-related statistics.

burglary The illegal entry into any building with the intent to commit a crime, such as theft.

capital crime A crime punishable by death or life imprisonment.

capital punishment The death penalty.

case in chief One side's trial evidence. In a criminal trial, the prosecution presents its evidence first. After it rests its case, the defense presents its evidence.

case law Law made by judges interpreting constitutions, statutes, and other case law; judge-made law.

citizen review boards An official group, staffed by ordinary citizens, authorized to review complaints of police misconduct.

civil case A lawsuit between individuals or organizations, which normally seeks monetary compensation for damages.

civil court A court that handles civil cases.

civilian review boards *See* **citizen review boards**.

commissioner An attorney who acts as a judge.

common law 1. The unwritten law in England that evolved over centuries and is the basis for U.S. law. 2. Case law in the United States as opposed to statutory law.

community policing A type of policing that stresses community interaction with the police. Also called community-based policing or community-oriented policing.

conspiracy The crime of two or more people agreeing to commit a crime. Most jurisdictions also require an overt act toward committing the crime. It is considered an **inchoate crime**.

contempt of court It consists of two types: civil and criminal. Civil contempt typically occurs when a person fails to obey a court order and is held in contempt until the order is obeyed. Criminal contempt is a crime that punishes an offender for disrupting or attacking the integrity of the court.

corrections The part of the criminal justice system that deals with convicted criminals; it includes jails, prisons, parole, and probation.

crime An illegal act punishable upon conviction in a court.

crime rate The amount of crime per so many people in the population.

criminal lawyer A prosecutor or defense attorney.

criminal negligence Doing an act with an extreme lack of care for the consequences. It is a state of mind requirement for certain crimes, e.g., involuntary manslaughter.

criminal procedure The rules for processing someone through the criminal justice system.

criminology The study of crime. A **criminologist** studies crime.

cross-examination The questioning of an opponent's witnesses at trial.

cyberbullying A form of bullying that takes place on the Internet.

deadly force Force that poses a high risk of death or serious injury to its human target.

death row A separate section of a prison reserved for inmates awaiting execution.

defendant The accused in a criminal trial.

defense attorney The attorney for the accused.

delinquent A minor who commits a **delinquent act**.

delinquent act In most states, this means an act that if done by an adult would be a crime. Some states, however, also include status offenses as delinquent acts.

determinate sentence A prison sentence for a specific length of time, e.g., five years. A **fixed sentence**.

deterrence The idea that fear of punishment will prevent crimes. For example, some people might be deterred from robbing banks because they know that bank robbers go to jail. **Specific deterrence** is the effect of preventing an offender from repeating the crime by punishing the offender. **General deterrence** is the effect of preventing the general population from committing crimes by punishing offenders.

direct examination An attorney's initial questioning of his or her own witness.

discretion The power to choose.

discretionary jurisdiction The power of some appeals courts, such as the U.S. Supreme Court, to accept or refuse to hear particular appeals. *See* **writ of certiorari**.

disturbing the peace The misdemeanor of willfully bothering other people by making a lot of noise.

DNA Deoxyribonucleic acid, the building block in every cell, is different in every human (except identical twins). From small amounts of blood, skin, or hair at a crime scene, a DNA profile can be made, which can be used to identify who was at the scene.

driving under the influence The crime of operating a motor vehicle while under the influence of drugs or alcohol.

due process In the Fifth and 14th amendments, the basic requirement that no person can be deprived of life, liberty, or property without a fair trial. This means that fair procedures must be used.

embezzlement The crime of stealing another's property that has been entrusted to you. E.g., a bank teller might embezzle money from the bank.

en banc The full bench of judges. Each federal circuit court has from six to 27 judges, but for most cases the judges hear cases in panels of three. When all the judges hear a case together, they hear it *en banc*.

entrapment The affirmative defense that the defendant would not have committed the crime if the police had not enticed the defendant.

evidence The means of determining facts in a trial. Testimony, physical objects, and exhibits are examples of evidence.

exclusionary rule A judicial rule that prevents the government from introducing illegally obtained evidence at a criminal trial.

ex post facto law A law passed criminalizing an act committed by a person before the law was passed.

extort To obtain money or property by threats of harm or of exposure of past deeds.

extortion The crime of obtaining money or property by threatening to harm another or to expose another's past deeds; intimidation. *See* **extort**.

fact finder The one responsible for deciding the facts of a particular case and coming to a verdict; either a judge or jury.

false imprisonment The crime of making a false arrest or unlawfully taking someone into custody.

felony A serious crime usually punished by one or more years of imprisonment in a state or federal penitentiary.

felony murder The rule that if any person is killed during a felony, the criminal can be charged with murder.

fitness hearing A special hearing in juvenile court to determine whether a juvenile should be tried in adult court.

fixed sentence *See* **determinate sentence**.

forfeiture The confiscation of assets either used in or derived from illegal activity.

forgery The crime of falsely signing a document with the intent to defraud.

fraud The crime of obtaining another's property through lies and deceit.

general intent The voluntary intent to do a prohibited act.

habeas corpus, writ of A court order requiring authorities to release a prisoner because the court has found that the prisoner is being illegally detained.

hacking The act of electronically breaking into or disrupting computer systems.

hearing Any court proceeding, such as a trial.

homicide Literally, human killing. The crimes of homicide range from different degrees of murder to different kinds of manslaughter.

hypothetical A made-up example.

impanel To select a jury.

incarceration rate The number of prisoners per 100,000 population.

inchoate crime A group of crimes that penalize planning, preparing, or aiding after the fact the commission of a crime. Examples of inchoate crimes are accessory after the fact, attempt, conspiracy, and solicitation.

incorrigible Juveniles who cannot be controlled by their parents may be labeled this.

indentured servant In American history, a person who contracted in return for transportation to America to work for free for a set number of years, usually two to seven.

indeterminate sentence A prison sentence of an indefinite period of time, for example "one year to 30 years." Under this sentence, prisoners are released when the parole board determines they are rehabilitated.

Internet crime Any crime committed using a computer or computer network.

interrogation Questioning.

involuntary manslaughter A killing caused by criminal negligence or an unintended killing that takes place during a misdemeanor offense.

jurisdiction 1. Power, authority, control. 2. The geographical area over which particular courts or police departments have power.

jurisprudence The philosophy of law, or the science that studies the principles of law.

jury tampering The crime of threatening or wrongfully trying to influence jurors.

larceny The unlawful taking of another's property with the intention of permanently depriving the owner of its possession and use; theft.

lawyer *See* **attorney**.

lynching A form of mob violence that punishes an accused person without a legal trial. The word comes from the American Revolution and a Colonel Charles Lynch of Virginia, who urged crowds to beat and frighten Tories, supporters of Britain.

magistrate A court officer who issues warrants; normally a lower-court judge who handles pretrial proceedings or presides over misdemeanor trials.

malice aforethought A state of mind requirement for murder. It is either an intent to kill or an intent to do an extremely dangerous act with a conscious disregard for the consequences.

marshal A law-enforcement officer who normally performs duties connected with a court.

mayhem The crime of mutilating or cutting off a part of someone's body.

mens rea Guilty mind; the state of mind requirement for crimes.

Miranda **warning** An advisory statement about the rights of suspects that police must read to suspects in custody before questioning them. The Supreme Court first required this statement in its *Miranda v. Arizona* decision in 1966.

misdemeanor A crime less serious than a felony, usually punished by a fine or imprisonment up to one year in a local jail.

mitigate To make less serious. Mitigating circumstances are circumstances surrounding a crime that tend to make it less serious.

Model Penal Code A criminal code composed by legal experts at the American Law Institute as a standard that legislatures may want to adopt. Unless sections of it are adopted by jurisdictions, it has no legal authority.

motion A formal request made to a court.

motion to suppress A request that the court exclude particular evidence from the trial because it was illegally obtained.

murder The unlawful killing of another person with malice aforethought.

nolo contendere A plea of no contest. (Latin for "I will not contest it.") It has the same effect as a guilty plea except that the person does not admit guilt. Thus if someone files a lawsuit against the person, the person has not admitted guilt.

notary, or notary public An official authorized to verify signatures on documents or attest to affidavits.

obstruction of justice The crime of interfering with the administration of justice.

organized crime A group that uses a business-like structure, with a boss and subordinates, to carry out crime on an ongoing basis.

overrule To rule that something is not valid. E.g., the judge overruled the objection.

pardon An act by the governor or president that forgives all or part of a prisoner's sentence.

parens patriae The idea that the state takes the role of parents to protect juveniles.

parole The conditional release of a prisoner before the end of a prison term.

parole board A board appointed by the governor that determines when prisoners may be released on parole.

penal Subject to punishment. A **penal code** is a list of laws defining crimes.

penitentiary A state or federal maximum-security prison.

peremptory challenge During jury selection, an attorney's rejection of a prospective juror that requires no reason be given to the court. Each side has a limited number of these challenges.

perjury The crime of lying while testifying under oath.

plaintiff The party in a lawsuit who sues the other party.

plea bargain An agreement struck between a criminal defendant and prosecutor. In exchange for a guilty plea from the defendant, the prosecutor will either (1) drop one of several charges, (2) lower the charge, or (3) recommend a light sentence.

precedent An issue of law previously decided by a court that other courts follow.

probable cause Evidence that an independent, cautious person would have good reason to believe.

probation An alternative to prison. This sentence requires the offender to follow certain conditions, usually under the supervision of a probation officer.

prosecute To try someone for a crime.

prosecution The government's side in a criminal case.

prosecutor The government's attorney who presents the case against a criminal defendant.

prosecutorial discretion The prosecutor's authority to decide what charges to bring and how to pursue a criminal case.

prostitution The act of engaging in a sexual act with another in exchange for money or other compensation. It is a crime in most jurisdictions.

public defender An attorney working for a government agency (the public defender's office) that defends criminal suspects who cannot afford their own attorney.

rape According to the UCR, the carnal knowledge of a female forcibly and against her will.

receiving stolen property The crime of buying or getting property that the buyer knows is stolen.

recidivism The committing of further crimes by offenders after they have been punished for previous convictions.

redirect examination An attorney's requestioning of his or her own witness after cross-examination.

rehabilitation Helping convicted offenders change their lives so that they can lead productive lives in society.

restitution Direct payments made from criminal to victim as compensation for a crime.

relevant Pertinent, appropriate, related to the subject at hand.

robbery The taking of a person's property by violence or threat of violence; forcible stealing.

search In *Katz v. United States* (1967), the Supreme Court defined a search as any governmental intrusion into something in which a person has a reasonable expectation of privacy.

seizure Any taking into possession, custody, or control. Property may be seized, but so may people. An arrest is one form of seizure.

sentence A punishment for a crime.

sheriff A county law-enforcement officer.

sodomy Homosexual or oral copulation.

solicitation The crime of asking, ordering, or encouraging another to commit a crime. It is classified as an **inchoate crime**.

specific intent The intent to do a prohibited act on purpose; the intent required for certain crimes, such as theft, which requires the specific intent of never returning the property.

status offense An offense, such as truancy or running away from home, that would not be a crime if committed by an adult.

statute A written law; a law enacted by the legislature.

statute of limitations A limit placed on the amount of time that a criminal action may be taken.

statutory law See statute.

sting operation Undercover police work that sets up a situation to catch criminals in the act.

street crime A class of crimes usually involving force or violence, such as murder, assault, robbery, or rape.

strict liability The imposition of criminal responsibility regardless of a person's intent.

subornation of perjury The crime of persuading another person to commit perjury.

sustain To rule that something is valid. E.g., the judge sustained the objection.

testify To make statements as a witness under oath.

testimony Statements made by witnesses under oath.

theft See larceny.

training schools Large secure facilities that hold juveniles found delinquent.

treason The crime of a U.S. citizen helping an enemy of the United States.

UCR Uniform Crime Reporting program. A nationwide program headed by the FBI that collects police reports of crime.

vandalism The crime of intentionally defacing or destroying another person's property.

venue The location of a trial.

verdict The decision of guilty or not guilty made by the jury or judge.

victimless crimes Crimes, such as prostitution and possession of illegal drugs, in which everyone involved chooses to be involved.

victimology The branch of criminology that studies crime victims.

vigilantes Persons who illegally take the law into their own hands and punish suspected lawbreakers.

voir dire During jury selection, the questioning of prospective jurors.

voluntary manslaughter The intentional killing of another person done under extreme provocation and in the heat of anger.

warrant A court order issued by a judge authorizing a search, an arrest, or a seizure of evidence of a crime.

white-collar crime A class of property crimes that are usually job-related, such as embezzlement, bribery, and consumer fraud.

witness tampering The crime threatening a witness or wrongfully persuading a witness not to testify.

writ A written court order.

writ of certiorari An order from an appeals court stating that the court will hear a case. These writs are granted by appeals courts that have discretionary jurisdiction.

Photo Credits

All photographs, cartoons, and opinion polls are reprinted with the permission of the followiing:

TABLE OF CASES

Below are the titles of cases cited in the book. Each is followed by its legal citation, the year it was decided, and the pages the case can be found on in *Criminal Justice in America*.

INDEX

perjury, 22–23, 402, 403
plea bargaining, 185–186, 402
police, 75–152; code of silence, 139–140, 146; community, 83–85; corruption, 139–140; history of, 76–77; minorities and, 80; policing of, 145–147; units of local police, 78–80; use of force, 141–142; women, 80; work, 79–80
preliminary hearing, 187
pre-release programs, 273
principal (of crime), 16
prison, 242–260; alternatives to, 262–275; conditions, 245–251; gangs, 251; history of, 224–225; overcrowding, 245–248; population, 253–257; private, 244; revolts, 249–251; security levels, 242–244; staying out of, 261. *See also* sentencing
probable cause, 106–108, 110, 116–119, 319, 357–360, 398, 402; hearing, 165, 187–188. *See also* Fourth Amendment
probation, 264–265, 327, 402; revoking of, 266–268
problem-oriented policing, 84
Prohibition, 50, 139
property crimes, 66–67. *See also* burglary; fraud; theft; white-collar crimes
prosecutors, 160–161, 196, 402; discretion of, 181–183, 402. *See also* lawyers, plea bargaining
public defenders, 162, 402. *See also* defense attorneys, lawyers, plea bargaining
public trial, right to. *See* trial
punishment: history of, 224–225; purpose of, 222–223. *See also* fines; prison; sentencing

Q–R

racial discrimination, 371–375; arrest and, 372; as cause of crime, 347; capital punishment and, 280, 374–375; jury verdicts and, 372–374; juvenile system and, 342–343; plea bargains and, 372; profiling, 136–138; sentencing and, 238–241, 374
rational choice and crime, 351–352
reasonable suspicion, 110, 116–119
receiving stolen property, 14–15, 402
rehabilitation, 222, 256, 402
restitution, 68, 69, 222, 402
retribution, 223
RICO, 17–18
robbery, 14, 64–65, 402

S

Sarbanes-Oxley Act, 58
San Francisco Vigilance Committee, 379–380
school: crime in, 380–383; gangs and, 380–381; safety measures, 382–383; searches, 318–320; shootings, 382
SDPD, 84–85
search and seizure, 105–121, 402; checklist, 122; defined, 106–108; schools and, 318–319
Second Amendment, 105, 361–362, 398self-defense, 36, 40–41.
self-incrimination. *See* Fifth Amendment
sentencing, 222–241, 402; crack cocaine, 238–241; factors in, 226–227; guidelines, 228–229; proportionate, 236–238; truth in, 252–253; race as a factor, 233–234. *See also* community corrections;

community service; determinate sentences; fines; indeterminate sentences; mandatory sentences; prison; punishment; three strikes
showups, 91–93
Singleton, Lawrence, 259–260
Sirhan, Sirhan, 258–259
Sixth Amendment, 105, 161, 165–168, 190, 232–235, 398
solicitation, 18, 402
speedy trial. *See* trial
spousal abuse. *See* domestic violence
Stand Your Ground laws, 42
Stanford Prison Experiment, 250
states and crime, 365
statute of limitations, 38, 403
sting operations, 46, 403
stop and frisk, 116–119
strict liability, 11, 403
Supreme Court, 353–370; state level, 365, 370

T

terrorism, responses to: racial profiling, 137–138; Patriot Act, 357, 360
theft, 14–15
three strikes, 186, 237–238, 252–253
throw-downs, 91–93
trace evidence, 98
trial, 194–218: mental capacity for, 191; pretrial, 179–193; procedures, 194–195; right to public, 167; right to speedy, 166–167. *See also* Sixth Amendment
truth in sentencing, 252–253
Tucker, Karla Faye, 284–285

U–V

UCR, 52–53, 403
veterans courts, 157
victims, 63–73; age of, 63; compensation of, 68–69; rights of, 71–73; property crimes and, 66–67; violent crimes and, 64–65
vigilantes, 377–380, 403
violent crime: causes of, 346–352; history of, 48–51; rate of, 53; schools and, 380–383; solutions to, 392–394; victims of, 64–65. *See also* domestic violence; gangs; homicide; robbery

W–Z

warrant, 110–112, 403; exceptions to, 113–122, 357–359
white-collar crime, 57–60, 403
Wilson, James Q., 84, 254, 349–350
witness: compel to testify, right to, 167–168; confront, right to, 167, 398; credibility of, 217; cross-examination of, 194, 209, 400; direct examination of, 208–209, 400; expert, 196, 208; eye-, 91–93; protection programs, 24, 71; tampering, 23–24, 403. *See also* Fifth Amendment; evidence
writ of certiorari. *See* certiorari
writ of habeas corpus. *See* habeas corpus